# First World War

and Army of Occupation

# War Diary

France, Belgium and Germany

52 DIVISION
Divisional Troops
Royal Army Medical Corps
1/1 Lowland Field Ambulance
19 August 1916 - 30 April 1919

WO95/2894/1

The Naval & Military Press Ltd
www.nmarchive.com
**Published in association with The National Archives**

Published by

The Naval & Military Press Ltd

Unit 10 Ridgewood Industrial Park,

Uckfield, East Sussex,

TN22 5QE England

Tel: +44 (0) 1825 749494

www.naval-military-press.com

www.nmarchive.com

*This diary has been reprinted in facsimile from the original. Any imperfections are inevitably reproduced and the quality may fall short of modern type and cartographic standards.*

# Contents

| Document type | Place/Title | Date From | Date To |
|---|---|---|---|
| Heading | WO95/2894 (1) | | |
| Heading | 1-1st (Lowland) Fld Ambulance 1918 Apl-1919 Apl | | |
| Heading | War Diary Of Lowland Field Ambulance R.A.M.C. (T) Vol XXXV From 1/4/16 To 30/4/16 | | |
| War Diary | | 17/04/1918 | 17/04/1918 |
| War Diary | Camp Fournier Marseilles | 18/04/1918 | 18/04/1918 |
| War Diary | Rue | 22/04/1918 | 28/04/1918 |
| War Diary | Les Tourbieres | 29/04/1918 | 29/04/1918 |
| War Diary | M 661000 Sheet 36a 1/40,000 | 30/04/1918 | 30/04/1918 |
| Miscellaneous | Number Of Report 143 | 05/04/1918 | 05/04/1918 |
| Miscellaneous | In The Field | 05/03/1918 | 05/03/1918 |
| Miscellaneous | Field Return | | |
| Miscellaneous | | | |
| Miscellaneous | In The Field | 27/04/1918 | 27/04/1918 |
| Miscellaneous | Field Return. | 27/04/1918 | 27/04/1918 |
| Heading | May 1918 1/1st Lowland F.A. | | |
| Heading | War Diary Of 1/1st Lowland Field Ambulance RAMC (T) 32nd (Lowland) Division Vol XXXVI From 1st May 1918 To 31st May 1918 | | |
| War Diary | M6.b 10.0 Sheet 36A 1/40000 | 01/05/1918 | 07/05/1918 |
| War Diary | Villers-Au-Bois | 08/05/1918 | 31/05/1918 |
| Miscellaneous | | | |
| Miscellaneous | In The Field | 04/05/1918 | 04/05/1918 |
| Miscellaneous | Field Return | 04/05/1918 | 04/05/1918 |
| Miscellaneous | | | |
| Miscellaneous | In The Field | 11/05/1918 | 11/05/1918 |
| Miscellaneous | Field Return | 11/05/1918 | 11/05/1918 |
| Miscellaneous | | | |
| Miscellaneous | In The Field | 18/05/1918 | 18/05/1918 |
| Miscellaneous | Field Return | 18/05/1918 | 18/05/1918 |
| Miscellaneous | | | |
| Miscellaneous | In The Field | 25/05/1918 | 25/05/1918 |
| Miscellaneous | Field Return | 25/05/1918 | 25/05/1918 |
| Miscellaneous | | | |
| Miscellaneous | In The Field | 31/05/1918 | 31/05/1918 |
| Miscellaneous | Field Return. | 31/05/1918 | 31/05/1918 |
| Miscellaneous | Appendix I | 10/05/1918 | 10/05/1918 |
| Miscellaneous | Appendix II May 1918 War Diary of 1/1 Low F.A. RAMC (T) | 15/05/1918 | 15/05/1918 |
| Miscellaneous | Appendix III May 1918 War Diary of 1/1 Low F.A. RAMC (T) | 19/05/1918 | 19/05/1918 |
| Heading | 1/1 Lowland Fd Amb Vol 3 June 1918 | | |
| War Diary | Villers-Au-Bois (Army Map B 1/40000 X 19.c.9.9) | 01/06/1918 | 06/06/1918 |
| War Diary | Villers-Au-Bois | 07/06/1918 | 10/06/1918 |
| War Diary | Villers-Au-Bois X19.c.9.9 Map B 1/40000 | 11/06/1918 | 11/06/1918 |
| War Diary | Villers-Au-Bois | 12/06/1918 | 30/06/1918 |
| Miscellaneous | Appendix I June 1918 War Diary of 1/1 Low Fd. Amb RAMC (T) | 01/06/1918 | 01/06/1918 |
| Miscellaneous | Appendix II June 1918 War Diary of 1/1st Low Fd Amb RAMC (T) | 08/06/1918 | 08/06/1918 |

| | | | |
|---|---|---|---|
| Miscellaneous | Appendix III june 1918 War Diary of 1/1st Low Fd Amb RAMC (T) | | |
| Miscellaneous | Appendix IV June 1918 War Diary of 1/1st Law Fd Amb R.A.M.C. (T) | 21/06/1918 | 21/06/1918 |
| Miscellaneous | Appendix V Month of June 1918 War Diary of 1/1st Law Fd Amb R.A.M.C. (T) | | |
| Miscellaneous | War Diary (July 1918) A.D.M.S. 52nd Div Appendix VI | | |
| Miscellaneous | Appendix VII (June 1918) War Diary 1/1st Low Fd Amb R.A.M.C. (T) | 30/06/1918 | 30/06/1918 |
| Miscellaneous | Field Return | 04/06/1918 | 04/06/1918 |
| Miscellaneous | In The Field | 04/06/1918 | 04/06/1918 |
| Miscellaneous | | | |
| Miscellaneous | Field Return | 14/06/1918 | 14/06/1918 |
| Miscellaneous | In The Field | 14/06/1918 | 14/06/1918 |
| Miscellaneous | | | |
| Miscellaneous | Field Return | 30/06/1918 | 30/06/1918 |
| Miscellaneous | In The Field | 21/06/1918 | 21/06/1918 |
| Miscellaneous | | | |
| Miscellaneous | Field Return | 28/06/1918 | 28/06/1918 |
| Miscellaneous | In The Field | 28/06/1918 | 28/06/1918 |
| Miscellaneous | | | |
| Heading | War Diary (July 1918) 1/1st Low Fd Amb Vol 4 | | |
| War Diary | Villers-Au-Bois An Map B 1/40,000 X 19.c.9.9 | 01/07/1918 | 22/07/1918 |
| War Diary | Barlin P. de C Q 3 A 3 6 | 23/07/1918 | 29/07/1918 |
| War Diary | Ecoivres F.13.a.8.2 | 30/07/1918 | 31/07/1918 |
| Miscellaneous | Appendix 1 War Diary of 1/1st Low Fd Amb July 1918 | 06/07/1918 | 06/07/1918 |
| Miscellaneous | Appendix II War Diary of 1/1st Low Fd Amb July 1918 | 07/07/1918 | 07/07/1918 |
| Miscellaneous | Appendix III July 1918 War Diary of 1/1st Low Fd Amb | | |
| Miscellaneous | Appendix IV July 1918 War Diary of 1/1st Law Fd Amb | 14/07/1918 | 14/07/1918 |
| Miscellaneous | Appendix V July 1918 War Diary of 1/1st Law Fd Amb | | |
| Miscellaneous | War Diary (July 1918) A.D.M.S. 52nd Div Appendix VI | 20/07/1918 | 20/07/1918 |
| Miscellaneous | Appendix VII July 1918 War Diary of 1/1st Low Fd Amb | 22/07/1918 | 22/07/1918 |
| Miscellaneous | Appendix VIII Marching Out State | 29/07/1918 | 29/07/1918 |
| Miscellaneous | Field Return | 08/07/1918 | 08/07/1918 |
| Miscellaneous | In The Field | 05/07/1918 | 05/07/1918 |
| Miscellaneous | | | |
| Miscellaneous | Field Return | 12/07/1918 | 12/07/1918 |
| Miscellaneous | In The Field | 12/07/1918 | 12/07/1918 |
| Miscellaneous | | | |
| Miscellaneous | Field Return | 19/07/1918 | 19/07/1918 |
| Miscellaneous | In The Field | 19/07/1918 | 19/07/1918 |
| Miscellaneous | | | |
| Miscellaneous | Field Return | 20/07/1918 | 20/07/1918 |
| Miscellaneous | In The Field | 26/07/1918 | 26/07/1918 |
| Miscellaneous | | | |
| Heading | War Diary Of 1/1st Lowland Field Ambulance RAMC (T) Aug 1918 Vol XXXIX | | |
| War Diary | Ecoivres F13.a.8.2 (Map B 1/40000) | 01/08/1918 | 08/08/1918 |
| War Diary | Ecoivres | 08/08/1918 | 18/08/1918 |
| War Diary | Cambligneul W 14 D 55 Sh 36 B 1/40000 | 19/08/1916 | 19/08/1916 |
| War Diary | Cambligneul | 20/08/1918 | 20/08/1918 |

| | | | |
|---|---|---|---|
| War Diary | Cambligneul (W 14 d 5.5) | 20/08/1918 | 20/08/1918 |
| War Diary | Lattre St Quentin J 23 d 9.2 Sh 51a | 21/08/1918 | 22/08/1918 |
| War Diary | Bretencourt R 26 b 1.2 Sh 51c 1/40000 | 23/08/1918 | 23/08/1918 |
| War Diary | Bretencourt | 23/08/1918 | 23/08/1918 |
| War Diary | Le Fermont R 21 C82 Sh 51c | 23/08/1918 | 24/08/1918 |
| War Diary | Le Fermont | 24/08/1918 | 24/08/1918 |
| War Diary | Ficheux M 31 b 2.8 Sh 51 B 1/40,000 | 24/08/1918 | 24/08/1918 |
| War Diary | M 31 b 2.8 | 24/08/1918 | 24/08/1918 |
| War Diary | M 31 b 2.8 Ficheux | 24/08/1918 | 26/08/1918 |
| War Diary | Mercatel M 30 c 2.2 Sh 51B 1/40,000 | 27/08/1918 | 27/08/1918 |
| War Diary | Mercatel M 35 a 2.8 | 28/08/1918 | 29/08/1918 |
| War Diary | Mercatel M 35 a 2.8 Sh 51B | 29/08/1918 | 29/08/1918 |
| War Diary | Mercatel M 35 a 2.8 | 30/08/1918 | 31/08/1918 |
| Miscellaneous | Appendix I War Diary of 1/1st Lowland Fld Ambulance 52nd (Lowland Division) Aug 1918 | 28/08/1918 | 28/08/1918 |
| Miscellaneous | Appendix II War Diary of 1/1st Lowland Fld Ambulance 52nd (Lowland Division) Aug 1918 | 28/08/1918 | 28/08/1918 |
| Miscellaneous | Field Return | 02/08/1918 | 02/08/1918 |
| Miscellaneous | In The Field | 02/08/1918 | 02/08/1918 |
| Miscellaneous | | | |
| Miscellaneous | R.E B 213 W.E 2nd Augt 1918 | | |
| Miscellaneous | Field Return | 09/08/1918 | 09/08/1918 |
| Miscellaneous | In The Field | 09/08/1918 | 09/08/1918 |
| Miscellaneous | | | |
| Miscellaneous | Field Return | 16/08/1918 | 16/08/1918 |
| Miscellaneous | In The Field | 16/08/1918 | 16/08/1918 |
| Miscellaneous | | | |
| Miscellaneous | AF B 213 | 16/08/1918 | 16/08/1918 |
| Miscellaneous | Field Return. | 23/08/1918 | 23/08/1918 |
| Miscellaneous | In The Field | 23/08/1918 | 23/08/1918 |
| Miscellaneous | A.F.B. 213 | 23/08/1918 | 23/08/1918 |
| Miscellaneous | In The Field | 23/08/1918 | 23/08/1918 |
| Miscellaneous | | | |
| Miscellaneous | A.F.B. 213 | 23/08/1918 | 23/08/1918 |
| Miscellaneous | Field Return | 30/08/1918 | 30/08/1918 |
| Miscellaneous | A.F.B. 213 | 30/08/1918 | 30/08/1918 |
| Miscellaneous | In The Field | 30/08/1918 | 30/08/1918 |
| Miscellaneous | | | |
| Heading | War Diary Of 1/1st Lowland Field Ambulance RAMC Sept 1918 Vol 6 | | |
| Miscellaneous | T1d23 Sh 61B | 01/09/1918 | 01/09/1918 |
| War Diary | T 14 B 51 Sh 51B | 01/09/1918 | 02/09/1918 |
| War Diary | T 22 b 2.8 | 02/09/1918 | 03/09/1918 |
| War Diary | U20 d 55 | 03/09/1918 | 03/09/1918 |
| War Diary | U20 d 55 Sh 51B Bullecourt | 03/09/1918 | 03/09/1918 |
| War Diary | U 20 d 55 Sh 51B | 04/09/1918 | 06/09/1918 |
| War Diary | B 3 b.50 Sheet 57c | 07/09/1918 | 08/09/1918 |
| War Diary | B 9.a.3.8 Sh 57c N.W. 1/20,000 | 09/09/1918 | 15/09/1918 |
| War Diary | D 1 d 68 Sh 57c NE 1/20000 | 16/09/1918 | 25/09/1918 |
| War Diary | D15.b.5.0 | 26/09/1918 | 26/09/1918 |
| War Diary | D15.b.50 Sh 57c | 26/09/1918 | 29/09/1918 |
| War Diary | D29c 85 Sh 57c | 29/09/1918 | 30/09/1918 |
| Miscellaneous | Appendix I War Diary of 1/1st Lowland Fld Ambulance RAMC (T) Aug 1918 | 11/04/1918 | 11/04/1918 |
| Miscellaneous | Appendix II War Diary of 1/1st Lowland Fld Ambulance RAMC (T) Sept 1918 | 21/09/1918 | 21/09/1918 |

| | | | |
|---|---|---|---|
| Heading | War Diary Of 1/1st Lowland Field Ambulance R.A.M.C. Vol XLI From 1/10/18 To 31/10/18 | | |
| War Diary | E 28 c 56 Sh 57c N.E. | 01/10/1918 | 06/10/1918 |
| War Diary | J 9 b 68 Sh 57c NE 1/20000 | 06/10/1918 | 07/10/1918 |
| War Diary | Villers Sir Simon I 5 a 26 Sheet 51c | 08/10/1918 | 12/10/1918 |
| War Diary | Les 4 Vents (Len 1/100000 2 H 5.6) | 13/10/1918 | 13/10/1918 |
| War Diary | Les 4 Vents | 14/10/1918 | 22/10/1918 |
| War Diary | M 27d 77 Sh 44a 1/40000 | 22/10/1918 | 22/10/1918 |
| War Diary | P25 C 1.4 Sheet 44a 1/40000 | 23/10/1918 | 23/10/1918 |
| War Diary | P25 C.1.4 Henin-Lietard | 23/10/1918 | 23/10/1918 |
| War Diary | M2d 35 Sh 44 1/40000 Coutiches | 24/10/1918 | 25/10/1918 |
| War Diary | Coutiches | 26/10/1918 | 26/10/1918 |
| War Diary | Lecelles I 29 c 8.6 Sh 44/40000 | 27/10/1918 | 28/10/1918 |
| War Diary | Rosult O.2.a.4.1 Sh 44 1/40000 | 28/10/1918 | 31/10/1918 |
| Miscellaneous | Field Return | 05/10/1918 | 05/10/1918 |
| Miscellaneous | A.F.B. 213 | 05/10/1918 | 05/10/1918 |
| Miscellaneous | In The Field | 05/10/1918 | 05/10/1918 |
| Miscellaneous | | | |
| Miscellaneous | Field Return | 12/10/1918 | 12/10/1918 |
| Miscellaneous | A.F.B. 213 | 12/10/1918 | 12/10/1918 |
| Miscellaneous | In The Field | 12/10/1918 | 12/10/1918 |
| Miscellaneous | | | |
| Miscellaneous | Field Return | | |
| Miscellaneous | A.F.B. 213 | 26/10/1918 | 26/10/1918 |
| Miscellaneous | | | |
| Miscellaneous | Field Return | 14/10/1918 | 14/10/1918 |
| Miscellaneous | AF B 213 | 19/10/1918 | 19/10/1918 |
| Miscellaneous | In The Field | 19/10/1918 | 19/10/1918 |
| Miscellaneous | | | |
| Heading | War Diary of 1/1st Lowland Field Ambulance Vol XLII From 1/11/18 To 30/11/18 | | |
| War Diary | Rosult O.2.a.4.1 Sh 44 1/400000 | 01/11/1918 | 09/11/1918 |
| War Diary | Etablissement Thermal P17 b 88 Sh 44 1/40000 | 09/11/1918 | 09/11/1918 |
| War Diary | Bonsecours L 10 C 65 Sh 44 1/40000 | 10/11/1916 | 10/11/1916 |
| War Diary | Bonsecours Hotel de La Cornette L10 Sh 44 1/40000 | 10/11/1918 | 10/11/1918 |
| War Diary | Sirault I 1 b71 Sh 45 1/40000 | 11/11/1918 | 29/11/1918 |
| War Diary | Chaussee Nd Louvignies Sh 38 W5b 4.6 1/40000 | 30/11/1918 | 30/11/1918 |
| Miscellaneous | Field Return | 02/11/1918 | 02/11/1918 |
| Miscellaneous | AF B 213 | 02/11/1918 | 02/11/1918 |
| Miscellaneous | In The Field | 02/11/1918 | 02/11/1918 |
| Miscellaneous | | | |
| Miscellaneous | Field Return | 16/11/1918 | 16/11/1918 |
| Miscellaneous | A.F.B. 213 | 16/11/1918 | 16/11/1918 |
| Miscellaneous | In The Field | 16/11/1918 | 16/11/1918 |
| Miscellaneous | | | |
| Miscellaneous | Field Return | 04/11/1918 | 04/11/1918 |
| Miscellaneous | A.F.B. 213 | 09/11/1919 | 09/11/1919 |
| Miscellaneous | In The Field | 09/11/1918 | 09/11/1918 |
| Miscellaneous | | | |
| Miscellaneous | Field Return | 30/11/1918 | 30/11/1918 |
| Miscellaneous | B 213 | 30/11/1918 | 30/11/1918 |
| Miscellaneous | In The Field | 30/11/1918 | 30/11/1918 |
| Miscellaneous | | | |
| Miscellaneous | Field Return | 23/11/1918 | 23/11/1918 |
| Miscellaneous | A.F.B. 213 | 23/11/1918 | 23/11/1918 |
| Miscellaneous | In The Field | 23/11/1918 | 23/11/1918 |

| | | | |
|---|---|---|---|
| Miscellaneous | | | |
| Heading | War Diary Of 1/1st Lowland Field Ambulance Vol XLIII<br>From 1/12/18 To 31/12/18 | | |
| War Diary | Chaussee N.D Louvignies W5b 4.6 Sh 38 | 01/12/1918 | 31/12/1918 |
| Miscellaneous | Routine Treatment For Scabies Appendix I | | |
| Miscellaneous | Field Return | 07/12/1915 | 07/12/1915 |
| Miscellaneous | B 213 | 01/12/1918 | 01/12/1918 |
| Miscellaneous | In The Field | 07/12/1918 | 07/12/1918 |
| Miscellaneous | | | |
| Miscellaneous | Field Return | 14/12/1918 | 14/12/1918 |
| Miscellaneous | B 213 | 14/12/1918 | 14/12/1918 |
| Miscellaneous | In The Field | 14/12/1918 | 14/12/1918 |
| Miscellaneous | | | |
| Miscellaneous | Field Return | 21/12/1918 | 21/12/1918 |
| Miscellaneous | B 213 | 21/12/1918 | 21/12/1918 |
| Miscellaneous | In The Field | 21/12/1918 | 21/12/1918 |
| Miscellaneous | | | |
| Miscellaneous | Field Return | 28/12/1918 | 28/12/1918 |
| Miscellaneous | B 213 | 28/12/1918 | 28/12/1918 |
| Miscellaneous | In The Field | 28/12/1918 | 28/12/1918 |
| Miscellaneous | | | |
| Heading | 1/1 Lowland Fd Amb Vol 10 Jan 1919 | | |
| War Diary | Chaussee N.D. Louvignies Sh 36 W 5b 46 | 01/01/1919 | 06/01/1919 |
| War Diary | Chaussee N.D. Louvignies | 06/01/1919 | 09/01/1919 |
| War Diary | Chaussee N.D. Louvignies Sh 38 W5b 4.6 | 09/01/1919 | 31/01/1919 |
| Miscellaneous | Field Return | 04/01/1919 | 04/01/1919 |
| Miscellaneous | B 213 | 04/01/1919 | 04/01/1919 |
| Miscellaneous | In The Field | 04/01/1919 | 04/01/1919 |
| Miscellaneous | | | |
| Miscellaneous | Field Return | 11/04/1919 | 11/04/1919 |
| Miscellaneous | B 213 | 11/01/1919 | 11/01/1919 |
| Miscellaneous | In The Field | 11/01/1919 | 11/01/1919 |
| Miscellaneous | | | |
| Miscellaneous | Field Return | 18/01/1919 | 18/01/1919 |
| Miscellaneous | B 213 | 18/01/1919 | 18/01/1919 |
| Miscellaneous | In The Field | 18/01/1919 | 18/01/1919 |
| Miscellaneous | | | |
| Miscellaneous | Field Return | 25/01/1919 | 25/01/1919 |
| Miscellaneous | R.A.S.C. Section | | |
| Miscellaneous | In The Field | 25/01/1919 | 25/01/1919 |
| Miscellaneous | | | |
| Heading | 1/1st Low Fd Amb War Diary Feb 1919 Vol 11 | | |
| War Diary | Chausee N-D Louvignies Sh 38 W 5.b.46 | 01/02/1919 | 28/02/1919 |
| Miscellaneous | Field Return | 01/02/1919 | 01/02/1919 |
| Miscellaneous | R.A.S.C. Sect | 01/02/1919 | 01/02/1919 |
| Miscellaneous | In The Field | 01/02/1919 | 01/02/1919 |
| Miscellaneous | | | |
| Miscellaneous | Field Return | 08/02/1919 | 08/02/1919 |
| Miscellaneous | R.A.S.C. Section | 08/02/1919 | 08/02/1919 |
| Miscellaneous | In The Field | 08/02/1919 | 08/02/1919 |
| Miscellaneous | | | |
| Miscellaneous | Field Return | 15/02/1919 | 15/02/1919 |
| Miscellaneous | R.A.S.C. Section | 15/02/1919 | 15/02/1919 |
| Miscellaneous | In The Field | 15/02/1919 | 15/02/1919 |
| Miscellaneous | | | |
| Miscellaneous | Field Return | 22/02/1919 | 22/02/1919 |

| | | | |
|---|---|---|---|
| Miscellaneous | R.A.S.C. Section | 22/02/1919 | 22/02/1919 |
| Miscellaneous | In The Field | 22/02/1919 | 22/02/1919 |
| Miscellaneous | | | |
| Heading | War Diary March 1919 Vol 12 | | |
| War Diary | Chausee N.D Louvignies Sh 38 W5b46 | 01/03/1919 | 15/03/1919 |
| War Diary | Chaussee N.D. Louvignies | 15/03/1919 | 16/03/1919 |
| War Diary | Soignies | 17/03/1919 | 31/03/1919 |
| Miscellaneous | Field Return | 01/03/1919 | 01/03/1919 |
| Miscellaneous | R.A.S.C. Section | 01/03/1919 | 01/03/1919 |
| Miscellaneous | Chaussee N.D. | 01/03/1919 | 01/03/1919 |
| Miscellaneous | | | |
| Miscellaneous | Field Return | 08/03/1919 | 08/03/1919 |
| Miscellaneous | R.A.S.C. Section | 05/03/1919 | 05/03/1919 |
| Miscellaneous | Chaussee N.D. Louvignies | 08/03/1919 | 08/03/1919 |
| Miscellaneous | | | |
| Miscellaneous | Field Return | 15/03/1919 | 15/03/1919 |
| Miscellaneous | | 15/03/1919 | 15/03/1919 |
| Miscellaneous | | | |
| Miscellaneous | Field Return | | |
| Miscellaneous | RASC H T Section | | |
| Miscellaneous | Soignies | 22/03/1919 | 22/03/1919 |
| Miscellaneous | | | |
| Miscellaneous | Field Return | 29/03/1919 | 29/03/1919 |
| Miscellaneous | | | |
| Miscellaneous | Soignies | 29/03/1919 | 29/03/1919 |
| Miscellaneous | | | |
| Heading | 1/1 Lowland F. A. April 1919 | | |
| War Diary | Soignies | 01/04/1919 | 30/04/1919 |
| Miscellaneous | Field Return | 05/04/1919 | 05/04/1919 |
| Miscellaneous | 1/1 Lowland Fld Ambc | 05/04/1919 | 05/04/1919 |
| Miscellaneous | Soignies | 05/03/1919 | 05/03/1919 |
| Miscellaneous | | | |
| Miscellaneous | Field Return | 12/04/1919 | 12/04/1919 |
| Miscellaneous | RASC H.T. | | |
| Miscellaneous | RASC MT | | |
| Miscellaneous | | | |
| Miscellaneous | Soignies | 12/04/1919 | 12/04/1919 |
| Miscellaneous | | | |
| Miscellaneous | Field Return | | |
| Miscellaneous | RASC HT | 12/04/1919 | 12/04/1919 |
| Miscellaneous | Soignies | 19/04/1919 | 19/04/1919 |
| Miscellaneous | | | |
| Miscellaneous | Field Return | 26/04/1919 | 26/04/1919 |
| Miscellaneous | R.A.S.C. | 26/04/1919 | 26/04/1919 |
| Miscellaneous | Soignies | 26/04/1919 | 26/04/1919 |
| Miscellaneous | | | |

W095

2894

11

52ND DIVISION

1-1ST(LOWLAND) FLD AMBULANCE

~~APR - DEC 1918~~

1918 APL – 1919 APL

Vol I 52

War Diary
of
1/1st London Field Ambulance
RAMC (T)
Vol XXXV

140/2900

11/4/Apr 1918

From 1/4/16 to 30/4/16

[illegible]
of 1/1st LFA RAMC (T)

| Place | Date | Hour | Summary of Events and Information |
|---|---|---|---|
| | 17/4/18 | | Arrived off MARSEILLES about 0700 in hazy weather, got through the mine field & berthed at quayside about 1000. Heavy rain came on & some of the troops got very wet during disembarkation. This unit disembarked at 1545 & marched to Camp FOURNIER, to tents. Camp small & not very comfortable for men. Capt R STANSFIELD reported for duty. JWL |
| CAMP FOURNIER MARSEILLES | 18/4/18 | | Unit marches out to-day at 1330 to entrain at 1427. Train is timed to leave at 1627 & baggage & 4 days rations are being got together by baggage party already detailed. JWL |

Instructions regarding War Diaries and Intelligence Summaries are contained in F. S. Regs., Part II. and the Staff Manual respectively. Title pages will be prepared in manuscript.

# WAR DIARY

or

~~INTELLIGENCE SUMMARY.~~

(Erase heading not required.)

407 Army Form C. 2118.

1/1st Lowland Field Ambulance
52nd (Lowland) Division

| Place | Date | Hour | Summary of Events and Information | Remarks and references to Appendices |
|---|---|---|---|---|
| RUE | 22/4/18 | | Train arrived at NOYELLES SUR SOMME yesterday forenoon 21/4/18 about 8 or 10 hours overdue. Unit detrained & marched to rest camp on outskirts of village to have a rest & a hot meal. Baggage was sent on by motor lorry to our destination RUE at about 1200. An officer to look out for billets for personnel and the 2 i/c Capt REID were sent on with this lorry & the baggage party. Main body of unit marched off from NOYELLES at 1500 for RUE. Marching in strength RAMC Off 9 OR 180, ASC (att) OR 44 | |
| | | | 2 RAMC + 4 ASC failed to leave MARSEILLES & ~~their~~ absence was reported to RTO there and to Camp Commandant at Camp Fournier. After a hot meal in the Public Square officers & men were distributed to billets. J.W.L | |
| RUE | 22/4/18 (Contd) | | Visited the billets occupied by the men to day & found them unsatisfactory & quite unsuitable for continued occupation in most cases. There are 5 in all, marked Y6 C2, B2, A11 & A17. The two first named are lofts in a farm yard and in a wood yard & are passable. B2 is a stone floored barn over-run with rats & mice which ate & destroyed some of the men's equipment. A11 is a loft in a farm yard not water tight or wind tight approached by a thin ladder & with a large part of the flooring removed. A17 is a stable inches thick with horse manure in an incredibly dirty & insanitary farm yard. J.W.L | |

A7092. Wt. W12839/M1293 750,000. 1/17. D. D & L., Ltd. Forms/C2118/14.

Instructions regarding War Diaries and Intelligence Summaries are contained in F. S. Regs., Part II. and the Staff Manual respectively. Title pages will be prepared in manuscript.

# WAR DIARY
*or*
~~INTELLIGENCE SUMMARY.~~
(*Erase heading not required.*)

408 Army Form C. 2118.

1/1st Lowland Field Ambulance
52nd Lowland Division.

| Place | Date | Hour | Summary of Events and Information | Remarks and references to Appendices |
|---|---|---|---|---|
| RUE | 23/4/18 | | After some difficulty ~~a billet~~ accommodation for about 90 men was found in a house at the Sugar factory of Mons Girard & a room suitable for use as a hospital ward also. Men in A11 & A17 were accordingly transferred this afternoon & arrangements made to admit to hospital walk cases from the brigade & treat those likely to be of short duration instead of sending them on to Hospital at ABBEVILLE. Arrangements were also made to park the horses & vehicles being drawn at ABBEVILLE to-day on their arrival to-night. Arranged also with Lt Col McLACHLAN who is in command at the staging camp for Infantry & transport to have the use of 7 tents for transport personnel so that they should be near their animals. J.W.L. | |
| RUE | 24/4/18 | | Removed transport personnel from billet Y6 to the tents at staging camp arranged for yesterday. Transport complete arrived last night about 2000. Received ADMS R 50/11 d/24/4/18 at 1800 this evening instructing me "to arrange for collection of all sick of 156th Bde units before & up to time of entrainment tomorrow 25th inst, & giving train timings. Sent 1 horse ambulance wagon to report to Bde HQ at St FIRMIN to-night ~~&~~ to follow them in to train timed to leave at 8-44 A.M. to-morrow. Got the use of a car & arranged with O.C. units to send a with VI wagon | |

D. D. & L., London, E.C.
(A8001) Wt. W1771/M2031 750,000 5/17 Sch. 52 Forms/C2118/14

Instructions regarding War Diaries and Intelligence Summaries are contained in F. S. Regs., Part II. and the Staff Manual respectively. Title pages will be prepared in manuscript.

# WAR DIARY
-or-
~~INTELLIGENCE~~ SUMMARY.
*(Erase heading not required.)*

409 Army Form C. 2118.

1/1st Lowland Field Ambulance
52nd Lowland Division

| Place | Date | Hour | Summary of Events and Information | Remarks and references to Appendices |
|---|---|---|---|---|
| RUE | 24/4/18 | | to report to each HQ. to-morrow as follows.<br>4th R S at RUE at 1000<br>7th R Scots at St QUENTIN at 1100 (report at St QUENTIN church) [illegible] guide.<br>7th S Rifles at St FIRMIN at 1400<br>8th S. Rifles at CHAMPNEUF at 1600<br>No. 2 Coy. 7th R Scots at St QUENTIN church at 1930 (for [illegible] train) J.W.L. | |
| RUE | 25/4/18 | | Ambulance reported as arranged. Units entrained & got off without accident. J.W.L. | |
| RUE | 26/4/18 | | Received instructions late to-night to send 1 Off + 2 men with 1 bicycle to be at HQ 155 Inf Brigade at 0845 to-morrow to act as billetting party for this unit + 52nd Divisional Sanitary Section. HQ 155 Inf Bde is 6 miles off at NOUVION J.W.L. | |
| RUE | 27/4/18 | | Capt. MACKENZIE + 2 O.R. duly left this morning as detailed for billetting purposes with 155 Inf Bde Units. Officers + NCOs attended a lecture on poison gas by the Divl Chemical adviser at HQ of Divl Train at LANNOY this morning at 0900. Received RAMC + 155 Inf Bde administrative Instructions regarding move to-morrow. In accordance with ADMS instructions contained in R 42/5 d/24/4/18 Capt. R. STANSFIELD M.C. R.A.M.C. (T.C.) was sent to report to O.C. 1/3rd Low Fld Amb. for duty yesterday J.W.L. | |

D. D. & L., London, E.C. (A8001) Wt. W1771/M2031 750,000 5/17 Sch. 82 Forms C2118/14

Instructions regarding War Diaries and Intelligence Summaries are contained in F. S. Regs., Part II. and the Staff Manual respectively. Title pages will be prepared in manuscript.

# WAR DIARY

~~or~~

~~INTELLIGENCE SUMMARY.~~

(*Erase heading not required.*)

410 Army Form C. 2118.

1/1st Lowland Field Ambulance
52nd (Lowland) Division

| Place | Date | Hour | Summary of Events and Information | Remarks and references to Appendices |
|---|---|---|---|---|
| RUE | 28 4/18 | | Necessary billetting certificates were completed & handed to Area Commandant. This unit leaves to-night by train at 2034 for AIRE. Necessary steps have been taken to ensure that private & any other claims are settled before leaving & to have the billets inspected after vacation to make sure that they are left in a clean condition, & that no equipment is left. J.W.L. | |
| Les Tourbieres | 29 4/18 | | Unit paraded at 1900 last night for entraining. OC of this unit acted as OC train with Lieut PHILLIPS, assistant APM 52nd Div., as Adjutant. Train left promptly & arrived at AIRE about 0500 but had to wait for 2 hours till preceding train cleared. Capt. MACKENZIE (the officer sent in advance) met train & guided the unit to billets at Les TOURBIERES. Horse transport wagons were got off train expeditiously & followed the unit. J.W.L. | |
| M6b10,0 Sheet 36A 1/40000 | 30 4/18 | | The 3 horsed ambulance wagons of the unit were sent round Bde units stationed in the neighbourhood of MAMETZ to collect any sick, & returned with them in the forenoon to Ambulance HQ. where tents had been erected for hospital purposes. Those not likely to be fit for duty in 4 days time were evacuated by motor ambulance to 51st C.C.S. at AIRE. Three motor ambulances reported for duty last night with this unit.<br>John W. Leitch Lt Col<br>OC 1/1st Lowland Fld Amb<br>R.A.M.C.(T) | |

D. D. & L., London, E.C.
(A8001) Wt. W1771/M2031 750,000 5/17 Sch. 52 Forms/C2.118/14

Perforated Sheet giving detail of personnel and horses wanting to complete, shown on Army Form B. 213.

Number of Report 143

| Detail of Wanting to Complete. | Drivers. | | | | | | | | | Farriers | | | | Wheelers | | | | | | | Fitters & Turners (R. E.) | | Fitters | | | Electricians | | | Engine Drivers | | | | | | | | | | | | | | | Armament Artificers | | | | | W.O.'s and N.C.O.'s (by ranks) not included in trade columns. | | | | | | | | | | | TOTAL to agree with wanting to complete | | Horses | | | |
|---|---|---|---|---|---|---|---|---|---|---|---|---|---|---|---|---|---|---|---|---|---|---|---|---|---|---|---|---|---|---|---|---|---|---|---|---|---|---|---|---|---|---|---|---|---|---|---|---|---|---|---|---|---|---|---|---|---|---|---|---|---|---|---|---|---|
| | R. A. | R. E. | A. S. C. | Car | Lorry | Steam | Gunners | Smith Gunners | Range Takers | Serjeants | Corporals | Shoeing, or Shoeing and Carriage Smiths | Cold Shoers | R. A. | H. T. | M. T. | Saddlers or Harness Makers | Blacksmiths | Bricklayers and Masons | Carpenters and Joiners | Wood | Iron | R. A. | Wireless | Plumbers | Ordinary | W. T. | Signalmen | Loco. | Field | Air Line Men | Permanent Line Men | Operators, Telegraph | Cablemen | Brigade Section Pioneers | General-duty Pioneers | Signallers | Instrument Repairers | Motor Cyclists | Motor Cyclist Artificers | Telephonists | Clerks | Machine Gunners | Fitters | Range Finders | Armourers | Storemen | Privates | | | | | | | | | | | | Officers | Other Ranks | Riding | Draught | Heavy Draught | Pack |
| CAVALRY | | | | | | | | | | | | | | | | | | | | | | | | | | | | | | | | | | | | | | | | | | | | | | | | | | | | | | | | | | | | | | | | | |
| R. A. | | | | | | | | | | | | | | | | | | | | | | | | | | | | | | | | | | | | | | | | | | | | | | | | | | | | | | | | | | | | | | | | | |
| R. E. | | | | | | | | | | | | | | | | | | | | | | | | | | | | | | | | | | | | | | | | | | | | | | | | | | | | | | | | | | | | | | | | |
| INFANTRY | | | | | | | | | | | | | | | | | | | | | | | | | | | | | | | | | | | | | | | | | | | | | | | | | | | | | | | | | | | | | | | | |
| R. A. M. C. | | | 16 | | | | | | | | | | | | | | | | | | | | | | | | | | | | | | | | | | | | | | | | | | | | | | | | | | | | | | | | | 2 | | | | | |
| A. O. C. | | | | | | | | | | | | | | | | | | | | | | | | | | | | | | | | | | | | | | | | | | | | | | | | | | | | | | | | | | | | | | | | |
| A. V. C. | | | | | | | | | | | | | | | | | | | | | | | | | | | | | | | | | | | | | | | | | | | | | | | | | | | | | | | | | | | | | | | | |

Remarks :—

John W. Leitch Lt Col Signature of Commander.

1/1 Low Fd Ambce Unit.

52 Div Formation to which attached.

5/4/18. Date of Despatch.

(26149.) Wt. W. 10698/4046. 500,000. 10/15. M.R.Co., Ltd. Forms/B. 213/6.

[P.T.O.

*For information of the A.G.'s Office at the Base.*

Officers and men who have become casuals, been transferred or joined since last report.

Place In the Field Date 5th March 1918.

| Regtl. Number | Rank | Name | Corps | Nature of casualty, or name of unit from or to which transferred | Date of being struck off or coming on the ration return | Remarks* |
|---|---|---|---|---|---|---|
| 316039 | Sgt. | Davidson J. | RAMC(T) 1/1st Low. Fd Amb | Returned from course with 156 M.G.C. on 1·4·18 | | |
| 316028 | Pte | Purvis J.G. | -do- | attached ADMS 52 Div for duty | off 1·4·18 | Auth: A.D.M.S. 52 Division |
| 4916 | Dr | Mohd. el Sayed Ibrahim | Native A.S.C. att 1/1st Low. Fd Amb | Sick to Hospital | off 1·4·18 | |
| 4869 | " | Massoar Hassan Mohd | -do- | Transferred to AHTD LUDD. Auth:- 156 Bde Administrative Instruction No 5 of 31.3.18. | off 2·4·18 | |
| 5669 | " | Ahmed Khalifa Amran | -do- | | | |
| 5956 | " | Morice Mohd Ahmed | -do- | | | |
| 5990 | " | Mohmed Ahmed Yousal | -do- | | | |
| 5991 | " | Abdel Magid Aly Abd. | -do- | | | |
| 5994 | " | Zaid Mohd Mohd | -do- | | | |
| 6048 | " | Abdel Aziz Khalifa Mohd | -do- | | | |
| 7252 | " | Abdel Rahman Ismail | -do- | | | |
| 7255 | " | Said Mohd el Mousai | -do- | | | |
| 7256 | " | Mohd Ismail Farris | -do- | | | |
| 7257 | " | Abdel Rahim Awad | -do- | | | |
| 8049 | " | Abdel Seleman Ahmed Baner | -do- | | | |
| 8052 | " | Boghati Abou Zaid Embabi | -do- | | | |
| 8056 | " | Ahmed Khalifa Aly | -do- | | | |
| 8469 | " | Aly Ibrahim Yousef | -do- | | | |
| 8553 | " | Abrilam Mohd Behmans | -do- | | | |
| | | Strength Officers | TF | 7 | | |
| | | | TC | 1 | | |
| | | WO | | 1 | | |
| | | QMS | | 1 | | |
| | | S/Sgts | | | | |
| | | Sgts | | 10 | | |
| | | L/Sgts | | 1 | | |
| | | Cpls | TF | 6 | | |
| | | | Reg | 2 | | |
| | | L/C | | 6 | | |
| | | Ptes | | | | |

* State whether absence is of a permanent or temporary nature, adding, in the case of casuals from wounds or disease, any available information for communication to the relatives.

No. of Report 1/13   **FIELD RETURN.**   Army Form B. 213.

(To be furnished by all arms, services and departments (except A.S.C. units) to the A. G.'s Office at the Base in accordance with Field Service Regulations, Part II.)

RETURN showing numbers RATIONED by, and Transport on charge of, [illegible] at [illegible]   5th April 18. Date.

| Detail | Personnel: Officers | Personnel: Other ranks | Personnel: Natives | Animals: Horses: Riding | Animals: Horses: Draught | Animals: Horses: Heavy Draught | Animals: Horses: Pack | Animals: Mules: Large | Animals: Mules: Small | Animals: Camels | Animals: Oxen | Guns, carriages and limbers, showing description | Ammunition wagons and limbers | Machine guns | Aircraft, showing description | Horsed: 4 Wheeled | Horsed: 2 Wheeled | Mechanical: Motor Cars | Mechanical: Tractors | Mechanical: Lorries, showing description | Mechanical: Trucks, showing description | Mechanical: Trailers | Motor Bicycles | Bicycles. | Remarks |
|---|---|---|---|---|---|---|---|---|---|---|---|---|---|---|---|---|---|---|---|---|---|---|---|---|---|
| Effective Strength of Unit | 8 | (a) 184 | | | | | | | | | | | | | | | | | | | | | | | (a) Includes 1 OR with Div HQ 1 OR at Div Concert Party |
| Details, *by Arms* attached to unit as in War Establishment:— | | | | | | | | | | | | | | | | | | | | | | | | | |
| A.S.C. (HT) | | 48 | | | | | | | | | | | | | | | | | | | | | | | |
| Total | 8 | 232 | | | | | | | | | | | | | | | | | | | | | | | |
| War Establishment | 10 | [illegible] | | | | | | | | | | | | | | | | | | | | | | | |
| Wanting to complete (Detail of Personnel and Horses below) | | | | | | | | | | | | | | | | | | | | | | | | | |
| Surplus | 2 | 14 | | | | | | | | | | | | | | | | | | | | | | | |
| *Attached (not to include the details shown above) | | | | | | | | | | | | | | | | | | | | | | | | | |
| Civilians:— Employed with the Unit | | | | | | | | | | | | | | | | | | | | | | | | | |
| Accompanying the Unit | | | | | | | | | | | | | | | | | | | | | | | | | |
| TOTAL RATIONED ... | 2 | 23[illegible] | | | | | | | | | | | | | | | | | | | | | | | |

* In the case of field ambulances, hospitals or depots, the number of patients are to be included here, the names being shown in A. F. A. 36.

James Leitch Lt Col   Signature of Commander.

5/4/18   Date of Despatch.

Demands made on this sheet should consist of personnel required from the Base only, and should not include any demands for personnel which can be completed by promotions or appointments within the **unit.**

Perforated Sheet giving detail of personnel and horses wanting to complete, shown on Army Form B. 213.

No. of Report 164

| Detail of Wanting to Complete. | Drivers: R.A. | Drivers: R.E. | Drivers: A.S.C.(M.T.) | Drivers: Car | Drivers: Lorry | Drivers: Steam | Gunners | Smith Gunners | Range Takers | Farriers: Serjeants | Farriers: Corporals | Shoeing, or Shoeing and Carriage Smiths | Cold Shoers | Wheelers: R.A. | Wheelers: H.T. | Wheelers: M.T. | Saddlers or Harness Makers | Blacksmiths | Bricklayers and Masons | Carpenters and Joiners | Fitters & Turners (R.E.): Wood | Fitters & Turners (R.E.): Iron | Fitters: R.A. | Fitters: Wireless | Plumbers | Electricians: Ordinary | Electricians: W.T. | Signalmen | Engine Drivers: Loco. | Engine Drivers: Field | Air Line Men | Permanent Line Men | Operators, Telegraph | Cablemen | Brigade Section Pioneers | General-duty Pioneers | Signallers | Instrument Repairers | Motor Cyclist | Motor Cyclist Artificers | Telephonists | Clerks | Machine Gunners | Armament Artificers: Fitters | Armament Artificers: Range Finders | Armourers | Storemen | Privates | W.O.'s and N.C.O.'s (by ranks) not included in trade columns: Sgt. ASC (MT) | W.O.'s and N.C.O.'s: Cpl. ASC (MT) | W.O.'s and N.C.O.'s: S/Sgt. RAMC. | W.O.'s and N.C.O.'s | W.O.'s and N.C.O.'s | W.O.'s and N.C.O.'s | W.O.'s and N.C.O.'s | | | | | TOTAL to agree with wanting to complete: Officers | TOTAL to agree with wanting to complete: Other Ranks | Horses: Riding | Horses: Draught | Horses: Heavy Draught | Horses: Pack |
|---|---|---|---|---|---|---|---|---|---|---|---|---|---|---|---|---|---|---|---|---|---|---|---|---|---|---|---|---|---|---|---|---|---|---|---|---|---|---|---|---|---|---|---|---|---|---|---|---|---|---|---|---|---|---|---|---|---|---|---|---|---|---|---|---|---|
| CAVALRY | | | | | | | | | | | | | | | | | | | | | | | | | | | | | | | | | | | | | | | | | | | | | | | | | | | | | | | | | | | | | | | | | |
| R.A. | | | | | | | | | | | | | | | | | | | | | | | | | | | | | | | | | | | | | | | | | | | | | | | | | | | | | | | | | | | | | | | | | |
| R.E. | | | | | | | | | | | | | | | | | | | | | | | | | | | | | | | | | | | | | | | | | | | | | | | | | | | | | | | | | | | | | | | | | |
| INFANTRY | | | | | | | | | | | | | | | | | | | | | | | | | | | | | | | | | | | | | | | | | | | | | | | | | | | | | | | | | | | | | | | | | |
| R.A.M.C. | | | 11 | | | | | | | | | | | | | | | | | | | | | | | | | | | | | | | | | | | | | | | | | | | | | | 1 | 1 | 1 | | | | | | | | | 2 | 14 | 6 | | | |
| A.O.C. | | | | | | | | | | | | | | | | | | | | | | | | | | | | | | | | | | | | | | | | | | | | | | | | | | | | | | | | | | | | | | | | | |
| A.V.C. | | | | | | | | | | | | | | | | | | | | | | | | | | | | | | | | | | | | | | | | | | | | | | | | | | | | | | | | | | | | | | | | | |
| | | | | | | | | | | | | | | | | | | | | | | | | | | | | | | | | | | | | | | | | | | | | | | | | | | | | | | | | | | | | | | | | | | |
| | | | | | | | | | | | | | | | | | | | | | | | | | | | | | | | | | | | | | | | | | | | | | | | | | | | | | | | | | | | | | | | | | | |

Remarks :— 11 Dr. A.S.C. (M.T.) Drivers.
2 Pte. R.A.M.C. Drivers.
13 O.R. A.S.C. (M.T.) required to complete, including 1 Sgt., 1 Cpl.
1 S/Sgt. R.A.M.C. required to complete.

[illegible] Signature of Commander.

[illegible] Field Ambce. R.A.M.C. (T) Unit.

[illegible] Division Formation to which attached.

20th April 1918 Date of Despatch.

(6305) Wt. W2927/M2226. 1,250,000. 6/17. McA. & W., Ltd. (E1348). Forms B2138/8.

[P.T.O.

*For information of the A.G.'s Office at the base.*

Officers and men who have become casuals, been transferred or joined since last report.

Place *In the Field* Date *27th April 1918*

| Regtl. Number | Rank | Name | Corps | Nature of casualty, or name of unit from or to which transferred | Date of being struck off or coming on the ration return | Remarks* |
|---|---|---|---|---|---|---|
| | Capt. | Stansfield R | R.A.M.C. (T.C.) | Joined unit as reinforcement from Hospital | On 3/4/18 | |
| | " | Stansfield R | -do- | To duty with 1/3 Lowl. Fd. Amb. | Off 26/4/18 | |
| 316097 | Pte. | Dickson D | R.A.M.C. (T) 1/1st Low. Fd. Amb. | Deprived of 7 days pay using insolent language to an N.C.O. | 22/4/18 | |
| 316253 | " | Sloan D | -do- | Transfers allotment of 6 per diem from Miss Maggie Sloan, 36 Rockbank St. Mile-end Glasgow to Master Walter Sloan, 36 Rockbank St. Mile-end Glasgow from 24.4.18 | | |
| 31308 | Pte. | McEwan J | R.A.M.C. | (1) Fined 5/- drunk in town. (2) Deprived of 3 days pay and forfeits 4 days pay under R.W. - Absent without leave from 18.4.18 to 24.4.18 | 25/4 | |
| 61143 | " | Gehan G | -do- | (1) Fined 2/6 drunk in town. (2) Deprived of 3 day's pay and forfeits 4 days pay under R.W. - Absent without leave from 18.4.18 to 24.4.18 | 25/4/18 | |
| T/37104 | Dr. | Ackroyd J | A.S.C. (H.T.) att. | Absent without | 25/4/18 | |
| T/35682 | Dr. | Littlewood W | 1/1st Low. Fd. Amb. | leave from 18.4.18 to 24.4.18 | 25/4/18 | |
| T/34282 | Dr. | Farrell W | -do- | Each deprived of 3 days pay and each | 25/4/18 | |
| T4/086[illegible] | Dr. | Bird L ~~Morgan D~~ | -do- | forfeit 4 days pay under R.W. | 25/4/18 | |
| T4/0375[illegible] | Dr. | Morgan D | -do- | Sick to Hospital | Off 25/4/18 | |

Strength

| | | | |
|---|---|---|---|
| Officers | R.A.M.C. (T.F.) | 7 | |
| | R.A.M.C. (T.C.) | 1 | 8 |
| W.O. | | 1 | |
| Q.M.S. | | 1 | |
| S. Sgts. | | 1 | |
| Sgts. | | 10 | |
| L/Sgts. | | 1 | |
| Cpls. | T.F. | 6 | |
| | Reg. | 2 | |
| L/Cpls. | | 6 | |
| Ptes. | | 156 | 184 |

* State whether absence is of a permanent or temporary nature, adding, in the case of casuals from wounds or disease, any available information for communication to the relatives.

**To be made up to and for Saturday in each week**

No. of Report 144

# FIELD RETURN.

Army Form B. 213

(To be furnished by all arms, services, and departments (except A.S.C. units) to the A.G.'s Office at the Base in accordance with Field Service Regulations, Part II.)

RETURN showing numbers (a) Effective strength of Unit. (b) Rationed by Unit. [illegible] Lond. F. Ambce. at In the Field B.E.F. 27th April 1918. Date.

| DETAIL | Personnel: Officers | Personnel: Other ranks | Personnel: Natives | Animals: Horses: Riding | Animals: Horses: Draught | Animals: Horses: Heavy Draught | Animals: Horses: Pack | Animals: Mules: Large | Animals: Mules: Small | Guns, showing description | Ammunition wagons | Machine guns | Aircraft, showing description | Horsed: 4 Wheeled | Horsed: 2 Wheeled | Mechanical: Motor Cars | Mechanical: Tractors | Mechanical: Lorries, showing description | Mechanical: Trucks, showing description | Mechanical: Trailers | Motor Bicycles | Bicycles | Motor Ambulances | REMARKS |
|---|---|---|---|---|---|---|---|---|---|---|---|---|---|---|---|---|---|---|---|---|---|---|---|---|
| Effective Strength of Unit...... | 8 | (a) 184 | | | | | | | | | | | | | | | | | | | | | | (a) Includes 2 O.R. att. D.H.Q. |
| Details *by Arms* attached to unit as in War Establishment:— | | | | | | | | | | | | | | | | | | | | | | | | |
| A.S.C. (M.T.) attached | | 47 | | 8 | 7 | 20 | | | | | | | | 13 | 4 | | | | | | | 1 | | |
| Total | 8 | 231 | | 8 | 7 | 20 | | | | | | | | 13 | 4 | | | | | | | 1 | | |
| War Establishment | 10 | 231 x | | 14 | 7 | 20 | | | | | | | | 13 | 4 | | | | | | 2 | 1 | 7 | x Includes R.A.M.C., A.S.C. (H.T.) and A.S.C. (M.T.) |
| Wanting to complete (Detail of Personnel and Horses below) | 2 | 13 (b) | | 6 | | | | | | | | | | | | | | | | | 2 | | 7 | (b) A.S.C. (M.T.) including 1 Sgt. + 7 Cpl. |
| Surplus | | 13 (c) | | | | | | | | | | | | | | | | | | | | | | (c) Includes 2 Pts. R.A.M.C. 11 Pts. A.S.C. (H.T.) |
| *Attached (not to include the details shown above)........ | | 4 | | | | | | | | | | | | | | | | | | | | | | |
| Civilians:— Employed with the Unit...... | | | | | | | | | | | | | | | | | | | | | | | | Lieut. Rationed in F. Ambce. |
| Accompanying the Unit...... | | | | | | | | | | | | | | | | | | | | | | | | |
| TOTAL RATIONED...... | 8 | 233 | | 8 | 7? | 20 | | | | | | | | | | | | | | | | | | |

* In the case of field ambulances, hospitals or depots, the number of patients are to be included here, the names being shown in A.F.A. 36.

[illegible] Signature of Commander.

27th April 1918 Date of Despatch.

May 1918.

160/2983.

1/1st Lowland F.A.

91

Vol 2

# War Diary

of

1/1st Lowland Field Ambulance RAMC(T)

52nd (Lowland) Division

Vol XXXVI

from 1st May 1918 to 31st May 1918

John W. Leitch Lt Col

O.C. 1/1st LFA. RAMC(T)

411 Army Form C. 2118.

# WAR DIARY
or
~~INTELLIGENCE SUMMARY.~~
(Erase heading not required.)

Instructions regarding War Diaries and Intelligence Summaries are contained in F. S. Regs., Part II. and the Staff Manual respectively. Title pages will be prepared in manuscript.

1/1st Lowland Field Ambulance
52nd (Lowland) Division.

| Place | Date | Hour | Summary of Events and Information | Remarks and references to Appendices |
|---|---|---|---|---|
| M6 b 10,0 Sheet 36A 1/40000 | 1/5/18 | | Difficulty has been experienced in obtaining supply of drugs & dressings on indent since arrival in this area. Indent countersigned by ADMS 52nd Division was not met by No 1 Base Depot M.S. when presented yesterday on the ground that it was not countersigned also by DDMS Corps. Forwarded this indent to ADMS under letter F 38 d 30/4/18 for favour of countersignature by DDMS. Indent was returned to me to-day by ADMS to have column for amount of stores on hand filled in. This was done & indent returned completed as requested with further indents similarly completed. Drew cash on imprest from Field Cashier XI Corps to-day for payment of NCOs & men. Sent 1 Offr (Capt J.W. BURTON) + 25 O.R. to report to OC detachment 15th Field Ambulance at LIGNE for 1 week's duty to assist in making of Corps Rest Camp in accordance with ADMS instructions (W 55 d 1/5/18). They will be rationed by this (1/1st Lowland) Field Ambulance. J.W.L. | |
| M6 b 10,0 Sheet 36A 1/40000 | 2/5/18 | | In consequence of indents for drugs & medical stores being delayed so long before being met I have had to advise MOs i/c Battalions of 155th Bde to apply to nearest CCS for such things as Boric & White lint to tide them over till this ambulance can get its indents met. Cf. letter F 50 of even date to MO i/c 1/8 Scot Rifles. J.W.L. | |

D. D. & L., London, E.C. (A8001) Wt. W1771/M2031 750,000 5/17 Sch. 52 Forms C2.118/14

Instructions regarding War Diaries and Intelligence Summaries are contained in F. S. Regs., Part II. and the Staff Manual respectively. Title pages will be prepared in manuscript.

# WAR DIARY

~~or~~

~~INTELLIGENCE SUMMARY.~~

(*Erase heading not required.*)

412 Army Form C. 2118.

1/1st Lowland Field Ambulance
52nd Lowland Division:

| Place | Date | Hour | Summary of Events and Information | Remarks and references to Appendices |
|---|---|---|---|---|
| MG, b100, Sheet 36A/40000 | 3/5/18 | | Received A.D.M.S. wire SR 9 d/3 5/18 intimating 52nd Div Warning Order that Division less R.A. would be transferred to 18th Corps on 6th, 7th & 8th inst. All ranks are being practised in quick adjustment of S.B.R.s whilst at work in billets in accordance with Divisional orders. Visited 1/3rd Highland Field Ambulance to-day at Ham with a view to getting information about Field Ambulance work on this front. Took Capt MACKENZIE, my 2nd in Command, with me & obtained a lot of useful information from the O.C., Lt.Col. FOGGEY, & his 2 in C Lt HAMSON (a former sergeant of ~~the~~ 1/1st Lowland Field Amb). JWL | |
| ML, b100, Sh 36A/40000 | 4/5/18 | | Received indents for medical stores & dressings to-night from A.D.M.S. office about 1800. That for drugs & dressings is now a fortnight old and the supply of bandages 3", white lint, boric lint, & jaconet, has been cut down to 500, 25 lb, 25 lb & 5 yds respectively – a quite inadequate supply (or allowance) in present circumstances. The amounts ~~that~~ indented for were 1200, 100 lb, 100 lb & 20 yds. No other roller bandages but the 3" size was asked for. Wrote a letter of protest but on second thoughts did not forward it as we will move | |

D. D. & L., London, E.C.
(A5001) Wt. W1771/M2031 750,000 5/17 Sch. 52 Forms/C2118/14

Instructions regarding War Diaries and Intelligence Summaries are contained in F. S. Regs., Part II. and the Staff Manual respectively. Title pages will be prepared in manuscript.

# WAR DIARY

or

~~INTELLIGENCE SUMMARY.~~

(Erase heading not required.)

413 Army Form C. 2118.

1/1st Lowland Field Ambulance
52nd (Lowland) Division

| Place | Date | Hour | Summary of Events and Information | Remarks and references to Appendices |
|---|---|---|---|---|
| M6 b 10,0 Sh 36A 1/40000 | 4 5/18 (Contd) | | into another Corps area in a few days. No supply of drugs or dressings has been received since leaving Egypt: Received RAMC O.O. No 1 d/4 5/18 about 2200 for move to NEUVILLE St VAAST & separate instructions to send 1 Off + 1 OR with bicycle + 3 days rations to go with lorry leaving GRANDE PLACE, AIRE at 1100 tomorrow as billetting party for this unit + Div. San. Sect. Detailed Capt LENNIE for this duty. Made weekly inspection of billets this forenoon. J.W.L. | |
| M6 b 10,0 Sh 36A 1/40000 | 5 5/18 | | Received ADMS SR9 d/5 5/18, time table for Entrainment. Capt LENNIE left as arranged. Detailed Capt BROWNE + 120 OR of this unit to attend the gas school at MAMETZ at 1500 for gas test + experience in accordance with instructions received from ADMS late last night. Capts MACKENZIE + YERLING and 12 O.R. were sent yesterday. J.W.L. | |
| M6 b.10,0 Sh 36A 1/40000 | 6 5/18 | | Received copy of 156th Inf Bde Order 34 respecting entraining of Bde units on 8th. This unit is due at AIRE station at 0808 & leaves at 0908. Received also copy of 52nd Div. Train Order for movement of the transport by road to DIVION tomorrow + on following day (8th) to NEUVILLE ST VAAST. Sent letter F75 of even date to ADMS advising him of proposed appointments to acting ranks in this unit | |

D. D. & L., London, E.C. (A8001) Wt. W1771/M2031 750,000 5/17 Sch. 52 Forms/C2118/14

414 Army Form C. 2118.

Instructions regarding War Diaries and Intelligence Summaries are contained in F. S. Regs., Part II. and the Staff Manual respectively. Title pages will be prepared in manuscript.

# WAR DIARY

or

~~INTELLIGENCE SUMMARY.~~

(Erase heading not required.)

1/1st Lowland Field Ambulance
52nd (Lowland) Division

| Place | Date | Hour | Summary of Events and Information | Remarks and references to Appendices |
|---|---|---|---|---|
| M6.b.10.0 Sh. 36A 1/40000 | 6/5/18 | | Also letter to Capt. BURTON at LIGNE instructing him to rejoin his unit with his party of 25 O.R. tomorrow unless he received orders to the contrary from higher authority. J.W.L. | |
| do | 7/5/18 | | Transport moved off from camp at 1000 to-day, marching out state as under. ASC (HT), 46; horses, riding, 8 draught 37; vehicles, 4-wheeled 13, 2-wheeled, 4. A proportion of the drivers acted as brakesmen. I detailed Capt. BROWNE RAMC(T), who was being sent as MO for the Brigade transport during the march, to act as Unit Transport Officer. Three more motor ambulances reported to-night for duty with this ambulance — 2 Sunbeam cars, & 1 Ford car. Received also from OC 52nd Sanitary Section the motor bicycle lent by this unit. Issued copies of arrangements for collection of sick of brigade units tomorrow, Letter F81 d/7 5/18 to 156th Bde HQ, 1/4th RS, 1/7th RS, 1/7th SR, 1/8th SR, 156 LTMB, & 412th Fld. Coy. RE. Sent copies of Billeting Certificate & Distribution List duly signed by Maire of BLESSY to Bde HQ. for transmission to Branch Requisition Officer. Capt. J.W. BURTON & 25 O.R. duly reported back from duty at Corps Rest Camp LIGNE. J.W.L. | |

D. D. & L., London, E.C.
(A5001) Wt. W1771/M2031 750,000 5/17 Sch. 52 Forms C2.118/14

Instructions regarding War Diaries and Intelligence Summaries are contained in F. S. Regs., Part II. and the Staff Manual respectively. Title pages will be prepared in manuscript.

# WAR DIARY
or
~~INTELLIGENCE SUMMARY.~~

(*Erase heading not required.*)

415 Army Form C. 2118.

1/1st Lowland Field Ambulance
52nd (Lowland) Division

| Place | Date | Hour | Summary of Events and Information | Remarks and references to Appendices |
|---|---|---|---|---|
| VILLERS-AU-BOIS | 8 5/18 | | Unit arrived at ACQ station about 1330 – about 20 minutes behind scheduled time. Marching in strength. RAMC, Off 8, OR. 181. Capt W F MACKENZIE was detailed by me to act as MO with the two motor ambulances left at AIRE station till remainder of Bde left with 2nd train due to leave AIRE at 1808 to-night & thereafter to bring the two motor ambulances on by road. Found on arrival here that NEUVILLE ST VAAST was a heap of bricks & rubble & that Capt. LENNIE (the unit billeting officer) had not managed to secure billets for us until after our train arrived at ACQ. He came down to the station about 1400 with the information that through the ADMS he had at last got billets in VILLERS-AU-BOIS & huts for a Hospital, ~~at~~ and that we were to go there. Reported arrival to ADMS about 1700 & learned from him that this unit would form a Divisional Rest station. Jw L. | |
| Villers-au-Bois | 9 5/18 | | This camp has been left in a rather untidy state. Have had fatigue parties busy since breakfast washing out the floors of huts & cleaning up generally. Am having the kitchens gutted out & ovens improvised from corrugated iron sheets built in by members of the unit. Have arranged a general scheme to provide a dining, reading, & recreation room (combined) | |

Instructions regarding War Diaries and Intelligence Summaries are contained in F. S. Regs., Part II. and the Staff Manual respectively. Title pages will be prepared in manuscript.

# WAR DIARY
or
# ~~INTELLIGENCE SUMMARY.~~

(Erase heading not required.)

416 Army Form C. 2118.

1/1st Lowland Field Ambulance
52nd (Lowland) Division

| Place | Date | Hour | Summary of Events and Information | Remarks and references to Appendices |
|---|---|---|---|---|
| Villers-au-Bois | 9/5/18 (Contd.) | | for patients, a Nissen hut for officers patients with beds, & another Nissen hut as a mess room & anteroom for officer patients. This completes the accommodation at the Dressing Station taken over here. At Douglas Camp I have arranged accommodation for patients O.R. & they will come for meals, tilizen with at hut, to the general dining rooms. Detailed Pte Glendye to act as landscape gardener & to make flower beds & plots about the huts. Detailed Capt J.W. BURTON to report to-day to D.D.M.S. Corps, for temporary duty in accordance with instructions of A.D.M.S. In the late forenoon the A.D.M.S. called & informed me that an attack was expected & that I had better hold the rest camp matter up & prepare to take in "gassed" cases & lightly wounded. There will be accommodation for some 300 men (for short residence only) between the Huts at Dressing Station & at Douglas Camp. Sent Ambulance car to Red Cross stores, HAM-in-ARTOIS, for Medical stores, comforts & hot water bottles urgently required by the 3 Divisional ambulances in case of a hostile attacks. J.W.L. | |
| Villers-au-Bois Army Map B 1/40000 X.19.C.9.9 | 10/5/18 | | Sent Capt R.A. LENNIE 1 sgt. & 9 ptes RAMC with some dressings & equipment to SAVY to form a Detraining centre for Walking Wounded at 0400 in accordance with A.D.M.S. instructions. Written instructions given Capt LENNIE in my F93 d/10/5/18 (see Appendix I) Detailed Bearer Division under Capt. J. BROWN to be ready to proceed to assistance of 1/2nd | APPENDIX I. |

D. D. & L., London, E.C.
(A8001) Wt. W1771/M2031 750,000 5/17 Sch. 52 Forms C2118/14

Instructions regarding War Diaries and Intelligence Summaries are contained in F. S. Regs., Part II. and the Staff Manual respectively. Title pages will be prepared in manuscript.

# WAR DIARY
~~or~~
~~INTELLIGENCE SUMMARY.~~
(*Erase heading not required.*)

417 Army Form C. 2118.

1/1st Lowland Field Ambulance
52nd (Lowland) Division

| Place | Date | Hour | Summary of Events and Information | Remarks and references to Appendices |
|---|---|---|---|---|
| Villers-au-Bois | 10/5/18 | | L.F.A. at AUX REITZ if called upon. J.W.L. | |
| do | 11/5/18 | | 4 O.R. proceeded to-day on 14 days leave to U.K. under divisional arrangements. ~~also~~ Short leave is being granted to 52nd Division only at present as a special concession. Went to Ham-in-Artois to get Red Cross Stores required for formation of Rest Camp. One Foden Thresh Disinfector reported to-day for duty with this Ambulance. J.W.L. | |
| Villers-au-Bois | 12/5/18 | | Thresh disinfector was sent to-day to O/c Baths BERTHONVAL FARM in accordance with A.D.M.S. instructions. Managed to get the blankets & clothing of all patients in hospital disinfected before it went. Sent 1 Ford Motor Ambulance to report to OC Detraining Centre for duty in emergencies in accordance with A.D.M.S. instructions. Met the RMOs of ~~7~~ 156th Bde at H.Q. 1/7th Scot. Rifles MONT St. ELOY at 1100 to demonstrate to them the ~~[illegible]~~ Thomas outfit & application of Thomas Splint for fractures of the thigh. Red cross stores arrived to-day. J.W.L. | |
| Villers-au-Bois | 13/5/18 | | The expected enemy attack has not yet materialized & I have taken the chance of proceeding with the rest camp plans. These have had to be delayed, however, owing to the number of acute cases sent here by ambulances ~~[illegible]~~ of the Division instead of to the C.C.S. Sent letter F121 of even date to ADMS asking whether some definition of the category "slight sick cases" to be taken by this ambulance or | |

D. D. & L., London, E.C.
(A8001) Wt. W1771/M2031 750,000 5/17 Sch. 32 Forms/C2118/14

Instructions regarding War Diaries and Intelligence Summaries are contained in F. S. Regs., Part II. and the Staff Manual respectively. Title pages will be prepared in manuscript.

# WAR DIARY
or
~~INTELLIGENCE SUMMARY.~~
(Erase heading not required.)

418 Army Form C. 2118.

1/1st Lowland Field Ambulance
52nd (Lowland) Division

| Place | Date | Hour | Summary of Events and Information | Remarks and references to Appendices |
|---|---|---|---|---|
| Villers-au-Bois | 13/5/18 | | transfer from other ambulances could be given. Motor ambulance sent by me to be at 8th C.C.S. WAVRANS at 0800 to bring back dentist in accordance with A.D.M.S. W 119 d/12/5/18 returned with Capt. Ward who stated that his orders were to go to 60th Field Ambulance De La HAIE to day & to this ambulance on Wednesday. I arranged to send him on, therefore, to De La Haie (about 2 Kilos) & send any dental cases from this Division there for treatment to-day. In all some 16 cases were thus sent ~~[illegible]~~ & treated. Admitted 4 cases of Scabies from 51st Division sent here as notified to me in A.D.M.S. W126 d/13/5/18. Late in the evening I received A.D.M.S. W128 that Evacuation Table No. 1 would read "Scabies will now be sent to Div. Rest Stn. 1st L.F.A. J.W.L. | |
| VILLERS-AU-BOIS | 14/5/18 | | Rest camp is gradually coming into being. Floor plots have been made at the dressing station & a large oven improvised in place of the very makeshift fire-place & hot plate which previously existed. Sick parades & the number of cases transferred to rest camp which have to be evacuated as unsuitable for treatment as convalescents (i.e. too acutely ill to be fit for duty in 2 or 3 weeks time) hamper the work of the "Rest" Station. Some 21 cases of "scabies" have been sent down to | |

D. D. & L., London, E.C. (A8001) Wt. W1771/M2031 750,000 5/17 Sch. 52 Forms/C2118/14

WAR DIARY

~~or~~

~~INTELLIGENCE SUMMARY.~~

(Erase heading not required.)

Instructions regarding War Diaries and Intelligence Summaries are contained in F. S. Regs., Part II. and the Staff Manual respectively. Title pages will be prepared in manuscript.

419 Army Form C. 2118.

1/1st Lowland Field Ambulance
52nd (Lowland) Division

| Place | Date | Hour | Summary of Events and Information | Remarks and references to Appendices |
|---|---|---|---|---|
| VILLERS-AU BOIS. | 14 5/18 (Contd.) | | day for admission + the diagnosis in 15 of them has been altered by me to "Phthiriasis" after examination. Arrangements are in progress for the improvising of a Serbian barrel & the giving of a hot bath to cases of true scabies. JWL | |
| Do | 15 5/18 | | In accordance with ADMS W119 d/12 5/18 I sent motor ambulance to be at 8th CCS WAVRANS at 0800 for dental surgeon. It returned empty + I then sent it back to No. 12 Stationary Hospital St. POL, but it again returned without a dental surgeon. In both cases the dental surgeons replied that their instructions were to be at 1/1st LFA + 60th Fld Amb on Tuesdays Thursdays + Saturdays. Forwarded their minutes along with mine to ADMS. Serbian barrel (improvised) has been completed + is in use to-day. A shelter is being erected over a full sized Zinc bath which I obtained last night through the Town Major. Wrote report, F139 (ADMS) of even date on "arrangements made for treating scabies" in reply to his R410/7 of even date. (See APPENDIX II) JWL | APPENDIX II |
| VILLERS-AU BOIS | 16 5/18 | | Improvised Serbian barrel is working efficiently. Attended lecture on gas at 1/3rd LFA to-day given to MOs of Division by Col ELLIOT. Numbers in this "Rest Stn" are now 120. Sick parades attend daily from Details camp + other units in neighbourhood. JWL | |

Instructions regarding War Diaries and Intelligence Summaries are contained in F. S. Regs., Part II. and the Staff Manual respectively. Title pages will be prepared in manuscript.

# WAR DIARY
~~or~~
~~INTELLIGENCE SUMMARY.~~
(*Erase heading not required.*)

420 Army Form C. 2118.

1/1st Lowland Field Ambulance
52nd (Lowland) Division

| Place | Date | Hour | Summary of Events and Information | Remarks and references to Appendices |
|---|---|---|---|---|
| VILLERS-AU BOIS | 17 5/18 | | Capt. A. VERLING RAMC (T.C.) left to-day for London to report to W.O. for discharge on expiry of his contract. This leaves 5 officers (including the 2 i/c) at this Amb. HQ. the 6th, Capt LENNIE, is O/c the Detraining Centre & the 7th Capt. BURTON is on temporary duty at 18th Corps HQ. Sent No 316294 Pte P.G. CARRUTHERS of this unit to report for temporary duty as a clerk in A.D.M.S. office in reply to special request from A.D.M.S. Pte Carruthers reported there last night. J.W.L. | |
| VILLERS-AU-BOIS | 18 5/18 | | Received Copy No 6 of Medical Arrangements No 2. In accordance with A.D.M.S. wire W151 d/17 5/18 representatives from this Field Ambulance were sent to attend a transport demonstration by 51st DIVISION at 1445 to-day. They were duly impressed with the condition of harness, wagons, & animals shown them at each unit's transport. In particular two wagons were shown them at the Train, one of which might easily have gained a prize at a trade exhibition in the halls of an International Exhibition. Axles, chains on tail board, & all brass & steel work was burnished brightly; & paint & wood-work was as nearly perfect as could be. The lesson intended to be learned from the demonstration has not been stated. J.W.L. | |
| VILLERS-AU-BOIS | 19/5/18 | | Sent 1 G.S. wagon to day to MINGOVAL to O/c DETRAINING centre for walking wounded in accordance with A.D.M.S. instructions in his SR 42 d/18 5/18. Forwarded | |

D. D. & L., London, E.C.
(A8001) Wt. W1771/M2031 750,000 5/17 Sch. 52 Forms/C2118/14

421 Army Form C. 2118.

# WAR DIARY

~~or~~

~~INTELLIGENCE SUMMARY.~~

(Erase heading not required.)

Instructions regarding War Diaries and Intelligence Summaries are contained in F. S. Regs., Part II. and the Staff Manual respectively. Title pages will be prepared in manuscript.

1/1st Lowland Field Ambulance
52nd (Lowland) Division

| Place | Date | Hour | Summary of Events and Information | Remarks and references to Appendices |
|---|---|---|---|---|
| VILLERS-AU-BOIS. | 19/5/18 (Contd) | | letter F170 of even date to A.D.M.S. showing detail of stores with which the wagon was loaded (see APPENDIX III). Received A.D.M.S. letter R497/4 d/18/5/17 forwarding DDMS XVIII Corps instructions to the effect that Divisional Rest stations should now keep up to 100 cases. There are already 136 patients here. Sent 2 oxygen cylinders with key & valve to OC 1/2nd LFA in accordance with A.D.M.S. R510/3 d 19/5/18. JWL | APPENDIX III |
| VILLERS-AU-BOIS | 20/5/18 | | Sent Capt W. F. MACKENZIE to 118 Chinese Labour Coy Camp at 0845 to inspect morning sick etc in accordance with A.D.M.S. R493/1 d/19/5/18. He will visit that camp daily until further orders. Sent 2 pairs leather & 4 prs cotton gloves & 2 ground sheets to orderly in charge of Foden Disinfector at BERTHONVAL FARM in accordance with A.D.M.S. R530/4 of even date. JWL | |
| VILLERS-AU-BOIS | 21/5/18 | | Capt MOWBERRY Dental surgeon from 12th Stationary Hospital ST POL visited today for duty in accordance with instructions. JWL | |
| VILLERS-AU-BOIS | 22/5/18 | | Visited BRCS at OUVE-WIRQUIN to get mosquito netting authorized by ADMS & DDMS. Visited the Retraining centre (now moved to MINGOVAL) on outward journey, & left 100 tin mugs for patients there on return journey. JWL | |
| VILLERS-AU-BOIS | 23/5/18 | | Called at 20th DIV HQ at 1030 accompanied by 1 other officer of this unit for purpose of being shown round the Divisional ambulances in accordance | |

D. D. & L., London, E.C.
(A8001) Wt. W1771/M2031 750,000 5/17 Sch. 52 Forms C2118/14

Instructions regarding War Diaries and Intelligence Summaries are contained in F. S. Regs., Part II. and the Staff Manual respectively. Title pages will be prepared in manuscript.

# WAR DIARY

~~or~~

~~INTELLIGENCE SUMMARY.~~

*(Erase heading not required.)*

422 Army Form C. 2118.

1/1st Lowland Field Ambulance
52nd (Lowland) Division

| Place | Date | Hour | Summary of Events and Information | Remarks and references to Appendices |
|---|---|---|---|---|
| VILLERS-AU-BOIS | 23/5/18 (Contd) | | with R539/4 of A.D.M.S. 52nd Division d/22 5/18. Saw A.D.M.S. 20th Div. who had a programme ready for us & went on to 61st Field Ambulance at ABLAIN-ST-NAZAIRE. After being shown round by the O.C., Lt Col McLELLAN, I left Capt LENNIE (the officer who accompanied me) to be taken to A.D.S. & remain the night for instruction, & proceeded to 62nd F.A. & then to 60th F.A. where was the Rest Camp of 20th Division. Got back to my own H.Q. about 1800. I found the O.C. of all 3 Field Ambulances most willing to show me all the arrangements for dealing with sick & wounded & to answer any questions I felt inclined to ask. Capt. Harry A.C. SWERTZ (T.C.) reported for duty with this Ambulance late to-night. J.W.L. | |
| VILLERS-AU-BOIS | 24/5/18 | | Demonstrated the application of "Thomas" Splint as laid down in Circular detailing the drill by numbers to N.C.Os of this unit at 1030. Capt H.A.C. SWERTZ was also present. Afterwards I sent Capt SWERTZ to report to O.C. 1/5th R.S.F. for duty as M.O. vice Capt S. CHURCHILL RAMC (T.C.) time expired. Capt SWERTZ has already had 2 years service as a T.C. Officer & is not new to work with a Battalion as M.O. The M.T. drivers lent to this ambulance were returned to | 2 |

D. D. & L., London, E.C.
(A8001) Wt. W1771/M2031 750,000 5/17 Sch. 52 Forms C2118/14

Instructions regarding War Diaries and Intelligence Summaries are contained in F. S. Regs., Part II. and the Staff Manual respectively. Title pages will be prepared in manuscript.

# WAR DIARY
or
~~INTELLIGENCE SUMMARY.~~
*(Erase heading not required.)*

423 Army Form C. 2118.

1/1st Lowland Field Ambulance
52nd (Lowland) Division

| Place | Date | Hour | Summary of Events and Information | Remarks and references to Appendices |
|---|---|---|---|---|
| VILLERS-AU-BOIS | 24/5/18 | | H.Q. 52nd M.T. Coy yesterday in accordance with instruction of A.D.M.S. Ambulance Cars & drivers of 52nd Division have now arrived from Egypt & 7 have reported with their cars for duty with this unit. Capt LENNIE reported back from his visit to A.D.S. 61st Field Ambulance to-night. JWL | |
| VILLERS-AU-BOIS | 25/5/18 | | Capt R.A. LENNIE O/c Entraining Centre visited his station at MINGOVAL to-day. He is now staying at HQ of this ambulance on account of shortage of M.O.s in accordance with A.D.M.S. letter R 544/4 d/21.5.18 & is visiting the Entraining Centre periodically. JWL<br>Detailed Capt J. BROWNE to proceed at 1000 to-day to H.Q. 73rd Field Ambulance for visit to A.D.S. of that unit for purpose of gaining information in accordance with A.D.M.S. R 539/4 d/22.5.18. Capt W.F. MACKENZIE ceases visiting 118th Chinese Labour Corps Camp after to-day; A.D.M.S. R 493/1 d/25.5.18 JWL | |
| VILLERS-AU-BOIS | 26/5/18 | | Received A.D.M.S. R 589/4 d/25.5.18 notifying probable reopening of R.A.M.C. School of instruction at ELNES. JWL | |
| VILLERS-AU-BOIS | 27/5/18 | | There was some shelling of the town & neighbourhood early this morning & one shell large fell just outside the dispensary. Some bottles were broken including one with strong $H_2SO_4$ but fortunately there were no casualties. | |

D. D. & L., London, E.C. (A5001) Wt. W1771/M2031 750,000 5/17 Sch. 52 Forms C2. 8/14

Instructions regarding War Diaries and Intelligence Summaries are contained in F. S. Regs., Part II. and the Staff Manual respectively. Title pages will be prepared in manuscript.

# WAR DIARY

~~or~~

~~INTELLIGENCE SUMMARY.~~

(*Erase heading not required.*)

424 Army Form C. 2118.

1/1st Lowland Field Ambulance
52nd (Lowland) Division

| Place | Date | Hour | Summary of Events and Information | Remarks and references to Appendices |
|---|---|---|---|---|
| VILLERS-AU-BOIS | 27/5/18 (Contd) | | Seed potatoes, cabbage plants, etc drawn yesterday from agricultural (Civil) farm at BERTHONVAL are being planted to-day in the ground prepared for them. Shelling continued intermittently throughout the day - chiefly high explosive & shrapnel bursting at a considerable height & directly overhead. It would appear that the enemy was attempting to register for his artillery | |
| | | 2030 | Sent 36 bearers & one sgt to report to O.C. 1/3rd L.F.A. Main Dressing Stn AUX RIETZ in accordance with A.D.M.S. SR 79 of even date. Returned 20 prs cotton & 20 prs leather gloves to D.A.D.O.S. in accordance with A.D.M.S. instruction | J.W.L. |
| VILLERS-AU-BOIS. | 28/5/18 | | There was a considerable amount of bombing by enemy planes in neighbourhood last night: little or no shelling. Report is confirmed that a shell (enemy) fell in a hut occupied by personnel of 1/2nd Lowland Field Ambulance at MONT ST ELOY yesterday morning killing 12 & more or less severely wounding 17 others. Sent 1 off (Capt. J. BROWN) & 2 N.C.Os of this unit to-day to attend R.A.M.C. school of instruction at ELNES in accordance with A.D.M.S. instructions in R 589/4 d 27/5/18. Rendered Report F230 d/28/5/18 to A.D.M.S. on the method adopted in this unit to ensure that all personnel were made acquainted with Unit, Divisional, etc, orders. in reply to his R 581/1 d/25/5/18. | J.W.L. |
| VILLERS-AU-BOIS. | 29/5/18 | | Examined some 40 men of 986th Div Employment Coy & returned completed rolls to O.C. | |

Instructions regarding War Diaries and Intelligence Summaries are contained in F. S. Regs., Part II. and the Staff Manual respectively. Title pages will be prepared in manuscript.

# WAR DIARY

or

~~INTELLIGENCE SUMMARY.~~

(Erase heading not required.)

425 Army Form C. 2118.

1/1st Lowland Field Ambulance
52nd (Lowland) Division

| Place | Date | Hour | Summary of Events and Information | Remarks and references to Appendices |
|---|---|---|---|---|
| VILLERS-AU-BOIS | 29 5/18 (Cont'd) | | In accordance with A.D.M.S. letter R621/17 d/27 5/18. Had 6 Hospital Marquees brought by motor ambulances from ESTREE-CAUCHIE in accordance with A.D.M.S. W286 of even date received about 1930. Only erected three of them, however, before 2200 as they were not camouflaged in any way & we have not so far been able to get "Cutch" from Ordnance for staining canvas. Wrote ~~A.D.M.S.~~ letter F234 to ADMS advising him of this & asking whether supply of Cutch & of red paint or cloth for large Geneva crosses could be expedited. J.W.S. | |
| VILLERS-AU-BOIS | 30 5/18 | | In accordance with A.D.M.S. RC41/5 d/29 5/18 I sent Capt W.F. MACKENZIE this morning to report for temporary duty with 1/2nd L.F.A at MONT ST ELOY. This leaves myself, Capt A.D. DOWNES, & the Q.M. (Capt REID) available for duty with this ambulance. The others are employed as follows. Capt MACKENZIE as above; Capt LENNIE O/c Entraining Centre (but stays at H.Q. + visits periodically until his presence is required continuously at Entraining centre, MINGOVAL); Capt. BURTON att. for duty temporarily to D.D.M.S. at Corps H.Q. Capt. BROWN at R.A.M.C. school, ELNES. Supply of Cutch arrived to-day & is being applied to the Tents. Have managed to procure 2 lb of red paint & have improvised a large Geneva Cross on the ground | |

D. D. & L., London, E.C. (A8001) Wt. W1771/M2031 750,000 5/17 Sch. 52 Forms/C2118/14

426 Army Form C. 2118.

Instructions regarding War Diaries and Intelligence Summaries are contained in F. S. Regs., Part II. and the Staff Manual respectively. Title pages will be prepared in manuscript.

# WAR DIARY
*or*
# ~~INTELLIGENCE SUMMARY.~~

(*Erase heading not required.*)

1/1st Lowland Field Ambulance
52nd (Lowland) Division

| Place | Date | Hour | Summary of Events and Information | Remarks and references to Appendices |
|---|---|---|---|---|
| VILLERS-AU-BOIS | 30 5/18 (Contd) | | by utilizing the concrete floors of two small huts which I found among the grass. These, when whitewashed, show up the red cross very well indeed. J.W.L. | |
| VILLERS-AU-BOIS (ARMY MAP B 1/40000 X19.C.4.4) | 31 5/18 | | Supply of cutch received yesterday sufficed to completely darken 4 marquees, & the remaining two were camouflaged with mud. All six were erected & ready for use by 22.00 last night. This place is being intermittently shelled still, & a M.T. wagon driver was brought in this afternoon unconscious from being blown up in his wagon by a H.E. shell in the M.T. park. The shells are not numerous but are landing all round in dangerous proximity to the dressing station, on the road through the village & past our transport. There have been no casualties to patients or personnel so far. By instructions of A.D.M.S. I sent 1 officer (Capt A.D. DOWNES) to 20th Divl Gas Centre, CARENCY, to-night to remain there till Friday morning, 4/7/18. Lieut HAMAKER of Res. Corps. USA att B.E.F. was sent by OC 62nd Field Amb. to replace him in accordance with arrangements. The two NCOs sent to RAMC School of Instruction reported back for duty late to-night. They brought a note from the Adj. simply stating that they were returned. Capt BROWNE has not been returned. | |

John W. Leitch Lt Col
O.C. 1/1st L.F.A. R.A.M.C.(T).

D. D. & L., London, E.C.
(A8001) Wt. W1771/M2031 750,000 5/17 Sch. 52 Forms C2118/14

Demands made on this sheet should consist of personnel required from the Base only, and should not include any demands for personnel which can be completed by promotions or appointments within the **unit.**

**Perforated Sheet giving detail of personnel and horses wanting to complete, shown on Army Form B. 213.**

No. of Report 145.

| Detail of Wanting to Complete. | Drivers: R.A. | Drivers: R.E. | Drivers: A.S.C. (M.T.) | Drivers: Car | Drivers: Lorry | Drivers: Steam | Gunners | Smith Gunners | Range Takers | Farriers: Serjeants | Farriers: Corporals | Shoeing, or Shoeing and Carriage Smiths | Cold Shoers | Wheelers: R.A. | Wheelers: H.T. | Wheelers: M.T. |
|---|---|---|---|---|---|---|---|---|---|---|---|---|---|---|---|---|
| CAVALRY | | | | | | | | | | | | | | | | |
| R.A. | | | | | | | | | | | | | | | | |
| R.E. | | | | | | | | | | | | | | | | |
| INFANTRY | | | | | | | | | | | | | | | | |
| R.A.M.C. | | | 8 | | | | | | | | | | | | | |
| A.O.C. | | | | | | | | | | | | | | | | |
| A.V.C. | | | | | | | | | | | | | | | | |
| | | | | | | | | | | | | | | | | |
| | | | | | | | | | | | | | | | | |

| Detail of Wanting to Complete. | Saddlers or Harness Makers | Blacksmiths | Bricklayers and Masons | Carpenters and Joiners | Fitters & Turners (R.E.): Wood | Fitters & Turners (R.E.): Iron | Fitters: R.A. | Fitters: Wireless | Plumbers | Electricians: Ordinary | Electricians: W.T. | Signalmen | Engine Drivers: Loco. | Engine Drivers: Field | Air Line Men | Permanent Line Men | Operators, Telegraph |
|---|---|---|---|---|---|---|---|---|---|---|---|---|---|---|---|---|---|
| CAVALRY | | | | | | | | | | | | | | | | | |
| R.A. | | | | | | | | | | | | | | | | | |
| R.E. | | | | | | | | | | | | | | | | | |
| INFANTRY | | | | | | | | | | | | | | | | | |
| R.A.M.C. | | | | | | | | | | | | | | | | | |
| A.O.C. | | | | | | | | | | | | | | | | | |
| A.V.C. | | | | | | | | | | | | | | | | | |
| | | | | | | | | | | | | | | | | | |
| | | | | | | | | | | | | | | | | | |

| Detail of Wanting to Complete. | Cablemen | Brigade Section Pioneers | General-duty Pioneers | Signallers | Instrument Repairers | Motor Cyclist | Motor Cyclist Artificers | Telephonists | Clerks | Machine Gunners | Armament Artificers: Fitters | Armament Artificers: Range Finders | Armourers | Storemen | Privates |
|---|---|---|---|---|---|---|---|---|---|---|---|---|---|---|---|
| CAVALRY | | | | | | | | | | | | | | | |
| R.A. | | | | | | | | | | | | | | | |
| R.E. | | | | | | | | | | | | | | | |
| INFANTRY | | | | | | | | | | | | | | | |
| R.A.M.C. | | | | | | | | | | | | | | | |
| A.O.C. | | | | | | | | | | | | | | | |
| A.V.C. | | | | | | | | | | | | | | | |
| | | | | | | | | | | | | | | | |
| | | | | | | | | | | | | | | | |

| Detail of Wanting to Complete. | W.O.'s and N.C.O.'s (by ranks) not included in trade columns: Sgts (M.T.) A.S.C. | W.O.'s and N.C.O.'s: Cpls (M.T.) A.S.C. | | | | | | | | | | TOTAL to agree with wanting to complete: Officers | TOTAL: Other Ranks | Horses: Riding | Horses: Draught | Horses: Heavy Draught | Horses: Pack |
|---|---|---|---|---|---|---|---|---|---|---|---|---|---|---|---|---|---|
| CAVALRY | | | | | | | | | | | | | | | | | |
| R.A. | | | | | | | | | | | | | | | | | |
| R.E. | | | | | | | | | | | | | | | | | |
| INFANTRY | | | | | | | | | | | | | | | | | |
| R.A.M.C. | 1 | 1 | | | | | | | | | | 2 | 10 | 6 | | | |
| A.O.C. | | | | | | | | | | | | | | | | | |
| A.V.C. | | | | | | | | | | | | | | | | | |
| | | | | | | | | | | | | | | | | | |
| | | | | | | | | | | | | | | | | | |

Remarks :— 11 Dr. A.S.C. (H.T.) surplus
10 O.R. A.S.C. (M.T.) including 1 Sgt + 1 Cpl required to complete.

John W. Leitch Lt Col. Signature of Commander.

1/1 Low. Fd. Ambce. R.A.M.C. (T.F.) Unit.

52 Div. Formation to which attached.

4th May 1918. Date of Despatch.

(6305) Wt. W2927/M2226. 1,250,000. 6/17. McA. & W., Ltd. (E1348). Forms B2138/8.

[P.T.O.

*For information of the A.G.'s Office at the base.*

A.S.C.

Officers and men who have become casuals, been transferred or joined since last report.

Place In the Field Date 4th May 1918

| Regtl. Number | Rank | Name | | Corps | Nature of casualty, or name of unit from or to which transferred | Date of being struck off or coming on the ration return | Remarks* |
|---|---|---|---|---|---|---|---|
| T4/161021 | Dr. | Arrowsmith | J | 52 Div Train A.S.C. | from Div Train for duty with Train Wagons attd. | on 28 4/18 | |
| T4/161021 | Dr. | Arrowsmith | J | -do- | Retd to Div Train with Wagon | off 3 5/18 | |
| M2/162166 | " | Scott | W. | XI Corps Troops MT Coy A.S.C. | attached for duty with 3 | on 30 4/18 | |
| M2/055913 | " | Nicholls | D.H. | -do. | Ambce motor Cars | on 30 4/18 | |
| M2/269418 | " | Loisby | H.S. | -do- | Car nos. 15966: 19553: 14376. | on 30 4/18 | |

* State whether absence is of a permanent or temporary nature, adding, in the case of casuals from wounds or disease, any available information for communication to the relatives.

*For information of the A.G.'s Office at the base.*

Officers and men who have become casuals, been transferred or joined since last report.

Place In the Field    Date 4th May 1918.

| Regtl. Number | Rank | Name | Corps | Nature of casualty, or name of unit from or to which transferred | Date of being struck off or coming on the ration return | Remarks* |
|---|---|---|---|---|---|---|
| 316201 | Sgt. | Bain J. | R.A.M.C.(T) 1/1st Low. Fd. Ambce. | Re-engaged under Mil. Ser. Act from 23.3.18. Bounty £15 claimed on AFW3428 on 28.4.18. | | |
| 316010 | A/L/Cpl. Pte. | Campbell D. | -do- | Re-engaged under Mil. Ser. Act from 16.4.18. Bounty of £15 claimed on AFW3428 on 28.4.18. | | |
| 31308 | Pte. | McEwan J. | R.A.M.C. | Sick to Hosp. | Off 1/5/18 | |
| 316131 | " | Henderson R. | RAMC 1/1st Low. Fd. Amb. | Sick to Hosp. | Off 3/5/18. | |
| 316170 | Cpl. | Kenny E.W. | -do- | Continues to draw addl. pay @ 6d. per diem as dispensers from 1.4.18 to 30.4.18 | | |
| 316168 | Sgt. | Meldrum A.A. | -do- | | | |
| 316277 | Pte. | Sloan D. | -do- | Continues to draw working pay @ 1/- per diem less 5d. Corps Pay as shoemaker from 1.4.18 to 30.4.18 | | |
| 316264 | " | Edington A. | -do- | Continues to draw working pay @ 1/- per diem less 5d. Corps Pay as Regt. Tailor from 1.4.18 to 30.4.18 | | |
| 316076 | " | Harvey A. | -do- | Continues to draw addl. pay @ 6d. per diem less 5d. Corps Pay as asst. Coy. acct. 1.4.18 to 30.4. | | |
| 42101 | " | Ward J. | R.A.M.C. | Absent from Billet without leave. 7 days C.C. | 3/5/18 | |
| 45956 | " | Finlay J. | -do- | Absent from Billet without leave. 7 days C.C. | 3/5/18 | |
| 56142 | " | Adams G. | -do- | Absent from Billet without leave. 7 days C.C. | 3/5/18. | |
| | | Strength. | | | | |
| | | Officers T.F. | 7 | | | |
| | | T.C. | 1 8 | | | |
| | | W.O. | 1 | | | |
| | | Q.M.S. | 1 | | | |
| | | S/Sgt. | 1 | | | |
| | | Sgt. | 10 | | | |
| | | Q.M.S. | 1 | | | |
| | | Cpls. T.F. | 6 | | | |
| | | — Reg. | 2 | | | |
| | | L/Cpls. | 6 | | | |
| | | Ptes. | 154 182 | | | |
| | | Category 'A' RAMC. O.R. | 182 | | | |

* State whether absence is of a permanent or temporary nature, adding, in the case of casuals from wounds or disease, any available information for communication to the relatives.

**To be made up to and for Saturday in each week**

No. of Report 185

## FIELD RETURN.

Army Form B. 213

(To be furnished by all arms, services, and departments (except A.S.C. units) to the A.G.'s Office at the Base in accordance with Field Service Regulations, Part II.)

RETURN showing numbers (a) Effective strength of Unit. (b) Rationed by Unit. 1/2nd Low Fd Ambce R.A.M.C. at In the Field 4th May 1918 Date.

| DETAIL | Personnel | | | Animals | | | | | | Guns and transport vehicles | | | | | | | | | | | | | | REMARKS |
|---|---|---|---|---|---|---|---|---|---|---|---|---|---|---|---|---|---|---|---|---|---|---|---|---|
| | | | | Horses | | | | Mules | | | | | | Horsed | | Mechanical | | | | | | | | |
| | Officers | Other ranks | Natives | Riding | Draught | Heavy Draught | Pack | Large | Small | Guns, showing description | Ammunition wagons | Machine guns | Aircraft, showing description | 4 Wheeled | 2 Wheeled | Motor Cars | Tractors | Lorries, showing description | Trucks, showing description | Trailers | Motor Bicycles | Bicycles | Motor Ambulances | |
| Effective Strength of Unit...... | 8 | (a) 182 | | | | | | | | | | | | | | | | | | | | | | (a) Includes 1 OR att Div Concert Party<br>" 1 OR at D.H.Q. |
| Details *by Arms* attached to unit as in War Establishment:— | | | | | | | | | | | | | | | | | | | | | | | | |
| A.S.C. (H.T.) attached | – | 47 | | 8 | 17 | 20 | | | | | | | | 13 | 4 | | | | | | | 1 | | |
| A.S.C. (M.T.) attached | – | 3 | | | | | | | | | | | | | | | | | | | 2(b) | | 3 | 1 cycle temp. att 52 Div San Sect. |
| Total | 8 | 232 | | 8 | 17 | 20 | | | | | | | | 13 | 4 | | | | | | 2 | 1 | 3 | |
| War Establishment | 10 | 231 | | 14 | 17 | 20 | | | | | | | | 13 | 4 | | | | | | 2 | 1 | 7 | |
| Wanting to complete (Detail of Personnel and Horses below) | 2 | 10(c) | | 6 | | | | | | | | | | | | | | | | | | | 4 | A.S.C. (M.T.) Including 1 Cpl M Cble. |
| Surplus | | 11(d) | | | | | | | | | | | | | | | | | | | | | | A.S.C. (H.T.) |
| *Attached (not to include the details shown above)........ | | 4 | | | | | | | | | | | | | | | | | | | | | | Sick retained in Fd Ambce. |
| Civilians:— Employed with the Unit...... | | | | | | | | | | | | | | | | | | | | | | | | |
| Accompanying the Unit...... | | | | | | | | | | | | | | | | | | | | | | | | |
| TOTAL RATIONED...... | 8 | 234 | | 8 | 17 | 20 | | | | | | | | [illegible] | [illegible] | | | | | | | | | |

* In the case of field ambulances, hospitals or depots, the number of patients are to be included here, the names being shown in A.F.A. 36.

[illegible signature] Lt Col. Signature of Commander.

4th May 1918 Date of Despatch.

Perforated Sheet giving detail of personnel and horses wanting to complete, shown on Army Form B. 213.

Number of Report 146.

| Detail of Wanting to Complete. | Drivers. | | | | | | Gunners | Smith Gunners | Range Takers | Farriers | | Shoeing, or Shoeing and Carriage Smiths | Cold Shoers | Wheelers | | | Saddlers or Harness Makers | Blacksmiths | Bricklayers and Masons | Carpenters and Joiners | Fitters & Turners (R. E.) | | Fitters | | Plumbers | Electricians | | Signalmen |
|---|---|---|---|---|---|---|---|---|---|---|---|---|---|---|---|---|---|---|---|---|---|---|---|---|---|---|---|---|
| | R. A. | R. E. | A. S. C. M.T. | Car | Lorry | Steam | | | | Serjeants | Corporals | | | R. A. | H. T. | M. T. | | | | | Wood | Iron | R. A. | Wireless | | Ordinary | W. T. | |
| CAVALRY | | | | | | | | | | | | | | | | | | | | | | | | | | | | |
| R. A. | | | | | | | | | | | | | | | | | | | | | | | | | | | | |
| R. E. | | | | | | | | | | | | | | | | | | | | | | | | | | | | |
| INFANTRY | | | | | | | | | | | | | | | | | | | | | | | | | | | | |
| R. A. M. C. | | | 5 | | | | | | | | | | | | | | | | | | | | | | | | | |
| A. O. C. | | | | | | | | | | | | | | | | | | | | | | | | | | | | |
| A. V. C. | | | | | | | | | | | | | | | | | | | | | | | | | | | | |

| Detail of Wanting to Complete. | Engine Drivers | | Air Line Men | Permanent Line Men | Operators, Telegraph | Cablemen | Brigade Section Pioneers | General-duty Pioneers | Signallers | Instrument Repairers | Motor Cyclists | Motor Cyclist Artificers | Telephonists | Clerks | Machine Gunners | Armament Artificers | | Armourers | Storemen | Privates | W.O's. and N.C.O's (by ranks) not included in trade columns. | | | | | | | | | | | TOTAL to agree with wanting to complete | | Horses | | | |
|---|---|---|---|---|---|---|---|---|---|---|---|---|---|---|---|---|---|---|---|---|---|---|---|---|---|---|---|---|---|---|---|---|---|---|---|---|---|
| | Loco. | Field | | | | | | | | | | | | | | Fitters | Range Finders | | | | Sgt ASC MT | Cpls ASC MT | | | | | | | | | | Officers | Other Ranks | Riding | Draught | Heavy Draught | Pack |
| CAVALRY | | | | | | | | | | | | | | | | | | | | | | | | | | | | | | | | | | | | | |
| R. A. | | | | | | | | | | | | | | | | | | | | | | | | | | | | | | | | | | | | | |
| R. E. | | | | | | | | | | | | | | | | | | | | | | | | | | | | | | | | | | | | | |
| INFANTRY | | | | | | | | | | | | | | | | | | | | | | | | | | | | | | | | | | | | | |
| R. A. M. C. | | | | | | | | | | | | | | | | | | | | 1 | 1 | 1 | | | | | | | | | | 2 | 8 | 6 | - | - | |
| A. O. C. | | | | | | | | | | | | | | | | | | | | | | | | | | | | | | | | | | | | | |
| A. V. C. | | | | | | | | | | | | | | | | | | | | | | | | | | | | | | | | | | | | | |

Remarks :—

John Sutch Lt.Col. Signature of Commander.

1/1st Low. Fd. Ambce. R.A.M.C. (T.) Unit.

52 Div. Formation to which attached.

11th May 1918. Date of Despatch.

(26149.) Wt. W. 10698/4046. 500,000. 10/15. M.R.Co.,Ltd. Forms/B. 213/6.

[P.T.O.

For information of the A. G.'s Office at the Base.

**Officers and men who have become casuals, been transferred or joined since last report.**

Place In the Field Date 11th May 1918.

| Regtl. Number | Rank | Name | | Corps | Nature of casualty, or name of unit from or to which transferred | Date of being struck off or coming on the ration return | Remarks* |
|---|---|---|---|---|---|---|---|
| – | Capt | Burton | J.W. | R.A.M.C.(T.F.) 4th Low[l]d Amb | To temp duty at H.Q. 18 Corps | off 8/5/18 | |
| 316157 | Pte | Carson | H.L. | -do- | To H.Q. 18 Corps Amb | off 8/5/18 | |
| 316261 | " | Rennie | J.A. | -do- | To temp duty at A.D.M.S. office | off 8/5/18 | |
| 316324 | " | Smellie | T.A. | -do- | 14 days C.C. Insolence to a NCO | 7/5/18 | |
| 410014 | " | Bickers | J.G. | -do- | Sick to H/o | off 7/5/18 | |
| 316098 | " | Gallacher | G | -do- | Voluntary allot. at 6d per diem to J. Gallacher Crookedholme Hurlford Kilmarnock started from 4.5.18 | | |
| 316255 | " | Hay | J | -do- | Increase of 1d per day in rates of pay on completion of 3rd year of service | 23.4.18 | |
| 316252 | " | McLean | J | -do- | | 22.4.18 | |
| 316259 | " | Reid | J | -do- | | 24.4.18 | |
| 316250 | " | McLeod | J. | -do- | | 21.4.18 | |
| 316270 | " | McNab | A | -do- | | 26.4.18 | |
| 316285 | " | Campbell | W | -do- | | 29.4.18 | |
| 316264 | " | Edington | A | -do- | | 24.4.18 | |
| 316256 | " | Nisbet | A | -do- | | 23.4.18 | |
| 316293 | " | Donald | W. | -do- | | 3.5.18 | |
| 316279 | " | Miller | R. | -do- | | 28.4.18 | |
| 316249 | " | Brown | G. | -do- | | 21.4.18 | |
| 316291 | " | McIntyre | J. | -do- | | 1.5.18 | |
| 316273 | " | Sloan | D. | -do- | | 29.4.18 | |
| 316297 | L/Cpl | Donovan | W | -do- | | 30.5.18 | |
| 316305 | Pte | Mirrlees | W | -do- | | 11.5.18 | |
| 316300 | " | Harvey | A | -do- | | 10.5.18 | |
| 316303 | " | Cowie | J | -do- | | 10.5.18 | |
| 316246 | " | Auld | J | -do- | | 21.4.18 | |
| 316301 | " | Hendry | J. | -do- | | 10.5.18 | |
| 316245 | " | Gillies | A. | -do- | | 21.4.18 | |
| 316276 | " | McKay | J | -do- | | 28.4.18 | |
| 316287 | " | Wallbeler | H. | -do- | | 29.4.18 | |
| 316281 | " | Hosie | W | -do- | | 28.4.18 | |
| 316021 | " | Craig | [illegible] | -do- | Retained in service under M.S.A. | 4/5/18 | Claim for bounty forwarded |
| 316022 | Cpl. | Nicol | R. | -do- | Retained in service under M.S.A. | 4/5/18 | Claim for bounty forwarded. |
| 316067 | Sgt. | Anderson | J. | -do- | Appointed a/S/Sgt with pay from 28.2.18 vice S/Sgt W. Steele to E.L.C. Base Depot KANTARA | | |
| 316229 | L/Sgt | McGregor | J | -do- | Appointed a/Sgt with pay from 28.2.18 vice Sgt Anderson J appointed a/S/Sgt. | | |
| 32830 | Cpl | Scott | T | -do- | Appointed a/L/Sgt with pay from 28.2.18 vice L/Sgt McGregor J. appointed a/Sgt. | | |
| 316021 | L/Cpl | Fothergill | W.D. | -do- | Appointed a/Cpl with pay from 28.2.18 vice Cpl Scott T appointed a/L/Sgt. | | |
| Strength. | | Officers | T.F. / T.C. | 7 / 1 — 8 | | | |
| | | W.O. | | 1 | | | |
| | | Q.M.S. | | 1 | All of R.A.M.C. Category "A" | | |
| | | S/Sgts | | 2 | | | |
| | | Sgts | | 10 | | | |
| | | L/Sgts | | 1 | | | |
| | | Cpls | T.F. / Reg. | 7 | | | |
| | | L/Cpls | | 5 | | | |
| | | Ptes | | 153 — 181 | | | |

* State whether absence is of a permanent or temporary nature, adding, in the case of casuals from wounds or disease, any available information for communication to the relatives.

*For information of the A.G.'s Office at the Base.*

A.S.C.

Officers and men who have become casuals, been transferred or joined since last report.

Place In the Field Date 11 May 1918

| Regtl. Number | Rank | Name | | Corps | Nature of casualty, or name of unit from or to which transferred | Date of being struck off or coming on the ration return | Remarks* |
|---|---|---|---|---|---|---|---|
| T4/ 247082 | 2 Cpl | Baillie | L. | A.S.C. att [illegible] Amb. | [illegible] to [illegible] | off 6 5/18 | |
| T4/ 058708 | Dr | Daniels | Jn. | -do- | 14 days C.C. Forfeits 1 G.C. Badge | 5 5/18 | |
| T4/ 254270 | " | Harris | F. | -do- | 14 days C.C. Forfeits 1 G.C. Badge | 5 5/18 | |
| T4/ 266080 | " | Sloan | W. | -do- | Deprived of 3 days pay | 10 5/18 | |
| T4/ 213831 | " | Miller | J. | -do- | Deprived of 3 days pay | 10 5/18 | |
| M2/ 156512 | Pte | Pilgrim | G. | A.S.C. M.T. | Joined unit | on 7 5/18 | |
| M2/ 148289 | " | Pentecost | A. | -do- | for duty with 3 [illegible] | on 7 5/18 | |
| M2/ 140430 | " | Rowland | W. | -do- | -do- | on 7 5/18 | |
| M2/ 162466 | " | Cook | W | -do- | Temp att C.R.A. 53 Div. [illegible] car | off 8 5/18 | |

* State whether absence is of a permanent or temporary nature, adding, in the case of casuals from wounds or disease, any available information for communication to the relatives.

No. of Report 146

# FIELD RETURN.

Army Form B. 213.

(To be furnished by all arms, services and departments (except A.S.C. units) to the A. G.'s Office at the Base in accordance with Field Service Regulations, Part II.)

RETURN showing numbers RATIONED by, and Transport on charge of, 1/4th Low. Fd. Ambce at In the Field 11th May 1918 Date.

| DETAIL | Personnel: Officers | Personnel: Other ranks | Personnel: Natives | Animals: Horses: Riding | Animals: Horses: Draught | Animals: Horses: Heavy Draught | Animals: Horses: Pack | Animals: Mules: Large | Animals: Mules: Small | Animals: Camels | Animals: Oxen | Guns, carriages, and limbers, and transport vehicles: Guns, carriages and limbers, showing description | Ammunition wagons and limbers | Machine guns | Aircraft, showing description | Horsed: 4 Wheeled | Horsed: 2 Wheeled | Mechanical: Motor Cars | Mechanical: Tractors | Mechanical: Lorries, showing description | Mechanical: Trucks, showing description | Mechanical: Trailers | Motor Bicycles | Bicycles. | Motor Ambces. | REMARKS |
|---|---|---|---|---|---|---|---|---|---|---|---|---|---|---|---|---|---|---|---|---|---|---|---|---|---|---|
| Effective Strength of Unit | (a) 8 | (b) 181 | | | | | | | | | | | | | | | | | | | | | | 1 | | (a) Includes 1 officer [illegible] att 18 Corps HQrs |
| Details, *by Arms* attached to unit as in War Establishment:— | | | | | | | | | | | | | | | | | | | | | | | | | | (b) Includes 3 O.R. att A.H.Q. 1 O.R. att 18 Corps HQ. (Amb). |
| A.S.C. (H.T.) att. | | 46 | | 8 | 17 | 20 | | | | | | | | | | 13 | 4 | | | | | | | | | |
| A.S.C. (M.T.) att. | | 6* | | | | | | | | | | | | | | | | | | | | | 2 | | 6 | * 1 MT driver with car [illegible] att C.R.A. 52 Div. |
| Total | 8 | 233 | | 8 | 17 | 20 | | | | | | | | | | 13 | 4 | | | | | | 2 | 1 | 6 | |
| War Establishment | 10 | 231 | | 14 | 17 | 20 | | | | | | | | | | 13 | 4 | | | | | | 2 | 1 | 7 | |
| Wanting to complete (Detail of Personnel and Horses below) | 2 | 8(c) | | 6 | - | - | | | | | | | | | | - | - | | | | | | - | - | 1 | (c) 1 O.R. RAMC 7 O.R. ASC (MT) |
| Surplus | - | 10(d) | | | | | | | | | | | | | | | | | | | | | | | | (d) A.S.C. (H.T.) |
| *Attached (not to include the details shown above) | | 2 | | | | | | | | | | | | | | | | | | | | | | | | Sick Rationed. |
| Civilians:— Employed with the Unit | | | | | | | | | | | | | | | | | | | | | | | | | | |
| Accompanying the Unit | | | | | | | | | | | | | | | | | | | | | | | | | | |
| TOTAL RATIONED ... | 7 | 230 | | 8 | 17 | 20 | | | | | | | | | | | | | | | | | | | | |

* In the case of field ambulances, hospitals or depots, the number of patients are to be included here, the names being shown in A. F. A. 36.

[illegible] Lt-Col. Signature of Commander.

11th May 1918 Date of Despatch.

Demands made on this sheet should consist of personnel required from the Base only, and should not include any demands for personnel which can be completed by promotions or appointments within the unit.

Perforated Sheet giving detail of personnel and horses wanting to complete, shown on Army Form B. 213.

No. of Report 147

| Detail of Wanting to Complete. | Drivers: R.A. | Drivers: R.E. | Drivers: A.S.C. | Drivers: Car | Drivers: Lorry | Drivers: Steam | Gunners | Smith Gunners | Range Takers | Farriers: Serjeants | Farriers: Corporals | Shoeing, or Shoeing and Carriage Smiths | Cold Shoers | Wheelers: R.A. | Wheelers: H.T. | Wheelers: M.T. | Saddlers or Harness Makers | Blacksmiths | Bricklayers and Masons | Carpenters and Joiners | Fitters & Turners (R.E.): Wood | Fitters & Turners (R.E.): Iron | Fitters: R.A. | Fitters: Wireless | Plumbers | Electricians: Ordinary | Electricians: W.T. | Signalmen | Engine Drivers: Loco. | Engine Drivers: Field | Air Line Men | Permanent Line Men | Operators, Telegraph | Cablemen | Brigade Section Pioneers | General-duty Pioneers | Signallers | Instrument Repairers | Motor Cyclist | Motor Cyclist Artificers | Telephonists | Clerks | Machine Gunners | Armament Artificers: Fitters | Armament Artificers: Range Finders | Armourers | Storemen | Privates | W.O.'s and N.C.O.'s (by ranks) not included in trade columns | | | | | | | | | | TOTAL to agree with wanting to complete: Officers | TOTAL: Other Ranks | Horses: Riding | Horses: Draught | Horses: Heavy Draught | Horses: Pack |
|---|---|---|---|---|---|---|---|---|---|---|---|---|---|---|---|---|---|---|---|---|---|---|---|---|---|---|---|---|---|---|---|---|---|---|---|---|---|---|---|---|---|---|---|---|---|---|---|---|---|---|---|---|---|---|---|---|---|---|---|---|---|---|---|---|
| CAVALRY | | | | | | | | | | | | | | | | | | | | | | | | | | | | | | | | | | | | | | | | | | | | | | | | | | | | | | | | | | | | | | | | |
| R.A. | | | | | | | | | | | | | | | | | | | | | | | | | | | | | | | | | | | | | | | | | | | | | | | | | | | | | | | | | | | | | | | | |
| R.E. | | | | | | | | | | | | | | | | | | | | | | | | | | | | | | | | | | | | | | | | | | | | | | | | | | | | | | | | | | | | | | | | |
| INFANTRY | | | | | | | | | | | | | | | | | | | | | | | | | | | | | | | | | | | | | | | | | | | | | | | | | | | | | | | | | | 3 / 2 | · | 6 | · | · | · |
| R.A.M.C. | | | | | | | | | | | | | | | | | | | | | | | | | | | | | | | | | | | | | | | | | | | | | | | | | | | | | | | | | | | | | | | | |
| A.O.C. | | | | | | | | | | | | | | | | | | | | | | | | | | | | | | | | | | | | | | | | | | | | | | | | | | | | | | | | | | | | | | | | |
| A.V.C. | | | | | | | | | | | | | | | | | | | | | | | | | | | | | | | | | | | | | | | | | | | | | | | | | | | | | | | | | | | | | | | | |
| | | | | | | | | | | | | | | | | | | | | | | | | | | | | | | | | | | | | | | | | | | | | | | | | | | | | | | | | | | | | | | | | |
| | | | | | | | | | | | | | | | | | | | | | | | | | | | | | | | | | | | | | | | | | | | | | | | | | | | | | | | | | | | | | | | | |

Remarks :—

James Little Lt Col. Signature of Commander.

1st Lows. Fd. Ambce. [illegible] Unit,

57th Division Formation to which attached.

18th May 1918. Date of Despatch.

[P.T.O.

D. D. & L. London, E.C.
(7422) Wt. W14775/M1553 1,000,000 2/17 (E934) Forms B213/8

*For information of the A.G.'s Office at the base.*

A.S.C.

Officers and men who have become casuals, been transferred or joined since last report.

Place In the Field  Date 18th May 1918.

| Regtl. Number | Rank | Name | Corps | Nature of casualty, or name of unit from or to which transferred | Date of being struck off or coming on the ration return | Remarks* |
|---|---|---|---|---|---|---|
| T4/039036 | Dr. | Ledgard. | A.S.C. (H.T.) att 1/1st L.F.A. | Sick to Hosp. | off 12 5/18 | |
| T4/085897 | " | Beavis | -do- | Sick to Hosp. | off 16 5/18 | |
| - | " | Wilkins - | A.S.C. M.T. | att. for duty with Amb Car | on 12 5/18 | Car No. 14166 |
| - | " | Wilkins - | -do- | Temp. att ADMS Office | | |
| - | " | Wilkins - | -do- | to duty with another Unit | off 16 5/18 | |
| M3/1665 | a/Sgt. | Yeatman J.G. | A.S.C. 52 Div. M.T. Coy. | Joined as | on 17 5/18 | |
| M2/080315 | Cpl. | Pounder J.J. | -do- | reinforcements | -do- | |
| M1/08945 | Pte. | Austin A.C. | -do- | for duty with | -do- | |
| M2/300394 | " | Marsh J.H. | -do- | Ambce Motor | -do- | |
| M2/100031 | " | Sims F. | -do- | Cars | -do- | |
| M2/096100 | " | Davies L. | -do- | -do- | -do- | |
| M2/018995 | " | Massie R. | 8th M.A.C. | -do- | -do- | |
| T4/245543 | Dr. | Savage | A.S.C. (H.T.) att 1/1st L.F.A. | Retained in Service under M.S.A from 30.11.17. Bounty claimed (£15). | | |
| | | | | | | |

*State whether absence is of a permanent or temporary nature, adding, in the case of casuals from wounds or disease, any available information for communication to the relatives.

*For information of the A.G.'s Office at the base.*

Officers and men who have become casuals, been transferred or joined since last report.

Place In the Field Date 18th May 1918.

| Regtl. Number | Rank | Name | | Corps | Nature of casualty, or name of unit from or to which transferred | Date of being struck off or coming on the ration return | Remarks* |
|---|---|---|---|---|---|---|---|
| - | Capt. | Verling | a | R.A.M.C. (T.C.) | To London to report at War Office. Ter. of contract | | off 17 5/18. |
| 316131 | Pte. | Henderson | R | R.A.M.C.(T) 1/2 Low. Fd. Amb. | Rejoined from Hospital | on 17 5/18 | |
| 316309 | " | Murray | D. | -do- | Increase of 1d per | 12.5.18 | |
| 316308 | " | Colville | W. | -do- | day in rate of pay | 12.5.18 | |
| 316206 | " | Hunter | Jn. | -do- | on completion of third | 3.5.18 | |
| 52839 | a/L/Sgt. | Scott | Y. | -do- | year of service | 6.2.18 | |
| 316029 | Pte. | Ritchie | G. | -do- | Retained in service under M.S.A. from 13/5/18 Bounty of £15 claimed | | |
| 316034 | " | Leask | J. | -do- | Retained in service under M.S.A. from 8/5/18 Bounty of £15 claimed | | |
| 316027 | " | Bradford | B. | -do- | Retained in service under M.S.A. from 9/5/18 Bounty of £15 claimed | | |
| 316038 | " | Purvis | Ja. | -do- | Retained in service under M.S.A. from 13/5/18 Bounty of £15 claimed. | | |
| 316155 | " | Hanlon | W. | -do- | Allotment of 9d per diem to Miss Edith Hanlon, 348 Cumbernauld Rd. Glasgow. to be stopped from 14 5/18. | | |
| | | | | | | | |
| | | Strength | | Officers T.C. T.F. | 7 | 7 | |
| | | | | W.O. | 1 | | |
| | | | | Q.M.S. | 1 | | |
| | | | | S/Sgts. | 2 | | |
| | | | | Sgts. | 10 | | |
| | | | | L/Sgts. (Reg.) | 1 | | |
| | | | | Cpls. T.F. Reg. | 7 1 | | |
| | | | | L/Cpls. | 5 | | |
| | | | | Ptes. | 154 | 182 | |

All "other ranks" R.A.M.C. Category "A"

*State whether absence is of a permanent or temporary nature, adding, in the case of casuals from wounds or disease, any available information for communication to the relatives.

**To be made up to and for Saturday in each week**

No. of Report 147.

# FIELD RETURN.

Army Form B. 213

(To be furnished by all arms, services, and departments (except A.S.C. units) to the A.G.'s Office at the Base in accordance with Field Service Regulations, Part II.)

RETURN showing numbers (a) Effective strength of Unit. (b) Rationed by Unit. 1 Low. Fd. Ambce. at In the Field 18th May 1918. Date.

| DETAIL | Personnel | | | Animals | | | | | | Guns and transport vehicles. | | | | | | | | | | | Motor Bicycles | Bicycles | Motor Ambulances | REMARKS |
|---|---|---|---|---|---|---|---|---|---|---|---|---|---|---|---|---|---|---|---|---|---|---|---|---|
| | | | | Horses | | | | Mules | | | | | | Horsed | | Mechanical | | | | | | | | |
| | Officers | Other ranks | Natives | Riding | Draught | Heavy Draught | Pack | Large | Small | Guns, showing description | Ammunition wagons | Machine guns | Aircraft, showing description | 4 Wheeled | 2 Wheeled | Motor Cars | Tractors | Lorries, showing description | Trucks, showing description | Trailers | | | | |
| Effective Strength of Unit...... | (a) 7 | (b) 182 | | | | | | | | | | | | | | | | | | | | 1 | | (a) Includes, 1 officer temp. att. Hqrs 18th Corps. |
| Details *by Arms* attached to unit as in War Establishment:— | | | | | | | | | | | | | | | | | | | | | | | | (b) Includes. 1 O.R. att. Div. Concert Pty. " 1 O.R. att. D.H.Q. |
| A.S.C. (H.T.) att. | | 44 | | 8 | 17 | 20 | | | | | | | | 12 | 4 | | | | | | | | | " 2 O.R. att. A.D.M.S. office " 1 O.R. att. 18 Corps Hq. |
| A.S.C. (M.T.) att. | | 13 | | | | | | | | | | | | | | | | | | | 2 | | 7 | " 11 O.R. on short leave to U.K. " 1 O.R. att. Bde. Hq. |
| | | | | | | | | | | | | | | | | | | | | | | | | (c) 1 Horse Amb. Wagon rendered unserviceable and beyond repair (accident) |
| Total | 7 | 239 | | 8 | 17 | 20 | | | | | | | | 12 | 4 | | | | | | 2 | 1 | 7 | |
| War Establishment | 10 | 231 | | 14 | 17 | 20 | | | | | | | | 13 | 4 | | | | | | 2 | 1 | 7 | |
| Wanting to complete (Detail of Personnel and Horses below) | 3 | | | 6 | | | | | | | | | | 1(c) | | | | | | | | | | |
| Surplus | | 8(d) | | | | | | | | | | | | | | | | | | | | | | (d) A.S.C. (H.T.) |
| *Attached (not to include the details shown above)........... | | 96 | | | | | | | | | | | | | | | | | | | | | | Sick rationed. |
| Civilians:— Employed with the Unit ...... | | | | | | | | | | | | | | | | | | | | | | | | |
| Accompanying the Unit ...... | | | | | | | | | | | | | | | | | | | | | | | | |
| TOTAL RATIONED...... | 6 | 318 | | 8 | 17 | 20 | | | | | | | | | | | | | | | | | | |

* In the case of field ambulances, hospitals or depots, the number of patients are to be included here, the names being shown in A. F. A. 36.

[signature] Lt. Col. Signature of Commander.

18th May 1918. Date of Despatch.

Demands made on this sheet should consist of personnel required from the Base only, and should not include any demands for personnel which can be completed by promotions or appointments within the unit.

Perforated Sheet giving detail of personnel and horses wanting to complete, shown on Army Form B. 213.

No. of Report 148.

| Detail of Wanting to Complete. | Drivers | | | | | | Gunners | Smith Gunners | Range Takers | Farriers | | Shoeing, or Shoeing and Carriage Smiths | Cold Shoers | Wheelers | | |
|---|---|---|---|---|---|---|---|---|---|---|---|---|---|---|---|---|
| | R.A. | R.E. | A.S.C. | Car | Lorry | Steam | | | | Serjeants | Corporals | | | R.A. | H.T. | M.T. |
| CAVALRY | | | | | | | | | | | | | | | | |
| R.A. | | | | | | | | | | | | | | | | |
| R.E. | | | | | | | | | | | | | | | | |
| INFANTRY | | | | | | | | | | | | | | | | |
| R.A.M.C. | | | | | | | | | | | | | | | | |
| A.O.C. | | | | | | | | | | | | | | | | |
| A.V.C. | | | | | | | | | | | | | | | | |
| | | | | | | | | | | | | | | | | |
| | | | | | | | | | | | | | | | | |

| Detail of Wanting to Complete. | Saddlers or Harness Makers. | Blacksmiths | Bricklayers and Masons | Carpenters and Joiners | Fitters & Turners (R.E.) | | Fitters | | Plumbers | Electricians | | Signalmen | Engine Drivers | | Air Line Men | Permanent Line Men | Operators, Telegraph | Cablemen |
|---|---|---|---|---|---|---|---|---|---|---|---|---|---|---|---|---|---|---|
| | | | | | Wood | Iron | R.A. | Wireless | | Ordinary | W.T. | | Loco. | Field | | | | |
| CAVALRY | | | | | | | | | | | | | | | | | | |
| R.A. | | | | | | | | | | | | | | | | | | |
| R.E. | | | | | | | | | | | | | | | | | | |
| INFANTRY | | | | | | | | | | | | | | | | | | |
| R.A.M.C. | | | | | | | | | | | | | | | | | | |
| A.O.C. | | | | | | | | | | | | | | | | | | |
| A.V.C. | | | | | | | | | | | | | | | | | | |
| | | | | | | | | | | | | | | | | | | |
| | | | | | | | | | | | | | | | | | | |

| Detail of Wanting to Complete. | Brigade Section Pioneers | General-duty Pioneers | Signallers | Instrument Repairers | Motor Cyclist | Motor Cyclist Artificers | Telephonists | Clerks | Machine Gunners | Armament Artificers | | Armourers | Storemen | Privates |
|---|---|---|---|---|---|---|---|---|---|---|---|---|---|---|
| | | | | | | | | | | Fitters | Range Finders | | | |
| CAVALRY | | | | | | | | | | | | | | |
| R.A. | | | | | | | | | | | | | | |
| R.E. | | | | | | | | | | | | | | |
| INFANTRY | | | | | | | | | | | | | | |
| R.A.M.C. | | | | | | | | | | | | | | |
| A.O.C. | | | | | | | | | | | | | | |
| A.V.C. | | | | | | | | | | | | | | |
| | | | | | | | | | | | | | | |
| | | | | | | | | | | | | | | |

| Detail of Wanting to Complete. | W.O.'s. and N.C.O.'s. (by ranks) not included in trade columns | | | | | | | | | | | TOTAL to agree with wanting to complete | | Horses | | | |
|---|---|---|---|---|---|---|---|---|---|---|---|---|---|---|---|---|---|
| | | | | | | | | | | | | Officers | Other Ranks | Riding | Draught | Heavy Draught | Pack |
| CAVALRY | | | | | | | | | | | | | | | | | |
| R.A. | | | | | | | | | | | | | | | | | |
| R.E. | | | | | | | | | | | | | | | | | |
| INFANTRY | | | | | | | | | | | | | | | | | |
| R.A.M.C. | | | | | | | | | | | | 3 | - | 6 | - | - | - |
| A.O.C. | | | | | | | | | | | | | | | | | |
| A.V.C. | | | | | | | | | | | | | | | | | |
| | | | | | | | | | | | | | | | | | |
| | | | | | | | | | | | | | | | | | |

Remarks :—

John W. Leitch Lt Col Signature of Commander.

1/1st Low Fd Ambce R.A.M.C (T) Unit.

52nd Division Formation to which attached.

25th May 1918 Date of Despatch.

D. D. & L. London, E.C.
(7422) Wt. W14775/M1553 1,000,000 2/17 (E934) Forms B213/8

[P.T.O.

R.S.C.

*For information of the A.G.'s Office at the base.*

Officers and men who have become casuals, been transferred or joined since last report.

Place In the Field Date 25th May 1918

| Regtl. Number | Rank | Name | Corps | Nature of casualty, or name of unit from or, to which transferred | Date of being struck off or coming on the ration return | Remarks* |
|---|---|---|---|---|---|---|
| T/34282 | Pte. | Farrell W. | A.S.C. (H.T.) att 1/1st Low. Fd. Amb. | 14 days CC. | 18/5/18 | |
| M2/048938 | - | Massie R. | 8th M.A.C. | 8th To M.A.C. | 22/5/18 | |
| M2/080045 | Sgt. | Brocklehurst H. | 52nd A.S.C. Div. M.T. Coy | Joined as | on 23/5/18 | |
| M2/134510 | Cpl | Langton P.J. | - do - | reinforcements | - do - | |
| M2/135890 | Pte. | Boorman H. | - do - | for duty with | - do - | |
| M2/138402 | " | Ames J. | - do - | Amb. Motor | - do - | |
| M2/117219 | " | Guthrie J.H. | - do - | Cars | - do - | |
| M2/135982 | " | Lewis C.H. | - do - | - do - | - do - | |
| M2/049455 | - | Dunkanson C. | - do - | - do - | - do - | |
| M2/135958 | - | Brooks C.A. | - do - | - do - | - do - | |
| M2/203296 | - | Croft C.R. | - do - | - do - | - do - | |
| M2/139160 | - | Baker W. | - do - | - do - | - do - | |
| M2/135999 | - | Blackwell J.G. | - do - | - do - | - do - | |
| M2/135944 | - | Cutting J. | - do - | - do - | - do | |
| M3/1065 | 2 Sgt. | Yeakman O.C. | - do - | To. 52nd Div. M.T. Coy. | 23/5/18 | |
| M2/080315 | Cpl | Pounder J.G. | - do - | - do - | - do - | |
| M/300384 | Pte. | Marsh J.H. | - do - | - do - | - do - | |
| M2/103031 | " | Sims J. | - do - | - do - | - do - | |
| M2/046400 | - | Davies L. | - do - | - do - | - do - | |
| M2/149259 | - | Pentecost H. | - do - | - do - | - do - | |
| M2/149420 | - | Rowland W. | - do - | - do - | - do - | |
| M2/055213 | - | Nicholls D.H. | - do - | - do - | - do - | |
| M2/269418 | - | Loasby H.W. | - do - | - do - | - do - | |
| M2/162166 | - | Cook W. | - do - | - do - | - do - | |
| M2/156512 | - | Pilgrim C. | - do - | - do - | - do - | |
| | | | | | | |
| | | | | | | |

*State whether absence is of a permanent or temporary nature, adding, in the case of casuals from wounds or disease, any available information for communication to the relatives.

*For information of the A.G.'s Office at the base.*

Officers and men who have become casuals, been transferred or joined since last report.

Place In the Field Date 25th May 1918

| Regtl. Number | Rank | Name | Corps | Nature of casualty, or name of unit from or to which transferred | Date of being struck off or coming on the ration return | Remarks* |
|---|---|---|---|---|---|---|
| – | Capt | Swerky H.A.C | R.A.M.C. (T.C) | Joined Unit as reinforcement from Base | On 23 5/18 | |
| – | Capt | Swerky H.A.C | R.A.M.C. (T.C) | To duty as R.M.O with 5th R.S.F | Off 24 5/18 | |
| 110567 | Pte. | Edwards W.H | R.A.M.C. att 1st Low. Fd. Amb | Granted War Pay of 1d per day on | 3 4/18 | |
| 97534 | " | Riley W | – do – | completion of first year of service | 2 4/18 | |
| 316313 | " | Hope A | R.A.M.C(T) 1st Low Fd. Amb | Increase of 1d | 14 5/18 | |
| 316316 | " | Barclay H | – do – | per day in rate | 14 5/18 | |
| 316329 | " | Porter J.P. | – do – | of pay on | 20 5/18 | |
| 316261 | " | Rennie J.D | – do – | completion of | 24 4/18 | |
| 316334 | " | Smellie T. | – do – | third year of service | 24 5/18 | |
| 316038 | " | McCauslane J.B | – do – | Retained in service under M.S.A. from 22 5/18 – Bounty of £15 claimed. | | |
| 410014 | Pte. | Beckers J.L | – do – | Rejoined Unit from Hosp | 24 5/18 | |
| | Strength | Officers | T.C. – T.F 4 | | | |
| | | W.O. | 1 | | | |
| | | Q.M.S | 1 | | | |
| | | S/Sgts | 2 | | | |
| | | Sgts | 10 | | | |
| | | L/Sgt (Reg) | 1 | | | |
| | | Cpls (T.F) (Reg) | 4 1 | | | |
| | | L/Cpls | 5 | | | |
| | | Ptes | 155 | 183. | | |
| | All other ranks R.A.M.C. Category "A" | | | | | |

*State whether absence is of a permanent or temporary nature, adding, in the case of casuals from wounds or disease, any available information for communication to the relatives.

**To be made up to and for Saturday in each week**

No. of Report 148

# FIELD RETURN.

Army Form B. 213

(To be furnished by all arms, services, and departments (except A.S.C. units) to the A.G.'s Office at the Base in accordance with Field Service Regulations, Part II.)

RETURN showing numbers (*a*) Effective strength of Unit. (*b*) Rationed by Unit. 1/1st Low. Fd. Ambce RAMC(T) at In the Field 25th May 1918 Date.

| DETAIL | Personnel | | | Animals | | | | | | Guns and transport vehicles. | | | | | | | | | | | | | | REMARKS |
|---|---|---|---|---|---|---|---|---|---|---|---|---|---|---|---|---|---|---|---|---|---|---|---|---|
| | | | | Horses | | | | Mules | | | | | | Horsed | | Mechanical | | | | | | | | |
| | Officers | Other ranks | Natives | Riding | Draught | Heavy Draught | Pack | Large | Small | Guns, showing description | Ammunition wagons | Machine guns | Aircraft, showing description | 4 Wheeled | 2 Wheeled | Motor Cars | Tractors | Lorries, showing description | Trucks, showing description | Trailers | Motor Bicycles | Bicycles | Motor Ambulances | |
| Effective Strength of Unit...... Details *by Arms* attached to unit as in War Establishment:— | (a) 4 | (b) 183 | | | | | | | | | | | | | | | | | | | | 1 | | (a) Includes 1 Officer temp att. Hqrs 18th Corps. (b) Includes 1 O.R. att Div. Concert Pty, 1 O.R. att. D.H.Q., 2 O.R. att A.D.M.S. office, 1 O.R. att 18th Corps Hqrs |
| A.S.C. (H.T.) att. | | 44 | | 8 | 14 | 20 | | | | | | | | 13 | 4 | | | | | | | | | 15 O.R. RAMC absent leave U.K. |
| A.S.C. (M.T.) att. | | 13 | | | | | | | | | | | | | | | | | | | 2 | | 4 | 4 O.R. A.S.C.(H.T.) absent leave to U.K. |
| Total | 4 | 240 | | 8 | 14 | 20 | | | | | | | | 13 | 4 | | | | | | 2 | 1 | 4 | |
| War Establishment | 10 | 231 | | 8 | 14 | 20 | | | | | | | | 13 | 4 | | | | | | 2 | 1 | 4 | |
| Wanting to complete (Detail of Personnel and Horses below) | 3 | | | 4 | | | | | | | | | | | | | | | | | | | | |
| Surplus | | 9 (d) | | | | | | | | | | | | | | | | | | | | | | (d) 8 A.S.C. (H.T.) & 1 RAMC(T) |
| *Attached (not to include the details shown above)........... | | 136 | | | | | | | | | | | | | | | | | | | | | | Sick rationed in Fd. Amb. |
| Civilians:— Employed with the Unit ...... | | | | | | | | | | | | | | | | | | | | | | | | |
| Accompanying the Unit ...... | | | | | | | | | | | | | | | | | | | | | | | | |
| TOTAL RATIONED...... | 6 | 352 | | 8 | 14 | 20 | | | | | | | | | | | | | | | | | | |

* In the case of field ambulances, hospitals or depots, the number of patients are to be included here, the names being shown in A.F.A. 36.

John W. Leitch Lt. Col. Signature of Commander.

25th May 1918 Date of Despatch.

Demands made on this sheet should consist of personnel required from the Base only, and should not include any demands for personnel which can be completed by promotions or appointments within the unit.

Perforated Sheet giving detail of personnel and horses wanting to complete, shown on Army Form B. 213.

No. of Report 149.

| Detail of Wanting to Complete. | Drivers R.A. | Drivers R.E. | Drivers A.S.C. | Drivers Car | Drivers Lorry | Drivers Steam | Gunners | Smith Gunners | Range Takers | Farriers Serjeants | Farriers Corporals | Shoeing, or Shoeing and Carriage Smiths | Cold Shoers | Wheelers R.A. | Wheelers H.T. | Wheelers M.T. |
|---|---|---|---|---|---|---|---|---|---|---|---|---|---|---|---|---|
| CAVALRY | | | | | | | | | | | | | | | | |
| R.A. | | | | | | | | | | | | | | | | |
| R.E. | | | | | | | | | | | | | | | | |
| INFANTRY | | | | | | | | | | | | | | | | |
| R.A.M.C. | | | | | | | | | | | | | | | | |
| A.O.C. | | | | | | | | | | | | | | | | |
| A.V.C. | | | | | | | | | | | | | | | | |

| Detail of Wanting to Complete. | Saddlers or Harness Makers. | Blacksmiths | Bricklayers and Masons | Carpenters and Joiners | Fitters & Turners (R.E.) Wood | Fitters & Turners (R.E.) Iron | Fitters R.A. | Fitters Wireless | Plumbers | Electricians Ordinary | Electricians W.T. | Signalmen | Engine Drivers Loco. | Engine Drivers Field | Air Line Men | Permanent Line Men | Operators, Telegraph | Cablemen |
|---|---|---|---|---|---|---|---|---|---|---|---|---|---|---|---|---|---|---|
| CAVALRY | | | | | | | | | | | | | | | | | | |
| R.A. | | | | | | | | | | | | | | | | | | |
| R.E. | | | | | | | | | | | | | | | | | | |
| INFANTRY | | | | | | | | | | | | | | | | | | |
| R.A.M.C. | | | | | | | | | | | | | | | | | | |
| A.O.C. | | | | | | | | | | | | | | | | | | |
| A.V.C. | | | | | | | | | | | | | | | | | | |

| Detail of Wanting to Complete. | Brigade Section Pioneers | General-duty Pioneers | Signallers | Instrument Repairers | Motor Cyclist | Motor Cyclist Artificers | Telephonists | Clerks | Machine Gunners | Armament Artificers Fitters | Armament Artificers Range Finders | Armourers | Storemen | Privates |
|---|---|---|---|---|---|---|---|---|---|---|---|---|---|---|
| CAVALRY | | | | | | | | | | | | | | |
| R.A. | | | | | | | | | | | | | | |
| R.E. | | | | | | | | | | | | | | |
| INFANTRY | | | | | | | | | | | | | | |
| R.A.M.C. | | | | | | | | | | | | | | |
| A.O.C. | | | | | | | | | | | | | | |
| A.V.C. | | | | | | | | | | | | | | |

| Detail of Wanting to Complete. | W.O.'s and N.C.O.'s (by ranks) not included in trade columns | | | | | | | | | | | TOTAL to agree with wanting to complete: Officers | TOTAL to agree with wanting to complete: Other Ranks | Horses: Riding | Horses: Draught | Horses: Heavy Draught | Horses: Pack |
|---|---|---|---|---|---|---|---|---|---|---|---|---|---|---|---|---|---|
| CAVALRY | | | | | | | | | | | | | | | | | |
| R.A. | | | | | | | | | | | | | | | | | |
| R.E. | | | | | | | | | | | | | | | | | |
| INFANTRY | | | | | | | | | | | | | | | | | |
| R.A.M.C. | | | | | | | | | | | | 3 | - | - | - | - | - |
| A.O.C. | | | | | | | | | | | | | | | | | |
| A.V.C. | | | | | | | | | | | | | | | | | |

Remarks :—

John W. Leitch Lt Col. Signature of Commander.

1st Lowland Field Ambulance Unit.

52nd Division Formation to which attached.

31st May 1918. Date of Despatch.

[P.T.O.

D. D. & L. London, E.C.
(7422) Wt. W14775/M1553 1,000,000 2/17 (E934) Forms B213/8

*For information of the A.G.'s Office at the base.*

---

Officers and men who have become casuals, been transferred or joined since last report.

Place In the Field Date 31st. May 1918.

| Regtl. Number | Rank | Name | Corps | Nature of casualty, or name of unit from or to which transferred | Date of being struck off or coming on the ration return | Remarks* |
|---|---|---|---|---|---|---|
| T4/043531 | Dr. | Davies G. J. | A.S.C. (H.T.) att. 1/1st. Lo. Fd. Amb. | sick to Hospl. (dental) | 30/5/18. | Tempy. |
| | | | | | | |
| | | | | | | |
| | | | | | | |
| | | | | | | |
| | | | | | | |
| | | | | | | |
| | | | | | | |
| | | | | | | |
| | | | | | | |
| | | | | | | |
| | | | | | | |
| | | | | | | |
| | | | | | | |
| | | | | | | |
| | | | | | | |
| | | | | | | |
| | | | | | | |
| | | | | | | |
| | | | | | | |
| | | | | | | |
| | | | | | | |
| | | | | | | |
| | | | | | | |
| | | | | | | |
| | | | | | | |
| | | | | | | |
| | | | | | | |

*State whether absence is of a permanent or temporary nature, adding, in the case of casuals from wounds or disease, any available information for communication to the relatives.

*For information of the A.G.'s Office at the base.*

---

Officers and men who have become casuals, been transferred or joined since last report.

Place In the Field Date 31st May 1918.

| Regtl. Number | Rank | Name | Corps | Nature of casualty, or name of unit from or to which transferred | Date of being struck off or coming on the ration return | Remarks* |
|---|---|---|---|---|---|---|
| | Capt. | W. G. Mackenzie | R.A.M.C.(T) 1/1st Lon. Fd. Amb. | Tempy attchd. 2nd Lon. F.A. | 31/5/18. | Tempy |
| 328024 | Pte. | Le Roy A. | — do — | Sick to Hospl. (dental) | 27/5/18. | Tempy |

Strength.

| | T.F. | M. |
|---|---|---|
| Officers | | |
| W.O. | 1 | |
| Q.M.S. | 1 | |
| S./Sgts. | 2 | |
| Sgts. | 10 | |
| L/Sgt. (Reg) | 1 | |
| Cpls. (T.F.) | M | |
| Cpls. (Reg) | 1 | |
| L/Cpls. | 5 | |
| Ptes. | 154 | 182. |

All other ranks R.A.M.C. Category A

*State whether absence is of a permanent or temporary nature, adding, in the case of casuals from wounds or disease, any available information for communication to the relatives.

**…be made up to and for Saturday in each week**

No. of Report 140

# FIELD RETURN.

Army Form B. 213

(To be furnished by all arms, services, and departments (except A.S.C. units) to the A.G.'s Office at the Base in accordance with Field Service Regulations, Part II.)

RETURN showing numbers (*a*) Effective strength of Unit. (*b*) Rationed by Unit. 1st Low. Fd. Ambce RAMC (T) at In the Field 31st May, 1918. Date.

| DETAIL | Personnel: Officers | Personnel: Other ranks | Personnel: Natives | Animals: Horses: Riding | Animals: Horses: Draught | Animals: Horses: Heavy Draught | Animals: Pack | Animals: Mules: Large | Animals: Mules: Small | Guns, showing description | Ammunition wagons | Machine guns | Aircraft, showing description | Horsed: 4 Wheeled | Horsed: 2 Wheeled | Mechanical: Motor Cars | Mechanical: Tractors | Mechanical: Lorries, showing description | Mechanical: Trucks, showing description | Mechanical: Trailers | Motor Bicycles | Bicycles | Motor Ambulances | REMARKS |
|---|---|---|---|---|---|---|---|---|---|---|---|---|---|---|---|---|---|---|---|---|---|---|---|---|
| Effective Strength of Unit...... | (a) 4 | (b) 182 | | | | | | | | | | | | | | | | | | | | 1. | | (a) Includes 1 Officer tempy. attchd. 18th Corps H.Q. – 1 Officer tempy. attchd 1/2nd Low. Fd. Ambce. – 1 Officer attending R.A.M.C. School ELNES –<br>(b) Includes 1.O.R. att. Div. Concert Pty. 1.O.R. " Div. H.Q. 1.O.R. " 52nd Div. Train HQ 2.O.R. " A.D.M.S. Office. 1.O.R. " 18th Corps H.Q. 4.O.R. RAMC. short leave UK 5.O.R. A.S.C.(HT) " " " 2 O.R. attending RAMC School – ELNES |
| Details *by Arms* attached to unit as in War Establishment:— | | | | | | | | | | | | | | | | | | | | | | | | |
| A.S.C. (H.T.) attached | - | 43 | | 8 | 14 | 20 | | | | | | | | 13 | 4 | | | | | | | | | |
| A.S.C. (M.T.) attached | - | 13 | | | | | | | | | | | | | | | | | | | 2 | | 4. | |
| Total | 4. | 238 | | 8 | 14 | 20 | | | | | | | | 13 | 4 | | | | | | 2 | 1 | 4. | |
| War Establishment | 10 | 231 | | 8 | 14 | 20 | | | | | | | | 13 | 4. | | | | | | 2 | 1 | 4. | |
| Wanting to complete (Detail of Personnel and Horses below) | 3 | - | | | | | | | | | | | | | | | | | | | | | | |
| Surplus | - | (c) 4. | | | | | | | | | | | | | | | | | | | | | | (c) 4 ASC(HT) |
| *Attached (not to include the details shown above)........... | - | 119 | | | | | | | | | | | | | | | | | | | | | | Sick rationed in 1st Amb. |
| Civilians :— Employed with the Unit ...... | | | | | | | | | | | | | | | | | | | | | | | | |
| Accompanying the Unit ...... | | | | | | | | | | | | | | | | | | | | | | | | |
| TOTAL RATIONED...... | 4 | 324 | | 8 | 14 | 20 | | | | | | | | | | | | | | | | | | |

* In the case of field ambulances, hospitals or depots, the number of patients are to be included here, the names being shown in A.F.A. 36.

[signature] Lt. Col. Signature of Commander. 31st May 1918 Date of Despatch.

VOL XXXVI

APPENDIX II (May 1918)
War Diary of 1/1st L.F.A. R.A.M.C.(T.)



Capt R.A. Lennie, 1/1st Low. F.A.

You will proceed forthwith as O/c Party of 1 N.C.O and 9 Privates to SAVY - LENS MAP 2.g.6.2 - to arrange accommodation, light refreshment, etc. for walking wounded.

Equipment and dressings sent with you to carry out duties will be :-

White Dressing Box with loose dressings,
2 Bowls for lotions, dissecting forceps, probe and straight scissors.
One Medical Companion and Water Bottle
Bovril for 200 patients.
Two dixies for hot water and Bovril.

You should get into touch with RTO, Light Railway, and the Town Major, and should return the Amb^ce Car by which you travel, at once, with a message to me stating any additional equipment you may find it necessary to have by you owing to numbers of wounded coming in. Motor cyclist or Amb^ce Car will be sent between 0800 and 0900, for report as to progress. Your men should take tea and sugar and breakfast ration with them.

Johnson Fitch
Lt.-Colonel,
O.C. 1st L. F. A. R. A. M. C. (T).

APPENDIX II VOL XXXVI (MAY 1918)
WAR DIARY of 1/1 LOW. F.A. RAMC (T)

HEADQUARTERS,
1/1ST LOWLAND
FIELD AMBULANCE.
No. F 139
Date 15 - 5 - 18

ADMS
52 DIV

Sir,

In reply to your R 410/7, d/15/5/18 I have the honour to report as follows:-

Since receipt of your W 128, d/13/5/18, received by me late that evening, that "Scabies" would now be sent to 1/1 Low. F.A. materials for formation of an improvised Serbian Barrel and provision of hot baths for such cases, have been collected, and it is expected to have both of these in operation to-morrow. Meantime arrangements have been made with O/c Div Baths to have any cases sent over there under charge of one or more orderlies, RAMC, for baths and disinfection of clothing. A number were sent there to-day under this arrangement. The usual application of sulphur ointment or liq. calc. sulphurate after careful opening up of any burrows found has been carried out. The general application of picric acid has been employed as part of the treatment in accordance with recent practice. Indeed, this has been rendered necessary by the difficulty of obtaining sulphur and sulphur ointment on indent sent by me to Depôts of Med. Stores in France. Cases admitted as scabies are seen personally by me as well as by MO doing duty.

I have the honour to be
Sir
Your obedient servant
John W. Leitch LT. COL
OC. 1/1 LOW. F.A., RAMC (T)

(MAY 1918) APPENDIX III VOL XXXVI

A.D.M.S. WAR DIARY of

52 Div 1/1 Low. F.A. RAMC(T)

HEADQUARTERS,
1/1ST LOWLAND
FIELD AMBULANCE.

No. F 170

Date 19.5.18

Ref. your S.P. 42 d/18/5/18 one G.S. wagon has to-day been despatched to MINGOVAL for use of O/c Detraining Centre, loaded with u/m stores:-

| | | | |
|---|---|---|---|
| F.M. Pannier Jars | 1 | Sheets ground | 30 |
| Med. Companion | 1 | Stools, camp | 1 |
| Water bottles | 2 | Stretchers, Amb^{ce} | 6 |
| Reserve Dr. Box | 1 | Stoves portable | 1 |
| Blankets G.S. | 80 | Table, camp | 1 |
| Boxes stationery | 1 | " , Operating | 1 |
| " dressing | 2 | Tents " | 1 |
| Flags, sig. with poles | 2 | " D C L | 2 |
| Lamps Operating | 1 | Jackets sleeping | 20 |
| Mattress (Op. Table) | 1 | Trousers pyjamas | 20 |
| Panniers A to G filled as per F.S. manual | | Panniers MC | 1 |
| | | Horrocks Test Box | 1 |

John M. Leitch Lt.-Colonel.

O.C. 1st L. F. A. R. A. M. C. (T)

17
June 1918

1/1 Lowland Fd Amb
Vol 3
140/3076.

427 Army Form C. 2118.

# WAR DIARY
~~or~~
# ~~INTELLIGENCE SUMMARY.~~
(*Erase heading not required.*)

Instructions regarding War Diaries and Intelligence Summaries are contained in F. S. Regs., Part II. and the Staff Manual respectively. Title pages will be prepared in manuscript.

1/1st Lowland Field Ambulance
52nd (Lowland) Division

| Place | Date | Hour | Summary of Events and Information | Remarks and references to Appendices |
|---|---|---|---|---|
| VILLERS-AU-BOIS (Army Map B 1/40000 X19. c. 9.9.) | 1/6/18 | | It is found that many of the cases sent to this Rest Station as "Scabies" by R.M.Os, A.D.S. & M.D.S. are not true scabies but a phtheiriasis due sometimes to pediculosis but more often to an irritation of the skin from a mixture of sweat & dirt. Pimples & even boils appear in the areas scratched. Admissions to this ambulance continue to be very large – from 40 to 50 per day, but cases returned to duty after a short residence are proportionately numerous. S/Sr SEARLE W.O. i/c transport, reported the breaking of pole of an ambulance wagon sent to M.D.S. of 1/2nd L.F.A. at MONT ST ELOY this afternoon to bring back patients for Rest Camps. The accident was due to a flaw in the wood & the wagon was in draught at the time. Patients, personnel, & animals, however, escaped without injury. Sent Weekly Health Report to A.D.M.S. (See copy APPENDIX I) Jn L | APPENDIX I. |
| VILLERS-AU-BOIS (Map B 1/40000 X19. c. 9.9.) | 2/6/18 | | Forwarded amendments to A.F. B213 for last month showing portion of O.R. who had been granted 14 days leave to U.K.; in accordance with his R 687/9 of even date. The number for the month were R.A.M.C. 21, A.S.C. 5. sent on leave to U.K., of whom reported back from leave R.A.M.C. 4, A.S.C. nil Jn L | |
| Do. | 3/6/18 | | Sent 1 N.C.O. & 21 men with picks & shovels to report to O.C. 1/2nd L.F.A. for work on a new M.D.S. in accordance with his instructions in R 697/4 d/2/6/18. Received copy | |

D. D. & L., London, E.C. (A8001) Wt. W1771/M2031 750,000 5/17 Sch. 52 Forms C2118/14

Instructions regarding War Diaries and Intelligence Summaries are contained in F. S. Regs., Part II. and the Staff Manual respectively. Title pages will be prepared in manuscript.

# WAR DIARY
*or*
# INTELLIGENCE SUMMARY.
(*Erase heading not required.*)

428 Army Form C. 2118.

1/1st Lowland Field Ambulance
52nd (Lowland) Division

| Place | Date | Hour | Summary of Events and Information | Remarks and references to Appendices |
|---|---|---|---|---|
| VILLERS-AU-BOIS X19 C99 Map B 1/40000 | 3 6/18 (Contd) | | of A.D.M.S. instructions to the three Field Ambulances that "in future all cases sent as Scabies to the 1st L.F.A. would be shown as admitted only in that unit's returns, & that those which did not turn out to be Scabies would also be shown in that unit's returns under the changed diagnosis. Received also A.D.M.S. instructions to the effect that my Weekly Health Report would refer to direct admissions only to this Ambulance & would include only 52nd Div. Sent 100 suits Pyjamas on loan to Corps Skin Centre ESTREE-CAUCHIE by motor ambulance this afternoon in accordance with A.D.M.S. R 704/3 of even date. Capt A D DOWNES reported back from visit to Gas centre & Ambulances of 20th Division. J.W.L. | |
| VILLERS-AU-BOIS X19 C99 Map B 1/40000 | 4 6/18 | | Lieut HAMAKER left this morning to report to O.C. 62nd Field Ambulance on the return to this ambulance of Capt. A.D. DOWNES. Sent letter F 253 to A.D.M.S. in reply to his R 692/4 d/2.6.18 giving draft of chit suggested by D.D.M.S. for use by M.T. Drivers when taking equipment with patients to C.C.S. Capt J BROWNE reported back from R.A.M.C. school of instruction ELNES. The proposed course had not been held but he had been detained on account of a possible attack. J.W.L. | |
| VILLERS-AU-BOIS X19.C99 Map B 1/40000 | 5 6/18 | | Nothing to note. J.W.L. | |
| | 6 6/18 | | Called on A.D.M.S. to explain the great difficulty I had in dealing with the number of so-called "Scabies" cases. Many of these are really due to the irritation of lice, etc. & only very | |

D. D. & L., London, E.C. (A800,) Wt. W1771/M2031 750,000 5/17 Sch. 52 Forms/C2118/14

429 Army Form C. 2118.

Instructions regarding War Diaries and Intelligence Summaries are contained in F. S. Regs., Part II. and the Staff Manual respectively. Title pages will be prepared in manuscript.

# WAR DIARY

~~or~~

~~INTELLIGENCE SUMMARY.~~

(Erase heading not required.)

1/1st Lowland Field Ambulance
52nd Lowland Division

| Place | Date | Hour | Summary of Events and Information | Remarks and references to Appendices |
|---|---|---|---|---|
| VILLERS-AU-BOIS Map B 1/40000 | 6/6/18 | | rarely can they be said to be due to acarus scabiei. Yet they are labelled "Scabies" by R.M.O.s & a F.M. card is attached to them at the 2nd or 3rd L.F.A. & they are sent forthwith to the Divisional Rest station. It is impossible that friction can be avoided when the diagnosis is changed at the Divisional Rest station, & the man given a bath & sent back to duty. Cases of all sorts continue to pour into the rest station at the rate of 40-50 per day & it is impossible to keep the numbers down to the prescribed limits. The personnel left me is fully employed & the A.D.M.S. allowed me to make use of convalescent patients in order to make up the working party for the new M.D.S. of 2nd L.F.A. to 40. required by his letter R 697/4 d/5 6/18. Detailed Capt R.A. LENNIE to proceed this forenoon to 1/7th Royal Scots for duty as M.O. in accordance with A.D.M.S. instructions to me to detail an officer for this duty. D.D.M.S. 18th Corps & A.A.G. 52nd Division visited this Ambulance & Rest Station & made a minute inspection this afternoon. | J.W.Y. |
| VILLERS-AU-BOIS. | 7 6/18 | | P.U.O. has become epidemic. It began with the N.F. Pioneers & has now affected many of my transport drivers & some of the RAMC personnel. | J.W.Y. |
| do | 8 6/18 | | Feel feverish myself to-day & have had to leave most things to my 2nd in | |

D. D. & L., London, E.C.
(A8001) Wt. W1771/M2031 750,000 5/17 Sch. 52 Forms/C2118/14

Instructions regarding War Diaries and Intelligence Summaries are contained in F. S. Regs., Part II. and the Staff Manual respectively. Title pages will be prepared in manuscript.

# WAR DIARY
or
~~INTELLIGENCE SUMMARY.~~
(Erase heading not required.)

430 Army Form C. 2118.

1/1st Lowland Field Ambulance
52nd (Lowland) Division

| Place | Date | Hour | Summary of Events and Information | Remarks and references to Appendices |
|---|---|---|---|---|
| VILLERS-AU-BOIS | 8/6/18 | | command. Wrote Weekly Health Report & forwarded copies to A.D.M.S. & B.G.C. 156th Bde. (Copy APPENDIX II) | APPENDIX II |
| do | 9/6/18 | | Still feeling unfit & have had to remain in bed most of the day. A.D.M.S. visited this Hospital in the afternoon & went round the huts & tents with Capt DOWNES. Two American M.O.s reported to-night from A.D.M.S. to be put up by this mess for the night & report to him at 0900 to-morrow. JWL | |
| VILLERS-AU-BOIS. | 10/6/18 | | The two American M.O.s have been detailed for duty with this unit. Their names are 1st Lt. L.N. HOST M.R.C. U.S.A. & 1st Lt. C.E. HAMILTON M.R.C. U.S.A. & particulars regarding them were to-day forwarded to A.D.M.S. in letter F286. Wrote letter F287 of even date to A.D.M.S. in reply to his letter of enquiry as to reasons for two men suffering from "Incontinence of urine" being evacuated to C.C.S. The numbers of cases admitted to this ambulance direct & on transfer have averaged between 50 & 60 daily for the past week. The average ~~number~~ in hospital every night has been over 170. Patients arrive at all hours up to 10 p.m. & it is very difficult to deal with them in a scattered camp only meant for a small dressing station & with no provision for a Rest Camp except a few Nissen huts (not hospital pattern) & six | |

D. D. & L., London, E.C. (A8001) Wt. W1771/M2031 750,000 5/17 Sch. 52 Forms C2118/14

431 Army Form C. 2118.

Instructions regarding War Diaries and Intelligence Summaries are contained in F. S. Regs., Part II. and the Staff Manual respectively. Title pages will be prepared in manuscript.

# WAR DIARY
—or—
~~INTELLIGENCE SUMMARY.~~
(Erase heading not required.)

1/1st Lowland Field Ambulance
52nd (Lowland) Division

| Place | Date | Hour | Summary of Events and Information | Remarks and references to Appendices |
|---|---|---|---|---|
| | | | hospital marquees. J.W.L. | |
| VILLERS-AU-BOIS: X19.c.9.9. Map B 1/40000. | 11/6/18 | | It is very difficult to get supplies here apparently. Indents on A.S.C. for quicklime for lime-washing & for making Liq. Calc. Sulphurat. sent a fortnight ago have not been met by the A.S.C. who referred us to the R.E., who again referred us to the Ordnance, who referred us back to the A.S.C. Wrote letter F292 of even date to A.D.M.S. on the subject. This is merely one instance of the delay & difficulty we have found since coming to France. J.W.L. | |
| VILLERS-AU-BOIS | 12/6/18 | – | Capt J. BROWNE & Cpl W.D. FOTHERGILL left by motor ambulance to carry with party from Fd. ambulances of this Division proceeding to WAVRANS for 1 week's course at RAMC school of Instruction to begin to-morrow. J.W.L. | |
| VILLERS-AU-BOIS. | 13/6/18 | | Sorted out men sent down for "examination by eye specialist", & for examination by Ear Throat & Nose Specialist. There are always more eye examination cases sent down than the numbers allotted to this Division to be sent by ambulance car to PERNES on Fridays, ~~viz~~ viz 5. J.W.L. | |
| VILLERS-AU-BOIS. | 14/6/18 | | Detailed Lt L.N. HOST to report to O.C. 1/3rd L.F.A. for temporary duty this forenoon. J.W.L. | |
| | 15/6/18 | | Sent 6 O.R. to report to O.C. 1/3rd L.F.A. for duty with Bearer Subdivision of this unit presently on detached duty with 1/3rd L.F.A. to replace some of those sent down with P.U.O. Sent Weekly Health Report to ADMS. (Copy APPENDIX III) J.W.L. | APPENDIX III |

D. D. & L., London, E.C. (A8001) Wt. W1771/M2031 750,000 5/17 Sch. 52 Forms/C2118/14

Instructions regarding War Diaries and Intelligence Summaries are contained in F. S. Regs., Part II. and the Staff Manual respectively. Title pages will be prepared in manuscript.

# WAR DIARY
or
~~INTELLIGENCE SUMMARY.~~
(Erase heading not required.)

432

Army Form C. 2118.

1/1st Lowland Field Ambulance
52nd (Lowland) Division

| Place | Date | Hour | Summary of Events and Information | Remarks and references to Appendices |
|---|---|---|---|---|
| VILLERS-AU-BOIS | 16/6/18 | | Received through A.D.M.S. last night a letter of enquiry as to why two indents (attached) of No. 1 Coy 11th Tank Corps dated 1st & 9th June had not been met. Enquiry showed that these indents had not been received by this ambulance & that the only indent which had been received by me from this 11th Tank Corps was on 27th May & had been supplied them on 28th May after I had sent it to A.D.M.S. for his approval & countersignature. Wrote letter F 303a d/16/6/18 to A.D.M.S. drawing attention to these facts. These vagrant bodies of Corps & Divisional Troops who are "supplied by the nearest Field Ambulance" are as a rule very lavish in their use of drugs & dressings etc. & have no scruples in drawing the same supplies from all the Field Ambulances of a Division – if they can. J.W.L. | |
| VILLERS-AU-BOIS | 17/6/18 | | Nothing to note J.W.L. | |
| " | 18/6/18 | | Forwarded to A.D.M.S. report of Bacteriologist on examination of throat swab sent him from a recent case of P.U.O. admitted to this unit. It was to the effect that a diplococcus like the Pneumococcus had been found in great abundance but the Bacillus of Influenza had not been found. He had found the Pneumococcus in abundance in all cases he had examined lately of P.U.O. & considered it to be a variety of the Pneumococcus. J.W.L. | |

Instructions regarding War Diaries and Intelligence Summaries are contained in F. S. Regs., Part II. and the Staff Manual respectively. Title pages will be prepared in manuscript.

# WAR DIARY

or

~~INTELLIGENCE SUMMARY.~~

(Erase heading not required.)

433 Army Form C. 2118.

1/1st Lowland Field Ambulance
52nd (Lowland) Division

| Place | Date | Hour | Summary of Events and Information | Remarks and references to Appendices |
|---|---|---|---|---|
| VILLERS-AU BOIS | 19/6/18 | | Handed over to 11th Yanks Battalion the drugs & dressings drawn by this unit on indent countersigned by A.D.M.S. Received A.D.M.S. R 955/2 of even date instructing me to have 10 Corps Units in neighbourhood supervised in sanitary matters & short report submitted by Sunday of each week. Capt. A.D. DOWNES reports for duty as M.O. 1/4 KOSB. J.W.L. | |
| VILLERS-AU BOIS | 20/6/18 | | Nothing to note. J.W.L. | |
| | 21/6/18 | | Received report of Capt. McKenzie ~~D.A.D.M.S.~~ on Sanitary condition of camps of the 10 Corps units noted in his R955/2 d 19/6/18. (see copy APPENDIX IV). Received ADMS R987/4 of even date at a late hour this evening that VILLERS SUBURBAN & RISPIN camps would be handed over tomorrow for use as an extension of 1/1st L.F.A. & that I should inspect these camps with a view to using them to best advantage. One section of a Canadian Field Ambulance to report to me for duty discipline & rations. J.W.L. | APPENDIX IV |
| VILLERS-AU BOIS | 22/6/18 | | Capt. J. BROWNE & 1 O.R. reported back from RAMC School WAVRANS. [illegible] J.W.L. Visited the three camps to be used as an extension & decided to use VILLERS camp for Acute P.U.O. cases (O.R.), officers quarters of RISPIN camp for officers with P.U.O. & mens quarters for convalescents (O.R.), & to leave SUBURBAN camp for the present as it was some distance off & was found to be occupied by 1/5th A & S.H. J.W.L. Forwarded to A.D.M.S. Weekly health report APPENDIX V & original copy of Capt. MacKenzie's Report App IV J.W.L. | APPENDIX V |
| VILLERS-AU BOIS | 23/6/18 | | Received ADMS R987/4 d 23/6/18 that scheme for extending my accommodation was now in abeyance & that my accommodation was now to be 200, that cases of P.U.O. were now | |

2353 Wt. W2514/1454 700,000 5/15 D. D. & L. A.D.S.S./Forms/C. 2118.

Instructions regarding War Diaries and Intelligence Summaries are contained in F. S. Regs., Part II. and the Staff Manual respectively. Title pages will be prepared in manuscript.

# WAR DIARY

~~or~~

~~INTELLIGENCE SUMMARY.~~

(Erase heading not required.)

434 Army Form C. 2118.

1/1st Lowland Field Ambulance
52nd (Lowland) Division

| Place | Date | Hour | Summary of Events and Information | Remarks and references to Appendices |
|---|---|---|---|---|
| VILLERS-AU-BOIS | 23/6/18 (Contd.) | | either be evacuated or sent to duty. In accordance with instructions received late last night 1 Off. + 53 O.R. suffering from P.U.O. were evacuated to AUBIGNY-LIGNY group of C.C.S. by midnight. Bearer party returned from 1/3rd L.F.A. Jw. L. | |
| VILLERS-AU-BOIS. | (Contd.) | | Two Soyer Stoves were to-day handed over to detachment of 1/2nd L.F.A. at Les 4 Vents in accordance with instructions contained in A.D.M.S. R1029/4 d/23 6/18. There were sent from the detraining centre of 1/1st L.F.A. at MINGOVAL, in accordance with A.D.M.S. R987/4 d/21 6/18 the [illegible] from Detraining Centre were handed over on that date 21/6/18 to same unit + 1 water cart with horses + driver sent to report from this H.qrs. The personnel at MINGOVAL has now been reduced to 1 N.C.O + 2 men - the ~~three~~ seven others having been returned for duty with this unit. Jw. L. | |
| VILLERS-AU-BOIS. | 24/6/18 | | The party of 6 O.R. reporting daily for duty in construction of Delousing Plant at CAMBLAIN L'ABBE was not sent to-day. The engineers did not appear yesterday & nothing was done. Notified A.D.M.S. (letter F335 d/23 6/18) that I would not send them until further instructions. 1 N.C.O. + 40 men are still going daily to MOUNT ST ELOI for duty in constructing the new Dressing Station there. | |
| VILLERS-AU-BOIS | 25/6/18 | | Attended Medical Board as President to examine Dental cases from 1/5th 1/6th & 1/7th H.L.I. & had proceedings in duplicate forwarded to A.D.M.S. Lt. L.N. HOST reported back from duty with 1/3rd L.F.A. Jw. L. | |

2353 Wt. W2514/1454 700,000 5/15 D. D. & L. A.D.S.S./Forms/C. 2118.

Instructions regarding War Diaries and Intelligence Summaries are contained in F. S. Regs., Part II. and the Staff Manual respectively. Title pages will be prepared in manuscript.

# WAR DIARY

~~or~~

~~INTELLIGENCE SUMMARY.~~

(Erase heading not required.)

435 Army Form C. 2118.

1/1st Lowland Field Ambulance
52nd (Lowland) Division

| Place | Date | Hour | Summary of Events and Information | Remarks and references to Appendices |
|---|---|---|---|---|
| VILLERS-AU-BOIS. | 26/6/18 | | S/Sgt. HAY Instructor in Cookery visited this ambulance to-day in accordance with instructions notified me in A.D.M.S. R 957/1 d/19/6/18. Received A.D.M.S. R 1088/4 of even date to arrange for supervision of sanitation of detachment of 52nd M.T. Coy. at Billet No. 33 ACQ, & that their sick would report daily at ambulance between 7 & 8 AM. Sent 4 G.S. wagons with 12 hours rations for men thereon to report to 1/2nd L.F.A. in accordance with instructions of A.D.M.S. to-day & daily as necessary. Jno. 1. | |
| VILLERS-AU-BOIS | 27/6/18 | | Received note S20 d/27/6/18 from O.C. 1/2nd L.F.A. that the 4 G.S. wagons would not be required by him further. Resubmitted the names of Capt. W F MACKENZIE & Capt. J. BROWNE to A.D.M.S. for promotion to rank of A/Major letter F 360 d/27/6/18 Jno. 2. | |
| VILLERS-AU-BOIS. | 28/6/18 | | O.C. leaves to-day on 14 days leave to U.K.. Capt. W F MACKENZIE takes command during his absence. Jno. W. Leitch Lt Col. | |
| " | 29/6/18 | | Weekly Health Report forwarded. See appendix. WFM | Ap VI |
| | | | Div. Rest Station inspected by A.D.M.S. 52nd Div. | |
| | 30/6/18 | | Received A.D.M.S. Order W 393 d/30/6/18:- All slightly sick cases to be retained to number of 150. Ordinary P.U.O. cases accordingly retained. Weekly Sanitary Report on small units in area is forwarded to ADMS. WFM | Ap VII |
| | | | W F Mackenzie Capt. | |

2353 Wt. W2544/1454 700,000 5/15 D. D. & L. A.D.S.S./Forms/C. 2118.

VOL XXXVII

Appendix I. (June 1918)

War Diary of 1st/2nd Lowland Fd Amb. R.A.M.C. (T)

## Weekly Health Report

31-5-18 / 1-6-18

(a) Principal causes of admissions during w/e 1/6/18.

| | Total | Increase | Decrease |
|---|---|---|---|
| Pyrexia N.Y.D. | 49 | 10 | – |
| I.C.T. | 10 | – | 1 |
| Malaria | 25 | 10 | – |
| Phthiriasis & skin diseases | 20 | 6 | – |
| Abscess & Whitlow | 5 | – | – |
| Scabies | 18 | – | 6 |
| Diarrhoea | 14 | 13 | – |

(b) Total sick admissions 284.

(c) Infectious diseases 4.

General remarks. –

There is an increase of total admissions this week of 33. The numbers admitted from 155th, 156th and 157th Bdes. respectively are 46 – 19 – 91. The admissions from the 156th Bde shew 1 dysentery each from 4th R.S. and 8th S.R., probably both recurrent cases. Two diarrhoeas came from 4th R.S., and the total Pyrexias from the Brigade were 5. With regard to the 155th Bde the increase in numbers would appear to be chiefly among Scabies and Skin Eruptions 7 each. Seven others sent as Scabies in which the diagnosis was changed in the Field Ambce, the men were given a bath, their clothes disinfected and returned to duty the next day. The 154th Bde. increase in numbers was mainly due to Scabies of which they had 9 cases – Skin Eruptions 3 and other slight eruptions sent as Scabies (19 in all), where the men were bathed, clothes disinfected and returned to duty the next day. The increase in Malaria is chiefly accounted for by 5th Royal Irish from which 14 cases were received. There has been a large number of dental cases evacuated this week, 32 in all, of which 6 came from 155th, two from 156th and 6 from 157th Bdes. respectively, the remainder from Divisional and Corps troops. There were 14 cases of Diarrhoea from 65th Bde R.F.A. The 5 cases of Dysentery came from Units of this Division and are probably recurrent cases. The analysis shews the need for frequent bathing and washing of clothing of men with skin eruptions. A considerable number of cases sent as Scabies are very mild and would appear not to be due to Scabies, but to irritation by dirt or dust ground into the skin and brought on chiefly by scratching. I would recommend that M.O.s be encouraged to have men found with skin eruptions, to wash their clothes at every opportunity, keep their nails clean as well as having a bath. Disinfection of clothing does not get rid of the dirt and irritating grit in the clothing.

John W. [illegible] Lt Col

Vol XXXVII

Appendix II (June 1918)

War Diary of 1st Low. Fd Amb. R.A.M.C.(T)

A.D.M.S.

52nd Division

## Weekly Health Report.

The report of last week has been altered to exclude Corps Troops so as to draw a comparison.

(a) Principal causes of admission during W/E 8.6.18. for 52nd Div.

| | Total | Increases | Decreases. |
|---|---|---|---|
| P.U.O. | 46. | 33 | - |
| Phthiriasis | 15. | 15. | - |
| I.C.T. | 12. | 9. | - |
| Pediculosis | 10. | 10. | - |

(b) Total Sick Admissions 132.

(c) Infectious Diseases NIL.

General Remarks.

The admissions of the 155th, 156th & 157th Bdes. and Divisional Troops are respectively 11, 27, 25 and 69, these admissions are only to the Rest Station and are therefore misleading. The chief diseases are P.U.O. and skin eruptions due chiefly to irritation of Lice and possibly dirt and perspiration in the skin. There has been an epidemic of P.U.O. among Divisional Troops in billets in Villers-au-Bois, in some cases all the men in a billet have been attacked. The disease would seem to be infectious as well as contagious. In every case the patients have been isolated, their clothing disinfected and steps taken regarding the billet for disinfection.

It is suggested that R.M.O's. might reduce their admissions to hospital of so called Scabies by

1. When in the line where water is scarce, men affected should
   (a) Keep their nails moderately short, but not cut or bitten into the quick, as this tends to make the nail ragged. The nail then should be smoothed after paring with the blade of knife or scissors, and mourning bands can

be cleaned by use of the point.

(b) Every opportunity should be taken of washing the hand and any itchy parts of body with soap and water, when these can be obtained.

(c) The seams of the fork of the trousers and under-clothing should be examined daily for lice or nits by the men themselves. Any living lice found should be killed and nits scraped off with a knife, after which Oxford Powder should be dusted in way of the seams. Only

(d) Sulphur or other ointments should be sparingly used, if at all. They tend to collect dust and dirt and so further soil the skin and clothing.

(e) The term Scabies should ~~not~~ be used, unless the burrows of the insect have actually been seen. Most cases of so called Scabies are really due to Pediculosis. Further, when a man has been pronounced Scabies by his M.O. at sick parade, he considers himself bound to scratch himself

(f) Some cases of desquammation of the skin between the fingers and superficial crusting are apt to be mistaken for the burrows of the insect. The use of the Lense from Tin A., in No 1. Field Medical Pannier, will clear up any doubt

2\. (a) When battalions are out of the line, men should then wash their clothing themselves in soap and water, incidentally this cleans the hands and nails

(b) Have hot baths as often as possible at Divisional Baths.

(c) Carry out all measures above detailed for time they are in the trenches.

8/6/18 Johnson Kutch Lt Col

Vol XXXVII

Appendix III (June 1918)

War Diary of 1/1st Low. Fd. Amb. R.A.M.C.(T)

A. D. M. S.

52nd Division.

Weekly Health Report

(a) Principal causes of admissions during week ending 15.6.18 for 52 Div

| | Total | Increase | Decrease |
|---|---|---|---|
| P.U.O. | 41 | - | 5 |
| Phtheriasis | 10 | - | 5 |
| Dental Cases | 10 | - | - |
| Scabies | 2 | 2 | - |

(b) Total Sick Admissions 80

(c) Infectious Diseases NIL

General Remarks:- Admissions by Bdes. are as follows:-

| | Total | Increase | Decrease |
|---|---|---|---|
| 155 Brigade | 18 | 7 | - |
| 156 Brigade | 14 | - | 13 |
| 157 Brigade | 16 | - | 9 |
| Div. Troops | 32 | - | 37 |

The cases of 155 Bde. consisted of P.U.O 3, Scabies 1, Phtheriasis, I.C.T. and other skin diseases 5, Dental Cases 6, Jaundice 1, Balanitis 1, N.Y.D 1.

Those of 156 Bde consisted of PUO 9, Phtheriasis, I.C.T. etc 2, Dental 2 other Diseases 1.

Those of 157 Bde consisted of PUO 6, Scabies 1, Phtheriasis I.C.T. etc 7 Diarrhoea 1, Dental 1.

Divisional Troops PUO 23, Malaria 1, Phtheriasis etc 2, other diseases 3, Dental 1 Venereal 1, accidental 1. The bulk of the Pyrexias came from A.S.C. and 1/1st L.F.A. 13 cases, A.D.C. and 1/3 L.F.A. 3 cases. Other diseases were unimportant from a health point of view. The Pyrexia epidemic would seem to have reached its maximum and to be now diminishing in violence.

[illegible] Lt. Col

R.M.O. 156 Bde.

VOL XXXVII

Appendix IV (June 1918)
War Diary of 1/1st Low. Fd Amb.
RAMC(T)

O. C. 1/1st Low. Fd. Amb.

I have to submit the following report in respect of the sanitation of camps visited under your orders.–

I. 52nd Div. Reinforcement Camp
II. 43rd Area Employment Coy
III. 169th Labour Coy.
IV. O.O. XVIII Corps Troops
V. Army Troops Coy R.E.
VI. XVIII Corps Salvage Coy.
VII. 16th Canadian Concert Party.
VIII. Town Major Villers-au-Bois
IX. Camp Comdt. Villers-au-Bois
X. No. 2 Labour Coy, La Pendu.

Camps I. & IX "Villers & Lispin" are in urgent need of sanitary effort. The cook-houses are almost devoid of tables. There are no meat safes. Grease traps are inadequate. Latrines are very defective. Many latrine lids are awanting. Fire buckets have been used as urinals. There is much refuse of very old standing lying about. A permanent Sanitary Squad in each camp is required. Huts recently occupied by isolation cases of P.U.O. have been disinfected and new latrines are being dug.

Camps II & VIII – Good.
Camp III Good
Camps IV & VI Very Good.
Camp V. Bad. New latrine required. Cookhouse dirty, food scraps inside and out.
Camp VII Execrable. Untreated tins scattered everywhere. No cookhouse, or cover on table. Using a public latrine which is very defective.
Camp X. Very good, but still use cresolised bucket latrine (on concrete base) and buries faeces in pit.

A general addition required to latrines is the fixation of a sheet of tin on the inside, opposite each seat to divert the stream of urine which in so many cases flows through the joints in the wood front.

[signature]
Capt. R.A.M.C.(T)
1/1st Low. Fd. Amb.

21st June 1918

VOL XXXVII

Appendix V (Month of June 1918)
War Diary of 1/1st Low Fd Amb RAMC (7)

A. D. M. S.
52nd. Division

## Weekly Health Report

(a) Principal causes of admission during week ending 22.6.18. for 52nd Division

| | Total | Increase | Decrease |
|---|---|---|---|
| P.U.O. | 78 | 37 | - |
| Phthiriasis | 6 | - | 4 |
| Dental Cases | 7 | - | 3 |
| Scabies | 2 | - | - |

(b) Total Sick Admissions 114 34

(c) Infectious Diseases 1 1

(d) General Remarks:- Admissions by Bdes. are as follows:

| | Total | Increase | Decrease |
|---|---|---|---|
| 155 Brigade | 78 | 60 | - |
| 156 Brigade | 7 | - | 7 |
| 157 Brigade | 19 | 3 | - |
| Div. Troops | 10 | - | 22 |

The only feature in the weeks admissions is the increase of cases of P.U.O. The case of infectious disease noted was one of suspected Dysentery from 4th. K.O.S.B. There has been one case of Jaundice admitted, but in my opinion it is not the epidemic infectious type.

John W. Leitch Lieut Col.
S.M.O. 156 Bde.

A. D. M. S.
52nd Division

appendix VI (June 1918)

Vol XXXVII War Diary 1/1st Low Fd Amb · RAMC (T)

Weekly Health Report.

(A) Principal causes of admissions during W/E 29/6/18 for 52nd Div

| | Total | Increase | Decrease |
|---|---|---|---|
| P.U.O. | 40 | - | 35 |
| Phthiriasis | 5 | - | 1 |
| Scabies | 4 | 2 | - |
| (b) Total sick admissions | 66 | - | 48 |
| (c) Infectious Diseases | 2 | 1 | - |

(d) General Remarks: Admissions by Bdes. are as follows.

| | Total | Increase | Decrease |
|---|---|---|---|
| 155th Bde | 14 | - | 64 |
| 156 " | 4 | - | - |
| 157 " | 16 | - | 3 |
| Div. Troops. | 29 | 19 | - |

The ~~only~~ feature of the weeks admissions is the decrease of P.U.O. The cases of infectious diseases were suspected Dysentery from 1/7th N.F. and 1/4th K.O.S.B

[illegible signature]
Capt.

Appendix VII (June 1918)
War Diary 1/1 Low Fd Amb R.A.M.C (T)

Vol
XXXVII

A. D. M. S.

52nd Division

Reference A.D.M.S. 52nd Div., No. R955/2,
I have to report that the Units detailed have been visited with exception of No. 2 Labour Company LA PENDU.

Rispin Camp is vacant in greater part. A latrine requires attention; also tables for the cookhouse are required.

Villers Camp (now occupied) considerable improvement is noted generally. Soakage pits are inadequate, tables are required for cookhouses. These defects in latrines have been brought to notice of O.C. The permanent staff of two pioneers does not appear to be adequate.

Canadian Concert Party are much improved but have no soakage pit and are cooking outside. Dining hut should be cleared of baggage, kits etc, defects have been indicated.

Fergusson Mackenzie
Capt.

30.6.18

**To be made up to and for Saturday in each week**

No. of Report 150.

# FIELD RETURN.

Army Form B. 213

(To be furnished by all arms, services, and departments (except A.S.C. units) to the A.G.'s Office at the Base in accordance with Field Service Regulations, Part II.)

RETURN showing numbers (*a*) Effective strength of Unit. (*b*) Rationed by Unit. 1st Lowland Field Ambulance RAMC at In the Field 4th June. 1918. Date.

| DETAIL. | Personnel: Officers | Personnel: Other ranks | Personnel: Natives | Animals: Horses: Riding | Animals: Horses: Draught | Animals: Horses: Heavy Draught | Animals: Horses: Pack | Animals: Mules: Large | Animals: Mules: Small | Guns, showing description | Ammunition wagons | Machine guns | Aircraft, showing description | Horsed: 4 Wheeled | Horsed: 2 Wheeled | Mechanical: Motor Cars | Mechanical: Tractors | Mechanical: Lorries, showing description | Mechanical: Trucks, showing description | Mechanical: Trailers | Motor Bicycles | Bicycles | Motor Ambulances | REMARKS |
|---|---|---|---|---|---|---|---|---|---|---|---|---|---|---|---|---|---|---|---|---|---|---|---|---|
| Effective Strength of Unit...... | (a) 6 | (b) 182 | | | | | | | | | | | | | | | | | | | | 1. | | Includes (A) 1 Officer tempy. attchd. XVIII Corps H.Q. 1 " " 1/2nd Low. Fd Amb. (b) Includes 1 O.R. attchd. Div. Concert Party. 1 " " Div. H.Q. 1 " " 52nd Div. Train HQ 1 " " XVIII Corps. HQ 18 " on short leave to U.K. |
| Details *by Arms* attached to unit as in War Establishment:— | | | | | | | | | | | | | | | | | | | | | | | | |
| A.S.C. (HT) attchd. | - | (c) 43 | | 8 | 14 | 20 | | | | | | | | 13 | 4 | | | | | | | | | |
| A.S.C. (MT) -do- | - | (d) 13. | | | | | | | | | | | | | | | | | | | 2 | | 4. | (c) Includes 4 O.R. on short leave to U.K. (d) Includes 1 O.R. attchd. A.D.M.S. Office |
| Total | 6 | 238 | | 8 | 14 | 20 | | | | | | | | 13 | 4 | | | | | | 2 | 1 | 4. | |
| War Establishment | 10 | 231 | | 8 | 14 | 20 | | | | | | | | 13 | 4 | | | | | | 2 | 1 | 4. | |
| Wanting to complete (Detail of Personnel and Horses below) | 4 | - | | - | - | - | | | | | | | | - | - | | | | | | - | - | - | |
| Surplus | - | 4. | | | | | | | | | | | | | | | | | | | | | | A.S.C. (HT) |
| *Attached (not to include the details shown above)............ | 1 | 141 | | | | | | | | | | | | | | | | | | | | | | Sick rationed in Fd. Amb. |
| Civilians:— Employed with the Unit ...... | | | | | | | | | | | | | | | | | | | | | | | | |
| Accompanying the Unit ...... | | | | | | | | | | | | | | | | | | | | | | | | |
| TOTAL RATIONED...... | 5 | 348 | | 8 | 14 | 20 | | | | | | | | | | | | | | | | | | |

* In the case of field ambulances, hospitals or depots, the number of patients are to be included here, the names being shown in A. F. A. 36.

J. McW. Leitch Lt. Col. Signature of Commander. 4th June 1918 Date of Despatch.

*For information of the A.G.'s Office at the base.*

Officers and men who have become casuals, been transferred or joined since last report.

Place In the Field Date 4th June 1918

| Regtl. Number | Rank | Name | Corps | Nature of casualty, or name of unit from or to which transferred | Date of being struck off or coming on the ration return | Remarks* |
|---|---|---|---|---|---|---|
| | Capt | Rennie R.L. | R.A.M.C.(T) 1/3rd Low. Fd. Amb. | to duty with 1/3rd R. Scots as R.M.O. | 4/6/18 | |
| | Pte | Carruthers P.G.C. | -do- | Returned from attchd duty with A.D.M.S. | 4/6/18 | |
| 318229 | " | Cochrane R.R. | -do- | War pay increased to 3d per day from | 29/5/18 | |
| 318328 | " | Kinnear T. | -do- | -do- | 2/6/18 | |
| 318313 | " | Hampton J. | -do- | -do- | 1/6/18 | |
| | | Undernoted proceeded on leave to UK | | | | Authority |
| 316084 | S/Sgt | Thompson W | R.A.M.C.(T) 1/3rd Low. Fd. Amb. | 4 weeks time expired leave to UK | 1/6/18 | A.D.M.S. R.421/10/T.E. |
| 316060 | Pte | Lawson W | -do- | 14 days leave to UK | 2/6/18 | |
| 316064 | L/Cpl | Lamb D | -do- | -do- | 4/6/18 | |
| 316238 | Pte | McDonald W | -do- | -do- | 5/6/18 | |
| | | Undernoted returned from leave from UK | | | | |
| 316205 | L/Cpl | McDonald R | R.A.M.C.(T) 1/3rd Low. Fd. Amb. | returned from 14 days leave to UK | 4/6/18 | |
| 316065 | Pte | Dunlop D | -do- | -do- | 4/6/18 | |
| 61353 | " | Worsley J | -do- | -do- | 4/6/18 | |
| 316221 | Sergt | Cowan G.S. | -do- | -do- | 6/6/18 | |
| 316215 | Pte | McLennan W | -do- | -do- | 5/6/18 | |
| Strength | | Officers T.F. | 6 | | | |
| | | W.O. | 1 | | | |
| | | QMS | 1 | | | |
| | | S/Sgts | 2 | | | |
| | | Sgts | 10 | | | |
| | | L/Sgt (Reg) | 1 | | | |
| | | Cpls (T.F.) (Reg) | 4<br>1 | | | |
| | | L/Cpls | 5 | | | |
| | | Ptes. 154 | 182 | | | |

All other ranks R.A.M.C. Category "A"

*State whether absence is of a permanent or temporary nature, adding, in the case of casuals from wounds or disease, any available information for communication to the relatives.

R.S.C. (H.T.)

*For information of the A.G.'s Office at the base.*

Officers and men who have become casuals, been transferred or joined since last report.

Place In the Field Date 4th June 1918

| Regtl. Number | Rank | Name | Corps | Nature of casualty, or name of unit from or to which transferred | Date of being struck off or coming on the ration return | Remarks* |
|---|---|---|---|---|---|---|
| T/34[illegible]1014 | Dr. | Ackroyd J. | R.S.C.(H.T.) A.C. 1st Lon. Fd. Amb. | Sick to hospl. | off 6/6/18 | |
| T4/063331 | " | Davies G.J. | -do- | returned from hospl. | on 6/6/18 | |
| | | Undernoted returned from leave from UK | | | | |
| T/[illegible]953 | Dr. | Butler [illegible] | R.S.C.(H.T.) A.C. 1st Lon. Fd. Amb. | 14 days leave UK. | 4/6/18 | |
| T4/[illegible]7008 | " | McMillan P. | -do- | -do- | 5/6/18. | |

*State whether absence is of a permanent or temporary nature, adding, in the case of casuals from wounds or disease, any available information for communication to the relatives.

Demands made on this sheet should consist of personnel required from the Base only, and should not include any demands for personnel which can be completed by promotions or appointments within the unit.

Perforated Sheet giving detail of personnel and horses wanting to complete, shown on Army Form B. 213.

No. of Report 150.

| Detail of Wanting to Complete | Drivers | | | | | | | | | Farriers | | | | Wheelers | | | | | | | Fitters & Turners (R.E.) | | Fitters | | | Electricians | | | Engine Drivers | | | | | | | | | | | | | | | Armament Artificers | | | | | W.O's. and N.C.O's. (by ranks) not included in trade columns | | | | | | | | | | | TOTAL to agree with wanting to complete | | Horses | | | |
|---|---|---|---|---|---|---|---|---|---|---|---|---|---|---|---|---|---|---|---|---|---|---|---|---|---|---|---|---|---|---|---|---|---|---|---|---|---|---|---|---|---|---|---|---|---|---|---|---|---|---|---|---|---|---|---|---|---|---|---|---|---|---|---|---|---|
| | R.A. | R.E. | A.S.C. | Car | Lorry | Steam | Gunners | Smith Gunners | Range Takers | Serjeants | Corporals | Shoeing, or Shoeing and Carriage Smiths | Cold Shoers | R.A. | H.T. | M.T. | Saddlers or Harness Makers | Blacksmiths | Bricklayers and Masons | Carpenters and Joiners | Wood | Iron | R.A. | Wireless | Plumbers | Ordinary | W.T. | Signalmen | Loco. | Field | Air Line Men | Permanent Line Men | Operators, Telegraph | Cablemen | Brigade Section Pioneers | General-duty Pioneers | Signallers | Instrument Repairers | Motor Cyclist | Motor Cyclist Artificers | Telephonists | Clerks | Machine Gunners | Fitters | Range Finders | Armourers | Storemen | Privates | | | | | | | | | | | | Officers | Other Ranks | Riding | Draught | Heavy Draught | Pack |
| CAVALRY | | | | | | | | | | | | | | | | | | | | | | | | | | | | | | | | | | | | | | | | | | | | | | | | | | | | | | | | | | | | | | | | | |
| R.A. | | | | | | | | | | | | | | | | | | | | | | | | | | | | | | | | | | | | | | | | | | | | | | | | | | | | | | | | | | | | | | | | | |
| R.E. | | | | | | | | | | | | | | | | | | | | | | | | | | | | | | | | | | | | | | | | | | | | | | | | | | | | | | | | | | | | | | | | | |
| INFANTRY | | | | | | | | | | | | | | | | | | | | | | | | | | | | | | | | | | | | | | | | | | | | | | | | | | | | | | | | | | | | | | | | | |
| R.A.M.C. | | | | | | | | | | | | | | | | | | | | | | | | | | | | | | | | | | | | | | | | | | | | | | | | | | | | | | | | | | | | 4 | - | - | - | - | - |
| A.O.C. | | | | | | | | | | | | | | | | | | | | | | | | | | | | | | | | | | | | | | | | | | | | | | | | | | | | | | | | | | | | | | | | | |
| A.V.C. | | | | | | | | | | | | | | | | | | | | | | | | | | | | | | | | | | | | | | | | | | | | | | | | | | | | | | | | | | | | | | | | | |
| | | | | | | | | | | | | | | | | | | | | | | | | | | | | | | | | | | | | | | | | | | | | | | | | | | | | | | | | | | | | | | | | | | |
| | | | | | | | | | | | | | | | | | | | | | | | | | | | | | | | | | | | | | | | | | | | | | | | | | | | | | | | | | | | | | | | | | | |

Remarks :—

John W. Leitch Lt. Col. Signature of Commander.

1/1st Low. Fd. Amb. R.A.M.C.(T) Unit,

52nd Division Formation to which attached.

9th June 1918 Date of Despatch.

D. D. & L. London, E.C.
(7422) Wt. W14775/M1553 1,000,000 2/17 (E934) Forms B213/8

[P.T.O.

**To be made up to and for Saturday in each week**

# FIELD RETURN.

Army Form B. 213

No. of Report 151

(To be furnished by all arms, services, and departments (except A.S.C. units) to the A.G.'s Office at the Base in accordance with Field Service Regulations, Part II.)

RETURN showing numbers (a) Effective strength of Unit. (b) Rationed by Unit. [illegible] at In the Field 14th June 1918. Date.

| DETAIL | Personnel: Officers | Personnel: Other ranks | Personnel: Natives | Horses: Riding | Horses: Draught | Horses: Heavy Draught | Horses: Pack | Mules: Large | Mules: Small | Guns, showing description | Ammunition wagons | Machine guns | Aircraft, showing description | Horsed: 4 Wheeled | Horsed: 2 Wheeled | Mechanical: Motor Cars | Mechanical: Tractors | Mechanical: Lorries, showing description | Mechanical: Trucks, showing description | Mechanical: Trailers | Motor Bicycles | Bicycles | Motor Ambulances | REMARKS |
|---|---|---|---|---|---|---|---|---|---|---|---|---|---|---|---|---|---|---|---|---|---|---|---|---|
| Effective Strength of Unit...... | (a) 8 | (b) 80 | | | | | | | | | | | | | | | | | | | | 1 | | (a) includes 1 [illegible] … at R.A.M.C. School. (b) includes 1 O.R. [illegible] … 9 O.R. on [illegible] leave to U.K. … |
| Details *by Arms* attached to unit as in War Establishment:— | | | | | | | | | | | | | | | | | | | | | | | | |
| A.S.C. (H.T.) | - | (c) 43 | | 8 | 17 | 19 | | | | | | | | 13 | 4 | | | | | | | | | |
| A.S.C. (M.T.) | | (d) 13 | | | | | | | | | | | | | | | | | | | 2 | | 7 | |
| Total | 8 | 235 | | 8 | 17 | 19 | | | | | | | | 13 | 4 | | | | | | 2 | 1 | 7 | [illegible] |
| War Establishment | 10 | 231 | | 8 | 17 | 20 | | | | | | | | 13 | 4 | | | | | | 2 | 1 | 7 | |
| Wanting to complete (Detail of Personnel and Horses below) | 2 | (e) 2 | | - | - | 1 | | | | | | | | - | - | | | | | | - | - | - | |
| Surplus | - | 6 | | | | | | | | | | | | | | | | | | | | | | A.S.C. (M.T.) |
| *Attached (not to include the details shown above)...... | 1 | 144 | | | | | | | | | | | | | | | | | | | | | | [illegible] rationed [illegible] |
| Civilians:— Employed with the Unit...... | | | | | | | | | | | | | | | | | | | | | | | | |
| Accompanying the Unit...... | | | | | | | | | | | | | | | | | | | | | | | | |
| TOTAL RATIONED...... | 9 | 350 | | 8 | 17 | 19 | | | | | | | | | | | | | | | | | | |

* In the case of field ambulances, hospitals or depots, the number of patients are to be included here, the names being shown in A.F.A. 36.

[illegible] Signature of Commander.

14th June 1918. Date of Despatch.

[P.T.O.

*For information of the A.G.'s Office at the base.*

Officers and men who have become casuals, been transferred or joined since last report.

Place In the Field Date 14th June 1918

| Regtl. Number | Rank | Name | | Corps | Nature of casualty, or name of unit from or to which transferred | Date of being struck off or coming on the ration return | Remarks* |
|---|---|---|---|---|---|---|---|
| | | | | R.A.M.C.(T) | | | |
| 316023 | Pte | Ritchie | D. | 1st Low. Fd Ambce | Credit ration | allce @ 2/1d | per day |
| 316230 | Pte | Anderson | J. | -do- | from 12.5.18 to | 26.5.18. | leave |
| 316235 | " | McCartney | J. | -do- | to U.K. 14 | days | |
| 316227 | " | Stewart | J.R. | -do- | | | |
| 316205 | Cpl | McDonald | R. | -do- | Credit ration | allce @ 2/1d | per day. |
| 316065 | Pte | Dunlop | D. | -do- | from 15.5.18 to | 29.5.18. | |
| | | | | | leave to U.K. | | |
| 61353 | " | Worsley | J. | -do- | 14 days. | | |
| 316221 | Sgt | Cowan | G. | -do- | Credit ration | allce @ 2/1d | per day |
| | | | | | from 18.5.18 to 1.6.18. | leave | |
| 316215 | Pte | McLennan | W. | -do- | to U.K. 14 days | | |
| 316225 | Sgt | Allison | W.S. | -do- | Credit ration | allce @ | 2/1d per day |
| 316228 | Pte | Martin | M. | -do- | from 21.5.18 to | 4.6.18. | |
| | | | | | leave to U.K. | | |
| 316219 | " | Smith | J. | -do- | 14 days. | | |
| 316241 | Cpl | Fothergill | W.D. | -do- | Credit ration | allce @ | 2/1d per day |
| 316046 | Pte | O'Neill | E. | -do- | from 24.5.18 | to 7.6.18. | |
| | | | | | leave to U.K. | | |
| 316054 | " | Hunter | J. | -do- | 14 days. | | |
| 316055 | " | Cant | E. | -do- | Credit ration | allce @ | 2/1d per |
| 316051 | " | McIntyre | R. | -do- | day from 27.5.18 | to 10.6.18. | |
| | | | | | leave to U.K. | | |
| 316044 | " | Pinkerton | J. | -do- | 14 days. | | |
| 316057 | " | McAllister | G. | -do- | Credit ration | allce @ | 2/1d per day |
| 316058 | " | Brown | W. | -do- | from 30.5.18 | to 13.6.18 | |
| 316048 | " | Murray | H. | -do- | leave to U.K. 14 days. | | |
| 316089 | S/Sgt | Thompson | W. | -do- | Credit ration from 1/6/18 to 1/7/18. | allce @ 2/1d 31 days to | per day U.K. (Mine ca.) |
| 316060 | Pte | Lawson | W. | -do- | Credit ration from 2/6/18 to 16/6/18 | allce @ 2/1d leave to U.K. | per day 14 days. |
| 316061 | Cpl | Lamb | A. | -do- | Credit ration from 4/6/18 to 18/6/18 | allce @ 2/1d leave to U.K. | per day, 14 days. |
| 316278 | Pte | McDonald | W. | -do- | Credit ration from 5.6.18 to 19/6/18 | allce @ 2/1d leave to U.K. | per day, 14 days. |
| 316241 | " | McKean | J. | -do- | Credit ration from 10/6/18 to 24/6/18 | allce @ 2/1d leave to U.K. | per day 14 days. |
| 316270 | Sgt | McGregor | J. | -do- | Credit ration from 14/6/18 to 28/6/18 | allce @ 2/1d leave to U.K. | per day 14 days. |

* State whether absence is of a permanent or temporary nature, adding, in the case of casuals from wounds or disease, any available information for communication to the relatives.

*For information of the A.G.'s Office at the base.*

A.S.C.

Officers and men who have become casuals, been transferred or joined since last report.

Place In the Field Date 14th June 1918.

| Regtl. Number | Rank | Name | Corps | Nature of casualty, or name of unit from or to which transferred | Date of being struck off or coming on the ration return | Remarks* |
|---|---|---|---|---|---|---|
| T4/234350 | Dr. | Burgess A.J. | A.S.C. (H.T.) att 1/1st Lancs Fd. Amb. | Sick to Hosp. | off 8 6/18. | |
| T4/045309 | S.S.M. | Searle W.J. | -do- | Proceeded on 14 days leave to UK. | 8 6/18 | |
| M2/049455 | Pte | Dunkason G | A.S.C. (M.T.) att 1/1st Lancs Fd Amb. | Proceeded on 14 days leave to UK | 12 6/18. | |
| T4/247009 | Dr. | McDonald D. | A.S.C. (H.T.) att 1/1st Lancs Fd Amb. | Returned from 14 days leave to UK. | 8 6/18 | |
| T/35061 | " | Cooper T. | -do- | Returned from 14 days leave to UK. | 10 6/18 | |
| T/25953 | " | Butler G | -do- | Credit ration allce @ 2/1 per day [illegible] 6/18. leave to UK. 14 days. | | |
| T4/247008 | " | McMillan P. | -do- | Credit ration allce @ 2/1 per day [illegible] 6/18. leave to UK. 14 days. | | |
| T4/247009 | " | McDonald D | -do- | Credit ration allce @ 2/1 per day [illegible] 6/18. leave to UK. 14 days. | | |
| T/35061 | " | Cooper T.H. | -do- | Credit ration allce @ 2/1 per day [illegible] 6/18. leave to UK. 14 days. | | |
| T4/[illegible] | " | [illegible] | -do- | Credit ration allce @ 2/1 per day [illegible] 6/18. leave to UK. 14 days. | | |
| T4/045309 | S.S.M. | Searle W.J. | -do- | Credit ration allce @ 2/1 per day [illegible] 6/18. leave to UK. 14 days. | | |
| M2/049455 | Pte | Dunkason G | A.S.C. (M.T.) att 1/1st Lancs Fd Amb. | Credit ration allce. @ 2/1 per day [illegible] 6/18. leave to UK. 14 days. | | |

* State whether absence is of a permanent or temporary nature, adding, in the case of casuals from wounds or disease, any available information for communication to the relatives.

*For information of the A.G.'s Office at the base.*

Officers and men who have become casuals, been transferred or joined since last report.

Place In the Field Date 14th June 1918

| Regtl. Number | Rank | Name | Corps | Nature of casualty, or name of unit from or to which transferred | Date of being struck off or coming on the ration return | Remarks* |
|---|---|---|---|---|---|---|
| — | Capt | Mackenzie D.F. | R.A.M.C.(T.) 1 Lowl. Fd. Amb. | Returned from temp. duty with 1/1 [illegible] F.A. | on 9 6/18 | |
| — | Capt | Browne J. | -do- | To R.A.M.C. School for course of instruction | 13 6/18 | Temp |
| 3160[illegible] | Cpl | Fothergill W.D. | -do- | -do- | 11 6/18 | Temp |
| 316039 | Sgt | Davidson J.A. | -do- | To Cadet School UK. candidate for commission | 8 6/18 | Permanent |
| 3160[illegible] | Pte | Tait F. | -do- | Temp. att. D.D.M.S. 1st Army | 8 6/18 | Temp |
| 316029 | " | Bradford A.A. | -do- | Sick to Hosp. | 11 6/18 | Permanent |
| | Lieut | Hamilton G.E. | Medical Reserve Corps U.S.A. | Joined unit | on 11 6/18 | |
| | Lieut | Host E.F. | -do- | as reinforcements | on 11 6/18 | |
| | | Undermentioned proceeded on leave to UK | | | | |
| 3160[illegible] | Pte | McKean J. | R.A.M.C.(T.) 1 Lowl. Fd. Amb. | 14 days leave to UK | 10 6/18 | |
| [illegible] | Sgt | McGregor J. | -do- | -do- | 14 6/18 | |
| | | Undermentioned returned from leave to UK | | | | |
| [illegible] | Sgt | Allison H.W. | R.A.M.C.(T.) 1 Lowl. Fd. Amb. | Returned from 14 days leave to UK | 8 6/18 | |
| [illegible] | Pte | Martin D. | -do- | -do- | 8 6/18 | |
| 3160[illegible] | " | Faith J. | -do- | -do- | 8 6/18 | |
| 3160[illegible] | Cpl | Fothergill W.D. | -do- | -do- | 10 6/18 | |
| 316046 | Pte | O'Neill E. | -do- | -do- | 10 6/18 | |
| 3160[illegible] | " | Hunter J. | -do- | -do- | 10 6/18 | |
| 316053 | " | Gant G. | -do- | -do- | 12 6/18 | |
| 316051 | " | McIntyre R. | -do- | -do- | 12 6/18 | |
| 3160[illegible] | " | Pinkerton J. | -do- | -do- | 12 6/18 | |

Strength: Officers T.F. 6, MRCUSA 2 — 8

W.O. 1
A.M.S. 1
Q/Sgts 2
Sgts 9
Sgt (Reg) 1
Cpls (Reg) 7
L/Cpls 5
Ptes 153 — 180

All other ranks R.A.M.C. category "A"

* State whether absence is of a permanent or temporary nature, adding, in the case of casuals from wounds or disease, any available information for communication to the relatives.

Demands made on this sheet should consist of personnel required from the Base only, and should not include any demands for personnel which can be completed by promotions or appointments within the unit.

Perforated Sheet giving detail of personnel and horses wanting to complete, shown on Army Form B. 213.

No. of Report 151

| Detail of Wanting to Complete. | Drivers R.A. | Drivers R.E. | Drivers A.S.C. | Drivers Car | Drivers Lorry | Drivers Steam | Gunners | Smith Gunners | Range Takers | Farriers Serjeants | Farriers Corporals | Shoeing, or Shoeing and Carriage Smiths | Cold Shoers | Wheelers R.A. | Wheelers H.T. | Wheelers M.T. | Saddlers or Harness Makers | Blacksmiths | Bricklayers and Masons | Carpenters and Joiners | Fitters & Turners (R.E.) Wood | Fitters & Turners (R.E.) Iron | Fitters R.A. | Fitters Wireless | Plumbers | Electricians Ordinary | Electricians W.T. | Signalmen | Engine Drivers Loco. | Engine Drivers Field | Air Line Men | Permanent Line Men | Operators, Telegraph | Cablemen | Brigade Section Pioneers | General-duty Pioneers | Signallers | Instrument Repairers | Motor Cyclist | Motor Cyclist Artificers | Telephonists | Clerks | Machine Gunners | Armament Artificers Fitters | Armament Artificers Range Finders | Armourers | Storemen | Privates | W.O.'s and N.C.O.'s (by ranks) not included in trade columns | | | | | | | | | | | TOTAL to agree with wanting to complete Officers | TOTAL to agree with wanting to complete Other Ranks | Horses Riding | Horses Draught | Horses Heavy Draught | Horses Pack |
|---|---|---|---|---|---|---|---|---|---|---|---|---|---|---|---|---|---|---|---|---|---|---|---|---|---|---|---|---|---|---|---|---|---|---|---|---|---|---|---|---|---|---|---|---|---|---|---|---|---|---|---|---|---|---|---|---|---|---|---|---|---|---|---|---|---|
| CAVALRY | | | | | | | | | | | | | | | | | | | | | | | | | | | | | | | | | | | | | | | | | | | | | | | | | | | | | | | | | | | | | | | | | | |
| R.A. | | | | | | | | | | | | | | | | | | | | | | | | | | | | | | | | | | | | | | | | | | | | | | | | | | | | | | | | | | | | | | | | | | |
| R.E. | | | | | | | | | | | | | | | | | | | | | | | | | | | | | | | | | | | | | | | | | | | | | | | | | | | | | | | | | | | | | | | | | | |
| INFANTRY | | | | | | | | | | | | | | | | | | | | | | | | | | | | | | | | | | | | | | | | | | | | | | | | 2 | | | | | | | | | | | | 2 | 2 | - | - | 1 | |
| R.A.M.C. | | | | | | | | | | | | | | | | | | | | | | | | | | | | | | | | | | | | | | | | | | | | | | | | | | | | | | | | | | | | | | | | | | |
| A.O.C. | | | | | | | | | | | | | | | | | | | | | | | | | | | | | | | | | | | | | | | | | | | | | | | | | | | | | | | | | | | | | | | | | | |
| A.V.C. | | | | | | | | | | | | | | | | | | | | | | | | | | | | | | | | | | | | | | | | | | | | | | | | | | | | | | | | | | | | | | | | | | |
| | | | | | | | | | | | | | | | | | | | | | | | | | | | | | | | | | | | | | | | | | | | | | | | | | | | | | | | | | | | | | | | | | | |
| | | | | | | | | | | | | | | | | | | | | | | | | | | | | | | | | | | | | | | | | | | | | | | | | | | | | | | | | | | | | | | | | | | |

Remarks :—

[signature] Lt-Col. Signature of Commander.

4 Low. Fd Ambce. R.A.M.C. (T.) Unit.

53 Division Formation to which attached.

14th June 1918. Date of Despatch.

(6305) Wt. W2927/M2226. 1,250,000. 6/17. McA. & W., Ltd. (E1348). Forms B2188/8.

[P

**To be made up to and for Saturday in each week**

No. of Report 952

# FIELD RETURN.

Army Form B. 213

(To be furnished by all arms, services, and departments (except A.S.C. units) to the A.G.'s Office at the Base in accordance with Field Service Regulations, Part II.)

RETURN showing numbers (*a*) Effective strength of Unit. (*b*) Rationed by Unit. 1/1st Low. Fd. Amb. R.A.M.C. at In the Field 21st June 1918 Date.

| DETAIL | Personnel: Officers | Personnel: Other ranks | Personnel: Natives | Animals: Horses: Riding | Animals: Horses: Draught | Animals: Horses: Heavy Draught | Animals: Horses: Pack | Animals: Mules: Large | Animals: Mules: Small | Guns, showing description | Ammunition wagons | Machine guns | Aircraft, showing description | Horsed: 4 Wheeled | Horsed: 2 Wheeled | Mechanical: Motor Cars | Mechanical: Tractors | Mechanical: Lorries, showing description | Mechanical: Trucks, showing description | Mechanical: Trailers | Motor Bicycles | Bicycles | Motor Ambulances | REMARKS |
|---|---|---|---|---|---|---|---|---|---|---|---|---|---|---|---|---|---|---|---|---|---|---|---|---|
| Effective Strength of Unit...... | (a) 8 | (b) 180 | | | | | | | | | | | | | | | | | | | | 1 | | (a) Includes 1 officer attached XVIII Corps HQrs. 1 " " " 1/3 Low. Fd. Amb. 1 " att. R.A.M.C. School 1 " on leave to U.K. |
| Details *by Arms* attached to unit as in War Establishment:— | | | | | | | | | | | | | | | | | | | | | | | | |
| A.S.C. (H.T.) | | (c) 42 | | 8 | 17 | 19 | | | | | | | | 13 | 4 | | | | | | | | | (b) Includes 1 O.R. att. Div Concert Party. 1 " " D.H.Q. 1 " " HQ. 52 Div Train |
| A.S.C. (M.T.) | | (d) 13 | | | | | | | | | | | | | | | | | | | 2 | | 7 | 1 " " XVIII Corps HQrs. 1 " " [illegible] 1 " at RAMC. School 4 " on leave to U.K. |
| | | | | | | | | | | | | | | | | | | | | | | | | (c) Includes 2 O.R. on leave to U.K. |
| Total | 8 | 235 | | 8 | 17 | 19 | | | | | | | | 13 | 4 | | | | | | 2 | 1 | 7 | (d) Includes 1 O.R. att. ADMS 52 DIV 1 O.R. leave to U.K. |
| War Establishment | 10 | 231 | | 8 | 17 | 20 | | | | | | | | 13 | 4 | | | | | | 2 | 1 | 7 | (e) R.A.M.C. |
| Wanting to complete (Detail of Personnel and Horses below) | 2 | 2 (e) | | – | – | 1 | | | | | | | | – | – | | | | | | – | – | – | |
| Surplus | | 6 | | | | | | | | | | | | | | | | | | | | | | A.S.C. (H.T.). |
| *Attached (not to include the details shown above)........ | 5 | 218 | | | | | | | | | | | | | | | | | | | | | | Sick rationed in Fd Amb. |
| Civilians :— Employed with the Unit...... | | | | | | | | | | | | | | | | | | | | | | | | |
| Accompanying the Unit...... | | | | | | | | | | | | | | | | | | | | | | | | |
| TOTAL RATIONED...... | 8 | 436 | | 8 | 17 | 19 | | | | | | | | | | | | | | | | | | |

* In the case of field ambulances, hospitals or depots, the number of patients are to be included here, the names being shown in A.F.A. 36.

[illegible signature] Lt-Col. Signature of Commander.

21st June 1918. Date of Despatch.

For information of the A.G.'s Office at the base.

Officers and men who have become casuals, been transferred or joined since last report.

Place In the Field A. S. C. Date 21st June 1918.

| Regtl. Number | Rank | Name | Corps | Nature of casualty, or name of unit from or to which transferred | Date of being struck off or coming on the ration return | Remarks* |
|---|---|---|---|---|---|---|
| T4/245543 | Dr | Savage A. | A. S. C. (H.T.) att 1/1 Low H Amb | Advanced to 6d rate A.S.C. Corps Pay as Saddler ~~wef~~ from Farr Baillie sick to Hp. | | 7/5/18 vice 6/7/18. Auth 52nd Div Train ASC T117d/11/6/18 |
| T4/245543 | Dr | Savage A | - do - | Retained in the service under M.S.A. 1916 | from 1-12-17. | |
| T4/246064 | " | Sloan W. B. | - do - | Returned from 14 days leave to U.K. | 17/6/18. | |

* State whether absence is of a permanent or temporary nature, adding, in the case of casuals from wounds or disease, any available information for communication to the relatives.

*For information of the A.G.'s Office at the base.*

**Officers and men who have become casuals, been transferred or joined since last report.**

Place: In the Field    Date: 21st June 1918

| Regtl. Number | Rank | Name | Corps | Nature of casualty, or name of unit from or to which transferred | Date of being struck off or coming on the ration return | Remarks* |
|---|---|---|---|---|---|---|
| – | Capt. | Host L.P. | Medical Reserve Corps U.S.A. | to temp. duty with 1/3 Low. Fd Amb. | 15/6/18 | Tempy. |
| – | Capt. | Holmes A.D. | RAMC(T) 1/1 Low. Fd Amb. | to [illegible] duty with 1/4 KOSB as MO. | 20/6/18 | Permanent |
| – | Lieut. Q.M. | Reed A.K. | -do- | Proceeded on 14 days leave to UK. | 20/6/18 | |
| 316066 | Pte | Lumsday W. | -do- | Proceeded on 14 days leave to UK. | 19/6/18 | |
| 316070 | " | McMillan R. | -do- | Proceeded on 14 days leave to UK. | 18/6/18 | |
| 316048 | " | Murray F.H. | -do- | Returned from 14 days leave to UK. | 19/6/18 | |
| 316051 | " | McAllister G. | -do- | -do- | 17/6/18 | |
| 316058 | " | Brown W. | -do- | -do- | 17/6/18 | |
| 316060 | " | Lawson W. | -do- | -do- | 20/6/18 | |
| [illegible] | | [illegible] W. | -do- | Credit rations allce @ 2/1d per diem from 19/6/18 to 1-7-18 14 days leave to UK. | | |
| 316048 | | McMillan R. | -do- | Credit rations allce @ 2/1d per diem from 19/6/18 to 2-7-18 14 days leave to UK. | | |
| ~~[illegible]~~ | | ~~Murray F.H.~~ | ~~-do-~~ | ~~Credit ration allce @ 2/1d per diem from to 14 days leave to UK.~~ | | |
| ~~[illegible]~~ | | ~~[illegible]~~ | ~~-do-~~ | | | |
| ~~[illegible]~~ | | ~~[illegible]~~ | ~~-do-~~ | ~~-do-~~ | | |
| ~~[illegible]~~ | | ~~[illegible]~~ | ~~-do-~~ | ~~Credit ration allce @ 2/1d per diem from to 14 days leave to UK.~~ | | |

| Strength | | | |
|---|---|---|---|
| Officers | T.F. | 6 | |
| | M.R.C. U.S.A. | 2 | 8. |
| W.O. | | 1 | |
| Q.M.S. | | 1 | |
| S/Sgts | | 2 | |
| Sgts | | 9 | |
| N.C.Os (Reg) | | 1 | |
| Cpls (Reg) | | 1/5 | |
| L/Cpls | | 5 | |
| Ptes | | 153 | 180. |

All other ranks RAMC Category 'A'

* State whether absence is of a permanent or temporary nature, adding, in the case of casuals from wounds or disease, any available information for communication to the relatives.

Demands made on this sheet should consist of personnel required from the Base only, and should not include any demands for personnel which can be completed by promotions or appointments within the unit.

Perforated Sheet giving detail of personnel and horses wanting to complete, shown on Army Form B. 213.

No. of Report 152

| Detail of Wanting to Complete. | Drivers R.A. | Drivers R.E. | Drivers A.S.C. | Drivers Car | Drivers Lorry | Drivers Steam | Gunners | Smith Gunners | Range Takers | Farriers Serjeants | Farriers Corporals | Shoeing, or Shoeing and Carriage Smiths | Cold Shoers | Wheelers R.A. | Wheelers H.T. | Wheelers M.T. | Saddlers or Harness Makers | Blacksmiths | Bricklayers and Masons | Carpenters and Joiners |
|---|---|---|---|---|---|---|---|---|---|---|---|---|---|---|---|---|---|---|---|---|
| CAVALRY | | | | | | | | | | | | | | | | | | | | |
| R.A. | | | | | | | | | | | | | | | | | | | | |
| R.E. | | | | | | | | | | | | | | | | | | | | |
| INFANTRY | | | | | | | | | | | | | | | | | | | | |
| R.A.M.C. | | | | | | | | | | | | | | | | | | | | |
| A.O.C. | | | | | | | | | | | | | | | | | | | | |
| A.V.C. | | | | | | | | | | | | | | | | | | | | |
| | | | | | | | | | | | | | | | | | | | | |
| | | | | | | | | | | | | | | | | | | | | |

| Detail of Wanting to Complete. | Fitters & Turners (R.E.) Wood | Fitters & Turners (R.E.) Iron | Fitters R.A. | Fitters Wireless | Plumbers | Electricians Ordinary | Electricians W.T. | Signalmen | Engine Drivers Loco. | Engine Drivers Field | Air Line Men | Permanent Line Men | Operators, Telegraph | Cablemen | Brigade Section Pioneers | General-duty Pioneers | Signallers | Instrument Repairers | Motor Cyclist | Motor Cyclist Artificers | Telephonists |
|---|---|---|---|---|---|---|---|---|---|---|---|---|---|---|---|---|---|---|---|---|---|
| CAVALRY | | | | | | | | | | | | | | | | | | | | | |
| R.A. | | | | | | | | | | | | | | | | | | | | | |
| R.E. | | | | | | | | | | | | | | | | | | | | | |
| INFANTRY | | | | | | | | | | | | | | | | | | | | | |
| R.A.M.C. | | | | | | | | | | | | | | | | | | | | | |
| A.O.C. | | | | | | | | | | | | | | | | | | | | | |
| A.V.C. | | | | | | | | | | | | | | | | | | | | | |
| | | | | | | | | | | | | | | | | | | | | | |
| | | | | | | | | | | | | | | | | | | | | | |

| Detail of Wanting to Complete. | Clerks | Machine Gunners | Armament Artificers Fitters | Armament Artificers Range Finders | Armourers | Storemen | Privates | W.O.'s and N.C.O.'s (by ranks) not included in trade columns | | | | | | | | | | | TOTAL to agree with wanting to complete Officers | TOTAL Other Ranks | Horses Riding | Horses Draught | Horses Heavy Draught | Horses Pack |
|---|---|---|---|---|---|---|---|---|---|---|---|---|---|---|---|---|---|---|---|---|---|---|---|---|
| CAVALRY | | | | | | | | | | | | | | | | | | | | | | | | |
| R.A. | | | | | | | | | | | | | | | | | | | | | | | | |
| R.E. | | | | | | | | | | | | | | | | | | | | | | | | |
| INFANTRY | | | | | | | | | | | | | | | | | | | | | | | | |
| R.A.M.C. | | | | | | | 2 | | | | | | | | | | | | 3 | 2 | | 1 | | |
| A.O.C. | | | | | | | | | | | | | | | | | | | | | | | | |
| A.V.C. | | | | | | | | | | | | | | | | | | | | | | | | |
| | | | | | | | | | | | | | | | | | | | | | | | | |
| | | | | | | | | | | | | | | | | | | | | | | | | |

Remarks :—

[illegible] Lt-Col Signature of Commander.

1/1 Lowl. Fd Ambce R.A.M.C.(T) Unit.

52nd (Low.) Division Formation to which attached.

20th June 1918. Date of Despatch.

(6305) Wt. W2927/M2226. 1,250,000. 6/17. McA. & W., Ltd. (E1348). Forms B213S/8.

[P.T.O.

**To be made up to and for Saturday in each week**

No. of Report 153

# FIELD RETURN.

Army Form B. 213

(To be furnished by all arms, services, and departments (except A.S.C. units) to the A.G.'s Office at the Base in accordance with Field Service Regulations, Part II.)

RETURN showing numbers (a) Effective strength of Unit. (b) Rationed by Unit. 1st Low. Fd Ambce. L.A. 660 at In the Field 28th June 1918. Date.

| DETAIL | Personnel: Officers | Personnel: Other ranks | Personnel: Natives | Animals: Horses: Riding | Animals: Horses: Draught | Animals: Horses: Heavy Draught | Animals: Horses: Pack | Animals: Mules: Large | Animals: Mules: Small | Guns, showing description | Ammunition wagons | Machine guns | Aircraft, showing description | Horsed: 4 Wheeled | Horsed: 2 Wheeled | Mechanical: Motor Cars | Mechanical: Tractors | Mechanical: Lorries, showing description | Mechanical: Trucks, showing description | Mechanical: Trailers | Motor Bicycles | Bicycles | Motor Ambulances | REMARKS |
|---|---|---|---|---|---|---|---|---|---|---|---|---|---|---|---|---|---|---|---|---|---|---|---|---|
| Effective Strength of Unit...... | (a) 7 | (b) 177 | | | | | | | | | | | | | | | | | | | | 1 | | (a) Includes 1 officer at XVII Corps HQ.<br>" 1 " on leave to U.K. |
| Details *by Arms* attached to unit as in War Establishment:— | | | | | | | | | | | | | | | | | | | | | | | | (b) Includes 1 O.R. at Div Concert Party.<br>2 " " D.H.Q.<br>1 " " Hq. Div Train<br>1 " " XVII Corps Hq.<br>9 " on leave to U.K.<br>1 " at [illegible] 1st Army |
| A.S.C. (H.T.) | | (c) 42 | | 7 | 17 | 19 | | | | | | | | 13 | 4 | | | | | | | | | |
| A.S.C. (M.T.) | | (d) 13 | | | | | | | | | | | | | | | | | | | 2 | | 7 | (c) Includes 2 O.R. leave to U.K.<br>(d) " 1 O.R. " " "<br>" 1 " at [illegible] 53 Div. |
| Total | 7 | 232 | | 7 | 17 | 19 | | | | | | | | 13 | 4 | | | | | | 2 | 1 | 7 | (e) R.A.M.C. |
| War Establishment | 10 | 231 | | 8 | 17 | 20 | | | | | | | | 13 | 4 | | | | | | 2 | 1 | 7 | |
| Wanting to complete (Detail of Personnel and Horses below) | 3 | 5 (e) | | 1 | * | 1 | | | | | | | | – | – | | | | | | – | – | – | * 1 Charger to Mob Vet Sec since last return. |
| Surplus | | 6 | | | | | | | | | | | | | | | | | | | | | | A.S.C. (H.T.) |
| *Attached (not to include the details shown above)*.......... | – | 66 | | | | | | | | | | | | | | | | | | | | | | Sick rationed in Fd Amb. |
| Civilians:— Employed with the Unit ...... | | | | | | | | | | | | | | | | | | | | | | | | |
| Accompanying the Unit ...... | | | | | | | | | | | | | | | | | | | | | | | | |
| TOTAL RATIONED...... | 7 | 279 | | 7 | 17 | 19 | | | | | | | | | | | | | | | | | | |

* In the case of field ambulances, hospitals or depots, the number of patients are to be included here, the names being shown in A. F. A. 36.

[illegible] Signature of Commander.

28th June 1918. Date of Despatch.

*For information of the A.G.'s Office at the base.*
A.S.C.

Officers and men who have become casuals, been transferred or joined since last report.

Place In the Field Date 28th June 1918.

| Regtl. Number | Rank | Name | Corps | Nature of casualty, or name of unit from or to which transferred | Date of being struck off or coming on the ration return | Remarks* |
|---|---|---|---|---|---|---|
| T4/045309 | S.S.M. | Searle W.J. | A.S.C. (H.T.) att. 1/1st Low. Fd. Amb. | Retd. from 14 days leave to U.K. | on 25/6/18. | |
| T/35711 | Dr. | McLaren P. | -do- | Granted 14 days from 26.6.18 to | leave to U.K. 10.7.18. via | Boulogne |
| T/35711 | " | McLaren D | -do- | Credit ration @ 2/1d per day for | allce above period | |
| T4/185778 | - | Loudon H | -do- | att. Special Hosp. at Camblain L'Abbé | 23/6/18 | Temp. |
| T4/254279 | - | Harris F | -do- | Entry in AFB 213 "Forfeiture of 1 G.C. Badge" | d/11/5/18. | Hereby cancelled. |

*State whether absence is of a permanent or temporary nature, adding, in the case of casuals from wounds or disease, any available information for communication to the relatives.

*For information of the A.G.'s Office at the base.*

Officers and men who have become casuals, been transferred or joined since last report.

Place In the Field　　　　Date 28th June 1918.

| Regtl. Number | Rank | Name | | Corps | Nature of casualty, or name of unit from or to which transferred | Date of being struck off or coming on the ration return | Remarks* |
|---|---|---|---|---|---|---|---|
| 450092 | Cpl | Luce | J. | R.A.M.C. att 1/1st Low Fd Amb. | War pay increased to 3d per day from | | |
| 316399 | Pte | Beattie | R. | R.A.M.C.(T) 1/1st Low Fd Amb | War pay increased to 3d per day from 10.5.18. | | |
| 316352 | " | Lawrie | J. | -do- | War pay increased to 3d per day from 2.6.15. | | |
| 328053 | " | Marshall | G.S. | -do- | War pay increased to 3d per day from 21.6.18. | | |
| 316306 | " | Stark | J. | -do- | War Pay increased to 3d per day from 11.5.18. | | |
| 318265 | " | Queenan | P. | -do- | War Pay increased ~~from~~ to 3 per day from 25.5.18. | | |
| 316219 | " | Faith | J. | -do- | Corps Pay reduced to 4d - Stoppage of Pay as Bugler from 20 6/18 Auth O/c RAMC Rec. 62/188/18 d/ 6 6/18 | | |
| 316099 | " | Golder | J. | -do- | -do- | -do- | -do- |
| 316064 | L/Cpl | Lamb | D. | -do- | Returned from 14 days leave to UK. | on 22 6/18 | |
| 316238 | Pte | McDonald | W. | -do- | Returned from 14 days leave to UK. | on 22 6/18 | |
| — | Capt | Browne | J. | -do- | Returned from course of instruction at RAMC School | on 23 6/18 | |
| ~~316[illegible]~~ | Cpl | Fothergill | W.D. | -do- | | on 23 6/18 | |
| 316076 | Pte | Harvey | Alex. | -do- | Granted 14 days leave to UK. from 23.6.18 to 7.6.18 credit ration allce @ 2/1d per diem for above period | | |
| 316077 | " | McGillivray | W. | -do- | | | |
| 316191 | " | Stillhouse | J. | -do- | Sick to Hosp. | off 24 6/18 | |
| 316129 | " | White | A. | -do- | Sick to Hosp. | off 26 6/18 | |
| 316038 | " | McAuslane | J.B. | -do- | Sick to Hosp. | off 28 6/18. | |
| 316293 | " | Donald | W.S. | -do- | Temp att ADMS office | off 26 6/18. | Temp. |
| 316168 | Sgt | Meldrum | A.A. | -do- | Granted 14 days leave to UK. from 26.6.18 to 10.7.18 credit ration allce @ 2/1 per d. for above period | | |
| 316074 | Pte | Johnstone | A. | -do- | | | |
| 316232 | L/C | Stewart | J. | -do- | Granted 28 days reengagement leave to UK. from 27.6.18 to 24.7.18. Credit ration allce @ 2/1 p.d. during above period. | | |
| · | Lieut | Hoste | L.N. | M.R.C. U.S.A. | Retd from temp duty with 1/3 Low Fd Amb on 27.6.18. | | |
| 316241 | Pte | McKean | T. | 1/1st Low Fd Amb. RAMC(T) | Retd from 14 days leave to UK. | on 28 6/18. | |
| 316023 | A/S/M | Ritchie | D. | -do- | Tobe Temp S.M. from 25.5.17 Auth O/c RAMC Records 5/20/18 d/ 20/6/18 | | |
| 316207 | Pte | Stanley | R. | -do- | Awarded 5 days C.B. | 22 6/18. | |

Strength:- Officers:- R.A.M.C. T.F. 5; M.R.C. U.S.A. 2 — 7.

| | |
|---|---|
| W.O. | 1 |
| Q.M.S. | 1 |
| S/Sgts | 2 |
| Sgts | 9 |
| L/Sgts. | 1 |
| Cpls. | 3 |
| L/Cpls. | 5 |
| Ptes. | 155 — 177 |

All O.R. RAMC Category 'A'

*State whether absence is of a permanent or temporary nature, adding, in the case of casuals from wounds or disease, any available information for communication to the relatives.

Demands made on this sheet should consist of personnel required from the Base only, and should not include any demands for personnel which can be completed by promotions or appointments within the unit.

Perforated Sheet giving detail of personnel and horses wanting to complete, shown on Army Form B. 213.

No. of Report 150

| Detail of Wanting to Complete. | Drivers R.A. | Drivers R.E. | Drivers A.S.C. | Drivers Car | Drivers Lorry | Drivers Steam | Gunners | Smith Gunners | Range Takers | Farriers Serjeants | Farriers Corporals | Shoeing, or Shoeing and Carriage Smiths | Cold Shoers | Wheelers R.A. | Wheelers H.T. | Wheelers M.T. | Saddlers or Harness Makers. | Blacksmiths | Bricklayers and Masons | Carpenters and Joiners | Fitters & Turners (R.E.) Wood | Fitters & Turners (R.E.) Iron | Fitters R.A. | Fitters Wireless | Plumbers | Electricians Ordinary | Electricians W.T. | Signalmen | Engine Drivers Loco. | Engine Drivers Field | Air Line Men | Permanent Line Men | Operators, Telegraph | Cablemen | Brigade Section Pioneers | General-duty Pioneers | Signallers | Instrument Repairers | Motor Cyclist | Motor Cyclist Artificers | Telephonists | Clerks | Machine Gunners | Armament Artificers Fitters | Armament Artificers Range Finders | Armourers | Storemen | Privates | W.O.'s and N.C.O.'s (by ranks) not included in trade columns | | | | | | | | | | | TOTAL to agree with wanting to complete Officers | TOTAL Other Ranks | Horses Riding | Horses Draught | Horses Heavy Draught | Horses Pack |
|---|---|---|---|---|---|---|---|---|---|---|---|---|---|---|---|---|---|---|---|---|---|---|---|---|---|---|---|---|---|---|---|---|---|---|---|---|---|---|---|---|---|---|---|---|---|---|---|---|---|---|---|---|---|---|---|---|---|---|---|---|---|---|---|---|---|
| CAVALRY. | | | | | | | | | | | | | | | | | | | | | | | | | | | | | | | | | | | | | | | | | | | | | | | | | | | | | | | | | | | | | | | | | |
| R.A. | | | | | | | | | | | | | | | | | | | | | | | | | | | | | | | | | | | | | | | | | | | | | | | | | | | | | | | | | | | | | | | | | |
| R.E. | | | | | | | | | | | | | | | | | | | | | | | | | | | | | | | | | | | | | | | | | | | | | | | | | | | | | | | | | | | | | | | | | |
| INFANTRY | | | | | | | | | | | | | | | | | | | | | | | | | | | | | | | | | | | | | | | | | | | | | | | | | | | | | | | | | | | | | | | | | |
| R.A.M.C. | | | | | | | | | | | | | | | | | | | | | | | | | | | | | | | | | | | | | | | | | | | | | | | | 5 | | | | | | | | | | | | 3 | 5 | 1 | - | 1 | |
| A.O.C. | | | | | | | | | | | | | | | | | | | | | | | | | | | | | | | | | | | | | | | | | | | | | | | | | | | | | | | | | | | | | | | | | |
| A.V.C. | | | | | | | | | | | | | | | | | | | | | | | | | | | | | | | | | | | | | | | | | | | | | | | | | | | | | | | | | | | | | | | | | |

Remarks :—

[signature] Capt
Signature of Commander.

for Lieut-Col. O.C. 1/1 Low. Fd. Ambce
Unit.

52 Division
Formation to which attached.

28th June 1918.
Date of Despatch.

D. D. & L. London, E.C.
(7422) Wt. W14775/M1553 1,000,000 2/17 (E934) Forms B213/8.

[P.T.O.

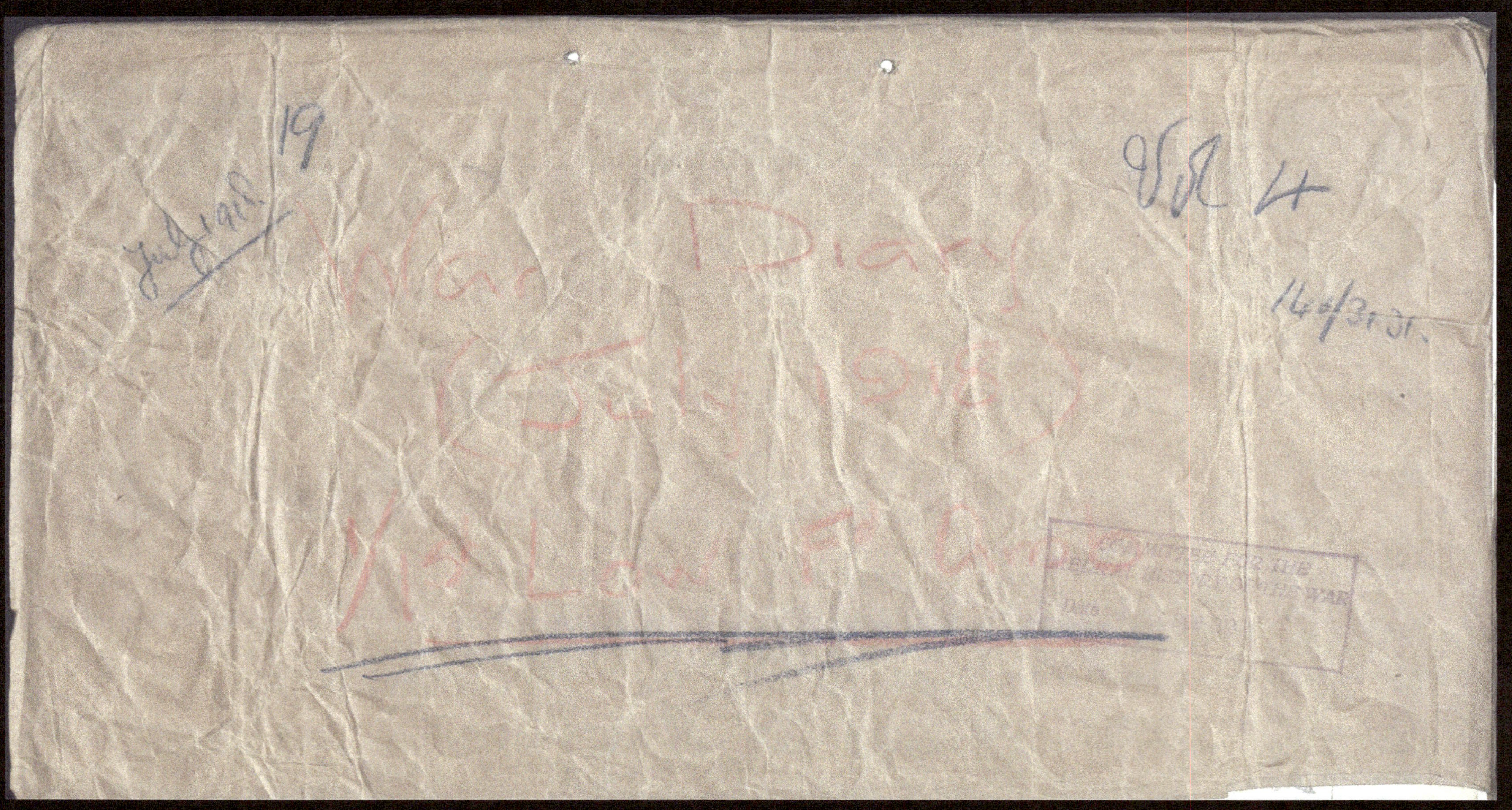
19
Vol 4
War Diary
(July 1918)

Page 436

Army Form C. 2118.

# WAR DIARY
*or*
~~INTELLIGENCE SUMMARY.~~
*(Erase heading not required.)*

Instructions regarding War Diaries and Intelligence Summaries are contained in F. S. Regs., Part II. and the Staff Manual respectively. Title pages will be prepared in manuscript.

1/1st Lowland Field Ambulance

| Place | Date | Hour | Summary of Events and Information | Remarks and references to Appendices |
|---|---|---|---|---|
| VILLERS-AU-BOIS Map B 1/40000 X19c99 | 1/7/18 | | R.1173/9 (ADMS 52nd Divn) calling for report on total possible accommodation for patients. This report was today rendered as Offrs 4. OR 300 | |
| " | 2/7/18 | | One Private on strength. Recd ADMS 52nd Div R1168/1:- Ordering retention of all P.U.O. cases unless their medical condition renders evacuation absolutely necessary. | |
| " | 3/7/18 | | Lieut NUNN S. J. M.R.C., U.S.A. joins as reinforcement & is taken on strength. 1 Pte off strength. | |
| " | 4/7/18 | | Secret order ADMS 52nd Div SR125 of date Summary of medical arrangements Battle Stations & procedure. | |
| " | 5/7/18 | | Under ADMS R1238/4 arrangements made to inspect medically all drafts to this Division | |
| " | do | | Under ADMS R1235/4 all ambulance drivers M.T. make themselves acquainted with alternative routes avoiding prescribed cross-roads. A.D.M.S. S.R. 123 of date Secret:- procedure on receipt of order "man Battle Stations". | |
| | do | | Order placed with newsagent for supply of newspapers for patients cost furnished by Dipping Fund. | |

D. Dugmore Mackenzie Capt

D. D. & L., London, E.C. (A8004) Wt. W1771/M2 31 750,000 5/17 Sch. 52 Forms/C2118/14

Page 437

Army Form C. 2118.

# WAR DIARY

*or*

~~INTELLIGENCE SUMMARY.~~

*(Erase heading not required.)*

1/1st Lowland Fd Ambce
RAMC T

Instructions regarding War Diaries and Intelligence Summaries are contained in F. S. Regs., Part II. and the Staff Manual respectively. Title pages will be prepared in manuscript.

| Place | Date | Hour | Summary of Events and Information | Remarks and references to Appendices |
|---|---|---|---|---|
| VILLERS-AU-BOIS MAP B X19c99 | 6/7/18 | | Under R1176/4 (ADMS 52nd Div) LIEUT. C.E. HAMILTON M.R.C., U.S.A. takes over medical charge of 52nd MG Battalion | No 1 Weekly Health Report |
| do | 7/7/18 | | Rec'd ADMS S.R. 128 Battle Stations procedure | No 2 Weekly Sanitary Report. |
| do | 8/7/18 | | ADMS R1294 of date details 40 men working Party to 3rd Lowland Fd Ambce. Secret ADMS 52nd Div S.R. 125 amendments Medical Locations. | |
| do | 9/7/18 | | Capt A.D. DOWNES withdrawn from 1/4th KOSB on relief by LT. W.H. HOST M.R.C. U.S.A. Q.M.S J.K. TAYLOR off strength on promotion to S/M & reposting. | |
| | " | | ADMS R.1318/9 Winter hutting accommodation needs asked | |
| do | 10/7/18 | | Nothing to report. | |
| | 11/7/18 | | Nothing to report | |

D. D. & L., London, E.C.
(A8004) Wt. W1771/M2·31 750,000 5/17 Sch. 52 Forms/C2118/14

Page 438

Army Form C. 2118.

# WAR DIARY
or
~~INTELLIGENCE SUMMARY.~~
(Erase heading not required.)

Instructions regarding War Diaries and Intelligence Summaries are contained in F. S. Regs., Part II. and the Staff Manual respectively. Title pages will be prepared in manuscript.

1/1st Lowland Fd Ambce
RAMC T

| Place | Date | Hour | Summary of Events and Information | Remarks and references to Appendices |
|---|---|---|---|---|
| VILLERS-AU-BOIS MAP B. X 19.C.9.9. | 12/7/18 | | ADMS R/1311/4 of date:- Owing to subsidence of P.U.O. epidemic Gargling now omitted & concert halls may now be taken into use. [initials] | |
| do | 13/7/18 | | 1 Pte on strength. | No. 3 Weekly Health Report. |
| do | 14/7/18 | | Lt Colonel J. W. LEITCH D.S.O. on return from Leave resumes command of unit. [signature] Major | No. 4 Sanitary Report |
| do | 15/7/18 | | D.D.M.S. VIII Corps visited this ambulance during the afternoon & made a minute inspection of the camp. J.W.L. | |
| do | 16/7/18 | | Called on A.D.M.S. at his request at 1030 to-day to take over his duties on proceeding on 14 day's leave to U.K. Returned in time for lunch, & in afternoon went round the unit's camp accompanied by Major Mackenzie & the Quartermaster (Capt Reid). I shall stay at Div. H.Q. while acting as A.D.M.S. & Major Mackenzie will act for me in the ambulance. John W. Leitch | |

D. D. & L., London, E.C.
(A8004) Wt. W1771/M2 31 750,000 5/17 Sch. 52 Forms/C2118/14

Page 439

Army Form C. 2118.

1/1st Lowland Fd Ambce RAMC T

# WAR DIARY
*or*
# ~~INTELLIGENCE SUMMARY.~~
(*Erase heading not required.*)

Instructions regarding War Diaries and Intelligence Summaries are contained in F. S. Regs., Part II. and the Staff Manual respectively. Title pages will be prepared in manuscript.

| Place | Date | Hour | Summary of Events and Information | Remarks and references to Appendices |
|---|---|---|---|---|
| VILLERS-AU-BOIS. MAP "B" X.19.C.9.9 | 16/7/18 | | A.D.M.S. 52nd Div No. R.1440/4 ~~ordering~~ 16 bearers to report to 1/3 Lowland Fd ambulance complied with. NBm | |
| | 17/7/18 | | Nothing to note. NBm | |
| | 18/7/18 | | Heavy bomb fell in proximity to Rest Station (Enemy aircraft, no casualties, slight damage. Form of Weekly Sanitary Report circulated by D.D.M.S. VIII Corps passed to units in this area having no M.O. & of strength over 20 NBm | Ap. V |
| | 19/7/18 | | A.D.M.S. No S.R. 143/1 Rec'd Warning "move" Major J. BROWNE South Wales Mounted Brig Fd Amb. att 1/1 Lowland Fd Amb to ~~Hosp~~ C.C.S. struck off strength. A.D.M.S. S.R 143/7 rec'd Disposal ~~[illegible]~~ of Equipment, Stores & patients, & notifying affiliation of This unit to 156 Inf Brig. for move NBm | |
| | 20/7/18 | | Secret B.M. 200 156 Inf. Brig. Rec'd :– Details of Relief<br>Called at 156 Inf Brig HQrs to discuss "medical arrangements" for forthcoming Orders for move.<br>52nd Div Train Order B.602 rec'd :– "Supplies" & movement of Train wagon.<br>Rec'd 156 Inf Brig Order No.44 :– Details of Relief, Routes & order of march, Timings. NBm<br>Weekly Health Report forwarded. | Ap. VI |

D. D. & L., London, E.C. (A8004) Wt. W1771/M2 31 750,000 5/17 Sch. 52 Forms/C2118/14

Instructions regarding War Diaries and Intelligence Summaries are contained in F. S. Regs., Part II. and the Staff Manual respectively. Title pages will be prepared in manuscript.

# WAR DIARY
*or*
# ~~INTELLIGENCE SUMMARY.~~
*(Erase heading not required.)*

Page 40 Army Form C. 2118.

1/1st Lowland Fd Ambce

| Place | Date | Hour | Summary of Events and Information | Remarks and references to Appendices |
|---|---|---|---|---|
| VILLERS-AU-BOIS MAP "B" X.19.c.9.9. | 21/7/18 | | Rec'd R.A.M.C. Operation Order No. 6 :- "Information, moves, Evacuation" | |
| | | | Rec'd 156 Inf Brig Order 45 :- move arrangements, medical arrangements | |
| | | | 16 Bearers returned from 1/3rd Lowland Fd Ambce | |
| | | | Handed over 52 Divisional Rest Station to 25th Fd Ambce | |
| | | | Weekly Sanitary Report forwarded to ADMS 52nd Div. [initials] | ~~A.P.~~ |
| | 22/7/18 | | Handed over W.W.D.P. Mingoval to 25th Fd Ambce. Relief Completed. | |
| | | | Unit marched out 16.25. Marching out State to ADMS 52nd | Ap. VII |
| | | | Division & 156 Inf Brigade. Arrived BARLIN at 1900. [initials] | |
| | | | Unit billeted in unoccupied miners cottages. | |
| BARLIN P. de C. Q3 a 36 | 23/7/18 | | Rec'd B.M. 242 even date 156 Inf Brig:- Warning move at short notice. | |
| | | | Attended conference at 156 Inf Hqrs:- Discussion on move by Tactical Train [initials] | |
| | | | Rec'd BM 248 d 23/7/18 156 Inf Brig:- Orders re foregoing. | |
| | 24/7/18 | | Rec'd B.M. 250 of even date 156 Inf Brig:- Orders relative to foreshadowed | |
| | | | move at short notice by Tactical Train or Bus. Reconnoitred | |
| | | | route of march & reported thereon. [initials] | |
| | | | Two limbered wagons allotted loaded with cooks utensils & medical | |
| | | | stores on a skeleton basis, & reported details of this to A.D.M.S. 52nd Div. [initials] | |
| | 25/7/18 | | Rec'd 156 Inf Brig S.C. 671 d 25/7/18 re distribution & transport of rations | |
| | | | in event of a move; also B.M. 263 d/25/7/18 156 Inf Brig amending B.M. 250 | |
| | | | Ferguson Mackenzie | |

D. D. & L., London, E.C. (A8004) Wt. W1771/M2 31 750,000 5/17 Sch. 52 Forms/C2118/14

Instructions regarding War Diaries and Intelligence Summaries are contained in F. S. Regs., Part II. and the Staff Manual respectively. Title pages will be prepared in manuscript.

# WAR DIARY

*or*

~~INTELLIGENCE SUMMARY.~~

*(Erase heading not required.)*

1/1st Lowland Fd Ambce

Page 440 Army Form C. 2118.

| Place | Date | Hour | Summary of Events and Information | Remarks and references to Appendices |
|---|---|---|---|---|
| BARLIN P. de C. Q 3 a 3.6 | 25/7/18 | | Rec'd 156 Inf. Brig S.C. 653:- further amendments to move rationing. RDm | |
| do | 26/7/18 | | Rec'd BM 278 156th Inf Brig:- Orders re Dress & Fighting Order. RDm | |
| do | 27/7/18 | | Nothing to note RDm | |
| do | 28/7/18 | | Nothing to note RDm | |
| do | 29/7/18 | | Rec'd. 156 Inf. Brig. Order. No. 46 of date:- move by road, march Table for 30th July 1918 with medical arrangements. | |
| | | | Rec'd B.M. 310, 156th Inf. Brig. Destination changed. Advance Party 1 Off. + 1 O.R. proceed. | |
| ECOIVRES F.13.a.8.2. | 30/7/18 | | Unit marched out at 1000 & arrived at Ecoivres 1530 | App No VIII |
| | | | Rec'd. on arrival R.A.M.C. Op. Order. No. 7 d/30/7/18:- Reliefs, Evacuation &c | |
| | | | Rec'd B.M. No 47 156 Brig:- Reliefs, Guides, Precautions &c | |
| do | 31/7/18 | | Rec'd "Amendment to RAMC Op. Order No. 7" d/30/7/18:- This unit to remain at present location dealing with sick of Division. | |

D. D. & L., London, E.C. (A8004) Wt. W1771/M2 31 750,000 5/17 Sch. 52 Forms/C2118/14

Instructions regarding War Diaries and Intelligence Summaries are contained in F. S. Regs., Part II. and the Staff Manual respectively. Title pages will be prepared in manuscript.

# WAR DIARY
*or*
# ~~INTELLIGENCE SUMMARY.~~

*(Erase heading not required.)*

Page 442

Army Form C. 2118.

1/1st Lowland Fd Ambce

| Place | Date | Hour | Summary of Events and Information | Remarks and references to Appendices |
|---|---|---|---|---|
| ECOIVRES F13a8.2. | 31/7/18 | | Capt. J.W. BURTON returned from temporary duty with DDMS VIII Corps<br>Lieut. S.J. NUNN sent for duty with 1/2nd Lowland Fd Ambce under ADMS 52nd Div No. R.1614/5 d/31/7/18.<br>Ferguson Mackenzie<br>Major for O.C.<br>1/1st Lowland Fd Ambce | |

D. D. & L., London, E.C.
(A8004) Wt. W1771/M2 31 750,000 5/17 Sch. 52 Forms/C2118/14

Vol. XXXVIII Appendix 1. - War Diary of 1/1st Low Fd Amb JULY 1918

(A) Principal causes of admissions during week.

| | Total | Increase | Decrease |
|---|---|---|---|
| P.U.O. | 25 | - | 15 |
| Scabies | 8 | 4 | - |
| Dental | 14 | 13 | - |
| (b) Total Sick Admissions | 48 | 12 | - |
| (c) Infectious Diseases | – | – | 2 |

(d) General Remarks:- Admissions by Brigades are as follows;

| | Total | Increase | Decrease |
|---|---|---|---|
| 155th Bde. | 20 | 6 | - |
| 156th " | 13 | - | 6 |
| 157th " | 14 | 1 | - |
| Div. Troops | 28 | - | 1 |

The features of the weeks admissions are the increase of Dental cases, and the decrease of P.U.O.



Fergusson Mackenzie
Capt.
OC 1/1st Low Fd. Amb

Appendix II (July 1918)

Vol. XXXVIII

WAR DIARY 1/1st LOW FD AMB

A.D.M.S.

52 Division

Weekly Sanitary Report on

small Units, detachments etc in VILLERS au BOIS Area

I have to report that many improvements have been carried out in VILLERS CAMP and sanitary work is still actively in progress.

[illegible] CAMP shows improvement.

The Billet occupied by Canadian Concert Party is now vacant. New grease trap is required by Army Troops Coy R.E. In other Units points have been indicated, for improvement, to Officers concerned.

[illegible] Mackenzie
Capt.
S.O. 1/1 Low Fd Ambce.

F 359

7.7.18.

VoL XXXVIII APPDIX III July 1918

WAR DIARY 1/1st Low Fd Amb

D.D.M.S. – 52nd Div

Weekly Health Report for 52nd Div. W/E 13.7.18

(a) Principal causes of admissions during week.

| | Total | Increase | Decrease |
|---|---|---|---|
| P.U.O. | 20 | - | 5 |
| Scabies | 6 | - | 2 |
| Dental | 9 | - | 5 |
| (b) Total sick admissions | 75 | - | 3 |
| (c) Infectious Diseases | 2 | 2 | - |

(d) General Remarks:- Admissions by Brigades are as follows;

| | Total | Increase | Decrease |
|---|---|---|---|
| 155th Bde. | 12 | - | 8 |
| 156th " | 29 | 16 | - |
| 157th " | 8 | - | 9 |
| Div. Troops. | 26 | - | 2 |

The increase in 156th Bde. is mainly attributable to [illegible]. There is not however in this case any one notable disease accounting for change.

[illegible signature]
Major
for OC 1/1st Low Fd. Amb

Vol. XXXVIII Appendix IV Jun 1918 War Diary of 1/1st Low. Fd. Amb.

A.D.M.S. 52nd Div.

Weekly Sanitary Report – Small Units 1
Area

I have to report that Units detailed by you, have been visited by me, and a Sanitary Diary has been opened in the Orderly Rooms of the majority of them, and notes for guidance made therein.

The following Units have left the area:–

16th Canadian Concert Party.

139th Labour Coy.

A.T. Coy, R.E.

At VILLERS camp 52nd Div. Reinforcements appear to be defeated in sanitary effort by the fact that the permanent staff is too small. The greater part of cooking and conservancy falls on a constantly changing personnel, who have no knowledge of requirements or of the facilities in existence. Cooking should be centralised. There are at present half a dozen or more cooking parties. Control is difficult, responsibility cannot be placed, and it is not reasonable to expect a like number of tables, meat safes, grease traps etc.

Rispin Camp, now occupied by M.G. detachment is supervised by the M.O. of 52nd M.G. Btn.

No. 2 Labour Coy, LA PENOU are worked by their own M.O. periodically. Sanitation is good. The bucket system of latrines is in use. Screening has been suggested to render this fly proof.

Water, kitchen, soakage points have been drawn attention to at Salvage and Ordnance Units.

14/7/18.

[illegible signature]
for O.C. 1/1st Low. Fd. Amb. RAMC

Vol XXXVIII Appendix V War Diary July 1918 of 1/1st Low Fd Amb

UNIT ......................................

WEEKLY SANITARY REPORT.

Week ending, Saturday.............1918.

1. Map location of Unit and M.I.Room.
2. Strength of Unit.
3. How many latrines and what type.
   (a)

   (b) How many existing latrines are inefficient.
   (c) How many latrines are not fitted with automatic lid-closing. in good repair.
4. (a) How many urinals and what type.
   (b) How many night urinals are provided.
   (c) How many existing Urinals are inefficient (i.e. without baffle plates, with wet standings etc.
5. How is excreta disposed of.
6. How many Cookhouses (including all Officers' Kitchens) are not:-
   (a) Clean.
   (b) Provided with clean table.
   (c) Provided with efficient food safe.
   (d) Provided with a receptacle (with lid) for dry refuse.
   (e) Provided with an efficient grease trap (with lid) in immediate neighbourhood.
   (f) Provided with ovens.
7. (a) What type of incinerator.
   (b) Whether efficient.
   (c) Is refuse bay provided.
8. WATER. (a) Source.
   (b) Amount of Bleaching powder used.
   (c) Is water duty personnel competent and permanent.
   (d) Condition of Water Carts.
   (e) How often cleaned - Dates of cleaning
   (f) What deficiencies in the following equipment:-Padlock (in working order)
   Tins of clarifying powder - 3.
   do. fresh bleaching powder-3.
   Rubber washers (packed in French chalk)
   Spanner No.287 (for differential pump.)
   Carriage brush. Tank brush.
   Washing brush.
   Covers for clarifying reels - 3.
   (g) Are the parts mentioned in (f) kept on the cart in the places provided for them.
   (h) Dates on which water in water carts tested by M.O.
   (i) How often are water bottles cleansed.

9. **FOOD.**
(a) Is diet sufficiently varied.
(b) Is supply of fresh vegetables supplemented from Canteen funds.
(c) How many cooks (including Officers mess Cooks) are not in possession of two suits of overalls.
(d) Average % of fresh meat supplied.

10. **ABLUTION.** (c) Are dining rooms provided
(a) How many benches.
(b) Are soap traps and filter pits (clarification sets) efficient.
(c) Are standings provided.

11. **BATHING.**
(a) Facilities.
(b) Number bathed.

12. How is manure dealt with. (Vide G.R.O. 1088 of 30/6/18.

13. Result of Contagious and Infectious Disease inspection. (All inspections held during the month to be included, also in the separate monthly report.) Dates of inspections, numbers inspected and findings to be given.

14. **DRAFTS.** (a) General physique.
(b) Freedom from lice and scabies.
(c) If fully inoculated.

15. **DELOUSING.**
Numbers deloused during week.

16. **INOCULATION.**
Numbers inoculated during week.

17. Number of men seen in M. I. Room.
do. do. sent to Hosp. with Pyrexia.
do. do. do. do. Scabies.
do. do. do. do. I. C. T.
do. do. do. do. Other Diseases

18. **C.O's REMARKS.**
What steps (in detail) have been taken:-
(a) To provide new sanitary appliances and facilities.

(b) To remedy any existing defects.

---

I have personally inspected all sanitation of the Unit, as shewn in the above report during the week.

Signature of M.O. ..........................

.........1918. ..........................

Vol XXXVIII War Diary (July 1918)

A.D.M.S. 52nd D.v.

Appendix VI

Weekly Health Report for 52nd Div. W/E 20.7.18

Principal causes of admissions during week.

| | Total | Increase | Decrease |
|---|---|---|---|
| P.U.O. | 5 | - | 15 |
| Scabies | 16 | 10 | - |
| Dental | 9 | - | - |
| (b) Total Sick Admissions | 65 | - | 10 |
| c) Infectious Diseases | - | - | 2 |

d) General Remarks:- Admissions by Brigades are as follows.

| | Total | Increase | Decrease |
|---|---|---|---|
| 155th Bde | 24 | 12 | - |
| 156th " | 9 | - | 20 |
| 157th " | 19 | 11 | - |
| Div. Troops. | 13 | - | 13 |

The features of the week are the steady declension of P.U.O.

Increase of 155th Bde due to 1/4th R.S.F. with 13 cases of which 8 are Scabies or Phthiriasis. Increase of 157th is merely due to same diseases

[illegible]
Major [illegible]
O/C 1/1st Low. Fd. Amb.

Vol. XXXVIII Appendix VII (July 1918) War Diary

Marching Out State of 1/1st Low Fd Amb

1/1st Low. Fd. Ambce. R.A.M.C.(T).

| Unit | Officers | Other Ranks | | Animals | Wagons | | Motor Amb Cars | Motor Cycles | | Remarks |
|---|---|---|---|---|---|---|---|---|---|---|
| | | R.A.M.C. | A.S.C. | | 4 wheeled | 2 wheeled | | | | |
| 1/1st Low. Fd. Amb. and A.S.C. (HT) + (MT) attached. | (a) 5 | 139 | * 52 | (b) 44 | (c) 14 | 4 | 6 | 1 | | (a) Includes 1 Chaplain<br>(b) Includes 2 Horses of Train Wagon<br>(c) Includes Train Wagon.<br>* Includes Train Driver |



[signature]
Major
for Lt.-Colonel,
O.C. 1st L. F. A. R. A. M. C. (T).

Vol XXXVIII Appendix VIII (July 1918) War Diary of 1/1st Low Fd Amb.

Marching Out State

1/1st. Low Fd. Amb.

| Unit | Officers | O.R. RAMC. | O.R. A.S.C. | Animals | Wagons 4 Wheeled | Wagons 2 Wheeled | Motor Ambce Cars | Motor Cycles | Remarks |
|---|---|---|---|---|---|---|---|---|---|
| 1/1st. Low. Fd. Amb and A.S.C. H.T. & M.T. attached | (a) 5 | 139. | * 44 | (b) 39. | (c) 14 | 4 | 7 | 1 | (a) Includes one Chaplain (b) Includes 2 horses Train Wagon (c) Includes Train wagons * Includes Train Drivers |

Field
29.7.18

[signature] Major
for Cb. 1/1st Low Fd. Amb.

**To be made up to and for Saturday in each week**

No. of Report ____________

# FIELD RETURN.

Army Form B. 213

(To be furnished by all arms, services, and departments (except A.S.C. units) to the A.G.'s Office at the Base in accordance with Field Service Regulations, Part II.)

RETURN showing numbers (*a*) Effective strength of Unit. (*b*) Rationed by Unit. [illegible] at [illegible] [illegible] July 1918 Date.

| DETAIL | Personnel: Officers | Personnel: Other ranks | Personnel: Natives | Animals: Horses: Riding | Horses: Draught | Horses: Heavy Draught | Horses: Pack | Mules: Large | Mules: Small | Guns, showing description | Ammunition wagons | Machine guns | Aircraft, showing description | Horsed: 4 Wheeled | Horsed: 2 Wheeled | Mechanical: Motor Cars | Tractors | Lorries, showing description | Trucks, showing description | Trailers | Motor Bicycles | Bicycles | Motor Ambulances | REMARKS |
|---|---|---|---|---|---|---|---|---|---|---|---|---|---|---|---|---|---|---|---|---|---|---|---|---|
| Effective Strength of Unit...... | (a) 5 | (b) 14 | | | | | | | | | | | | | | | | | | | | 1 | | (a) Includes 1 officer att XVIII Corps H.Q. / [illegible] on leave |
| Details *by Arms* attached to unit as in War Establishment:— | | | | | | | | | | | | | | | | | | | | | | | | (b) Includes 1 O.R. att [illegible] / [illegible] |
| A.S.C. (H.T.) | | 41 (c) | | 7 | 17 | 20 | | | | | | | | 10 | 4 | | | | | | | | | 1 " " [illegible] / 1 " " H.Q. XVIII Corps / 1 " " [illegible] |
| A.S.C. (M.T.) | | 136 (d) | | | | | | | | | | | | | | | | | | | 2 | | 7 | 10 on leave [illegible] |
| | | | | | | | | | | | | | | | | | | | | | | | | (c) Includes 3 O.R. on leave to U.K. |
| | | | | | | | | | | | | | | | | | | | | | | | | (d) " 1 O.R. att [illegible] |
| Total | 6 | 233 | | 7 | 17 | 20 | | | | | | | | 13 | 4 | | | | | | 2 | 1 | 7 | |
| War Establishment | 10 | 231 | | 8 | 17 | 20 | | | | | | | | 13 | 4 | | | | | | 2 | 1 | 7 | |
| Wanting to complete (Detail of Personnel and Horses below) | 2 | 53 | | 1 | | 4 | | | | | | | | | | | | | | | | | | * to [illegible] |
| Surplus | | 5 | | | | | | | | | | | | | | | | | | | | | | |
| *Attached (not to include the details shown above)......... | 1 | 90 | | | | | | | | | | | | | | | | | | | | | | A.S.C. (M.T.) |
| Civilians:— Employed with the Unit...... | 1 | | | | | | | | | | | | | | | | | | | | | | | Not rationed |
| Accompanying the Unit...... | | | | | | | | | | | | | | | | | | | | | | | | Drivers |
| TOTAL RATIONED...... | 1 | 308 | | 7 | 17 | 20 | | | | | | | | | | | | | | | | | | |

* In the case of field ambulances, hospitals or depots, the number of patients are to be included here, the names being shown in A.F.A. 36.

[illegible] Signature of Commander. [illegible] July 1918 Date of Despatch.

*For information of the A.G.'s Office at the base.*

A.S.C.

Officers and men who have become casuals, been transferred or joined since last report.

Place In the Field Date 5th July 1918.

| Regtl. Number | Rank | Name | Corps | Nature of casualty, or name of unit from or to which transferred | Date of being struck off or coming on the ration return | Remarks* |
|---|---|---|---|---|---|---|
| [illegible] | Dr | Farrell | A.S.C. att 1/1 [illegible] Fd. Amb | Sick to Hosp. | Off 1/7/18 | |
| [illegible] | " | Carwood | -do- | Granted 14 days leave to U.K. from 3.7.18 to 17.7.18. | | |
| [illegible] | " | Carwood | -do- | Credit ration allce @ 2/1 p.d. from 3.7.18 to 17.7.18. 14 days leave to U.K. | | |
| | " | [illegible] | -do- | Retd from [illegible] duty at [illegible] | on 3/7/18 | |
| [illegible] | Dr | Dunkason | A.S.C. MT att 1/1 [illegible] F Amb | Returned from 14 days leave to U.K. | on 1/7/18 | |
| [illegible] | " | [illegible] | -do- | Increase of [illegible] Pay @ [illegible] per day from 11.12.17. | | |
| | | | | | | |

* State whether absence is of a permanent or temporary nature, adding, in the case of casuals from wounds or disease, any available information for communication to the relatives.

*For information of the A.G.'s Office at the base.*

Officers and men who have become casuals, been transferred or joined since last report.

Place In the Field Date 5th July 1918.

| Regtl. Number | Rank | Name | Corps | Nature of casualty, or name of unit from or to which transferred | Date of being struck off or coming on the ration return | Remarks* |
|---|---|---|---|---|---|---|
| — | Lt.-Col. | J. A. Lenton | R. A. M. C. (T) 1st Low. Fd. Amb. | Granted 14 days leave to U.K. from 29.6.18 to 13.7.18. | | |
| | [illegible] | [illegible] L. | R. A.M.C. (T) | Joined unit as reinforcement | on 1/7/18 | |
| 31024 | Pte | [illegible] A. | R. A. M. C. (T) 1st Low. Fd. Amb. | Rejoined unit from Hospital | on 3/7/18 | |
| — | Lieut. | [illegible] J. J. | M. R. C. U. S. A. | Joined unit as reinforcement | on 4/7/18 | |
| 316079 | Cpl. | Ross D. | R. A. M. C. (T) 1st Low. Fd. Amb. | Granted 14 days leave to U.K. from 30.6.18 to 14.7.18 | | |
| [illegible] | Cpl. | Ross D | -do- | Credit ration allce @ 1/- p.d. from 30.6.18 to 14.7.18. 14 days leave to U.K. | | |
| [illegible] | Pte | Gallacher G | -do- | Granted 14 days leave to U.K. from 30.6.18 to 14.7.18 | | |
| [illegible] | Pte. | Gallacher G. | -do- | Credit ration allce @ 1/- p.d. from 30.6.18 to 14.7.18. 14 days leave to U.K. | | |
| 316073 | " | Cowie J. | -do- | Granted 14 days leave to U.K. from 3.7.18 to 17.7.18. | | |
| 316076 | " | Cowie J. | -do- | Credit ration allce @ 1/- p.d. from 3.7.18 to 17.7.18. 14 days leave to U.K. | | |
| [illegible] | " | Glendey S. | -do- | Granted 14 days leave to U.K. from 3.7.18 to 17.7.18. | | |
| [illegible] | " | Glendey S. | -do- | Credit ration allce @ 3/6 p.d. from 3.7.18 to 17.7.18 14 days leave to U.K. | | |
| [illegible] | Cpl. | [illegible] R. | -do- | Granted 28 days leave to U.K. from 4.7.18 to 31.7.18. | | |
| [illegible] | Cpl. | [illegible] R. | -do- | Credit ration allce @ 3/6 p.d. from 4.7.18 to 31.7.18. 28 days leave to U.K. | | |
| [illegible] | [illegible] | [illegible] W. | -do- | Returned from 14 days leave to U.K. | on 3/7/18 | |
| [illegible] | Cpl | McGregor J. | -do- | -do- | on 3/7/18 | |
| [illegible] | Pte | [illegible] W. | -do- | -do- | on 4/7/18 | |
| [illegible] | Pte | McMillan R. | -do- | -do- | on 5/7/18 | |
| | | Strength | Officers | T.F. 5 / M.R.C. U.S.A. 3 | 8 | |
| | | | W.O. | 1 | | |
| | | | Q.M.S. | 1 | | |
| | | | S. Sgts | 2 | | |
| | | | Sgts | 10 | | |
| | | | L/Sgts | 1 | | |
| | | | Cpls | 8 | | |
| | | | L/Cpls | 6 | | |
| | | | Ptes | 150 | 179 | |
| | | All Category "A" | | | | |

* State whether absence is of a permanent or temporary nature, adding, in the case of casuals from wounds or disease, any available information for communication to the relatives.

Demands made on this sheet should consist of personnel required from the Base only, and should not include any demands for personnel which can be completed by promotions or appointments within the unit.

Perforated Sheet giving detail of personnel and horses wanting to complete, shown on Army Form B. 213.

No. of Report 154

| Detail of Wanting to Complete. | Drivers: R.A. | Drivers: R.E. | Drivers: A.S.C. | Drivers: Car | Drivers: Lorry | Drivers: Steam | Gunners | Smith Gunners | Range Takers | Farriers: Serjeants | Farriers: Corporals | Shoeing, or Shoeing and Carriage Smiths | Cold Shoers | Wheelers: R.A. | Wheelers: H.T. | Wheelers: M.T. | Saddlers or Harness Makers | Blacksmiths | Bricklayers and Masons | Carpenters and Joiners | Fitters & Turners (R.E.): Wood | Fitters & Turners (R.E.): Iron | Fitters: R.A. | Fitters: Wireless | Plumbers | Electricians: Ordinary | Electricians: W.T. | Signalmen | Engine Drivers: Loco. | Engine Drivers: Field |
|---|---|---|---|---|---|---|---|---|---|---|---|---|---|---|---|---|---|---|---|---|---|---|---|---|---|---|---|---|---|---|
| CAVALRY | | | | | | | | | | | | | | | | | | | | | | | | | | | | | | |
| R.A. | | | | | | | | | | | | | | | | | | | | | | | | | | | | | | |
| R.E. | | | | | | | | | | | | | | | | | | | | | | | | | | | | | | |
| INFANTRY | | | | | | | | | | | | | | | | | | | | | | | | | | | | | | |
| R.A.M.C. | | | | | | | | | | | | | | | | | | | | | | | | | | | | | | |
| A.O.C. | | | | | | | | | | | | | | | | | | | | | | | | | | | | | | |
| A.V.C. | | | | | | | | | | | | | | | | | | | | | | | | | | | | | | |
| | | | | | | | | | | | | | | | | | | | | | | | | | | | | | | |
| | | | | | | | | | | | | | | | | | | | | | | | | | | | | | | |

| Detail of Wanting to Complete. | Air Line Men | Permanent Line Men | Operators, Telegraph | Cablemen | Brigade Section Pioneers | General-duty Pioneers | Signallers | Instrument Repairers | Motor Cyclist | Motor Cyclist Artificers | Telephonists | Clerks | Machine Gunners | Armament Artificers: Fitters | Armament Artificers: Range Finders | Armourers | Storemen | Privates | W.O.'s and N.C.O.'s (by ranks) not included in trade columns | | | | | | | | | | | TOTAL to agree with wanting to complete: Officers | TOTAL to agree with wanting to complete: Other Ranks | Horses: Riding | Horses: Draught | Horses: Heavy Draught | Horses: Pack |
|---|---|---|---|---|---|---|---|---|---|---|---|---|---|---|---|---|---|---|---|---|---|---|---|---|---|---|---|---|---|---|---|---|---|---|---|
| CAVALRY | | | | | | | | | | | | | | | | | | | | | | | | | | | | | | | | | | | |
| R.A. | | | | | | | | | | | | | | | | | | | | | | | | | | | | | | | | | | | |
| R.E. | | | | | | | | | | | | | | | | | | | | | | | | | | | | | | | | | | | |
| INFANTRY | | | | | | | | | | | | | | | | | | | | | | | | | | | | | | | | | | | |
| R.A.M.C. | | | | | | | | | | | | | | | | | | 3 | | | | | | | | | | | | 2 | 3 | 1 | - | 1 | - |
| A.O.C. | | | | | | | | | | | | | | | | | | | | | | | | | | | | | | | | | | | |
| A.V.C. | | | | | | | | | | | | | | | | | | | | | | | | | | | | | | | | | | | |
| | | | | | | | | | | | | | | | | | | | | | | | | | | | | | | | | | | | |
| | | | | | | | | | | | | | | | | | | | | | | | | | | | | | | | | | | | |

Remarks :—

[illegible] Captain — Signature of Commander.

[illegible] C.A.D. 6(T) — Unit.

[illegible] Division — Formation to which attached.

5th July 1918 — Date of Despatch.

[P.T.O.

(6305) Wt. W2927/M2226. 1,250,000. 6/17. McA. & W., Ltd. (E1348). Forms B2138/8.

**To be made up to and for Saturday in each week**

No. of Report 155

# FIELD RETURN.

Army Form B. 213

(To be furnished by all arms, services, and departments (except A.S.C. units) to the A.G.'s Office at the Base in accordance with Field Service Regulations, Part II.)

RETURN showing numbers (a) Effective strength of Unit. (b) Rationed by Unit. [illegible] at [illegible] 12th July 1918 Date.

| DETAIL | Personnel: Officers | Personnel: Other ranks | Personnel: Natives | Animals: Horses: Riding | Animals: Horses: Draught | Animals: Horses: Heavy Draught | Animals: Horses: Pack | Animals: Mules: Large | Animals: Mules: Small | Guns, showing description | Ammunition wagons | Machine guns | Aircraft, showing description | Horsed: 4 Wheeled | Horsed: 2 Wheeled | Mechanical: Motor Cars | Mechanical: Tractors | Mechanical: Lorries, showing description | Mechanical: Trucks, showing description | Mechanical: Trailers | Motor Bicycles | Bicycles | Motor Ambulances | REMARKS |
|---|---|---|---|---|---|---|---|---|---|---|---|---|---|---|---|---|---|---|---|---|---|---|---|---|
| Effective Strength of Unit...... | (a) 8 | (b) 177 | | | | | | | | | | | | | | | | | | | | 1 | | (a) Includes 1 off. Corps att. VIII Corps Hq. 1 off. [illegible] att. 52 M.G. Bn. 1 off. on leave to UK |
| Details *by Arms* attached to unit as in War Establishment:— | | | | | | | | | | | | | | | | | | | | | | | | |
| A.S.C. H.T. att. | | (c) 41 | | 6 | 17 | 20 | | | | | | | | 13 | 4 | | | | | | | | | (b) Includes 1 O.R. att. Div. [illegible] Hq. 2 " " [illegible] 1 " " Div. Train 1 " " VIII Corps Hq. 19 " on leave to UK. |
| A.S.C. M.T. att. | | (d) 13 | | | | | | | | | | | | | | | | | | | 2 | | 7 | (c) Includes 2 O.R. on leave to UK. (d) [illegible] 1 O.R. att. [illegible] |
| Total | 8 | 231 | | 6 | 17 | 20 | | | | | | | | 13 | 4 | | | | | | 2 | 1 | 7 | 1 Rider [illegible] Vet Section since last return |
| War Establishment | 10 | 231 | | 8 | 17 | 20 | | | | | | | | 13 | 4 | | | | | | 2 | 1 | 7 | |
| Wanting to complete (Detail of Personnel and Horses below) | 2 | 5* | | 2 | - | - | | | | | | | | - | - | | | | | | - | - | - | * R.A.M.C. |
| Surplus | | 5** | | | | | | | | | | | | | | | | | | | | | | ** A.S.C. (H.T.) |
| *Attached (not to include the details shown above)......... | 1 | | | | | | | | | | | | | | | | | | | | | | | Chaplain |
| Civilians:— Employed with the Unit...... | 1 | 125 | | | | | | | | | | | | | | | | | | | | | | Sick admitted |
| Accompanying the Unit...... | | | | | | | | | | | | | | | | | | | | | | | | |
| TOTAL RATIONED...... | 7 | 329 | | 6 | 17 | 20 | | | | | | | | | | | | | | | | | | |

* In the case of field ambulances, hospitals or depots, the number of patients are to be included here, the names being shown in A.F.A. 36.

[illegible] Major Signature of Commander. 12th July 1918. Date of Despatch.

*For information of the A.G.'s Office at the base.*

A.S.C.

Officers and men who have become casuals, been transferred or joined since last report.

Place In the Field    Date 12. 7. 18

| Regtl. Number | Rank | Name | Corps | Nature of casualty, or name of unit from or to which transferred | Date of being struck off or coming on the ration return | Remarks* |
|---|---|---|---|---|---|---|
| T4/044551 | Dr. | Lloyd W. | A.S.C. (M.T.) att. 1/1st [illegible] | Returned from 14 days leave in UK. | on 7/7/18. | |
| T4/038273 | " | Drew J. | -do- | Granted 14 days leave to U.K. from 10.7.18 to 24.7.18. Credit ration allce @ 2/1d. pd. from 10.7.18 to 24.7.18. 14 days in UK. via Boulogne. | | |
| | | | | | | |
| | | | | | | |
| | | | | | | |
| | | | | | | |
| | | | | | | |
| | | | | | | |
| | | | | | | |
| | | | | | | |
| | | | | | | |
| | | | | | | |
| | | | | | | |
| | | | | | | |
| | | | | | | |
| | | | | | | |
| | | | | | | |
| | | | | | | |
| | | | | | | |
| | | | | | | |
| | | | | | | |
| | | | | | | |
| | | | | | | |
| | | | | | | |
| | | | | | | |
| | | | | | | |
| | | | | | | |
| | | | | | | |
| | | | | | | |

* State whether absence is of a permanent or temporary nature, adding, in the case of casuals from wounds or disease, any available information for communication to the relatives.

*For information of the A.G.'s Office at the base.*

Officers and men who have become casuals, been transferred or joined since last report.

Place In the Field Date 13th July 1918.

| Regtl. Number | Rank | Name | | Corps | Nature of casualty, or name of unit from or to which transferred | Date of being struck off or coming on the ration return | Remarks* |
|---|---|---|---|---|---|---|---|
| 316182 | Dr. | Tait | R. | R.A.M.C. T. 1/Low. Fd. Amb. | To duty at D.M.S. Office | off 3/7/18 | Permanent. |
| – | Lieut. | Hamilton | G.G. | M.R.C. U.S.A. | To duty with 52 M.G. Bn. as M.O. | off 4/7/18 | Tempy. |
| 316203 | Q.M.S. | Taylor | J.K. | R.A.M.C.(T.F.) 1/Low. Fd. Amb. | To be T/S.M. from 11.3.18. (Auth: O i/c RAMC Records 5/375 d/ 7/7/18) | | |
| 316203 | T/S.M. | Taylor | J.K. | -do- | Posted for duty to No 8 Stat. Hosp. | off 10/7/18 | (Auth: O i/c RAMC Records 5/375 d/7 |
| – | Capt. | Downes | A.D. | -do- | Returned from duty with 1/4 K.O.S.B. | on 10/7/18 | |
| – | Lieut. | Host | L.N. | M.R.C. U.S.A. | To duty with 1/4 K.O.S.B. as M.O. | off 10/7/18 | Permanent. |
| 316064 | Cpl. | Laing | D. | R.A.M.C. T. 1/Low. Fd. Amb. | married - Janet Miller Clark at 26 Mansfield St. Partick Glasgow on 14.6.18 Present address of wife - c/o Clark, 26 Mansf St. Partick Glasgow. | | |
| 316161 | L/Cpl. | Campbell | J. | -do- | married - Janet Watson Turner Watt at Muiravonside Parish Church on 28.6.18. Present address of wife: - VIEWVALE Manuel, by Linlithgow. | | |
| – | Hon Capt & Q.M. | Reid A.M. | | -do- | Returned from 14 days leave to UK. | on 6/7/18 | |
| 316046 | Pte | Harvey | A. | -do- | Returned from 14 days leave to UK. | on 9/7/18 | |
| 3160[illegible] | " | McGillivray | W. | -do- | Returned from 14 days leave in UK. | on 9/7/18 | |
| 316168 | Cpl. | Meldrum | A.A. | -do- | Returned from 14 days leave in UK. | on 12/7/18 | |
| 316083 | Pte | McGillies | J.D. | -do- | Granted 14 days leave to UK. 10.7.18 to 24.7.18. | | |
| 316095 | " | Crawford | R. | -do- | Credit ration allce @ 2/1d p.d. from 10.7.18 to 24.7.18. | | |
| 316092 | " | Binning | G. | -do- | 14 days leave to UK. via Boulogne. | | |
| 31606[illegible] | S/Sgt | Anderson | J. | -do- | Granted 28 days leave to UK. from 11.7.18 to 8.8.18 Credit ration allce for above period of 28 days @ 2/1 | | |
| 316089 | Pte | Hay | A.R. | -do- | Granted 14 days leave to UK from 7.7.18 to | | |
| 316112 | " | Raeburn | A. | -do- | 21.7.18. Credit ration allce @ 2/1d p.d. from 7.7. | | |
| 316136 | " | Muir | D.S. | -do- | to 21.7.18. 14 days in U.K. | | |
| 316175 | " | McGregor | M.R. | -do- | -do- | -do- | |
| 316114 | Ptes | Thomson | W.C. | -do- | Granted 14 days leave in UK. from 13.7.18 to 27.7 | | |
| 316125 | " | Brownlie | J. | -do- | Credit rat. allce. @ 2/1 per d. for above period of 14 | | |

Strength

| | | | | |
|---|---|---|---|---|
| Officers | TF | 6 | | |
| | MRC. USA. | 2 | 8 | |
| | W.O. | 1 | | |
| | S/Sgts | 2 | | |
| | Sgts | 10 | | |
| | L/Sgts | 1 | | |
| | Cpls | 8 | | |
| | L/Cpls | 6 | | |
| | Ptes | 149 | 177 | |

All R.A.M.C. Category "A"

* State whether absence is of a permanent or temporary nature, adding, in the case of casuals from wounds or disease, any available information for communication to the relatives.

Demands made on this sheet should consist of personnel required from the Base only, and should not include any demands for personnel which can be completed by promotions or appointments within the **unit.**

Perforated Sheet giving detail of personnel and horses wanting to complete, shown on Army Form B. 213.

No. of Report 155

| Detail of Wanting to Complete. | Drivers: R.A. | Drivers: R.E. | Drivers: A.S.C. | Drivers: Car | Drivers: Lorry | Drivers: Steam | Gunners | Smith Gunners | Range Takers | Farriers: Serjeants | Farriers: Corporals | Shoeing, or Shoeing and Carriage Smiths | Cold Shoers |
|---|---|---|---|---|---|---|---|---|---|---|---|---|---|
| CAVALRY | | | | | | | | | | | | | |
| R.A. | | | | | | | | | | | | | |
| R.E. | | | | | | | | | | | | | |
| INFANTRY | | | | | | | | | | | | | |
| R.A.M.C. | | | | | | | | | | | | | |
| A.O.C. | | | | | | | | | | | | | |
| A.V.C. | | | | | | | | | | | | | |
| | | | | | | | | | | | | | |
| | | | | | | | | | | | | | |

| Detail of Wanting to Complete. | Wheelers: R.A. | Wheelers: H.T. | Wheelers: M.T. | Saddlers or Harness Makers | Blacksmiths | Bricklayers and Masons | Carpenters and Joiners | Fitters & Turners (R.E.): Wood | Fitters & Turners (R.E.): Iron | Fitters: R.A. | Fitters: Wireless | Plumbers | Electricians: Ordinary | Electricians: W.T. | Signalmen |
|---|---|---|---|---|---|---|---|---|---|---|---|---|---|---|---|
| CAVALRY | | | | | | | | | | | | | | | |
| R.A. | | | | | | | | | | | | | | | |
| R.E. | | | | | | | | | | | | | | | |
| INFANTRY | | | | | | | | | | | | | | | |
| R.A.M.C. | | | | | | | | | | | | | | | |
| A.O.C. | | | | | | | | | | | | | | | |
| A.V.C. | | | | | | | | | | | | | | | |
| | | | | | | | | | | | | | | | |
| | | | | | | | | | | | | | | | |

| Detail of Wanting to Complete. | Engine Drivers: Loco. | Engine Drivers: Field | Air Line Men | Permanent Line Men | Operators, Telegraph | Cablemen | Brigade Section Pioneers | General-duty Pioneers | Signallers | Instrument Repairers | Motor Cyclist | Motor Cyclist Artificers | Telephonists | Clerks | Machine Gunners | Armament Artificers: Fitters | Armament Artificers: Range Finders | Armourers | Storemen | Privates |
|---|---|---|---|---|---|---|---|---|---|---|---|---|---|---|---|---|---|---|---|---|
| CAVALRY | | | | | | | | | | | | | | | | | | | | |
| R.A. | | | | | | | | | | | | | | | | | | | | |
| R.E. | | | | | | | | | | | | | | | | | | | | |
| INFANTRY | | | | | | | | | | | | | | | | | | | | |
| R.A.M.C. | | | | | | | | | | | | | | | | | | | | 5 |
| A.O.C. | | | | | | | | | | | | | | | | | | | | |
| A.V.C. | | | | | | | | | | | | | | | | | | | | |
| | | | | | | | | | | | | | | | | | | | | |
| | | | | | | | | | | | | | | | | | | | | |

| Detail of Wanting to Complete. | W.O.'s and N.C.O.'s (by ranks) not included in trade columns | | | | | | | | | | TOTAL to agree with wanting to complete: Officers | TOTAL: Other Ranks | Horses: Riding | Horses: Draught | Horses: Heavy Draught | Horses: Pack |
|---|---|---|---|---|---|---|---|---|---|---|---|---|---|---|---|---|
| CAVALRY | | | | | | | | | | | | | | | | |
| R.A. | | | | | | | | | | | | | | | | |
| R.E. | | | | | | | | | | | | | | | | |
| INFANTRY | | | | | | | | | | | | | | | | |
| R.A.M.C. | | | | | | | | | | | 2 | 5 | 2 | . | - | |
| A.O.C. | | | | | | | | | | | | | | | | |
| A.V.C. | | | | | | | | | | | | | | | | |
| | | | | | | | | | | | | | | | | |
| | | | | | | | | | | | | | | | | |

Remarks :—

[illegible] Major Signature of Commander.

1st Low. Fd. Ambce. R.A.M.C. (T) Unit.

52 Division Formation to which attached.

12th July 1918. Date of Despatch.

(6305) Wt. W2927/M2226. 1,250,000. 6/17. McA. & W., Ltd. (E1348). Forms B2138/8.

[P.T.O.

**To be made up to and for Saturday in each week**

No. of Report 156

# FIELD RETURN.

Army Form B 213

(To be furnished by all arms, services, and departments (except A.S.C. units) to the A.G.'s Office at the Base in accordance with Field Service Regulations, Part II.)

RETURN showing numbers (a) Effective strength of Unit. (b) Rationed by Unit. 4/Lon. Fd. Ambce. at In the Field 19th July 1918. Date.

| DETAILS. | *Personnel | | | | | Animals | | | | | | Guns and transport vehicles | | | | | | | | | | | | | | | REMARKS (Number of Acting W.O.'s and N.C.O.'s included in effective strength to be shown in this column.) |
|---|---|---|---|---|---|---|---|---|---|---|---|---|---|---|---|---|---|---|---|---|---|---|---|---|---|---|---|
| | | | | | | Horses | | | | Mules | | Guns, showing description | Ammunition wagons | Machine guns | Aircraft, showing description | Horsed | | Mechanical | | | | | Motor Bicycles | Bicycles | Motor Ambulances | |
| | Officers | Other Ranks | | | | Riding | Draught | Heavy Draught | Pack | Large | Small | | | | | 4 Wheeled | 2 Wheeled | Motor Cars | Tractors | Lorries, showing description | Trucks, showing description | Trailers | | | | |
| Effective Strength of Unit ... ... | (a) 7 | (b) 178 | | | | | | | | | | | | | | | | | | | | | | 1 | | (a) Includes 1 off. at VIII Corps [illegible] / 1 off. at [illegible] / 1 off. at C.H.S. |
| Details by Arms attached to Unit as in War Establishment ... ... ... | | | | | | | | | | | | | | | | | | | | | | | | | | |
| A.S.C. (H.T.) | | (c) 44 | | | | 6 | 17 | 19 | | | | | | | | 13 | 4 | | | | | | | | | (b) Includes 1 o.r. at [illegible] / 2 o.r. at C.H.S. / 1 o.r. at [illegible] / 1 o.r. at VIII Corps / 24 o.r. on [illegible] |
| A.S.C. (M.T.) | | (d) 13 | | | | | | | | | | | | | | | | | | | | | 2 | | 7 | |
| TOTAL ... ... | 7 | 232 | | | | 6 | 14 | 19 | | | | | | | | 13 | 4 | | | | | | 2 | 1 | 7 | (c) Includes 2 o.r. on leave |
| War Establishment ... ... ... | 10 | 234 | | | | 8 | 17 | 20 | | | | | | | | 13 | 4 | | | | | | 2 | 1 | 7 | (d) Includes 1 o.r. at [illegible] |
| Wanting to complete ... ... ... (Detail of Personnel and Horses below.) | 3 | 4* | | | | 2 | - | 1 | | | | | | | | | | | | | | | | | | * R.A.M.C. |
| SURPLUS ... ... (Detail of Personnel and Horses below.) | - | 5** | | | | | | | | | | | | | | | | | | | | | | | | ** A.S.C. (H.T.) |
| †Attached (not to include the details shown above) ... ... ... | 1 | | | | | | | | | | | | | | | | | | | | | | | | | Chaplain |
| Attached for Rations only ... ... | 2 | 133 | | | | | | | | | | | | | | | | | | | | | | | | Sick Rationed |
| Civilians Employed with and Accompanying the Unit ... ... ... | | | | | | | | | | | | | | | | | | | | | | | | | | |
| ‡Detached from and struck off effective strength of own Unit ... ... | | | | | | | | | | | | | | | | | | | | | | | | | | |
| ‡Detached from but retained on effective strength of own unit... ... ... | | | | | | | | | | | | | | | | | | | | | | | | | | |
| TOTAL RATIONED ... | 10 | 309 | | | | 6 | 17 | 19 | | | | | | | | | | | | | | | | | | |

* Blank columns to be used for W.A.A.C. Natives or as may be required.

† In the case of field ambulances, hospitals or depots, the number of patients are to be included here, the names being shown in A.F.A. 36.
‡ These details to be enumerated by arms.

[illegible] Major for Signature of Commander.

19th July 1918 Date of Despatch.

*For information of the A.G.'s Office at the base.*

A.S.C.

Officers and men who have become casuals, been transferred or joined since last report.

Place In the Field    Date 19 - 7 - 18.

| R'gtl. Number | Rank | Name | Corps | Nature of casualty, or name of unit from or to which transferred. | Date of being struck off or coming on the ration return. | Remarks * |
|---|---|---|---|---|---|---|
| T4/247002 | Dr. | Davidson A. | A.S.C. HT att 1/3 L.F.A. | Granted 14 days leave to U.K. from 14-7-18 to 28-7-18, via Boulogne. Credit ration allce for above period of 14 days at 2/1 per diem. | | |
| T4/[illegible] | Cpl. | Wilson T | -do- | Granted 14 days leave to U.K. from 17-7-18 to 31-7-18, via Boulogne. Credit rat. allce for above period of 14 days @ 2/1 per diem. | | |
| T/[illegible]5711 | Dr. | McLaren [illegible] | -do- | Retd from 14 days leave to U.K. on 13/7/18 | | |
| T4/036374 | - | [illegible] J | -do- | Retd from 14 days leave to U.K. on 19/7/18 | | |

* State whether absence is of a permanent or temporary nature, adding, in the case of casuals from wounds or disease any available information for communication to the relatives.

*The perforated sheet is not to be used to record casualties; additional sheets, preferably foolscap, to be attached when necessary. These sheets to be carefully numbered and the number of attached sheets to be noted here.*

*For information of the A.G.'s Office at the base.*

Officers and men who have become casuals, been transferred or joined since last report.

Place In the Field Date 19th July 1918.

| Regtl. Number | Rank | Name | Corps | Nature of casualty, or name of unit from or to which transferred. | Date of being struck off or coming on the ration return. | Remarks * |
|---|---|---|---|---|---|---|
| – | Capt a/Major | Browne J. | R.A.M.C. (T) 1/Lowland Fd. Amb. | Sick to Hosp | off 19/7/18 | |
| | Pte | White A | -do- | Retd from Hosp on 14/7/18 | | |
| 316109 | " | McDougall W | -do- | Granted 14 days leave to UK from 14.7.18 to 28.7.18. Credit not allce @ 2/1 per day for that pd. | | |
| 316104 | " | Love A | -do- | -do- | -do- | -do- |
| 316132 | Sgt | Thomson G.A. | -do- | -do- | -do- | -do- |
| 316179 | " | Kenny E. | -do- | Granted 14 days leave to UK from 17.7.18 to 31.7.18. Credit [illegible] allce @ 2/1 per d for that period | | |
| 316119 | Pte | Wallace R | -do- | | | |
| 316150 | " | Anderson T.B. | -do- | | | |
| 316003 | " | McKelvie W | -do- | Granted 28 days leave to UK from 18.7.18 to 15.8.18. Credit not allce 2/1 pd. for that period of 28 days. | | |
| 316101 | " | Graham R. | do. | Granted 14 days leave to UK from 20.7.18 to 3.8.18. Cred. not allce @ 2/1 pd. for that period. | | |
| 316006 | " | Crawford S. | -do- | Granted 30 days leave to UK from 20.7.18 to 19.8.18. Credit not allce for that period of 30 days | | |
| 316074 | Pte | Johnstone A | -do- | Retd from 14 days leave in UK | | on 14/7/18. |
| 316078 | Cpl | Ross D | -do- | -do- | -do- | on 16.7.18 |
| 316098 | Pte | Gallacher C | -do- | -do- | -do- | on 16.7.18 |
| 316093 | " | Currie J | -do- | -do- | -do- | on 19.7.18 |
| | Lieut Col. | Smith J.M. | -do- | Acting as A.D.M.S. in Div. | | Temporary |

Strength. Officers T.F. 6
M.R.C. U.S.A. 1 — 7

W.O. 1
Q.M.Sgts 2
Sgts 10
L/Sgts 1
Cpls 8
L/Cpls 6
Pte 150 — 178

All Category 'A'.

* State whether absence is of a permanent or temporary nature, adding, in the case of casuals from wounds or disease any available information for communication to the relatives.

*The perforated sheet is not to be used to record casualties ; additional sheets, preferably foolscap, to be attached when necessary. These sheets to be carefully numbered and the number of attached sheets to be noted here.*

Perforated Sheet giving detail of personnel and horses wanting to complete or surplus, shown on Army Form B. 213.

No. of Report 156.

| Detail of Wanting to Complete or Surplus. | Drivers. R.A. | Drivers. R.E. | Drivers. A.S.C. | Drivers. Car | Drivers. Lorry | Drivers. Steam | Gunners | Gunners Howitzer | Smith Gunners | Range Takers | Farriers Serjeants | Farriers Corporals | Shoeing or Shoeing and Carriage Smiths | Cold Shoers | Wheelers R.A. | Wheelers H.T. | Wheelers M.T. | Saddlers or Harness Makers | Blacksmiths | Bricklayers and Masons | Carpenters and Joiners | Fitters & Turners (R.E.) Wood | Fitters & Turners (R.E.) Iron | Fitters R.A. | Fitters Wireless. | Plumbers | Electricians Ordinary | Electricians W.T. | Signalmen. | Engine Drivers Loco. | Engine Drivers Field | Air Line Men. | Permanent Line Men | Operators, Telegraph | Cablemen | Brigade Section Pioneers | General-duty Pioneers | Signallers | Instrument Repairers | Motor Cyclist | Motor Cyclist Artificers | Telephonists | Clerks | Machine Gunners | Armament Artificers Fitters | Armament Artificers Range Finders | Armourers | Storemen | Privates | W.O's and N.C.O's (by ranks) not included in trade columns. | | | | | | | | | | | TOTAL to agree with wanting to complete or surplus Officers | TOTAL to agree with wanting to complete or surplus Other Ranks | Horses Riding | Horses Draught | Horses Heavy Draught | Horses Pack |
|---|---|---|---|---|---|---|---|---|---|---|---|---|---|---|---|---|---|---|---|---|---|---|---|---|---|---|---|---|---|---|---|---|---|---|---|---|---|---|---|---|---|---|---|---|---|---|---|---|---|---|---|---|---|---|---|---|---|---|---|---|---|---|---|---|---|---|
| CAVALRY— Deficiency | | | | | | | | | | | | | | | | | | | | | | | | | | | | | | | | | | | | | | | | | | | | | | | | | | | | | | | | | | | | | | | | | | |
| Surplus | | | | | | | | | | | | | | | | | | | | | | | | | | | | | | | | | | | | | | | | | | | | | | | | | | | | | | | | | | | | | | | | | | |
| R.A.— Deficiency | | | | | | | | | | | | | | | | | | | | | | | | | | | | | | | | | | | | | | | | | | | | | | | | | | | | | | | | | | | | | | | | | | |
| Surplus | | | | | | | | | | | | | | | | | | | | | | | | | | | | | | | | | | | | | | | | | | | | | | | | | | | | | | | | | | | | | | | | | | |
| R.E.— Deficiency | | | | | | | | | | | | | | | | | | | | | | | | | | | | | | | | | | | | | | | | | | | | | | | | | | | | | | | | | | | | | | | | | | |
| Surplus | | | | | | | | | | | | | | | | | | | | | | | | | | | | | | | | | | | | | | | | | | | | | | | | | | | | | | | | | | | | | | | | | | |
| INFANTRY— Deficiency | | | | | | | | | | | | | | | | | | | | | | | | | | | | | | | | | | | | | | | | | | | | | | | | | | | | | | | | | | | | | | | | | | |
| Surplus | | | | | | | | | | | | | | | | | | | | | | | | | | | | | | | | | | | | | | | | | | | | | | | | | | | | | | | | | | | | | | | | | | |
| R.A.M.C.— Deficiency | | | | | | | | | | | | | | | | | | | | | | | | | | | | | | | | | | | | | | | | | | | | | | | | | 4 | | | | | | | | | | | | 2 | 4 | 2 | - | 1 | |
| Surplus | | | | | | | | | | | | | | | | | | | | | | | | | | | | | | | | | | | | | | | | | | | | | | | | | | | | | | | | | | | | | | | | | | |
| A.O.C.— Deficiency | | | | | | | | | | | | | | | | | | | | | | | | | | | | | | | | | | | | | | | | | | | | | | | | | | | | | | | | | | | | | | | | | | |
| Surplus | | | | | | | | | | | | | | | | | | | | | | | | | | | | | | | | | | | | | | | | | | | | | | | | | | | | | | | | | | | | | | | | | | |
| A.V.C.— Deficiency | | | | | | | | | | | | | | | | | | | | | | | | | | | | | | | | | | | | | | | | | | | | | | | | | | | | | | | | | | | | | | | | | | |
| Surplus | | | | | | | | | | | | | | | | | | | | | | | | | | | | | | | | | | | | | | | | | | | | | | | | | | | | | | | | | | | | | | | | | | |
| Deficiency | | | | | | | | | | | | | | | | | | | | | | | | | | | | | | | | | | | | | | | | | | | | | | | | | | | | | | | | | | | | | | | | | | |
| Surplus | | | | | | | | | | | | | | | | | | | | | | | | | | | | | | | | | | | | | | | | | | | | | | | | | | | | | | | | | | | | | | | | | | |
| Deficiency | | | | | | | | | | | | | | | | | | | | | | | | | | | | | | | | | | | | | | | | | | | | | | | | | | | | | | | | | | | | | | | | | | |
| Surplus | | | | | | | | | | | | | | | | | | | | | | | | | | | | | | | | | | | | | | | | | | | | | | | | | | | | | | | | | | | | | | | | | | |

Remarks :—

[illegible] Major [illegible] Signature of Commander.

Unit.

52 Division Formation to which attached.

19th July 1918. Date of Despatch

(16523.) Wt. W6016—PP 1432. 1,500m. 3/18. D & S. (E1256) Forms B213/8.

**To be made up to and for Saturday in each week**

Army Form B 213

# FIELD RETURN.

No. of Report 157

(To be furnished by all arms, services, and departments (except A.S.C. units) to the A.G.'s Office at the Base in accordance with Field Service Regulations, Part II.)

RETURN showing numbers (*a*) Effective strength of Unit. (*b*) Rationed by Unit. 4th Div. Fd. Ambce at In the Field 20th July 1918 Date.

| Details. | *Personnel: Officers | Other Ranks | | | Animals: Horses: Riding | Draught | Heavy Draught | Pack | Mules: Large | Small | Guns and transport vehicles: Guns, showing description | Ammunition wagons | Machine guns | Aircraft, showing description | Horsed: †4 Wheeled | ‡2 Wheeled | Mechanical: Motor Cars | Tractors | Lorries, showing description | Trucks, showing description | Trailers | Motor Bicycles | Bicycles | Motor Ambulances | Remarks (Number of Acting W.O.'s and N.C.O.'s included in effective strength to be shown in this column.) |
|---|---|---|---|---|---|---|---|---|---|---|---|---|---|---|---|---|---|---|---|---|---|---|---|---|---|
| Effective Strength of Unit ... ... | (a) 7 | (b) 178 | | | | | | | | | | | | | | | | | | | | | 1 | | (a) Includes 1 officer a/a[illegible]. " 1 officer VIII Corps Hq. 1 officer 52 M.G. Bn. |
| Details by Arms attached to Unit as in War Establishment ... ... | | | | | | | | | | | | | | | | | | | | | | | | | (b) Includes 1 O.R. att. Div. Com. Hq. |
| A.S.C. (H.T.) | | (c) 40 | | | 6 | 17 | 19 | | | | | | | | 13 | 4 | | | | | | | | | " 3 " " Div. Hqrs |
| A.S.C. (M.T.) | | (d) 13 | | | | | | | | | | | | | | | | | | | | 2 | | 7 | " 1 " " Div. Train " 32 " on leave " 1 " at 57 C.C.S. (c) Includes 4 O.R. on leave |
| Total ... ... | 7 | 231 | | | 6 | 17 | 19 | | | | | | | | 13 | 4 | | | | | | 2 | 1 | 7 | (d) Excludes 1 O.R. att. [illegible] |
| War Establishment ... ... | 10 | 231 | | | 8 | 17 | 20 | | | | | | | | 13 | 4 | | | | | | 2 | 1 | 7 | * R.A.M.C. |
| Wanting to complete (Detail of Personnel and Horses below.) | 3 | 4 * | | | 2 | · | 1 | | | | | | | | | | | | | | | | | | ** A.S.C. (H.T.) |
| Surplus ... (Detail of Personnel and Horses below.) | | 4 ** | | | | | | | | | | | | | | | | | | | | | | | |
| †Attached (not to include the details shown above) ... ... | 1 | | | | | | | | | | | | | | | | | | | | | | | | Chaplain |
| Attached for Rations only ... | 1 | 6 | | | | | | | | | | | | | | | | | | | | | | | Sick Rationed |
| Civilians Employed with and Accompanying the Unit ... | | | | | | | | | | | | | | | | | | | | | | | | | |
| ‡Detached from and struck off effective strength of own Unit ... | | | | | | | | | | | | | | | | | | | | | | | | | |
| ‡Detached from but retained on effective strength of own unit... ... | | | | | | | | | | | | | | | | | | | | | | | | | |
| Total Rationed ... | 6 | 194 | | | 6 | 17 | 19 | | | | | | | | | | | | | | | | | | |

* Blank columns to be used for W.A.A.C. Natives or as may be required.

† In the case of field ambulances, hospitals or depots, the number of patients are to be included here, the names being shown in A.F.A. 36.

‡ These details to be enumerated by arms.

[illegible] Major Signature of Commander.

26th July 1918 Date of Despatch.

A.S.C.

*For information of the A.G.'s Office at the base.*

Officers and men who have become casuals, been transferred or joined since last report.

Place In the Field    Date 26.7.18

| Regtl. Number | Rank | Name | | Corps | Nature of casualty, or name of unit from or to which transferred. | Date of being struck off or coming on the ration return. | Remarks * |
|---|---|---|---|---|---|---|---|
| T2/135999 | Pte | Blackwell | G. | A.S.C. M.T. att 1/1st Lows Fd Amb | Forfeits 5 days pay also 1 G.C. Badge | 17 2/18. | See AFB2069 |
| T4/247003 | Dr. | Davidson | J. | A.S.C. H.T. att 1/1 Lows Fd Amb. | Granted 14 days leave to U.K. 5.8.18. via Boulogne | | from 22.7.18 to |
| | | | | Credit Rat. allce @ 2/1d p.d. to 5.8.18. | for 14 days | | from 22.7.18 |
| T4/07[illegible] | " | Green | A | A.S.C. H.T. att 1/1 Lows Fd Ambce | Sick to Hosp. | off 24 7/18. | |

* State whether absence is of a permanent or temporary nature, adding, in the case of casuals from wounds or disease any available information for communication to the relatives.

*The perforated sheet is not to be used to record casualties ; additional sheets, preferably foolscap, to be attached when necessary. These sheets to be carefully numbered and the number of attached sheets to be noted here.*

*For information of the A.G.'s Office at the base.*

Officers and men who have become casuals, been transferred or joined since last report.

Place In the Field Date 26th July 1918.

| Regtl. Number | Rank | Name | | Corps | Nature of casualty, or name of unit from or to which transferred. | Date of being struck off or coming on the ration return. | Remarks * |
|---|---|---|---|---|---|---|---|
| 316078 | Cpl. | Ross | D. | R.A.M.C.(T) 1/1 Lowl. Fd. Amb. | married Helen Bryden McDowall, Lorne Place Bellshill Rd. Uddingston on 6th July 1918. at The Manse Uddingston, Glasgow. Present address of wife:- C/o McDowall Lorne Place, Bellshill Rd Uddingston, Glasgow | | |
| 316078 | Cpl. | Ross | D. | -do- | allotment of 4d p.d. to Jas. Ross, 13 Greenrigg St. Uddingston to be increased to 6d p.d. and transferred to Mrs Helen Bryden Ross C/o McDowall. Lorne Place Uddingston Glasgow from 6-7-18. | | |
| 316078 | Cpl. | Ross | D. | -do- | Voluntary allotment @ 1/- p.d. from 6.7.18 to Mrs Helen Bryden Ross C/o McDowall, Lorne Place, Uddingston Glasgow. | | |
| 316299 | Pte | Beattie | R.B. | -do- | awarded 5 days C.C. | 18/7/18. | See AFB 2069. |
| 316103 | Pte | Johnstone | R. | -do- | Granted 14 days leave to UK. from 21.7.18 to 4.8.18 | | |
| 316128 | " | Young | H.B. | -do- | Credit rat. allce @ 2/1 p.d. for above period. | | |
| 316099 | " | Golder | J. | -do- | Granted 14 days leave to UK. from 22.7.18 to 5.8.18 Credit rat. allce @ 2/1 p.d. for above period | | |
| 316096 | " | Darkes | F. | -do- | Granted 14 days leave to UK. from 23.7.18 to 6.8.18 | | |
| 316124 | " | Murray | D. | -do- | Credit rat. allce @ 2/1 p.d. for above period | | |
| 316129 | " | White | A. | -do- | Granted 14 days leave to UK. from 24.7.18 to 7.8.18 | | |
| 316094 | " | Cherrie | T. | -do- | Credit rat. allce @ 2/1 p.d. for above period | | |
| 316088 | " | McKellar | H. | -do- | Granted 14 days leave to UK. from 25.7.18 to 8.8.18 | | |
| 316097 | " | Dickson | D. | -do- | Credit rat. allce @ 2/1 p.d. for above period | | |
| 316100 | " | Gough | T.C. | -do- | Granted 14 days leave to UK. from 26.7.18 to 9.8.18 | | |
| 316156 | " | Shaw | P. | -do- | Credit rat. allce @ 2/1 p.d. for above period. | | |
| 316066 | Sgt | Campbell | J.S. | -do- | Granted 31 days leave to UK. from 27.7.18 to 27.8.18 Credit rat. allce @ 2/1 p.d. for above period | | |
| 316110 | Pte | Paterson | A. | -do- | Granted 14 days leave to UK. from 27.7.18 to 10.8.18 Credit rat. allce @ 2/1 p.d. for above period | | |
| 316134 | Pte | Glendye | D. | -do- | Retd. from 14 days in UK. on 20/7/18. | | |
| 316086 | " | Ellis | W.L. | -do- | -do- | -do- | on 25.7.18 |
| 316084 | " | Rankine | Jn. | -do- | -do- | -do- | " -do- |
| 316089 | " | May | A. | -do- | -do- | -do- | " -do- |
| 316117 | " | Raeburn | A. | -do- | -do- | -do- | " -do- |
| 316136 | " | Muir | D.S. | -do- | -do- | -do- | " -do- |
| 316175 | " | McGregor | W.R. | -do- | -do- | -do- | " -do- |

| | | |
|---|---|---|
| Strength Off | T.F. | 6 |
| | MRC U.S.A. | 1 — 7 |
| | W/O | 1 |
| | S/Sgts | 2 |
| | Sgts | 10 |
| | L/Sgts | 1 |
| | Cpls | 8 |
| | L/Cpls | 6 |
| | Ptes. | 150 — 178 |

All Category 'A'

* State whether absence is of a permanent or temporary nature, adding, in the case of casuals from wounds or disease any available information for communication to the relatives.

*The perforated sheet is not to be used to record casualties ; additional sheets, preferably foolscap, to be attached when necessary. These sheets to be carefully numbered and the number of attached sheets to be noted here.*

Perforated Sheet giving detail of personnel and horses wanting to complete or surplus, shown on Army Form B. 213.

No. of Report 157.

| Detail of Wanting to Complete or Surplus. | Drivers. R.A. | Drivers. R.E. | Drivers. A.S.C. | Drivers. Car | Drivers. Lorry | Drivers. Steam | Gunners | Gunners Howitzer | Smith Gunners | Range Takers | Farriers Serjeants | Farriers Corporals | Shoeing or Shoeing and Carriage Smiths | Cold Shoers | Wheelers R.A. | Wheelers H.T. | Wheelers M.T. | Saddlers or Harness Makers | Blacksmiths | Bricklayers and Masons | Carpenters and Joiners | Fitters & Turners (R.E.) Wood | Fitters & Turners (R.E.) Iron | Fitters R.A. | Fitters Wireless. | Plumbers | Electricians Ordinary | Electricians W.T. | Signalmen. | Engine Drivers Loco. | Engine Drivers Field | Air Line Men. | Permanent Line Men | Operators, Telegraph | Cablemen | Brigade Section Pioneers | General-duty Pioneers | Signallers | Instrument Repairers | Motor Cyclist | Motor Cyclist Artificers | Telephonists | Clerks | Machine Gunners | Armament Artificers Fitters | Armament Artificers Range Finders | Armourers | Storemen | Privates | W.O.'s and N.C.O.'s (by ranks) not included in trade columns. | | | | | | | | | | TOTAL to agree with wanting to complete or surplus. Officers | TOTAL Other Ranks | Horses Riding | Horses Draught | Horses Heavy Draught | Horses Pack |
|---|---|---|---|---|---|---|---|---|---|---|---|---|---|---|---|---|---|---|---|---|---|---|---|---|---|---|---|---|---|---|---|---|---|---|---|---|---|---|---|---|---|---|---|---|---|---|---|---|---|---|---|---|---|---|---|---|---|---|---|---|---|---|---|---|---|
| CAVALRY— DEFICIENCY | | | | | | | | | | | | | | | | | | | | | | | | | | | | | | | | | | | | | | | | | | | | | | | | | | | | | | | | | | | | | | | | | | |
| SURPLUS | | | | | | | | | | | | | | | | | | | | | | | | | | | | | | | | | | | | | | | | | | | | | | | | | | | | | | | | | | | | | | | | | | |
| R.A.— DEFICIENCY | | | | | | | | | | | | | | | | | | | | | | | | | | | | | | | | | | | | | | | | | | | | | | | | | | | | | | | | | | | | | | | | | | |
| SURPLUS | | | | | | | | | | | | | | | | | | | | | | | | | | | | | | | | | | | | | | | | | | | | | | | | | | | | | | | | | | | | | | | | | | |
| R.E.— DEFICIENCY | | | | | | | | | | | | | | | | | | | | | | | | | | | | | | | | | | | | | | | | | | | | | | | | | | | | | | | | | | | | | | | | | | |
| SURPLUS | | | | | | | | | | | | | | | | | | | | | | | | | | | | | | | | | | | | | | | | | | | | | | | | | | | | | | | | | | | | | | | | | | |
| INFANTRY— DEFICIENCY | | | | | | | | | | | | | | | | | | | | | | | | | | | | | | | | | | | | | | | | | | | | | | | | | | | | | | | | | | | | | | | | | | |
| SURPLUS | | | | | | | | | | | | | | | | | | | | | | | | | | | | | | | | | | | | | | | | | | | | | | | | | | | | | | | | | | | | | | | | | | |
| R.A.M.C.— DEFICIENCY | | | | | | | | | | | | | | | | | | | | | | | | | | | | | | | | | | | | | | | | | | | | | | | | | 4 | | | | | | | | | | | 3 | 4 | 2 | - | 1 | |
| SURPLUS | | | | | | | | | | | | | | | | | | | | | | | | | | | | | | | | | | | | | | | | | | | | | | | | | | | | | | | | | | | | | | | | | | |
| A.O.C.— DEFICIENCY | | | | | | | | | | | | | | | | | | | | | | | | | | | | | | | | | | | | | | | | | | | | | | | | | | | | | | | | | | | | | | | | | | |
| SURPLUS | | | | | | | | | | | | | | | | | | | | | | | | | | | | | | | | | | | | | | | | | | | | | | | | | | | | | | | | | | | | | | | | | | |
| A.V.C.— DEFICIENCY | | | | | | | | | | | | | | | | | | | | | | | | | | | | | | | | | | | | | | | | | | | | | | | | | | | | | | | | | | | | | | | | | | |
| SURPLUS | | | | | | | | | | | | | | | | | | | | | | | | | | | | | | | | | | | | | | | | | | | | | | | | | | | | | | | | | | | | | | | | | | |
| DEFICIENCY | | | | | | | | | | | | | | | | | | | | | | | | | | | | | | | | | | | | | | | | | | | | | | | | | | | | | | | | | | | | | | | | | | |
| SURPLUS | | | | | | | | | | | | | | | | | | | | | | | | | | | | | | | | | | | | | | | | | | | | | | | | | | | | | | | | | | | | | | | | | | |
| DEFICIENCY | | | | | | | | | | | | | | | | | | | | | | | | | | | | | | | | | | | | | | | | | | | | | | | | | | | | | | | | | | | | | | | | | | |
| SURPLUS | | | | | | | | | | | | | | | | | | | | | | | | | | | | | | | | | | | | | | | | | | | | | | | | | | | | | | | | | | | | | | | | | | |

Remarks :—

[illegible] Major R.C.  Signature of Commander.

p/Low Fd. Ambce R.A.M.C. (T.)  Unit.

52 Div  Formation to which attached.

26. 7. 18.  Date of Despatch.

(16523.) Wt. W6016—PP 1432. 1,500m. 8/18. D & S. (E1256) Forms B213S/8.

[P.T.O.

29

9/R 5

aug. 1918

War Diary Vol XXXIX
of
1/1st Lowland Field Ambulance
RAMC(T)

from
1/8/18

to
31/8/18



[illegible] Lt Col
OC 1/1st LFA
1/9/18

Instructions regarding War Diaries and Intelligence Summaries are contained in F. S. Regs., Part II. and the Staff Manual respectively. Title pages will be prepared in manuscript.

# WAR DIARY

or

~~INTELLIGENCE SUMMARY.~~

(*Erase heading not required.*)

443 Army Form C. 2118.

1/1st Lowland Field Ambulance

| Place | Date | Hour | Summary of Events and Information | Remarks and references to Appendices |
|---|---|---|---|---|
| ECOIVRES F13, a 8.2 (Map B 1/40000) | 1/8/18 | | Col returns to duty with the Ambulance from a/ADMS vice Col A.J. MACDOUGALL who returned to-day from 14 days leave in U.K. Officers doing duty with this unit are now as follows:- a/Lt Col J.W. LEITCH in command, a/MAJOR W.F. MACKENZIE commanding C Section Capt A.D. DOWNES commanding B Section during absence of Major J. BROWNE sick in hospital Capt J.W. BURTON 1/1st Lowland Field Ambulance & Capt & Qr Mr A.M. REID. Capt R.A. LENNIE 1/1st Lowland Field Ambulance who was admitted to hospital on 24th July from temporary duty with 7th Royal Scots was evacuated to-day & is off strength. JWL | |
| do | 2/8/18 | | Went round billets & hospital buildings occupied by this unit & arranged a number of improvements chief of which was provision of dining hall & tables for personnel. As accommodation is not large enough there will have to be two tables at each meal. Flies are very numerous all over the ~~camp~~ billets. JWL | |
| do | 3/8/18 | | Made usual daily inspection of billets & transport lines. Two small huts have been granted this unit to-day by Town Major for use of overflow of transport personnel. Lime washing & cleaning out of kitchens & billets is being proceeded with. Detailed Major MACKENZIE to improve the camps | |

D. D. & L., London, E.C. (A8004) Wt. W1771/M2 31 750,000 5/17 Sch. 52 Forms/C2118/14

444 Army Form C. 2118.

Instructions regarding War Diaries and Intelligence Summaries are contained in F. S. Regs., Part II. and the Staff Manual respectively. Title pages will be prepared in manuscript.

# WAR DIARY
or
~~INTELLIGENCE SUMMARY.~~
*(Erase heading not required.)*

1/1st Lowland Field Ambulance

| Place | Date | Hour | Summary of Events and Information | Remarks and references to Appendices |
|---|---|---|---|---|
| ECOIVRES F13 a 8 2. Map B 1/40000 | 3/8/18 (Contd) | | of the following units in regard to sanitation: 1/1st Mobile Vet Sect. at F13c, 52nd Div. Train at F14c, & 52nd Div. Reception Camp at Billet 51 ECOIVRES. A.D.M.S. inspected ~~camp~~ Hospital, billets, & transport lines. & drew attention to various details but did not express himself regarding the improvements which were being carried out. Capt. J.W. BURTON reports for temporary duty with 19th Bde R.G.A at G.8.c.0,1 (Map B) as M.O. & is off strength as from tomorrow, 4th Aug. J.W.L. | |
| do | 4/8/18 | | Lt DOBIE 413th Field Coy R.E. called to see what floors required cement & to make a report thereon. Gutters at Horse standings of this unit are being paved with cobble stones by transport personnel. Transport personnel mess is now in working order & fly proof receptacles are being made out of boxes. The A.S.C. M.T. personnel have now also been provided with a mess room. Main mess room at H.Q. is not yet completed but work is being pushed on as fast as possible. Sent 1 N.C.O. & 36 Bearers to report to O.C. 1/2nd L.F.A. in accordance with A.D.M.S. instructions for duty with that unit. J.W.L. | |
| do | 5/8/18 | | Two fire-places for dixies in the main kitchen have been rebuilt & whole kitchen cleaned out & white washed. Flies are still very numerous. | |

D. D. & L., London, E.C. (A8004) Wt. W1771/M2·31 750,000 5/17 Sch. 52 Forms/C2118/14

Instructions regarding War Diaries and Intelligence Summaries are contained in F. S. Regs., Part II. and the Staff Manual respectively. Title pages will be prepared in manuscript.

# WAR DIARY

or

~~INTELLIGENCE SUMMARY.~~

(Erase heading not required.)

445 Army Form C. 2118.

1/1st Lowland Field Ambulance.

| Place | Date | Hour | Summary of Events and Information | Remarks and references to Appendices |
|---|---|---|---|---|
| F13 a82 Map, B 1/40000 ECOIVRES. | 5/8/18 (Contd.) | | of fly traps & fly papers seem difficult to get. Arsenic traps cannot well be used in the kitchen. Hut for hanging quarters of meat in has now been completed & is in use. Cement for floor has not yet been obtained. JWY. | |
| do | 6/8/18. | | Wrote A.D.M.S. for authority to draw 6 carts of gravel from Fosse 9 for use in filling up holes in, & generally improving, the horse standings; as a good deal of water collects in wet weather under the horses' feet. Obtained a chaff cutter left by 235th Divisional Train some time ago in care of a farm near, occupied by Mons. Ségard, for use of this unit during its stay here. Sent a large quantity of salvaged matter to Divl Salvage dump during the last 2 or 3 days. Received authority to draw the R.E. Stores indented for on 2nd from AUX RIETZ dump. Have found an old 250 gallon corrugated water tank which I intend making into an improvised disinfector of the Serbian barrel type with a wooden grating in the bottom to hold the clothing above the water level. Have also managed to get two Tubs for use in washing clothes of personnel, & hospital cases. JWY. | |
| do | 7/8/18 | | Material indented for on 2nd was drawn from RE dump at AUX RIETZ yesterday | |

D. D. & L., London, E.C.
(A8004) Wt. W1771/M2 31 750,000 5/17 Sch. 52 Forms/C2118/14

446 Army Form C. 2118.

Instructions regarding War Diaries and Intelligence Summaries are contained in F. S. Regs., Part II. and the Staff Manual respectively. Title pages will be prepared in manuscript.

# WAR DIARY
~~or~~
~~INTELLIGENCE SUMMARY.~~
*(Erase heading not required.)*

1/1st Lowland Field Ambulance

| Place | Date | Hour | Summary of Events and Information | Remarks and references to Appendices |
|---|---|---|---|---|
| ECOIVRES F 13.a.82 Map B 1/40000 | 7/8/18 | | afternoon & floor of meat hut has been cemented to-day. Only 1 barrel of cement was allowed (of the 2 barrels indented for) & it was partially spoiled owing to water having got into it. The "dolly tubs" are in use to-day & seem to be proving a success. The mess room for personnel at main Billet was completed yesterday & is in use to-day. Efforts are being made to have accumulations of garbage found to be breeding flies freely in surrounding areas dealt with by units concerned, or by Town Major & Sanitary Section where ground is not now in occupation. A book is being kept in the orderly room of each unit visited by Major MACKENZIE & an entry made in it regarding any points requiring attention after his visit. Sample of water taken from water cart after its return from filling up was found to have been satisfactorily chlorinated with only 1 measure of bleaching powder. A/Major J. BROWNE reported for duty from Hosp (42 CCS) [illegible] | |
| do | 8/8/18 | | A.D.M.S. visited this ambulance to-day ~~& went~~ to inspect a farmyard at No. 47 in this Street which I had asked should be put out of bounds to | |

D. D. & L., London, E.C.
(A8004) Wt. W1771/M2 31 750,000 5/17 Sch. 52 Forms/C2118/14

Instructions regarding War Diaries and Intelligence Summaries are contained in F. S. Regs., Part II. and the Staff Manual respectively. Title pages will be prepared in manuscript.

# WAR DIARY
or
~~INTELLIGENCE SUMMARY.~~
(*Erase heading not required.*)

~~449~~ 447 Army Form C. 2118.

1/1st Lowland Field Ambulance

| Place | Date | Hour | Summary of Events and Information | Remarks and references to Appendices |
|---|---|---|---|---|
| ECOIVRES. | 8/8/18 (Cont'd) | | British Troops owing to the very unfavourable report Major MACKENZIE had made as to its sanitary condition. In the evening the Town Major called & informed me that the owner, or occupier, of this farm was called Wavelet & had proved a very troublesome, grasping, individual, well known for his insanitary & filthy farm but litigious & difficult to deal with. J.W.L. | |
| do. | 9/8/18 | | Received A.D.M.S. R1778/1 d/8/8/18 instructing me to detail MAJOR MACKENZIE & 3 O.R. (N.C.O.s if possible) to attend the 10th Course at 1st Army School of Instruction at No. 1 C.C.S. PERNES, from 11th to 24th August. This will leave myself, Major J. BROWNE, & Capt. A.D. DOWNES available for duty with the unit, although I have to show 8 officers on my effective strength of whom <u>none</u> are on leave. The value of this course of "instruction" is not apparent – unless for Junior officers – if the experience of the last course counts for anything. J.W.L. | |
| do. | 10/8/18 | | Syllabus of 10th Course at 1st Army RAMC School of Instruction received. It is noted that officers & O.R. have instruction daily in <u>Squad</u> drill by the "instructor", & that there is also instruction given on the arrest of haemorrhage, the use | |

D. D. & L., London, E.C. (A8004) Wt. W1771/M2 31 750,000 5/17 Sch. 52 Forms/C2118/14

Instructions regarding War Diaries and Intelligence Summaries are contained in F. S. Regs., Part II. and the Staff Manual respectively. Title pages will be prepared in manuscript.

448 Army Form C. 2118.

# WAR DIARY

or

~~INTELLIGENCE SUMMARY.~~

(Erase heading not required.)

1/1st Lowland Field Ambulance

| Place | Date | Hour | Summary of Events and Information | Remarks and references to Appendices |
|---|---|---|---|---|
| ECOIVRES | 10/8/18 (Contd.) | | of the triangular bandage, & the application of Thomas' Splints & rifle splint. There are also lectures, or demonstrations, in nursing by the Sister &c. but there is no instruction in stretcher drill or handling of injured; though possibly this will be given incidentally. A successful concert was given to-night at HQ of this unit. J.w.L | |
| do | 11/8/18 | | Major MACKENZIE, Sgt ALLISON, Sgt G.H. THOMSON, & Cpl W.R. DONALD proceeded to 1st Army RAMC School of Instruction, PERNES. J.w.L | |
| do | 12/8/18 | | MAJOR J BROWNE will visit surrounding details of units of this Division with a view to supervision of their sanitation during MAJOR MACKENZIE'S absence at School of Instruction. Capt. R.A. LENNIE reported for duty with this unit to-day on discharge from Hospital (7 CCS). The number of flies has notably diminished. The use of formalin solution in improvised traps in the kitchens, & improvised arsenic traps elsewhere, together with freer use of fly papers has helped, though no doubt the vigorous destruction of breeding dumps of rubbish round about by burying in pits & sealing with canvas has been more efficacious. These are methods which were practised in Egypt & Palestine with great success by this Division but seem to be | |

D. D. & L., London, E.C. (A8004) Wt. W1771/M2 31 750,000 5/17 Sch. 52 Forms/C2118/14

Instructions regarding War Diaries and Intelligence Summaries are contained in F. S. Regs., Part II. and the Staff Manual respectively. Title pages will be prepared in manuscript.

# WAR DIARY

~~or~~

~~INTELLIGENCE SUMMARY.~~

(*Erase heading not required.*)

449 Army Form C. 2118.

1/1st Lowland Field Ambulance

| Place | Date | Hour | Summary of Events and Information | Remarks and references to Appendices |
|---|---|---|---|---|
| ECOIVRES | 12/8/18 | | unknown – or at least not made use of in France. The horse manure is swept up daily from the street opposite this ambulance by fatigue party of the unit in addition to the usual daily sweeping of the street by Divisional fatigue party under the Town Major's Sanitary men. Additional fireplaces have been built in the kitchens & the old ones repaired & rebuilt where necessary. Meat safes & fly proof presses have been constructed by members of the unit for all kitchens, & a large bread press (fly proof) for the Qr. Master's store. The floor of the kitchen at the hospital has now been cemented & is much more easily kept clean. All the kitchens & men's billets have been white washed, or treated with white distemper obtained from B.R.C.S. The gutters at the stables have been paved with cobble stones & other sanitary improvements carried out there. Improvised disinfector spoken of in my note of 6/8/18 has been completed at hospital (the school buildings) & will be in use as soon as the fireplace built under it dries sufficiently to allow a fire to be made. Capt R.A. LENNIE reported for duty from Hospital (7th C.C.S.) J.W.L. | |
| do | 13/8/18. | | Improvised disinfector was found to leak badly after fire under it had been set going. | |

D. D. & L., London, E.C. (A8004) Wt. W1771/M2 31 750,000 5/17 Sch. 52 Forms/C2118/14

Instructions regarding War Diaries and Intelligence Summaries are contained in F. S. Regs., Part II. and the Staff Manual respectively. Title pages will be prepared in manuscript.

# WAR DIARY
~~or~~
~~INTELLIGENCE SUMMARY.~~
*(Erase heading not required.)*

450 Army Form C. 2118.

1/1st Lowland Field Ambulance

| Place | Date | Hour | Summary of Events and Information | Remarks and references to Appendices |
|---|---|---|---|---|
| ECOIVRES | 13/8/18 (Contd) | | some leaking place having been stopped by tar and lead. Another (smaller) tank is being set up in its place. J.W.L. | |
| do | 14/8/18 | | Chaplain G.C. CLAIRMONT attached to this unit reported to 1/7th Scott Rifles for duty with that Battalion. Disinfector is in use & can deal with 10 blankets per hour very efficiently. J.W.L. | |
| do | 15/8/18 | | Received RAMC O.O. No 8 d/15 8/18 detailing reliefs of Divisional Ambulances & moves. This unit is to take over from 1/2nd Highland F.A. at CAMBLIGNEUL & to send a holding party to-day under arrangements between O's.C concerned. Proceeded with Capt. R.A. LENNIE 1 NCO & 4 men by ambulance car to CAMBLIGNEUL saw Lt. Col MILLER 1/2nd Highland F.A. & found that he was not leaving his present site until 18th Inst & was then going to St CATHERINE'S. Left the N.C.O. & 4 men & returned in car with Capt LENNIE. Arranged with 155th Bde H.Q. to collect sick of that Bde in accordance with ADMS instructions. Wrote letter to H.Q. 157th Bde that I would send an ambulance daily between 10 & 11 a.m. to Mt St ELOY from 17th till further orders to | |

D. D. & L., London, E.C.
(A8004) Wt. W1771/M2 31 750,000 5/17 Sch. 52 Forms/C2118/14

Instructions regarding War Diaries and Intelligence Summaries are contained in F. S. Regs., Part II. and the Staff Manual respectively. Title pages will be prepared in manuscript.

# WAR DIARY

or

~~INTELLIGENCE SUMMARY.~~

(Erase heading not required.)

457

Army Form C. 2118.

1/1st Lowland Field Ambulance

| Place | Date | Hour | Summary of Events and Information | Remarks and references to Appendices |
|---|---|---|---|---|
| ECOIVRES | 15/8/18 contd | | collect sick from 157th Bde in accordance with instructions of ADMS. This unit has also to collect sick from 56th Bde R.F.A. in ACQ & from the D.A.C. in FREVIN CAPELLE. Div L. | |
| do | 16/8/18 | | In accordance with A.D.M.S. R1901/5 d/15/8/18 to detail M.O. for temporary duty with 1/3rd L.F.A. I sent Capt R.A. LENNIE to report to O.C. that unit this forenoon. The 1/1st LOWLAND F.A. is now left with myself, Major J BROWNE & Capt. A.D. DOWNES as medical officers available to carry on the work of the ambulance, collect sick, see sick parades of the following units, (& also supervise their sanitation): 52nd Divl Train, 52nd Divl Reception Camp, 1/1st Mobile Veterinary Section, 155th & 157th Inf Brigade Transport Lines. The remaining 4 medical officers are detached for duties elsewhere but must still be shown on the "effective strength" of this unit. There are no officers on leave of any kind at present. A "traverse" built of earth inside corrugated iron walls is being erected by this unit across the middle of the larger horse standing situated at the fork of Station road | |

D. D. & L., London, E.C.
(A8004) Wt. W1771/M2·31 750,000 5/17 Sch. 52 Forms/C2118/14

Instructions regarding War Diaries and Intelligence Summaries are contained in F. S. Regs., Part II. and the Staff Manual respectively. Title pages will be prepared in manuscript.

# WAR DIARY
or
~~INTELLIGENCE SUMMARY.~~
(Erase heading not required.)

452

Army Form C. 2118.

1/1st Lowland Field Ambulance
52nd (Lowland) Division

| Place | Date | Hour | Summary of Events and Information | Remarks and references to Appendices |
|---|---|---|---|---|
| ECOIVRES ~~16/8/18~~ | 16/8/18 Contd. | | & ECOIVRES-ACQ road in order to limit the effect of a direct hit by aeroplane bomb, or a shell. In reply to A.D.M.S. R 1902/7d/15 8/18 forwarded letter F541 showing No, Rank, name, unit, No of days in Amb. & the diagnosis of the 15 men evacuated to C.C.S by this unit from 52nd Division on 15/8/18. Full use has been made of the Divisional Rest Station & no patient likely to be fit for duty within 14 days has been evacuated to C.C.S. J.W.L. | |
| do. | 17/8/18. | | No. 341010 S/S HAMPSON A.F. 1/3rd West Lancs Fld Amb. reported to-day for duty with this unit, in accordance with instructions of A.G's No. 59/66/29/18. Received 155th Inf Bde Orders No 107 d/17 8/18 detailing times of move of units of Bde to CAUCOURT area. J.W.L. | |
| do | 18/8/18 | | Received A.D.M.S. SR 173/7 of even date instructing this unit to remain in its present location till 19th inst. Visited CAMBLIGNEUL & arranged with O.C. 1/2nd HIGHLAND Fld Amb. there to send an officer (Capt DOWNES) of this unit down there to-night with 2 motor ambulances & some dressing station personnel & stores to look after the sick who might require hospital care before arrival of this unit tomorrow. There is already a holding party of 1 N.C.O. & 2 men of this unit at CAMBLIGNEUL J.W.L. | |

D. D. & L., London, E.C. (A8004) Wt. W1771/M2 31 750,000 5/17 Sch. 52 Forms/C2118/14

Instructions regarding War Diaries and Intelligence Summaries are contained in F. S. Regs., Part II. and the Staff Manual respectively. Title pages will be prepared in manuscript.

# WAR DIARY

~~or~~

~~INTELLIGENCE SUMMARY.~~

(*Erase heading not required.*)

453 Army Form C. 2118.

1/1st Lowland Field Ambulance
52nd (Lowland) Division.

| Place | Date | Hour | Summary of Events and Information | Remarks and references to Appendices |
|---|---|---|---|---|
| CAMBLIGNEUL<br>W14 d 5.5<br>Sh 36 B 1/40000 | 19/8/18 | | Handed over billets etc at ECOIVRES to representative of Town Major shortly after 9 A.M to-day & received certificate from him that same had been left in a clean & sanitary condition. Arrived at billets of 1/2nd Highland Field Amb with main body of unit by march route via A.C.Q. & CAMBLAIN L'ABBE at 10-45. Found 1/2nd Highland Field Amb. had lost 14 of their horses by enemy aeroplane bombs last night. Proceeded at once to collect materials to improvise splinter-proof walls round horse lines & standings, & to dig zig zag trenches near huts occupied by personnel & patients. R.E. material is scarce, but C.R.E. has agreed to provide some hurdles though he is unable to supply stakes. Some old bedding wire & delapidated sheets of corrugated iron found round about billets & huts will also help. Latrines (deep pit) are not fly proof & we have closed one & are proceeding with the digging of a new pit latrine. | |
| | | | J.W.L. | |
| CAMBLIGNEUL | 20/8/18 | | Capt REID (Quartermaster) recollected seeing some stakes near ECOIVRES which had been left by a Battalion of this Division on moving out & with the aid of these & the wooden battens of an old corrugated iron shelter a protective standing | |

D. D. & L., London, E.C.
(A8004) Wt. W1771/M2 31 750,000 5/17 Sch. 52 Forms/C2118/14

454

Instructions regarding War Diaries and Intelligence Summaries are contained in F. S. Regs., Part II. and the Staff Manual respectively. Title pages will be prepared in manuscript.

# WAR DIARY

or

~~INTELLIGENCE SUMMARY.~~

*(Erase heading not required.)*

Army Form C. 2118.

1/1st Lowland Field Ambulance
52nd Lowland Division

| Place | Date | Hour | Summary of Events and Information | Remarks and references to Appendices |
|---|---|---|---|---|
| CAMBLIGNEUL (W14 d 5.5) | 20/8 (Contd) | | for 20 horses was half completed by 8 p.m. last night. The remaining horses were put into two barns the walls of which were well built of stone & afforded protection from splinters. Work on revetments & shelter trenches is being carried on to-day. A.D.M.S. called ~~between~~ 12 & 1 o'clock to-day & went round the hospital huts, cookhouse, latrines, grease trap at cookhouse. He called attention to the fact that a patient in the hospital (newly arrived) had unduly long hair, that the latrines were not fly proof & that refuse likely to breed flies was being dumped beside the incinerator at the ground of [illegible] site which seems to be used as a public incinerator but is in the ambulance area. He made no comment on the work being done for protection against bombs. Capt J.W. BURTON rejoined from 19th Bn RGA. J.W.L. Received orders in the late afternoon that Division would concentrate on night of 20/21st, & later received ADMS SR 181 & 182, 155th Inf Bde Order 108, & a number of other orders instructions & telegrams all ~~relating to~~ connected with move, copies Medical arrangements, evacuation of sick & wounded etc. J.W.L. | |
| LATTRE ST QUENTIN J23 d 9.2 Sh 51c | 21/8/18 | | Unit marched out from billets at CAMBLIGNEUL at 11.45 last night with transport & reached starting point (Road junction E1 a 2 2 Sh. 51c) at 12.25 a.m. in | |

D. D. & L., London, E.C. (A8004) Wt. W1771/M2 31 750,000 5/17 Sch. 52 Forms/C2118/14

Instructions regarding War Diaries and Intelligence Summaries are contained in F. S. Regs., Part II. and the Staff Manual respectively. Title pages will be prepared in manuscript.

# WAR DIARY

or

~~INTELLIGENCE SUMMARY.~~

(*Erase heading not required.*)

455 Army Form C. 2118.

1/1st Lowland Field Ambulance
52nd (Lowland) Division

| Place | Date | Hour | Summary of Events and Information | Remarks and references to Appendices |
|---|---|---|---|---|
| LATTRE ST QUENTIN (J23d92 Sh51c) | 21/8/18 (Contd.) | | in accordance with instructions to be there at 12.30 A.M. (night of 20/21st) to march in rear of 155th Bde as far as HERMAVILLE. The 3 horsed Ambulance wagons were detailed one to accompany each Batt. on the march & report to the ambulance HQ at LATTRE ST QUENTIN afterwards. 1 ambulance motor wagon + 2 clerks were sent to report to O.C. 1/2nd Lowland F.A. at AGNEZ LES DUISANS in accordance with A.D.M.S. orders. The remaining motor ambulance wagons + motor cyclist were sent on in advance of the unit. Excluding these the marching out strength was as undernoted:– | |

| O/R | Personnel RAMC | Personnel ASC | chargers | riders | Horses H.D. | Horses L.D. | Vehicles 4 wh. | Vehicles 2 wh. | cycles* |
|---|---|---|---|---|---|---|---|---|---|
| 5 | 147 | 47 | 4 | 2 | 23 | 17 | 4 | 14 | 1 |

* 1 Motor cycle + driver at A.D.M.S. office as dispatch rider.

Stores taken over from 1/2nd Highland Fd Amb at CAMBLIGNEUL were handed over to Billet Warden for Area Commandant.

Wrote letter to F 575 d/21/8/18 to 156th Bde HQ that I would send an ambulance motor to B.H.R. daily between 1000 + 1100 to collect sick from units of 156th Bde in accordance with A.D.M.S. orders, + sent letter F 577 of same date to A.D.M.S. giving return of stores taken over + handed over during move. J.W.L.

1845 Sent 1 ambulance motor wagon to report to O.C. 52nd Div Artillery ~~division~~ for temporary duty in accordance with A.D.M.S. instructions just received. J.W.L.

D. D. & L., London, E.C. (A8004) Wt. W1771/M2 31 750,000 5/17 Sch. 52 Forms/C2118/14

456 Army Form C. 2118.

# WAR DIARY
or
~~INTELLIGENCE SUMMARY.~~
(Erase heading not required.)

Instructions regarding War Diaries and Intelligence Summaries are contained in F. S. Regs., Part II. and the Staff Manual respectively. Title pages will be prepared in manuscript.

1/1st Lowland Field Ambulance
52nd Lowland Division

| Place | Date | Hour | Summary of Events and Information | Remarks and references to Appendices |
|---|---|---|---|---|
| LATTRE ST QUENTIN Sh 51c J23.d.9.2. | 22/8/18 | | A.D.M.S. called this afternoon on his return from reconnoitring tour in view of warning order of move. He instructed me to send 2 officers + 2 Bearer subdivisions to 2/3rd N. MIDLAND Fld AMB. at R15 b5.3, Sh 51c by means of 1/1st Lowland F.A. motor ambulances + 6 more to be lent temporarily by 1/2nd Low. F.A. Also 4 Clerks to Corps Main Dressing Station LE BAC DU SUD Q31 d6.7. Sh 51c. ~~&~~ 90 blankets 5 wheeled stretchers (+ 5 more to be sent from 1/2nd Low Fld Amb.) to ~~be~~ accompany the Bearer Subdivision to M.D.S. at R15 b5.3 above mentioned along with 5 ambulance wagons of 1/1st Lowland Fld Amb. ~~[illegible]~~ mentioned to have stores + personnel at that MDS by 1800 to-night, + detailed MAJOR MACKENZIE + Capt BURTON with 74 O.R. (including 2 sgts.) as personnel. (B+C section bearers made up to section strength from bearers of A section). | |
| | | 1830 | Received 156th Bde + ~~[illegible]~~ A.D.M.S. orders to move to BRETONCOURT + report on arrival to A.D.M.S. at CHATEAU there. Marched out with remainder of unit from ~~B~~ LATTRE ST QUENTIN at 2015. Marching out state as undernoted:- | |

| Offs | Personnel | | Chargers | Riders | Horses | | Vehicles | | Motor Cycle | Cycle |
|---|---|---|---|---|---|---|---|---|---|---|
| | RAMC | ASC | | | LD | HD | 2 axle | 1 axle | | |
| 4 | 71 | 38 | 4 | 2 | 17 | 23 | 14 | 4 | 1 | 1 |

The 52nd Divisional Artillery were bombed by enemy aeroplanes last night nearly

D. D. & L., London, E.C. (A8004) Wt. W1771/M2 31 750,000 5/17 Sch. 52 Forms/C2118/14

Instructions regarding War Diaries and Intelligence Summaries are contained in F. S. Regs., Part II. and the Staff Manual respectively. Title pages will be prepared in manuscript.

# WAR DIARY

~~or~~

~~INTELLIGENCE SUMMARY.~~

(*Erase heading not required.*)

457 Army Form C. 2118.

1/1st Lowland Field Ambulance
52nd (Lowland) Division

| Place | Date | Hour | Summary of Events and Information | Remarks and references to Appendices |
|---|---|---|---|---|
| LATTRE ST QUENTIN Sh 51c. J23d9.2 | 22/8/18 | | the whole way from ACQ to their new location near BEAUMETZ & 1 off + 3 O.R. were brought to this ambulance about 4 A.M. to-day by the motor ambulance of this unit attached to them last night for temporary duty. 1 officer + 5 O.R. were brought down this afternoon suffering from slighter wounds for A.T. Serum. After receiving this they were able to be returned for duty except one with a small scalp wound (already suppurating) who was sent to C.C.S. The officer informed me that about 70 bombs in all were dropped on them on the way but practically all the casualties occurred from one or two which landed right amongst them as they were parking at BEAUMETZ. One of the 4 who were brought in this morning died on way down to C.C.S. J.w.L. | |
| BRETONCOURT R26b1.2 Sh 51c 1/40000 | 23/8/18. | | Route taken was through WANQUENTIN + BEAUMETZ LES LOGES; bivouac ground was reached about 0130. There was bright moonlight the whole way + the roads in neighbourhood were very congested with long lines of traffic of all kinds proceeding towards BRETONCOURT district. Enemy planes came over + bombed dumps + billets but did not seem to notice the traffic. A good many of our own planes were overhead also. Reported by orderly to A.D.M.S. + bivouacked on ground allotted to us. Called at A.D.M.S. office in the forenoon + learned that 2 were to take over from 2/1st North Midland Fld. Ambulance | |

Instructions regarding War Diaries and Intelligence Summaries are contained in F. S. Regs., Part II. and the Staff Manual respectively. Title pages will be prepared in manuscript.

# WAR DIARY
or
~~INTELLIGENCE SUMMARY.~~
(Erase heading not required.)

458 Army Form C. 2118.

1/1st Lowland Field Ambulance
52nd Lowland Division

| Place | Date | Hour | Summary of Events and Information | Remarks and references to Appendices |
|---|---|---|---|---|
| BRETONCOURT | 23/8/18 (Contd) | | at LE FERMENT R21 c 8,2 Sh 51c & dated on received R.A.M.C. O.O. No 10 d/23 8/18. Moved into R21 c 82 at 1400 & took over from 2/1st N MIDLAND F.A. at 1700 in accordance with R.A.M.C. O.O. No. 10. Saw a number of sick from surrounding units in afternoon. Marching out strength as under. | |

| Off | Personnel RAMC | ASC (HT/MT) | Transport etc |
|---|---|---|---|
| 5 * | 54 | 38 | as in note 22/8/18. |

* Includes 2 Chaplains (1 R.C. & 1 Presbyterian) attached to unit for rations etc arriving at BRETONCOURT this morning.

Detailed Major Brown & 17 O.R. Tent subdivision to report to Corps M.D.S. at BAC DU SUD to-day.

| Place | Date | Hour | Summary of Events and Information | Remarks and references to Appendices |
|---|---|---|---|---|
| LE FERMONT R21 c 82 Sh 51c | 23/8/18 | 2000 | Sent remaining motor cyclist for temporary duty with 1/2nd Lowland F.A. in accordance with A.D.M.S. letter R2010/1 d/23 8/18. Any letters of an urgent nature requiring use of a motor cyclist to be sent to A.D.M.S. Office for despatch. JWL | |
| do | 24/8/18 | 0900 | Received R.A.M.C. O.O. No. 11 d 24/8/18 at 0630 this morning to form an A.D.S. at MERCATEL in vacated R.A.P. at M35 a 29 (Sh. 51B); remainder of ambulance less personnel at Corps M.D.S. to concentrate in vicinity of 1/2nd Lowland Field Ambulance at M31 b 28 (Sh 51C). Sent Capt. A.D. DOWNES with part of Tent subdivision (7 O.R.) & Dressing station | |

D. D. & L., London, E.C. (A8004) Wt. W1771/M2 31 750,000 5/17 Sch. 52 Forms/C2118/14

459 Army Form C. 2118.

Instructions regarding War Diaries and Intelligence Summaries are contained in F. S. Regs., Part II. and the Staff Manual respectively. Title pages will be prepared in manuscript.

# WAR DIARY
~~or~~
~~INTELLIGENCE SUMMARY.~~
*(Erase heading not required.)*

1/1st Lowland Field Ambulance
52nd Lowland Division

| Place | Date | Hour | Summary of Events and Information | Remarks and references to Appendices |
|---|---|---|---|---|
| LE FERMONT | 24/8/18 (Contd) | | equipment by motor ambulances at 9 A.M. instructing Capt DOWNES to have Capt BURTON & the 72 bearers presently with 1/2nd L.F.A at M31 (Ficheux) sent on to his dressing station at M35. Reported same to A.D.M.S. by orderly. Packed remainder of ambulance transport & prepared to move to M31 in accordance with instructions of A.D.M.S. Evacuated 8 gassed cases to C.M.D.S. & 3 sick to Corps Rest Station by motor ambulance. J.W.L. | |
| FICHEUX ~~MERCATEL~~ M31 b 2 8 Sh. 51B 1/40000 | 24/8/18 | 2000 | Marched out from LE FERMONT at 1000 & reached M31 b 28 at 1130. Parked transport immediately S of 1/2nd L.F.A. dressing station there. Marching out strength as under. 15 OR reported back from C.M.D.S. MAJOR BROWNE was sent to 3rd Canadian C.C.S. for temporary duty & 2 chiefs remain at C.M.D.S. | |

| Off. | Personnel R.A.M.C. | Personnel A.S.C. | Chargers | Riders | Horses H.D. | Horses L.D. | Vehicles 1 Axle | Vehicles 2 Axle | Cycle |
|---|---|---|---|---|---|---|---|---|---|
| 4 * | 47 | 39 | 4 | 2 | 23 | 17 | 4 | 14 | 1 |

* includes two chaplains

Received word that the 2 motor cycles of this unit (both on detached duty) had broken down owing to accidents on the roads. Neither of the drivers was hurt.

Received note from A.D.M.S. that 156 + 157 Bdes were on a line N.E. of HENIN, this line being roughly N26 central to T9b09 & that A.D.S. should be pushed forward; (2) that nothing was known of the roads from MERCATEL ~~HENIN~~ + BOISLEUX ST MARQ to HENIN & these should be reconnoitred with a view to use by Ambulance motor cars; (3) that 156

D. D. & L., London, E.C. (A8001) Wt. W1771/M2031 750,000 5/17 Sch. 52 Forms/C2118/14

460 Army Form C. 2118.

Instructions regarding War Diaries and Intelligence Summaries are contained in F. S. Regs., Part II. and the Staff Manual respectively. Title pages will be prepared in manuscript.

# WAR DIARY

~~or~~

~~INTELLIGENCE SUMMARY.~~

*(Erase heading not required.)*

1/1st Lowland Field Ambulance
52nd Lowland Division

| Place | Date | Hour | Summary of Events and Information | Remarks and references to Appendices |
|---|---|---|---|---|
| M31 b 28 | 24/8/18 | | Bde H.Q. was in S6b58. Proceeded to A.D.S. at M35 by motor car & found that Capt DOWNES had got into touch with 1/7th SR & 1/7 RS but could not find 1/4th R.S. Walked down to 156 Bde HQ by sunken road & ROSS LANE & found that they were very near H.Q. of 1/7th R.S. but in S5b58 not S6b58. Gen. LEGGAT informed me that Batt H.Q. were situated as follows 1/7th SR at N31 a 28, 1/7th RS at T1a22 & 1/4th R.S. at ~~T6~~ T1,60,5. He expressed satisfaction at the way in which evacuation of wounded was going on & informed me that so far as he knew the road running in a S.E. direction from M30c09 was good down to CRUCIFIX in S6d, but that roads from M30c09 to NEUVILLE VITASSE & from M30c21 to HENIN were impassable for ambulances owing to shell holes & barbed wire. Reported to A.D.M.S. accordingly, stating that I did not think it desirable to move the A.D.S. further forward than its present site in M35 till these roads were cleared & made passable. Sent Capt COLES & some bearers who had reported to me at M31 from 1/3rd L.F.A. to A.D.S. to assist Capt DOWNES & Capt BURTON there. Received note from O.C. 1/2nd L.F.A. that he had closed his dressing station at M31b28 at 2-30 p.m. Occupied this station but did not open up. About 1030 a fire broke out near BLAIRVILLE direction caused by A.E. bombs & ambulances going down to C.M.D.S. were stopped & sent back to this H.Q. Eight | |

D. D. & L., London, E.C.
(A8001) Wt. W1771/M2031 750,000 5/17 Sch. 52 Forms/C2118/14

Instructions regarding War Diaries and Intelligence Summaries are contained in F. S. Regs., Part II. and the Staff Manual respectively. Title pages will be prepared in manuscript.

# WAR DIARY
or
# INTELLIGENCE SUMMARY.
(Erase heading not required.)

461 Army Form C. 2118.

1/1st Lowland Field Ambulance
52nd (Lowland) Division

| Place | Date | Hour | Summary of Events and Information | Remarks and references to Appendices |
|---|---|---|---|---|
| M31 b 2 8 FICHEUX | 24/8/18 (Contd) | | wounded were brought in to this HQ (5 from A.E. bombs of whom 2 were serious & 3 from A.E. machine gun bullets) & a dressing station was at once opened up here for their treatment & evacuation. J.W.L. | |
| do | 25/8/18 | | The fire last night was due to a column of 7 motor lorries bringing up 6" How. shells & ammunition, having been hit by 3 A.E. bombs & set on fire. Motor ambulances from A.D.S. & here were delayed 3 hours before getting down to C.M.D.S. at BAC DU SUD with their loads of wounded from A.D.S. at M35 & this dressing station at M31 a 2 8. A.D.M.S. called. There was a good deal of sneezing among the personnel of this unit at 7 p.m & again at 9 p.m. apparently due to gas shelling of our front line. Wind was in a favourable direction for gas drifting this way. Visited A.D.S. at M35 this afternoon & found evacuation had gone on very well & there had been no congestion in spite of the delay on the roads & the distance to BAC DU SUD where C.M.D.S. is. A total of 166 wounded & gassed cases had been evacuated in addition to sick to 1200 to-day. All clear at A.D.S. at 1720 J.W.L. | |
| do | 26/8/18 | | Received R.A.M.C. O.O. No. 12 d/25 8/18 at 0130 this morning and proceeded at once by motor ambulance to A.D.S. Gave the O.C. there (Capt DOWNES) the position of 155th Bde H.Q. (in ROSS LANE just before coming to 156th Bde HQ) & instructed him to get in touch & send out ~~bearers~~ additional bearers to clear AID POSTS formed by | |

D. D. & L., London, E.C. (A8001) Wt. W1771/M2031 750,000 5/17 Sch. 52 Forms/C2118/14

Instructions regarding War Diaries and Intelligence Summaries are contained in F. S. Regs., Part II. and the Staff Manual respectively. Title pages will be prepared in manuscript.

# WAR DIARY
~~or~~
~~INTELLIGENCE SUMMARY.~~
(Erase heading not required.)

462 Army Form C. 2118.

1/1st Lowland Field Ambulance
52nd (Lowland) Division

| Place | Date | Hour | Summary of Events and Information | Remarks and references to Appendices |
|---|---|---|---|---|
| FICHEUX M31 b 2 8. | 26/8/18 (Contd) | | battalions of 155th Bde in addition to those of 156th Bde. O.C. A.D.S. informed me that he ~~could~~ now got motor ambulances to M30 c 31 but that road from this point to M36 b 6 5 was too rough for cars. Road to CRUCIFIX in S 6 d was good. Got back to FICHEUX Dressing station at 0400. A.D.M.S. called early in forenoon & asked to see the accommodation at this Dressing Station. D.D.M.S. XVII Corps also called here before midday & saw A.D.M.S. while he was here. A.D.M.S. 57th Division called here in afternoon. Received note from O.C. A.D.S. at M35 d by car at 1600 saying that the evacuation route from forward battalions was now getting very long & that as A.D.M.S. had asked him to keep as many of 1/3rd L.F.A. bearers at his A.D.S. as possible he feared his bearers would not be able to cope with the work. He had 1 N.C.O. + 8 bearers at ~~the~~ AID POST of 1/7th S.R. & two relay posts each of 4 bearers between that and A.D.S. all these were 1/1st L.F.A. bearers & he had sent 20 more bearers out there to clear 1/4th R.S.F 1/5th R.S.F & 1/4th K.O.S.B. this morning. They were provided with wheeled stretchers. Also, 1 N.C.O. + 12 men were with 1/7th R.S. + 8 bearers with 1/4th R.S. These 21 O.R. belonged to 1/3rd L.F.A. | |
| | | | A.D.M.S. called about 4-30 in a Div. motor car & took me with him to A.D.S. to reconnoitre roads, ~~which~~ we found these to be as stated by Capt DOWNES. & went down | |

D. D. & L., London, E.C.
(A8001) Wt. W1771/M2031 750,000 5/17 Sch. 52 Forms/C2118/14

463 Army Form C. 2118.

Instructions regarding War Diaries and Intelligence Summaries are contained in F. S. Regs., Part II. and the Staff Manual respectively. Title pages will be prepared in manuscript.

# WAR DIARY

~~or~~

~~INTELLIGENCE SUMMARY.~~

(Erase heading not required.)

1/1st Lowland Field Ambulance
52nd Lowland Division

| Place | Date | Hour | Summary of Events and Information | Remarks and references to Appendices |
|---|---|---|---|---|
| FICHEUX M31b28 | 24/8/18 (Contd.) | | the good road to CRUCIFIX at S6d, then along road towards HENIN to 157th Bde HQ at T2a22, returned to 156th Bde HQ at T1b15, & then to 1/2nd L.F.A. at S6d91 where I waited to arrange about an A.D.S. with O.C. of that unit while A.D.M.S. went on. Found 1/2nd L.F.A. had already an A.D.S. at T3a3.5 which was not very good & could not be enlarged as place was still under shell fire & patients had to be carried to a relay post near 157th Bde HQ in T2a52. As this was the only feasible route owing to roads north & East being ~~blocked~~ impassable for motor ambulances I arranged to give O.C. 1/2nd L.F.A. what assistance he required in bearers & ambulances for evacuating wounded from 156th Bde who were swinging round EAST of HENIN. Reached M31 Dressing station about 9 p.m. by ambulance car & found all ready to move to MERCATEL in accordance with written orders given to MAJOR MACKENZIE at 8 p.m. during my absence. Left 1 Cpl & 2 men to hold Dressing Station at M31b28 till morning (ambulances (if any) should arrive), & bivouacked for the night with unit (less personnel at A.D.S., M.D.S. & 1 Tent subdivision at C.M.D.S.) in M30c22 Sh 51B. | |
| | | | Sent a brief written report on situation to A.D.M.S. by orderly who brought RAMC O.O. No. 12 at 0130 this morning in accordance with his written request. | |
| | | | The tent subdivision less MAJOR BROWNE & 2 clerks reported back for duty with this ambulance this afternoon from C.M.D.S. BAC DU SUD. | |

D. D. & L., London, E.C. (A8001) Wt. W1771/M2031 750,000 5/17 Sch. 52 Forms/C2118/14

Instructions regarding War Diaries and Intelligence Summaries are contained in F. S. Regs., Part II. and the Staff Manual respectively. Title pages will be prepared in manuscript.

# WAR DIARY
~~or~~
# ~~INTELLIGENCE SUMMARY.~~
*(Erase heading not required.)*

464 Army Form C. 2118.

1/1st Lowland Field Ambulance
52nd Lowland Division

| Place | Date | Hour | Summary of Events and Information | Remarks and references to Appendices |
|---|---|---|---|---|
| FICHEUX M31 b28 | 26/8/18 (Contd) | | Wounded evacuated for 24 hours ending 1200 to-day. Offs 5 OR 144 Gassed off. nil OR 2 total Off 5 OR 146 | JWL |
| MERCATEL M30 c 22. Sh. 51B | 27/8/18 | | Received letter SC 26 d/26/8/18 from a/Staff Capt. 156 Bde at 0130 that he was unable to say where Battn HQ. were at present & asking me to send 3 orderlies to him at Bde H.Q. T1 b16, with returning orderly so that he might send them forward with guides as soon as Battn HQ. were fixed. Complied. Received R.A.M.C. OO. No 13 d/27/8/18 at 0715 & proceeded to A.D.S. just formed by 1/3rd L.F.A. at HENIN to arrange with O.C. 1/3rd L.F.A. for evacuation of 156th Bde through that A.D.S. & to lend him cars & bearers as required. Found a number of 157th cases awaiting evacuation & brought back a car load which I sent straight on to C.M.D.S. at BAC DU SUD. New Corps M.D.S. is to open at BLAIRVILLE at 1200 to-day. Sent on Motor Lorry (as soon as it reported to me) to 1/3rd L.F.A. at HENIN for walking wounded. Returned Capt COLES to that unit for duty & sent on also 5 of my 7 Motor Ambulances & 1 N.C.O. & all available bearers, 19 in all, to HENIN (A.D.S. of 1/3rd LFA) for duty. Sent note to Sgt. McGREGOR i/c Bearers at his post in sunken road at N26 a 9.5 (approximately) to instruct | |

D. D. & L., London, E.C. (A8001) Wt. W1771/M2031 750,000 5/17 Sch. 52 Forms/C2118/14

465 Army Form C. 2118.

Instructions regarding War Diaries and Intelligence Summaries are contained in F. S. Regs., Part II. and the Staff Manual respectively. Title pages will be prepared in manuscript.

# WAR DIARY
~~or~~
~~INTELLIGENCE~~ SUMMARY.

(*Erase heading not required.*)

1/1st Lowland Field Ambulance
52nd Lowland Division

| Place | Date | Hour | Summary of Events and Information | Remarks and references to Appendices |
|---|---|---|---|---|
| MERCATEL M30 c.2.2. Sh. 51B 1/40000 | 27/8/18 (Contd) | | all bearers & relay posts between that & MERCATEL to report to H.Q. & to carry on all evacuations now to A.D.S. at HENIN. bearers to collect all wounded west of his post, on the way, & bring them to MERCATEL. Arranged to have the wounded (now mostly walking cases) collected at H.Q at M30 c.2.2. fed, & sent on to A.D.S. at M35 a.28. for dressing & evacuation by motor ambulance or commandeered returning motor lorry (with a Medical orderly). Wounded for 24 hours ending 1200 to-day:- Off 5; OR. 104; Gassed nil. The Cpl & 2 men left at FICHEUX, M31 a.28., as a holding party reported back this afternoon; that dressing station having been taken over by 2/2 Wessex F.A. Commandeered a returning empty motor wagon & sent down 30 walking wounded (in charge of an orderly to station by motor ambulance) who had found their way from various points in front to this A.D.S. & transport lines. JWL | |
| MERCATEL M35 a 28 | 28/8/18 | | Moved my H.Q. to this A.D.S as there is better accommodation for orderly room etc when things are quieter. Transport lines remain at M30 c.2.2 under charge of the Q.M. Capt A.M.REID. Wounded for 24 hours ending 1200 to-day were:- Off 1, OR, 70, of whom 1 off & 68 O.R. were admitted before midnight 27th/28th In accordance with instructions this unit is now receiving only sick of 156th Bde & a few from other units of other formations who straggle in. The Division was relieved in the line last night & 156th Bde is bivouacked in M35 a.; 155 Bde in M28d; | |

D. D. & L., London, E.C. (A8001) Wt. W1771/M2031 750,000 5/17 Sch. 52 Forms/C2118/14

466 Army Form C. 2118.

Instructions regarding War Diaries and Intelligence Summaries are contained in F. S. Regs., Part II. and the Staff Manual respectively. Title pages will be prepared in manuscript.

# WAR DIARY
or
# INTELLIGENCE SUMMARY.
(Erase heading not required.)

1/1st Lowland Field Ambulance
52nd Lowland Division

| Place | Date | Hour | Summary of Events and Information | Remarks and references to Appendices |
|---|---|---|---|---|
| MERCATEL M35a28 | 28/8/18 (Contd) | | & 157th Bde in M34d. In accordance with my instruction Capt DOWNES & Capt. BURTON have given me each a written report covering the days when they were each on detached duty. These reports are attached as APPENDICES I & II. Jw? | APPENDICES I & II. |
| do | 29/8/18 | | Sent MAJOR MACKENZIE & 38 O.R. (Personnel of B & C tent subdivisions) by 5 motor ambulances to report for duty with 45th & 46th CCS's respectively at BAC DU SUD in accordance with A.D.M.S. SR 101 d/28/8/18 received by me last night. As there seemed to be some doubt as to the number of officers to be sent, I wrote letter F 892 of even date to A.D.M.S. asking whether it was intended that only 1 officer should be sent or that 3 officers should be sent, & pointing out that to send 3 officers would leave myself only as a medical officer with the ambulance. The D.A.D.M.S., Major BROWNE, called by motor car in reply to this & it was finally agreed that I should send these two other officers down but that they should call at D.D.M.S. XVII Corps office, BRETONCOURT, on the way for instructions. All 3 officers reported back in the afternoon to their H.Q. for duty in accordance with instructions of D.D.M.S. It would appear that the ambiguity arose from D.D.M.S. office wire being sent "Tent subdivision less officer" instead of "less officers". Sent also 1 N.C.O. & 15 men in accordance with A.D.M.S. letter S.R. 203 issued at 2345 last night & received by me this morning to WARLUZEL, Sh 51c O27, to load tents on lorries. They reported back late this afternoon. | |
| | | 2000 | Sent 2 officers (MAJOR MACKENZIE & Capt BURTON) with 25 O.R., bearers, | |

D. D. & L., London, E.C.
(A8001) Wt. W1771/M2031 750,000 5/17 Sch. 52 Forms/C2118/14

Instructions regarding War Diaries and Intelligence Summaries are contained in F. S. Regs., Part II. and the Staff Manual respectively. Title pages will be prepared in manuscript.

# WAR DIARY
or
~~INTELLIGENCE SUMMARY.~~
(Erase heading not required.)

467

Army Form C. 2118.

1/1st Lowland Field Ambulance
52nd Lowland Division

| Place | Date | Hour | Summary of Events and Information | Remarks and references to Appendices |
|---|---|---|---|---|
| MERCATEL M35 a 28 Sh. 51B. | 29/8/18 (Contd) | | to report to O.C 1/3rd L.F.A at site of new C.M.D.S at BOIRY BECQUERELLE for temporary duty. ~~Sent No 316309 Pte David Murray by motor amb~~ in accordance with verbal instructions of A.D.M.S. Sent No. 316309 Pte DAVID MURRAY to report to O.C. 410th Fld Coy RE at S 2 a 8.6 for temporary duty with water test case Poisons, in accordance with A.D.M.S. letter M.O. 35 of even date. J.W.L. | |
| MERCATEL M35 a 2.8 | 30/8/18 | | Pte MURRAY returned about midnight having been unable to find 410th Fd Coy RE. Sent him + No 316189 Pte CARSON J.B. (who was student demonstrator in Chemistry in Alan Glen's School, Glasgow, when war broke out) by motor ambulance to ADMS with note for interview re testing of water for poisons, + both were detained for attached duty in connection therewith. Received S.R. 203, d/29/8/18 that C.M.D.S opens at 6 a.m. to-day at BOIRY BECQUERELLE; Sh. 51B T.1.c.3.8.; Collected 250 to 300 suits of S.D. clothing + 1 bale of putties (broken) for gassed cases from Dressing station at M31 b 2 8 where they had been left by 1/3rd L.F.A. + forwarded them by ambulance motor to 1/3rd L.F.A. at C.M.D.S., obtaining receipt for same. Capt J.W. BURTON + 26 O.R. reported back from 1/3rd L.F.A. MAJOR MACKENZIE + 1 O.R. still remain there. Sent an orderly to 156th Bde H.Q. to form the connecting link between Bde HQ + the Fld Ambulance or A.D.S. or Bearer Officer. | |
| | | 2100 | Held Medical Board in accordance with instructions received to-day from A.D.M.S. on No. 18865 L/Cpl James Moffat 1/4th Royal Scots + forwarded proceedings in duplicate to A.D.M.S. along with correspondence attached. J.W.L. | |

D. D. & L., London, E.C.
(A8001) Wt. W1771/M2031 750,000 5/17 Sch. 52 Forms/C2118/14

468 Army Form C. 2118.

Instructions regarding War Diaries and Intelligence Summaries are contained in F. S. Regs., Part II. and the Staff Manual respectively. Title pages will be prepared in manuscript.

# WAR DIARY
or
# ~~INTELLIGENCE SUMMARY.~~
(Erase heading not required.)

| Place | Date | Hour | Summary of Events and Information | Remarks and references to Appendices |
|---|---|---|---|---|
| MERCATEL M35 a.2.8. | 31/8/18 | | Received R.A.M.C.O.O. No. 14 d/30.8.18. Detailed Capt J.W. BURTON as Bearer Officer to report to 156th Bde H.Q. 76 O.R. (bearers of B & C sections made up to strength from A section) will form two 2 bearer subdivisions with 156th Bde. Reconnoitred new camping ground. | |
| | | 1300 | Sent 4 motor ambulances & 2 horsed ambulances with 1 orderly (wagon) to report to O.C. 1/2nd L.F.A. Capt BURTON reported back from Bde H.Q. ~~B~~ 152th Bde is to move out at 1600. 3 Sgts each with a party of 4 bearers & 2 stretchers will rendezvous at T4.c.4.4. at 1845 to meet the Battalions. Remainder of bearers under a sgt. will report to A.D.S. (1/2nd L.F.A.) before 2100 to be under command ~~&~~ at the disposal of Capt. BURTON as bearer officer RAMC 156th Bde. Received A.D.M.S. W502 of even date that relief of 2/3rd London Field ambulance by 1/2nd Lowland F.A would be by midnight 31/1 and that location of A.D.S. was T23a 5.7 not T22 b.8.6. as given in R.A.M.C. O.O. No 14. Sent 1 motor ambulance with a wagon orderly to be posted at Cross Roads N33.d.3.9. for ~~troops~~ in HENIN HILL area in accordance with A.D.M.S. W503 of even date. Unit marched out at 1500 leaving a small holding party of 1 off. + 3 O.R. at dressing station M35.a.2.8. to deal with sick still straggling in. Marching out strength: | |

| Off | RAMC | ASC HT | ASC MT | Horses HD | Horses LD | Wagons 2 cycle | Wagons 1 cycle | Motor Ambs | Motor Cycles | Cycles |
|---|---|---|---|---|---|---|---|---|---|---|
| 3 | 98 | 33 | 5 | 17 | 17 | 11 | 4 | 1* | 0 | 1 |

* 1 Motor ambulance in Workshops temporarily

Notified A.D.M.S. location of new camp. viz. T.1.d.2.3. Sh 51B.

Johnson [illegible] Lt Col
O.C. 1/1st Lowland Fd. Amb.

D. D. & L., London, E.C. (A8001) Wt. W1771/M2031 750,000 5/17 Sch. 52 Forms/C2118/14

APPENDIX I Vol XXXIX (Aug 1918) 28/8/18.

War Diary of 1/1st Lowland Fld Ambulance
52nd (Lowland) Div.

24/8/18 – 11 a.m. Took over R.A.P. M35 a 2.8/51B as A.D.S. of 1/1 LFA. R.M.O. 1/7 S.R. just moving out, some wounded were waiting for evacuation.

4 p.m. Sgt McGregor with a party of 1 Corporal and 16 O.R. sent forward to 1/7 S.R. R.A.P. at M 36 B 56 – 1 NCO + 8 bearers remaining there + 2 Relay posts formed – consisting of 4 bearers each – between the R.A.P. & A.D.S.

1 LCpl + 12 bearers of 1/3 L.F.A. at 1/7 R.S.
8 bearers of 1/2 L.F.A. at 1/4 R.S.

25/8/18 – No alteration

26/8/18 – 4 a.m. As soon as A.D.M.S. orders were received re attack by 155 Bde, 2 bearers of 1/3 L.F.A. were sent to 155 Bde Hdqrs with a note asking them to let me know situation of Bat. Hdqrs of Units of 155 Bde in order to get in touch with RAP's.

6 a.m. Wire received from H.Q. 1/5 R.S.F. asking for bearers & giving M 36 B 5.6 (i.e. RAP 1/7 S.R.) as place to meet guides. Immediately Sgt. McGregor + 12 bearers with 6 stretchers were sent out. He placed 8 bearers at RAP 1/5 RSF situated at N 26 c 0 8 + 4 bearers as a relay post between there & M 36 B 5.6. He then returned to A.D.S. & reported.

About 8 a.m. a message was received from 155 Bde Hdqrs that Battle Hdqrs of both battalions was located at N 26 c 0 8 & saying they would be glad of bearers as soon as possible.

Sgt McGregor was sent out again with 20 bearers & 10 stretchers with instructions to double all the Relay Posts between the A.D.S. & RAP's at N 26 c 0 8, utilising the RAP of 1/7 S.R. as a relay post. When this was done there was now 4 relay posts (including RAP 1/7 S.R.) with 8 bearers in each & Sgt McGregor at the RAP's of 155 Bde at N 26 c 0 8 + 16 bearers. This was carried out by about 10.30 am.

About 12 noon RAP's moved forward. After clearing the wounded Sgt McGregor moved forward to N 26 a 9 5 & sent forward bearers to new RAP's which were formed, he then notified me where he was & that he was in touch with RAP's & he had a chain of relay posts to A.D.S. Motor Ambulances were sent to M 30 c 3.0 to which point patients were brought by stretcher carriers from next relay. ~~...~~ At night Horse ambulance wagons went forward along the chain as far as possible to help in evacuation.

On 27th stretcher cases were sent down to ADS at HENIN run by 1/2 + 1/3 L.F.A. – walking cases were directed back to own ADS & relay posts called in.

[illegible] Capt.

APPENDIX [illegible] VOL XXXIII [illegible]
War Diary of 1/1st [illegible]
52nd ([illegible]) Div

To OC

1/1 Low. Fld. Amb.

Sir

In accordance with instructions received from you I reported to OC. ADS. 2/3 North Midland Field Amb. at 6 pm. on 22nd August.

I had with me 2 N.C.O's and 30 bearers of 1/1 Low. Fld Amb. The OC. ADS told me to billet my party for the night in trenches near the ADS. He stated he would detail them as required.

Six men were sent out to a R.A.P. (location unknown) by O.C. next morning early and did not rejoin me.

On the 23rd wounded commenced arriving at A.D.S. about 6.30 A.M. and had practically ceased at 8.30 A.M. I suggested to O.C. A.D.S. that I should go with 6 bearers in a car to Southern R.A.P. (J10 a 88) and see if wounded were lying there as it seemed that too few cases were coming down. He agreed. Before leaving I received a message from A.D.M.S. 52nd Division ordering me to send bearers to J.5 b 8.2 where there were 50 cases waiting evacuation

(2)

This point was near where I proposed going, so I set off with 1 N.C.O. and 6 bearers in a car to BOISLEUT AU MONT (S. 10 a 88). On arriving at the R.A.P. (BOISLEUT AU MONT) I found a large number of wounded of all classes lying waiting dressing and evacuation. The M.O. there who was attached to 1/6 D.L.I. was moving back to his unit (who had gone to reserve) and did not know where any of the Battalions of the 156th Brigade were situated. He was receiving wounded also from the 56th Div. and some from the Guards Div. I sent Corporal Edwards and 2 men to (S 5 d 82) where he found the M.O. 1/4th R.S. who had a number of cases to evacuate. I communicated with the A.D.S and asked for cars, dressings, and all the bearers possible. I sent Corporal Edwards out again giving him roughly the line of the 156th Brigade and told him to find the remaining R.A.P. this he did and soon complete chains were formed between my post and Battalions.

As I had no Medical Comforts I borrowed from surrounding units and was able to feed the patients.

I obtained an adjacent

(3)

dug-out. 25 Suit gas clothing. Gassed cases were numerous and severe. Evacuation by car was uncertain and arrangements with Local Heavy Artillery lorries were lent and additional cars obtained from the Guards Division. On several occasions the area was Shelled heavily and Gassed.

About 4 pm. Col Jobson Scott of 1/2nd Low Fld Amb came, and I explained the situation to him. He promised, and sent to me all the stores &c necessary and supplied 24 additional bearers. Evacuation proceeding smoothly after this time, and I was relieved by 1/2nd Low Fld Amb at 9 AM on the 24th and ordered by ADMS to proceed to ADS 1/1 Low Fld Amb at (M.35 a 28) and report there for duty, the bearers following.

I was most ably assisted by all ranks of 1/1 and 1/2 Low. Fld. Amb.

Jack W Bunton Capt
RAMC T

28/8/18

**To be made up to and for Saturday in each week**

No. of Report 158

# FIELD RETURN.

Army Form B. 213

(To be furnished by all arms, services, and departments (except A.S.C. units) to the A.G.'s Office at the Base in accordance with Field Service Regulations, Part II.)

RETURN showing numbers (*a*) Effective strength of Unit. (*b*) Rationed by Unit. 1/Lowl. Fd. Ambce. at In the Field 2nd Augt 1918 Date.

| DETAILS. | *Personnel: Officers | Other Ranks | | | | Animals: Horses: Riding | Draught | Heavy Draught | Pack | Mules: Large | Small | Guns and transport vehicles: Guns, showing description | Ammunition wagons | Machine guns | Aircraft, showing description | Horsed: † 4 Wheeled | 2 Wheeled | Mechanical: Motor Cars | Tractors | Lorries, showing description | Trucks, showing description | Trailers | Motor Bicycle | Bicycles | Motor Ambulances | REMARKS (Number of Acting W.O.'s and N.C.O.'s included in effective strength to be shown in this column.) |
|---|---|---|---|---|---|---|---|---|---|---|---|---|---|---|---|---|---|---|---|---|---|---|---|---|---|---|
| Effective Strength of Unit ... ... | (a) 7 | (b) 178 | | | | | | | | | | | | | | | | | | | | | | 1 | | (a) Includes 1 officer [illegible] at 52 M.G. " 1 [illegible] att. [illegible] |
| Details by Arms attached to Unit as in War Establishment ... ... | | | | | | | | | | | | | | | | | | | | | | | | | | (b) Includes 1 O.R. at [illegible] " 2 " at 52 D.H.Q. " 1 " " Div. Train |
| A.S.C. (H.T.) | | (c) 40 | | | | 6 | 17 | 16 | | | | | | | | 13 | 4 | | | | | | | | | " 1 " " 42 C.C.S. |
| A.S.C. (M.T.) | | (d) 13 | | | | | | | | | | | | | | | | | | | | | 2 | | 7 | " 28 O.R. on leave to U.K. " 2 " " " to Rest. (c) Includes 5 O.R. on leave to U. (d) Includes 1 O.R. att. D.H.Q. |
| TOTAL ... | 7 | 231 | | | | 6 | 17 | ◊ 16 | | | | | | | | 13 | 4 | | | | | | 2 | 1 | 7 | ◊ 3 Hy. Draft to Mob. Vety Sect. [illegible] |
| War Establishment ... ... | 10 | 231 | | | | 8 | 17 | 20 | | | | | | | | 13 | 4 | | | | | | 2 | 1 | 7 | |
| Wanting to complete ... ... ... (Detail of Personnel and Horses below.) | 3 | * 4 | | | | 2 | - | 4 | | | | | | | | - | - | | | | | | - | - | - | * R.A.M.C. |
| SURPLUS ... (Detail of Personnel and Horses below.) | - | ** 4 | | | | | | | | | | | | | | | | | | | | | | | | ** A.S.C. (H.T.) |
| †Attached (not to include the details shown above) ... ... | 1 | | | | | | | | | | | | | | | | | | | | | | | | | Chaplain |
| Attached for Rations only ... | | 10 | | | | | | | | | | | | | | | | | | | | | | | | Sick Rationed |
| Civilians Employed with and Accompanying the Unit ... ... | | | | | | | | | | | | | | | | | | | | | | | | | | |
| ‡Detached from and struck off effective strength of own Unit ... | | | | | | | | | | | | | | | | | | | | | | | | | | |
| ‡Detached from but retained on effective strength of own unit... ... | | | | | | | | | | | | | | | | | | | | | | | | | | |
| TOTAL RATIONED ... | 6 | 200 | | | | 6 | 17 | 16 | | | | | | | | | | | | | | | | | | |

* Blank columns to be used for W.A.A.C. Natives or as may be required.

† In the case of field ambulances, hospitals or depots, the number of patients are to be included here, the names being shown in A.F.A. 36.
‡ These details to be enumerated by arms.

[illegible] Leitch Lieut-Col. Signature of Commander.

2nd Augt 1918. Date of Despatch.

*For information of the A.G.'s Office at the base.*

A.S.C.

Officers and men who have become casuals, been transferred or joined since last report.

Place In the Field Date 2/8/18.

| Regtl. Number | Rank | Name | Corps | Nature of casualty, or name of unit from or to which transferred. | Date of being struck off or coming on the ration return. | Remarks * |
|---|---|---|---|---|---|---|
| T/SR/[illegible] | Dr. | Ash B. | A.S.C. (H.T.) att. [illegible] | Granted 14 days leave to UK via Boulogne from 25.7.18 to 8.8.18. Cr. [illegible] allowance for that period | | |
| T/35682 | - | Littlewood W. | -do- | Granted 14 days leave to UK via Calais from 30.7.18 to 13.8.18. Cr. [illegible] allce. [illegible] for that period | | |
| T4/038213 | Dr. | Drew J. | -do- | Rets from 14 days leave in UK | on 27/7/18. | |
| T4/[illegible]47002 | - | Davidson A. | -do- | -do- | on 1/8/18. | |
| T/35061 | - | Cooper Y. | -do- | 10 days C.C. | on 31/7/18 | |
| T4/058708 | - | Daniels Ed. | -do- | -do- | -do- | |

* State whether absence is of a permanent or temporary nature, adding, in the case of casuals from wounds or disease any available information for communication to the relatives.

*The perforated sheet is not to be used to record casualties; additional sheets, preferably foolscap, to be attached when necessary. These sheets to be carefully numbered and the number of attached sheets to be noted here.*

*For information of the A.G.'s Office at the base.*

Officers and men who have become casuals, been transferred or joined since last report.

Place In the Field  Date 2nd Augt 1918.

| Regtl. Number | Rank | Name | Corps | Nature of casualty, or name of unit from or to which transferred. | Date of being struck off or coming on the ration return. | Remarks * |
|---|---|---|---|---|---|---|
| – | Lieut Col. | J. W. Leitch D.S.O. | R.A.M.C.(T) 1/1st Lows. Fd Amb. | Retd. from temp duty as A.D.M.S. | on 2 8/18 | |
| – | Capt. | J. W. Burton | -do- | Retd from duty at D.D.M.S. office | on 1 8/18 | |
| – | Lieut | J. J. Nunn | M.R.C. U.S.A | To temp. duty with 1/2 Low Fd Amb. | off 1 8/18 | Tempy. |
| 316143 | Pte | L. Scott | R.A.M.C.(T.F.) 1/1st Lows Fd Amb. | Granted 14 days leave in U.K. from 28.7.18 to 11.8.18. Credit ration allce @ 2/1d pd. for that period | | |
| 316147 | " | W. C. Eadie | -do- | Granted 14 days leave in U.K. from 29.7.18 to 12.8.18. | | |
| 316163 | " | R. F. Edgecombe | -do- | Credit rat. allce @ 2/1d p.d. for that period | | |
| 316159 | " | A. L. Tinto | (do) | Granted 14 days leave in U.K. from 30.7.18 to 13.8.18. Credit rat. allce @ 2/1d pd. for that period. | | |
| 316153 | " | A. V. Hanlon | -do- | Granted 14 days leave in U.K. from 31.7.18 to 14.8.18 | | |
| 316154 | " | R. Brown | -do- | Credit rat. allce @ 2/1d pd. for that period. | | |
| 316151 | " | J. Candlish | -do- | Granted 14 days leave to U.K. from 1.8.18 to 15.8.18 | | |
| 316148 | " | D. W. Laird | -do- | Credit rat. allce @ 2/1d pd. for that period. | | |
| 316157 | " | M. E. Carson | -do- | Granted 14 days leave in U.K. from 2.8.18 to 16.8.18 Credit rat. allce @ 2/1d pd. for that period. | | |
| 316201 | Sgt. | J. Main | -do- | Granted 31 days leave in U.K. from 3.8.18 to 3.9.18 Credit rat. allce @ 2/1d pd. for that period | | |
| 316165 | Pte | R. Findlay | -do- | Granted 14 days leave to U.K. from 3.8.18 to 17.8.18 Credit rat. allce @ 2/1d pd. for that period. | | |
| 316076 | Pte | A. Harvey | -do- | Continues to draw addl. pay @ 6d pd. less 4d late R.A.M.C. [illegible] as acct. Cy. Acct. 7–31 7/18 | | |
| 316158 | Sgt. | A. A. Meldrum | -do- | Continues to draw addl pay @ 6d per d. as Dispenser from 10.7.18 to 31.7.18. | | |
| 316179 | " | E. V. Kenny | -do- | Continues to draw addl pay @ 6d per d. as Dispenser from 1.7.18 to 17.7.18. | | |
| 316273 | Pte | D. Sloan | -do- | Continues to draw Working pay @ 1/- per d. less 4d Corps Pay from 1–31.7.18 as Shoemaker | | |
| 316264 | " | R. Edington | -do- | Continues to draw Working pay @ 1/- p.d. less 4d Corps Pay from 1–31.7.18 as Tailor. | | |
| 316114 | " | A. C. Thomson | -do- | married Margaret Pattison Struthers at Union House, Camelon By Falkirk on 17.7.18 | | |
| | | | | Present address of Wife:– C/o Struthers, Union House Camelon By Falkirk | | |
| 316073 | " | Jn Cowie | -do- | married Janet Boyd, at the Manse, Coatbridge on 10.7.18. | | |
| | | | | Present address of Wife:– C/o Boyd 25 Eglinton St. Coatbridge | | |
| | Strength | Officers | R.A.M.C. T.F. | 5 | | |
| | | | M.R.C. U.S.A. | 2 | 7 | |
| | | | W.O. | 1 | | |
| | | | S/Sgts | 2 | | |
| | | | Sgts | 10 | | |
| | | | A/Sgts | 1 | | |
| | | | Cpls | 8 | | |
| | | | | 6 | | |
| | | | L/Cpls | | | |
| | | | Ptes | 150 | 178 | |

* State whether absence is of a permanent or temporary nature, adding, in the case of casuals from wounds or disease any available information for communication to the relatives.

*The perforated sheet is not to be used to record casualties: additional sheets, preferably foolscap, to be attached when necessary. These sheets to be carefully numbered and the number of attached sheets to be noted here.*

Perforated Sheet giving detail of personnel and horses wanting to complete or surplus, shown on Army Form B. 213.

No. of Report 158

| Detail of Wanting to Complete or Surplus. | Drivers R.A. | Drivers R.E. | Drivers A.S.C. | Drivers Car | Drivers Lorry | Drivers Steam | Gunners | Gunners Howitzer | Smith Gunners | Range Takers | Farriers Serjeants | Farriers Corporals | Shoeing or Shoeing and Carriage Smiths | Cold Shoers | Wheelers R.A. | Wheelers H.T. | Wheelers M.T. | Saddlers or Harness Makers | Blacksmiths | Bricklayers and Masons | Carpenters and Joiners |
|---|---|---|---|---|---|---|---|---|---|---|---|---|---|---|---|---|---|---|---|---|---|
| CAVALRY—DEFICIENCY | | | | | | | | | | | | | | | | | | | | | |
| SURPLUS | | | | | | | | | | | | | | | | | | | | | |
| R.A.—DEFICIENCY | | | | | | | | | | | | | | | | | | | | | |
| SURPLUS | | | | | | | | | | | | | | | | | | | | | |
| R.E.—DEFICIENCY | | | | | | | | | | | | | | | | | | | | | |
| SURPLUS | | | | | | | | | | | | | | | | | | | | | |
| INFANTRY—DEFICIENCY | | | | | | | | | | | | | | | | | | | | | |
| SURPLUS | | | | | | | | | | | | | | | | | | | | | |
| R.A.M.C.—DEFICIENCY | | | | | | | | | | | | | | | | | | | | | |
| SURPLUS | | | | | | | | | | | | | | | | | | | | | |
| A.O.C.—DEFICIENCY | | | | | | | | | | | | | | | | | | | | | |
| SURPLUS | | | | | | | | | | | | | | | | | | | | | |
| A.V.C.—DEFICIENCY | | | | | | | | | | | | | | | | | | | | | |
| SURPLUS | | | | | | | | | | | | | | | | | | | | | |
| DEFICIENCY | | | | | | | | | | | | | | | | | | | | | |
| SURPLUS | | | | | | | | | | | | | | | | | | | | | |
| DEFICIENCY | | | | | | | | | | | | | | | | | | | | | |
| SURPLUS | | | | | | | | | | | | | | | | | | | | | |

| Detail of Wanting to Complete or Surplus. | Fitters & Turners (R.E.) Wood | Fitters & Turners (R.E.) Iron | Fitters R.A. | Fitters Wireless | Plumbers | Electricians Ordinary | Electricians W.T. | Signalmen | Engine Drivers Loco. | Engine Drivers Field | Air Line Men | Permanent Line Men | Operators, Telegraph | Cablemen | Brigade Section Pioneers | General-duty Pioneers | Signallers | Instrument Repairers | Motor Cyclist | Motor Cyclist Artificers | Telephonists | Clerks | Machine Gunners |
|---|---|---|---|---|---|---|---|---|---|---|---|---|---|---|---|---|---|---|---|---|---|---|---|
| CAVALRY—DEFICIENCY | | | | | | | | | | | | | | | | | | | | | | | |
| SURPLUS | | | | | | | | | | | | | | | | | | | | | | | |
| R.A.—DEFICIENCY | | | | | | | | | | | | | | | | | | | | | | | |
| SURPLUS | | | | | | | | | | | | | | | | | | | | | | | |
| R.E.—DEFICIENCY | | | | | | | | | | | | | | | | | | | | | | | |
| SURPLUS | | | | | | | | | | | | | | | | | | | | | | | |
| INFANTRY—DEFICIENCY | | | | | | | | | | | | | | | | | | | | | | | |
| SURPLUS | | | | | | | | | | | | | | | | | | | | | | | |
| R.A.M.C.—DEFICIENCY | | | | | | | | | | | | | | | | | | | | | | | |
| SURPLUS | | | | | | | | | | | | | | | | | | | | | | | |
| A.O.C.—DEFICIENCY | | | | | | | | | | | | | | | | | | | | | | | |
| SURPLUS | | | | | | | | | | | | | | | | | | | | | | | |
| A.V.C.—DEFICIENCY | | | | | | | | | | | | | | | | | | | | | | | |
| SURPLUS | | | | | | | | | | | | | | | | | | | | | | | |
| DEFICIENCY | | | | | | | | | | | | | | | | | | | | | | | |
| SURPLUS | | | | | | | | | | | | | | | | | | | | | | | |
| DEFICIENCY | | | | | | | | | | | | | | | | | | | | | | | |
| SURPLUS | | | | | | | | | | | | | | | | | | | | | | | |

| Detail of Wanting to Complete or Surplus. | Armament Artificers Fitters | Armament Artificers Range Finders | Armourers | Storemen | Privates | W.O.'s and N.C.O.'s (by ranks) not included in trade columns. | | | | | | | | | | | TOTAL to agree with wanting to complete or surplus Officers | TOTAL Other Ranks | Horses Riding | Horses Draught | Horses Heavy Draught | Horses Pack |
|---|---|---|---|---|---|---|---|---|---|---|---|---|---|---|---|---|---|---|---|---|---|---|
| CAVALRY—DEFICIENCY | | | | | | | | | | | | | | | | | | | | | | |
| SURPLUS | | | | | | | | | | | | | | | | | | | | | | |
| R.A.—DEFICIENCY | | | | | | | | | | | | | | | | | | | | | | |
| SURPLUS | | | | | | | | | | | | | | | | | | | | | | |
| R.E.—DEFICIENCY | | | | | | | | | | | | | | | | | | | | | | |
| SURPLUS | | | | | | | | | | | | | | | | | | | | | | |
| INFANTRY—DEFICIENCY | | | | | | | | | | | | | | | | | | | | | | |
| SURPLUS | | | | | | | | | | | | | | | | | | | | | | |
| R.A.M.C.—DEFICIENCY | | | | | 4 | | | | | | | | | | | | 3 | 4 | 2 | - | 4 | |
| SURPLUS | | | | | | | | | | | | | | | | | | | | | | |
| A.O.C.—DEFICIENCY | | | | | | | | | | | | | | | | | | | | | | |
| SURPLUS | | | | | | | | | | | | | | | | | | | | | | |
| A.V.C.—DEFICIENCY | | | | | | | | | | | | | | | | | | | | | | |
| SURPLUS | | | | | | | | | | | | | | | | | | | | | | |
| DEFICIENCY | | | | | | | | | | | | | | | | | | | | | | |
| SURPLUS | | | | | | | | | | | | | | | | | | | | | | |
| DEFICIENCY | | | | | | | | | | | | | | | | | | | | | | |
| SURPLUS | | | | | | | | | | | | | | | | | | | | | | |

Remarks :—

[illegible] Lieut Col. Signature of Commander.

1/Low. Fd. Ambce. R.A.M.C. (T.F.) Unit.

52 Division Formation to which attached.

2nd Augt 1918. Date of Despatch.

(16523.) Wt. W6016—PP 1432. 1,500m. 3/18. D & S. (E1256) Forms B213/8. [P.T.O.

A.F. B 213 W/E. 2nd Aug 1918.

| No | Rk | Name | Unit | Casualty | Remarks |
|---|---|---|---|---|---|
| 316093 | Pte | Donald W. | R.A.M.C. [illegible] Trans. | Retd from duty [illegible] | on 29-7-18. |
| 316232 | L/Cpl | Stewart J. | -do- | Retd from 28 days leave in U.K. | on 29-7-18 |
| 316083 | Pte | McGrillen M. | -do- | " from [illegible] leave | -do- |
| 316095 | " | Crawford E. | -do- | in U.K. | -do- |
| 316072 | " | Binning G. | -do- | -do- | -do- |
| 316114 | " | Thomson W. | -do- | -do- | on 30-7-18 |
| 316125 | " | Brunstone J. | -do- | -do- | -do- |
| 316104 | " | Love A.L. | -do- | -do- | on 1-8-18 |
| 316119 | " | McDougall W. | -do- | -do- | -do- |
| 316179 | Cpl | Kenny E. | -do- | -do- | on 2-8-18 |
| 316180 | Pte | Anderson T.B. | -do- | -do- | -do- |
| 316118 | " | Wallace R. | -do- | -do- | -do- |
| 316122 | Pte | [illegible] R. | -do- | Retd from 28 days leave U.K. | -do- |

**To be made up to and for Saturday in each week**

No. of Report 155

# FIELD RETURN.

Army Form B 213

(To be furnished by all arms, services, and departments (except A.S.C. units) to the A.G.'s Office at the Base in accordance with Field Service Regulations, Part II.)

RETURN showing numbers (*a*) Effective strength of Unit. (*b*) Rationed by Unit. [illegible] at In the Field. 9th Augt 1918. Date.

| Details. | *Personnel: Officers | Other Ranks | | | | Animals: Horses: Riding | Draught | Heavy Draught | Pack | Mules: Large | Small | Guns and transport vehicles: Guns, showing description | Ammunition wagons | Machine guns | Aircraft, showing description | Horsed: 4 Wheeled | 2 Wheeled | Mechanical: Motor Cars | Tractors | Lorries, showing description | Trucks, showing description | Trailers | Motor Bicycles | Bicycles | Motor Ambulances | Remarks (Number of Acting W.O.'s and N.C.O.'s included in effective strength to be shown in this column.) |
|---|---|---|---|---|---|---|---|---|---|---|---|---|---|---|---|---|---|---|---|---|---|---|---|---|---|---|
| Effective Strength of Unit ... ... | (a) 7 | (b) 180 | | | | | | | | | | | | | | | | | | | | | | 1 | | (a) Includes 1 officer at [illegible] / " 1 / " 1 |
| Details by Arms attached to Unit as in War Establishment ... ... ... | | | | | | | | | | | | | | | | | | | | | | | | | | |
| A.S.C. (H.T.) | | (c) 40 | | | | 6 | 17 | 6 | | | | | | | | 13 | 4 | | | | | | | | | (b) Includes 1 O.R. at [illegible] / " 1 " / " 1 " |
| A.S.C. (H.T.) | | (d) 13 | | | | | | | | | | | | | | | | | | | | | | | | " 35 " |
| | | | | | | | | | | | | | | | | | | | | | | | 2 | | 7 | " 44 " |
| | | | | | | | | | | | | | | | | | | | | | | | | | | (c) Includes 4 O.R. leave to U.K. / 1 O.R. " to Rest Camp. |
| Total ... ... | 7 | 233 | | | | 6 | 17 | 6 | | | | | | | | 13 | 4 | | | | | | 2 | 1 | 7 | (d) " 1 O.R. [illegible] / " 1 O.R. on leave to U.K. |
| War Establishment ... ... ... | 10 | 231 | | | | 5 | 17 | 20 | | | | | | | | 13 | 4 | | | | | | 2 | 1 | 7 | |
| Wanting to complete ... ... ... (Detail of Personnel and Horses below.) | 3 | * 2 | | | | 2 | - | 4 | | | | | | | | - | - | | | | | | - | - | - | * R.A.M.C. |
| Surplus ... ... (Detail of Personnel and Horses below.) | | ** 4 | | | | | | | | | | | | | | | | | | | | | | | | ** A.S.C. (H.T.) |
| †Attached (not to include the details shown above) ... ... ... ... | | 30 | | | | | | | | | | | | | | | | | | | | | | | | Sick rationed |
| Attached for Rations only ... ... | 1 | | | | | | | | | | | | | | | | | | | | | | | | | Chaplain |
| Civilians Employed with and Accompanying the Unit ... ... ... | | | | | | | | | | | | | | | | | | | | | | | | | | |
| ‡Detached from and struck off effective strength of own Unit ... ... | | | | | | | | | | | | | | | | | | | | | | | | | | |
| ‡Detached from but retained on effective strength of own unit... ... ... | | | | | | | | | | | | | | | | | | | | | | | | | | |
| Total Rationed ... | 8 | [illegible] | | | | 6 | 17 | 6 | | | | | | | | 4 | | | | | | | | | | |

* Blank columns to be used for W.A.A.C. Natives or as may be required.

† In the case of field ambulances, hospitals or depots, the number of patients are to be included here, the names being shown in A.F.A. 36.
‡ These details to be enumerated by arms.

[illegible] Signature of Commander.

9th Augt 1918. Date of Despatch.

*For information of the A.G.'s Office at the base.*

Officers and men who have become casuals, A.S.C. been transferred or joined since last report.

Place In the Field Date 9th Aug 1918.

| Regtl. Number | Rank | Name | Corps | Nature of casualty, or name of unit from or to which transferred. | Date of being struck off or coming on the ration return. | Remarks * |
|---|---|---|---|---|---|---|
| M2/117210 | Dr | Guthrie J.A. | A.S.C. (M.T.) att. 1/1 Low'd Fd Amb | Granted 14 days leave to UK. via Calais 5.8.18 – 19.8.18. Credit rat. allce @ 3/- for that period | | |
| T4/[illegible]2015 | Dr | [illegible] J. | A.S.C. (H.T.) att. [illegible] | Granted 14 days leave to UK. via Calais 8.8.18 to 22.8.18. Credit rat. allce @ [illegible] for that period. | | |
| T4/[illegible] | Cpl. [illegible] | Wilson Y. | -do- | Returned from 14 days in UK. | On 3 8/18 | |
| T4/[illegible] | Dr | Davidson J. | -do- | Retd from 14 days in UK. | on | |
| T4/[illegible] | Dr | [illegible] | -do- | To Army Rest Camp for 14 days | off 7 8/18 | Temp. |

* State whether absence is of a permanent or temporary nature, adding, in the case of casuals from wounds or disease any available information for communication to the relatives.

*The perforated sheet is not to be used to record casualties; additional sheets, preferably foolscap, to be attached when necessary. These sheets to be carefully numbered and the number of attached sheets to be noted here.*

*For information of the A.G.'s Office at the base.*

Officers and men who have become casuals, been transferred or joined since last report.

Place In the Field Date 9th Augt 1918.

| Regtl. Number | Rank | Name | Corps | Nature of casualty, or name of unit from or to which transferred. | Date of being struck off or coming on the ration return. | Remarks * |
|---|---|---|---|---|---|---|
| – | Major | Browne J. | R.A.M.C.(T) 1/1st Low. F.A. | Retd from Hosp. on 8/8/18 | | |
| – | Capt | Burton J.W. | -do- | To temp. duty with [illegible] Bde R.F.A. | | off 4/8/18 Temp. |
| 316100 | Pte | McTavish D. | -do- | Granted 14 days leave to UK. 4.8.18 – 18.8.18 | | |
| 316171 | " | Hill J. | -do- | Credit rat. allce @ 2/1d p.d. for that period | | |
| 316140 | " | [illegible] A. | -do- | Granted 14 days leave to UK. 5.8.18 – 19.8. Credit rat. allce @ 2/1d p.d. for that period | | |
| 316188 | " | Johnstone W. | -do- | Granted 14 days leave to UK. 6.8.18 – 20.8 | | |
| 316179 | " | [illegible] | -do- | Credit rat. allce @ 2/1d p.d. for that period | | |
| 316186 | " | Calder [illegible] | -do- | Granted 14 days leave to UK. 7.8.18 – 21.8 | | |
| 316193 | " | [illegible] | -do- | Credit rat. allce @ 2/1d p.d. for that period | | |
| 342[illegible] | " | [illegible] | -do- | Granted 14 days leave to UK. 8.8.18 to 22.8.18. Credit rat. allce @ 2/1d for that period | | |
| 42191 | " | Ward G. | -do- | Granted 14 days leave to UK. 9.8.18 – 23.8.18 | | |
| 316250 | " | [illegible] C. | -do- | Credit rat. allce @ 2/1d p.d. for that period | | |
| [illegible] | " | [illegible] | -do- | Granted 21 days leave to UK. 10.8.18 to 10.9.18. Credit rat. allce @ 2/1d p.d. for that period | | |
| 316101 | " | Graham R. | -do- | Retd from 14 days leave in U.K | on 7/8/18 | |
| 316103 | " | Johnstone R. | -do- | | " | |
| 316124 | " | Young J.B. | -do- | | " | |
| 316099 | " | Golden J. | -do- | Retd from 14 days in UK on 8/8/18 | | |
| | " | Barrow? D. | -do- | Retd from H.D. C.C.S. on 8/8/18 | | |
| 316[illegible]4 | " | [illegible] D. | -do- | Retd from duty at A.D.M.S. office on 9/8/18. | | |
| 316119 | " | [illegible] J. | -do- | Joined as reinforcements | on 4.8.18 | |
| 419101 | " | [illegible] | [illegible] | | -do- | |

The following entry should have appeared on B213 to [illegible] 12/7/18

| Regtl. Number | Rank | Name | Corps | Nature of casualty, or name of unit from or to which transferred. | Date of being struck off or coming on the ration return. | Remarks * |
|---|---|---|---|---|---|---|
| 316086 | Pte | Elkins? A.G. | R.A.M.C.(T) 1/1st Low. F. Ambce | Granted 14 days leave to UK. 6.7.18 – 20.7.18 | | |
| 316084 | " | [illegible] J. | | Credit rat. allce @ 2/1d p.d. for that period | | |
| 316099 | " | Golden J. | RAMC(T) 1/1st Low. F. Ambce | Married Margaret [illegible] at Cambuslang on 27.7.18. Present address of wife: [illegible] Clydeford Rd, Cambuslang, Glasgow. | | |
| 42130 | Pte | Ferry? G.A. | RAMC(T) 1/1st Low. F. Amb | Deprived of 14 days pay. Forfeits 1 G.C. Badge. | 4/8/18 | See AFB 2069 attached. |

Strength. Officers TF 6, MRCUSA 2 = 8.

| | |
|---|---|
| W.O. | 1 |
| QMS | 1 |
| S/Sgts | 1 |
| Sgts | 10 |
| [illegible] | 1 |
| Cpls | 10 |
| LCpls | 5 |
| Ptes | 151 |
| | 180 |

All Category "A".

* State whether absence is of a permanent or temporary nature, adding, in the case of casuals from wounds or disease any available information for communication to the relatives.

*The perforated sheet is not to be used to record casualties; additional sheets, preferably foolscap, to be attached when necessary. These sheets to be carefully numbered and the number of attached sheets to be noted here.*

Perforated Sheet giving detail of personnel and horses wanting to complete or surplus, shown on Army Form B. 213.

No. of Report 158.

| Detail of Wanting to Complete or Surplus. | Drivers. | | | | | | Gunners | Gunners Howitzer | Smith Gunners | Range Takers | Farriers | | Shoeing or Shoeing and Carriage Smiths | Cold Shoers |
|---|---|---|---|---|---|---|---|---|---|---|---|---|---|---|
| | R.A. | R.E. | A.S.C. | Car | Lorry | Steam | | | | | Serjeants | Corporals | | |
| CAVALRY— DEFICIENCY | | | | | | | | | | | | | | |
| SURPLUS | | | | | | | | | | | | | | |
| R.A.— DEFICIENCY | | | | | | | | | | | | | | |
| SURPLUS | | | | | | | | | | | | | | |
| R.E.— DEFICIENCY | | | | | | | | | | | | | | |
| SURPLUS | | | | | | | | | | | | | | |
| INFANTRY— DEFICIENCY | | | | | | | | | | | | | | |
| SURPLUS | | | | | | | | | | | | | | |
| R.A.M.C.— DEFICIENCY | | | | | | | | | | | | | | |
| SURPLUS | | | | | | | | | | | | | | |
| A.O.C.— DEFICIENCY | | | | | | | | | | | | | | |
| SURPLUS | | | | | | | | | | | | | | |
| A.V.C.— DEFICIENCY | | | | | | | | | | | | | | |
| SURPLUS | | | | | | | | | | | | | | |
| DEFICIENCY | | | | | | | | | | | | | | |
| SURPLUS | | | | | | | | | | | | | | |
| DEFICIENCY | | | | | | | | | | | | | | |
| SURPLUS | | | | | | | | | | | | | | |

| Detail of Wanting to Complete or Surplus. | Wheelers | | | Saddlers or Harness Makers | Blacksmiths | Bricklayers and Masons | Carpenters and Joiners | Fitters & Turners (R.E.) | | Fitters | | Plumbers | Electricians | | Signalmen. | Engine Drivers | |
|---|---|---|---|---|---|---|---|---|---|---|---|---|---|---|---|---|---|
| | R.A. | H.T. | M.T. | | | | | Wood | Iron | R.A. | Wireless. | | Ordinary | W.T. | | Loco. | Field |
| CAVALRY— DEFICIENCY | | | | | | | | | | | | | | | | | |
| SURPLUS | | | | | | | | | | | | | | | | | |
| R.A.— DEFICIENCY | | | | | | | | | | | | | | | | | |
| SURPLUS | | | | | | | | | | | | | | | | | |
| R.E.— DEFICIENCY | | | | | | | | | | | | | | | | | |
| SURPLUS | | | | | | | | | | | | | | | | | |
| INFANTRY— DEFICIENCY | | | | | | | | | | | | | | | | | |
| SURPLUS | | | | | | | | | | | | | | | | | |
| R.A.M.C.— DEFICIENCY | | | | | | | | | | | | | | | | | |
| SURPLUS | | | | | | | | | | | | | | | | | |
| A.O.C.— DEFICIENCY | | | | | | | | | | | | | | | | | |
| SURPLUS | | | | | | | | | | | | | | | | | |
| A.V.C.— DEFICIENCY | | | | | | | | | | | | | | | | | |
| SURPLUS | | | | | | | | | | | | | | | | | |
| DEFICIENCY | | | | | | | | | | | | | | | | | |
| SURPLUS | | | | | | | | | | | | | | | | | |
| DEFICIENCY | | | | | | | | | | | | | | | | | |
| SURPLUS | | | | | | | | | | | | | | | | | |

| Detail of Wanting to Complete or Surplus. | Air Line Men. | Permanent Line Men | Operators, Telegraph | Cablemen | Brigade Section Pioneers | General duty Pioneers | Signallers | Instrument Repairers | Motor Cyclist | Motor Cyclist Artificers | Telephonists | Clerks | Machine Gunners | Armament Artificers | | Armourers | Storemen | Privates |
|---|---|---|---|---|---|---|---|---|---|---|---|---|---|---|---|---|---|---|
| | | | | | | | | | | | | | | Fitters | Range Finders | | | |
| CAVALRY— DEFICIENCY | | | | | | | | | | | | | | | | | | |
| SURPLUS | | | | | | | | | | | | | | | | | | |
| R.A.— DEFICIENCY | | | | | | | | | | | | | | | | | | |
| SURPLUS | | | | | | | | | | | | | | | | | | |
| R.E.— DEFICIENCY | | | | | | | | | | | | | | | | | | |
| SURPLUS | | | | | | | | | | | | | | | | | | |
| INFANTRY— DEFICIENCY | | | | | | | | | | | | | | | | | | |
| SURPLUS | | | | | | | | | | | | | | | | | | |
| R.A.M.C.— DEFICIENCY | | | | | | | | | | | | | | | | | | 2 |
| SURPLUS | | | | | | | | | | | | | | | | | | |
| A.O.C.— DEFICIENCY | | | | | | | | | | | | | | | | | | |
| SURPLUS | | | | | | | | | | | | | | | | | | |
| A.V.C.— DEFICIENCY | | | | | | | | | | | | | | | | | | |
| SURPLUS | | | | | | | | | | | | | | | | | | |
| DEFICIENCY | | | | | | | | | | | | | | | | | | |
| SURPLUS | | | | | | | | | | | | | | | | | | |
| DEFICIENCY | | | | | | | | | | | | | | | | | | |
| SURPLUS | | | | | | | | | | | | | | | | | | |

| Detail of Wanting to Complete or Surplus. | W.O.'s and N.C.O.'s (by ranks) not included in trade columns. | | | | | | | | | TOTAL to agree with wanting to complete or surplus | | Horses | | | |
|---|---|---|---|---|---|---|---|---|---|---|---|---|---|---|---|
| | | | | | | | | | | Officers | Other Ranks | Riding | Draught | Heavy Draught | Pack |
| CAVALRY— DEFICIENCY | | | | | | | | | | | | | | | |
| SURPLUS | | | | | | | | | | | | | | | |
| R.A.— DEFICIENCY | | | | | | | | | | | | | | | |
| SURPLUS | | | | | | | | | | | | | | | |
| R.E.— DEFICIENCY | | | | | | | | | | | | | | | |
| SURPLUS | | | | | | | | | | | | | | | |
| INFANTRY— DEFICIENCY | | | | | | | | | | | | | | | |
| SURPLUS | | | | | | | | | | | | | | | |
| R.A.M.C.— DEFICIENCY | | | | | | | | | | 2 | 2 | 2 | - | 4 | |
| SURPLUS | | | | | | | | | | | | | | | |
| A.O.C.— DEFICIENCY | | | | | | | | | | | | | | | |
| SURPLUS | | | | | | | | | | | | | | | |
| A.V.C.— DEFICIENCY | | | | | | | | | | | | | | | |
| SURPLUS | | | | | | | | | | | | | | | |
| DEFICIENCY | | | | | | | | | | | | | | | |
| SURPLUS | | | | | | | | | | | | | | | |
| DEFICIENCY | | | | | | | | | | | | | | | |
| SURPLUS | | | | | | | | | | | | | | | |

Remarks :—

Lt Col. Signature of Commander.

OC [illegible] Fd. Ambce. R.A.M.C.(T) Unit.

52 Div Formation to which attached.

9th Aug 1918. Date of Despatch.

(16523.) Wt. W6016—PP 1432. 1,500m. 3/18. D & S. (E1256) Forms B213/8.

[P.T.O.

**To be made up to and for Saturday in each week**

No. of Report 159.

# FIELD RETURN.

Army Form B 213

(To be furnished by all arms, services, and departments (except A.S.C. units) to the A.G.'s Office at the Base in accordance with Field Service Regulations, Part II.)

RETURN showing numbers (*a*) Effective strength of Unit. (*b*) Rationed by Unit. [illegible] at In the Field 16 Aug 1918 Date.

| Details. | *Personnel: Officers | Other Ranks | | | | Animals: Horses: Riding | Draught | Heavy Draught | Pack | Mules: Large | Small | Guns and transport vehicles: Guns, showing description | Ammunition wagons | Machine guns | Aircraft, showing description | Horsed: 4 Wheeled | 2 Wheeled | Mechanical: Motor Cars | Tractors | Lorries, showing description | Trucks, showing description | Trailers | Motor Bicycles | Bicycles | Motor Ambulances | Remarks (Number of Acting W.O.'s and N.C.O.'s included in effective strength to be shown in this column.) |
|---|---|---|---|---|---|---|---|---|---|---|---|---|---|---|---|---|---|---|---|---|---|---|---|---|---|---|
| Effective Strength of Unit ... ... | (a) 8 | (b) 130 | | | | | | | | | | | | | | | | | | | | | | 1 | | (a) Includes 1 Off. [illegible] |
| Details by Arms attached to Unit as in War Establishment ... ... ... | | | | | | | | | | | | | | | | | | | | | | | | | | (b) Includes 1 O.R. [illegible] |
| A.S.C. (H.T.) | | (c) 30 | | | | 6 | 17 | 16 | | | | | | | | 13 | 4 | | | | | | | | | [illegible] |
| " (M.T.) | | | | | | | | | | | | | | | | | | | | | | | 2 | | 7 | (c) Includes [illegible] — do — |
| Total ... ... | 8 | [illegible] | | | | 6 | 17 | 16 | | | | | | | | 13 | 4 | | | | | | 2 | 1 | 7 | [illegible] Div. Train. |
| War Establishment ... ... ... | 10 | 251 | | | | 8 | 17 | 20 | | | | | | | | 13 | 4 | | | | | | 2 | | 7 | |
| Wanting to complete ... ... ... (Detail of Personnel and Horses below.) | 1 | 8 | | | | 2 | | 4 | | | | | | | | | | | | | | | | | | 8 R.A.M.C. |
| Surplus ... ... (Detail of Personnel and Horses below.) | | 5 | | | | | | | | | | | | | | | | | | | | | | | | 5 A.S.C. (H.T.) |
| †Attached (not to include the details shown above) ... ... ... ... | | 16 | | | | | | | | | | | | | | | | | | | | | | | | Sick rationed. |
| Attached for Rations only ... ... | | | | | | | | | | | | | | | | | | | | | | | | | | |
| Civilians Employed with and Accompanying the Unit ... ... ... | | | | | | | | | | | | | | | | | | | | | | | | | | |
| ‡Detached from and struck off effective strength of own Unit ... ... | | | | | | | | | | | | | | | | | | | | | | | | | | |
| ‡Detached from but retained on effective strength of own unit... ... ... | | | | | | | | | | | | | | | | | | | | | | | | | | |
| Total Rationed ... | 5 | 208 | | | | 6 | 17 | 16 | | | | | | | | | | | | | | | | | | |

* Blank columns to be used for W.A.A.C. Natives or as may be required.

† In the case of field ambulances, hospitals or depots, the number of patients are to be included here, the names being shown in A.F.A. 36.

‡ These details to be enumerated by arms.

[illegible] Lt Col. Signature of Commander.

16 Aug 1918 Date of Despatch.

*For information of the A.G.'s Office at the base.*

Officers and men who have become casuals, been transferred or joined since last report.

Place In the Field Date 16th Aug 1918

| Regtl. Number | Rank | Name | | Corps | Nature of casualty, or name of unit from or to which transferred. | Date of being struck off or coming on the ration return. | Remarks * |
|---|---|---|---|---|---|---|---|
| - | Capt | Lennie | R.A. | 1/4 Lon. R.A. Ramet | Reld from Hospt | 13/8/18. | |
| | 1st Lt | Nunn | L.J. | MRC USA att 1/4 [illegible] | To duty with RFA 9 Bde [illegible] | 14/8/18. | |
| 316054 | Pte | Hunter | J. | 1/4 [illegible] Ramet | [illegible] as candidate for RAF auth. [illegible] | [illegible] 20/7/18. | RAF [illegible] |
| 410196 | C.Q.M.S. | Hemphill | J. | Ramet. | Reinforcement from [illegible] Depot | 13/8/18. | |
| 67353 | Pte | [illegible] | T. | [illegible] | [illegible] days C.O. | 12/8/18. | [illegible] AF B 2069. |
| 316232 | L/c | Stewart | J. | [illegible] Ramet | Commencement [illegible] allot. [illegible] per day in favour of mother Mrs Jeanie Stewart from 15/8/18. | | |
| 419101 | Pte | [illegible] | W. | - do - | [illegible] Ration allce [illegible] per day for period of leave to UK 14 - 28/8/18. | | |
| 316054 | " | Hunter | J. | - do - | [illegible] Ration allce [illegible] per day [illegible] proceeding to England as candidate for RAF. | | |
| | Capt. Hon. | MacKenzie | [illegible] | do. | Proceeded to No [illegible] for course of instruction | 11/8/18 | |
| 316225 | Sgt | Allison | H. | | | | |
| 316122. | Sgt | Thomson | E.H. | | | | |
| 316293 | Cpl | Donald | W. [illegible] | | | | |
| 316100 | Pte | Gough | T.C. | | Forfeits 1 days | | |
| 316156 | " | Sharp | P. | - do - | Pay under R.W. | 12/8/18. | |
| 316110 | " | Paterson | A. | - do | Forfeits 2 days | 13/8/18 | |
| 316143 | " | Scott. | E. | do | Pay under R.W. | 14/8/18 | |
| 316147 | " | [illegible] | A.S. | do | | 15/8/18 | |

Strength. Officers. T.F. 7
MRC USA. 1 8
W.O. 1
[illegible] 4
[illegible] 1
Sgts. 10
L/Sgts. 1
Cpls 10
L/C
Ptes. 150. 180.

All Category "A"

* State whether absence is of a permanent or temporary nature, adding, in the case of casuals from wounds or disease any available information for communication to the relatives.

*The perforated sheet is not to be used to record casualties ; additional sheets, preferably foolscap, to be attached when necessary. These sheets to be carefully numbered and the number of attached sheets to be noted here.*

Perforated Sheet giving detail of personnel and horses wanting to complete or surplus, shown on Army Form B. 213.

No. of Report 159.

| Detail of Wanting to Complete or Surplus. | Drivers. R.A. | Drivers. R.E. | Drivers. A.S.C. | Drivers. Car | Drivers. Lorry | Drivers. Steam | Gunners | Gunners Howitzer | Smith Gunners | Range Takers | Farriers Serjeants | Farriers Corporals | Shoeing or Shoeing and Carriage Smiths | Cold Shoers | Wheelers R.A. | Wheelers H.T. | Wheelers M.T. | Saddlers or Harness Makers | Blacksmiths | Bricklayers and Masons | Carpenters and Joiners | Fitters & Turners (R.E.) Wood | Fitters & Turners (R.E.) Iron | Fitters R.A. | Fitters Wireless. | Plumbers | Electricians Ordinary | Electricians W.T. | Signalmen. | Engine Drivers Loco. | Engine Drivers Field | Air Line Men. | Permanent Line Men | Operators, Telegraph | Cablemen | Brigade Section Pioneers | General-duty Pioneers | Signallers | Instrument Repairers | Motor Cyclist | Motor Cyclist Artificers | Telephonists | Clerks | Machine Gunners | Armament Artificers Fitters | Armament Artificers Range Finders | Armourers | Storemen | Privates | W.O.'s and N.C.O.'s (by ranks) not included in trade columns. | TOTAL to agree with wanting to complete or surplus. Officers | TOTAL to agree with wanting to complete or surplus. Other Ranks | Horses Riding | Horses Draught | Horses Heavy Draught | Horses Pack |
|---|---|---|---|---|---|---|---|---|---|---|---|---|---|---|---|---|---|---|---|---|---|---|---|---|---|---|---|---|---|---|---|---|---|---|---|---|---|---|---|---|---|---|---|---|---|---|---|---|---|---|---|---|---|---|---|
| CAVALRY—DEFICIENCY | | | | | | | | | | | | | | | | | | | | | | | | | | | | | | | | | | | | | | | | | | | | | | | | | | | | | | | | |
| SURPLUS | | | | | | | | | | | | | | | | | | | | | | | | | | | | | | | | | | | | | | | | | | | | | | | | | | | | | | | | |
| R.A.—DEFICIENCY | | | | | | | | | | | | | | | | | | | | | | | | | | | | | | | | | | | | | | | | | | | | | | | | | | | | | | | |
| SURPLUS | | | | | | | | | | | | | | | | | | | | | | | | | | | | | | | | | | | | | | | | | | | | | | | | | | | | | | | |
| R.E.—DEFICIENCY | | | | | | | | | | | | | | | | | | | | | | | | | | | | | | | | | | | | | | | | | | | | | | | | | | | | | | | |
| SURPLUS | | | | | | | | | | | | | | | | | | | | | | | | | | | | | | | | | | | | | | | | | | | | | | | | | | | | | | | |
| INFANTRY—DEFICIENCY | | | | | | | | | | | | | | | | | | | | | | | | | | | | | | | | | | | | | | | | | | | | | | | | | | | | | | | |
| SURPLUS | | | | | | | | | | | | | | | | | | | | | | | | | | | | | | | | | | | | | | | | | | | | | | | | 3 | | 1 | 2 | 2 | | 4 | |
| R.A.M.C.—DEFICIENCY | | | | | | | | | | | | | | | | | | | | | | | | | | | | | | | | | | | | | | | | | | | | | | | | | 1-QMTS. | | | | | | |
| SURPLUS | | | | | | | | | | | | | | | | | | | | | | | | | | | | | | | | | | | | | | | | | | | | | | | | | | | | | | | |
| A.O.C.—DEFICIENCY | | | | | | | | | | | | | | | | | | | | | | | | | | | | | | | | | | | | | | | | | | | | | | | | | | | | | | | |
| SURPLUS | | | | | | | | | | | | | | | | | | | | | | | | | | | | | | | | | | | | | | | | | | | | | | | | | | | | | | | |
| A.V.C.—DEFICIENCY | | | | | | | | | | | | | | | | | | | | | | | | | | | | | | | | | | | | | | | | | | | | | | | | | | | | | | | |
| SURPLUS | | | | | | | | | | | | | | | | | | | | | | | | | | | | | | | | | | | | | | | | | | | | | | | | | | | | | | | |
| DEFICIENCY | | | | | | | | | | | | | | | | | | | | | | | | | | | | | | | | | | | | | | | | | | | | | | | | | | | | | | | |
| SURPLUS | | | | | | | | | | | | | | | | | | | | | | | | | | | | | | | | | | | | | | | | | | | | | | | | | | | | | | | |
| DEFICIENCY | | | | | | | | | | | | | | | | | | | | | | | | | | | | | | | | | | | | | | | | | | | | | | | | | | | | | | | |
| SURPLUS | | | | | | | | | | | | | | | | | | | | | | | | | | | | | | | | | | | | | | | | | | | | | | | | | | | | | | | |

Remarks :—

Lt Col. Signature of Commander.

1/1 Low Fd Amb RAMC T. Unit.

52nd Div Formation to which attached.

16 Aug 1918 Date of Despatch.

(16523.) Wt. W6016—PP 1432. 1,500m. 3/18. D & S. (E1256) Forms B213S/8.

[P.T.O.

HEADQUARTERS, [illegible] LOWLAND [illegible] AMBULANCE.

AF B 213 W/E 16/8/18

| No | Rk. | Name | Unit | Casualty | |
|---|---|---|---|---|---|
| 316255 | Pte | May. J. | 1/2 Ld Fd Amce. | Granted 14 days leave to UK. 11/8/18 to 25/8/18. Credit ration allce @ 2/1 per day for that period. | |
| 316256 | " | Nisbet A. | -do- | Granted 14 days leave to UK 12/8/18 to 26/8/18. Credit ration allce at 2/1 per day for that period. | |
| 316259 | " | Reid. J.S. | do. | Granted leave to UK for 14 days 13/8/18 to 27/8/18. Credit ration allce at 2/1 per day for that period. | |
| 316261 | " | Rennie J.D. | do. | Granted 14 days leave to UK 14/8/18 to 28/8/18. Credit ration allce at 2/1 per day for that period. | |
| 316264 | Pte | Edington A. | do. | Granted 14 days leave to UK 16/8/18 to 30/8/18. Credit ration allce @ 2/1 per day for that period. | |
| 316010 | L/c | Campbell D | do | Granted 31 days leave to UK. 17/8/18 to 17/9/18. Credit ration allce @ 2/1 per day for that period. | |
| 316252 | Pte. | McLean. J. | do. | Granted 14 days leave to UK, 18/8/18 to 1/9/18. Credit ration allce @ 2/1 per day for that period. | |
| 316067. | S/S | Anderson J. | -do- | Rejd. from 28 days leave to UK. | " 10/8/18. |
| 316094 | Pte | Christie T | do | " " 14 " " " " | " " |
| 316129 | " | White A | do | " " 14 " " " " | " " |
| 316124 | " | Murray D. | do | " " 14 " " " " | " " |
| 316096 | " | Dankes H | do | " " 14 " " " " | " " |
| 316097 | " | Dickson D | do | " " 14 " " " " | " 11/8/18 |
| 316098 | " | McKellar J | do. | " " 14 " " " " | " " |
| 316100 | " | Gough T.C. | do. | " " 14 " " " " | " 12/8/18 |
| 316156 | " | Sharp P. | do. | " " 14 " " " " | " " |
| 316110 | " | Paterson A | do. | " " 14 " " " " | " 13/8/18. |
| 316143 | " | Scott L. | do | " " 14 " " " " | " 14/8/18. |
| 316163 | " | Edgecombe H | do | " " 14 " " " " | " 14/8/18. |
| 316153 | " | Tinto A | do | " " 14 " " " " | " 15/8/18 |
| 316147 | " | Eadie W | do | " " 14 " " " " | " 15/8/18. |

To be made up to and for Saturday in each week

No. of Report 160

# FIELD RETURN.

Army Form B 213

(To be furnished by all arms, services, and departments (except A.S.C. units) to the A.G.'s Office at the Base in accordance with Field Service Regulations, Part II.)

RETURN showing numbers (a) Effective strength of Unit. (b) Rationed by Unit. 1st Low. Fld Amb. at In the Field 23rd August 1918 Date.

| Details. | Personnel* Officers | Personnel* Other Ranks | | | Animals Horses Riding | Draught | Heavy Draught | Pack | Mules Large | Small | Guns and transport vehicles Guns, showing description | Ammunition wagons | Machine guns | Aircraft, showing description | Horsed 4 Wheeled | 2 Wheeled | Mechanical Motor Cars | Tractors | Lorries, showing description | Trucks, showing description | Trailers | Motor Bicycles | Bicycles | Motor Ambulances | Remarks (Number of Acting W.O.'s and N.C.O.'s included in effective strength to be shown in this column.) |
|---|---|---|---|---|---|---|---|---|---|---|---|---|---|---|---|---|---|---|---|---|---|---|---|---|---|
| Effective Strength of Unit ... ... | (a) 8 | (b) 179 | | | | | | | | | | | | | | | | | | | | * | 1 | | (a) Includes 1 Officer @ 1/4 R.S.F.<br>" 1 " 1/3rd L.F.A. |
| Details by Arms attached to Unit as in War Establishment ... ... | | | | | | | | | | | | | | | | | | | | | | | | | (b) " 1 O.R. Div. Concert Party<br>" 2 " " H.Q.<br>" 1 " " TRAIN<br>" 25 " Leave to U.K.<br>" 1 " Army Rest Camp |
| A.S.C. (H.T.) | | (c) 39 | | | 6 | 17 | 21 | | | | | | | | 13 | 4 | | | | | | | | | |
| " (M.T.) | | (d) 13 | | | | | | | | | | | | | | | | | | | | 2 | | 7 | (c) " 4 " Leave to U.K.<br>(d) " 1 " Div. H.Q. |
| Total ... ... | 8 | 231 | | | 6 | 17 | 21 | | | | | | | | 13 | 4 | | | | | | 2 | 1 | 7 | |
| War Establishment ... ... ... | 10 | 231 | | | 8 | 17 | 20 | | | | | | | | | | | | | | | 2 | 1 | 7 | |
| Wanting to complete ... ... (Detail of Personnel and Horses below.) | 2 | *3 | | | 2 | . | . | | | | | | | | | | | | | | | | | | * Ramc |
| Surplus ... ... (Detail of Personnel and Horses below.) | | ø3 | | | | | 1 | | | | | | | | | | | | | | | | | | ø A.S.C. (H.T.) |
| †Attached (not to include the details shown above) ... ... ... | | | | | | | | | | | | | | | | | | | | | | | | | |
| Attached for Rations only ... ... | | | | | | | | | | | | | | | | | | | | | | | | | |
| Civilians Employed with and Accompanying the Unit ... ... | | | | | | | | | | | | | | | | | | | | | | | | | |
| ‡Detached from and struck off effective strength of own Unit ... ... | | | | | | | | | | | | | | | | | | | | | | | | | |
| ‡Detached from but retained on effective strength of own unit... ... | | | | | | | | | | | | | | | | | | | | | | | | | |
| Total Rationed ... | 6 | 195 | | | 6 | 17 | 21 | | | | | | | | | | | | | | | | | | |

* Blank columns to be used for W.A.A.C. Natives or as may be required.

† In the case of field ambulances, hospitals or depots, the number of patients are to be included here, the names being shown in A.F.A. 36.

‡ These details to be enumerated by arms.

Lt. Col. Signature of Commander.

23rd August 1918 Date of Despatch.

For information of the A.G.'s Office at the base.

Officers and men who have become casuals, been transferred or joined since last report.

Place In the Field Date 23rd August 1918

| Regtl. Number | Rank | Name | | Corps | Nature of casualty, or name of unit from or to which transferred. | Date of being struck off or coming on the ration return. | Remarks * |
|---|---|---|---|---|---|---|---|
| | Capt. | Lennie | R.A. | 1/3 Low. Fd. Amb. RAMC (T.F.) | To duty with 1/3 Low. Fd. Amb. | 16/8/18. | Tempy. |
| | " | Barton | J.W. | do. | Returned from duty 19th Bde. R.G.A. | 21/8/18 | |
| | Major | Mackenzie | W.J. | do | Returned from Rear School of Instruction | 22/8/18 | |
| 341010 | S/Sgt. | Hampson | R.F. | 43 W. Lancs Fd. Amb. | Transferred to this Amb. for duty | 18/8/18. | Permanent |
| 415196 | Cpl. | Hemphill | W.J. | RAMC (T) | To duty with 1/3 Low. Fd. Amb. | 20/8/18 | do. |
| 316225 | Sergt. | Allison | A.W. | 1/1st Low. Fd. Amb. RAMC (T) | Returned from Rear School of Instruction | 22/8/18 | |
| 316122 | " | Thomson | J.A. | do. | do. | do. | |
| 316293 | Cpl. | Donald | W.S. | do. | do. | do. | |
| 316154 | Pte | Brown | R. | do. | Forfeits | 17.8.18. | |
| 316158 | " | Hanlon | C.W. | do. | 2 | do. | |
| 316151 | " | Candlish | J. | do | days pay | 18.8.18. | |
| 316003 | | McKechnie | W. | do. | under | do. | |
| 316148 | | Laird | D.W. | do. | R.W. | do. | |
| 325024 | | Le Roy | H. | do. | 14 days C.B. | 20.8.18. | |
| 316352 | | Laurie | J. | do. | do. | do. | |
| 316143 | | Scott | L. | do. | do. | do. | |
| 316165 | | Findlay | R. | do. | Forfeits 2 days pay under R.W. | do. | |

T.C. 1
T.F. 6
Strength Officers M.R.C. U.S.A. 1 8

W.O. 1
S/Sgt. 1
S/Sgts 2
Sgts 4
L/Sgt 1
Cpls. 10
L/Cpls 5
Ptes 149 179

All Category "A".

* State whether absence is of a permanent or temporary nature, adding, in the case of casuals from wounds or disease any available information for communication to the relatives.

*The perforated sheet is not to be used to record casualties; additional sheets, preferably foolscap, to be attached when necessary. These sheets to be carefully numbered and the number of attached sheets to be noted here.*

A.F.B. 213.

W. E. 23·8·18.

| No. | Rank | Name | | Unit | Casualty | | Date |
|---|---|---|---|---|---|---|---|
| 316262 | Pte | Adamson | W. | 1/1 L.F.A. Ramc(T) | Granted 14 days leave to UK. Ration allowance @ 2/1 per day for that period | | 19·8·18 = 2·9·18. |
| 410023 | L/Cpl | Reeves | F. | do. | do. | do. | 20·8·18 = 3·9·18. |
| 318265 | Pte. | Queenan | P. | do. | do. | do. | do. |
| 410038 | " | Jackson | F. | do. | do | do. | 22·8·18 = 5·9·18. |
| 410054 | " | Parkins | L. | do. | do. | do. | 23·8·18 = 6·9·18 |
| 316293 | Cpl. | Donald | W.S. | do. | do. | do. | do. |
| 410044 | Pte | Beckers | J.H. | do. | do. | do. | do. |
| 42136 | | Ferry | E. | do. | do. | do. | 25·8·18 = 8·9·18. |
| 310021 | | Craig | J. | do. | Granted 31 days leave to UK. Ration allowance @ 2/1 per day for that period. | | 24·8·18 = 25·9·18. |
| 329815 | Pte | Southern | G. | Ramc. | Joined as Reinforcements from Base | | 21·8·18. |
| 40150 | | Quigley | J. | do. | do. | | do. |

*For information of the A.G.'s Office at the base.*

Officers and men who have become casuals, been transferred or joined since last report.

Place In the Field    Date 23rd August 1918

| Regtl. Number | Rank | Name | | Corps | Nature of casualty, or name of unit from or to which transferred. | Date of being struck off or coming on the ration return. | Remarks * |
|---|---|---|---|---|---|---|---|
| | Capt. | Lennie | R.A. | [illegible] RAMC (T.F.) | To duty with 1/3 Low. Fd Amb. | 16/8/18. | Tempy. |
| | | Barton | J.W. | do. | Returned from duty 19th Bde. R.G.A. | 21/8/18 | |
| | Major | MacKenzie | W.J. | do | Returned from RAMC School of Instruction | 22/8/18 | |
| 341010 | St Sgt. | Hampson | R.F. | 1/3 W. Lancs Fd. Amb. | Transferred to this Amb. for duty | 18/8/18. | Permanent |
| 410196 | QMS | Hemphill | W.J. | RAMC (T) | To duty with 1/3 Low Fd Amb. | 20/8/18 | — do. — |
| 316225 | Sergt | Allison | A.W. | 1/1st Low. Fld. Amb. RAMC (T) | Returned from RAMC School of Instruction | 22/8/18 | |
| 316122 | " | Thomson | G.A. | do. | do. | do. | |
| 316293 | Cpl. | Donald | D.S. | do. | do. | do. | |
| 316154 | Pte | Brown | R. | do. | Forfeits | 17. 8. 18. | |
| 316158 | " | Hanlon | C.W. | do. | 2 | do. | |
| 316151 | " | Candlish | J | do | days pay | 15. 8. 18. | |
| 316003 | | McKechnie | W. | do. | under | do. | |
| 316148 | | Laird | D.W. | do. | R. W. | do. | |
| 325024 | | Le Roy | H. | do. | 14 days C.C. | 20. 8. 18. | |
| 316352 | | Laurie | J. | do. | do. | do. | |
| 316143 | | Scott | L. | do. | do. | do. | |
| 316165 | | Findlay | R. | do. | Forfeits 2 days pay under R.W. | do | |

T.C. 1
T.F. 6

Strength Officers M.R.C. U.S.A. 1 8

W.O. 1
QMS 1
S/Sgts 2
Sgts 11
L/Sgts 1
Cpls. 10
L/Cpls 5
Ptes 149 179

All Category "A".

* State whether absence is of a permanent or temporary nature, adding, in the case of casuals from wounds or disease any available information for communication to the relatives.

*The perforated sheet is not to be used to record casualties; additional sheets, preferably foolscap, to be attached when necessary. These sheets to be carefully numbered and the number of attached sheets to be noted here.*

Perforated Sheet giving detail of personnel and horses wanting to complete or surplus, shown on Army Form B. 213.

No. of Report ____________

| Detail of Wanting to Complete or Surplus. | Drivers. R.A. | Drivers. R.E. | Drivers. A.S.C. | Drivers. Car | Drivers. Lorry | Drivers. Steam | Gunners | Gunners Howitzer | Smith Gunners | Range Takers | Farriers Serjeants | Farriers Corporals | Shoeing or Shoeing and Carriage Smiths | Cold Shoers | Wheelers R.A. | Wheelers H.T. | Wheelers M.T. | Saddlers or Harness Makers | Blacksmiths | Bricklayers and Masons | Carpenters and Joiners | Fitters & Turners (R.E.) Wood | Fitters & Turners (R.E.) Iron | Fitters R.A. | Fitters Wireless. | Plumbers | Electricians Ordinary | Electricians W.T. | Signalmen. | Engine Drivers Loco. | Engine Drivers Field | Air Line Men. | Permanent Line Men | Operators, Telegraph | Cablemen | Brigade Section Pioneers | General-duty Pioneers | Signallers | Instrument Repairers | Motor Cyclist | Motor Cyclist Artificers | Telephonists | Clerks | Machine Gunners | Armament Artificers Fitters | Armament Artificers Range Finders | Armourers | Storemen | Privates | W.O.'s and N.C.O.'s (by ranks) not included in trade columns. | | | | | | | | | | | TOTAL to agree with wanting to complete or surplus Officers | TOTAL Other Ranks | Horses Riding | Horses Draught | Horses Heavy Draught | Horses Pack |
|---|---|---|---|---|---|---|---|---|---|---|---|---|---|---|---|---|---|---|---|---|---|---|---|---|---|---|---|---|---|---|---|---|---|---|---|---|---|---|---|---|---|---|---|---|---|---|---|---|---|---|---|---|---|---|---|---|---|---|---|---|---|---|---|---|---|
| CAVALRY— DEFICIENCY | | | | | | | | | | | | | | | | | | | | | | | | | | | | | | | | | | | | | | | | | | | | | | | | | | | | | | | | | | | | | | | | | | |
| SURPLUS | | | | | | | | | | | | | | | | | | | | | | | | | | | | | | | | | | | | | | | | | | | | | | | | | | | | | | | | | | | | | | | | | | |
| R.A.— DEFICIENCY | | | | | | | | | | | | | | | | | | | | | | | | | | | | | | | | | | | | | | | | | | | | | | | | | | | | | | | | | | | | | | | | | | |
| SURPLUS | | | | | | | | | | | | | | | | | | | | | | | | | | | | | | | | | | | | | | | | | | | | | | | | | | | | | | | | | | | | | | | | | | |
| R.E.— DEFICIENCY | | | | | | | | | | | | | | | | | | | | | | | | | | | | | | | | | | | | | | | | | | | | | | | | | | | | | | | | | | | | | | | | | | |
| SURPLUS | | | | | | | | | | | | | | | | | | | | | | | | | | | | | | | | | | | | | | | | | | | | | | | | | | | | | | | | | | | | | | | | | |
| INFANTRY— DEFICIENCY | | | | | | | | | | | | | | | | | | | | | | | | | | | | | | | | | | | | | | | | | | | | | | | | | | | | | | | | | | | | | | | | | | |
| SURPLUS | | | | | | | | | | | | | | | | | | | | | | | | | | | | | | | | | | | | | | | | | | | | | | | | | | | | | | | | | | | | | | | | | | |
| R.A.M.C.— DEFICIENCY | | | | | | | | | | | | | | | | | | | | | | | | | | | | | | | | | | | | | | | | | | | | | | | | | 3 | | | | | | | | | | | | 2 | 3 | 2 | | | |
| SURPLUS | | | | | | | | | | | | | | | | | | | | | | | | | | | | | | | | | | | | | | | | | | | | | | | | | | | | | | | | | | | | | | | | | | |
| A.O.C.— DEFICIENCY | | | | | | | | | | | | | | | | | | | | | | | | | | | | | | | | | | | | | | | | | | | | | | | | | | | | | | | | | | | | | | | | | | |
| SURPLUS | | | | | | | | | | | | | | | | | | | | | | | | | | | | | | | | | | | | | | | | | | | | | | | | | | | | | | | | | | | | | | | | | | |
| A.V.C.— DEFICIENCY | | | | | | | | | | | | | | | | | | | | | | | | | | | | | | | | | | | | | | | | | | | | | | | | | | | | | | | | | | | | | | | | | | |
| SURPLUS | | | | | | | | | | | | | | | | | | | | | | | | | | | | | | | | | | | | | | | | | | | | | | | | | | | | | | | | | | | | | | | | | | |
| DEFICIENCY | | | | | | | | | | | | | | | | | | | | | | | | | | | | | | | | | | | | | | | | | | | | | | | | | | | | | | | | | | | | | | | | | | |
| SURPLUS | | | | | | | | | | | | | | | | | | | | | | | | | | | | | | | | | | | | | | | | | | | | | | | | | | | | | | | | | | | | | | | | | | |
| DEFICIENCY | | | | | | | | | | | | | | | | | | | | | | | | | | | | | | | | | | | | | | | | | | | | | | | | | | | | | | | | | | | | | | | | | | |
| SURPLUS | | | | | | | | | | | | | | | | | | | | | | | | | | | | | | | | | | | | | | | | | | | | | | | | | | | | | | | | | | | | | | | | | | |

Remarks :—

Lt. Col. Signature of Commander.

1/1st Low. Fld. Ambce. RAMC (T.F.) Unit.

52nd Division Formation to which attached.

23rd Aug. 1918. Date of Despatch.

(16523.) Wt. W6016—PP 1432. 1,500m. 3/18. D & S. (E1256) Forms B213S/8.

[P.T.O.

A.F.B. 213

A.S.C.

W.E. 23. 8. 18.

| No. | Rank | Name. | Unit | Casualty. | Date. | Remark |
|---|---|---|---|---|---|---|
| T/14642 | Dvr. | Appleyard F. | A.S.C. (H.T.) att. of Low. Fld Amb. Rame(T.F.) | Granted 14 days leave to U.K. Ration allowance @ 2/1 per day for that period | 24. 8. 18 to 7. 9. 18. | |

**To be made up to and for Saturday in each week**

No. of Report 161

# FIELD RETURN.

Army Form B 213

(To be furnished by all arms, services, and departments (except A.S.C. units) to the A.G.'s Office at the Base in accordance with Field Service Regulations, Part II.)

RETURN showing numbers (a) Effective strength of Unit. (b) Rationed by Unit. 1st Lowland Field Ambce at In the Field 30/8/18 Date.

| DETAILS. | *Personnel: Officers | Other Ranks | | | | Animals: Horses: Riding | Draught | Heavy Draught | Pack | Mules: Large | Small | Guns and transport vehicles: Guns, showing description | Ammunition wagons | Machine guns | Aircraft, showing description | Horsed: 4 Wheeled | 2 Wheeled | Mechanical: Motor Cars | Tractors | Lorries, showing description | Trucks, showing description | Trailers | Motor Bicycles | Bicycles | Motor Ambulances | REMARKS (Number of Acting W.O.'s and N.C.O.'s included in effective strength to be shown in this column.) |
|---|---|---|---|---|---|---|---|---|---|---|---|---|---|---|---|---|---|---|---|---|---|---|---|---|---|---|
| Effective Strength of Unit ... ... | (a) 8 | (b) 130 | | | | | | | | | | | | | | | | | | | | | | 1 | | (a) Includes 1 Officer @ 4th R.S.; 1 " " 1/3 L.F.A |
| Details by Arms attached to Unit as in War Establishment ... ... | | | | | | | | | | | | | | | | | | | | | | | | | | 1 3 Low CCS; 1 1/3 LFA; (b) 1 OR @ Div Concert P.; 1 " Farm |
| A S C. (H.T.) | | (c) 38 | | | | 6 | 17 | 21 | | | | | | | | 13 | 4 | | | | | | | | | 2 @ Div Hdqrs; 29 Leave to U.K. |
| (M.T.) | | (d) 12 | | | | | | | | | | | | | | | | | | | | | | | 7 | (c) 1 Army Rest Camp; 4 OR Leave to UK; (d) 1 " do |
| TOTAL ... | 8 | 230 | | | | 6 | 17 | 21 | | | | | | | | 13 | 4 | | | | | | | 1 | 7 | |
| War Establishment ... ... | 10 | 231 | | | | 8 | 17 | 20 | | | | | | | | 13 | 4 | | | | | | 2 | 1 | 7 | |
| Wanting to complete ... ... (Detail of Personnel and Horses below.) | 2* | 2 | | | | 2 | | | | | | | | | | | | | | | | | 2 | | | * Rame |
| SURPLUS ... (Detail of Personnel and Horses below.) | | ⊕2 | | | | | | 1 | | | | | | | | | | | | | | | | | | ⊕ ASC (HT) |
| †Attached (not to include the details shown above) ... ... | | | | | | | | | | | | | | | | | | | | | | | | | | |
| Attached for Rations only ... | | | | | | | | | | | | | | | | | | | | | | | | | | |
| Civilians Employed with and Accompanying the Unit ... ... | | | | | | | | | | | | | | | | | | | | | | | | | | |
| ‡Detached from and struck off effective strength of own Unit ... | | | | | | | | | | | | | | | | | | | | | | | | | | |
| ‡Detached from but retained on effective strength of own unit... ... | | | | | | | | | | | | | | | | | | | | | | | | | | |
| TOTAL RATIONED ... | 4 | 191 | | | | 6 | 17 | 21 | | | | | | | | | | | | | | | | | | |

* Blank columns to be used for W.A.A.C. Natives or as may be required.

† In the case of field ambulances, hospitals or depots, the number of patients are to be included here, the names being shown in A.F.A. 36.
‡ These details to be enumerated by arms.

Lt Col
Signature of Commander.

30 August 1918
Date of Despatch.

A.F.B 213 W.E 30-8-18

| No | Rank | Name | Unit | Casualty | Date | Remarks |
|---|---|---|---|---|---|---|
| 410045 | Pte | Hodgson E.R. | 1/1 Low. Hd. Amb Ramc (T.F.) | Granted 14 days leave to U.K. Ration Allowance @ 2/1 per day for that period | 26-8-18 to 9-9-18 | |
| 328030 | | Carson S. | do | do | 28-8-18 - 11-9-18 | |
| 316279 | | Miller R.W. | do | do | do | |
| 328053 | | Marshall G.W. | do | do | 29-8-18 - 12-9-18 | |
| 316249 | | Brown G.F. | do | do | do | |
| 316245 | | Willis H. | do | do | do | |
| 316281 | | Hosie W. | do | do | do | |
| 316285 | | Campbell W. | do | do | 30-8-18 - 13-9-18 | |
| 316287 | | Gallacher H. | do | do | do | |
| 316273 | | Sloan D. | do | do | 31-8-18 - 14-9-18 | |
| 316296 | | Hunter J. | do | do | 1-9-18 - 15-9-18 | |
| 316303 | | Cowie J. | do | do | do | |
| 316276 | | McKay J. | do | do | do | |
| 316024 | | Leask J. | do | Granted 30 days leave to U.K. Ration Allowance @ 2/1 per day for that period | 31-8-18 to 30-9-18 | |
| 316188 | | Johnson J.Y. | do | Returned from Leave 14 days to U.K. | 24-8-18 | |
| 316189 | | Carson J.B. | do | do | do | |
| 316186 | | Hilder F. | do | do | do | |
| 316193 | | Stewart W. | do | do | do | |
| 34251 | | Toon J.A. | do | do | 27-8-18 | |
| 42191 | | Ward T. | do | do | 25-8-18 | |
| 316250 | | McLeod A. | do | do | do | |
| 316255 | | May J. | do | do | 27-8-18 | |
| 316256 | | Nisbet A. | do | do | 29-8-18 | |
| 316259 | | Reid J.S. | do | do | do | |
| 316066 | Sgt | Campbell J.S. | do | Returned from Leave 31 days to U.K. | 29-8-18 | |

A.S.C.

A.F.B 213 WE 30-8-18.

| No | Rank | Name | | Unit | Casualty | Date |
|---|---|---|---|---|---|---|
| T3/024605 | Dvr | Chinner | E. | ASC (HT) att 1/1 Low. Fd amb | To Hospital Sick while on Leave | 16/8/18 |
| T/36536 | " | Jeggo | C. | do | 14 days C.C | 27/8/18 |
| T4/199997 | " | Clapperton | R. | do. | 10 days C.C. | do. |
| T4/044551 | " | Lloyd | W. | do | do. | do. |
| M1/08845 | Pte | Austin | S.C. | ASC (MT) att 1/1 Low F amb. | To Hospital | 20/8/18. |
| T4/245523 | Dvr | Brasenell | W.J. | ASC (H.T) att 1/1 Low F amb. | Granted 14 days leave to UK. Ration Allce @ 2/1 per day for that period | 27.8.18 - 10.9.18 |
| M2/134510 | Cpl | Langton | P.J. | ASC (MT) att 1/1 Low Fd amb. | do. | 26.8.18 - 9.9.18 |
| T4/042229 | Sgt | Turner | W. | ASC (HT) att 1/1 L F A | do. | 1.9.18 - 15.9.18 |
| T4/242015 | Dvr | Lockhart | J. | do. | Returned from 14 days leave to UK. | 27.8.18 |

*For information of the A.G.'s Office at the base.*

Officers and men who have become casuals, been transferred or joined since last report.

Place In the Field Date 30th August 1918

| Regtl. Number | Rank | Name | Corps | Nature of casualty, or name of unit from or to which transferred. | Date of being struck off or coming on the ration return. | Remarks * |
|---|---|---|---|---|---|---|
| | Major | Browne J | Ramc (T.F.) 1/1 Low Fd Amb Co | To duty with 3rd Can. C.C.S. | 24/8/18 | Temp |
| | " | Mackenzie W.F. | do | To duty with 1/3 Low Fd Amb Co | 30/8/18 | do |
| 316131 | Pte | Henderson R | do | To Hospital Sick | 19/8/18 | |
| 318313 | " | Hampton J | do | do | do | |
| 70100 | " | Wrigley J | do | 7 days C.C | 29/8/18 | |
| 316256 | " | Nisbet A | do | Forfeits one days pay under R.W. | 30/8/18 | |
| 61353 | " | Worsley T | do | War Pay increased to 3d per day from 16/7/18 | 16/7/18 | |
| 112200 | " | Pender W | do | War Pay increased to 1d per day from 13/4/18 | 13/4/18 | |
| | | Strength Officers | T.C. 1, T.F. 6, M.C. U.S.A. 1 — 8 | | | |
| | | | W.O. 1, Qm.S 1, S/Sgts 2, Sgts 10, L/Sgts 1, Cpls 10, L/Cpl 5, Ptes 150 — 180 | | | |

All Category "A"

| Regtl. Number | Rank | Name | Corps | Nature of casualty |
|---|---|---|---|---|
| 316100 | Pte | Gough T.C. | Ramc (T.F.) 1/1 Low Fld Amb. | Forfeits one days pay under Royal Warrant not two days pay as stated on A.F.B. 213 dated 16/8/18 and 23/8/18 |
| 316156 | Pte | Sharp P | do | |
| 316110 | | Paterson A | do | |
| 316143 | | Scott L | do | |
| 316147 | | Eadie W | do | |
| 316154 | | Brown R | do | |
| 316153 | | Hanlon W | do | |
| 316151 | | Candlish J | do | |
| 316003 | | McKechnie W | do | |
| 316148 | | Laird D.W. | do | |
| 316165 | | Findlay R | do | |

* State whether absence is of a permanent or temporary nature, adding, in the case of casuals from wounds or disease any available information for communication to the relatives.

*The perforated sheet is not to be used to record casualties; additional sheets, preferably foolscap, to be attached when necessary. These sheets to be carefully numbered and the number of attached sheets to be noted here.*

Perforated Sheet giving detail of personnel and horses wanting to complete or surplus, shown on Army Form B. 213.

No. of Report 161

| Detail of Wanting to Complete or Surplus. | Drivers. R.A. | Drivers. R.E. | Drivers. A.S.C. | Drivers. Car | Drivers. Lorry | Drivers. Steam | Gunners | Gunners Howitzer | Smith Gunners | Range Takers | Farriers Serjeants | Farriers Corporals | Shoeing or Shoeing and Carriage Smiths | Cold Shoers | Wheelers R.A. | Wheelers H.T. | Wheelers M.T. | Saddlers or Harness Makers | Blacksmiths | Bricklayers and Masons | Carpenters and Joiners |
|---|---|---|---|---|---|---|---|---|---|---|---|---|---|---|---|---|---|---|---|---|---|
| CAVALRY— Deficiency | | | | | | | | | | | | | | | | | | | | | |
| Surplus | | | | | | | | | | | | | | | | | | | | | |
| R.A.— Deficiency | | | | | | | | | | | | | | | | | | | | | |
| Surplus | | | | | | | | | | | | | | | | | | | | | |
| R.E.— Deficiency | | | | | | | | | | | | | | | | | | | | | |
| Surplus | | | | | | | | | | | | | | | | | | | | | |
| INFANTRY— Deficiency | | | | | | | | | | | | | | | | | | | | | |
| Surplus | | | | | | | | | | | | | | | | | | | | | |
| R.A.M.C.— Deficiency | | | | | | | | | | | | | | | | | | | | | |
| Surplus | | | | | | | | | | | | | | | | | | | | | |
| A.O.C.— Deficiency | | | | | | | | | | | | | | | | | | | | | |
| Surplus | | | | | | | | | | | | | | | | | | | | | |
| A.V.C.— Deficiency | | | | | | | | | | | | | | | | | | | | | |
| Surplus | | | | | | | | | | | | | | | | | | | | | |
| Deficiency | | | | | | | | | | | | | | | | | | | | | |
| Surplus | | | | | | | | | | | | | | | | | | | | | |
| Deficiency | | | | | | | | | | | | | | | | | | | | | |
| Surplus | | | | | | | | | | | | | | | | | | | | | |

| Detail of Wanting to Complete or Surplus. | Fitters & Turners (R.E.) Wood | Fitters & Turners (R.E.) Iron | Fitters R.A. | Fitters Wireless. | Plumbers | Electricians Ordinary | Electricians W.T. | Signalmen. | Engine Drivers Loco. | Engine Drivers Field | Air Line Men. | Permanent Line Men | Operators, Telegraph | Cablemen | Brigade Section Pioneers | General-duty Pioneers | Signallers | Instrument Repairers | Motor Cyclist | Motor Cyclist Artificers | Telephonists | Clerks | Machine Gunners | Armament Artificers Fitters | Armament Artificers Range Finders | Armourers | Storemen | Privates |
|---|---|---|---|---|---|---|---|---|---|---|---|---|---|---|---|---|---|---|---|---|---|---|---|---|---|---|---|---|
| CAVALRY— Deficiency | | | | | | | | | | | | | | | | | | | | | | | | | | | | |
| Surplus | | | | | | | | | | | | | | | | | | | | | | | | | | | | |
| R.A.— Deficiency | | | | | | | | | | | | | | | | | | | | | | | | | | | | |
| Surplus | | | | | | | | | | | | | | | | | | | | | | | | | | | | |
| R.E.— Deficiency | | | | | | | | | | | | | | | | | | | | | | | | | | | | |
| Surplus | | | | | | | | | | | | | | | | | | | | | | | | | | | | |
| INFANTRY— Deficiency | | | | | | | | | | | | | | | | | | | | | | | | | | | | 2 |
| Surplus | | | | | | | | | | | | | | | | | | | | | | | | | | | | |
| R.A.M.C.— Deficiency | | | | | | | | | | | | | | | | | | | | | | | | | | | | |
| Surplus | | | | | | | | | | | | | | | | | | | | | | | | | | | | |
| A.O.C.— Deficiency | | | | | | | | | | | | | | | | | | | | | | | | | | | | |
| Surplus | | | | | | | | | | | | | | | | | | | | | | | | | | | | |
| A.V.C.— Deficiency | | | | | | | | | | | | | | | | | | | | | | | | | | | | |
| Surplus | | | | | | | | | | | | | | | | | | | | | | | | | | | | |
| Deficiency | | | | | | | | | | | | | | | | | | | | | | | | | | | | |
| Surplus | | | | | | | | | | | | | | | | | | | | | | | | | | | | |
| Deficiency | | | | | | | | | | | | | | | | | | | | | | | | | | | | |
| Surplus | | | | | | | | | | | | | | | | | | | | | | | | | | | | |

| Detail of Wanting to Complete or Surplus. | W.O.'s and N.C.O.'s (by ranks) not included in trade columns. | | | | | | | | | | | TOTAL to agree with wanting to complete or surplus. Officers | TOTAL Other Ranks | Horses Riding | Horses Draught | Horses Heavy Draught | Horses Pack |
|---|---|---|---|---|---|---|---|---|---|---|---|---|---|---|---|---|---|
| CAVALRY— Deficiency | | | | | | | | | | | | | | | | | |
| Surplus | | | | | | | | | | | | | | | | | |
| R.A.— Deficiency | | | | | | | | | | | | | | | | | |
| Surplus | | | | | | | | | | | | | | | | | |
| R.E.— Deficiency | | | | | | | | | | | | | | | | | |
| Surplus | | | | | | | | | | | | | | | | | |
| INFANTRY— Deficiency | | | | | | | | | | | | 2 | 2 | 2 | | | |
| Surplus | | | | | | | | | | | | | | | | | |
| R.A.M.C.— Deficiency | | | | | | | | | | | | | | | | | |
| Surplus | | | | | | | | | | | | | | | | | |
| A.O.C.— Deficiency | | | | | | | | | | | | | | | | | |
| Surplus | | | | | | | | | | | | | | | | | |
| A.V.C.— Deficiency | | | | | | | | | | | | | | | | | |
| Surplus | | | | | | | | | | | | | | | | | |
| Deficiency | | | | | | | | | | | | | | | | | |
| Surplus | | | | | | | | | | | | | | | | | |
| Deficiency | | | | | | | | | | | | | | | | | |
| Surplus | | | | | | | | | | | | | | | | | |

Remarks :—

Lt. Col. Signature of Commander.

1/1st Lowland Fd. Amb. Reserve (T.F.) Unit.

52nd Division Formation to which attached.

30 August 1918 Date of Despatch.

(16523.) Wt. W6016—PP 1432. 1,500m. 3/18. D & S. (E1256) Forms B213/8.

[P.T.O.

Sept 1918 13

Vol XL

War Diary Vol 6

of

1/1st Lowland Field Ambulance RAMC

from 1/9/18 to 30/9/18



[illegible] Lieut Col
OC 1/1st LFA RAMC(T)

469 Army Form C. 2118.

Instructions regarding War Diaries and Intelligence Summaries are contained in F. S. Regs., Part II. and the Staff Manual respectively. Title pages will be prepared in manuscript.

# WAR DIARY

or

# ~~INTELLIGENCE SUMMARY.~~

(Erase heading not required.)

1/1st Lowland Field Ambulance
52nd Lowland Division

| Place | Date | Hour | Summary of Events and Information | Remarks and references to Appendices |
|---|---|---|---|---|
| T1 d 2 3 Sh 61B. | 1/9/18 | | Bearer party sent out last night consisting of 1 Off Capt BURTON N. & 68 O.R. & were sent as follows: 3 N.C.Os & 12 bearers to ~~4th~~ Battns 156th Bde 1 Sgt. & 52 O.R. to A.D.S. to report & await instructions from Capt BURTON. | |
| | | 1130 | Received ADMS SR 209 of even date to move my H.Q. forthwith to T14 a or b & report exact coordinates to his office on completion. Transport also to move. | |
| T14 b 51 Sh 51B | | 1600 | Arrived at present site at 1530 with unit & transport. Marching out strength as under: | |

| Chaplain | RAMC Off | RAMC O.R. | ASC HT | ASC MT | Horses H.D. | Horses L.D. | Wagons 2 axle | Wagons 1 axle | Ambulance Motor | Cycle Motor | Cycles |
|---|---|---|---|---|---|---|---|---|---|---|---|
| 1※ | 3 | 30 | ‡32 | 4‡ | 17 | 17 | 12φ | 4 | 1 | nil | 1 |

※ & Batman
φ includes train wagon
‡ 1 left on 14 days leave to U.K. before unit marched out.

Sent 1 Water cart (full) to report to A.D.S. T23 a 57 for use of O.C. & bearers 1/1st Lowland Fld. Amb.
Notified ADMS & O.C. train the exact coordinate of this HQ & transport.
Received R.H.M.C. O.O. No 15 d/1/9/18.

JWL

| Place | Date | Hour | Summary of Events and Information | Remarks and references to Appendices |
|---|---|---|---|---|
| T14 b 51 Sh 57B | 2/9/18 | | Ambulance motor car rejoined unit from post at Cross Roads N33 d 39, when the 157th Bde had moved out from HENIN HILL. There were about 60 casualties during the night among troops of 56th Div. (who had moved there from the line last night) from A.E. bombs & the car proved very useful in getting these to C.M.D.S. | |

470 Army Form C. 2118.

Instructions regarding War Diaries and Intelligence Summaries are contained in F. S. Regs., Part II. and the Staff Manual respectively. Title pages will be prepared in manuscript.

# WAR DIARY
or
~~INTELLIGENCE SUMMARY.~~

(Erase heading not required.)

1/1st Lowland Field Ambulance
52nd (Lowland) Division.

| Place | Date | Hour | Summary of Events and Information | Remarks and references to Appendices |
|---|---|---|---|---|
| T 14. b 5.1 | 2/9/18 (Contd) | | Prepared to move to neighbourhood of T 22 a 5.7 N. side of the road in accordance with A.D.M.S. instructions received this forenoon. | |
| T 22 b 2 8 | 2/9/18 | 1700 | Moved to present location this afternoon at 1400. Site at T 22 a 5.7 was on top of hill & would be very cold for the horses standing in the wind. Present site is in a dip & better sheltered from wind besides having a good entrance for transport from the road which is sunken. Collected 12 unserviceable stretchers from area about U 19 d & forwarded them to A.D.S. of 1/2nd L.F.A in U 20 d in accordance with A.D.M.S. instructions. | |
| | | 1730 | Received order from A.D.M.S. to send 2 cars at once + 2 horsed ambulances to A.D.S. 1/2nd L.F.A.; Complied. This makes 6 ambulance motor cars of 1/1st L.F.A on detached duty with 1/2nd L.F.A. at A.D.S. Major MACKENZIE reported back from 1/3rd L.F.A. (Corps M.D.S.) for duty with this unit | JWL |
| T22 b 2 8 | 3/9/18 | | Tested samples of water sent by A.D.M.S. from wells at T 24. a 7.5 & T 28. c 8.7. for poisons & for amount of chlorine required for sterilization. Notified Divisional Water Officer of the result viz. both free from metallic poisons: former requires 1 measure & the latter 2 measures of bleaching powder per 100 gallons. | |
| U 20 d 5 5. | 3/9/18 | 1400 | Moved Ambulance H.Q. & transport lines to this site in the forenoon in accordance with A.D.M.S instructions in W 551 of same date. Find it very difficult to move with only | |

D. D. & L., London, E.C. (A8001) Wt. W1771/M2031 750,000 5/17 Sch. 52 Forms/C2118/14

Instructions regarding War Diaries and Intelligence Summaries are contained in F. S. Regs., Part II. and the Staff Manual respectively. Title pages will be prepared in manuscript.

# WAR DIARY

~~or~~

~~INTELLIGENCE~~ ~~SUMMARY.~~

(Erase heading not required.)

471 Army Form C. 2118.

1/1st Lowland Field Ambulance
52nd (Lowland) Division

| Place | Date | Hour | Summary of Events and Information | Remarks and references to Appendices |
|---|---|---|---|---|
| U20 d 55 Sh 51B BULLECOURT | 3/9/18 (Contd) | | 1 horsed & 1 motor ambulance available for transporting the material to be carried additional to that for which the establishment was meant. We have now to carry 200 blankets & a varying number of extra stretchers for which there is no horse transport on the establishment. These have to be dumped and brought forward later unless the motor ambulances are available. It takes two motor ambulances to move the M.T. stores alone, eg. tyres, petrol, lubricating oil, etc. Wrote A.D.M.S. asking if I could have 2 of the motor ambulances of this Fld Amb kept at my disposal for possible move forward [illegible] of A.D.S. personnel & equipment by this Fld Amb. Visited QUEANT & A.D.S. 1/2nd L.F.A. J.W.L. | |
| U20 d 55 Sh 51B. | 4/9/18 | | A.D.M.S. replies to my letter that he considers 1 motor ambulance wagon sufficient for this unit in the meantime. To-day has been spent by personnel of this unit in salving material lying round about. Have brought in 2 wheeled stretcher carriages & a quantity of German Ambulance stores including 5 boxes for inhalation of oxygen with masks & oxygen cylinder complete, bandages woven from brown paper, & paper pulp absorbent dressings, antitetanic serum, etc. Enemy shelled neighbouring areas & back to CROISSILLES this afternoon with his long range guns. The usual bombing raids were made by enemy last night but no missiles fell in this camp. Reconnoitred direct road to QUEANT. J.W.L. | |

D. D. & L., London, E.C.
(A8001) Wt. W1771/M2031 750,000 5/17 Sch. 52 Forms/C2118/14

472

Army Form C. 2118.

Instructions regarding War Diaries and Intelligence Summaries are contained in F. S. Regs., Part II. and the Staff Manual respectively. Title pages will be prepared in manuscript.

# WAR DIARY

~~or~~

~~INTELLIGENCE SUMMARY.~~

*(Erase heading not required.)*

1/1st Lowland Field Ambulance
52nd (Lowland) ~~Division~~

| Place | Date | Hour | Summary of Events and Information | Remarks and references to Appendices |
|---|---|---|---|---|
| U 20 d 5.5 Sheet 57B | 5/9/18 | | A.D.S. 1/2nd LFA at QUEANT received some shells last night among their transport & lost some 10 horses killed & wounded besides one A.S.C. Driver killed. The whole of the transport of 1/2nd L.F.A. was in the open west of QUEANT town on site to which the A.D.S. & HQ of that unit moved on morning of 3rd inst from W of BULLECOURT. One riding horse & 4 of the 6 draught horses attached temporarily with the 2 horsed ambulances & 1 water cart from 1/1st L.F.A. stampeded. One draught horse was recovered this morning by S/Sgt Search A.S.C. of this ambulance transport among some artillery horses passing this camp on watering parade. The riding horse & the 3 other draught horses have not yet been found in spite of diligent search by this ambulance transport personnel. The H.Q., A.D.S. & transport lines of 1/2nd L.F.A. have now moved back to NOREUIL & are situated in C 10 c 91 Sheet 57c<br>Visited H.Q. 156th Bde to see Capt BURTON, O.C. bearers 1/1st L.F.A. He is at present situated in dugouts in sunken road at D1 a 4.9. with his bearers & close to Bde H.Q. He informed me that the arrangement of bearer officers & bearers with 156th Bde had worked very well indeed, & that B.G.C was well pleased with the evacuation arrangements so far as bearers were concerned. Considerable difficulty, however, had arisen in finding the A.D.S. owing to frequent moves of the A.D.S. under arrangement of 1/2nd L.F.A. Although the O.C. 1/2nd L.F.A. notified A.D.M.S. of his moves of A.D.S. ~~forwards~~ & backwards the | |

D. D. & L., London, E.C.
(A8001) Wt. W1771/M2031 750,000 5/17 Sch. 52 Forms/C2118/14

Instructions regarding War Diaries and Intelligence Summaries are contained in F. S. Regs., Part II. and the Staff Manual respectively. Title pages will be prepared in manuscript.

# WAR DIARY
or
~~INTELLIGENCE SUMMARY.~~
(Erase heading not required.)

473 Army Form C. 2118.

1/1st Lowland Field Ambulance
52nd (Lowland) Division

| Place | Date | Hour | Summary of Events and Information | Remarks and references to Appendices |
|---|---|---|---|---|
| U20 d 55 Sheet 51B | 5/9/18 Contd. | | information took hours to filter down through D.H.Q. & B.H.Q. to Bearer Officers with result that cases would be sent to A.D.S. only to find that it had moved. In addition to the runners supplied by this ambulance to 156th Bde H.Q. to form the connecting link with Bearer Officer, he had also found it necessary to keep 2 or 3 of his bearers employed in finding out & keeping in touch with the peripatetic A.D.S. New C.M.D.S. opens at U25 central at 9 a.m. to-day for walking wounded only: lying cases to be sent to T.1.c.5.5. as before. Received R.A.M.C. O.O. No. 15 of even date to move ambulance to T14d on relief by 2/1st London F.A + S.R. 213/1 to send 12 horses to 1/2nd L.F.A. at C.10.c.9.1 on completion of move of 1/1st Lowland F.A. transport. Had moved M.T. stores by 2 motor ambulances when I received A.D.M.S. W610 to cancel R.A.M.C.O.O. + SR 213/1 [initials] | |
| U20 d 55 Sheet 51B | 6/9/18 | | Sent Capt A.D. DOWNES to be temporarily attached to 1/2nd Lowland F.A at NOREUIL in accordance with A.D.M.S. W615 received late last night. 4 Ambulances (motor) of 1/1st Lowland F.A are at present with 1/2nd L.F.A. + also 2 horsed ambulances complete + 1 Water cart complete (for use of bearers with 156th Bde). Submitted the names of the following N.C.Os + men of this unit to A.D.M.S. for consideration with a view to immediate award for Gallantry in action during | |

D. D. & L., London, E.C. (A8001) Wt. W1771/M2031 750,000 5/17 Sch. 52 Forms/C2118/14

Instructions regarding War Diaries and Intelligence Summaries are contained in F. S. Regs., Part II. and the Staff Manual respectively. Title pages will be prepared in manuscript.

# WAR DIARY
or
~~INTELLIGENCE SUMMARY.~~
(Erase heading not required.)

474 Army Form C. 2118.

1/1st Lowland Field Ambulance
52nd (Lowland) Division

| Place | Date | Hour | Summary of Events and Information | Remarks and references to Appendices |
|---|---|---|---|---|
| U 20 d 5.5. Sh. 51B | 6/9/18 (Contd) | | the advance 24th - 27th August:- 316229 Sgt. McGREGOR J.; 22891 Cpl EDWARDS, J. 316235 Pte MACARTNEY, J. Received A.D.M.S. letter MO/112 ~~of even date~~ d/5/9/18 that Capt A.D. DOWNES was granted leave & might proceed as soon as possible out of my allotment. Wrote O.C. 1/2nd Lowland F.A. requesting him to instruct Capt A.D. DOWNES to report to-morrow to this HQ. Detailed 1 N.C.O. + 2 men to relieve similar party of 2/2nd London F.A. at Field Amb site BLAIRVILLE X4a in accordance with A.D.M.S. W618 of even date. J.W.L. | |
| Sh. B3.b.5.0 Sheet 57C | 7/9/18 | | Received R.A.M.C. OO No 16 d/6/9/18 at 0200 this morning. In accordance therewith I instructed the two horsed ambulances of this unit presently attached to 1/2nd Lowland Field Amb to report at once to H.Q. 155 Bde C.6.b.5.5. + H.Q. 156th Bde D.1.a.3.2. respectively to accompany these Bdes to concentration bivouacs in Corps Reserve. Moved HQ + transport of this Ambulance at 0800 to present site. March formation in column of 3s instead of in 4s as formerly. Capt A.D. DOWNES reported back from 1/2nd Lowland F.A. & proceeds to-day on 14 days leave to U.K. sailing on 9th inst. Set the personnel to work immediately to collect corrugated iron, wood, etc. from the trenches in the neighbourhood for the purpose of erecting bomb-protection - revetments for horses, + for formation of kitchens latrines etc. J.W.L. | |

D. D. & L., London, E.C. (A8001) Wt. W1771/M2031 750,000 5/17 Sch. 52 Forms/C2118/14

Instructions regarding War Diaries and Intelligence Summaries are contained in F. S. Regs., Part II. and the Staff Manual respectively. Title pages will be prepared in manuscript.

# WAR DIARY

~~or~~

~~INTELLIGENCE SUMMARY.~~

(Erase heading not required.)

475 Army Form C. 2118.

1/1st Lowland Field Ambulance
52nd (Lowland) Division

| Place | Date | Hour | Summary of Events and Information | Remarks and references to Appendices |
|---|---|---|---|---|
| B,3,b,5,0 Sheet 57c | 8/9/18 | | Erection of revetments for protection against bomb splinters is proceeding satisfactorily, & salvage generally of stores & munitions is being carried out. A.D.M.S. called this forenoon. Weather wet & stormy. The corrected coordinates of this Ambulance site is B9.a.3.8. Map 57c N.W. 1/20000, & not as stated in margin. J.W.L. | |
| B9,a,3,8. Sh 57c N.W. 1/20000 | 9/9/18 | | Visited 156th Bde H.Q. & 1/7th Royal Scots & 1/7th Scot. Rifles for purpose of inspecting, & giving advice on sanitation. Personnel & transport engaged in salvage & in erection of revetments & improvised huts for kitchen, harness, fodder etc. J.W.L. | |
| do. | 10/9/18 | | Weather has been very wet & stormy, & this has interfered with the erection of earthworks & shelters. The N.C.O. & 2 men sent to Fld Amb site at BLAIRVILLE reported back to-day for duty with this unit, the site having been taken over by 150th Fld. Ambulance under authority of XVII Corps. J.W.L. | |
| do | 11/9/18 | | Enemy aeroplanes visited the area between midnight & 0100 this morning & dropped a large number of bombs without doing any damage to personnel or animals so far as is known to me. Weather still wet, stormy, & cold. J.W.L. Personnel sent to S10 d 0.5 in two lots this afternoon for bath. No conveyances to baths were available. Only about 80 could be sent at 3-4 hour instead of 150 (places allotted) as there are 40 men on leave to U.K. & 40 at 45th & 46th C.C.S.'s on detached duty. The remainder, 9, attended between 5 & 6 p.m. Forwarded Memorandum in reply to ADMS. MO/192 d 11/9 see APPENDIX I. J.W.L. | APPENDIX I |

D. D. & L., London, E.C. (A8001) Wt. W1771/M2031 750,000 5/17 Sch. 52 Forms/C2118/14

Instructions regarding War Diaries and Intelligence Summaries are contained in F. S. Regs., Part II. and the Staff Manual respectively. Title pages will be prepared in manuscript.

# WAR DIARY
or
~~INTELLIGENCE SUMMARY.~~
(Erase heading not required.)

476 Army Form C. 2118.

1/1st Lowland Field Ambulance
52nd (Lowland) Division

| Place | Date | Hour | Summary of Events and Information | Remarks and references to Appendices |
|---|---|---|---|---|
| B9a.3.8. Sh 57c NW 1/20000 | 12/9/18 | | Very heavy rain last night & to-day with high wind. A.D.M.S called at 1400 to-day to examine men sent by R.M.O.s with a view to re-classification. All the material salved by this unit have been used in building huts for kitchen, fodder & harness, & for large bomb splinter shelters for 40 horses which is nearing completion, as well as for dug-out roofs for personnel. J.S.L. | |
| do | 13/9/18 | | Heavy rain continued throughout the night but to-day weather has improved. Lobby has cleared. Visited 1/7th Scot Rifles & 1/4th Royal Scots. Former have done good work in improvising box seats for deep pit latrines but these points are not in all cases fly proof. They have also erected a large oven near Batt. H.Q. capable of roasting for at least half a battalion, & have collected a score of large brass Howitzer cartridge cases (about 9" or 10" diam) for use as ablution basins. The 1/4th R.S kitchens are good with the exception of H.Q. Officers' mess kitchen which is very dirty & insanitary & to which I drew the attention of the orderly officer. Medical equipment of the Battalions has been made up during the past week with the exception of a few unexpendable stores still to come. J.S.L. | |
| do | 14/9/18. | | The hut for the kitchen has been completed & two good ovens with fire places for | |

D. D. & L., London, E.C. (A8001) Wt. W1771/M2031 750,000 5/17 Sch. 52 Forms/C2118/14

477 Army Form C. 2118.

# WAR DIARY

~~or~~

~~INTELLIGENCE SUMMARY.~~

(Erase heading not required.)

Instructions regarding War Diaries and Intelligence Summaries are contained in F. S. Regs., Part II. and the Staff Manual respectively. Title pages will be prepared in manuscript.

1/1st Lowland Field Ambulance
52nd (Lowland) Division

| Place | Date | Hour | Summary of Events and Information | Remarks and references to Appendices |
|---|---|---|---|---|
| B9 a 3 8.<br>Sh. 57c N.W. | 14/9/18<br>(Contd) | | Camp Kettles made. Bomb-protection revetments have been completed round a standing ~~suppo~~ capable of giving protection to 40 horses. J.W.L. | |
| do | 15/9/18. | | Received R.A.M.C. O.O. No. 17 d/14 9/18 instructing 1/1st Lowland Field Ambulance to take over A.D.S. at D1 d 6.8 from 2/2nd Wessex Field Ambulance & be responsible for evacuation from Collecting Posts & to the Corps Main Dressing Station. Relief to be completed by 2 p.m on 16th Inst. Called at 156th Bde H.Q. & arranged to detail 1 N.C.O. 5 bearers & 1 horsed Ambulance wagon to report to-morrow respectively to 1/7th Scot. Rifles at 0830, 1/4th Royal Scots at 0930, & 1/7th Royal Scots at 1030, the ambulance wagons to report to H.Q. 1/1st Lowland Field Ambulance at D1 d 6.8 on completion of moves of battalions. Visited A.D.S. at D1 d 6.8 & arranged about taking over to-morrow & to have guides at A.D.S. at 0900 to-morrow to conduct Bearers Officers & bearers of Bde (157th) taking over left subsection of Divisional line. The Officer & Bearers for Bde (155th) taking over the right section (or subsection?) of the line are taking over the Aid Posts there this morning. J.W.L. | |
| D1 d 6 8<br>Sh. 57c NE<br>1/20000 | 16/9/18 | | Moved advanced Dressing Station tent subdivision & equipment to A.D.S. by 0830 to-day & proceeded round R.A.P.s in left section, which were relieved during the forenoon. Relieved the car posts by 1100, & took over the A.D.S. at 1400 in accordance with instructions in R.A.M.C. O.O. No 17. As trolley used on light railway between D11 c 6.0 & D9 d 4.2 (near right car post) had been removed by Artillery units yesterday I moved the right | |

D. D. & L., London, E.C. (A8001) Wt. W1771/M2031 750,000 5/17 Sch. 52 Forms/C2118/14

Instructions regarding War Diaries and Intelligence Summaries are contained in F. S. Regs., Part II. and the Staff Manual respectively. Title pages will be prepared in manuscript.

# WAR DIARY
or
~~INTELLIGENCE SUMMARY.~~
(Erase heading not required.)

478 Army Form C. 2118.

1/1st Lowland Field Ambulance
52nd Lowland Division

| Place | Date | Hour | Summary of Events and Information | Remarks and references to Appendices |
|---|---|---|---|---|
| D1 d 68 Sh. 57c NE 1/20000 | 16/9/18 (Contd) | | car post forward from the latter point to D11 c 5.0. Notified A.D.M.S. & O.C. Bearer 155th Bde of the change. In accordance with instructions of A.D.M.S. Capt. SCOTT-WILSON R.A.M.C. reported to me for duty to-night from 1/3rd L.F.A. (Corps Main Dressing Station). Capt. J.M. MORGAN R.A.M.C. also reported to-night as a reinforcement in accordance with instructions of A.D.M.S. Stationed 1 N.C.O. 4 men & a horsed ambulance wagon at the Quarry V28 c 8.5 (Sh 57B SE 1/20000) for evacuation of cases from Support Bde (156th) & neighbouring units. J.Y.L. | |
| do. | 17/9/18 Contd | | Severe storm of lightning & rain between midnight & 2 a.m. this morning. Bombs were dropped on surrounding areas from 9 p.m. last night & there was considerable heavy artillery activity on both sides. Personnel are set to work to clean up the camp, make revetments for protection of the transport against bomb splinters & a beginning is made with a plan of turning one of the damaged huts into a hut for treating gassed cases on plan undernoted. | |

+ Gassed clothing thrown here after undressing in verandah

Entrance → [Part of hut destroyed by shell fire.] [Verandah] [Baths for Other Ranks] [Baths for officers] [Corridor] [Clean Clothing Room] [Dressing Room] [MEDICAL INSPECTION ROOM] → Exit

A. Window for orderly to hand out fresh clothing or pyjamas & ~~[illegible]~~
B. ditto for other ranks
C. Door into clothing store

X Gassed clothing thrown here after undressing in verandah. J.Y.L.

D. D. & L., London, E.C. (A8004) Wt. W1771/M2 31 750,000 5/17 Sch. 52 Forms/C2118/14

Instructions regarding War Diaries and Intelligence Summaries are contained in F. S. Regs., Part II. and the Staff Manual respectively. Title pages will be prepared in manuscript.

# WAR DIARY
*or*
# ~~INTELLIGENCE SUMMARY.~~
(*Erase heading not required.*)

477

Army Form C. 2118.

1/1st Lowland Field Ambulance
52nd Lowland Division

| Place | Date | Hour | Summary of Events and Information | Remarks and references to Appendices |
|---|---|---|---|---|
| D1 d 6.8. Sh. 57c NE 1/20000 | 18/9/18 | | Received over 100 wounded from 6 p.m. last night till 9 a.m. this morning including 11 Officers. Three of the officers died shortly after being brought to the Advanced Dressing Station one of them being Capt K.M. ROSS R.A.M.C. M.O. i/c 1/5th H.L.I. Sent Capt Scott Wilson through the night to do duty temporarily with 1/5th H.L.I. in place of Capt. ROSS. Lt Col MACDONALD & Major BELL of 4th Canadian Field Amb called this forenoon to arrange taking over of posts of left section of line by 2nd Canadian Div to-morrow night. Major LOMER D.A.D.M.S. 2nd Canadian Division called in early afternoon in connection with this matter also. Owing to the heavy rain during the night & to fresh shell holes the road from Right Car post at D11 c 5.0 could not be used by Motor ambulances after 0600 this morning & Car post was moved back to old position at D9 d 4.3. I have stationed a horsed ambulance wagon in lee of the slope S of about D17 a 9.5 to convey wounded from right section down to Right car post. | |
| do. | 19/9/18. | | PRONVILLE<br>Received A.D.M.S. SR/222 of even date that Canadian Corps is taking over Left Sector XVII Corps on night 19th/20th, this ambulance to conduct A.D.S. at its present location & to continue to evacuate from Right Section. a holding party of 4th Canadian Fld Amb being located at A.D.S. but not to take over. Received also A.D.M.S. SR 222 further to above ~~that~~ to reconnoitre ground for my transport S. of new Division boundary & report to him by 11 A.M. to-morrow. Left Post car was hit by high explosive on way down at 1900 & patients, driver & car orderly all more or less seriously wounded. One of the patients in the car died of wounds then received. J.W.L.<br>Reconnoitred ground as instructed & recommended to A.D.M.S. suitable ground available at C 18 b 5.4 | |

A7092. Wt W12839/M1293. 750,000. 1/17. D. D & L., Ltd. Forms/C2118/14.

Instructions regarding War Diaries and Intelligence Summaries are contained in F. S. Regs., Part II. and the Staff Manual respectively. Title pages will be prepared in manuscript.

# WAR DIARY
or
~~INTELLIGENCE SUMMARY.~~
(Erase heading not required.)

480 Army Form C. 2118.

1/1st Lowland Field Ambulance
52nd (Lowland) Division

| Place | Date | Hour | Summary of Events and Information | Remarks and references to Appendices |
|---|---|---|---|---|
| D1 d 6 8 Sh. 57c N.E. | 19/9/18 Contd. | | Sick & wounded passed through A.D.S. between midday yesterday & midday to-day were as follows<br>Sick 52nd Div. Off 3, O.R. 34; Others 3, 7. Wounded 52nd Div. Off 2, O.R. 111; Others –, 9. Total Sick & Wounded Off 8, O.R. 161<br>Capt Palmer C.A.M.C. called to-day with reference to taking over from this Field Ambulance tonight relief is to be completed by 9 p.m. to-night.<br>A second motor ambulance has been hit by enemy shell whilst standing at the left car post at INCHY this afternoon. A fresh car was sent out at 3-30 to take up duty in its place. Asked for use of 3 motor ambulances to-night till 0900 to-morrow & received them from 1/3rd L.F.A. In consequence of wire from 155 Bde HQ no. Bm 2000 d/19 9/18 time 2012 & A.D.M.S. minute Mo/329 appended sent for 2 motor ambulances 1/2nd L.F.A. to send to the place given viz. D10.c.6.4. as urgently requiring these. Lt Col ANDERSON 13th Canadian Fld Amb. called this afternoon. Left car post & posts in left section were taken over by 4th Canadian Fld Ambulance who will evacuate their cases to A.D.S. at CAGNICOURT. Motor ambulance & personnel of 1/1st Lowland Fld Amb. will remain at left car post till to-morrow. JwK | |
| do | 20/9/18 | | Received a wire at 0430 from Staff Capt. 155th Bde asking if ambulance could be sent to 155 Bde H.Q. for body of Lt Col GIBBONS. Replied in the negative as all the ambulances including the 5 got last night from 1/2nd & 1/3rd ambulances were busy evacuating cases between car post, A.D.S., & C.M.D.S. When things quietened about 0800 | |

A5092 Wt W12839/M1293 750,000. 1/17. D. D & L., Ltd. Forms/C2118/14.

Instructions regarding War Diaries and Intelligence Summaries are contained in F. S. Regs., Part II. and the Staff Manual respectively. Title pages will be prepared in manuscript.

# WAR DIARY

*or*

~~INTELLIGENCE SUMMARY.~~

*(Erase heading not required.)*

481 Army Form C. 2118.

1/1st Lowland Field Ambulance
52nd (Lowland) Division

| Place | Date | Hour | Summary of Events and Information | Remarks and references to Appendices |
|---|---|---|---|---|
| V1 d 68 Sh 57c NE | 20/9/18 (Cont'd) | | I sent a note to driver of Horsed Ambulance at D17 a 9.5 to call at 155 Bde HQ when relieved in early forenoon & bring down body of Lt Col GIBBONS to cemetery near A.D.S. but car orderly on reporting stated that body had been taken down before he got to 155 Bde HQ. Ambulance car & personnel from left car post reported back at A.D.S. this morning on relief by 4th Canadian F.A. party. Withdrew horsed ambulance & personnel from Quarry Post, V28 c 8.5 Sh 51B SE, this forenoon on learning that 156th Bde had moved from that area. No intimation had been received by me from Bde HQ of the intended move. Received A.D.M.S. letter S.R/225 of even date that 156th Bde would relieve 155th Bde to-night & sent Capt BURTON to report to Bde HQ & act as Bearer Officer about 2 p.m. He would have 58 O.R. as bearers including 20 O.R. of 1/2nd L.F.A. attached as a temporary measure by A.D.M.S. instructions. | |
| | | | Sick & wounded passed through A.D.S. for 24 hours ending 1200 to-day:- | |

| Sick | Off | OR | Wounded | Off | OR | Total | Off | OR |
|---|---|---|---|---|---|---|---|---|
| 52nd Div | | 35 | 52nd Div | 6 | 142 | | 6 | 177 |
| Other Formations | 1 | 6 | O.F. | – | 15 | | 1 | 21 |

J.W.L.

| Place | Date | Hour | Summary of Events and Information | Remarks and references to Appendices |
|---|---|---|---|---|
| | | 2000 | Received 156th Inf Bde Order No. ~~[illegible]~~ 56 d/20 9/18. | |
| do | 21/9/18 | | Visited 156th Bde HQ & went into medical arrangements with O.C. Bearers. Reported to A.D.M.S. the distribution of R.A.Ps, relay posts, ambulance car & wagon posts & personnel; & also the new posts formed. The 20 bearers of 1/2nd L.F.A. were withdrawn to-night by | |

Instructions regarding War Diaries and Intelligence Summaries are contained in F. S. Regs., Part II. and the Staff Manual respectively. Title pages will be prepared in manuscript.

# WAR DIARY ~~or~~ ~~INTELLIGENCE SUMMARY.~~

(Erase heading not required.)

482 Army Form C. 2118.

1/1st Lowland Field Ambulance
52nd (Lowland) Division

| Place | Date | Hour | Summary of Events and Information | Remarks and references to Appendices |
|---|---|---|---|---|
| D1d68 57c NE | 21/9/18 (Contd) | | order of A.D.M.S. All available fit men at this HQ including officers servants and men who had returned to-day from leave were sent out to replace them & by this means Capt Burton's party of bearers was made up to 51 O.R. Distribution is as in APPENDIX II. Sick & wounded passed through A.D.S. for 24 hours ending 1200 to-day. | APPENDIX II |

| Sick | Off | OR | Wounded | Off | OR | Total | Off | OR |
|---|---|---|---|---|---|---|---|---|
| 52nd Div | 1 | 13 | 52nd Div | 2 | 58 | 52nd Div | 3 | 71 |
| Other Formations | – | 10 | O.F. | – | 10 | O.F. | – | 20 |

J.W.L.

| Place | Date | Hour | Summary of Events and Information | Remarks and references to Appendices |
|---|---|---|---|---|
| do | 22/9/18 | | Hut for treating Gassed cases was completed to-day by the pioneers of this unit & is in use. A.D.M.S. 2nd Canadian Division & party visited this A.D.S. this forenoon. 157th Bde are taking over line to-night on right of 156th Bde from about E20.c.3.3 to E26c8.0 & will evacuate wounded through relay posts of 156th Bde to this A.D.S. The Aid Post at E19a83 has been made a combined Aid Post & Relay Post (No 5) & will be reinforced by 8 bearers of 1/2nd L.F.A. Similarly Relay Post No. 2 will be reinforced by 4 more bearers of 1/2nd L.F.A. as a reserve. Sent up 20 blankets 10 ground sheets & 10 sheets of pluvinine to-night for use of patients being carried down, & placed an extra car at the car post D15b55 & an extra ambulance at the horsed ambulance post at D.17.a.9.5. Sick & wounded passed through A.D.S. for 24 hours ending 1200 to-day:— | |

| Sick | Off | OR | Wounded | Off | OR | Total | Off | OR |
|---|---|---|---|---|---|---|---|---|
| 52nd Div | – | 25 | 52nd Div | 6 | 117 | 52nd Div | 6 | 142 |
| Other Formations | – | 9 | O.F. | 1 | 8 | O.F. | 1 | 17 |

J.W.L.

D. D. & L., London E.C. (10340) Wt W5300/P713 750,000 3/18 E 688 Forms/C2118/16.

483 Army Form C. 2118.

# WAR DIARY
or
~~INTELLIGENCE SUMMARY.~~
(Erase heading not required.)

Instructions regarding War Diaries and Intelligence Summaries are contained in F. S. Regs., Part II. and the Staff Manual respectively. Title pages will be prepared in manuscript.

1/1st Lowland Field Ambulance
52nd (Lowland) Division

| Place | Date | Hour | Summary of Events and Information | Remarks and references to Appendices |
|---|---|---|---|---|
| D1 d 68 57c NE | 23/9/18 | | Sick & wounded passed through A.D.S. for 24 hours ending 1200 to-day:- | |
| | | | Sick: 52nd Div — Off –, O.R. 17; Other Formations — Off –, O.R. 10. Wounded: 52nd Div — Off 38 (O.R.); O.F. — Off –, O.R. 14. Total: 52nd Division — Off –, O.R. 55; Other Formation — Off –, O.R. 24 | |
| | | | to let me have 20 O.R. from 1/2nd L.F.A. to-morrow | |
| | | | A.D.M.S called this morning & promised for fatigue work necessary in this camp while personnel of this unit were so busy owing to so many being on detached duty. No men can be sent on leave to U.K. at present as every fit man is required for duty. J.W.L. | |
| do | 24/9/18 | | Sick & wounded passed through A.D.S for 24 hours ending 1200 to day:- | |
| | | | Sick: 52nd Div — Off –, O.R. 32; Other Formations — Off –, O.R. 7. Wounded: 52nd Div — Off –, O.R. 24; Other Formations — Off 1, O.R. 5. Total: 52nd Div — Off –, O.R. 56; O.F. — Off 1, O.R. 12 | |
| | | | 1 N.C.O. & 20 men reported from 1/2nd L.F.A for temporary duty for to-day with this unit & did useful fatigue work filling in old German latrines about camp. 155th Bde took over from 156th Bde in the line last night & Bearer Officers Capt J.W. BURTON & his bearers reported back in camp this morning. J.W.L. | |
| do. | 25/9/18 | | Detailed Capt J.M MORGAN to report to O.C. 1/7th Royal Scots to day for temporary duty as M.O. vice Lt GALLAGHER MRC USA sick to hospital | |
| | | | Sick & wounded passed through this A.D.S for 24 hours ending 1200 to-day | |
| | | | Sick: 52nd Div — Off –, O.R. 23; Other Formation — Off 0, O.R. 16. Wounded: 52nd Div — Off 1, O.R. 38; O.F. — Off 0, O.R. 5. Total: 52nd Div — Off 4, O.R. 61; O.F. — Off 0, O.R. 21 | |

D. D. & L., London E.C.
(10340) W1 W5300/P713 750,000 3/18 E 688 Forms/C2118/16

484 Army Form C. 2118.

Instructions regarding War Diaries and Intelligence Summaries are contained in F. S. Regs., Part II. and the Staff Manual respectively. Title pages will be prepared in manuscript.

# WAR DIARY
or
# ~~INTELLIGENCE~~ SUMMARY.

(*Erase heading not required.*)

1/1st Lowland Field Ambulance
52nd (Lowland) Division

| Place | Date | Hour | Summary of Events and Information | Remarks and references to Appendices |
|---|---|---|---|---|
| D1 d 6.8. 57c N.E. | 25/9/18 (Contd) | | Reconnoitred road through D15 b, 16 c, + 22 b + d as far as it was practicable for (a) motor ambulances + (b) horsed ambulances in accordance with instructions of A.D.M.S. received by wire at 2130 last night + reported to him by 1200 to-day that it was practicable for motor ambulances in dry weather — by a track only — from D22 d as far as D30 a 5.0 + thence by fair road to BAPAUME - CAMBRAI road; also reported that road through D15 b + d, 21 b + d to junction with LAGNICOURT Road at J3 a 4.2 was practicable for motor ambulances for evacuation via LAGNICOURT to C.M.D.S. in U 25. Received to-night R.A.M.C. O.O. No 18. from which it appeared that 52nd Div would carry out operations at a date to be notified later + that O.C. 1/1st L.F.A. would be in charge of present A.D.S. at D1 d 5.9 + present car posts, + that left A.D.S. would close at D1 d 5.9 at 9 a.m. on 26/9/18 + open at D15 b 5.5 at same hour on 26/9/18. Detailed Capt J.W. BURTON to report to 156th Bde HQ. at 2.30 p.m. to day as Bearer Officer with that Bde + to take his Bearer subdivisions with him. | |
| D15 b 5.0. | 26/9/18 | | Sent tent subdivision personnel (1 tent subdivision with 1 officer) with equipment + 50 stretchers + other material in W.D. wagon + motor ambulance wagons to open new A.D.S. at site fixed viz. D15 b 5.0 (handed over for walking wounded to) Dressing station at D1 d 5.9 to O.C. 13th Canadian Field Ambulance. Had sent back transport except water carts + horsed ambulances + I proceeded to new A.D.S. after ... to C11 c 7.6. Major Mackenzie | |

D. D. & L., London E.C
(10340) Wt W5300/P713 750,000 3/18 E 688 Forms/C2118/16.

Instructions regarding War Diaries and Intelligence Summaries are contained in F. S. Regs., Part II. and the Staff Manual respectively. Title pages will be prepared in manuscript.

# WAR DIARY
~~or~~
# ~~INTELLIGENCE~~ SUMMARY.

*(Erase heading not required.)*

485 Army Form C. 2118.

1/1st Lowland Field Ambulance
52nd (Lowland) Division

| Place | Date | Hour | Summary of Events and Information | Remarks and references to Appendices |
|---|---|---|---|---|
| D15 b 5.0 Sh 57c | 26/9/18 (Contd) | | handing over, leaving the Q.M. (Capt. REID) and the chaplain (Rev. ARCHd MAIN C.F.) at the transport lines ~~still~~ on account of the want of ~~accommod~~ accommodation at new A.D.S. which was very much crowded out by the reserve Bn. of 63rd Div who had come in there last night. Owing to the congestion of the area the A.D.S. was not in operation until 1200. & the few cases which did come down were passed on to 13th Canadian Field ambulance at D1 d 5.4 by arrangement made with OC that ambulance, & notified by me to A.D.M.S. JWL | |
| do | 27/9/18 | | Sent situation report to A.D.M.S. at 0500 that things had been quiet so far as number of cases coming in was concerned. Total with wounded from time of opening until 0500 had only amounted to 35. Zero hour was 0520 to-day & cases poured down all day. Quite a large number of stretcher cases (both British & German troops) were carried down by German prisoners & this led to a temporary shortage of stretchers at the A.D.S. owing to the number of cases at the A.D.S. occupying stretchers. At 1700 there were still 200 patients on stretchers of whom 100 were wounded Germans. We had to send on a large number without taking note of them; but those we did manage to take a note of numbered 850 up to 7 pm to-night. Lt J.K. GUTHRIE M.R.C. USA reported about 0730 this morning for temporary duty with this unit. JWL | |

D. D. & L., London E.C.
(10346) Wt W5300/P713 750,000 3/18 E 688 Forms/C2118/16.

486 Army Form C. 2118.

# WAR DIARY
or
~~INTELLIGENCE~~ SUMMARY.
(*Erase heading not required.*)

Instructions regarding War Diaries and Intelligence Summaries are contained in F. S. Regs., Part II. and the Staff Manual respectively. Title pages will be prepared in manuscript.

1/1st Lowland Field Ambulance
52nd (Lowland) Division

| Place | Date | Hour | Summary of Events and Information | Remarks and references to Appendices |
|---|---|---|---|---|
| D15 b 5.0 Sh 57c 1/20000 | 28/9/18 | | Details by Divisions of wounded recorded & given Field medical card, during daylight on 27th Sept are as follows - | |
| | | | Off. / O.R. | |
| | | | 52nd Div 12 / 160 | |
| | | | 63rd 16 / 514 | |
| | | | 57th - / 12 | |
| | | | Corps Troops 3 / 22 | |
| | | | Artillery unit 2 / 23 | |
| | | | Canadians - / 62 | |
| | | | Total 33 / 793 Grand total = 859 [sic] | |
| | | | German Wounded Off. & O.R. recorded on card 33. | |
| | | | I estimate that at least 500 more were fed & passed on unrecorded as their wounds were already satisfactorily dressed. Many walking wounded were sent down unrecorded in the earlier part of the day by commandeered returning empty motor wagons - an orderly being sent with each wagon load to C.M.D.S. At 5 p.m. I informed A.D.M.S. by telephone that there were 230 cases still awaiting evacuation of whom 200 were stretcher cases occupying stretchers & 100 of these stretcher cases were German wounded. All British wounded were cleared to C.M.D.S. by 0100 this morning & the last of the German wounded were cleared by 04.00 this morning. I reported by telephone to A.D.M.S. at that hour that my A.D.S. was now clear. JWL. | |

D. D. & L., London E.C
(10340) Wt W5300/P713 750,000 3/18 E 688 Forms/C2118/16.

Instructions regarding War Diaries and Intelligence Summaries are contained in F. S. Regs., Part II. and the Staff Manual respectively. Title pages will be prepared in manuscript.

# WAR DIARY
*or*
# ~~INTELLIGENCE SUMMARY.~~
*(Erase heading not required.)*

487

Army Form C. 2118.

1/1st Lowland Field Ambulance
52nd (Lowland) Division

| Place | Date | Hour | Summary of Events and Information | Remarks and references to Appendices |
|---|---|---|---|---|
| D 15 b 5 0<br>Sh. 57c 1/20000 | 29/9/18 | | Reconnoitred site for new camp of this Ambulance which is to move to-day to the vicinity of D 28 b + d or D 29 a + c. Chose a position in D 29 C | |
| D 29 C 8 5 | " | 1615 | Moved into this site at 1300 to-day with personnel of this ambulance (less 2 tent subdivisions + 2 bearer subdivisions) + transport. Transport lines located in D 29 C 7 8. Notified new location to ADMS + to O.C. Divisional Train. Marching out strength as under:- | |

| Chaplain | RAMC Off | RAMC O.R. | ASC H.T. | ASC M.T. | HORSES L.D. | HORSES H.D. | HORSES Riders | WAGONS 4 wheel | WAGONS 2 wheel | MOTORS AMB CARS | MOTORS cycles | CYCLES | Wheeled stretcher carriages |
|---|---|---|---|---|---|---|---|---|---|---|---|---|---|
| 1 | 5 | 56 | 36 | 6* | 19 | 20 | 5 | 13 | 4* | 4 | 1* | 1# | 5 |

* 1 Car with driver out at Car post. 1 driver & motor cycle att ADMS., 2 cars with driver at Workshops.
3 O.R. M.T. on leave to U.K.

J.W.L.

| Place | Date | Hour | Summary of Events and Information | Remarks and references to Appendices |
|---|---|---|---|---|
| D 29 C 8 5<br>Sh. 57c 1/20000 | 30/9/18 | | Visited car post + 156th Bde HQ. Sent 1 ambulance car to Cross Roads E 28 C 2 9 at 1000 to-day to collect any sick of Bde Units. This was in response to a wire from B.HQ. received last night which asked for this to be done. Withdrew Bearer Officer + all personnel except 1 N.C.O. + 5 bearers with each Battn + 1 orderly at B.HQ. as runner. J.W.L. | |

John W. Leitch Lt Col
O.C. 1/1st Lowland Field Amb.
R.A.M.C.(T.)

D. D. & L., London E.C
(10340) Wt W5300/P713 750,000 3/18 E 688 Forms/C2118/16.

APPENDIX I VOL XL. (Sept 1918)
WAR DIARY of 1/1st LOWLAND F.D. AMBULANCE RAMC(T)

Confidential

A.D.M.S.
52 DIV/

Memorandum in accordance with your MO/192 d 11/9/18.

The ~~practical~~ tactical & other lessons to be learned from recent operations appear to me to be as follows:

(1) The A.D.S. when formed should not be hastily moved forward. It was found on more than one occasion, that although the o/c A.D.S. had notified A.D.M.S. of his intended move forward, time was not given for this information to reach bearer officers with brigades. The result was that wounded were sent to old site of A.D.S.

Considerable inconvenience might be obviated by calling forward a tent sub-division held in reserve to form a new A.D.S. in the forward area, as soon as that becomes necessary.

Wounded coming in after the new A.D.S. had ~~moved~~ formed would still be able to get attention at the site they expected.

(2) Closer co-operation with Brigade bearer officers should be observed before car relay posts are moved forward.

For example, one car relay post at cross roads at BULLECOURT moved forward in the direction of QUEANT before the left side of the line was cleared.

Cases brought to this cross roads found the car relay post gone, & had to be evacuated by commandeered returning motor lorry.

(3) Transport of a Field ambulance should not be taken to an A.D.S. Only a minimum of animals. eg. those required for water cart & horsed ambulance should be brought forward.

A.D.S. material & sufficient personnel to start A.D.S. can usually be sent forward by motor ambulances, or if the roads are impossible for ambulances owing to shell holes & it is considered advisable to form a post further forward a limber wagon can be utilised.

As regards improvements in training, organisation & equipment, I have nothing to suggest.

11/9/18

James [illegible] Lieut Col
1/1 Lowland Fd Amb
RAMC (T)

APPENDIX II Vol XL (Sept 1918)
War Diary of 1/1st Lowland Fld Ambulance RAMC(T)

Ref Maps 57c NE 1/20000

Medical arrangements for portion of 52nd Division (156th Bde in the line) on 21/9/18.

Relay Posts

No 1 D17 d 3 8. 7 bearers.

No 2 D18 c 5 8. 6 bearers 4 stretchers 11 blankets.

No 3 D18 d 2 6 (also Aid Post 7th SR) 1 NCO 9 bearers 4 stretchers 4 blankets.

No 4 E 19 a 0 9 10 bearers 7 stretchers 24 blankets

Aid Post E13 d 0 8 4th RS. 1 NCO 12 bearers 4 stretchers 6 blankets.

Aid Post E19 a 8 3 7th RS 1 NCO 6 bearers

Total Stretchers 19
Blankets 45
Bearers 53
(Plus 2 bearers who came down with later in day leaving bearers 51)

1 Horsed ambulance at D17 a 9 5

1 Motor ambulance at D15 b 5 5 (moved there to-day from former post at D9 d 4 3, S of PRONVILLE)

[illegible signature]

Oct 1918 — 25

140/3401

Vol 7

WAR DIARY

of

1/1st Lowland Field Ambulance

R.A.M.C.T.

Vol XLI

from 1/10/18

to 31/10/18

James Laird Lt Col
O.C. 1/1st L.F.A. R.A.M.C.(T)

Instructions regarding War Diaries and Intelligence Summaries are contained in F. S. Regs., Part II. and the Staff Manual respectively. Title pages will be prepared in manuscript.

# WAR DIARY

~~or~~

~~INTELLIGENCE SUMMARY.~~

(Erase heading not required.)

488 Army Form C. 2118.

1/1st Lowland Field Ambulance
52nd (Lowland) Division

| Place | Date | Hour | Summary of Events and Information | Remarks and references to Appendices |
|---|---|---|---|---|
| E28 c 5 6 Sh 57c NE | 1/10/18 | | Moved Ambulance, less 2 tent subdivisions & 3 NCOs & 15 bearers attached to Battalions 156th Bde, to this site to day in accordance with instructions in RAMC OO no 19 d/1 10/18 ADMS called in the afternoon after unit had moved in. Marching in strength as under:- | |

| Chaplain | RAMC Off | RAMC OR | ASC HT | ASC MT | Chargers | Riders | Horses LD | Horses HD | Vehicles [illegible] | Vehicles [illegible] | Motor Vehicles Ambces | Motor Vehicles Cycles | Cycle |
|---|---|---|---|---|---|---|---|---|---|---|---|---|---|
| 1 | 5 | 85 | 27 | 4.x | 4 | 2 | 19 | 20 | 4 | 13 | 2 x | 1 x | 1 |

x 4 Motor Ambulances with drivers sent to report to OC 1/2nd Lowland Fld Ambulance
1 " " in Workshop
1 Motor cycle & rider M.T. attached ADMS 3 OR M.T. on leave to U.K.

| Place | Date | Hour | Summary of Events and Information | Remarks and references to Appendices |
|---|---|---|---|---|
| | | 1930 | Visited ADS at F25 a 3 7 to see OC 1/2nd LFA who was to take it over to-day from 1/3 Field Ambulance in accordance with RAMC OO No 19 J.W.L. | |
| do | 2/10/18 | 1000 | Sent all my wheeled stretcher carriages (6 in charge of [illegible]) [illegible] motor ambulances [illegible] CANTAINGE F28 d 5 9 in response to report to OC 1/3rd LFA at car post ([illegible] A 25) to his urgent written request received at 0945. Detailed Major MACKENZIE to report to 156th Bde HQ L3 c 4 6 as Bearer Officer immediately after breakfast & to report to [illegible] Bde HQ at 0900 to bring [illegible] of Bde Unit motor ambulances to report at 156th [illegible]. Sent 1 Sgt 1 Cpl & 34 bearers with 16 stretchers during forenoon to report to 156th Bde HQ [illegible] further orders. Major McKENZIE reported back by lunch time & said that Bde HQ desired him to stay at Ambulance HQ until called for. The bearer party also returned in afternoon with similar instructions contained in SC 2/22 of same date. | |

D. D. & L., London E.C
(10340) Wt W5300/P713 750,000 3/18 E 688 Forms/C2118/16.

Instructions regarding War Diaries and Intelligence Summaries are contained in F. S. Regs., Part II. and the Staff Manual respectively. Title pages will be prepared in manuscript.

# WAR DIARY
or
# INTELLIGENCE SUMMARY.
(Erase heading not required.)

489 Army Form C. 2118.

1/1st Lowland Field Ambulance
52nd (Lowland) Division

| Place | Date | Hour | Summary of Events and Information | Remarks and references to Appendices |
|---|---|---|---|---|
| E28 c5.6 Sh 57c NE | 3/10/18 | | Personnel employed on camp fatigues. | JWL |
| do | 4/10/18 | | Established an evacuating post at E 23 d 5.1 to day in accordance with ADMS instructions in MO/538 of even date. Party consists of 1 NCO 4 men & 3 bell tents. Tent up later for shelter for use of patients going down in wet weather. | JWL |
| do | 5/10/18 | | Capt. THOMAS D MILLER RAMC TC reported to day for duty with this ambulance in accordance with instructions of A.D.M.S. in MO/550 of even date. | JWL |
| do | 6/10/18 | | Detailed Capt T.D. MILLER to report to 56th Bde R.F.A for temporary duty as M.O. vice Capt. INGHAM who proceeds on leave to U.K. Reference R.A.M.C. O.O. No 20 of even date detailing moves etc & sent Capt. J.W. BURTON with 1 O.R. & 1 bicycle to report in time to billeting party to TINQUES & due to leave LOUVERVAL with lorry conveying billeting parties ... Cross roads J.9.b. at 1300 to day | |
| | | 1200 | Capt MILLER returned to this unit, having been unable to find 56th Bde RFA at ~~address~~ site given him at A.D.M.S office. | |
| J9b68 Sh 57c NE 1/20000 | do | 1645 | Moved out from old area at 1400 & arrived at present site at 1600. Marching out strength as under:– | |

| Chaplain | Personnel Offs | Personnel RAMC | Personnel ASC | Chargers | Riders | Horses LD | Horses HD | Vehicles 2 wheeled | Vehicles 4 wheeled | Motor Vehicles Cars | Motor Vehicles Cycles | Cycles | Remarks |
|---|---|---|---|---|---|---|---|---|---|---|---|---|---|
| 1 | *6 | 92 | (a) 33 | 4 | 2 | 18 | 22(b) | (b) 14 | 4 | (c) 4 | 1(d) | - | |

* Includes 1 off temporarily attached from 2/2nd Wessex Fld Amb.
(a) Includes train driver & 6 M.T. A.S.C.
(b) Includes train wagon & horses.
(c) 2 cars at workshops & 1 attached A.D.M.S
(d) 1 cycle & M.T. driver att. A.D.M.S. as D.R.

JWL

(10340) W1 W3300/P713 750,000 3/18 E. 688 Forms/C2118/16. D. D. & L., London E.C

Instructions regarding War Diaries and Intelligence Summaries are contained in F. S. Regs., Part II. and the Staff Manual respectively. Title pages will be prepared in manuscript.

# WAR DIARY
or
# ~~INTELLIGENCE SUMMARY.~~
(Erase heading not required.)

490 Army Form C. 2118.

1/1st Lowland Field Ambulance
52nd (Lowland) ~~Field~~ Division

| Place | Date | Hour | Summary of Events and Information | Remarks and references to Appendices |
|---|---|---|---|---|
| J 9 b 6 8 Sh 57c 1/20000 | 7/10/18 | | Tent subdivision of this Fd. Amb. att. 46th C.C.S. reported back at 0130 to-day. Ambulance moved to-day to TINQUES in accordance with A.D.M.S. instructions in MO/572 d/6 10/18. Personnel entrain at VAULX VRAUCOURT in train departing at 1515 & due to arrive at TINQUES at 1750. All motor ambulances proceed by road. 1 Limber & officers' chargers entrain at FRENICOURT on train due to leave at 1415 & timed to arrive at 1650. Remainder of Horse transport proceeds by road under orders of OC Divl. train. Detailed MAJOR MACKENZIE to proceed in charge of the Horse Transport & [illegible] the orders of O.C. train relative thereto which were received by me through A.D.M.S. MO/573 issued at 0815 this morning.<br>Sent Lt GUTHRIE MRC USA to report to CRA 52nd Div. at CANTAING MILL, F27c23, this morning by returning ambulance car from C.M.D.S. in accordance with A.D.M.S. MO/557. J.W.L. | |
| VILLERS SIR SIMON I 5 a 2 6 Sheet 51c | 8/10/18 | | d/6 10/18 Train left VAULX VRAUCOURT at 1520 yesterday & arrived in TINQUES at 2320 — 3½ hours late on a 2¼ hours journey. It consisted of about 30 vehicles & at its best attained a speed of not more than 10 miles per hour. There was a double line of rail the whole way & apparently no congestion of traffic as only 3 trains passed going in opposite direction during the whole 8 hours journey. Unit arrived in billets at VILLERS SIR SIMON at 0130 this morning. The billets & accommodation provided by Town Major are the best this unit has yet struck in France & somewhat atoned for the depressing railway journey.<br>Wrote ADMS regarding the provision of baths & [illegible] for the Bde & hastening of necessary | |

D. D. & L., London E.C.
(10349) Wt W5300/P713 750,000 3/18 E 688 Forms/C2118/16.

491 Army Form C. 2118.

Instructions regarding War Diaries and Intelligence Summaries are contained in F. S. Regs., Part II. and the Staff Manual respectively. Title pages will be prepared in manuscript.

# WAR DIARY or INTELLIGENCE SUMMARY.

(Erase heading not required.)

1/1st Lowland Field Ambulance
52nd (Lowland) Division

| Place | Date | Hour | Summary of Events and Information | Remarks and references to Appendices |
|---|---|---|---|---|
| VILLERS SIR SIMON Isa 26, Sh. 57c | 8/10/18 (Contd) | | material to get the straps [illegible] at IZEL-LES-HAMEAU completed as soon as possible. Wrote A.D.M.S. also regarding personnel, 1 off & 19 O.R. of this Field Ambulance attached to 45 C.C.S. who have not yet rejoined their unit. J.W.L. | |
| do | 9/10/18 | | Major J. BROWNE & 19 O.R., tent subdivision of this Unit att. 45th C.C.S. were brought back to-day by 3 motor ambulance cars of this unit sent for them. 19 O.R. of this unit reported to day to 6th C.C.S. RUITZ for temporary duty in accordance with instructions of A.D.M.S. Major W. F. MACKENZIE was detailed this evening to proceed to 6th C.C.S. for temporary duty as M.O. with this tent subdivision. J.W.L. | |
| do | 10/10/18 | | Received A.D.M.S. No. R/13/1 d/9 10/18 to carry out the training of officers &c. during the period that this Division is in this area, & to use to the fullest extent officers who had been at the R.A.M.C. School of Instruction in instructing officers & O.R. in the latest methods as used at the school. Received also A.D.M.S. letter of even date regarding fitting of straps to motor ambulances for fracture cases when passing over rough roads. These have already been fitted to 6 cars but 1 car is not yet so fitted. Hinged doors are being fitted by the unit's joiners to Horsed ambulance wagons to protect | |

D. D. & L., London E.C
(10340) Wt W5300/P713 750,000 3/18 E 688 Forms/C2118/16.

Instructions regarding War Diaries and Intelligence Summaries are contained in F. S. Regs., Part II. and the Staff Manual respectively. Title pages will be prepared in manuscript.

# WAR DIARY
or
~~INTELLIGENCE~~ SUMMARY.
(Erase heading not required.)

492 Army Form C. 2118.

1/1st Lowland Field Ambulance
52nd (Lowland) Division

| Place | Date | Hour | Summary of Events and Information | Remarks and references to Appendices |
|---|---|---|---|---|
| VILLERS SIR SIMON | 10/10/18 | | the water tank tap from damage by men standing on it, in accordance with DDMS | |
| I 5 a 26 SE 57c | | | VIII Corps Standing Orders para 13. Metal work on the Horsed transport wagons is | |
| | | | being repainted as opportunity offers in accordance with G.R.O. 4809. It is found, however | |
| | | | that the paint does not adhere very well to the polished & burnished surfaces. Whilst under | |
| | | | VIII Corps in June the paint was scraped off the grease caps on axles, drag rope washers, | |
| | | | tail-board chains & other painted metal parts in accordance with instructions received, & | |
| | | | all these surfaces were polished and burnished at the cost of much time & trouble | |
| | | | Instructed Capt T.D. MILLER to report for temporary duty as M.O. i/c 1/4th R.S in relief of | |
| | | | Capt R.A. LENNIE who will report to this H.Q. prior to proceeding on leave to U.K. J.W.L. | |
| do. | 11/10/18 | | Capt R.A. LENNIE proceeded to day on 14 days leave to U.K. Dental facilities | |
| | | | for Off. & O.R. would appear to be inadequate to meet their needs as there was a | |
| | | | good deal of really necessary work to be overtaken before this Division took action prior | |
| | | | in operations & which has had to stand over for the past 2 months or more. Visited | |
| | | | 1/7th R.S & pointed out some defects in sanitation - eg lid of an officer's deep pit latrine | |
| | | | left wide open. Detailed Major J. BROWNE & "B" section to take over [illegible] and site | |
| | | | at LES 4 VENTS to-morrow as a D.R.S. in accordance with A.D.M.S. R 61/11 of even date & to leave | |
| | | | 1 N.C.O. & 4 men there overnight. Had a practice drill by the Fire Picket of this unit & | |
| | | | used the water pumped up by buckets for washing the transport wagons. J.W.L. | |
| do | 12/10/18 | | B Section with transport & 2 motor ambulances took over D.R.S at LES 4 VENTS from 2/4th ? A | |
| | | | In accordance with A.D.M.S. instructions I sent 1 Off (Capt A D DOWNES), 1 water cart, & 1 tent subdivision | |

D. D. & L., London E.C
(10346) Wt W5300/P713 750,000 3/18 E 688 Forms/C2118/16.

Instructions regarding War Diaries and Intelligence Summaries are contained in F. S. Regs., Part II. and the Staff Manual respectively. Title pages will be prepared in manuscript.

# WAR DIARY ~~or~~ ~~INTELLIGENCE SUMMARY.~~

(Erase heading not required.)

4~~9~~2 Army Form C. 2118.

1/1st Lowland Field Ambulance
52nd (Lowland) Division

| Place | Date | Hour | Summary of Events and Information | Remarks and references to Appendices |
|---|---|---|---|---|
| VILLERS SIR SIMON (I5 a 2 6 Sh. 51c) | 12/10/18 (contd.) | | 20 OR. of A section Tent subdivision) in 3 ambulance cars to report for temporary duty with C.M.D.S at FRESNICOURT, instructing 2 of the ambulance cars to proceed & report to O.C. 31st M.A.C at OLHAIN for temporary duty. ~~[illegible]~~ One water cart was also sent by road to join the tent subdivision at FRESNICOURT. As this reduces the personnel remaining at VILLERS SIR SIMON to 2 officers (myself & the Quartermaster) and 2 bearer subdivisions less those on leave to U.K. I called on A.D.M.S at LE CAUROY & was instructed by him to move Ambulance to Les 4 Vents & report to him when ready to open as a Divisional Rest Station. JWL | |
| LES 4 VENTS (Lens 1/100000 2.H. 5. 6.) | 13/10/18 | | Unit marched out from VILLERS SIR SIMON to-day ~~and~~ at 1030 & arrived here at 1415. Marching out strength as under:- | |

| Personnel | | | | | Horses | | | | Vehicles | | Motor Vehicles | | | Remarks |
|---|---|---|---|---|---|---|---|---|---|---|---|---|---|---|
| Chaplains | RAMC | | ASC | | Chargers | Riders | L.D. | H.D. | 2 axle | 1 axle | Cycles | Amb. Cars | cycle | |
| | Off | OR | HT | MT | | | | | | | | | | |
| 1 | 2 | 78 | 21 | 3 | 3 | 1 | 14 | 16 | 10 | 2 (c) | 1 (a) | 3 (b) | 1 | (a) Other cycle was brought back from A.D.M.S. office & sent to Les 4 Vents yesterday (b) 2 cars in workshops & 2 cars at 31 M.A.C. (c) 1 Water cart deficient but 1 on loan from 1/3rd L.F.A. |

Notified A.D.M.S of arrival & that this unit was now ready to receive cases as a Divisional Rest station. Out going unit (24th Field Ambulance) has stripped the place of tables, forms, stretchers, & blankets. Red cross stores were indented for yesterday through A.D.M.S & indent ~~passed~~ taken to D.D.M.S. office last night by Capt. BURTON. JWL

D. D. & L., London E.C. (19340) W1 W5300/P713 750,000 3/18 E 688 Forms/C2118/16.

Instructions regarding War Diaries and Intelligence Summaries are contained in F. S. Regs., Part II. and the Staff Manual respectively. Title pages will be prepared in manuscript.

# WAR DIARY
or
~~INTELLIGENCE SUMMARY.~~

(Erase heading not required.)

494

Army Form C. 2118.

1/1st Lowland Field Ambulance
52nd (Lowland) Division

| Place | Date | Hour | Summary of Events and Information | Remarks and references to Appendices |
|---|---|---|---|---|
| LES 4 VENTS | 14/10/18 | | The two cars sent to 31st M.A.C. on 12/10/18 reported back to this unit last night. Returned Water Cart lent by 1/3rd L.F.A. on afternoon of 12th. It would appear that the Medical unit (or units) at FRESNICOURT to which a tent subdivision with 1 off was sent on 12/10/18 is a Corps Rest Station not a Corps MAIN Dressing Station. Unit was employed to-day cleaning up camps & getting huts in order for reception of cases. Blankets & stretchers (for beds) promised from Corps. Reserves of these stores have not arrived but units' equipment will do for a beginning. Educational Officer 52nd Division called to-day & it was arranged that he should have the use of the hut set apart as patients' dining & recreation hall for lectures to patients & personnel: also that a small Library of books should be placed in care of this Field Ambulance for use of patients & personnel. There is a good incinerator built at this camp & the incineration of faeces was begun yesterday. J.W.L. | |
| do | 15/10/18 | | Forwarded indent for B.R.C.S. stores that were urgently required by B.R.C.S. car which happened to call here to-day – choosing the most urgent things already asked in my indent of 12th which was forwarded by A.D.M.S. to D.D.M.S. for favour of countersignature. Tables, forms, lamps, stretchers & blankets were removed by the out-going unit (24th Fld Amb.) for their new Rest Station to be formed at ST CATHERINES. A.D.M.S. called to-night & informed me that Corps would not grant me the use of | |

D. D. & L., London E.C
(10340) Wt W5300/P713 750,000 3/18 E 688 Forms/C2118/16.

Instructions regarding War Diaries and Intelligence Summaries are contained in F. S. Regs., Part II. and the Staff Manual respectively. Title pages will be prepared in manuscript.

# WAR DIARY
*or*
# ~~INTELLIGENCE~~ SUMMARY.
(*Erase heading not required.*)

495 Army Form C. 2118.

1/1st Lowland Field Ambulance
52nd (Lowland) Division

| Place | Date | Hour | Summary of Events and Information | Remarks and references to Appendices |
|---|---|---|---|---|
| LES 4 VENTS | 15/10/18 (Contd) | | stretchers & blankets meantime; also that he did not think it would be easy to get the 20 tables & 40 forms I indented for yesterday through Division, but that he would try to get me some wood to make them. I have however, just heard from my QM that he has to-night received about 50 stretchers to replace a similar number salved & returned to ordnance as unserviceable while we were in the 3rd Army. The assistance of VIII Corps is not therefore very necessary meantime. Capt A D DOWNES, OC tent subdivision of this unit sent to FRESNICOURT, informs me that there is a tent subdivision there from each Division in VIII Corps, that the OC is a Major, & that it is intended to make the camp there a Corps Rest Station with Division at tent subdivisions each receiving its own Divisional sick. Meantime they are being employed looking after some 200 Canadian sick left by the Canadian Corps Rest Station from whom VIII Corps took over. The equipment of a tent subdivision was sent there from this Field Ambulance to-day in 1 GS Wagon & 1 water cart was sent with the party on 12th inst. Jw. L. | |
| do | 16/10/18 | | Received A.D.M.S. R 82/3 d/15 10/18 returning my indent of 12/10/18 for B.R.C.S. stores & drawing my attention to Min 2 of D.D.M.S. which says that the present is not considered a suitable time for drawing these stores. Stores indented for yesterday arrived this forenoon from B.R.C.S. & we have now got Beatrice stoves to warm some of the Wards. 3 baths for bathing patients, some distemper paint, some baking | |

D. D. & L., London E.C
(10346) Wt W5300/P713 750,000 3/18 E. 688 Forms/C2118/16.

496 Army Form C. 2118.

Instructions regarding War Diaries and Intelligence Summaries are contained in F. S. Regs., Part II. and the Staff Manual respectively. Title pages will be prepared in manuscript.

# WAR DIARY
or
~~INTELLIGENCE SUMMARY.~~

*(Erase heading not required.)*

1/1st Lowland Field Ambulance
52nd (Lowland) Division

| Place | Date | Hour | Summary of Events and Information | Remarks and references to Appendices |
|---|---|---|---|---|
| LES 4 VENTS | 16/10/18 (Contd) | | cloth for making blinds for windows to prevent lights being visible at night & a few other necessaries. The baling cloth will enable us to sabve a number of blankets which are at present being used as blinds in the absence of any other suitable material. The joiners have been busy since coming here mending doors & patching windows & doing other minor but necessary repairs. A canteen has also been opened by this unit, & tailor's, shoemaker's, & barber's shops set up in suitable places. There are in residence to-night Off. Nil, O.R. 40. of whom the 19 received to-day have had a hot bath before being passed to the Wards & their clothing removed for disinfesting in the Delousers of Skin Centre at ESTREE CAUCHIE. There is no delouser at LES 4 VENTS — but the means of efficiency exhibited is otherwise good. J.W.L. | |
| Do | 17/10/18 | | Visited Tent Subdivision under Capt A.D. DOWNES at C.R.S. FRESNICOURT. They are in quite comfortable quarters & are being employed in cleaning up & distempering the Wards & in carrying out various improvements. Major CRAWFORD 37th Field Ambulance is in command & he informed me that he is to have 1 tent subdivision from each Division in the Corps, each of which will take the cases belonging to its Division. There are only about 20 patients left of those taken over, the remainder having been evacuated. The station is not yet open as a C.R.S. but the VIII Corps are giving him tables & forms & doing a considerable amount of R E work to the station. Cui bono ? 52nd D.R.S. here was receiving the day after taking over! J.W.L. | |

D. D. & L., London E.C
(10340) Wt W5300/P713 750,000 3/18 E 688 Forms/C2118/16.

Instructions regarding War Diaries and Intelligence Summaries are contained in F. S. Regs., Part II. and the Staff Manual respectively. Title pages will be prepared in manuscript.

# WAR DIARY
or
~~INTELLIGENCE SUMMARY.~~
(Erase heading not required.)

497 Army Form C. 2118.

1/1st Lowland Field Ambulance
52nd (Lowland) Division

| Place | Date | Hour | Summary of Events and Information | Remarks and references to Appendices |
|---|---|---|---|---|
| LES 4 VENTS | 18/10/18 | | Capt MORGAN of this unit, temporarily attached as M.O. to 1/7th R.S. has been transferred to 51st Div. Capt. MILLER of this unit, temporarily attached as M.O. to 1/4th R.S. has been sent to Hospital sick. Both are now off strength of this unit. J.W.L. | |
| do | 19/10/18 | | In accordance with ~~ADMS~~ RAMC O.O. No. 20 d/18 10/18 received by me last night 1 off + 2 bearer subdivisions with 3 Horsed ambulance wagons + 1 Limber are being sent to report to H.Q. 156th Bde at Chateau DE LA HAIE at 1500 to-day. In addition to this I am sending 24 stretchers 60 blankets + 30 Pluvinsin sheets for patients. Marching out strength:– 1 off + 57 O.R. RAMC. 1 sgt. 1 batman 4 drivers A.S.C.: Animals 6 ~~HD~~, 2 L.D. horses + 2 riding horses. Two H.D. horses + 1 driver have been lent to-day to Mme Dirion Henri, Camblignent to assist in ploughing her farm. Major MACKENZIE + 18 O.R. + 1 batman ASC returned to-day from No. 6 C.C.S. RUITZ in 3 motor ambces Cars of 1/1st L.F.A. sent for them in accordance with verbal instructions of DDMS VIII Corps J.W.L. | |
| do | 20/10/18 | | Heavy rain during night + fields too wet to-day for ploughing. Capt BURTON + the 2 bearer subdivisions with Horsed ambces + Limber moved forward to-day with 156th Bde from CHATEAU DE LA HAIE to BILLY MONTIGNY O 32 – O 33. There were 87 O.R. + 1 Off. patients resident in this D.R.S. last night. Visited VIII Corps Rest Station at FRESNICOURT to pay Tent Subdivision of this ambulance presently doing duty there + to try to arrange with O.C. (Major Crawford) to take over about 50 cases temporarily | |

D. D. & L., London E.C
(10340) Wt W3300/P713 750,000 3/18 E 688 Forms/C2118/16

498 Army Form C. 2118.

Instructions regarding War Diaries and Intelligence Summaries are contained in F. S. Regs., Part II. and the Staff Manual respectively. Title pages will be prepared in manuscript.

# WAR DIARY
*or*
# INTELLIGENCE SUMMARY.
*(Erase heading not required.)*

1/1st Lowland Field Ambulance
52nd (Lowland) Division

| Place | Date | Hour | Summary of Events and Information | Remarks and references to Appendices |
|---|---|---|---|---|
| LES 4 VENTS | 20/10/18 Contd | | of the 87 presently in this Divisional Rest Station in the event of a move. | |
| | | 2000. | Received A.D.M.S. W54 of even date to evacuate all my cases to ST POL & return all stores surplus to mobilization & G.R.O. stores to FRESNICOURT. Evacuation of patients & disposal of stores taken over is being carried out. JWL | |
| do | 21/10/18 | | Personnel of this Unit reported back from temporary duty at C.R.S. FRESNICOURT. JWL | |
| do | 22/10/18 | 0900 | Received at 0700 A.D.M.S. W77 d/21-10-18 to move to-day to RED MILL, LIEVIN & on 23rd to move to HENIN-LIETARD, P25 c.1.4. Ambulance Car sent to report to H.Q. RA in ST. ELOI to evacuate sick to AGNEZ LES DUISANS Group of C.C.S. & to remain until RA rejoin the Division. | |
| M27d77 Sh 44A/40000 | | 1800 | Sent an advanced party of cooks etc. & cooks stores in 2 motor ambulances to this location RED MILL LIEVIN & remainder marched in at 1600. Marching in strength:- | |

| Chaplain | Personnel RAMC Offs | Personnel RAMC OR | Personnel ASC H.T. | Personnel ASC M.T. | Horses Chargers | Horses Riders | Horses L.D. | Horses H.D. | Vehicles 2 axle | Vehicles 1 axle | Motors Ambces | Motors Cycles | Cycle | Wheeled Stretcher Carriages |
|---|---|---|---|---|---|---|---|---|---|---|---|---|---|---|
| 1 | 5 | 88 | 21 | 7 | 3 | 1 | 16 | 16 | *10 | 4 | ϕ6 | 2 | 1 | 7 |

* 3 Horsed Ambulances & 1 limber wagon out with Bearers with 156th Bde.
ϕ 1 Ambulance car on detached duty with 52nd Divisional Artillery. JWL

| Place | Date | Hour | Summary of Events and Information | Remarks and references to Appendices |
|---|---|---|---|---|
| P25 c1.4 Sheet 44A/40000 | 23/10/18 | | Moved ambulance by march route to this site, Hospital DARCY, HENIN-LIETARD this forenoon & took over from 1/2nd L.F.A. who moved out at 1330 to-day. Took over from 1/2nd L.F.A. 46 cases sick, & a number of sick rolled in from units (chiefly Labour Coys) in the | |

D. D. & L., London E.C. (10340) Wt W5300/P713 750,000 3/18 E 688 Forms/C2118/16.

Instructions regarding War Diaries and Intelligence Summaries are contained in F. S. Regs., Part II. and the Staff Manual respectively. Title pages will be prepared in manuscript.

# WAR DIARY

~~or~~

~~INTELLIGENCE SUMMARY.~~

(Erase heading not required.)

499 Army Form C. 2118.

1/1st Lowland Field Ambulance
52nd (Lowland) Division

| Place | Date | Hour | Summary of Events and Information | Remarks and references to Appendices |
|---|---|---|---|---|
| P25. C.1.4. HENIN-LIETARD | 23/10/18 | | neighbourhood during the afternoon so that by night time there were over 90 cases in the hospital. Marching in state same as on 22/10/18. Jw.L. | |
| M2 d 35 Sh 44 1/40000 COUTICHES | 24/10/18 | | Moved Ambulance, less 1 tent subdivision complete + 2 bearer subdivisions with 1 off att 156th Bde, to School at COUTICHES to day. Time of starting 1000 & route via AUBY, WARENDIN, LA PLACETTE, + FLINES. Marching out strength as under, + all reached destination at 1630. | |

| Chaplains | Personnel RAMC Off | RAMC OR | ASC H.T. | ASC M.T. | Horses Chargers | Horses Riders | Horses L.D. | Horses H.D. | Vehicles 2 axle | Vehicles 1 axle | Motors Ambulance | Motors Cycles | Cycle | Wheeled stretcher Carriages |
|---|---|---|---|---|---|---|---|---|---|---|---|---|---|---|
| 1 | 3 | 70 | 21 | 5 | 3 | 1 | 14 | 14 | 9 | 3 | 4* | 2 | 1 | 7 |

1 motor ambulance car sent [illegible] to A.D.M.S before moving out. Two other ambulance cars were sent out at same time to report one to O.C 1/3rd LFA at AUBY + other to O.C Bearers 156th BDE also at AUBY. They rejoined later in day but one of them had to be sent to Workshops for repairs when it returned. Major W.F. MCKENZIE + Capt. A.D. DOWNES were the officers left with tent subdivision at Hospital DARCY + there were also left there 1 G.S. Wagon, 1 Water Cart, + subsequently 2 of the 4 motor Ambulances.

Found on arrival that school at COUTICHES had been used as a hospital by the Germans + contained some enamelled hospital furniture but was left in a very dirty condition. All personnel on arrival were set to work + school + billets

D. D. & L., London E.C. (10340) W1 W5300/P713 750,000 3/18 E 688 Forms/C2118/16.

500 Army Form C. 2118.

Instructions regarding War Diaries and Intelligence Summaries are contained in F. S. Regs., Part II. and the Staff Manual respectively. Title pages will be prepared in manuscript.

# WAR DIARY
or
~~INTELLIGENCE SUMMARY.~~

(Erase heading not required.)

1/1st Lowland Field Ambulance
52nd (Lowland) Division

| Place | Date | Hour | Summary of Events and Information | Remarks and references to Appendices |
|---|---|---|---|---|
| COUTICHES M2 d 3 5 Sh 44 1/40000 | 24/10/18 (Contd) | | were thoroughly cleaned up, open latrines filled in & fresh latrines made. Capt BURTON reported back to this H.Q at COUTICHES with his bearers & transport less 2 horsed ambulance wagons sent for temporary duty with 24th Field Ambulance, ST AMAND, P.8 Sh 44 1/40000 in early morning of 23/10/18 in accordance with A.D.M.S W90 to Capt BURTON. Notified A.D.M.S of arrival, & that there was accommodation for 50 patients. JwL | |
| do | 25/10/18 | | A.D.M.S called [re] transport arrangements. Received note from ~~[illegible]~~ AREA COMMANDANT at HENIN LIETARD through O.C Detachment at HOSPITAL DARCY quoting his instructions under VIII Corps A305 d/23 10/18 that owing to delay action mines in HENIN-LIETARD area no troops would be billetted in Squares O 23, 24, 29, 30, 34, 35, & P 25. As Hospital DARCY is in P25 I went by ambulance car to HENIN-LIETARD and afterwards to A.D.M.S 52nd Div at FLINES. Received verbal instructions from A.D.M.S to withdraw Post at HENIN-LIETARD to-morrow. Sent Major BROWNE & 1 tent subdivision to report to C.C.S at ECOLE NORMALE 44 RUE D'ARRAS, DOUAI in accordance with A.D.M.S instructions received this afternoon. ~~Arrange~~ Sent written instructions to O.C Detachment at Hospital DARCY to-night by Despatch Rider to evacuate his cases by M.A.C cars to-morrow & move his tent subdivision by returning ambulance cars to H.Q at COUTICHES; section equipment in 1 G.S. Wagon & 1 water cart to be sent to O.C C.C.S at ECOLE NORMALE, DOUAI. Two Horsed Ambulance Cars reported back from temporary duty with 24th Fld Amb. JwL | |

D. D. & L., London E.C
(10340) Wt W5300/P713 750,000 3/18 E 688 Forms/C2118/16.

Instructions regarding War Diaries and Intelligence Summaries are contained in F. S. Regs., Part II. and the Staff Manual respectively. Title pages will be prepared in manuscript.

# WAR DIARY
or
# ~~INTELLIGENCE SUMMARY.~~
(*Erase heading not required.*)

501 Army Form C. 2118.

1/1st Lowland Field Ambulance
52nd (Lowland) Division

| Place | Date | Hour | Summary of Events and Information | Remarks and references to Appendices |
|---|---|---|---|---|
| COUTICHES | 26/10/18 | | Received A.D.M.S. R210/11 d/25/10/18 confirming verbal instructions to withdraw detachment at HENIN-LIETARD & this detachment less transport reported to this H.Q. this afternoon. D.D.M.S. VIII Corps called & was shown the arrangements, etc. J.W.L. | |
| LECELLES I29 c 8.6. Sh 44 1/40000 | 27/10/18 | | Moved ambulance, less 1 tent subdivision at DOUAI, to billets at this site to-day by march route under 156th Bde Order No. 64 dated 26/10/18. Marching in strength is under:- | |

| PERSONNEL | | | | | | | HORSES | | VEHICLES | | | | | |
|---|---|---|---|---|---|---|---|---|---|---|---|---|---|---|
| Chaplain | R.A.M.C | | A.S.C | | Chargers | Riders | LD | HD | Horsed | | Motor | | Cycle | Wheeled stretcher Carriages |
| | Off | OR | H.T. | M.T. | | | | | 2 wheels | 4 wheels | cars | Cycles | | |
| 1 | 4 | 123 | *28 | 5 | 4 | 2 | 16 | *20 | *13 | 3 | 3ϕ | 2 | 1 | 7 |

* Includes 1 driver 2 H.D. Horses & Train Wagon.
ϕ 3 cars in Workshops & 1 att. 52nd Divisional Artillery for duty.

Before moving out of COUTICHES German medical stores were left under charge of 1 NCO + 4 men of 1/2nd L.F.A. sent in accordance with A.D.M.S. SR 14 d/26/10/18 to take them over until orders for their disposal were received from D.D.M.S.

1800 Visited A.D.S. of 38th Fld Ambulance at I 28 d 5.2. & found that they were simply standing by for the night, having handed over to A.D.S. 36th Fld Ambulance at I 36 a 6.7. Visited latter & found they were doing the whole evacuation of the 12th Division & had 1 car post only (at J 34 a 6.5). It was stated that this was quite sufficient as casualties were few. Visited 156th Bde H.Q. & arranged to send

D. D. & L., London E.C
(10340) Wt W5300/P713 750,000 3/18 E 688 Forms/C2118/16.

502 Army Form C. 2118.

Instructions regarding War Diaries and Intelligence Summaries are contained in F. S. Regs., Part II. and the Staff Manual respectively. Title pages will be prepared in manuscript.

# WAR DIARY or INTELLIGENCE SUMMARY.

(Erase heading not required.)

1/1st Lowland Field Ambulance
52nd (Lowland) Division

| Place | Date | Hour | Summary of Events and Information | Remarks and references to Appendices |
|---|---|---|---|---|
| LECELLES I 29 c 8.6 Sh 44 1/40000 | 27/10/18 (Contd) | | 6 bearers & 2 wheeled stretcher carriages to each Battalion when they moved into the line in relief of 36th Bde. Received R.A.M.C. O.O. No 21 of even date. | JWL |
| do | 28/10/18 | | Visited A.D.S. at I 36 a 6.7 accompanied by Major MACKENZIE then proceeded to inspect House at J 32 a 2.1 which was said by officers of 36th Field Ambulance to be suitable for an A.D.S. & had been "reserved" by them for this purpose. Found enemy shells dropping near the road at J 32 a 2.3 so took the Field Road through this reserved A.D.S. to Car Post at J 34 a 6.5 & thence to broken bridge across the canal at J 29 c 5.5. Visited also M.D.S. of 36th Field Ambulance at O 2 a 4.1 & arranged to formally take over M.D.S. & A.D.S. from 36th Field Ambulance at 1900 to-night. | |
| | | 1400 | Moved ambulance, less tent subdivision at DOUAI, & 1 off with the Chaplain & 12 OR R.A.M.C. detailed to take over A.D.S. at I 36 a in relief of personnel of 36th F.A. there, to M.D.S. at O 2 a 4.1 (ROSULT) marching out strength as under:– | |

| Personnel RAMC Off | Personnel RAMC OR | Personnel ASC HT | Personnel ASC MT | Horses Chargers | Horses Riders | Horses LD | Horses HD | Horsed Vehicles 2 wheels | Horsed Vehicles 4 wheels | Motor Amb Cars | Cycles Motor | Cycles Push | Wheeled Stretcher Carriages |
|---|---|---|---|---|---|---|---|---|---|---|---|---|---|
| 3 | ϕ 106 | 28 | 3 | 4 | 2 | 16 | 20 | 13 | 3 | 3* | 2 | 1 | 1 |

* 1 Car at A.D.S. & 1 car at Car Post
ϕ 18 other ranks with Battalions

| Place | Date | Hour | Summary of Events and Information | Remarks and references to Appendices |
|---|---|---|---|---|
| ROSULT O 2 a 4.1 Sh 44 1/40000 | | 1630 | Capt D.F. BROWNE 1/3rd L.F.A. reported for temporary duty with this Field Ambulance & was sent on by me to report to MAJOR MACKENZIE at A.D.S. for duty. | JWL |

D. D. & L., London E.C.
(10340) Wt W5300/P713 750,000 3/18 E. 688 Forms/C2118/16.

503 Army Form C. 2118.

# WAR DIARY
or
# INTELLIGENCE SUMMARY.
*(Erase heading not required.)*

Instructions regarding War Diaries and Intelligence Summaries are contained in F. S. Regs., Part II. and the Staff Manual respectively. Title pages will be prepared in manuscript.

1/1st Lowland Field Ambulance
52nd Lowland Division.

| Place | Date | Hour | Summary of Events and Information | Remarks and references to Appendices |
|---|---|---|---|---|
| ROSULT O 2 a 41 Sh 44 1/40000 | 29/10/18 | | Enemy dropped some 5.9 shells at intervals during the night about 500 yds from ROSULT. 1/1st LFA took over formally from 36th Field Ambulance at 1900 last night & the latter unit moved out from ROSULT at 1120 to-day. A.D.M.S. 52nd Division called this forenoon. 11 cars of 31st M.A.C. reported to this H.Q last night under a Sgt. They are part of 12 cars attached for duty with 12th Division, the remaining car being still with 37th Field Amb. By instructions of A.D.M.S. 52nd Division 8 cars will remain with 1/1st L.F.A. & 3 cars were sent for duty with 1/3rd L.F.A. It is proposed to utilize the goods sheds at Railway Stn ROSULT as a temporary hospital for milder Influenza cases of this Division should there be an outbreak of this disease. The civil population in ROSULT are being given a considerable amount of medical attention for Influenza at present. They have been underfed for some time & take the disease badly. Their cattle have been taken away by the Germans & Ideal milk has to be supplied by this Ambulance especially for sick children. J.W.L. | |
| do | 30/10/18 | | Large shed measuring approximately 70 ft x 40 ft has been cleaned out & double-decked beds (used by previous unit in occupation for personnel) rearranged so as to provide 100 beds for Influenza patients in the event of an outbreak of this disease. An adjoining shed measuring approximately the same has been cleaned out & reserved for ordinary sick. Personnel are being accommodated in a third | |

Instructions regarding War Diaries and Intelligence Summaries are contained in F. S. Regs., Part II. and the Staff Manual respectively. Title pages will be prepared in manuscript.

# WAR DIARY
or
# ~~INTELLIGENCE SUMMARY.~~

(Erase heading not required.)

504 Army Form C. 2118.

1/1st Lowland Field Ambulance
52nd (Lowland) Division

| Place | Date | Hour | Summary of Events and Information | Remarks and references to Appendices |
|---|---|---|---|---|
| ROSULT O 2 a 4 1 Sh 44 1/40000 | 30/10/18 (Contd) | | shed of similar size. Bales of shavings left by the Germans have been used to provide "straw" for beds on the floors, which are bare earth. Wounded & seriously sick are being evacuated by M.A.C. cars to DOUAI after being provided with hot drinks etc at this M.D.S. Foul places & latrines left uncovered have been filled up & the general surroundings of the camp made sanitary. Wrote A.D.M.S. in answer to an inquiry that I considered the Galvanising shed at the Station, ROSULT, capable of being turned into Divisional Baths with the minimum of alterations. Sent indents for B.R.C.S stores & Medical & Ordnance stores necessary for equipment of A.D.S. & R.A.Ps in accordance with Standing Orders No 1 of D.D.M.S. VIII Corps & A.D.M.S. 52nd Div No R 305/3 d/30/10/18. It has been found necessary to utilize the cloth Distinguishing Flags carried on establishment — material for painting tin flags in accordance with D.D.M.S. VIII Corps instructions have not been obtainable owing to moves in recent mobile warfare. Capt R.A. LENNIE reported back from 14 days leave in U.K. [illegible] | |
| do | 31/10/18 | | A.D.M.S. called this forenoon. Visited A.D.S in afternoon. Tent subdivision & transport at DOUAI are at a Hospital for Refugees at the Ecole Normale there & not a C.C.S as stated in note of 25th on p. 500. ADMS R 261/1 d/28/10/18 informed me that O.C. had been instructed by D.D.M.S. VIII Corps to return this tent subdivision to their H.Q. but this has not yet been done. | |

Johnston Keith Lt Col
OC 1/1st L.F.A. R.A.M.C.(T)

D. D. & L., London E.C
(10340) Wt W5300/P713 750,000 3/18 E 688 Forms/C2118/16.

**To be made up to and for Saturday in each week**

No. of Report 166

# FIELD RETURN.

Army Form B. 213

(To be furnished by all arms, services, and departments (except A.S.C. units) to the A.G.'s Office at the Base in accordance with Field Service Regulations, Part II.)

RETURN showing numbers (*a*) Effective strength of Unit. (*b*) Rationed by Unit. 1/1st Low. Fd. Ambce [?] at In the Field 5th Octr. 1918 Date.

| Details. | *Personnel: Officers | Other Ranks | | | | Animals – Horses: Riding | Draught | Heavy Draught | Pack | Mules: Large | Small | Guns and transport vehicles: Guns, showing description | Ammunition wagons | Machine guns | Aircraft, showing description | Horsed: † 4 Wheeled | 2 Wheeled | Mechanical: Motor Cars | Tractors | Lorries, showing description | Trucks, showing description | Trailers | Motor Bicycles | Bicycles | Motor Ambulances | Remarks (Number of Acting W.O.'s and N.C.O.'s included in effective strength to be shown in this column.) |
|---|---|---|---|---|---|---|---|---|---|---|---|---|---|---|---|---|---|---|---|---|---|---|---|---|---|---|
| Effective Strength of Unit ... ... | (a) 8 | (b) 177 | | | | | | | | | | | | | | | | | | | | | | 1 | | (a) Includes 1 officer at 1/4th R. Scots; 1 at 1/7th -do-; 1 at 45 C.C.S. (b) 19 OR at -do-; 19 OR at 46 C.C.S.; 1 OR at Div. Concert Party; 1 OR at Div. Train; 1 OR at Div. HQ; 1 OR at 413th [?] Coy. R.E.; 2 OR at C.M.D.S.; 1 OR at BHQ; 6 OR at 1/4th R. Scots; 6 OR at 1/7th -do-; 6 OR at 1/7th S. Rifles; 27 OR on leave to U.K. |
| Details by Arms attached to Unit as in War Establishment ... ... | | | | | | | | | | | | | | | | | | | | | | | | | | |
| A.S.C. (H.T. [?]) | | (c) 36 | | | | 6 | 18 | 20 | | | | | | | | 13 | 3 | | | | | | | | | |
| A.S.C. M.T. | | (d) 12 | | | | | | | | | | | | | | | | | | | | | 2 | | 7 | |
| Total ... ... | 8 | 225 | | | | 6 | 18 | 20 | | | | | | | | 13 | 3 | | | | | | 2 | 1 | 7 | (c) 8 OR; 1 OR at 217th Coy A.S.C. |
| War Establishment ... ... ... | 10 | 231 | | | | 8 | 14 | 20 | | | | | | | | 13 | 4 | | | | | | 2 | 1 | 7 | (d) 2 OR on leave to U.K.; 3 OR at Div. M.T. Coy; 1 OR at D.H.Q. |
| Waiting to complete ... ... (Detail of Personnel and Horses below.) | 2 | & 6 | | | | 2 | - | - | | | | | | | | - | 1 | | | | | | - | - | - | & 5 RAMC & 1 ASC (Corp. SS [?]) |
| Surplus ... ... (Detail of Personnel and Horses below.) | - | - | | | | - | 1 | - | | | | | | | | - | - | | | | | | - | - | - | |
| †Attached (not to include the details shown above) ... ... | 1 | | | | | | | | | | | | | | | | | | | | | | | | | 1 Off. MRC USA tempy attd. |
| Attached for Rations only ... ... | 1 | | | | | | | | | | | | | | | | | | | | | | | | | 1 Chaplain |
| Civilians Employed with and Accompanying the Unit ... ... | | | | | | | | | | | | | | | | | | | | | | | | | | |
| ‡Detached from and struck off effective strength of own Unit ... ... | | | | | | | | | | | | | | | | | | | | | | | | | | |
| ‡Detached from but retained on effective strength of own unit... ... ... | | | | | | | | | | | | | | | | | | | | | | | | | | |
| Total Rationed ... | 4 [?] | 127 | | | | 6 | 18 | 20 | | | | | | | | | | | | | | | | | | |

* Blank columns to be used for W.A.A.C. Natives or as may be required.

† In the case of field ambulances, hospitals or depots, the number of patients are to be included here, the names being shown in A.F.A. 36.

‡ These details to be enumerated by arms.

John W. Leitch Lieut Colonel Signature of Commander.

4th October 1918 Date of Despatch.

A.F. B.213. R.S.C. 5th Oct. 1918

| No. | Rank | Name | Nature of Casualty | Date |
|---|---|---|---|---|
| T4/245543 | Dr. | Savage H. | Granted 6th rate R.S.C. pay as shoeing smith from 7/6/18. Vice Shoeing Smith Baillie to Hosp. sick (This cancels entry in B.213 of 21/9/18. Original Vet. off. certificate attached in accordance with ASC/14119/1827 - 11/8/18) | |
| T4/247752 | Dr. | Jones T.A. | Granted 14 days leave to U.K. via Boulogne. Credit ration allowance at 2/1 p.d. for that period | 3 10/18 to 17/18 |
| T4/043531 | Dr. | Davies G. | Returned from 14 days leave to U.K. | 30 9/18 |
| T4/086455 | " | Bird S.L. | — do — | 30 9/18 |
| T2/11442 | Dr. | Appleyard T. | War pay increased to 4d p.d. from | 4 10/18 |
| M2/135982 | Pte. | Lewis G.H. | Granted 14 days leave to U.K. via Boulogne. Credit ration allowance at 2/1 p.d. for that period. | 30 9/18 - 14 10/18 |
| M2/080045 | Sgt. | Brackhurst H. | to Hosp. sick whilst on leave to U.K. (This N.C.O was granted leave to U.K. via Boulogne from 15.9.18 to 29.9.18) | 24 9/18 |
| M2/049455 | Pte. | Dunkason E. | Granted extension of leave to 30 9/18. (authy. W.O. 1539/16169 B.) This man was granted 14 days special leave to U.K. via Boulogne from 8.9.18 to 22.9.18. Credit ration allce. at 2/1 p.d. for that period. | 18 9/18 |
| M2/135958 | Pte. | Brooks C.A. | Married Miss Alice Elizabeth Brudge on 1 10/18 at Parish Church Shanklin, Isle of Wight. Transfers allot. from Mother to Wife. Present address of Wife 'Dunedin' Florence Rd. Shanklin I. of W. | |

For information of the A.G.'s Office at the base.

Officers and men who have become casuals, been transferred or joined since last report.

Place: On the Field    Date: 3rd October 1918.

| Regtl. Number | Rank | Name | Corps | Nature of casualty, or name of unit from or to which transferred. | Date of being struck off or coming on the ration return. | Remarks * |
|---|---|---|---|---|---|---|
| [illegible] | Pte. | Adamson W. | 1st Low. Fd. Amb. RAMC (T) | To Hosp. sick | 1/10/18 | |
| [illegible] | " | Crawford G. | do | do | 4/10/18 | |
| [illegible] | Cpl. | [illegible] C.V. | do | [illegible] | 30/9/18 | |
| [illegible] | Pte. | Gallacher C. | do | [illegible] | 1/10/18 | inclusive |
| [illegible] | " | Eadie W.S.C. | do | [illegible] | 1/10/18 | inclusive |
| [illegible] | " | Parkinson H. | do | [illegible] | 4/10/18 | |
| [illegible] | " | Sloan D. | do | [illegible] | | |
| [illegible] | " | Sloan D. | do | [illegible] | | |
| [illegible] | " | Willis A. | do | [illegible] | | |
| [illegible] | " | Southern G. | do | [illegible] | 3.10.18 to 17.10.18 | |
| [illegible] | " | Pinkerton [illegible] | do | do | 4.10.18 to 18.10.18 | |
| [illegible] | " | McAllister G. | do | do | do | |
| [illegible] | " | Brown W. | do | do | do | |
| [illegible] | " | Murray [illegible] | do | do | do | |
| [illegible] | " | Lawson W. | do | do | 5.10.18 to 19.10.18 | |
| [illegible] | S/M. | Ritchie D. | do | [illegible] | [illegible] | |
| [illegible] | Cpl. | McFadden [illegible] | do | Returned from 14 days leave U.K. | 30/9/18 | |
| [illegible] | Pte. | Murray David | do | do | do | |
| [illegible] | " | Fenwick W. | do | do | 1/10/18 | |
| [illegible] | " | McEnemy R. | do | do | do | |
| [illegible] | " | [illegible] A.C. | do | do | do | |
| [illegible] | " | Bowie G. | do | do | 2/10/18 | |
| [illegible] | Cpl. | Dewar [illegible] | do | do | 3/10/18 | |
| [illegible] | Pte. | Harvey R. | do | do | do | |
| [illegible] | " | Leask [illegible] | do | Returned from 14 days leave to U.K. | do | |
| [illegible] | " | Lawrie [illegible] | do | Returned from 14 days leave to U.K. | [illegible] | |
| 23490 | " | Forrest A.S. | do | do | do | |
| [illegible] | " | Rankin [illegible] | do | do | do | |
| [illegible] | " | Bain [illegible] | do | Returned from 14 days leave to U.K. | do | |

* State whether absence is of a permanent or temporary nature, adding, in the case of casuals from wounds or disease any available information for communication to the relatives.

*The perforated sheet is not to be used to record casualties; additional sheets, preferably foolscap, to be attached when necessary. These sheets to be carefully numbered and the number of attached sheets to be noted here.*

Perforated Sheet giving detail of personnel and horses wanting to complete or surplus, shown on Army Form B. 213.

No. of Report 166.

| Detail of Wanting to Complete or Surplus. | Drivers. R.A. | Drivers. R.E. | Drivers. A.S.C. | Drivers. Car | Drivers. Lorry | Drivers. Steam | Gunners | Gunners Howitzer | Smith Gunners | Range Takers | Farriers Serjeants | Farriers Corporals | Shoeing or Shoeing and Carriage Smiths | Cold Shoers | Wheelers R.A. | Wheelers H.T. | Wheelers M.T. | Saddlers or Harness Makers | Blacksmiths | Bricklayers and Masons | Carpenters and Joiners | Fitters & Turners (R.E.) Wood | Fitters & Turners (R.E.) Iron | Fitters R.A. | Fitters Wireless. | Plumbers | Electricians Ordinary | Electricians W.T. | Signalmen. | Engine Drivers Loco. | Engine Drivers Field | Air Line Men. | Permanent Line Men | Operators, Telegraph | Cablemen | Brigade Section Pioneers | General-duty Pioneers | Signallers | Instrument Repairers | Motor Cyclist | Motor Cyclist Artificers | Telephonists | Clerks | Machine Gunners | Armament Artificers Fitters | Armament Artificers Range Finders | Armourers | Storemen | Privates | W.O.'s and N.C.O.'s (by ranks) not included in trade columns. M.T. Sergt. | | | | | | | | | | | TOTAL, to agree with wanting to complete or surplus Officers | TOTAL Other Ranks | Horses Riding | Horses Draught | Horses Heavy Draught | Horses Pack |
|---|---|---|---|---|---|---|---|---|---|---|---|---|---|---|---|---|---|---|---|---|---|---|---|---|---|---|---|---|---|---|---|---|---|---|---|---|---|---|---|---|---|---|---|---|---|---|---|---|---|---|---|---|---|---|---|---|---|---|---|---|---|---|---|---|---|---|
| CAVALRY—DEFICIENCY | | | | | | | | | | | | | | | | | | | | | | | | | | | | | | | | | | | | | | | | | | | | | | | | | | | | | | | | | | | | | | | | | | |
| SURPLUS | | | | | | | | | | | | | | | | | | | | | | | | | | | | | | | | | | | | | | | | | | | | | | | | | | | | | | | | | | | | | | | | | | |
| R.A.—DEFICIENCY | | | | | | | | | | | | | | | | | | | | | | | | | | | | | | | | | | | | | | | | | | | | | | | | | | | | | | | | | | | | | | | | | | |
| SURPLUS | | | | | | | | | | | | | | | | | | | | | | | | | | | | | | | | | | | | | | | | | | | | | | | | | | | | | | | | | | | | | | | | | | |
| R.E.—DEFICIENCY | | | | | | | | | | | | | | | | | | | | | | | | | | | | | | | | | | | | | | | | | | | | | | | | | | | | | | | | | | | | | | | | | | |
| SURPLUS | | | | | | | | | | | | | | | | | | | | | | | | | | | | | | | | | | | | | | | | | | | | | | | | | | | | | | | | | | | | | | | | | | |
| INFANTRY—DEFICIENCY | | | | | | | | | | | | | | | | | | | | | | | | | | | | | | | | | | | | | | | | | | | | | | | | | | | | | | | | | | | | | | | | | | |
| SURPLUS | | | | | | | | | | | | | | | | | | | | | | | | | | | | | | | | | | | | | | | | | | | | | | | | | | | | | | | | | | | | | | | | | | |
| R.A.M.C.—DEFICIENCY | | | | | | | | | | | | 1 | | | | | | | | | | | | | | | | | | | | | | | | | | | | | | | | | | | | | | 1 | | | | | | | | | | | 2 | 5 | 2 | | | |
| SURPLUS | | | | | | | | | | | | | | | | | | | | | | | | | | | | | | | | | | | | | | | | | | | | | | | | | | | | | | | | | | | | | | | | 1 | | |
| A.O.C.—DEFICIENCY | | | | | | | | | | | | | | | | | | | | | | | | | | | | | | | | | | | | | | | | | | | | | | | | | | | | | | | | | | | | | | | | | | |
| SURPLUS | | | | | | | | | | | | | | | | | | | | | | | | | | | | | | | | | | | | | | | | | | | | | | | | | | | | | | | | | | | | | | | | | | |
| A.V.C.—DEFICIENCY | | | | | | | | | | | | | | | | | | | | | | | | | | | | | | | | | | | | | | | | | | | | | | | | | | | | | | | | | | | | | | | | | | |
| SURPLUS | | | | | | | | | | | | | | | | | | | | | | | | | | | | | | | | | | | | | | | | | | | | | | | | | | | | | | | | | | | | | | | | | | |
| DEFICIENCY | | | | | | | | | | | | | | | | | | | | | | | | | | | | | | | | | | | | | | | | | | | | | | | | | | | | | | | | | | | | | | | | | | |
| SURPLUS | | | | | | | | | | | | | | | | | | | | | | | | | | | | | | | | | | | | | | | | | | | | | | | | | | | | | | | | | | | | | | | | | | |
| DEFICIENCY | | | | | | | | | | | | | | | | | | | | | | | | | | | | | | | | | | | | | | | | | | | | | | | | | | | | | | | | | | | | | | | | | | |
| SURPLUS | | | | | | | | | | | | | | | | | | | | | | | | | | | | | | | | | | | | | | | | | | | | | | | | | | | | | | | | | | | | | | | | | | |

Remarks :—

John W. Leitch Lt. Col. Signature of Commander.

1/1st Lowland Field Ambulance Unit.

52nd Division Formation to which attached.

4th October 1918 Date of Despatch.

(16523.) Wt. W6016—PP 1432. 1,500m. 3/18. D & S. (E1256) Forms B2138/3.

[P.T.O.

Additional information regarding "wanting to complete," and sufficient information to explain the difference between the present and previous week's effective strength is to be entered in this space.

Where the return of specific individuals is desired a note is to be made hereon.

REMARKS.

Any further remarks necessary may be entered here.

Strength of Officers (T.F.) 6
(T.C.) 2
8

Strength of W.O.s NCOs & Men.

W.O. 1
Q.M.S. 1
C/Sgts 2
Sgts 9
L/Sgt 1
Cpls 10
L/Cpls 5
Ptes 115
144

All Category 'A'

Explanation of R.A. effective strength.

| Drivers. | Gunners. | Signallers. | Artificers. | N.C.O's. | Total. |
|---|---|---|---|---|---|
| | | | | | |

**To be made up to and for Saturday in each week**

No. of Report 164

# FIELD RETURN.

Army Form B. 213

(To be furnished by all arms, services, and departments (except A.S.C. units) to the A.G.'s Office at the Base in accordance with Field Service Regulations, Part II.)

RETURN showing numbers (a) Effective strength of Unit. (b) Rationed by Unit. 1/1st Lowland Field Ambulance at In the Field 12th Oct. 18 Date.

| Details. | *Personnel | | | | | Animals | | | | | | Guns and transport vehicles | | | | | | | | | | | | | | Remarks |
|---|---|---|---|---|---|---|---|---|---|---|---|---|---|---|---|---|---|---|---|---|---|---|---|---|---|---|
| | | | | | | Horses | | | | Mules | | | | | | Horsed | | Mechanical | | | | | | | | |
| | Officers | Other Ranks | | | | Riding | Draught | Heavy Draught | Pack | Large | Small | Guns, showing description | Ammunition wagons | Machine guns | Aircraft, showing description | 4 Wheeled | 2 Wheeled | Motor Cars | Tractors | Lorries, showing description | Trucks, showing description | Trailers | Motor Bicycles | Bicycles | Motor Ambulances | (Number of Acting W.O.'s and N.C.O.'s included in effective strength to be shown in this column.) |
| Effective Strength of Unit | (a) 9 | (b) 177 | | | | | | | | | | | | | | | | | | | | | | 1 | | (a) Includes 1 Officer att. 1/4th R. Scots<br>" 1 " " 1/9th do.<br>" 1 " " 6th C.C.S.<br>" 1 " on Leave to U.K. |
| Details by Arms attached to Unit as in War Establishment | | (c) | | | | | | | | | | | | | | | | | | | | | | | | (b) " 10 O.R. att. 6th C.C.S.<br>" 1 " " D.H.Q.<br>" 1 " " Div. Con. Pa<br>" 1 " " Div. Train<br>" 18 " on Leave to U.K. |
| A.S.C. (HT) | | 36 | | | | 6 | 18 | 20 | | | | | | | | 13 | 3 | | | | | | 2 | | 4 | |
| A.S.C. (MT) | | (d) 11 | | | | | | | | | | | | | | | | | | | | | | | | (c) " 6 " "<br>" 1 " att. 6th C.C.S.<br>" 1 " " 217 Coy A.S.C.<br>(d) " 1 " on Leave. U.K.<br>" 1 " att. D.H.Q. |
| Total | 9 | 224 | | | | 6 | 18 | 20 | | | | | | | | 13 | 3 | | | | | | 2 | 1 | 4 | (c) " 1 " " 6 CCS |
| War Establishment | 10 | 231 | | | | 8 | 14 | 20 | | | | | | | | 13 | 4 | | | | | | 2 | 1 | 4 | |
| Wanting to complete (Detail of Personnel and Horses below.) | 1 | 7a | | | | 2 | | | | | | | | | | | 1 | | | | | | | | | a 5. RAMC & 2 ASC M.T. |
| Surplus (Detail of Personnel and Horses below.) | | | | | | | 4 | | | | | | | | | | | | | | | | | | | |
| †Attached (not to include the details shown above) | 1 | | | | | | | | | | | | | | | | | | | | | | | | | Chaplain att. |
| Attached for Rations only | | | | | | | | | | | | | | | | | | | | | | | | | | |
| Civilians Employed with and Accompanying the Unit | | | | | | | | | | | | | | | | | | | | | | | | | | |
| ‡Detached from and struck off effective strength of own Unit | | | | | | | | | | | | | | | | | | | | | | | | | | |
| ‡Detached from but retained on effective strength of own unit | | | | | | | | | | | | | | | | | | | | | | | | | | |
| Total Rationed | 10 | [illegible] | | | | 6 | 18 | 20 | | | | | | | | | | | | | | | | | | |

* Blank columns to be used for W.A.A.C. Natives or as may be required.

† In the case of field ambulances, hospitals or depots, the number of patients are to be included here, the names being shown in A.F.A. 36.

‡ These details to be enumerated by arms.

John W. Leitch Lt. Col. Signature of Commander.

12th Oct. 18 Date of Despatch.

A.F.B. 213.

15th Oct 1918

R.S.C. Att.

| No. | Rank | Name | | Nature of Casualty | Date |
|---|---|---|---|---|---|
| M2/049455 | Pte. | Duncason | C. | Transferred to Home Establishment | from 1 10/18. |
| T4/254249 | Dr. | Harris | J. | Proceeded on 14 days leave to U.K. via Boulogne. Credit ration allce. for period @ 2/ | 7-10-18 to pd. 21-10-18 |
| T4/057408 | " | Daniels | G.H. | — do — | — do — |
| T1SR/562. | " | Foster | W.H. | — do — | 8-10-18 to 22-10-18 |
| T4/240091 | " | Robertson | G.B. | — do — | 11-10-18 to 25-10-18 |
| T/29314 | Dr. | Sutton | C. | Returned from 14 days leave U.K | 5 10/18 |
| T/36536. | " | Jeggo | C. | — do — | — do — |
| T4/185446 | " | Lowden | H. | — do — | 6 10/18 |
| T4/199947 | " | Clapperton | R. | — do — | 6 10/18 |
| T4/213931 | " | Miller | C. C. | — do — | 6 10/18 |
| T4/213601 | " | Burton | W. | — do — | 6 10/18 |

*For information of the A.G.'s Office at the base.*

Officers and men who have become casuals, been transferred or joined since last report.

Place In the Field　　　　Date 12th Oct. 1918

| Regtl. Number | Rank | Name | Corps | Nature of casualty, or name of unit from or to which transferred. | Date of being struck off or coming on the ration return. | Remarks * |
|---|---|---|---|---|---|---|
| | Capt. | [illegible] Miller | R.A.M.C.(T) | Joined as reinforcement from Base. | 5/10/18 | [illegible] |
| | " | do. | do. | To duty with 1/4 R.S. as R.M.O. | 11/10/18 | Tempy. |
| | " | R. L. Rennie | do. | Returned from duty with 1/4 R.S. | 11/10/18 | |
| | " | - do - | do. | Proceeded on 14 days leave to U.K. via Boulogne | 13.10.18 | – 27.10.18. |
| | Major | [illegible] Browne. | do. | Returned from duty with 45 C.C.S. | 9/10/18 | |
| | " | W. F. Mackenzie | do. | To duty with 6 C.C.S. | 9/10/18 | Tempy. |
| [illegible] | Pte. | McIntyre C. | do. | Granted 3 days extension of leave ending 2/10 | | Auth. [illegible] |
| [illegible] | L/Cpl. | Mitchelson D. | do. | " " " | | Auth. [illegible] |
| [illegible] | Pte. | McIntyre R. | do. | Granted 14 days leave to U.K. Credit ration allce. at [illegible] for that period. via Boulogne | 6.10.18 | – 20.10.18. |
| [illegible] | " | McMillan R. | do. | do. | | do. |
| [illegible] | " | Partington H. | do. | do. | 8.10.18 | to 22.10.18. |
| [illegible] | L/Cpl. | Hampson W. J. | do. | do. | 11.10.18 | to 25.10.18. |
| [illegible] | Cpl. | McDonald R. | do. | Granted six weeks leave to U.K. credit ration allce. for that period @ 2/- pd. via Boulogne | 12.10.18 | – 23.11.18. |
| [illegible] | Pte. | McIntyre C. | do. | Returned from leave | 5/10/18 | |
| [illegible] | L/Cpl. | Mitchelson D. J. | do. | do. | do. | |
| [illegible] | Cpl. | Dewar C. | do. | do. | do. | |
| [illegible] | Pte. | Murray J. B. | do. | do. | do. | |
| [illegible] | " | Smellie W. A. | do. | do. | 6/10/18. | |
| [illegible] | " | Pender W. | do. | do. | do. | |
| [illegible] | " | Peter W. | do. | do. | do. | |
| [illegible] | " | McEwen H. | do. | do. | do. | |
| [illegible] | " | Edwards W. J. | do. | do. | 7/10/18 | |
| [illegible] | " | Gosling J. J. | do. | do. | do. | |
| [illegible] | " | Gee D. | do. | do. | do. | |
| [illegible] | " | Morris E. | do. | do. | do. | |
| [illegible] | " | Stanley R. | do. | do. | 8/10/18. | |

* State whether absence is of a permanent or temporary nature, adding, in the case of casuals from wounds or disease any available information for communication to the relatives.

*The perforated sheet is not to be used to record casualties ; additional sheets, preferably foolscap, to be attached when necessary. These sheets to be carefully numbered and the number of attached sheets to be noted here.*

Additional information regarding "wanting to complete," and sufficient information to explain the difference between the present and previous week's effective strength is to be entered in this space.

Where the return of specific individuals is desired a note is to be made hereon.

REMARKS.

Any further remarks necessary may be entered here.

Strength of Officers (T.F.) 6.
(T.C.) 3
9.

Strength of W.O.'s, N.C.O's and men.

W.O. 1
Q.M.S. 1
S/Sgts. 2
Sgts. 9.
L/Sgt. 1
Cpls. 10.
L/Cpls. 5
Ptes. 148
147

All category "A".

| Explanation of R.A. effective strength. | | | | | | |
|---|---|---|---|---|---|---|
| | Drivers. | Gunners. | Signallers. | Artificers. | N.C.O's. | Total. |
| | | | | | | |

Perforated Sheet giving detail of personnel and horses wanting to complete or surplus, shown on Army Form B. 213.

No. of Report 164.

| Detail of Wanting to Complete or Surplus. | Drivers. R.A. | Drivers. R.E. | Drivers. A.S.C. | Drivers. Car | Drivers. Lorry | Drivers. Steam | Gunners | Gunners Howitzer | Smith Gunners | Range Takers | Farriers Serjeants | Farriers Corporals | Shoeing or Shoeing and Carriage Smiths | Cold Shoers | Wheelers R.A. | Wheelers H.T. | Wheelers M.T. | Saddlers or Harness Makers | Blacksmiths | Bricklayers and Masons | Carpenters and Joiners | Fitters & Turners (R.E.) Wood | Fitters & Turners (R.E.) Iron | Fitters R.A. | Fitters Wireless. | Plumbers | Electricians Ordinary | Electricians W.T. | Signalmen. | Engine Drivers Loco. | Engine Drivers Field | Air Line Men. | Permanent Line Men | Operators, Telegraph | Cablemen | Brigade Section Pioneers | General-duty Pioneers | Signallers | Instrument Repairers | Motor Cyclist | Motor Cyclist Artificers | Telephonists | Clerks | Machine Gunners | Armament Artificers Fitters | Armament Artificers Range Finders | Armourers | Storemen | Privates | W.O's and N.C.O's (by ranks) not included in trade columns. Sgt H.T. A.S.C. | | | | | | | | | | TOTAL to agree with wanting to complete or surplus Officers | TOTAL Other Ranks | Horses Riding | Horses Draught | Horses Heavy Draught | Horses Pack |
|---|---|---|---|---|---|---|---|---|---|---|---|---|---|---|---|---|---|---|---|---|---|---|---|---|---|---|---|---|---|---|---|---|---|---|---|---|---|---|---|---|---|---|---|---|---|---|---|---|---|---|---|---|---|---|---|---|---|---|---|---|---|---|---|---|---|
| CAVALRY— DEFICIENCY | | | | | | | | | | | | | | | | | | | | | | | | | | | | | | | | | | | | | | | | | | | | | | | | | | | | | | | | | | | | | | | | | | |
| SURPLUS | | | | | | | | | | | | | | | | | | | | | | | | | | | | | | | | | | | | | | | | | | | | | | | | | | | | | | | | | | | | | | | | | |
| R.A.— DEFICIENCY | | | | | | | | | | | | | | | | | | | | | | | | | | | | | | | | | | | | | | | | | | | | | | | | | | | | | | | | | | | | | | | | | |
| SURPLUS | | | | | | | | | | | | | | | | | | | | | | | | | | | | | | | | | | | | | | | | | | | | | | | | | | | | | | | | | | | | | | | | | |
| R.E.— DEFICIENCY | | | | | | | | | | | | | | | | | | | | | | | | | | | | | | | | | | | | | | | | | | | | | | | | | | | | | | | | | | | | | | | | | |
| SURPLUS | | | | | | | | | | | | | | | | | | | | | | | | | | | | | | | | | | | | | | | | | | | | | | | | | | | | | | | | | | | | | | | | | |
| INFANTRY— DEFICIENCY | | | | | | | | | | | | | | | | | | | | | | | | | | | | | | | | | | | | | | | | | | | | | | | | | | | | | | | | | | | | | | | | | |
| SURPLUS | | | | | | | | | | | | | | | | | | | | | | | | | | | | | | | | | | | | | | | | | | | | | | | | | | | | | | | | | | | | | | | | | |
| R.A.M.C.— DEFICIENCY | | | | | 1 | | | | | | | | 1 | | | | | | | | | | | | | | | | | | | | | | | | | | | | | | | | | | | | | 1 | | | | | | | | | | 1 | 52 | | | | |
| SURPLUS | | | | | | | | | | | | | | | | | | | | | | | | | | | | | | | | | | | | | | | | | | | | | | | | | | | | | | | | | | | | | | | 1 | | |
| A.O.C.— DEFICIENCY | | | | | | | | | | | | | | | | | | | | | | | | | | | | | | | | | | | | | | | | | | | | | | | | | | | | | | | | | | | | | | | | | |
| SURPLUS | | | | | | | | | | | | | | | | | | | | | | | | | | | | | | | | | | | | | | | | | | | | | | | | | | | | | | | | | | | | | | | | | |
| A.V.C.— DEFICIENCY | | | | | | | | | | | | | | | | | | | | | | | | | | | | | | | | | | | | | | | | | | | | | | | | | | | | | | | | | | | | | | | | | |
| SURPLUS | | | | | | | | | | | | | | | | | | | | | | | | | | | | | | | | | | | | | | | | | | | | | | | | | | | | | | | | | | | | | | | | | |
| DEFICIENCY | | | | | | | | | | | | | | | | | | | | | | | | | | | | | | | | | | | | | | | | | | | | | | | | | | | | | | | | | | | | | | | | | |
| SURPLUS | | | | | | | | | | | | | | | | | | | | | | | | | | | | | | | | | | | | | | | | | | | | | | | | | | | | | | | | | | | | | | | | | |
| DEFICIENCY | | | | | | | | | | | | | | | | | | | | | | | | | | | | | | | | | | | | | | | | | | | | | | | | | | | | | | | | | | | | | | | | | |
| SURPLUS | | | | | | | | | | | | | | | | | | | | | | | | | | | | | | | | | | | | | | | | | | | | | | | | | | | | | | | | | | | | | | | | | |

Remarks :—

Johnson Leitch Lt. Col. Signature of Commander.

1/1st Lowland Field Ambulance. Unit.

52nd Division Formation to which attached.

10th Oct. 1918. Date of Despatch.

(16523.) Wt. W6016—PP 1432. 1,500m. 3/18. D & S. (E1256) Forms B2138/8.

[P.T.O.

**To be made up to and for Saturday in each week**

No. of Report 169.

# FIELD RETURN.

Army Form B. 213

(To be furnished by all arms, services, and departments (except A.S.C. units) to the A.G.'s Office at the Base in accordance with Field Service Regulations, Part II.)

RETURN showing numbers (*a*) Effective strength of Unit. (*b*) Rationed by Unit. 1/1 Lowland Field Amb at In the Field 26th Oct. Date.

| DETAILS. | Personnel* Officers | Other Ranks | | | | Animals: Horses Riding | Draught | Heavy Draught | Pack* | Mules Large | Small | Guns and transport vehicles: Guns, showing description | Ammunition wagons | Machine guns | Aircraft, showing description | Horsed 4 Wheeled | 2 Wheeled | Mechanical: Motor Cars | Tractors | Lorries, showing description | Trucks, showing description | Trailers | Motor Bicycles | Bicycles | Motor Ambulances | REMARKS (Number of Acting W.O.'s and N.C.O.'s included in effective strength to be shown in this column.) |
|---|---|---|---|---|---|---|---|---|---|---|---|---|---|---|---|---|---|---|---|---|---|---|---|---|---|---|
| Effective Strength of Unit ... ... | (a) 7 | (b) 169. | | | | | | | | | | | | | | | | | | | | | | 1 | | (a) Includes 1 officer on leave<br>(b) " 1 [illegible] DHQ, [illegible]<br>and 1 @ Div. [illegible]<br>" 15 O.R. [illegible] to U.K. |
| Details by Arms attached to Unit as in War Establishment ... ... ... | | | | | | | | | | | | | | | | | | | | | | | | | | |
| A.S.C. H.T. | | (c) 35 | | | | 6 | 18 | 23 | | | | | | | | | | | | | | | | | | (c) " 1 " " " " " |
| A.S.C. M.T. | | (d) 11 | | | | | | | | | | | | | | 13 | 14 | | | | | | 3 | | 7. | (d) " 2 on leave to U.K.<br>" 1 @ DHQ |
| TOTAL ... ... | 7 | 21[illegible] | | | | 6 | [illegible] | 20 | | | | | | | | 13 | 14 | | | | | | 3 | 1 | 7 | |
| War Establishment ... ... ... | 10 | 2[illegible]1 | | | | 5 | 17 | 20 | | | | | | | | 13 | 14 | | | | | | 3 | 1 | 7. | |
| Wanting to complete ... ... ... (Detail of Personnel and Horses below.) | 3 | 1 16 | | | | [illegible] | | | | | | | | | | | | | | | | | | | | † 15 R.A.M.C., [illegible] |
| SURPLUS ... ... (Detail of Personnel and Horses below.) | | | | | | | 1 | | | | | | | | | | | | | | | | | | | |
| †Attached (not to include the details shown above) ... ... ... ... | 1 | | | | | | | | | | | | | | | | | | | | | | | | | Chaplain. |
| Attached for Rations only ... ... | | | | | | | | | | | | | | | | | | | | | | | | | | |
| Civilians Employed with and Accompanying the Unit ... ... ... | | | | | | | | | | | | | | | | | | | | | | | | | | |
| ‡Detached from and struck off effective strength of own Unit ... ... | | | | | | | | | | | | | | | | | | | | | | | | | | |
| ‡Detached from but retained on effective strength of own unit... ... ... | | 1 | | | | | | 2 | | | | | | | | | | | | | | | | | | [illegible] |
| TOTAL RATIONED ... | 7 | 118 | | | | [illegible] | | | | | | | | | | | | | | | | | | | | |

* Blank columns to be used for W.A.A.C. Natives or as may be required.

† In the case of field ambulances, hospitals or depots, the number of patients are to be included here, the names being shown in A.F.A. 36.

‡ These details to be enumerated by arms.

[illegible] Signature of Commander.

26/10/18. Date of Despatch.

M. 2513.

[illegible]

| No. | RK | NAME | | NATURE OF CASUALTY. | DATE. |
|---|---|---|---|---|---|
| T/35692 | Dvr | Littlewood | W. | Sick to Hospl | 19/10/18. |
| T/35061 | " | Cooper | J. | Granted 14 days leave to UK via Boulogne Credit ration allce for that period. 25/10/- to | 8/11/18 |
| T4/245543 | " | Savage | H. T. | Granted 14 days leave to UK via Boulogne Credit ration allce for that period 29/10 to 12/11/18 | |
| M2/135999 | Me | Boorman | H.J.G. | Granted 14 days leave to UK via Boulogne Credit ration allce for that period 21/10/- to 4/11/18. | |
| T4/247752. | Dr | Jones | T.A. | Retd. from leave. | 22/10/18 |
| T4/254279 (T4/058408) | Dr | Daniels | J.H. | -do- | 24/10/18 |
| | Dr | Harris | J. | -do- | 24/10/18 |

*For information of the A.G.'s Office at the base.*

Officers and men who have become casuals, been transferred or joined since last report.

Place ______________________ Date [illegible]

| Regtl. Number | Rank | Name | Corps | Nature of casualty, or name of unit from or to which transferred. | Date of being struck off or coming on the ration return. | Remarks * |
|---|---|---|---|---|---|---|
| [illegible] | [illegible] | [illegible] | [illegible] | [illegible] | [illegible] | |
| [illegible] | | [illegible] | | [illegible] | [illegible] | |
| [illegible] | | [illegible] | [illegible] | [illegible] | [illegible] | |
| [illegible] | | [illegible] | [illegible] | do | [illegible] | |
| [illegible] | | [illegible] | do | do | [illegible] | |
| [illegible] | 2" | Hudson E.R. | do | [illegible] | [illegible] | |
| [illegible] | [illegible] | [illegible] | [illegible] | [illegible] | [illegible] | [illegible] |
| [illegible] | Pte | [illegible] | R.A.M.C. T. | do. do. | [illegible] | [illegible] |
| 6016 | " | [illegible] | do | do. do. | [illegible] | [illegible] |
| [illegible] | Sgt | [illegible] | do. | do. do. | [illegible] | [illegible] |
| [illegible] | Pte | [illegible] | do. | [illegible] | [illegible] | |
| [illegible] | " | [illegible] | do | do | [illegible] | |
| [illegible] | " | [illegible] | do | do | " | |
| [illegible] | " | [illegible] | do | do | " | |
| [illegible] | " | [illegible] | do | do | " | |
| [illegible] | " | [illegible] | do | do | " | |
| [illegible] | " | [illegible] | R.A.M.C. | do | " | |
| 16057 | " | [illegible] | R.A.M.C. T | do. | " | |

STRENGTH. Officers T.F. 7. W.O., N.C.O. and men

| | | | |
|---|---|---|---|
| W.O. | 1. | [illegible] | 10. |
| [illegible] | 1. | [illegible] | 5. |
| [illegible] | [illegible] | [illegible] | |
| [illegible] | [illegible] | [illegible] | 141 |
| [illegible] | 1. | | 164. |

[illegible] Category "A".

* State whether absence is of a permanent or temporary nature, adding, in the case of casuals from wounds or disease any available information for communication to the relatives.

*The perforated sheet is not to be used to record casualties; additional sheets, preferably foolscap, to be attached when necessary. These sheets to be carefully numbered and the number of attached sheets to be noted here.*

Perforated Sheet giving detail of personnel and horses wanting to complete or surplus, shown on Army Form B. 213.

No. of Report 169.

| Detail of Wanting to Complete or Surplus. | Drivers. R.A. | Drivers. R.E. | Drivers. A.S.C. | Drivers. Car | Drivers. Lorry | Drivers. Steam | Gunners | Gunners Howitzer | Smith Gunners | Range Takers | Farriers Serjeants | Farriers Corporals | Shoeing or Shoeing and Carriage Smiths | Cold Shoers | Wheelers R.A. | Wheelers H.T. | Wheelers M.T. | Saddlers or Harness Makers | Blacksmiths | Bricklayers and Masons | Carpenters and Joiners | Fitters & Turners (R.E.) Wood |
|---|---|---|---|---|---|---|---|---|---|---|---|---|---|---|---|---|---|---|---|---|---|---|
| CAVALRY—DEFICIENCY | | | | | | | | | | | | | | | | | | | | | | |
| SURPLUS | | | | | | | | | | | | | | | | | | | | | | |
| R.A.—DEFICIENCY | | | | | | | | | | | | | | | | | | | | | | |
| SURPLUS | | | | | | | | | | | | | | | | | | | | | | |
| R.E.—DEFICIENCY | | | | | | | | | | | | | | | | | | | | | | |
| SURPLUS | | | | | | | | | | | | | | | | | | | | | | |
| INFANTRY—DEFICIENCY | | | | | | | | | | | | | | | | | | | | | | |
| SURPLUS | | | | | | | | | | | | | | | | | | | | | | |
| R.A.M.C.—DEFICIENCY | | | 1 | | | | | | | | 1 | | | | | | | | | | | |
| SURPLUS | | | | | | | | | | | | | | | | | | | | | | |
| A.O.C.—DEFICIENCY | | | | | | | | | | | | | | | | | | | | | | |
| SURPLUS | | | | | | | | | | | | | | | | | | | | | | |
| A.V.C.—DEFICIENCY | | | | | | | | | | | | | | | | | | | | | | |
| SURPLUS | | | | | | | | | | | | | | | | | | | | | | |
| DEFICIENCY | | | | | | | | | | | | | | | | | | | | | | |
| SURPLUS | | | | | | | | | | | | | | | | | | | | | | |
| DEFICIENCY | | | | | | | | | | | | | | | | | | | | | | |
| SURPLUS | | | | | | | | | | | | | | | | | | | | | | |

| Detail of Wanting to Complete or Surplus. | Fitters & Turners (R.E.) Iron | Fitters R.A. | Fitters Wireless. | Plumbers | Electricians Ordinary | Electricians W.T. | Signalmen. | Engine Drivers Loco. | Engine Drivers Field | Air Line Men. | Permanent Line Men | Operators, Telegraph | Cablemen | Brigade Section Pioneers | General-duty Pioneers | Signallers | Instrument Repairers | Motor Cyclist | Motor Cyclist Artificers | Telephonists | Clerks | Machine Gunners |
|---|---|---|---|---|---|---|---|---|---|---|---|---|---|---|---|---|---|---|---|---|---|---|
| CAVALRY—DEFICIENCY | | | | | | | | | | | | | | | | | | | | | | |
| SURPLUS | | | | | | | | | | | | | | | | | | | | | | |
| R.A.—DEFICIENCY | | | | | | | | | | | | | | | | | | | | | | |
| SURPLUS | | | | | | | | | | | | | | | | | | | | | | |
| R.E.—DEFICIENCY | | | | | | | | | | | | | | | | | | | | | | |
| SURPLUS | | | | | | | | | | | | | | | | | | | | | | |
| INFANTRY—DEFICIENCY | | | | | | | | | | | | | | | | | | | | | | |
| SURPLUS | | | | | | | | | | | | | | | | | | | | | | |
| R.A.M.C.—DEFICIENCY | | | | | | | | 6 | | | | | | | | | | | | | | |
| SURPLUS | | | | | | | | | | | | | | | | | | | | | | |
| A.O.C.—DEFICIENCY | | | | | | | | | | | | | | | | | | | | | | |
| SURPLUS | | | | | | | | | | | | | | | | | | | | | | |
| A.V.C.—DEFICIENCY | | | | | | | | | | | | | | | | | | | | | | |
| SURPLUS | | | | | | | | | | | | | | | | | | | | | | |
| DEFICIENCY | | | | | | | | | | | | | | | | | | | | | | |
| SURPLUS | | | | | | | | | | | | | | | | | | | | | | |
| DEFICIENCY | | | | | | | | | | | | | | | | | | | | | | |
| SURPLUS | | | | | | | | | | | | | | | | | | | | | | |

| Detail of Wanting to Complete or Surplus. | Armament Artificers Fitters | Armament Artificers Range Finders | Armourers | Storemen | Privates | W.O.'s and N.C.O.'s (by ranks) not included in trade columns. Sgt MT ASC | | | | | | | | | | | TOTAL to agree with wanting to complete or surplus Officers | TOTAL Other Ranks | Horses Riding | Horses Draught | Horses Heavy Draught | Horses Pack |
|---|---|---|---|---|---|---|---|---|---|---|---|---|---|---|---|---|---|---|---|---|---|---|
| CAVALRY—DEFICIENCY | | | | | | | | | | | | | | | | | | | | | | |
| SURPLUS | | | | | | | | | | | | | | | | | | | | | | |
| R.A.—DEFICIENCY | | | | | | | | | | | | | | | | | | | | | | |
| SURPLUS | | | | | | | | | | | | | | | | | | | | | | |
| R.E.—DEFICIENCY | | | | | | | | | | | | | | | | | | | | | | |
| SURPLUS | | | | | | | | | | | | | | | | | | | | | | |
| INFANTRY—DEFICIENCY | | | | | | | | | | | | | | | | | | | | | | |
| SURPLUS | | | | | | | | | | | | | | | | | | | | | | |
| R.A.M.C.—DEFICIENCY | | | | | 13 | 1 | | | | | | | | | | | 3 | 16 | 2 | | | |
| SURPLUS | | | | | | | | | | | | | | | | | | | | | | |
| A.O.C.—DEFICIENCY | | | | | | | | | | | | | | | | | | | | | | |
| SURPLUS | | | | | | | | | | | | | | | | | | | | | | |
| A.V.C.—DEFICIENCY | | | | | | | | | | | | | | | | | | | | | | |
| SURPLUS | | | | | | | | | | | | | | | | | | | | | | |
| DEFICIENCY | | | | | | | | | | | | | | | | | | | | | | |
| SURPLUS | | | | | | | | | | | | | | | | | | | | | | |
| DEFICIENCY | | | | | | | | | | | | | | | | | | | | | | |
| SURPLUS | | | | | | | | | | | | | | | | | | | | | | |

Remarks :—

[illegible] Major for Lt Col Signature of Commander.

1/ Lowland Fd Amb RAMC T. Unit.

52nd Div Formation to which attached.

26th Oct 1918 Date of Despatch.

(16523.) Wt. W6016—PP 1432. 1,500m. 3/18. D & S. (E1256) Forms B2138/8. [P.T.O.

**To be made up to and for Saturday in each week**

No. of Report 168

# FIELD RETURN.

Army Form B. 213

(To be furnished by all arms, services, and departments (except A.S.C. units) to the A.G.'s Office at the Base in accordance with Field Service Regulations, Part II.)

RETURN showing numbers (*a*) Effective strength of Unit. (*b*) Rationed by Unit. 1/ Lowland Field Ambulance at In the Field 14 Oct 1918 Date.

| Details. | *Personnel: Officers | Other Ranks | | | | Animals: Horses: Riding | Draught | Heavy Draught | Pack | Mules: Large | Small | Guns and transport vehicles: Guns, showing description | Ammunition wagons | Machine guns | Aircraft, showing description | Horsed: †4 Wheeled | 2 Wheeled | Mechanical: Motor Cars | Tractors | Lorries, showing description | Trucks, showing description | Trailers | Motor Bicycles | Bicycles | Motor Ambulances | Remarks (Number of Acting W.O.'s and N.C.O.'s included in effective strength to be shown in this column.) |
|---|---|---|---|---|---|---|---|---|---|---|---|---|---|---|---|---|---|---|---|---|---|---|---|---|---|---|
| Effective Strength of Unit ... ... | (a) 7 | (b) 175 | | | | | | | | | | | | | | | | | | | | | | 1 | | (a) Includes 1 off. [illegible] of following, [illegible] No. 4 [illegible] 8 C. Rstn, & leave to U.K.<br>(b) Includes 14 O.R. at No. 6 [illegible]<br>" 20 " " 8 C. Rest [illegible]<br>" 1 " " D.H.Q.<br>" 1 " " [illegible]<br>" 19 " on leave to U.K.<br>~~" 1 " [illegible]~~<br>(c) " 8 " on leave to U.K.<br>" 1 [illegible] at [illegible]<br>~~" 1 [illegible]~~<br>(d) " 1 " on leave to U.K.<br>" 1 " at D.H.Q. |
| Details by Arms attached to Unit as in War Establishment ... ... | | | | | | | | | | | | | | | | | | | | | | | | | | | |
| A.S.C. (H.T.) | | (c) 36 | | | | 6 | 18 | 20 | | | | | | | | 13 | 14 | | | | | | | | | |
| A.S.C. (M.T.) | | (d) 11 | | | | | | | | | | | | | | | | | | | | | 2 | | 7 | |
| Total ... | 17 | 222 | | | | 6 | 18* | 20* | | | | | | | | 13 | 14 | | | | | | 2 | 1 | 7 | |
| War Establishment ... ... | 10 | [illegible] | | | | 8 | 11 | 20 | | | | | | | | | | | | | | | 2 | 1 | 7 | * 2 H.D. [illegible] 8 C. R. Stn |
| Wanting to complete ... ... (Detail of Personnel and Horses below.) | 3 | 4 | | | | | | | | | | | | | | | | | | | | | | | | 7 - RAMC & 2 ASC MT |
| Surplus ... ... (Detail of Personnel and Horses below.) | | | | | | | 1 | | | | | | | | | | | | | | | | | | | |
| †Attached (not to include the details shown above) ... ... | 1 | | | | | | | | | | | | | | | | | | | | | | | | | Chaplain |
| Attached for Rations only ... ... | | | | | | | | | | | | | | | | | | | | | | | | | | |
| Civilians Employed with and Accompanying the Unit ... | | | | | | | | | | | | | | | | | | | | | | | | | | |
| ‡Detached from and struck off effective strength of own Unit ... | | | | | | | | | | | | | | | | | | | | | | | | | | |
| ‡Detached from but retained on effective strength of own unit... | | 1 | | | | | | 2 | | | | | | | | | | | | | | | | | | at [illegible] 52nd D. [illegible] Train |
| Total Rationed ... | 5 | 148 | | | | 6 | 16 | 20 | | | | | | | | | | | | | | | | | | |

* Blank columns to be used for W.A.A.C. Natives or as may be required.

† In the case of field ambulances, hospitals or depots, the number of patients are to be included here, the names being shown in A.F.A. 36.

‡ These details to be enumerated by arms.

[illegible] Lt Col. Signature of Commander.

14 Oct 1918 Date of Despatch.

AF B 213.

19 Oct 1918

A.S.C. att^d

| No | Rank. | Name. | | Nature of Casualty. | Date |
|---|---|---|---|---|---|
| M2/135999 | Pte | Blackwell | G.J. | Granted 14 days leave to UK via Boulogne. Credit ration allce @ 2/- per day for that period 14/10/18 to 27/10/18 | |
| CMT/15 | Dvr | Dobson | G. | do do 15/10/18 to 29/10/18 | |
| T/25953 | " | Butler. | F. | do do 16/10/18 to 30/10/18 | |
| M2/135962 | Pte | Lewis | G.H. | Rtd. from leave | 18/10/18. |
| TH/243601 | Dvr. | Barlow | W. | War pay increased to 4d from | 11/10/18 |
| T/35061 | " | Cooper | T H | do " | 13/10/18 |
| TH/245593 | " | Bracewell | W.J. | do " | 9/10/18. |

1 ASC sheet att[illegible]

*For information of the A.G.'s Office at the base.*

Officers and men who have become casuals, been transferred or joined since last report.

Place In the Field　　　　Date 14 Oct 1918

| Regtl. Number | Rank | Name | | Corps | Nature of casualty, or name of unit from or to which transferred. | Date of being struck off or coming on the ration return. | Remarks * |
|---|---|---|---|---|---|---|---|
| 316077 | Pte | Dickson | D | RAMC T. | Sick - To Hosp. | 13/10/18. | |
| 316041 | [illegible] | Fothergill | W.D. | do. | Granted 14 days Leave to U.K. via Boulogne. Credit ration allce [illegible] | | 11/10/18 to 25/10/18 |
| 316046 | Pte | O'Neil | E | do. | do | do | 11/10/18 to [illegible] 1/11/18. |
| 316055 | " | Cant | G. | do. | do. | do | [illegible] 1/11/18. |
| 316215 | " | McLennan | W. | do. | Granted 14 days leave to UK, via Boulogne. Credit ration allce [illegible] for that period. | | 16/10/18 to 30/10/18. |
| 316334 | " | Smellie | T.A. | do | Sick - To Hospl. | 17/10/18. | |
| 61443 | " | Gehan | G. | RAMC. | Returned from leave | 16/10/18 | |
| 70100 | " | Bigley | J. | do. | do | " | |
| 56142 | " | Adams | E. | do. | do | " | |
| 27891 | Cpl | Edwards | J. | do. | do | " | |
| | Capt | Millar | T.D. | RAMC T | Sick - to Hospl. | 18/10/18 | Temp'y att. 1/4 R.S. |
| | " | Morgan | J.M. | RAMC | To 5th D.I.S. | " | Temp'y att. 1/7 R.S. |

Strength:- Officers (TF) 6.
(T.C.) 3.

W.O. NCO & MEN.

| | | | |
|---|---|---|---|
| W.O. | 1. | Cpls | 10. |
| QMS. | 1. | L/Cpls | 5. |
| S/Sgts. | 2. | Ptes. | 146. |
| Sgts | 9. | Total. | 175. |
| L/Sgts. | 1. | | |

All category "A".

* State whether absence is of a permanent or temporary nature, adding, in the case of casuals from wounds or disease any available information for communication to the relatives.

*The perforated sheet is not to be used to record casualties ; additional sheets, preferably foolscap, to be attached when necessary. These sheets to be carefully numbered and the number of attached sheets to be noted here.*

Perforated Sheet giving detail of personnel and horses wanting to complete or surplus, shown on Army Form B. 213.

No. of Report 168

| Detail of Wanting to Complete or Surplus | Drivers R.A. | Drivers R.E. | Drivers A.S.C. | Drivers Car | Drivers Lorry | Drivers Steam | Gunners | Gunners Howitzer | Smith Gunners | Range Takers | Farriers Serjeants | Farriers Corporals | Shoeing or Shoeing and Carriage Smiths | Cold Shoers | Wheelers R.A. | Wheelers H.T. | Wheelers M.T. | Saddlers or Harness Makers | Blacksmiths | Bricklayers and Masons | Carpenters and Joiners |
|---|---|---|---|---|---|---|---|---|---|---|---|---|---|---|---|---|---|---|---|---|---|
| CAVALRY— DEFICIENCY | | | | | | | | | | | | | | | | | | | | | |
| SURPLUS | | | | | | | | | | | | | | | | | | | | | |
| R.A.— DEFICIENCY | | | | | | | | | | | | | | | | | | | | | |
| SURPLUS | | | | | | | | | | | | | | | | | | | | | |
| R.E.— DEFICIENCY | | | | | | | | | | | | | | | | | | | | | |
| SURPLUS | | | | | | | | | | | | | | | | | | | | | |
| INFANTRY— DEFICIENCY | | | | | | | | | | | | | | | | | | | | | |
| SURPLUS | | | | | | | | | | | | | | | | | | | | | |
| R.A.M.C.— DEFICIENCY | | | 1 | 1 | | | | | | | | 1 | | | | | | | | | |
| SURPLUS | | | | | | | | | | | | | | | | | | | | | |
| A.O.C.— DEFICIENCY | | | | | | | | | | | | | | | | | | | | | |
| SURPLUS | | | | | | | | | | | | | | | | | | | | | |
| A.V.C.— DEFICIENCY | | | | | | | | | | | | | | | | | | | | | |
| SURPLUS | | | | | | | | | | | | | | | | | | | | | |
| DEFICIENCY | | | | | | | | | | | | | | | | | | | | | |
| SURPLUS | | | | | | | | | | | | | | | | | | | | | |
| DEFICIENCY | | | | | | | | | | | | | | | | | | | | | |
| SURPLUS | | | | | | | | | | | | | | | | | | | | | |

| Detail of Wanting to Complete or Surplus | Fitters & Turners (R.E.) Wood | Fitters & Turners (R.E.) Iron | Fitters R.A. | Fitters Wireless. | Plumbers | Electricians Ordinary | Electricians W.T. | Signalmen. | Engine Drivers Loco. | Engine Drivers Field. | Air Line Men. | Permanent Line Men | Operators, Telegraph | Cablemen | Brigade Section Pioneers | General-duty Pioneers | Signallers | Instrument Repairers | Motor Cyclist | Motor Cyclist Artificers | Telephonists | Clerks | Machine Gunners |
|---|---|---|---|---|---|---|---|---|---|---|---|---|---|---|---|---|---|---|---|---|---|---|---|
| CAVALRY— DEFICIENCY | | | | | | | | | | | | | | | | | | | | | | | |
| SURPLUS | | | | | | | | | | | | | | | | | | | | | | | |
| R.A.— DEFICIENCY | | | | | | | | | | | | | | | | | | | | | | | |
| SURPLUS | | | | | | | | | | | | | | | | | | | | | | | |
| R.E.— DEFICIENCY | | | | | | | | | | | | | | | | | | | | | | | |
| SURPLUS | | | | | | | | | | | | | | | | | | | | | | | |
| INFANTRY— DEFICIENCY | | | | | | | | | | | | | | | | | | | | | | | |
| SURPLUS | | | | | | | | | | | | | | | | | | | | | | | |
| R.A.M.C.— DEFICIENCY | | | | | | | | | 6 | | | | | | | | | | | | | | |
| SURPLUS | | | | | | | | | | | | | | | | | | | | | | | |
| A.O.C.— DEFICIENCY | | | | | | | | | | | | | | | | | | | | | | | |
| SURPLUS | | | | | | | | | | | | | | | | | | | | | | | |
| A.V.C.— DEFICIENCY | | | | | | | | | | | | | | | | | | | | | | | |
| SURPLUS | | | | | | | | | | | | | | | | | | | | | | | |
| DEFICIENCY | | | | | | | | | | | | | | | | | | | | | | | |
| SURPLUS | | | | | | | | | | | | | | | | | | | | | | | |
| DEFICIENCY | | | | | | | | | | | | | | | | | | | | | | | |
| SURPLUS | | | | | | | | | | | | | | | | | | | | | | | |

| Detail of Wanting to Complete or Surplus | Armament Artificers Fitters | Armament Artificers Range Finders | Armourers | Storemen | Privates | W.O.'s and N.C.O.'s (by ranks) not included in trade columns. Sgt MT ASC | | | | | | | | | TOTAL to agree with wanting to complete or surplus Officers | TOTAL Other Ranks | Horses Riding | Horses Draught | Horses Heavy Draught | Horses Pack |
|---|---|---|---|---|---|---|---|---|---|---|---|---|---|---|---|---|---|---|---|---|
| CAVALRY— DEFICIENCY | | | | | | | | | | | | | | | | | | | | |
| SURPLUS | | | | | | | | | | | | | | | | | | | | |
| R.A.— DEFICIENCY | | | | | | | | | | | | | | | | | | | | |
| SURPLUS | | | | | | | | | | | | | | | | | | | | |
| R.E.— DEFICIENCY | | | | | | | | | | | | | | | | | | | | |
| SURPLUS | | | | | | | | | | | | | | | | | | | | |
| INFANTRY— DEFICIENCY | | | | | | | | | | | | | | | | | | | | |
| SURPLUS | | | | | | | | | | | | | | | | | | | | |
| R.A.M.C.— DEFICIENCY | | | | | | 1 | | | | | | | | | 3 | 7 | | 1 | | |
| SURPLUS | | | | | | | | | | | | | | | | | | | | |
| A.O.C.— DEFICIENCY | | | | | | | | | | | | | | | | | | | | |
| SURPLUS | | | | | | | | | | | | | | | | | | | | |
| A.V.C.— DEFICIENCY | | | | | | | | | | | | | | | | | | | | |
| SURPLUS | | | | | | | | | | | | | | | | | | | | |
| DEFICIENCY | | | | | | | | | | | | | | | | | | | | |
| SURPLUS | | | | | | | | | | | | | | | | | | | | |
| DEFICIENCY | | | | | | | | | | | | | | | | | | | | |
| SURPLUS | | | | | | | | | | | | | | | | | | | | |

Remarks :—

[illegible] Lt Col Signature of Commander.

1/Low W Amb Rame [illegible] Unit.

50th Div Formation to which attached.

19 Oct 1918 Date of Despatch.

(16523.) Wt. W6016—PP 1432. 1,500m. 3/18. D & S. (E1256) Forms B2138/3.

[P.T.O.

Nov. 1918 19

1/1 Lowland F.A. Amb.

War Diary
of
1/1st Lowland Field Ambulance 8
Vol XLII

140/3401

from 1/11/18 to 30/11/18



[illegible] Lt Col
OC 1/1st Lowland Field Amb
RAMC (T)

Instructions regarding War Diaries and Intelligence Summaries are contained in F. S. Regs., Part II. and the Staff Manual respectively. Title pages will be prepared in manuscript.

# WAR DIARY
~~or~~
## ~~INTELLIGENCE SUMMARY.~~
*(Erase heading not required.)*

505 Army Form C. 2118.

1/1st Lowland Field Ambulance
52nd (Lowland) Division

| Place | Date | Hour | Summary of Events and Information | Remarks and references to Appendices |
|---|---|---|---|---|
| ROSULT O.2.a.4.1. Sh.44 1/40000 | 1/11/18 | | Nothing to note. J.W.L. | |
| do | 2/11/18 | | Officer (Major LAMB) from 1/2nd L.F.A. reported for temporary duty with this Fld Amb. vice Officer (Capt. BROWN) of 1/3rd L.F.A. who was returned on relief to 1/3rd L.F.A. by ambulance car. J.W.L. | |
| do | 3/11/18 | | G.O.C. 52nd Div. accompanied by Lt Col MAUDE visited this Amb HQ today & inspected the arrangements. Visited A.D.S. in afternoon to see whether Car Post at NIVELLE could be moved forward to Canal Bridge at J.29.c.7.5. but found this still impracticable owing to enemy shelling, & not necessary for evacuation which was satisfactory. Two bursts of enemy shells (about 10 in all) landed near the A.D.S. during my visit & the house adjoining was rather badly damaged. J.W.L. | |
| do | 4/11/18 | | Received A.D.M.S. S.R. 18 d/3.11.18 timed at 0800 to-day to the effect that Bearers of 1/1st L.F.A. under Bearer Officer would accompany 156th Bde in case of an advance on the withdrawal of the enemy. Instructed Major MACKENZIE to act as Bearer Officer & to arrange with 156th Bde HQ as to time when he & Bearers should report. Visited A.D.S. car post at NIVELLE & R.A.P. of 1/7th S.R. at J.29.c.5.4. Visited Bde HQ & arranged to establish an additional car post before dusk to-night at P.5.a.9.1 & sent a 3rd wheeled stretcher carriage to M.O. i/c 1/7th S.R. for use of the outlying companies of that Battalion in evacuation of cases to car Posts. Returned by way of new Car Post, St AMAND & A.D.S. Received RAMC OO No. 22 d/4.11.18 timed at 1500. Three of the 8 | |

D. D. & L., London E.C.
(10340) Wt W5300/P713 750,000 3/18 E 688 Forms/C2118/16.

Instructions regarding War Diaries and Intelligence Summaries are contained in F. S. Regs., Part II. and the Staff Manual respectively. Title pages will be prepared in manuscript.

# WAR DIARY

~~or~~

~~INTELLIGENCE SUMMARY.~~

(Erase heading not required.)

506 Army Form C. 2118.

1/1st Lowland Field Ambulance
52nd (Lowland) Division

| Place | Date | Hour | Summary of Events and Information | Remarks and references to Appendices |
|---|---|---|---|---|
| ROSULT O2a41 | 4/11/18 (Contd) | | M.A.C. cars att this unit were ~~for~~ returned to 31st M.A.C. yesterday in accordance with instructions of D.D.M.S. & OC 31st M.A.C. JwL | |
| do | 5/11/18 | | Dental Surgeon Capt C.B. WHITE reported to this unit to-day for duty from 25th Field Ambulance in accordance with A.D.M.S. R 336/4 d/4 11/8. Withdrew car post which I had established temporarily at 1600 yesterday at P5a.91 for use of Bearer Officer 157th Bde as this is not now necessary owing to A.D.S. at P9c.9.8 having been taken over by 1/3rd L.F.A. from 24th Field Ambulance in accordance with R.A.M.C. O.O. d/4/11/8. JwL | |
| do | 6/11/18 | | Received No. R 405/7 of even date intimating the sudden death of Pte R. FINDLAY 1/1st L.F.A. last night at 156th Bde HQ. where he was attached as "runner" & instructing me to hold a post mortem examination & report cause of death. Arranged to have the body brought to this HQ. to-day & autopsy made to-night. Received R.A.M.C. O.O. No 23 issued at 1800 to-day that on receipt of the word "HUNT" the 52nd Div. would advance; an A.D.S. would at once be opened by 1/2nd L.F.A. at HAUTE RIVE J36.a.0.9. & cars wanted; A.D.S. 1/1st L.F.A. at I36a would close & the M.D.S. 1/1st L.F.A. at its present site O2a41. become a car relay post with 2 cars which would go up to J36a as cars come down. JwL | |
| do | 7/11/18 | | Reported to A.D.M.S. that autopsy on Pte R. FINDLAY showed death to be due to Carbon monoxide poisoning, & that a sample of blood from right ventricle had been taken for spectroscopic examination. Visited A.D.S. & instructed Major Mackenzie to report | |

D. D. & L., London E.C
(10340) W1 W5300/P713 750,000 3/18 E 688 Forms/C2118/16.

507 Army Form C. 2118.

Instructions regarding War Diaries and Intelligence Summaries are contained in F. S. Regs., Part II. and the Staff Manual respectively. Title pages will be prepared in manuscript.

# WAR DIARY
or
# ~~INTELLIGENCE SUMMARY.~~

*(Erase heading not required.)*

1/1st Lowland Field Ambulance
52nd (Lowland) Division

| Place | Date | Hour | Summary of Events and Information | Remarks and references to Appendices |
|---|---|---|---|---|
| ROSULT O2a41<br>Sheet 44 1/40000 | 7/11/18<br>(Contd) | | to 156th Bde HQ for orders regarding Bearers of 1/1st L.F.A. & to arrange to close the A.D.S.<br>on receipt of the word "HUNT", leaving 2 cars (that at A.D.S. + that at car post NIVELLE)<br>at the site of A.D.S as a car relay post with 1 N.C.O & 4 men. Major LAMB<br>1/2nd L.F.A was instructed to rejoin his unit to-night from A.D.S. JWL | |
| do | 8/11/18 | | Received A.D.M.S W 256 of even date "HUNT". Sent forward at once 38 O.R bearers to<br>A.D.S. I 36 a to report to Major MACKENZIE, the bearer officer 156th Bde. These<br>are additional to the 6 bearers of this unit already attached to each battalion with<br>2 Wheeled stretcher carriages (3 in the case of 1/7th S.R.). ~~[illegible]~~<br>Received R.A.M.C O.O No 24 of even date to clear this M.D.S. of all cases except<br>scabies on completion to send all M.A.C cars except 2 to the A.D.S. 1/3rd L.F.A<br>at P9C98, & notify O.C. of having done so. Evacuation would then be to P9C98.<br>Post to O2a & car relay post of this ambulance at I 36 a would be withdrawn<br>Evacuation of sick of 155th Bde would be undertaken by 1/1st L.F.A. & I wrote<br>155th Bde HQ that an ambulance would be sent for this purpose to B.HQ at<br>1000 tomorrow. Visited A.D.S 1/2nd L.F.A at J 36 a O.9 taking forward the 2 cars<br>from the Relay Post as the evacuation was difficult owing to the flooded condition of<br>the country. Found the A.D.S clear but left the two cars at A.D.S. for use in case<br>of need, with instructions to leave at 0700 tomorrow & take any cases down to new<br>M.D.S at P9C98, then travel via the relay post at I 36 a pick up personnel & stores<br>+ come on to H.Q of this ambulance at O2a41 (ROSULT STATION). all the cars | |

D. D. & L., London E.C
(10340) Wt W5300/P713 750,000 3/18 E 888 Forms/C2118/16.

Instructions regarding War Diaries and Intelligence Summaries are contained in F. S. Regs., Part II. and the Staff Manual respectively. Title pages will be prepared in manuscript.

# WAR DIARY
*or*
# ~~INTELLIGENCE SUMMARY.~~
*(Erase heading not required.)*

508 Army Form C. 2118.

1/1st Lowland Field Ambulance
52nd (Lowland) Division

| Place | Date | Hour | Summary of Events and Information | Remarks and references to Appendices |
|---|---|---|---|---|
| ROSULT O2a.41 | 8/11/18 (Contd) | | at MDS ROSULT (except scabies) were cleared by 1800, & 8 M.A.C. cars instructed to report for duty to OC 1/3rd L.F.A. at new M.D.S, P9c98. Received A.D.M.S. W267 of even date to move this ambulance to ETABLISSEMENT THERMAL, P17b88, tomorrow. Detailed Capt R.A.LENNIE to report to A.D.M.S. office at 0900 tomorrow to attend civilian sick in accordance with A.D.M.S. W264 of even date. | J.W.L. |
| do | 9/11/18 | | Sent one ambulance car to report to A.D.M.S. for duty in accordance with instructions. Moved ambulance less 1 off + 2 bearer subdivisions to P17b88. Marching out strength as under:– | |

| Personnel | | | | | Horses | | | | Vehicles | | Motors | | Cycles |
|---|---|---|---|---|---|---|---|---|---|---|---|---|---|
| Chaplain | R.A.M.C. Off | R.A.M.C. O.R. | A.S.C. H.T. | A.S.C. M.T. | [illegible] | Riding | L.D. | H.D. | 4 wheeled | 2 wheeled | Amb cars | Cycles | |
| 1 | *6 | 90 | 28 | ϕ12 | 4 | 2 | 17 | 20 | 13 | 4 | ϕ8 | — | 1 |

* Includes 1 dental surgeon attached.
ϕ Includes 3 O.R. + 2 cars attached from 31st M.A.C. for duty. Other motor cycle in workshops. 1 car + 1 motor cycle attached to A.D.M.S. for duty.

| Place | Date | Hour | Summary of Events and Information | Remarks and references to Appendices |
|---|---|---|---|---|
| ETABLISSEMENT THERMAL P17b88 [illegible] | | | Found on arrival that a Battalion of the Worcesters VIII Corps was also to be billetted in the Hotel Etablissement Thermal, & that a details party of 1 M.O. & 66 O.R. of 157th Bde still remained but were moving out at 1600. There is a sulphur spring at this place of a tepid heat & arrangements were at once made to give the 28 scabies cases brought with us in accordance with A.D.M.S. instructions the benefit of tepid sulphur water baths (the water smells distinctly of $H_2S$). Two fairly sound zones | |

D. D. & L., London E.C
(10340) Wt W5300/P713 750,000 3/18 E 688 Forms/C2118/16.

509 Army Form C. 2118.

Instructions regarding War Diaries and Intelligence Summaries are contained in F. S. Regs., Part II. and the Staff Manual respectively. Title pages will be prepared in manuscript.

# WAR DIARY
or
# INTELLIGENCE SUMMARY.

*(Erase heading not required.)*

1/1st Lowland Field Ambulance
52nd (Lowland) Division

| Place | Date | Hour | Summary of Events and Information | Remarks and references to Appendices |
|---|---|---|---|---|
| ETABLISSEMENT THERMAL P17b6 | 9/11/18 (Cont^d) | | or wor baths were found after a search twice made use of for the purpose of giving the scabies cases a "soak". Capt. R.A.LENNIE reported back to this HQ with motor car sent to ADMS this morning as D.H.Q was moving forward unexpectedly. Took over equipment (142 blankets 35 stretchers trome drugs & dressings of 24th Fld ambulance) at Dressing station P9C 9.8 from 1/3rd L.F.A in accordance with ADMS W273 d/8 11/18. Sent two men to act as guard for these. The 1/3rd L.F.A having moved forward. Received W281 of own date to move early tomorrow morning to BONSECOURS – L10 | [illegible] |
| BONSECOURS L10C65 Sh.44 1/40000 | 10/11/18 | | Moved out after breakfast, sending the ambulance cars forward first. Marching out strength as noted yesterday. One ambulance car broke a back spring & had to be sent to the workshop with its driver. Route was via HAUTE RIVE + HERCHIES. There was great congestion owing to units of VIII Division + 52nd Division being on the same route – the only one available – + the flooded condition of the country. Went forward by an ambulance car to BONSECOURS & received there W289 d/10 11/18 from Capt DOWNES whom I had sent on with the ambulance cars in the morning to find billets for the personnel + patients. Sent back to late HQ of 52nd Divn at MONT DE PERUWELZ for 4 cases left under charge of my orderly by instructions of ADMS before he moved this forenoon with DHQ to SIRAULT. Went forward to SIRAULT by ambulance car going via BLATON, STAMBRUGE, Loch 10, + HAUTRAGE | |

D. D. & L., London E.C
(10340) Wt W5300/P713 750,000 3/18 E 688 Forms/C2118/16.

510 Army Form C. 2118.

Instructions regarding War Diaries and Intelligence Summaries are contained in F. S. Regs., Part II. and the Staff Manual respectively. Title pages will be prepared in manuscript.

# WAR DIARY or INTELLIGENCE SUMMARY.

(Erase heading not required.)

1/1st Lowland Field Ambulance
52nd (Lowland) Division

| Place | Date | Hour | Summary of Events and Information | Remarks and references to Appendices |
|---|---|---|---|---|
| BONSECOURS HOTEL de la CORNETTE L10 Sh 44 1/40000 | 10/11/18 (Contd) | | Received verbal instructions from ADMS to move forward to HAPPART early to-morrow & to be responsible for the evacuation of 156th Bde to-morrow on arrival. Unit reached BONSECOURS about 1830 having been long delayed by preceding traffic on the roads. J.W.L. | |
| SIRAULT I.16.71 Sh 45 1/40000 | 11/11/18 | | Unit moved out of BONSECOURS at 0715 sent the motor ambulances on in advance with the Dentist (as billeting officer) this equipment & the 0800 orderly with despatches for ADMS Office at SIRAULT ~~with~~ as cars could only go the round about way. Unit marched via BLATON, STAMBRUGES, both 10 at H1d45 (Sh 45 1/40000) field touch to demolished canal bridge at H2c98 & on to HAPPART. On arrival there dispatch received from ADMS instructed me to proceed with unit to SIRAULT & intimated that hostilities would cease at ~~10~~ 1100 to day. Unit marched into SIRAULT at 1115 & got into billets. Proceeded to 156th Bde HQ at HERCHIES to establish touch with them & arranged to send ambulances at 1000 daily to BHQ to collect sick of units. Hospital formed at school I1C (opposite Church) by this unit with accommodation for about 40 sick. Ambulance HQ at I1b71. Dental surgeon has accommodation for working at I1d86. Marching in state of unit as under:- | |

| Personnel | | | | | Horses | | | | Vehicles | | Motor | | | Remarks |
|---|---|---|---|---|---|---|---|---|---|---|---|---|---|---|
| Chaplain | RAMC | | ASC | | Chargers | Riders | LD | HD | 2 wheels | 4 wheels | Ambce cars | Cycles | Cycles | |
| | Off | OR | HT | MT | | | | | | | | | | |
| 1 | 6 | 86* | 28 | 6 | 4 | 2 | 17 | 20 | 13 | 4 | 5ɸ | – | 1 | * 2 OR Opened at P9C.88. Sh 44<br>2 OR Gone on leave to UK<br>ɸ includes 2 MAC cars |

Three cars of this ambulance in workshops & one car with A.D.M.S. also 1 motor cycle J.W.L.

D. D. & L., London E.C
(10340) Wt W5300/P713 750,000 3/18 E 688 Forms/C2118/16.

Instructions regarding War Diaries and Intelligence Summaries are contained in F. S. Regs., Part II. and the Staff Manual respectively. Title pages will be prepared in manuscript.

# WAR DIARY
or
# INTELLIGENCE SUMMARY.
(Erase heading not required.)

511 Army Form C. 2118.

1/1st Lowland Field Ambulance
52nd (Lowland) Division

| Place | Date | Hour | Summary of Events and Information | Remarks and references to Appendices |
|---|---|---|---|---|
| SIRAULT I.16.7 | 12/11/18 | | By instructions of the ADMS the M.A.C cars attached to this Division are parked at the Church SIRAULT under his orders & the drivers to be rationed by this Fld. Amb. Evacuation of lighter sick & wounded is to DOUAI; of serious sick & wounded to No. 4 Canadian C.C.S. VALENCIENNES. Div. Fld. Ambce retain sick likely to be better in 4 days & all scabies cases of the Division etc. are sent to 1/1st L.F.A. to be retained by this unit. JWL | |
| do | 13/11/18 | | Detailed Capt. R.A. LENNIE with batman & 4 O.R. to report to Div Train at BAUDOUR to supervise disinfection of all ~~[illegible]~~ troops going on leave in accordance with instructions of A.D.M.S. in W.340 d/12/11/18 & R452/2 of [illegible] date. ~~the~~ Foot & mouth disease exists in the present area. Transport horses are to day assisting farmers (in whose stables they have horses stabled) in ploughing as the weather is suitable, & every effort is being made by this unit to assist in agricultural work. JWL | |
| do | 14/11/18 | | Weather still bright with frost at night. Ploughing continues & I estimate that about 6 acres of earth surface have been turned over in the two days besides carting of mangel wurzels etc. A.D.M.S. visited Hospital this afternoon. The cases of scabies we have had to ~~carry~~ retain have proved troublesome. They are not ill enough to be in bed yet have to be treated as "patients". They resent being made to march when the unit moves & get into mischief when the unit is in billets. JWL | |

D. D. & L., London E.C
(10340) Wt W5300/P713 750,000 3/18 E .688 Forms/C2118/16.

# WAR DIARY ~~or INTELLIGENCE SUMMARY.~~

(Erase heading not required.)

572 Army Form C. 2118.

Instructions regarding War Diaries and Intelligence Summaries are contained in F. S. Regs., Part II. and the Staff Manual respectively. Title pages will be prepared in manuscript.

1/1st Lowland Field Ambulance
52nd (Lowland) Division

| Place | Date | Hour | Summary of Events and Information | Remarks and references to Appendices |
|---|---|---|---|---|
| SIRAULT I.16.71 Sheet 45 | 15/11/18 | | Lt A. LINN R.A.M.C. T.C. reported to day for duty with this unit as a reinforcement from Base. JWL | |
| do. | 16/11/18 | | Sent Lt A. LINN at 0015 this morning in accordance with instructions of A.D.M.S. 52nd Div. received late last night to report immediately to A.D.M.S. VIII Div. at TERTRA. S/Sm W.J. SEARLE A.S.C. attached this ambulance reports this forenoon to 52nd Div Train for duty. A Warrant Officer, Class II, S/Sm. Bellchambers is sent in place of him. This change is not satisfactory from any point of view. The S/Sm sent as a W.O. Class II, was a Sgt. A.S.C. until yesterday, & the 2 Sgts. A.S.C. now att 1/1st L.F.A. are of at least equal service & have good records. The O.C. of this unit has not been consulted with regard to the change - which ~~[illegible]~~ does not appear to be for the good of the service. Surgeon Lieut-Commander C. ROSS. R.N. reported to-day for duty with this unit from 1/3rd Lowland Field Ambulance & has been sent for temporary duty as M.O. i/c 17th Northumberland Fusiliers (Pioneer Battalion) vice Capt EVANS RAMC who is proceeding on 14 days leave to U.K. ~~S/Sm W.J. SEARLE A.S.C. (att) reports to 52nd DHQ for duty~~ JWL | |
| do | 17/11/18 | | Detachment of 16 O.R. of this unit sent to day to attend thanksgiving service at ERBAUT in accordance with instructions received from A.D.M.S. last night. Capt. R.A. LENNIE reported back this afternoon from temporary duty at 52nd Divisional Train HQ at BAUDOUR. JWL | |
| do | 18/11/18 | | ~~Division~~ HQ moved from SIRAULT to day to NIMY (Chateau de la BRUYERE) N of MONS. | |

D. D. & L., London E.C
(10340) Wt W5300/P713 750,000 3/18 E 888 Forms/C2118/16.

Instructions regarding War Diaries and Intelligence Summaries are contained in F. S. Regs., Part II. and the Staff Manual respectively. Title pages will be prepared in manuscript.

# WAR DIARY
or
# ~~INTELLIGENCE SUMMARY.~~
(Erase heading not required.)

513 Army Form C. 2118.

1/1st Lowland Field Ambulance
52nd (Lowland) Division

| Place | Date | Hour | Summary of Events and Information | Remarks and references to Appendices |
|---|---|---|---|---|
| SIRAULT I.16.71 | 18/11/18 (contd) | | Moved HQ of this ambulance from SIRAULT Rly. Station to SIRAULT town near the church this afternoon. Exact location of Office is now I.1.c.6.3. Maps Sh 45 1/40000. JwL | |
| SIRAULT I.1.c.6.3. Sh 45 1/40000 | 19/11/18 | | Have arranged a Dining & Lecture Hall for the personnel. Billets are very cold as in many cases there are no fires, & floors are of stone, or tiled. Some are accommodated in barns. Some bales of shavings left by the Germans near BAUDOUR are being sent for, to be used as bedding for men billetted in places with stone or earth floors. ADMS R498/18 d/18 11/18 directs this unit to be responsible for the evacuation of sick from the 2 other Field Ambulances to C.C.S's. There are 5 M.A.C. cars with this Division for evacuation of sick – chiefly to DOUAI. These cars are parked with 1/1st L.F.A. C.C.S. at VALENCIENNES (& now also at MONS) take only serious cases. Owing to the state of the roads cars sent to C.C.S at DOUAI cannot return same day. JwL | |
| do | 20/11/18 | | In accordance with instructions contained in ADMS. R507/4 d/19 11/18 an examination of the personnel of this unit was made to-day for Scabies & result (a nil return) rendered to ADMS. In accordance with R516/1 of even date Petrol tins will not now be carried on Water Carts. This will obviate the need of the superstructures made to carry these petrol tins. It has been arranged to give popular lectures to the personnel of this unit in the dining & recreation hall as often as possible – Mondays, Wednesdays, & Fridays to begin with. The first was given to-night by Lt Col J.W. Leitch at 1930 on "Sound & the Perception of Sound". JwL | |
| do. | 21/11/18 | | Pte FAIRBRASS of this unit was detailed as R.A.M.C. orderly att 52nd Div. M.T. Coy at BRUAY in accordance with A.D.M.S. R503/4 d/19 11/18 & was sent there to-day by ambulance car. Major. | |

D. D. & L., London E.C
(10340) Wt W5300/P713 750,000 3/18 E 688 Forms/C2118/16.

514 Army Form C. 2118.

Instructions regarding War Diaries and Intelligence Summaries are contained in F. S. Regs., Part II. and the Staff Manual respectively. Title pages will be prepared in manuscript.

# WAR DIARY
*or*
# ~~INTELLIGENCE SUMMARY.~~
*(Erase heading not required.)*

1/1st Lowland Field Ambulance
52nd (Lowland) Division

| Place | Date | Hour | Summary of Events and Information | Remarks and references to Appendices |
|---|---|---|---|---|
| SIRAULT I.16.c.3 Sh.45 1/40000 | 21/11/18 (Contd) | | Mackenzie of this unit left to-day on 14 days to U.K. sailing from BOULOGNE on 23/11/18. In accordance with ADMS R522/1 d/20th a list was forwarded to him to-day of stores which it was not considered necessary to take with the unit to Germany. JWL | |
| do | 22/11/18 | | Pro forma showing list of men in this unit whose trades were connected with railway work or would render them suitable for employment in a Railway unit which might have to be formed quickly has been completed & was forwarded to-day direct to D.A.G. in accordance with instructions in A.D.M.S. R 575/1 d/19th. JWL | |
| do | 23/11/18 | | A syllabus of classes which it is proposed to hold next week on the following subjects has been prepared:- Dynamics & Trigonometry, English, French, History & Geography, Mathematics (including algebra & arithmetic). The second popular lecture held in this unit was given by Capt C.B. White, Dental Surgeon attached, at 1930 to-night on "Poultry Keeping"; it was as largely attended as the previous lecture. JWL | |
| do | 24/11/18 | | Sunday. Church Parade held at 1100 - the first there has been an opportunity of having as a unit for a very long time. Received A.D.M.S. circular letter forwarding educational conference reports for circulation to the 3 Fld Ambulances & appointing Rev A. MAIN to be Group Educational Officer for the Divisional R.A.M.C. He is already unit educational officer of 1/1st Lowland Field Amb. JWL | |
| do | 25/11/18 | | Sent Capt. C.B. WHITE Dental Surgeon to-day by motor ambulance car to report for duty with 1/3rd W.R. Fld Amb at LE FOREST (north of DOUAI) in accordance with A.D.M.S. R566/4 d/24th. As arranged last week unit classes began to-day; Dynamics at 1000, English at 1100, Mathematics at 1400, & French at | |

D. D. & L., London E.C
(10340) W1 W5300/P713 750,000 3/18 E 888 Forms/C2118/16.

515 Army Form C. 2118.

Instructions regarding War Diaries and Intelligence Summaries are contained in F. S. Regs., Part II. and the Staff Manual respectively. Title pages will be prepared in manuscript.

# WAR DIARY
*or*
~~INTELLIGENCE SUMMARY.~~
*(Erase heading not required.)*

1/1st Lowland Field Ambulance
52nd (Lowland) Division

| Place | Date | Hour | Summary of Events and Information | Remarks and references to Appendices |
|---|---|---|---|---|
| SIRAULT I1 c 6 3. Sh 45 1/40000 | 25/11/18 (Contd) | | 1500. The numbers attending these classes are respectively 13, 98, 75, & 49<br>The usual periodical inspection of horses & harness was held at 0930 to-day<br>by the O.C. this unit. In the evening a "Discussion" Class on Political &<br>social economy was held at 1900 under the chairmanship of Rev. A. MAIN C.F.<br>Unit Educational Officer. After the class the arrangements made for Postal<br>voters under the Representation of the People Act were explained by the O.C. JwL<br>The 2 men left as guard over stores taken over from 1/3rd L.F.A. East of ST AMAND reported back to this unit to-day. | |
| do | 26/11/18 | | Visited NEUFVILLES to-day accompanied by the Q.M., Capt. REID, & went<br>over area allotted to this unit. Reported to B.G.C. 156th Bde (with copy to A.D.M.S.)<br>on return. The first match of Football tournament was played this afternoon<br>at HERCHIES by a team from A & B Sections of this unit against a team from<br>No. 3 Coy 1/7th R.S. After a keen contest the result was 1 goal to 0 in favour<br>of the R.S. team. 10 minutes overtime both ways was played in order to get<br>a decision at all, & the goal was scored in the 19th minute of the overtime.<br>Have detailed Capt. R.A. LENNIE to act as understudy to the unit educational<br>Officer in accordance with A.D.M.S. circular letter of 24/11/18. JwL | |
| do | 27/11/18 | | Received A.D.M.S. R 613/11 d/27/11/18 that 1/1st L.F.A. would march ~~on~~ 28th Inst to NEUFVILLES<br>area & billets allotted by 156th Bde. Went by ambulance car to D.H.Q. to see A.D.M.S. regarding<br>accommodation for Hospital cases, etc. in area allotted. In evening went to 156th B.H.Q. to<br>see the B.G.C. whether it were possible to get part of the school for girls in NEUFVILLES for | |

D. D. & L., London E.C.
(10340) Wt W5300/P713 750,000 3/18 E 688 Forms/C2118/16.

516 Army Form C. 2118.

Instructions regarding War Diaries and Intelligence Summaries are contained in F. S. Regs., Part II. and the Staff Manual respectively. Title pages will be prepared in manuscript.

# WAR DIARY

or

# ~~INTELLIGENCE SUMMARY.~~

(*Erase heading not required.*)

1/1st Lowland Field Ambulance
52nd (Lowland) Division

| Place | Date | Hour | Summary of Events and Information | Remarks and references to Appendices |
|---|---|---|---|---|
| SIRAULT I.ccc S245 1/40000 | 27/11/18 (Contd) | | Hospital, but as there is a small school & other hall accommodation is very limited the matter could only be arranged by postponing movement of 1/1st L.F.A. until 30th. In the meantime I am to meet an officer from B.H.Q. at the Mairie at CHAUSSEE LOUVIGNY at 1000 on 29th & see whether the school there can be got for hospital purposes. Telephoned A.D.M.S. from B.H.Q. Unit held a very successful concert tonight from 1930 to 2200. J.W.L. | |
| do | 28/11/18 | | Nothing to note. J.W.L. | |
| do | 29/11/18 | | Visited CHAUSSEE N.D LOUVIGNIES today as arranged. Accommodation appears to be satisfactory & A.D.M.S. was informed accordingly. Received R671/4 of even date to move ambulance tomorrow to billets arranged. J.W.L. | |
| CHAUSSEE N.D LOUVIGNIES. S238 W5646 1/40000 | 30/11/18 | | Moved out with unit & transport & patients at 0800. Strength as under:— | |

| Chaplain | Personnel RAMC Off. | Personnel RAMC OR | Personnel ASC HT | Personnel ASC MT | Horses Riders | Horses LD | Horses HD | Vehicles 1 axle | Vehicles 2 axle | Motor Vehicles amb. | Motor Vehicles cycles | Cycle |
|---|---|---|---|---|---|---|---|---|---|---|---|---|
| 1 | 5 | 148 | 34* | 10ϕ | 6 | 19 | 21* | 4 | 14* | 6ϕ | 1ϕ | 1 |

* Includes 1 G.S. Wagon (train), 2 horses & 1 driver.
ϕ 1 Car & driver M.T. att. for duty to A.D.M.S.; 1 driver on leave to U.K.; & 1 driver deficient; 1 motor cycle at repair workshop.

The M.A.C. driver & car were sent to report for duty to 1/2nd L.F.A. before unit left at 0800.
21 Patients (scabies cases) marched with the unit.
Unit arrived at destination at 1330 & proceeded to allotted billets.

John W. Leitch Lt Col

D. D. & L., London E.C.
(10340) Wt W5300/P713 750,000 3/18 E 688 Forms/C2118/16.

**To be made up to and for Saturday in each week**

No. of Report 140.

# FIELD RETURN.

Army Form B. 213

(To be furnished by all arms, services, and departments (except A.S.C. units) to the A.G.'s Office at the Base in accordance with Field Service Regulations, Part II.)

RETURN showing numbers (*a*) Effective strength of Unit. (*b*) Rationed by Unit. [illegible] at [illegible] [illegible] Date.

| DETAILS. | *Personnel | | | | Animals | | | | | | Guns and transport vehicles | | | | | | | | | | | | | | | REMARKS |
|---|---|---|---|---|---|---|---|---|---|---|---|---|---|---|---|---|---|---|---|---|---|---|---|---|---|
| | | | | | Horses | | | | Mules | | | | | | Horsed | | Mechanical | | | | | | | | | (Number of Acting W.O.'s and N.C.O.'s included in effective strength to be shown in this column.) |
| | Officers | Other Ranks | | | Riding | Draught | Heavy Draught | Pack | Large | Small | Guns, showing description | Ammunition wagons | Machine guns | Aircraft, showing description | 4 Wheeled | 2 Wheeled | Motor Cars | Tractors | Lorries, showing description | Trucks, showing description | Trailers | Motor Bicycles | Bicycles | Motor Ambulances | |
| Effective Strength of Unit ... ... | (a) 7 | (b) 169 | | | | | | | | | | | | | | | | | | | | | 1 | | (a) Includes 1 at [illegible] and 1 at Refugee Hospl. |
| Details by Arms attached to Unit as in War Establishment ... ... ... | | 161 | | | | | | | | | | | | | | | | | | | | | | | (b) Includes 17 at 156 [illegible] / 19 " Refugee Hospt. / 16 on leave to U.K. / 2 [illegible] / 1 [illegible] |
| A.S.C. H.T. | | 25 | | | 6 | 14 | 20 | | | | | | | | 13 | 4 | | | | | | | | | (c) " 7 on leave to U.K. |
| A.S.C. M.T. | | (c) 10 | | | | | | | | | | | | | | | | | | | | 2 | – | 7 | 2 at Refugee Hospt. / (d) " 1 on leave to U.K. / [illegible] |
| TOTAL ... ... | 7 | 216 | | | 6 | 17 | 20 | | | | | | | | 13 | 4 | | | | | | 2 | 1 | 7 | |
| War Establishment ... ... ... | 10 | 231 | | | 6 | 17 | 20 | | | | | | | | 13 | 4 | | | | | | 2 | 1 | 7 | |
| Wanting to complete ... ... ... (Detail of Personnel and Horses below.) | 3 | 15 | | | 2 | · | · | | | | | | | | · | · | | | | | | · | · | | + 13 [illegible] |
| SURPLUS ... ... (Detail of Personnel and Horses below.) | | | | | | | | | | | | | | | | | | | | | | | | | |
| †Attached (not to include the details shown above) ... ... ... | 3 | | | | | | | | | | | | | | | | | | | | | | | | [illegible] |
| Attached for Rations only ... ... | [illegible] | 10 | | | | | | | | | | | | | | | | | | | | | | | [illegible] |
| Civilians Employed with and Accompanying the Unit ... ... ... | | | | | | | | | | | | | | | | | | | | | | | | | |
| ‡Detached from and struck off effective strength of own Unit ... ... | | | | | | | | | | | | | | | | | | | | | | | | | |
| ‡Detached from but retained on effective strength of own unit... ... ... | [illegible] | 10 | | | | | | | | | | | | | | | | | | | | | | | [illegible] |
| TOTAL RATIONED ... | 8 | 161 | | | 6 | 17 | 20 | | | | | | | | | | | | | | | | | | |

* Blank columns to be used for W.A.A.C. Natives or as may be required.

† In the case of field ambulances, hospitals or depots, the number of patients are to be included here, the names being shown in A.F.A. 36.

‡ These details to be enumerated by arms.

[illegible] Lt.-Col. Signature of Commander.

2 Nov 1918 Date of Despatch.

AF B213

W/E 2/11/18

ASC

| No | Rank | Name | | Corps | Casualty | |
|---|---|---|---|---|---|---|
| T1SR/562. | Dvr | Foster | C | ASC. | Retd from leave. | 26/10/18. |
| M2/135999 | Pte | Blackwell | G | ASC MT | do | 1/11/18. |
| M1/08555 | Sgt | Temple. | J. | do | Reinfor. from 5th Dvn MT ASC | 26/10/18. |
| T/35711 | Dvr | McLaren | P | ASC HT | Granted 14 days leave to UK via Boulogne. Condition [illegible] 31/10 - 14/11. | |
| T/32086 | Dvr | Fox | GW | do. | Granted 6d rate ASC pay as Shoe Smith from [illegible] vice [illegible]. [illegible] ASC [illegible]. Granted [illegible] of 10/- under [illegible] | |

*For information of the A.G.'s Office at the base.*

Officers and men who have become casuals, been transferred or joined since last report.

Place *In the Field.* Date *2nd Nov 1918*

| Regtl. Number | Rank | Name | | Corps | Nature of casualty, or name of unit from or to which transferred. | Date of being struck off or coming on the ration return. | Remarks * |
|---|---|---|---|---|---|---|---|
| | Capt | Barton | J. | R.A.M.C. | To [illegible] | 28 10/18 | Temporarily |
| | | Brown | D.A. | do. | From [illegible] | 29 10/18 | -do- |
| | | Lennie | R.A. | do. | Retd from leave | 31 10/18 | |
| 316352 | Pte | Laurie | J. | do. | Sick To Hospl. | 26 10/18. | |
| 316143 | " | Scott | L. | do. | -do- | 28 10/18 | |
| 419974 | " | Phillips | J. | do. | -do- | 27 10/18. | |
| 419764 | " | Phillips | J. | do. | Retd from Hospl. | 1 11/18. | |
| 317164 | " | Hatton | E.D. | do. | [illegible] Base | 30 10/18. | |
| 61443 | " | Gehan | J. | do. | Retd from Hospl | 1 11/18 | |
| 316077 | " | McGillivray | W. | do. | Granted 14 days leave to UK via Boulogne, [illegible] ration allce. for same period [illegible] pay | | 28 10/18 - 11 11/18 |
| 315073 | " | Lewis | J. | do. | -do- -do- | | 29 10/18 - 12 11/18. |
| 316074 | " | Johnstone | A. | do. | -do- -do- | | 30 10/18 - 13 11/18. |
| 316134 | " | Claridge | J. | do. | -do- -do- | | 1 11/18 - 15 11/18. |
| 316016 | " | Ellis | A.G. | do. | -do- -do- | | 3 11/18 - 17 11/18. |
| 316065 | " | Dunlop | D. | do. | Granted [illegible] leave to UK. via Boulogne, [illegible] allce. for same [illegible] day | | 3 11/18 - 18 11/18 |
| 316159 | " | Tinto | A.L. | do. | [illegible] to [illegible] | from | 14-9-18. |
| 316193 | " | Stewart | W.A. | do. | -do- | -do- | 23-10-18. |
| 316144 | " | Jenkins | A. | do. | -do- | -do- | 12-9-18. |
| 93315 | " | Tuck | A.C. | do. | [illegible] to 5 [illegible] | | 26-10-18. |
| 316058 | " | Brown | W. | do. | Granted 14 days extension of leave W.O. [illegible] D.N. 72463 [illegible] ration allce. for that period | | 18 10/18 - 22 10/18. |
| 401246 | " | Farrington | H. | do. | Retd. from leave. | 26 10/18. | |
| 316054 | " | Brown | J. | do. | -do- | 26 10/18. | |
| 45757 | " | Finlay | J. | -do- | -do- | 29 10/18. | |
| 341010 | S/S | Hampson | A.F. | do | -do- | 29 10/18. | |
| 316048 | Pte | Murray. | F.H. | do | -do- | 30 10/18. | |
| 316060 | Pte | Lawton | W. | do. | Married Miss [illegible] Kinnaird on [illegible] at 90 [illegible] St. Hamilton St. Glasgow. Present address [illegible] 41 John St. [illegible] Glasgow | | |

STRENGTH: Officers: T.F. 6, R.C. 1 — 7

W.O.' N.C.O.' & men.

| | | |
|---|---|---|
| W.O. | 1 | [illegible] 10 |
| C.M.S. | 1 | [illegible] 5 |
| S/Sgts | 2 | Ptes 141 |
| Sgts | 1 | |
| L/Sgts | 1 | 169 |

ALL CATEGORY "A".

* State whether absence is of a permanent or temporary nature, adding, in the case of casuals from wounds or disease any available information for communication to the relatives.

*The perforated sheet is not to be used to record casualties; additional sheets, preferably foolscap, to be attached when necessary. These sheets to be carefully numbered and the number of attached sheets to be noted here.*

Perforated Sheet giving detail of personnel and horses wanting to complete or surplus, shown on Army Form B. 213.

No. of Report 190.

| Detail of Wanting to Complete or Surplus. | Drivers. R.A. | Drivers. R.E. | Drivers. A.S.C. | Drivers. Car | Drivers. Lorry | Drivers. Steam | Gunners | Gunners Howitzer | Smith Gunners | Range Takers | Farriers Serjeants | Farriers Corporals | Shoeing or Shoeing and Carriage Smiths | Cold Shoers | Wheelers R.A. | Wheelers H.T. | Wheelers M.T. | Saddlers or Harness Makers | Blacksmiths | Bricklayers and Masons | Carpenters and Joiners | Fitters & Turners (R.E.) Wood | Fitters & Turners (R.E.) Iron | Fitters R.A. | Fitters Wireless. | Plumbers | Electricians Ordinary | Electricians W.T. | Signalmen. | Engine Drivers Loco. | Engine Drivers Field | Air Line Men. | Permanent Line Men | Operators, Telegraph | Cablemen | Brigade Section Pioneers | General-duty Pioneers | Signallers | Instrument Repairers | Motor Cyclist | Motor Cyclist Artificers | Telephonists | Clerks | Machine Gunners | Armament Artificers Fitters | Armament Artificers Range Finders | Armourers | Storemen | Privates | W.O's and N.C.O's (by ranks) not included in trade columns. | | | | | | | | | | | TOTAL to agree with wanting to complete or surplus Officers | TOTAL to agree with wanting to complete or surplus Other Ranks | Horses Riding | Horses Draught | Horses Heavy Draught | Horses Pack |
|---|---|---|---|---|---|---|---|---|---|---|---|---|---|---|---|---|---|---|---|---|---|---|---|---|---|---|---|---|---|---|---|---|---|---|---|---|---|---|---|---|---|---|---|---|---|---|---|---|---|---|---|---|---|---|---|---|---|---|---|---|---|---|---|---|---|---|
| CAVALRY—DEFICIENCY | | | | | | | | | | | | | | | | | | | | | | | | | | | | | | | | | | | | | | | | | | | | | | | | | | | | | | | | | | | | | | | | | | |
| SURPLUS | | | | | | | | | | | | | | | | | | | | | | | | | | | | | | | | | | | | | | | | | | | | | | | | | | | | | | | | | | | | | | | | | | |
| R.A.—DEFICIENCY | | | | | | | | | | | | | | | | | | | | | | | | | | | | | | | | | | | | | | | | | | | | | | | | | | | | | | | | | | | | | | | | | | |
| SURPLUS | | | | | | | | | | | | | | | | | | | | | | | | | | | | | | | | | | | | | | | | | | | | | | | | | | | | | | | | | | | | | | | | | | |
| R.E.—DEFICIENCY | | | | | | | | | | | | | | | | | | | | | | | | | | | | | | | | | | | | | | | | | | | | | | | | | | | | | | | | | | | | | | | | | | |
| SURPLUS | | | | | | | | | | | | | | | | | | | | | | | | | | | | | | | | | | | | | | | | | | | | | | | | | | | | | | | | | | | | | | | | | | |
| INFANTRY—DEFICIENCY | | | | | | | | | | | | | | | | | | | | | | | | | | | | | | | | | | | | | | | | | | | | | | | | | | | | | | | | | | | | | | | | | | |
| SURPLUS | | | | | | | | | | | | | | | | | | | | | | | | | | | | | | | | | | | | | | | | | | | | | | | | | | | | | | | | | | | | | | | | | | |
| R.A.M.C.—DEFICIENCY | | | 1 | | | | | | | | 1 | | | | | | | | | | | | | | | | | | | 6 | | | | | | | | | | | | | | | | | | 11 | 2 | | | | | | | | | | | | 3 | 15 | 2 | | | |
| SURPLUS | | | | | | | | | | | | | | | | | | | | | | | | | | | | | | | | | | | | | | | | | | | | | | | | | | | | | | | | | | | | | | | | | | |
| A.O.C.—DEFICIENCY | | | | | | | | | | | | | | | | | | | | | | | | | | | | | | | | | | | | | | | | | | | | | | | | | | | | | | | | | | | | | | | | | | |
| SURPLUS | | | | | | | | | | | | | | | | | | | | | | | | | | | | | | | | | | | | | | | | | | | | | | | | | | | | | | | | | | | | | | | | | | |
| A.V.C.—DEFICIENCY | | | | | | | | | | | | | | | | | | | | | | | | | | | | | | | | | | | | | | | | | | | | | | | | | | | | | | | | | | | | | | | | | | |
| SURPLUS | | | | | | | | | | | | | | | | | | | | | | | | | | | | | | | | | | | | | | | | | | | | | | | | | | | | | | | | | | | | | | | | | | |
| DEFICIENCY | | | | | | | | | | | | | | | | | | | | | | | | | | | | | | | | | | | | | | | | | | | | | | | | | | | | | | | | | | | | | | | | | | |
| SURPLUS | | | | | | | | | | | | | | | | | | | | | | | | | | | | | | | | | | | | | | | | | | | | | | | | | | | | | | | | | | | | | | | | | | |
| DEFICIENCY | | | | | | | | | | | | | | | | | | | | | | | | | | | | | | | | | | | | | | | | | | | | | | | | | | | | | | | | | | | | | | | | | | |
| SURPLUS | | | | | | | | | | | | | | | | | | | | | | | | | | | | | | | | | | | | | | | | | | | | | | | | | | | | | | | | | | | | | | | | | | |

Remarks :—

[illegible] Lt Col Signature of Commander.

1/Lon. 3d Amb. [illegible] Unit.

[illegible] DIV Formation to which attached.

2/11/18. Date of Despatch.

(16523.) Wt. W6016—PP 1432. 1,500m. 3/18. D & S. (E1256) Forms B2138/8.

[P.T.O.

**To be made up to and for Saturday in each week**

No. of Report 172

# FIELD RETURN.

Army Form B. 213

(To be furnished by all arms, services, and departments (except A.S.C. units) to the A.G.'s Office at the Base in accordance with Field Service Regulations, Part II.)

RETURN showing numbers (*a*) Effective strength of Unit. (*b*) Rationed by Unit. 1/Low. Fd. Ambce. at In the Field 16/11/18 Date.

| Details. | *Personnel: Officers | Other Ranks | | | | Animals: Horses: Riding | Draught | Heavy Draught | Pack | Mules: Large | Small | Guns and transport vehicles: Guns, showing description | Ammunition wagons | Machine guns | Aircraft, showing description | Horsed: 4 Wheeled | 2 Wheeled | Mechanical: Motor Cars | Tractors | Lorries, showing description | Trucks, showing description | Trailers | Motor Bicycles | Bicycles | Motor Ambulances | Remarks (Number of Acting W.O.'s and N.C.O.'s included in effective strength to be shown in this column.) |
|---|---|---|---|---|---|---|---|---|---|---|---|---|---|---|---|---|---|---|---|---|---|---|---|---|---|---|
| Effective Strength of Unit | (a) 7 | (B) 165 | | | | | | | | | | | | | | | | | | | | | | 1 | | (a) Includes 1 @ 1/4 R.S. 52 Div. Train; (B) Includes 5 @ 52 Div. Train; " 2 D.H.Q. + 1 Concert Pty; " 19 on leave to U.K. |
| Details by Arms attached to Unit as in War Establishment ... | | | | | | | | | | | | | | | | | | | | | | | | | | |
| A.S.C. H.T. | | (c) 35 | | | | 6 | 17 | 20 | | | | | | | | 13 | 4 | | | | | | | | | |
| A.S.C. M.T. | | (D) 12 | | | | | | | | | | | | | | | | | | | | | (E) 2 | - | 7 | (c) " 7 on leave to U.K.; (D) " 1 @ D.H.Q.; " 1 on leave to U.K.; (E) " 1 at Workshops |
| Total | 7 | 212 | | | | 6 | 17 | 20 | | | | | | | | 13 | 4 | | | | | | 2 | 1 | 7 | |
| War Establishment | 10 | 231 | | | | 8 | 17 | 20 | | | | | | | | 13 | 4 | | | | | | 2 | 1 | 7 | |
| Wanting to complete (Detail of Personnel and Horses below.) | 3 | 19+ | | | | 2 | | | | | | | | | | | | | | | | | | | | +17 R.A.M.C.; 1 A.S.C. H.T.; 1 " M.T. |
| Surplus (Detail of Personnel and Horses below.) | | | | | | | | | | | | | | | | | | | | | | | | | | |
| †Attached (not to include the details shown above) ... | | 27 (Patients) | | | | | | | | | | | | | | | | | | | | | | | | |
| Attached for Rations only | *2 | 7 | | | | | | | | | | | | | | | | | | | | | | | | * Chaplain & Dental Officer; * Dentist's Batman |
| Civilians Employed with and Accompanying the Unit ... | | | | | | | | | | | | | | | | | | | | | | | | | | |
| ‡Detached from and struck off effective strength of own Unit | | | | | | | | | | | | | | | | | | | | | | | | | | x 52 Div. Train |
| ‡Detached from but retained on effective strength of own unit... | | x 11 | | | | | 2x | | | | | | | | | | | | | | | | | | | x 10 M.A.C. Drivers, 1 Driver 52 Div. Train |
| Total Rationed | 7 | 215 | | | | 6 | 19 | 20 | | | | | | | | | | | | | | | | | | |

* Blank columns to be used for W.A.A.C. Natives or as may be required.

† In the case of field ambulances, hospitals or depots, the number of patients are to be included here, the names being shown in A.F.A. 36.

‡ These details to be enumerated by arms.

[illegible] Lt. Col. Signature of Commander.

16/11/18 Date of Despatch.

A.F.B.213

# A. S. C.  W/E 16/11/18

| No. | Rank | Name | | Casualty | Date |
|---|---|---|---|---|---|
| M2/135590 | Dr. | Boorman | H. | Returned from leave | 9-11-18 |
| T4/233892 | Sgt. | Allan | F. | -do- | 14-11-1[8] |
| T4/064551 | Dr. | Lloyd | W. | Granted leave to U.K. via Boulogne<br>Credit Ration allce. @ 2/4 p.o. for period<br>(14 days) | 16/11 - 30/11 |

*For information of the A.G.'s Office at the base.*

A.S.C. sheet attd.

Officers and men who have become casuals, been transferred or joined since last report.

Place In the Field  Date 16/11/18

| Regtl. Number | Rank | Name | | Corps | Nature of casualty, or name of unit from or to which transferred. | Date of being struck off or coming on the ration return. | Remarks * |
|---|---|---|---|---|---|---|---|
| 316163 | Pte. | Edgecombe | N.E. | R.A.M.C.(T.) | Sick to Hospital | 9 11/18 | |
| 316008 | " | Gallacher | C. | - do - | - do - | 14 11/18 | |
| 1240 | " | Fenwick | W. | - do - | G.S.W. Hand (L) | 11 11/18 | Remained at duty |
| 316018 | Cpl. | Ross | J. | - do - | Granted leave to U.K. via Boulogne. 14 days. Credit Ration allce. @ 2/4 p.d. 12 11/18 | - 26 11/18 | |
| 316054 | Pte. | Rankine | J. | - do - | - do - - do - | 13 11/18 - 27 11/18 | |
| 316089 | " | Hay | A. | - do - | - do - - do - | 14 11/18 - 28 11/18 | |
| 316232 | L/Cpl. | Stewart | J. | - do - | - do - - do - | 15 11/18 - 29 11/18 | |
| 316210 | Pte. | Faith | J. | - do - | Granted 42 days leave to U.K. via Boulogne Credit Ration allce. @ 2/4 p.d. | 17 11/18 - 29 12/18 | |
| 316190 | " | McTavish | D.B. | - do - | War pay increased to 4d from 20/10/18 | | |
| 316068 | " | Gourlay | W. | - do - | Returned from leave | 8 11/18 | |
| 316168 | Sgt. | Meldrum | A. | - do - | - do - | 12 11/18 | |
| 316076 | Pte. | Harvey | A. | - do - | - do - | 14 11/18 | |
| 46118 | Cpl. | Mead | L.E. | - do - | - do - | 14 11/18 | |

STRENGTH:- Officers T.F. 6, T.C. 1 = 7

W.O's N.C.O's Men

W.O. 1 Cpls. 10

Q.M.S. 1 L/Cpls. 4

S. Sgts. 2 Ptes. 138

Sgts. 8 165

L Sgts. 1

ALL CATEGORY "A"

* State whether absence is of a permanent or temporary nature, adding, in the case of casuals from wounds or disease any available information for communication to the relatives.

*The perforated sheet is not to be used to record casualties; additional sheets, preferably foolscap, to be attached when necessary. These sheets to be carefully numbered and the number of attached sheets to be noted here.*

Perforated Sheet giving detail of personnel and horses wanting to complete or surplus, shown on Army Form B. 213.

No. of Report 172

| Detail of Wanting to Complete or Surplus. | Drivers. R.A. | Drivers. R.E. | Drivers. A.S.C. | Drivers. Car | Drivers. Lorry | Drivers. Steam | Gunners | Gunners Howitzer | Smith Gunners | Range Takers | Farriers Serjeants | Farriers Corporals | Shoeing or Shoeing and Carriage Smiths | Cold Shoers | Wheelers R.A. | Wheelers H.T. | Wheelers M.T. | Saddlers or Harness Makers | Blacksmiths | Bricklayers and Masons | Carpenters and Joiners | Fitters & Turners (R.E.) Wood | Fitters & Turners (R.E.) Iron | Fitters R.A. | Fitters Wireless. | Plumbers | Electricians Ordinary | Electricians W.T. | Signalmen. | Engine Drivers Loco. | Engine Drivers Field | Air Line Men. | Permanent Line Men | Operators, Telegraph | Cablemen | Brigade Section Pioneers | General-duty Pioneers | Signallers | Instrument Repairers | Motor Cyclist | Motor Cyclist Artificers | Telephonists | Clerks | Machine Gunners | Armament Artificers Fitters | Armament Artificers Range Finders | Armourers | Storemen | Privates | W.O.'s and N.C.O.'s (by ranks) not included in trade columns. Cpl. R.A.M.C. | | | | | | | | | | | TOTAL to agree with wanting to complete or surplus Officers | TOTAL Other Ranks | Horses Riding | Horses Draught | Horses Heavy Draught | Horses Pack |
|---|---|---|---|---|---|---|---|---|---|---|---|---|---|---|---|---|---|---|---|---|---|---|---|---|---|---|---|---|---|---|---|---|---|---|---|---|---|---|---|---|---|---|---|---|---|---|---|---|---|---|---|---|---|---|---|---|---|---|---|---|---|---|---|---|---|---|
| CAVALRY—DEFICIENCY | | | | | | | | | | | | | | | | | | | | | | | | | | | | | | | | | | | | | | | | | | | | | | | | | | | | | | | | | | | | | | | | | | |
| SURPLUS | | | | | | | | | | | | | | | | | | | | | | | | | | | | | | | | | | | | | | | | | | | | | | | | | | | | | | | | | | | | | | | | | | |
| R.A.—DEFICIENCY | | | | | | | | | | | | | | | | | | | | | | | | | | | | | | | | | | | | | | | | | | | | | | | | | | | | | | | | | | | | | | | | | | |
| SURPLUS | | | | | | | | | | | | | | | | | | | | | | | | | | | | | | | | | | | | | | | | | | | | | | | | | | | | | | | | | | | | | | | | | | |
| R.E.—DEFICIENCY | | | | | | | | | | | | | | | | | | | | | | | | | | | | | | | | | | | | | | | | | | | | | | | | | | | | | | | | | | | | | | | | | | |
| SURPLUS | | | | | | | | | | | | | | | | | | | | | | | | | | | | | | | | | | | | | | | | | | | | | | | | | | | | | | | | | | | | | | | | | | |
| INFANTRY—DEFICIENCY | | | | | | | | | | | | | | | | | | | | | | | | | | | | | | | | | | | | | | | | | | | | | | | | | | | | | | | | | | | | | | | | | | |
| SURPLUS | | | | | | | | | | | | | | | | | | | | | | | | | | | | | | | | | | | | | | | | | | | | | | | | | | | | | | | | | | | | | | | | | | |
| R.A.M.C.—DEFICIENCY | | | | 1 | | | | | | | | 1 | | | | | | | | | | | | | | | | | | | | | | | | | | | | | | | | | | | | | 15 | 2 | | | | | | | | | | | 3 | 19 | 2 | | | |
| SURPLUS | | | | | | | | | | | | | | | | | | | | | | | | | | | | | | | | | | | | | | | | | | | | | | | | | | | | | | | | | | | | | | | | | | |
| A.O.C.—DEFICIENCY | | | | | | | | | | | | | | | | | | | | | | | | | | | | | | | | | | | | | | | | | | | | | | | | | | | | | | | | | | | | | | | | | | |
| SURPLUS | | | | | | | | | | | | | | | | | | | | | | | | | | | | | | | | | | | | | | | | | | | | | | | | | | | | | | | | | | | | | | | | | | |
| A.V.C.—DEFICIENCY | | | | | | | | | | | | | | | | | | | | | | | | | | | | | | | | | | | | | | | | | | | | | | | | | | | | | | | | | | | | | | | | | | |
| SURPLUS | | | | | | | | | | | | | | | | | | | | | | | | | | | | | | | | | | | | | | | | | | | | | | | | | | | | | | | | | | | | | | | | | | |
| DEFICIENCY | | | | | | | | | | | | | | | | | | | | | | | | | | | | | | | | | | | | | | | | | | | | | | | | | | | | | | | | | | | | | | | | | | |
| SURPLUS | | | | | | | | | | | | | | | | | | | | | | | | | | | | | | | | | | | | | | | | | | | | | | | | | | | | | | | | | | | | | | | | | | |
| DEFICIENCY | | | | | | | | | | | | | | | | | | | | | | | | | | | | | | | | | | | | | | | | | | | | | | | | | | | | | | | | | | | | | | | | | | |
| SURPLUS | | | | | | | | | | | | | | | | | | | | | | | | | | | | | | | | | | | | | | | | | | | | | | | | | | | | | | | | | | | | | | | | | | |

Remarks :—

[signature] Signature of Commander.

1/1 Low. Fd. Ambce. Unit.

52 Div. Formation to which attached.

16/11/18 Date of Despatch.

(16523.) Wt. W6016—PP 1432. 1,500m. 3/18. D & S. (E1256) Forms B2138/3.

[P.T.O.

**To be made up to and for Saturday in each week**

Army Form B. 213

# FIELD RETURN.

No. of Report ______

(To be furnished by all arms, services, and departments (except A.S.C. units) to the A.G.'s Office at the Base in accordance with Field Service Regulations, Part II.)

RETURN showing numbers (*a*) Effective strength of Unit. (*b*) Rationed by Unit. ______ at In the Field ______ 9/11/18 Date.

| Details. | *Personnel: Officers | Other Ranks | | | | Animals: Horses: Riding | Draught | Heavy Draught | Pack | Mules: Large | Small | Guns and transport vehicles: Guns, showing description | Ammunition wagons | Machine guns | Aircraft, showing description | Horsed: 4 Wheeled | 2 Wheeled | Mechanical: Motor Cars | Tractors | Lorries, showing description | Trucks, showing description | Trailers | Motor Bicycles | Bicycles | Motor Ambulances | Remarks (Number of Acting W.O.'s and N.C.O.'s included in effective strength to be shown in this column.) |
|---|---|---|---|---|---|---|---|---|---|---|---|---|---|---|---|---|---|---|---|---|---|---|---|---|---|---|
| Effective Strength of Unit ... ... | 7 | 167 | | | | | | | | | | | | | | | | | | | | | | 1 | | |
| Details by Arms attached to Unit as in War Establishment ... ... ... | | | | | | | | | | | | | | | | | | | | | | | | | | |
| A.S.C. H.T. | | 35 | | | | 6 | 17 | 30 | | | | | | | | 13 | 21 | | | | | | | | | |
| A.S.C. M.T. | | 12 | | | | | | | | | | | | | | | | | | | | | 2 | | 7 | |
| Total ... ... | 7 | 214 | | | | 6 | 17 | 30 | | | | | | | | 13 | 21 | | | | | | 2 | 1 | 7 | |
| War Establishment ... ... ... | 10 | 231 | | | | 8 | 17 | 30 | | | | | | | | 13 | 14 | | | | | | 2 | 1 | 7 | |
| Wanting to complete ... ... (Detail of Personnel and Horses below.) | 3 | 17* | | | | 2 | | | | | | | | | | | | | | | | | | | | *15 - R.A.M.C. 1 - A.S.C. M.T. |
| Surplus ... ... (Detail of Personnel and Horses below.) | | | | | | | | | | | | | | | | | | | | | | | | | | |
| †Attached (not to include the details shown above) ... ... ... | | 65 | (Patients) | | | | | | | | | | | | | | | | | | | | | | | |
| Attached for Rations only ... ... | 3 | 9 | | | | | | | | | | | | | | | | | | | | | | | | |
| Civilians Employed with and Accompanying the Unit ... ... | | | | | | | | | | | | | | | | | | | | | | | | | | |
| ‡Detached from and struck off effective strength of own Unit ... ... | | | | | | | | | | | | | | | | | | | | | | | | | | |
| ‡Detached from but retained on effective strength of own unit... ... ... | | 6 | | | | | | | | | | | | | | | | | | | | | | | | |
| Total Rationed ... ... | | | | | | 6 | | | | | | | | | | | | | | | | | | | | |

* Blank columns to be used for W.A.A.C. Natives or as may be required.

† In the case of field ambulances, hospitals or depots, the number of patients are to be included here, the names being shown in A.F.A. 36.

‡ These details to be enumerated by arms.

______ Lt Col Signature of Commander.

9/11/18 Date of Despatch.

W B 213

# A.S.C.

W/E 9/11/19

| No | Rank | NAME | | CASUALTY | DATE. |
|---|---|---|---|---|---|
| T4/036341 | Dvr | Cawood | [illegible] | Granted leave to UK via Boulogne. Subsist. [illegible] allce @ [illegible] for the period 7/11/19 - | 21/11/19. |
| T4/038273 | " | Drew. | J | do do. 9/11/19 - | 23/11/19. |
| M2/139160 | Mc | Baker. | S. | do. do. 11/11/19 - | 25/11/19. |
| GHT/12 | Dvr | Dobson | G. | Retd. from leave. | 4/11/19. |
| T/25953 | " | Butler | F | -do- | 4/11/19. |

*For information of the A.G.'s Office at the base.*

[illegible] sheet att'd

Officers and men who have become casuals, been transferred or joined since last report.

Place In the Field. Date [illegible]

| Regtl. Number | Rank | Name | | Corps | Nature of casualty, or name of unit from or to which transferred. | Date of being struck off or coming on the ration return. | Remarks * |
|---|---|---|---|---|---|---|---|
| | Capt | [illegible] | | [illegible] | [illegible] | 3/[illegible] | |
| | Major | [illegible] | J. | do | [illegible] | [illegible] | [illegible] |
| 316301 | Pte | [illegible] | J. | [illegible] | [illegible] | [illegible] | |
| 3164[illegible] | " | Raeburn | A | do. | - do. - do. | 5/[illegible] - 19/[illegible]. | |
| 316136 | " | M[illegible] | Q | do | - do. - do. | 6/[illegible] - 20/[illegible]. | |
| 316092 | " | Bunning | G | do | - do. - do. | 8/[illegible] - 22/[illegible]. | |
| 31[illegible] | L/Cpl | [illegible] | G. | do | [illegible] | [illegible] | |
| 316[illegible] | " | [illegible] | S | do | [illegible] | 5/[illegible] | |
| 316[illegible] | Pte | [illegible] | K | do | Died [illegible] | 6/[illegible] | [illegible] |
| [illegible] | | [illegible] | J.S. | do | [illegible] | 9/[illegible] | |
| 31[illegible] | [illegible] | [illegible] | [illegible] | do. | [illegible] £15 Bounty [illegible]. | | |
| [illegible] | Pte | [illegible] | [illegible] | do | [illegible] | [illegible] | |
| [illegible] | [illegible] | [illegible] | [illegible] | do | " " " | [illegible] | |
| 316[illegible] | Pte | [illegible] | D | do | [illegible] | [illegible] | [illegible] Glasgow. |
| 316[illegible] | [illegible] | [illegible] | [illegible] | do | [illegible] | [illegible] | |
| 316[illegible] | Pte | [illegible] | E | - do. | - do. - | [illegible] | |
| 316[illegible] | " | [illegible] | G. | - do. | - do. - | [illegible] | |
| 316[illegible] | [illegible] | [illegible] | [illegible] | - do | Reinforcement | [illegible] | [illegible] Hospital |

STRENGTH Officers [illegible]

[illegible]

167.

ALL CATEGORY A.

* State whether absence is of a permanent or temporary nature, adding, in the case of casuals from wounds or disease any available information for communication to the relatives.

*The perforated sheet is not to be used to record casualties; additional sheets, preferably foolscap, to be attached when necessary. These sheets to be carefully numbered and the number of attached sheets to be noted here.*

Perforated Sheet giving detail of personnel and horses wanting to complete or surplus, shown on Army Form B. 213.

No. of Report 171.

| Detail of Wanting to Complete or Surplus. | Drivers. R.A. | R.E. | A.S.C. | Car | Lorry | Steam | Gunners | Gunners Howitzer | Smith Gunners | Range Takers | Farriers Serjeants | Corporals | Shoeing or Shoeing and Carriage Smiths | Cold Shoers | Wheelers R.A. | H.T. | M.T. | Saddlers or Harness Makers | Blacksmiths | Bricklayers and Masons | Carpenters and Joiners | Fitters & Turners (R.E.) Wood | Iron | Fitters R.A. | Wireless. | Plumbers | Electricians Ordinary | W.T. | Signalmen. | Engine Drivers Loco. | Field | Air Line Men. | Permanent Line Men | Operators, Telegraph | Cablemen | Brigade Section Pioneers | General-duty Pioneers | Signallers | Instrument Repairers | Motor Cyclist | Motor Cyclist Artificers | Telephonists | Clerks | Machine Gunners | Armament Artificers Fitters | Range Finders | Armourers | Storemen | Privates | W.O.'s and N.C.O.'s (by ranks) not included in trade columns. 295 RAMC | | | | | | | | | | | TOTAL to agree with wanting to complete or surplus. Officers | Other Ranks | Horses Riding | Draught | Heavy Draught | Pack .... |
|---|---|---|---|---|---|---|---|---|---|---|---|---|---|---|---|---|---|---|---|---|---|---|---|---|---|---|---|---|---|---|---|---|---|---|---|---|---|---|---|---|---|---|---|---|---|---|---|---|---|---|---|---|---|---|---|---|---|---|---|---|---|---|---|---|---|---|
| CAVALRY— DEFICIENCY | | | | | | | | | | | | | | | | | | | | | | | | | | | | | | | | | | | | | | | | | | | | | | | | | | | | | | | | | | | | | | | | | | |
| SURPLUS | | | | | | | | | | | | | | | | | | | | | | | | | | | | | | | | | | | | | | | | | | | | | | | | | | | | | | | | | | | | | | | | | | |
| R.A.— DEFICIENCY | | | | | | | | | | | | | | | | | | | | | | | | | | | | | | | | | | | | | | | | | | | | | | | | | | | | | | | | | | | | | | | | | | |
| SURPLUS | | | | | | | | | | | | | | | | | | | | | | | | | | | | | | | | | | | | | | | | | | | | | | | | | | | | | | | | | | | | | | | | | | |
| R.E.— DEFICIENCY | | | | | | | | | | | | | | | | | | | | | | | | | | | | | | | | | | | | | | | | | | | | | | | | | | | | | | | | | | | | | | | | | | |
| SURPLUS | | | | | | | | | | | | | | | | | | | | | | | | | | | | | | | | | | | | | | | | | | | | | | | | | | | | | | | | | | | | | | | | | | |
| INFANTRY— DEFICIENCY | | | | | | | | | | | | | | | | | | | | | | | | | | | | | | | | | | | | | | | | | | | | | | | | | | | | | | | | | | | | | | | | | | |
| SURPLUS | | | | | | | | | | | | | | | | | | | | | | | | | | | | | | | | | | | | | | | | | | | | | | | | | | | | | | | | | | | | | | | | | | |
| R.A.M.C.— DEFICIENCY | | | | 1 | | | | | | | | | | | | | | | | | | | | | | | | | | | | | | | | | | | | | | | | | | 132 | | | | | | | | | | | | 3 | 172 | | | | |
| SURPLUS | | | | | | | | | | | | | | | | | | | | | | | | | | | | | | | | | | | | | | | | | | | | | | | | | | | | | | | | | | | | | | | | | | |
| A.O.C.— DEFICIENCY | | | | | | | | | | | | | | | | | | | | | | | | | | | | | | | | | | | | | | | | | | | | | | | | | | | | | | | | | | | | | | | | | | |
| SURPLUS | | | | | | | | | | | | | | | | | | | | | | | | | | | | | | | | | | | | | | | | | | | | | | | | | | | | | | | | | | | | | | | | | | |
| A.V.C.— DEFICIENCY | | | | | | | | | | | | | | | | | | | | | | | | | | | | | | | | | | | | | | | | | | | | | | | | | | | | | | | | | | | | | | | | | | |
| SURPLUS | | | | | | | | | | | | | | | | | | | | | | | | | | | | | | | | | | | | | | | | | | | | | | | | | | | | | | | | | | | | | | | | | | |
| DEFICIENCY | | | | | | | | | | | | | | | | | | | | | | | | | | | | | | | | | | | | | | | | | | | | | | | | | | | | | | | | | | | | | | | | | | |
| SURPLUS | | | | | | | | | | | | | | | | | | | | | | | | | | | | | | | | | | | | | | | | | | | | | | | | | | | | | | | | | | | | | | | | | | |
| DEFICIENCY | | | | | | | | | | | | | | | | | | | | | | | | | | | | | | | | | | | | | | | | | | | | | | | | | | | | | | | | | | | | | | | | | | |
| SURPLUS | | | | | | | | | | | | | | | | | | | | | | | | | | | | | | | | | | | | | | | | | | | | | | | | | | | | | | | | | | | | | | | | | | |

Remarks :—

[illegible] Signature of Commander.

[illegible] Unit.

58 Div Formation to which attached.

9/1/18 Date of Despatch.

(16523.) Wt. W6016—PP 1432. 1,500m. 3/18. D & S. (E1256) Forms B213S/3.

[P.T.O.

**To be made up to and for Saturday in each week**

# FIELD RETURN.

Army Form B. 213

No. of Report 154

4 (To be furnished by all arms, services, and departments (except A.S.C. units) to the A.G.'s Office at the Base in accordance with Field Service Regulations, Part II.)

RETURN showing numbers (*a*) Effective strength of Unit. (*b*) Rationed by Unit. 1st Lowland Field Ambce. at In the Field 30-11-18 Date.

| Details. | *Personnel | | | | Animals | | | | | | Guns and transport vehicles | | | | | | | | | | | | | | | Remarks |
|---|---|---|---|---|---|---|---|---|---|---|---|---|---|---|---|---|---|---|---|---|---|---|---|---|---|
| | | | | | Horses | | | | Mules | | | | | | Horsed | | Mechanical | | | | | | | | | |
| | Officers | Other Ranks | | | Riding | Draught | Heavy Draught | Pack | Large | Small | Guns, showing description | Ammunition wagons | Machine guns | Aircraft, showing description | 4 Wheeled | 2 Wheeled | Motor Cars | Tractors | Lorries, showing description | Trucks, showing description | Trailers | Motor Bicycles | Bicycles | Motor Ambulances | (Number of Acting W.O.'s and N.C.O.'s included in effective strength to be shown in this column.) |
| Effective Strength of Unit ... ... | (a) 7 | (b) 166 | | | | | | | | | | | | | | | | | | | | | 1 | | (a) Includes 1 O. 4 R.S.<br>" 1 on leave to U.K.<br>(b) Includes 4 at 52 Div. Train<br>" 1 " 52 D. H.Q.<br>" 1 " 52 Div. Concert<br>" 1 " 156 Bde. H.Q.<br>" 11 on leave to U.K. |
| Details by Arms attached to Unit as in War Establishment ... ... ... | | | | | | | | | | | | | | | | | | | | | | | | | |
| A.S.C. H.T. | | (c) 36 | | | 6 | 19 | 19 | | | | | | | | 13 | 4 | | | | | | | | | |
| A.S.C. M.T. | | (d) 12 | | | | | | | | | | | | | | | | | | | | (e) 2 | | 7 | (c) Includes 2 on leave to U.K.<br>(d) Includes 1 @ 52 D.H.Q.<br>" 1 on leave to U.K.<br>(e) 1 at Workshops |
| Total ... ... | 7 | 213 | | | 6 | 19 | 19 | | | | | | | | 13 | 4 | | | | | | 2 | 1 | 7 | |
| War Establishment ... ... ... | 10 | 231 | | | 8 | 17 | 20 | | | | | | | | 13 | 4 | | | | | | 2 | 1 | 7 | |
| Wanting to complete ... ... (Detail of Personnel and Horses below.) | 3 | (f) 19 | | | 2 | | 1 | | | | | | | | | | | | | | | | | | (f) 16 R.A.M.C.<br>2 A.S.C. (H.T.) [illegible]<br>1 A.S.C. (M.T.) |
| Surplus ... ... (Detail of Personnel and Horses below.) | | (g) 1 | | | | 2 | | | | | | | | | | | | | | | | | | | (g) 1 A.S.C. (H.T.) [illegible] |
| †Attached (not to include the details shown above) ... ... ... | | 39 | | | | | | | | | | | | | | | | | | | | | | | Patients |
| Attached for Rations only ... ... | 2 | | | | | | | | | | | | | | | | | | | | | | | | Chaplain + Town Major |
| Civilians Employed with and Accompanying the Unit ... ... | | | | | | | | | | | | | | | | | | | | | | | | | |
| ‡Detached from and struck off effective strength of own Unit ... | | | | | | | | | | | | | | | | | | | | | | | | | |
| ‡Detached from but retained on effective strength of own unit... ... | | (h) 7 | | | | | (i) 2 | | | | | | | | | | | | | | | | | | (h) 6 M.A.C. Drivers 1 O.R. 52 Div. Train<br>(i) 52 Div. Train |
| Total Rationed ... | 7 | 237 | | | 6 | 19 | 21 | | | | | | | | | | | | | | | | | | |

* Blank columns to be used for W.A.A.C. Natives or as may be required.

† In the case of field ambulances, hospitals or depots, the number of patients are to be included here, the names being shown in A.F.A. 36.

‡ These details to be enumerated by arms.

[signature] Lt. Col. —Signature of Commander.

30-11-18 Date of Despatch.

B.213

No. 174.

A.S.C.

WE 30.11.18

| No. | RANK | NAME | CASUALTY | DATE |
|---|---|---|---|---|
| T/35061 | Dr. | Cooper T.H. | To Hosp. U.K. (while on leave) | 12 11/18 |
| T4/036341 | Dr. | Lowrand J. | Returned from leave | 23 11/18 |
| T4/247091 | Dr. | Robertson J.B. | - do - | 26 11/18 |
| T4/038223 | . | Drew J. | - do - | 26 11/18 |

30 11/18.

John W. Leitch Lt. Col.
O.C. 1/1 Lans. Fd. Ambce.

A.S.C. Sheet A/4.

*For information of the A.G.'s Office at the base.*

Officers and men who have become casuals, been transferred or joined since last report.

Place In the Field Date 30.11.18

| Regtl. Number | Rank | Name | Corps | Nature of casualty, or name of unit from or to which transferred. | Date of being struck off or coming on the ration return. | Remarks * |
|---|---|---|---|---|---|---|
| 316003 | Pte. | Bowie J.R. | R.A.M.C.(T) | Sick to Hospital | 22/11/18 | |
| 316246 | " | Auld J. | -do- | -do- | 27/11/18 | |
| 316006 | " | Crawford G. | do. | Reinforcement from Base 26/11/18 | | |
| 316037 | Cpl. | Hislop R.P. | do. | Granted leave to U.K. via Calais 14 days. Credit Ration Allce. O2/4p.o. 1-12-18 – 15/12/18 | | |
| 316301 | Pte. | Hendry J. | do. | Retd. from leave | 22/11/18 | |
| 316136 | " | Muir Q.S. | -do- | -do- | 23/11/18 | |
| 316112 | " | Raeburn A. | do. | -do- | 23/11/18 | |
| 316093 | " | Binning G. | -do- | -do- | 24/11/18 | |
| 316205 | Cpl. | McDonald R. | -do- | -do- | 25/11/18 | |
| 308164 | Pte. | Hutton R. | do. | War pay increased to 4d from 15.9.18 | | |
| 410054 | " | Parkins L.C. | do. | -do- do. 4d " 6.11.18 | | |

Strength: Officers T.F. 6
T.C. 1
7

-do. W.O. N.C.O. & men

W.O. 1
Q.M.S. 1
S/Sgts. 2
Sgts. 8
L/Sgts. 1
Cpls. 10
L/Cpls. 4
PTES. 134 TOTAL = 166

ALL CATEGORY "A".

* State whether absence is of a permanent or temporary nature, adding, in the case of casuals from wounds or disease any available information for communication to the relatives.

*The perforated sheet is not to be used to record casualties; additional sheets, preferably foolscap, to be attached when necessary. These sheets to be carefully numbered and the number of attached sheets to be noted here.*

Perforated Sheet giving detail of personnel and horses wanting to complete or surplus, shown on Army Form B. 213.

No. of Report 174

| Detail of Wanting to Complete or Surplus | Drivers R.A. | Drivers R.E. | Drivers A.S.C. | Drivers Car | Drivers Lorry | Drivers Steam | Gunners | Gunners Howitzer | Smith Gunners | Range Takers | Farriers Serjeants | Farriers Corporals | Shoeing or Shoeing and Carriage Smiths | ~~Cold Shoers~~ Farr. Drivers | Wheelers R.A. | Wheelers H.T. | Wheelers M.T. |
|---|---|---|---|---|---|---|---|---|---|---|---|---|---|---|---|---|---|
| CAVALRY— DEFICIENCY | | | | | | | | | | | | | | | | | |
| SURPLUS | | | | | | | | | | | | | | | | | |
| R.A.— DEFICIENCY | | | | | | | | | | | | | | | | | |
| SURPLUS | | | | | | | | | | | | | | | | | |
| R.E.— DEFICIENCY | | | | | | | | | | | | | | | | | |
| SURPLUS | | | | | | | | | | | | | | | | | |
| INFANTRY— DEFICIENCY | | | | | | | | | | | | | | | | | |
| SURPLUS | | | | | | | | | | | | | | | | | |
| R.A.M.C.— DEFICIENCY | | | 1 | 1 | | | | | | | | 1 | | | | | |
| SURPLUS | | | | | | | | | | | | | | 1 | | | |
| A.O.C.— DEFICIENCY | | | | | | | | | | | | | | | | | |
| SURPLUS | | | | | | | | | | | | | | | | | |
| A.V.C.— DEFICIENCY | | | | | | | | | | | | | | | | | |
| SURPLUS | | | | | | | | | | | | | | | | | |
| DEFICIENCY | | | | | | | | | | | | | | | | | |
| SURPLUS | | | | | | | | | | | | | | | | | |
| DEFICIENCY | | | | | | | | | | | | | | | | | |
| SURPLUS | | | | | | | | | | | | | | | | | |

| Detail of Wanting to Complete or Surplus | Saddlers or Harness Makers | Blacksmiths | Bricklayers and Masons | Carpenters and Joiners | Fitters & Turners (R.E.) Wood | Fitters & Turners (R.E.) Iron | Fitters R.A. | Fitters Wireless. | Plumbers | Electricians Ordinary | Electricians W.T. | Signalmen. | Engine Drivers Loco. | Engine Drivers Field | Air Line Men. | Permanent Line Men | Operators, Telegraph | Cablemen | Brigade Section Pioneers | General-duty Pioneers | Signallers |
|---|---|---|---|---|---|---|---|---|---|---|---|---|---|---|---|---|---|---|---|---|---|
| CAVALRY— DEFICIENCY | | | | | | | | | | | | | | | | | | | | | |
| SURPLUS | | | | | | | | | | | | | | | | | | | | | |
| R.A.— DEFICIENCY | | | | | | | | | | | | | | | | | | | | | |
| SURPLUS | | | | | | | | | | | | | | | | | | | | | |
| R.E.— DEFICIENCY | | | | | | | | | | | | | | | | | | | | | |
| SURPLUS | | | | | | | | | | | | | | | | | | | | | |
| INFANTRY— DEFICIENCY | | | | | | | | | | | | | | | | | | | | | |
| SURPLUS | | | | | | | | | | | | | | | | | | | | | |
| R.A.M.C.— DEFICIENCY | | | | | | | | | | | | | | | | | | | | | |
| SURPLUS | | | | | | | | | | | | | | | | | | | | | |
| A.O.C.— DEFICIENCY | | | | | | | | | | | | | | | | | | | | | |
| SURPLUS | | | | | | | | | | | | | | | | | | | | | |
| A.V.C.— DEFICIENCY | | | | | | | | | | | | | | | | | | | | | |
| SURPLUS | | | | | | | | | | | | | | | | | | | | | |
| DEFICIENCY | | | | | | | | | | | | | | | | | | | | | |
| SURPLUS | | | | | | | | | | | | | | | | | | | | | |
| DEFICIENCY | | | | | | | | | | | | | | | | | | | | | |
| SURPLUS | | | | | | | | | | | | | | | | | | | | | |

| Detail of Wanting to Complete or Surplus | Instrument Repairers | Motor Cyclist | Motor Cyclist Artificers | Telephonists | Clerks | Machine Gunners | Armament Artificers Fitters | Armament Artificers Range Finders | Armourers | Storemen | Privates |
|---|---|---|---|---|---|---|---|---|---|---|---|
| CAVALRY— DEFICIENCY | | | | | | | | | | | |
| SURPLUS | | | | | | | | | | | |
| R.A.— DEFICIENCY | | | | | | | | | | | |
| SURPLUS | | | | | | | | | | | |
| R.E.— DEFICIENCY | | | | | | | | | | | |
| SURPLUS | | | | | | | | | | | |
| INFANTRY— DEFICIENCY | | | | | | | | | | | |
| SURPLUS | | | | | | | | | | | |
| R.A.M.C.— DEFICIENCY | | | | | | | | | | | 14 |
| SURPLUS | | | | | | | | | | | |
| A.O.C.— DEFICIENCY | | | | | | | | | | | |
| SURPLUS | | | | | | | | | | | |
| A.V.C.— DEFICIENCY | | | | | | | | | | | |
| SURPLUS | | | | | | | | | | | |
| DEFICIENCY | | | | | | | | | | | |
| SURPLUS | | | | | | | | | | | |
| DEFICIENCY | | | | | | | | | | | |
| SURPLUS | | | | | | | | | | | |

| Detail of Wanting to Complete or Surplus | W.O.'s and N.C.O.'s (by ranks) not included in trade columns: Sjt. R.A.M.C.(T) | | | | | | | | | | | TOTAL to agree with wanting to complete or surplus: Officers | TOTAL: Other Ranks | Horses Riding | Horses Draught | Horses Heavy Draught | Horses Pack |
|---|---|---|---|---|---|---|---|---|---|---|---|---|---|---|---|---|---|
| CAVALRY— DEFICIENCY | | | | | | | | | | | | | | | | | |
| SURPLUS | | | | | | | | | | | | | | | | | |
| R.A.— DEFICIENCY | | | | | | | | | | | | | | | | | |
| SURPLUS | | | | | | | | | | | | | | | | | |
| R.E.— DEFICIENCY | | | | | | | | | | | | | | | | | |
| SURPLUS | | | | | | | | | | | | | | | | | |
| INFANTRY— DEFICIENCY | | | | | | | | | | | | | | | | | |
| SURPLUS | | | | | | | | | | | | | | | | | |
| R.A.M.C.— DEFICIENCY | 2 | | | | | | | | | | | 3 | 19 | 2 | | 1 | |
| SURPLUS | | | | | | | | | | | | | 1 | | 2 | | |
| A.O.C.— DEFICIENCY | | | | | | | | | | | | | | | | | |
| SURPLUS | | | | | | | | | | | | | | | | | |
| A.V.C.— DEFICIENCY | | | | | | | | | | | | | | | | | |
| SURPLUS | | | | | | | | | | | | | | | | | |
| DEFICIENCY | | | | | | | | | | | | | | | | | |
| SURPLUS | | | | | | | | | | | | | | | | | |
| DEFICIENCY | | | | | | | | | | | | | | | | | |
| SURPLUS | | | | | | | | | | | | | | | | | |

Remarks :—

[illegible] Lt. Col. Signature of Commander.

1st Lowland Field Ambulance Unit.

52 Div. Formation to which attached.

30. 11. 18. Date of Despatch.

(16523.) Wt. W6016—PP 1432. 1,500m. 3/18. D & S. (E1256) Forms B2138/8.

[P.T.O.

**To be made up to and for Saturday in each week**

Army Form B. 213

No. of Report 153

# FIELD RETURN.

(To be furnished by all arms, services, and departments (except A.S.C. units) to the A.G.'s Office at the Base in accordance with Field Service Regulations, Part II.)

RETURN showing numbers (a) Effective strength of Unit. (b) Rationed by Unit. 1/1 Lowland Field Ambulance at In the Field 23-11-15 Date.

| Details. | *Personnel: Officers | Other Ranks | | | Animals: Horses: Riding | Draught | Heavy Draught | Pack | Mules: Large | Small | Guns and transport vehicles: Guns, showing description | Ammunition wagons | Machine guns | Aircraft, showing description | Horsed: †4 Wheeled | ‡2 Wheeled | Mechanical: Motor Cars | Tractors | Lorries, showing description | Trucks, showing description | Trailers | Motor Bicycles | Bicycles | Motor Ambulances | Remarks (Number of Acting W.O.'s and N.C.O.'s included in effective strength to be shown in this column.) |
|---|---|---|---|---|---|---|---|---|---|---|---|---|---|---|---|---|---|---|---|---|---|---|---|---|---|
| Effective Strength of Unit ... ... | (a) 7 | (b) 167 | | | | | | | | | | | | | | | | | | | | | 1 | | (a) Includes 1 ... R.S.<br>(a) " 1 on leave to U.K.<br>(b) Includes 4 at 52 Div. Train<br>" 1 " 156 Bde. H.Q.<br>" 2 " 52 D. H.Q.<br>" 1 " ... Lowland ...<br>" 15 on leave to U.K. |
| Details by Arms attached to Unit as in War Establishment ... ... | | | | | | | | | | | | | | | | | | | | | | | | | |
| A.S.C. H.T. | | (c) 36 | | | 6 | 19 | 19 | | | | | | | | 13 | 4 | | | | | | | | | |
| A.S.C. M.T. | | (d) 12 | | | | | | | | | | | | | | | | | | | | 2 | | 7 | (c) Includes 4 on leave in U.K.<br>(d) Includes 1 at D.H.Q. (52)<br>" 1 on leave to U.K. |
| Total ... ... | 7 | 215 | | | 6 | 19 | 19 | | | | | | | | 13 | 4 | | | | | | 2 | 1 | 7 | |
| War Establishment ... ... ... | 10 | 231 | | | 8 | 17 | 20 | | | | | | | | 13 | 4 | | | | | | 2 | 1 | 7 | |
| Wanting to complete ... ... (Detail of Personnel and Horses below.) | 3 | 16 (E) | | | 2 | . | 1 | | | | | | | | . | | | | | | | . | | . | (E) 15 R.A.M.C.<br>1 A.S.C. (H.T.)<br>1 A.S.C. (M.T.) |
| Surplus ... ... (Detail of Personnel and Horses below.) | | | | | | 2 | | | | | | | | | | | | | | | | | | | |
| †Attached (not to include the details shown above) ... ... ... | | 39 (=) | | | | | | | | | | | | | | | | | | | | | | | (=) Patients |
| Attached for Rations only ... ... | x 3 | + 1 | | | | | | | | | | | | | | | | | | | | | | | x Chaplain, Dentist & Quarter Master<br>+ Dentist's Batman |
| Civilians Employed with and Accompanying the Unit ... ... ... | | | | | | | | | | | | | | | | | | | | | | | | | |
| ‡Detached from and struck off effective strength of own Unit ... | | | | | | | | | | | | | | | | | | | | | | | | | |
| ‡Detached from but retained on effective strength of own unit... ... | | ø 7 | | | | | * 2 | | | | | | | | | | | | | | | | | | ø 6 M.A.C. Driver & 1 O.R. 52 Div. Train<br>* 52 Div. Train |
| Total Rationed ... | 8 | 231 | | | 6 | 19 | 21 | | | | | | | | | | | | | | | | | | |

* Blank columns to be used for W.A.A.C. Natives or as may be required.

† In the case of field ambulances, hospitals or depots, the number of patients are to be included here, the names being shown in A.F.A. 36.

" ‡ These details to be enumerated by arms.

[illegible] Lt. Col. Signature of Commander.

23-11-15 Date of Despatch.

A.F. B.213

No. 173

A. S. C. W/E 23/11/18

| No. | Rank | Name | | Casualty | Date. |
|---|---|---|---|---|---|
| T4/045309 | S.S/M. | Searle | W. | To Duty with 52 DIV. TRAIN | 16-11-18 |
| T2/10257 | A/C.S.M. | Bellelambers | C. | From 52 DIV. TRAIN VICE S.S/M Searle | 16-11-18 |
| T/05711 | Dr. | McLaren | P. | Returned from leave | 17-11-18 |
| T4/237009 | Dr Farr. | Ramsay | W.G. | Reinforcement from 52 DIV. Train | 18-11-18 |

23.11.18.

Lt. Col.

O.C. 1/1 Lowland Div. Ambce.

A.S.C. Sheet att'd

*For information of the A.G.'s Office at the base.*

Officers and men who have become casuals, been transferred or joined since last report.

Place In the Field    Date 23.11.18.

| Regtl. Number | Rank | Name | Corps | Nature of casualty, or name of unit from or to which transferred. | Date of being struck off or coming on the ration return. | Remarks * |
|---|---|---|---|---|---|---|
| — | Surgeon Lt Commr. | Ross C. (R.N.) | | Joined as Reinforcement | 16/11/18 | |
| | -do- | -do- | | To Duty with 17 N.F. as R.M.O. | " | |
| | Major | McKenzie | R.A.M.C.(T) | Granted 14 days leave to U.K. via Boulogne | 23·11·18 to 7·12·18 | |
| 139135? | Pte | Jay A | R.A.M.C. | Joined as Reinforcement from Base | 16/11/18 | |
| 4657? | " | Teal W | -do- | -do- | 16/11/18 | |
| 45293? | " | Youth? A | -do- | -do- | 16/11/18 | |
| 316097 | " | Dickson D | R.A.M.C.(T) | -do- | 20/11/18 | |
| 495139 | " | Fairbairn G | -do- | To Duty with 53 Div. M.T. Coy. | " | |
| 316306 | " | Stark J | -do- | To Base for transfer to Home Estab.? | 21/11/18 | D.A.G. letter C.R. No. 118100/6 A dated [illegible] |
| 316114 | " | Thomson A.C. | -do- | Granted leave to U.K. via Boulogne Credit Ration allce. 14 days @ 2/- p.d. | 18/11/18 – 2/12/18 | |
| 31608? | " | McGillies J | -do- | -do- | -do- | 21/11/18 – 5/12/18 |
| 316077 | " | McGillivray W. | -do- | Returned from leave | 16/11/18 | |
| 316073 | " | Cowie J | -do- | -do- | 17/11/18 | |
| 316074 | " | Johnstone A | -do- | -do- | 17/11/18 | |
| 316023 | S/M | Ritchie D. | -do- | -do- | 19/11/18 | |
| 316086 | Pte. | Ellice A.G. | -do- | -do- | 19/11/18 | |
| 316134 | " | Glendye S. | -do- | -do- | 20/11/18 | |
| 31618? | " | Carson J.G.? | -do- | War pay increased to 4d [illegible] | | 21/10/18 |
| 316191 | " | Hillhouse J. | -do- | -do- | -do- | 21/10/18 |
| 36059 | " | McEwan H | -do- | -do- | -do- | ?/7/18 |

STRENGTH:- OFFICERS T.M. 6, T.C. 1 = 7

W.Os. N.C.Os. & men

| | | | |
|---|---|---|---|
| W.O. | 1 | Cpls | 10 |
| Q.M.S. | 1 | L/Cpls | 4 |
| S.Sgts | 2 | | |
| Sgts | 5 | Ptes | 140 |
| L/Sgts | 1 | | [illegible] |

ALL CATEGORY A

* State whether absence is of a permanent or temporary nature, adding, in the case of casuals from wounds or disease any available information for communication to the relatives.

*The perforated sheet is not to be used to record casualties ; additional sheets, preferably foolscap, to be attached when necessary. These sheets to be carefully numbered and the number of attached sheets to be noted here.*

Perforated Sheet giving detail of personnel and horses wanting to complete or surplus, shown on Army Form B. 213.

No. of Report 173

| Detail of Wanting to Complete or Surplus. | Drivers. R.A. | Drivers. R.E. | Drivers. A.S.C. | Drivers. Car | Drivers. Lorry | Drivers. Steam | Gunners | Gunners Howitzer | Smith Gunners | Range Takers | Farriers Serjeants | Farriers Corporals | Shoeing or Shoeing and Carriage Smiths | Cold Shoers | Wheelers R.A. | Wheelers H.T. | Wheelers M.T. |
|---|---|---|---|---|---|---|---|---|---|---|---|---|---|---|---|---|---|
| CAVALRY— DEFICIENCY | | | | | | | | | | | | | | | | | |
| SURPLUS | | | | | | | | | | | | | | | | | |
| R.A.— DEFICIENCY | | | | | | | | | | | | | | | | | |
| SURPLUS | | | | | | | | | | | | | | | | | |
| R.E.— DEFICIENCY | | | | | | | | | | | | | | | | | |
| SURPLUS | | | | | | | | | | | | | | | | | |
| INFANTRY— DEFICIENCY | | | | | | | | | | | | | | | | | |
| SURPLUS | | | | | | | | | | | | | | | | | |
| R.A.M.C.— DEFICIENCY | | | | 1 | | | | | | | | 1 | | | | | |
| SURPLUS | | | | | | | | | | | | | | | | | |
| A.O.C.— DEFICIENCY | | | | | | | | | | | | | | | | | |
| SURPLUS | | | | | | | | | | | | | | | | | |
| A.V.C.— DEFICIENCY | | | | | | | | | | | | | | | | | |
| SURPLUS | | | | | | | | | | | | | | | | | |
| DEFICIENCY | | | | | | | | | | | | | | | | | |
| SURPLUS | | | | | | | | | | | | | | | | | |
| DEFICIENCY | | | | | | | | | | | | | | | | | |
| SURPLUS | | | | | | | | | | | | | | | | | |

| Detail of Wanting to Complete or Surplus. | Saddlers or Harness Makers | Blacksmiths | Bricklayers and Masons | Carpenters and Joiners | Fitters & Turners (R.E.) Wood | Fitters & Turners (R.E.) Iron | Fitters R.A. | Fitters Wireless. | Plumbers | Electricians Ordinary | Electricians W.T. | Signalmen. | Engine Drivers Loco. | Engine Drivers Field | Air Line Men. | Permanent Line Men |
|---|---|---|---|---|---|---|---|---|---|---|---|---|---|---|---|---|
| CAVALRY— DEFICIENCY | | | | | | | | | | | | | | | | |
| SURPLUS | | | | | | | | | | | | | | | | |
| R.A.— DEFICIENCY | | | | | | | | | | | | | | | | |
| SURPLUS | | | | | | | | | | | | | | | | |
| R.E.— DEFICIENCY | | | | | | | | | | | | | | | | |
| SURPLUS | | | | | | | | | | | | | | | | |
| INFANTRY— DEFICIENCY | | | | | | | | | | | | | | | | |
| SURPLUS | | | | | | | | | | | | | | | | |
| R.A.M.C.— DEFICIENCY | | | | | | | | | | | | | | | | |
| SURPLUS | | | | | | | | | | | | | | | | |
| A.O.C.— DEFICIENCY | | | | | | | | | | | | | | | | |
| SURPLUS | | | | | | | | | | | | | | | | |
| A.V.C.— DEFICIENCY | | | | | | | | | | | | | | | | |
| SURPLUS | | | | | | | | | | | | | | | | |
| DEFICIENCY | | | | | | | | | | | | | | | | |
| SURPLUS | | | | | | | | | | | | | | | | |
| DEFICIENCY | | | | | | | | | | | | | | | | |
| SURPLUS | | | | | | | | | | | | | | | | |

| Detail of Wanting to Complete or Surplus. | Operators, Telegraph | Cablemen | Brigade Section Pioneers | General-duty Pioneers | Signallers | Instrument Repairers | Motor Cyclist | Motor Cyclist Artificers | Telephonists | Clerks | Machine Gunners | Armament Artificers Fitters | Armament Artificers Range Finders | Armourers | Storemen | Privates |
|---|---|---|---|---|---|---|---|---|---|---|---|---|---|---|---|---|
| CAVALRY— DEFICIENCY | | | | | | | | | | | | | | | | |
| SURPLUS | | | | | | | | | | | | | | | | |
| R.A.— DEFICIENCY | | | | | | | | | | | | | | | | |
| SURPLUS | | | | | | | | | | | | | | | | |
| R.E.— DEFICIENCY | | | | | | | | | | | | | | | | |
| SURPLUS | | | | | | | | | | | | | | | | |
| INFANTRY— DEFICIENCY | | | | | | | | | | | | | | | | |
| SURPLUS | | | | | | | | | | | | | | | | |
| R.A.M.C.— DEFICIENCY | | | | | | | | | | | | | | | | 13 |
| SURPLUS | | | | | | | | | | | | | | | | |
| A.O.C.— DEFICIENCY | | | | | | | | | | | | | | | | |
| SURPLUS | | | | | | | | | | | | | | | | |
| A.V.C.— DEFICIENCY | | | | | | | | | | | | | | | | |
| SURPLUS | | | | | | | | | | | | | | | | |
| DEFICIENCY | | | | | | | | | | | | | | | | |
| SURPLUS | | | | | | | | | | | | | | | | |
| DEFICIENCY | | | | | | | | | | | | | | | | |
| SURPLUS | | | | | | | | | | | | | | | | |

| Detail of Wanting to Complete or Surplus. | W.O.'s and N.C.O.'s (by ranks) not included in trade columns. Sgt. T.R.A.M.C.(T) | | | | | | | | | | | TOTAL to agree with wanting to complete or surplus Officers | TOTAL to agree with wanting to complete or surplus Other Ranks | Horses Riding | Horses Draught | Horses Heavy Draught | Horses Pack |
|---|---|---|---|---|---|---|---|---|---|---|---|---|---|---|---|---|---|
| CAVALRY— DEFICIENCY | | | | | | | | | | | | | | | | | |
| SURPLUS | | | | | | | | | | | | | | | | | |
| R.A.— DEFICIENCY | | | | | | | | | | | | | | | | | |
| SURPLUS | | | | | | | | | | | | | | | | | |
| R.E.— DEFICIENCY | | | | | | | | | | | | | | | | | |
| SURPLUS | | | | | | | | | | | | | | | | | |
| INFANTRY— DEFICIENCY | | | | | | | | | | | | | | | | | |
| SURPLUS | | | | | | | | | | | | | | | | | |
| R.A.M.C.— DEFICIENCY | 2 | | | | | | | | | | | 3 | 17 | 2 | 2 | 1 | |
| SURPLUS | | | | | | | | | | | | | | | | | |
| A.O.C.— DEFICIENCY | | | | | | | | | | | | | | | | | |
| SURPLUS | | | | | | | | | | | | | | | | | |
| A.V.C.— DEFICIENCY | | | | | | | | | | | | | | | | | |
| SURPLUS | | | | | | | | | | | | | | | | | |
| DEFICIENCY | | | | | | | | | | | | | | | | | |
| SURPLUS | | | | | | | | | | | | | | | | | |
| DEFICIENCY | | | | | | | | | | | | | | | | | |
| SURPLUS | | | | | | | | | | | | | | | | | |

Remarks :—
B.213 gives A.S.C. (H.T.) Establishment strength as 36
but as this does not include a Farrier Cpl.
a deficiency of 1 Far. Cpl. is shown above.

John W. Leitch Lt. Col. Signature of Commander.

4 Lowland Field Ambce. Unit.

52 Div. Formation to which attached.

23-11-18. Date of Despatch.

(16523.) Wt. W6016—PP 1432. 1,500m. 3/18. D & S. (E1256) Forms B2138/8.

[P.T.O.

17
Dec 1918

VR 9
140/3481

War Diary
of
1/1st Lowland Field Ambulance
Vol XLIII

from 1/12/18 to 31/12/18

[illegible] Lt Col
OC 1/1st LFA R.A.M.C.(T)

517 Army Form C. 2118.

Instructions regarding War Diaries and Intelligence Summaries are contained in F. S. Regs., Part II. and the Staff Manual respectively. Title pages will be prepared in manuscript.

# WAR DIARY
or
~~INTELLIGENCE~~ SUMMARY.
(*Erase heading not required.*)

1/1st Lowland Field Ambulance
52nd (Lowland) Division

| Place | Date | Hour | Summary of Events and Information | Remarks and references to Appendices |
|---|---|---|---|---|
| CHAUSSEE N.D. LOUVIGNIES W5b4,6 Sh 38. | 1/12/18 | | Sunday! Presbyterian church service at 1400. Most of the day spent in getting personnel settled in billets. ADMS called in afternoon & was shown proposed arrangements – the school for hospital, a small hall with 2 annexes for a dining & recreation room, the ~~kitchen~~ places chosen for kitchen, officers' mess, sergeants' mess etc. Received R722/4 that 1 MAC car would report from 1/2nd L.F.A. for use in evacuating to C.C.S. J.W.L. | |
| do | 2/12/18 | | Forwarded to C.R.E. through A.D.M.S. indents for corrugated iron, bricks, & wood for making ovens, incinerator, tables, forms etc. Visited billets & made some redistribution with a view to better comfort of the men. An "Early Treatment" room has been established J.W.L. | |
| do | 3/12/18 | | Sent Sgt. Muldoon & 24 men to report for temporary duty to O.C. 1/2nd L.F.A. Mons Station in accordance with A.D.M.S. R729/4 d/2 12/18, 1 G.S. Wagon & 4 ambulance motors were also sent. Visited ADMS with regard to ~~their~~ the difficulty of this party marching daily to & from Mons, & with his approval arranged with O.C. 1/2nd L.F.A. that he (the latter) should find billets for them in Mons & should take personnel & horses on his ration strength. Sent Major BROWNE, Capt R.A. LENNIE & 12 O.R. of B Tent subdivision to-night in 3 motor cars (one of which came from 1/2nd L.F.A. at Mons for rations for party at 1/2nd L.F.A. for to-morrow by arrangement) to report to Cavalry Barracks MONS in accordance with A.D.M.S. R746/5 d/3 12/18 received by me this afternoon. They take with them also equipment for dealing with repatriated Prisoners of War. Sent 2 L.D. Horses to 413th Fld Coy R.E. in accordance with A.D.M.S. R740/1 of even date J.W.L. | |

D. D. & L., London E.C
(10340) Wt W5300/P713 750,000 3/18 E 688 Forms/C2118/16.

518 Army Form C. 2118.

Instructions regarding War Diaries and Intelligence Summaries are contained in F. S. Regs., Part II. and the Staff Manual respectively. Title pages will be prepared in manuscript.

# WAR DIARY
~~or~~
~~INTELLIGENCE SUMMARY.~~
*(Erase heading not required.)*

1/1st Lowland Field Ambulance
52nd (Lowland) Division

| Place | Date | Hour | Summary of Events and Information | Remarks and references to Appendices |
|---|---|---|---|---|
| CHAUSSEE N.D. LOUVIGNIES. W5b44 Sh 38. | 4/12/18 | | The M.A.C. car did not report for duty with this unit for evacuation purposes, and ADMS R771/4 received to-night intimates that the M.A.C. cars are being sent to their unit – 31st M.A.C. O.C. 1/2nd L.F.A. is to return one one of the 4 cars sent to him at MONS. Completed visiting the billets & making redistribution where such seemed desirable. A number of refugees with baggage were being sent by wagons of this unit to BAUDOUR & MONS. J.w.L. | |
| do | 5/12/18 | | Visited 52nd M.G. Batt. at CAMBRON St VINCENT & 52nd T.M.B. at THORICOURT in connection with applications from them for medical assistance. This unit is collecting sick daily from 156th Bde Units & from 52nd D.A.C. at MASNUY ST. PIERRE – all by horsed ambulances. Rations are drawn from BAUDOUR & ration wagon leaves before 0800 & is never back before 1700 – often 6 or 8 hours later. Sgt MELDRUM reported back this afternoon from 1/2nd L.F.A. with 23 men under arrest under a charge of failing to appear at a parade at 1800 last night of which they had been warned. Letter & charge sheet sent with Sgt Meldrum by O.C. 1/2nd L.F.A. Detailed S/S HAMPSON & men to be sent in their place by 3 motor ambulances immediately after breakfast to-morrow morning. J.w.L. | |

D. D. & L., London E.C.
(10340) Wt W5300/P713 750,000 3/18 E 688 Forms/C2118/16.

Instructions regarding War Diaries and Intelligence Summaries are contained in F. S. Regs., Part II. and the Staff Manual respectively. Title pages will be prepared in manuscript.

# WAR DIARY
or
# ~~INTELLIGENCE SUMMARY.~~
(*Erase heading not required.*)

579 Army Form C. 2118.

1/1st Lowland Field Ambulance
52nd (Lowland) Division

| Place | Date | Hour | Summary of Events and Information | Remarks and references to Appendices |
|---|---|---|---|---|
| CHAUSSEE N. D. LOUVIGNIES<br>W.5646 S138. | 6/12/18 | | Arranged to get supply of bricks from a M. Michel of this village who makes<br>bricks. He has kindly consented to give me 100 or so for nothing. They are<br>required for building ovens & dixie fireplaces etc for the unit. Visited Brasserie<br>at NEUFVILLES today to get barrel for making disinfector - no success as<br>manager not in & price was not known. Barrels very difficult to get here &<br>none can be found in the village in a serviceable condition. J.W.L. | |
| do | 7/12/18 | | Completed adjourned hearing of charge against 23 men at orderly room today.<br>21 received 14 days C.C. & remaining 2 dismissed. Advised O.C. 1/2nd L.F.A. &<br>ADMS of the result. Evidence available was unsatisfactory & conflicting. The<br>men had not been tactfully handled. 2nd Lt COWELL from 412th Coy R.E.<br>called to-day in accordance with instructions & was shown requirements for<br>baths etc. He arranged that I should send tomorrow to 412th R.E. at MASNUY<br>St PIERRE to draw the stores, wood corrugated iron, 2 bags cement, & a<br>barrel for making Serbian barrel. J.W.L. | |
| do | 8/12/18 | | Wagons came back without the cement & the barrel; which were not<br>available. ~~D.D.M.S. XXII Corps accompanied by D.A.D.M.S. & ADMS 52nd Div called to-day to~~<br>Wrote ADMS. asking authority to draw 1 arhtbin disinfector from 410th Fd Coy R.E.<br>J.W.L. | |

D. D. & L., London, E.C.
(A8001) Wt. W1771/M2031 750,000 5/17 Sch. 52 Forms/C2118/14

Instructions regarding War Diaries and Intelligence Summaries are contained in F. S. Regs., Part II. and the Staff Manual respectively. Title pages will be prepared in manuscript.

# WAR DIARY
or
# ~~INTELLIGENCE SUMMARY.~~
(Erase heading not required.)

520 Army Form C. 2118.

1/1st Lowland Field Ambulance
52nd (Lowland) Division

| Place | Date | Hour | Summary of Events and Information | Remarks and references to Appendices |
|---|---|---|---|---|
| CHAUSSEE N. D. LOUVIGNIES W5646 8238 | 9/12/18 | | DDMS XXII Corps & A.D.M.S. 52nd Division called to-day. Rode to JOURBISE to attend G.O.C's conference at 155th Bde H.Q. there at 1430 JWL | |
| do | 10/12/18 | | Sent to 410th Fld Coy R.E. at JOURBISE & received 1 improvised Serbian barrel. This was set up on prepared fireplace of bricks & clay in afternoon. A number of tables & forms have been made by unit joiners – partly from wood of old German double tier beds & partly from wood drawn from R.E. – for use in Dining & Lecture hall. Erection of bath shelter at the Hospital (Schoolhouse) from wood drawn from 412th R.E. is proceeding satisfactorily. Ovens & dixies fires at the kitchen are also being rapidly completed by members of the unit. Visited Chateau d'Louvignies & reported to A.D.M.S. as to possibility of using part of it for an extension of Hospital. Major W.F. MACKENZIE rejoined from 14 days leave in U.K. JWL | |
| do | 11/12/18 | | Two N.C.O.s 20 men & 1 G.S. Wagon left at 1300 by march route to report to O.C. 1/2nd L.F.A. at Station MONS in accordance with A.D.M.S. R862/4 d/10 12/18. This makes the R.A.M.C personnel of this unit now attached temporarily to 1/2nd L.F.A. up to 3 NCOs & 44 men with 2 G.S. Wagons 4 horses & 2 drivers A.S.C. The 2 off & 12 men still remain at the Cavalry Barracks MONS treating the sick & medically attending the repatriated P of W. of all nationalities. Lt DRUMMOND att 155th Bde gave the 2nd of a course of 3 lectures to this unit on | |

D. D. & L., London, E.C.
(A8001) Wt. W1771/M2031 750,000 5/17 Sch. 52 Forms/C2118/14

Instructions regarding War Diaries and Intelligence Summaries are contained in F. S. Regs., Part II. and the Staff Manual respectively. Title pages will be prepared in manuscript.

# WAR DIARY
*or*
# ~~INTELLIGENCE SUMMARY.~~
(*Erase heading not required.*)

521 Army Form C. 2118.

1/1st Lowland Field Ambulance
52nd (Lowland) Division

| Place | Date | Hour | Summary of Events and Information | Remarks and references to Appendices |
|---|---|---|---|---|
| CHAUSSEE N. D. LOUVIGNIES W.S.646 SL38 | 11/12/18 (Cont'd) | | "How to study nature" at 1400 in the Lecture hall of this unit. The attendance was as large as could be expected considering the number on duty & detached from the unit. JWL. | |
| do | 12/12/18 | | Notice boards marking "Limits of billetting area" have been set up in accordance with Divisional Orders & exact map locations of these sent to D.A.D.P.M. in reply to his request for same. Visited Detachment of this unit at Cavalry Barracks MONS. Received A.D.M.S. R866/4 of even date to take over medical & sanitary supervision of 412th Fld Coy. R.E. who were expected to move to LOUVIGNIES to-morrow. JWL | |
| do | 13/12/18 | | Lt DRUMMOND att 155 Bde HQ gave the last of the 3 lectures on "How to study nature" to this Field Ambulance at 1400 to-day. Good progress has been made with erection of bath shelter at Hospital. The improvised "Ash bin" disinfector has been in active use since yesterday & is working very well. A six seater box latrine over a deep pit has been got into use & others are being constructed as wood becomes available. A beginning has been made with erection of ovens for cookhouse – a few sheets of corrugated iron having been obtained from the R.E. Major DAVIES OC 412th Fld Coy. RE called to-night on arrival of his unit at CHATEAU d'LOUVIGNIES to ask if he could help us in any way. JWL. | |
| do | 14/12/18 | | Sent 1 NCO. & 19 men to report for temporary duty to OC 1/3rd L.F.A. at ECOLE NORMALE MONS in accordance with instructions in A.D.M.S. R899/4 d/13 12/18 JWL. | |

D. D. & L., London, E.C. (A8001) Wt. W1771/M2031 750,000 5/17 Sch. 52 Forms/C2118/14

Instructions regarding War Diaries and Intelligence Summaries are contained in F. S. Regs., Part II. and the Staff Manual respectively. Title pages will be prepared in manuscript.

# WAR DIARY
or
INTELLIGENCE SUMMARY.
(Erase heading not required.)

522 Army Form C. 2118.

1/1st Lowland Field Ambulance, 52nd (Lowland) Division

| Place | Date | Hour | Summary of Events and Information | Remarks and references to Appendices |
|---|---|---|---|---|
| CHAUSSE N.D. LOUVIGNIES W5b4.6. Sh 38 | 15/12/18 | | A.D.M.S. called & inspected hospital, kitchen, dining hall, latrines, & billetting & camp arrangements generally. J.W.L. | |
| do | 16/12/18 | | The classes on English, French, Mathematics & Dynamics in this unit are suspended from to-day owing to the numbers absent from the unit on detached duty. J.W.L. | |
| do | 17/12/18 | | Bath shelter for scabies and other patients has been completed & is in full use to-day. A scheme of routine treatment has been drawn out & copies given to Ward masters & orderlies. A copy has also been posted up in the baths (Appendix I). J.W.L. | APPENDIX I |
| do | 18/12/18 | | Nothing to note. | |
| do | 19/12/18 | | Capt. & Qm. REID proceeded to-day on 14 days leave to U.K. sailing on 22nd Dec. J.W.L. | |
| | | | A.D.M.S. visited | |
| do | 20/12/18 | | A large standard pattern grease trap is being made by the unit joiner for use at the kitchen. The ovens recently built are not raising enough heat on one side & will have to be taken down & rebuilt. 2 out of the 4 ovens built seem to be working satisfactorily. J.W.L. | |
| do | 21/12/18 | | Ordinary routine. | |
| do | 22/12/18 | | Received a note from Major BROWNE i/c Detachment of this unit at Returned P. of W. Centre, Cavalry Barracks MONS that by order of A.D.M.S. 52nd Division he was now att. | |

D. D. & L., London, E.C. (A8001) Wt. W1771/M2031 750,000 5/17 Sch. 52 Forms/C2118/14

Instructions regarding War Diaries and Intelligence Summaries are contained in F. S. Regs., Part II. and the Staff Manual respectively. Title pages will be prepared in manuscript.

# WAR DIARY
~~or~~
~~INTELLIGENCE SUMMARY.~~
*(Erase heading not required.)*

523 Army Form C. 2118.

1/1st Lowland Field Ambulance
52nd (Lowland) Division

| Place | Date | Hour | Summary of Events and Information | Remarks and references to Appendices |
|---|---|---|---|---|
| CHAUSSEE N.D. LOUVIGNIES WS646. Sh. 38. | 22/12/18 (Contd) | | 1/3rd L.F.A. for duty & Capt. R.A. LENNIE was similarly att. 1/2nd L.F.A. The 12 O.R. less 2 officers' servants, were remaining at Cavalry Barracks. The officers reported to 1/3rd & 1/2nd L.F.A. respectively on 20th Inst. J.W.L. | |
| do | 23/12/18 | | ~~Sunday~~. Ordinary routine duties carried out. J.W.L. | |
| do | 24/12/18 | | Some of the stores lent by this unit under instructions of A.D.M.S. to 1/2nd L.F.A. at MONS Station were returned last night. Wrote O.C. 1/2nd L.F.A. today ~~asking~~ giving a list of deficiencies asking when these might be expected. J.W.L. | |
| do | 25/12/18 | | Christmas day:- Work reduced to a minimum. Office work has been very heavy during the past few weeks. J.W.L. | |
| do | 26/12/18 | | M. le Maire has been pressing for the use of the school which we are now using as a hospital. Have told him that a house of 2 stories presently occupied by French refugee families might be considered for use as a hospital in place of the school provided the refugees can be accommodated elsewhere & the house given over entirely for hospital use. Surg. Lt. Commander ROSS reported for duty with this unit from 109th Bde R.F.A. J.W.L. | |
| do | 27/12/18 | | Received note from Major BROWNE that he has been detailed to take charge of the section 1/3rd L.F.A. at ~~MONTIGNY~~ LENS – the present Divisional Rest Stn. J.W.L. | |
| do | 28/12/18 | | The 2 G.S. Wagons & drivers attached temporarily to 1/2nd L.F.A. at Station MONS reported back to this unit yesterday (27th). The 20 O.R. temporarily attached 1/3rd L.F.A. ECOLE NORMALE, MONS rejoined | |

D. D. & L., London, E.C. (A8004) Wt. W1771/M2031 750,000 5/17 Sch. 52 Forms/C2118/14

Instructions regarding War Diaries and Intelligence Summaries are contained in F. S. Regs., Part II. and the Staff Manual respectively. Title pages will be prepared in manuscript.

# WAR DIARY
~~or~~
~~INTELLIGENCE~~ SUMMARY.
(Erase heading not required.)

524 Army Form C. 2118.

1/1st Lowland Field Ambulance
52nd Lowland Division

| Place | Date | Hour | Summary of Events and Information | Remarks and references to Appendices |
|---|---|---|---|---|
| CHAUSSEE N.D. LOUVIGNIES WS. b46 Sh. 38 | 28/12/18 (Contd.) | | unit to-day. Weather very wet. J.W.L. | |
| | 29/12/18 | | Ordinary routine duties carried out. J.W.L. | |
| | 30/12/18 | | Nothing to note. A 5-a-side football competition for members of the unit is being played as weather permits. J.W.L. | |
| | 31/12/18 | | A.D.M.S. visited. Dr. Jones A.S.C. was despatched from this unit to-day for demobilization under the arrangements for coalminers. There are 11 coalminers altogether in the unit. J.W.L. | |

James W. Leitch Lt Col
O.C. 1/1st Lowland Field Ambulance
R.A.M.C.(T.)

D. D. & L., London, E.C.
(A8001) Wt. W1771/M2031 750,000 5/17 Sch. 52 Forms/C2118/14

APPENDIX I (Decr 1918) War Diary of 1/1st Lowland Fld Ambce
Vol XLIII RAMC(T)

## ROUTINE TREATMENT for SCABIES

1/ On admission to Hospital Patients will be shown into first chamber of the Bath House and will undress. All his clothing – except. boots and leather articles – will be loosely bundled together and taken by the Orderly to the Disinfector. Boots and leather articles will be disinfected by a 2% solution of Eusol.

2/ Patient will enter the second chamber and thoroughly bath himself with soap and hot water, after which he will remain in the bath (Temp. about 100°) for half an hour.

Affected parts should be well soaked and hot water added as required, by Orderly to maintain the temperature.

N.B. Orderly will see that the patient steps out of the bath before hot water is added.

3/ Patient will rapidly dry himself, and enter chamber three, where Sulphur Ointment will be rubbed into affected parts by or under supervision of an Orderly until Ointment disappears.

Patient will then put on a clean suit of Pyjamas and go to his bed in the Ward, where he will remain for one hour.

4/ A second hot bath and rubbing with Sulphur Ointment will be given same day, and similarly two baths and Ointment rubbings on each of the three succeeding days – – ie 4 days in all.

5/ After eight baths and rubbings have been completed patient will be passed to the Convalescent Ward for Discharge or Transfer.

6/ Patients will be instructed to examine their clothing for live lice or unscorched NITS when clothing is returned to them from Disinfector and to bring to the Orderly's notice any such found.

7/ Above Routine Treatment will not be varied except by Order of the M.O. doing duty.

## PEDICULOSIS & OTHER SKIN DISEASES

Treatment will be as in Scabies except that there will be no rubbing with Ointment and only the Initial Hot Bath need be given.

After the patient's clothing has been satisfactorily disinfected he will be passed at once to the Convalescent Ward.

John W. Leitch Lt Col
OC 1/1 Low Fd Amb.

To be [illegible]de up to and for Saturday in each week

No. of Report 175 I

# FIELD RETURN.

Army Form B. 213

(To be furnished by all arms, services, and departments (except A.S.C. units) to the A.G.'s Office at the Base in accordance with Field Service Regulations, Part II.)

RETURN showing numbers (a) Effective strength of Unit. (b) Rationed by Unit. 1/1 Lowland Field Ambce at In the Field [illegible] 7-12-18 Date.

| DETAILS. | *Personnel: Officers | Other Ranks | | | Animals: Horses: Riding | Draught | Heavy Draught | Pack | Mules: Large | Small | Guns and transport vehicles: Guns, showing description | Ammunition wagons | Machine guns | Aircraft, showing description | Horsed: 4 Wheeled | 2 Wheeled | Mechanical: Motor Cars | Tractors | Lorries, showing description | Trucks, showing description | Trailers | Motor Bicycles | Bicycles | Motor Ambulances | REMARKS (Number of Acting W.O.'s and N.C.O.'s included in effective strength to be shown in this column.) |
|---|---|---|---|---|---|---|---|---|---|---|---|---|---|---|---|---|---|---|---|---|---|---|---|---|---|
| Effective Strength of Unit ... ... | (a) 7 | (b) 167 | | | | | | | | | | | | | | | | | | | | | 1 | | (a) Surgeon 1 on leave to U.K. Includes 1 @ 1/4 R.S. " 2 @ 1st Low. F.A. [illegible] [illegible] (b) Includes 1 @ 52 D.H.Q. " 1 @ 52 Div. [illegible] " 1 @ 156 Bde. H.Q. " 12 @ [illegible] " 25 @ 1/2 Low. Fd. Amb. " 1 @ 52 Div. Train " 5 on leave to U.K. |
| Details by Arms attached to Unit as in War Establishment ... ... | | | | | | | | | | | | | | | | | | | | | | | | | |
| A. S. C. (H.T.) | | (c) 35 | | | 6 | 17 | 19 | | | | | | | | 13 | 4 | | | | | | | | | (c) Includes 2 on leave to U.K. " 1 @ 1/2 Low. Fd. Amb. |
| A. S. C. (M.T.) | | (d) 11 | | | | | | | | | | | | | | | | | | | | 2 | | 7 | (d) Includes 1 @ 52 D.H.Q. (e) 1 @ Workshops |
| TOTAL ... ... | 7 | 213 | | | 6 | 17 | x 10 | | | | | | | | 13 | 4 | | | | | | 2 | 1 | 7 | (d) Includes 3 @ 1/2 Low. Fd. Am. (x) 2 at 1/2 L.F.A. |
| War Establishment ... ... ... | 10 | 231 | | | 8 | 17 | 20 | | | | | | | | 13 | 4 | | | | | | 2 | 1 | 7 | |
| Wanting to complete ... ... (Detail of Personnel and Horses below.) | 3 | (f) 19 | | | 2 | . | 1 | | | | | | | | . | . | | | | | | . | . | . | (f) 15 R.A.M.C. 2 A.S.C. (H.T.) Includes 1 Farr. Cpl. 2 A.S.C. (M.T.) |
| SURPLUS ... ... (Detail of Personnel and Horses below.) | | (g) 1 | | | | | | | | | | | | | | | | | | | | | | | (g) 1 A.S.C. (H.T.) Farr. [illegible] |
| †Attached (not to include the details shown above) ... ... ... | | 33 | | | | | | | | | | | | | | | | | | | | | | | Patients |
| Attached for Rations only ... ... | 1 | | | | | | | | | | | | | | | | | | | | | | | | Chaplain |
| Civilians Employed with and Accompanying the Unit ... ... | | | | | | | | | | | | | | | | | | | | | | | | | |
| ‡Detached from and struck off effective strength of own Unit ... | | | | | | | | | | | | | | | | | | | | | | | | | |
| ‡Detached from but retained on effective strength of own unit... ... | | | | | | | | | | | | | | | | | | | | | | | | | |
| TOTAL RATIONED ... | 4 | 193 | | | 6 | 17 | 17 | | | | | | | | | | | | | | | | | | |

* Blank columns to be used for W.A.A.C. Natives or as may be required.

† In the case of field ambulances, hospitals or depots, the number of patients are to be included here, the names being shown in A.F.A. 36.

‡ These details to be enumerated by arms.

[illegible] Lt. Col. Signature of Commander.

7. 12. 18 Date of Despatch.

No. 155

B 213 A.S.C. W.E. 7.12.18

| No. | RANK | NAME | CASUALTY | DATE |
|---|---|---|---|---|
| 39160 | Pte. | Baker W. | Sick to Hospital in U.K. (while on leave) | 16/11/18 |

[illegible] Lt. Col.
OC. [illegible]

2/12/18

A.S. 6 Sheet 4

*For information of the A.G.'s Office at the base.*

Officers and men who have become casuals, been transferred or joined since last report.

Place In the Field  Date 7.12.18

| Regtl. Number | Rank | Name | | Corps | Nature of casualty, or name of unit from or to which transferred. | Date of being struck off or coming on the ration return | Remarks * |
|---|---|---|---|---|---|---|---|
| 3162[illegible] | Pte. | Carruthers | P.S.E. | R.A.M.C. (T.) | Sick to Hosp. | 30.11.18 | |
| 31630[illegible] | | Colville | W. | do | Sick to Hosp. | 30.11.18 | |
| 4100[illegible] | | Jackson | F.S. | do | Reinforcement from Base | 1.12.18 | |
| 3160[illegible] | | Bowie | J. | do | Reinforcement from Hospital | 3.12.18 | |
| 4100[illegible] | | Hodgson | | do | Candidate for Commission Returned to Unit | 30.11.18 | |
| 3160[illegible] | | Rankine | J. | do | Returned from leave | 30.11.18 | |
| 3160[illegible] | Cpl. | [illegible] | J. | do | do | 30.11.18 | |
| 316232 | Cpl. | Stewart | J. | do | do | 4.12.18 | |
| 316225 | Pte. | McLennan | W. | do | do | 4.12.18 | |
| 31611[illegible] | | Johnson | A.C. | do | do | 5.12.18 | |
| 3160[illegible] | | Hay | A. | do | do | 2.12.18 | |
| 3160[illegible] | | Hay | A. | do | Married Miss Annie Dunlop Thomson at Glasgow on 21/?/18. Present address of wife C/o Thomson 17 [illegible] Street, Shawlands, Glasgow. From 21/?/18 transfer allotment from mother to wife, Mrs Annie Hay C/o Thomson 17 [illegible] Street, Shawlands, Glasgow. | | |
| 316[illegible] | Pte. | [illegible] Roy | H. | R.A.M.C. (T) | [illegible] pay increased to 4d from 2?.11.18 | | |
| 104[illegible] | " | [illegible] | R.J. | R.A.M.C. | do do 3d | 30.11.18 | |

Strength

Officers T.F. 6
T.C. 1
R.A.M.C. 1

W.O. NCOs & Men

| | |
|---|---|
| W.O. | 1 |
| Q.M.S. | 1 |
| S/Sgts | 2 |
| Sgts | 8 |
| L/Sgts | 1 |
| Cpls. | 10 |
| L/Cpls. | 4 |
| Ptes. | 140 |
| TOTAL | 167 |

All Category A

* State whether absence is of a permanent or temporary nature, adding, in the case of casuals from wounds or disease any available information for communication to the relatives.

*The perforated sheet is not to be used to record casualties; additional sheets, preferably foolscap, to be attached when necessary. These sheets to be carefully numbered and the number of attached sheets to be noted here.*

Perforated Sheet giving detail of personnel and horses wanting to complete or surplus, shown on Army Form B. 213.

No. of Report 175

| Detail of Wanting to Complete or Surplus | Drivers R.A. | Drivers R.E. | Drivers A.S.C. | Drivers Car | Drivers Lorry | Drivers Steam | Gunners | Gunners Howitzer | Smith Gunners | Range Takers | Farriers Serjeants | Farriers Corporals | Shoeing or Shoeing and Carriage Smiths | ~~Cold Shoers~~ FARR. DRIVER | Wheelers R.A. | Wheelers H.T. | Wheelers M.T. |
|---|---|---|---|---|---|---|---|---|---|---|---|---|---|---|---|---|---|
| CAVALRY—DEFICIENCY | | | | | | | | | | | | | | | | | |
| SURPLUS | | | | | | | | | | | | | | | | | |
| R.A.—DEFICIENCY | | | | | | | | | | | | | | | | | |
| SURPLUS | | | | | | | | | | | | | | | | | |
| R.E.—DEFICIENCY | | | | | | | | | | | | | | | | | |
| SURPLUS | | | | | | | | | | | | | | | | | |
| INFANTRY—DEFICIENCY | | | | | | | | | | | | | | | | | |
| SURPLUS | | | | | | | | | | | | | | | | | |
| R.A.M.C.—DEFICIENCY | | | 1 | 2 | | | | | | | | 1 | | | | | |
| SURPLUS | | | | | | | | | | | | | | 1 | | | |
| A.O.C.—DEFICIENCY | | | | | | | | | | | | | | | | | |
| SURPLUS | | | | | | | | | | | | | | | | | |
| A.V.C.—DEFICIENCY | | | | | | | | | | | | | | | | | |
| SURPLUS | | | | | | | | | | | | | | | | | |
| DEFICIENCY | | | | | | | | | | | | | | | | | |
| SURPLUS | | | | | | | | | | | | | | | | | |
| DEFICIENCY | | | | | | | | | | | | | | | | | |
| SURPLUS | | | | | | | | | | | | | | | | | |

| Detail of Wanting to Complete or Surplus | Saddlers or Harness Makers | Blacksmiths | Bricklayers and Masons | Carpenters and Joiners | Fitters & Turners (R.E.) Wood | Fitters & Turners (R.E.) Iron | Fitters R.A. | Fitters Wireless. | Plumbers | Electricians Ordinary | Electricians W.T. | Signalmen. | Engine Drivers Loco. | Engine Drivers Field | Air Line Men. | Permanent Line Men | Operators, Telegraph | Cablemen | Brigade Section Pioneers | General-duty Pioneers | Signallers |
|---|---|---|---|---|---|---|---|---|---|---|---|---|---|---|---|---|---|---|---|---|---|
| CAVALRY—DEFICIENCY | | | | | | | | | | | | | | | | | | | | | |
| SURPLUS | | | | | | | | | | | | | | | | | | | | | |
| R.A.—DEFICIENCY | | | | | | | | | | | | | | | | | | | | | |
| SURPLUS | | | | | | | | | | | | | | | | | | | | | |
| R.E.—DEFICIENCY | | | | | | | | | | | | | | | | | | | | | |
| SURPLUS | | | | | | | | | | | | | | | | | | | | | |
| INFANTRY—DEFICIENCY | | | | | | | | | | | | | | | | | | | | | |
| SURPLUS | | | | | | | | | | | | | | | | | | | | | |
| R.A.M.C.—DEFICIENCY | | | | | | | | | | | | | 6 | | | | | | | | |
| SURPLUS | | | | | | | | | | | | | | | | | | | | | |
| A.O.C.—DEFICIENCY | | | | | | | | | | | | | | | | | | | | | |
| SURPLUS | | | | | | | | | | | | | | | | | | | | | |
| A.V.C.—DEFICIENCY | | | | | | | | | | | | | | | | | | | | | |
| SURPLUS | | | | | | | | | | | | | | | | | | | | | |
| DEFICIENCY | | | | | | | | | | | | | | | | | | | | | |
| SURPLUS | | | | | | | | | | | | | | | | | | | | | |
| DEFICIENCY | | | | | | | | | | | | | | | | | | | | | |
| SURPLUS | | | | | | | | | | | | | | | | | | | | | |

| Detail of Wanting to Complete or Surplus | Instrument Repairers | Motor Cyclist | Motor Cyclist Artificers | Telephonists | Clerks | Machine Gunners | Armament Artificers Fitters | Armament Artificers Range Finders | Armourers | Storemen | Privates | W.O.'s and N.C.O.'s (by ranks) not included in trade columns. Sgts. R.A.M.C. | | | | | | | | | | | TOTAL to agree with wanting to complete or surplus Officers | TOTAL Other Ranks | Horses Riding | Horses Draught | Horses Heavy Draught | Horses Pack |
|---|---|---|---|---|---|---|---|---|---|---|---|---|---|---|---|---|---|---|---|---|---|---|---|---|---|---|---|---|
| CAVALRY—DEFICIENCY | | | | | | | | | | | | | | | | | | | | | | | | | | | | |
| SURPLUS | | | | | | | | | | | | | | | | | | | | | | | | | | | | |
| R.A.—DEFICIENCY | | | | | | | | | | | | | | | | | | | | | | | | | | | | |
| SURPLUS | | | | | | | | | | | | | | | | | | | | | | | | | | | | |
| R.E.—DEFICIENCY | | | | | | | | | | | | | | | | | | | | | | | | | | | | |
| SURPLUS | | | | | | | | | | | | | | | | | | | | | | | | | | | | |
| INFANTRY—DEFICIENCY | | | | | | | | | | | | | | | | | | | | | | | | | | | | |
| SURPLUS | | | | | | | | | | | | | | | | | | | | | | | | | | | | |
| R.A.M.C.—DEFICIENCY | | | | | | | | | | | 132 | | | | | | | | | | | | 3 | 19 | 2 | | 1 | |
| SURPLUS | | | | | | | | | | | | | | | | | | | | | | | | | | | | |
| A.O.C.—DEFICIENCY | | | | | | | | | | | | | | | | | | | | | | | | | | | | |
| SURPLUS | | | | | | | | | | | | | | | | | | | | | | | | | | | | |
| A.V.C.—DEFICIENCY | | | | | | | | | | | | | | | | | | | | | | | | | | | | |
| SURPLUS | | | | | | | | | | | | | | | | | | | | | | | | | | | | |
| DEFICIENCY | | | | | | | | | | | | | | | | | | | | | | | | | | | | |
| SURPLUS | | | | | | | | | | | | | | | | | | | | | | | | | | | | |
| DEFICIENCY | | | | | | | | | | | | | | | | | | | | | | | | | | | | |
| SURPLUS | | | | | | | | | | | | | | | | | | | | | | | | | | | | |

Remarks :—

[illegible] Lt. Col. Signature of Commander.

11th Lowland Field Ambulance Unit.

52 D.V. Formation to which attached.

7 · 12 · 18 Date of Despatch.

(16523.) Wt. W6016—PP 1432. 1,500m. 3/18. D & S. (E1256) Forms B213S/S.

[P.T.O.

**To be made up to and for Saturday in each week**

No. of Report 176

# FIELD RETURN.

Army Form B. 213

(To be furnished by all arms, services, and departments (except A.S.C. units) to the A.G.'s Office at the Base in accordance with Field Service Regulations, Part II.)

RETURN showing numbers (*a*) Effective strength of Unit. (*b*) Rationed by Unit. 1/1 Lon. Fd. Amb at In the Field 14/12/18. Date.

| Details. | *Personnel: Officers | Other Ranks | | | Animals: Horses: Riding | Draught | Heavy Draught | Pack | Mules: Large | Small | Guns and transport vehicles: Guns, showing description | Ammunition wagons | Machine guns | Aircraft, showing description | Horsed: 4 Wheeled | 2 Wheeled | Mechanical: Motor Cars | Tractors | Lorries, showing description | Trucks, showing description | Trailers | Motor Bicycles | Bicycles | Motor Ambulances | Remarks (Number of Acting W.O.'s and N.C.O.'s included in effective strength to be shown in this column.) |
|---|---|---|---|---|---|---|---|---|---|---|---|---|---|---|---|---|---|---|---|---|---|---|---|---|---|
| Effective Strength of Unit ... ... | 7 | 166 | | | | | | | | | | | | | | | | | | | | | | | [illegible] |
| Details by Arms attached to Unit as in War Establishment ... ... | | | | | | | | | | | | | | | | | | | | | | | | | [illegible] |
| A.S.C. H.T. | | 35 | | | 6 | 16 | 14 | | | | | | | | 13 | 4 | | | | | | | | | [illegible] |
| A.S.C. M.T. | | 11 | | | | | | | | | | | | | | | | | | | | 2 | 1 | 7 | [illegible] |
| Total ... ... | 7 | 212 | | | 6 | 16 | 14 | | | | | | | | 13 | 4 | | | | | | 2 | 1 | 7 | [illegible] |
| War Establishment ... ... ... | 10 | 231 | | | 8 | 17 | 20 | | | | | | | | 13 | 4 | | | | | | 2 | 1 | 7 | |
| Wanting to complete ... ... ... (Detail of Personnel and Horses below.) | 3 | 20 | | | 2 | 1 | 1 | | | | | | | | | | | | | | | | | | 16 - RANK. 2 - ASC 2 - ASC M.T |
| Surplus ... ... (Detail of Personnel and Horses below.) | | 1 | | | | | | | | | | | | | | | | | | | | | | | 1 - ASC M.T ([illegible]) |
| †Attached (not to include the details shown above) ... ... ... | | 22 | | | | | | | | | | | | | | | | | | | | | | | Patients |
| | 1 | | | | | | | | | | | | | | | | | | | | | | | | Chaplain |
| Attached for Rations only ... | | | | | | | | | | | | | | | | | | | | | | | | | |
| Civilians Employed with and Accompanying the Unit ... ... | | | | | | | | | | | | | | | | | | | | | | | | | |
| ‡Detached from and struck off effective strength of own Unit ... | | | | | | | | | | | | | | | | | | | | | | | | | |
| ‡Detached from but retained on effective strength of own unit... ... | | | | | | | | | | | | | | | | | | | | | | | | | |
| Total Rationed ... | 5 | 161 | | | 6 | 16 | 15 | | | | | | | | | | | | | | | | | | |

* Blank columns to be used for W.A.A.C. Natives or as may be required.

† In the case of field ambulances, hospitals or depots, the number of patients are to be included here, the names being shown in A.F.A. 36.

‡ These details to be enumerated by arms.

[illegible] Lt Col. Signature of Commander.

14/12/18. Date of Despatch.

B 213    A.S.C. Section    w/e 14/12/18

| No | Rk. | Name | | Remarks | |
|---|---|---|---|---|---|
| M2/036444 | Pte | Joyce | W.J. | Granted 14 days [illegible] U.K. [illegible] Credit [illegible] period | 12/12 - 26/12 |
| T/32015 | Dvr. | Fox | L.W. | — do — — do — | 12/12 - 26/12 |
| T4/044561 | " | Lloyd | W.S. | Retd from leave | 11/12 |
| T4/145543 | " | Savage | H.T. | — do — | 12/12 |

*For information of the A.G.'s Office at the base.*

A.S.C. sheet attached

Officers and men who have become casuals, been transferred or joined since last report.

Place In the Field Date 14/12/18.

| Regtl. Number | Rank | Name | Corps | Nature of casualty, or name of unit from or to which transferred. | Date of being struck off or coming on the ration return. | Remarks * |
|---|---|---|---|---|---|---|
| | Major | W. F. Mackenzie | R. an. C. S. | Retd. from leave | 11/12/18. | |
| 4[illegible]1178 | Cpl | Mead L. E. | do | Retd. to Base surplus to establishment | 9/12/18. | |
| 3[illegible]505 | Cpl | McDonald R. | do | | | |
| 316308 | Pte | Colville W. | do | Reinf. from Hospt | 9/12/18. | |
| 376098 | " | Galloch C. | do | " " Base | 11/12/18. | |
| 316083 | " | McCritchie J. | do | Retd from leave | 8/12/18. | |
| 316301 | " | Hendry J. | do | Sick to Hospt | 14/12/18. | |
| 16087 | Q.M.S. | Thomson W. | do | Commenced duties as QMS on 9/11/18 (vice QMS Taylor) & not 9/12/18 as notified. | | |

Strength: Officers T.F. 6 T.C. 1 / 7.

W.O. NCOs & men.

W.O. 1.
QMS 1.
S/Sgts 2.
Sgts 8.
L/Sgts 1.
Cpls 8.
L/Cpls 4.
Ptes 141
166.

All Category "A".

* State whether absence is of a permanent or temporary nature, adding, in the case of casuals from wounds or disease any available information for communication to the relatives.

*The perforated sheet is not to be used to record casualties ; additional sheets, preferably foolscap, to be attached when necessary. These sheets to be carefully numbered and the number of attached sheets to be noted here.*

Perforated Sheet giving detail of personnel and horses wanting to complete or surplus, shown on Army Form B. 213.

No. of Report ____________

| Detail of Wanting to Complete or Surplus. | Drivers: R.A. | Drivers: R.E. | Drivers: A.S.C. | Drivers: Car | Drivers: Lorry | Drivers: Steam | Gunners | Gunners Howitzer | Smith Gunners | Range Takers | Farriers: Serjeants | Farriers: Corporals | Shoeing or Shoeing and Carriage Smiths | Cold Shoers | Wheelers: R.A. | Wheelers: H.T. | Wheelers: M.T. | Saddlers or Harness Makers | Blacksmiths | Bricklayers and Masons | Carpenters and Joiners | Fitters & Turners (R.E.): Wood | Fitters & Turners (R.E.): Iron | Fitters: R.A. | Fitters: Wireless. | Plumbers | Electricians: Ordinary | Electricians: W.T. | Signalmen. | Engine Drivers: Loco. | Engine Drivers: Field | Air Line Men. | Permanent Line Men | Operators, Telegraph | Cablemen | Brigade Section Pioneers | General-duty Pioneers | Signallers | Instrument Repairers | Motor Cyclist | Motor Cyclist Artificers | Telephonists | Clerks | Machine Gunners | Armament Artificers: Fitters | Armament Artificers: Range Finders | Armourers | Storemen | Privates | W.O.'s and N.C.O.'s (by ranks) not included in trade columns. | | | | | | | | | | | TOTAL to agree with wanting to complete or surplus: Officers | TOTAL to agree with wanting to complete or surplus: Other Ranks | Horses: Riding | Horses: Draught | Horses: Heavy Draught | Horses: Pack |
|---|---|---|---|---|---|---|---|---|---|---|---|---|---|---|---|---|---|---|---|---|---|---|---|---|---|---|---|---|---|---|---|---|---|---|---|---|---|---|---|---|---|---|---|---|---|---|---|---|---|---|---|---|---|---|---|---|---|---|---|---|---|---|---|---|---|---|
| CAVALRY— DEFICIENCY | | | | | | | | | | | | | | | | | | | | | | | | | | | | | | | | | | | | | | | | | | | | | | | | | | | | | | | | | | | | | | | | | | | |
| SURPLUS | | | | | | | | | | | | | | | | | | | | | | | | | | | | | | | | | | | | | | | | | | | | | | | | | | | | | | | | | | | | | | | | | | | |
| R.A.— DEFICIENCY | | | | | | | | | | | | | | | | | | | | | | | | | | | | | | | | | | | | | | | | | | | | | | | | | | | | | | | | | | | | | | | | | | | |
| SURPLUS | | | | | | | | | | | | | | | | | | | | | | | | | | | | | | | | | | | | | | | | | | | | | | | | | | | | | | | | | | | | | | | | | | | |
| R.E.— DEFICIENCY | | | | | | | | | | | | | | | | | | | | | | | | | | | | | | | | | | | | | | | | | | | | | | | | | | | | | | | | | | | | | | | | | | | |
| SURPLUS | | | | | | | | | | | | | | | | | | | | | | | | | | | | | | | | | | | | | | | | | | | | | | | | | | | | | | | | | | | | | | | | | | | |
| INFANTRY— DEFICIENCY | | | | | | | | | | | | | | | | | | | | | | | | | | | | | | | | | | | | | | | | | | | | | | | | | | | | | | | | | | | | | | | | | | | |
| SURPLUS | | | 1 | 2 | | | | | | | | 1 | | | | | | | | | | | | | | | | | | | | | | | | | | | | | | | | | | | | | | | | | | | | | | | | | | | | | | | |
| R.A.M.C.— DEFICIENCY | | | | | | | | | | | | | | | | | | | | | | | | | | | | | | | | | | | | | | | | | | | | | | | | | | | | | | | | | | | | | | | | | | | |
| SURPLUS | | | | | | | | | | | | | | | | | | | | | | | | | | | | | | | | | | | | | | | | | | | | | | | | | | | | | | | | | | | | | | | | | | | |
| A.O.C.— DEFICIENCY | | | | | | | | | | | | | | | | | | | | | | | | | | | | | | | | | | | | | | | | | | | | | | | | | | | | | | | | | | | | | | | | | | | |
| SURPLUS | | | | | | | | | | | | | | | | | | | | | | | | | | | | | | | | | | | | | | | | | | | | | | | | | | | | | | | | | | | | | | | | | | | |
| A.V.C.— DEFICIENCY | | | | | | | | | | | | | | | | | | | | | | | | | | | | | | | | | | | | | | | | | | | | | | | | | | | | | | | | | | | | | | | | | | | |
| SURPLUS | | | | | | | | | | | | | | | | | | | | | | | | | | | | | | | | | | | | | | | | | | | | | | | | | | | | | | | | | | | | | | | | | | | |
| DEFICIENCY | | | | | | | | | | | | | | | | | | | | | | | | | | | | | | | | | | | | | | | | | | | | | | | | | | | | | | | | | | | | | | | | | | | |
| SURPLUS | | | | | | | | | | | | | | | | | | | | | | | | | | | | | | | | | | | | | | | | | | | | | | | | | | | | | | | | | | | | | | | | | | | |
| DEFICIENCY | | | | | | | | | | | | | | | | | | | | | | | | | | | | | | | | | | | | | | | | | | | | | | | | | | | | | | | | | | | | | | | | | | | |
| SURPLUS | | | | | | | | | | | | | | | | | | | | | | | | | | | | | | | | | | | | | | | | | | | | | | | | | | | | | | | | | | | | | | | | | | | |

Remarks :—

____________ Signature of Commander.

____________ Unit.

____________ Formation to which attached.

____________ Date of Despatch.

(16523.) Wt. W6016—PP 1432. 1,500m. 3/18. D & S. (E1256) Forms B2138/3. [P.T.O.

**To be made up to and for Saturday in each week**

No. of Report 177 — **FIELD RETURN.** — Army Form B. 213

(To be furnished by all arms, services, and departments (except A.S.C. units) to the A.G.'s Office at the Base in accordance with Field Service Regulations, Part II.)

RETURN showing numbers (a) Effective strength of Unit. (b) Rationed by Unit. 1/1 Low. Fd. Ambce. at In the Field 21/12/18 Date.

| Details. | *Personnel: Officers | Other Ranks | | | Animals: Horses: Riding | Draught | Heavy Draught | Pack | Mules: Large | Small | Guns and transport vehicles: Guns, showing description | Ammunition wagons | Machine guns | Aircraft, showing description | Horsed: 4 Wheeled | 2 Wheeled | Mechanical: Motor Cars | Tractors | Lorries, showing description | Trucks, showing description | Trailers | Motor Bicycles | Bicycles | Motor Ambulances | Remarks (Number of Acting W.O.'s and N.C.O.'s included in effective strength to be shown in this column.) |
|---|---|---|---|---|---|---|---|---|---|---|---|---|---|---|---|---|---|---|---|---|---|---|---|---|---|
| Effective Strength of Unit ... ... | (a) 7 | (b) 166 | | | | | | | | | | | | | | | | | | | | | 1 | | (a) 1 @ 14 R.S. + 1 on leave to U.K.<br>2 @ 1st Army P.O.W. Centre<br>(b) 46 @ 1/2 L.F. AMB.<br>12 @ 1st Army P.O.W. Centre<br>20 @ 1/3 L.F. AMB.<br>1 @ as 156 B.H.Q. - A.D.M.S. - Div. TRA<br>1 @ Concert Party<br>3 on leave to U.K. |
| Details by Arms attached to Unit as in War Establishment ... ... A.S.C. (H.T.) | | (c) 35 | | | 6 | 16 | 19 (x) | | | | | | | | 13 | 4 | | | | | | | | | (c) 2 @ 1/2 L.F. AMB.<br>2 on leave to U.K. |
| A.S.C. (M.T.) | | (d) 11 | | | | | | | | | | | | | | | | | | | | 2 | | 7 | (d) 1 on leave to U.K. & 1 @ D.H.Q.<br>1 @ 1/2 L.F. AMB.<br>(x) 4 @ 1/2 L.F. AMB. |
| Total ... ... | 7 | 212 | | | 6 | 16 | 19 | | | | | | | | 13 | 4 | | | | | | 2 | 1 | 7 | |
| War Establishment ... ... ... | 10 | 231 | | | 8 | 17 | 20 | | | | | | | | 13 | 4 | | | | | | 2 | 1 | 7 | |
| Wanting to complete ... ... ... (Detail of Personnel and Horses below.) | 3 | 20 | | | 2 | 1 | 1 | | | | | | | | | | | | | | | | | | 16 R.A.M.C. 2 A.S.C.(H.T.) 2 A.S.C.(M.T.) |
| Surplus ... ... (Detail of Personnel and Horses below.) | | 1 | | | | | | | | | | | | | | | | | | | | | | | 1. A.S.C. (H.T.) Lorry Driver |
| †Attached (not to include the details shown above) ... ... ... ... | | 20 | | | | | | | | | | | | | | | | | | | | | | | Patients |
| Attached for Rations only ... ... | 1 | 1 | | | | | | | | | | | | | | | | | | | | | | | Chaplain + Billet Warden |
| Civilians Employed with and Accompanying the Unit ... ... ... | | | | | | | | | | | | | | | | | | | | | | | | | |
| ‡Detached from and struck off effective strength of own Unit ... ... | | | | | | | | | | | | | | | | | | | | | | | | | |
| ‡Detached from but retained on effective strength of own unit... ... ... | | | | | | | | | | | | | | | | | | | | | | | | | |
| Total Rationed ... | 4 | 141 | | | 6 | 16 | 15 | | | | | | | | | | | | | | | | | | |

* Blank columns to be used for W.A.A.C. Natives or as may be required.

† In the case of field ambulances, hospitals or depots, the number of patients are to be included here, the names being shown in A.F.A. 36.
‡ These details to be enumerated by arms.

[illegible] Lt. Col. Signature of Commander. 21/12/18 Date of Despatch.

B 213 A.S.C. Section W E 21.12/18

| No. | Rank | Name | | Casualty | Date |
|---|---|---|---|---|---|
| T4/239009 | DR. FARR. | RAMSAY | W.G. | Granted leave to U.K. via Calais | 20/12/18 – 3/1/19. |
| | | | | (14 days) Credit Ration allce. @ 2/4 per day for that period | |
| T2/14647 | Dr. | Appleyard | J. | War pay increased to 4d from | 4/10/18 |
| T1.SR./5[illegible]63 | " | Foster | C.H. | do. do. 4d do. | 22/9/18 |

A.S.C. sheet att.d.

*For information of the A.G.'s Office at the base.*

Officers and men who have become casuals, been transferred or joined since last report.

Place In the Field                Date 21/12/18

| Regtl. Number | Rank | Name | | Corps | Nature of casualty, or name of unit from or to which transferred. | Date of being struck off or coming on the ration return. | Remarks * |
|---|---|---|---|---|---|---|---|
| 316009 | Pte. | Gallacher | C | R.A.M.C. (T.) | Sick to Hosp. | 16 12/18 | |
| 3162[illegible] | " | Auld | J | -do- | Reinforcement from Base | 17 12/18 | |
| 316[illegible] | | Dunlop | D | -do- | Retd. from leave | 19 12/18 | |
| 32[illegible]030 | " | Parsons | J | -do- | W.i. pay increased to 4d from 14/12/18 | | |
| [illegible]1005 | " | Jackson | J.L. | -do- | -do- do. 4d do. 9/9/18 | | |
| | L/Cpl. Q.M. | Reid | A. McK. | do. | Granted leave to U.K. via Boulogne 22-12-18 – 5-1-19 Credit Ration Allce @ 2/4 pd for that period (14 days) | | |

Strength: Officers T.F. 6, T.C. 1 } 7

W.O.s N.C.O.s & men

| | |
|---|---|
| W.O. | 1 |
| Q.M.S. | 1 |
| S Sgts. | 2 |
| Sgts. | 8 |
| L Sgts. | 1 |
| Cpls. | 8 |
| L/cpls. | 4 |
| Ptes. | 141 |
| TOTAL | 166 |

All Category "A"

* State whether absence is of a permanent or temporary nature, adding, in the case of casuals from wounds or disease any available information for communication to the relatives.

*The perforated sheet is not to be used to record casualties; additional sheets, preferably foolscap, to be attached when necessary. These sheets to be carefully numbered and the number of attached sheets to be noted here.*

Perforated Sheet giving detail of personnel and horses wanting to complete or surplus, shown on Army Form B. 213.

No. of Report 177

| Detail of Wanting to Complete or Surplus. | Drivers. R.A. | Drivers. R.E. | Drivers. A.S.C. | Drivers. Car M.T. A.S.C. | Drivers. Lorry | Drivers. Steam | Gunners | Gunners Howitzer | Smith Gunners | Range Takers | Farriers. ~~Serjeants~~ Driver | Farriers. Corporals | Shoeing or Shoeing and Carriage Smiths | Cold Shoers | Wheelers R.A. | Wheelers H.T. | Wheelers M.T. | Saddlers or Harness Makers | Blacksmiths | Bricklayers and Masons | Carpenters and Joiners | Fitters & Turners (R.E.) Wood | Fitters & Turners (R.E.) Iron | Fitters R.A. | Fitters Wireless. | Plumbers | Electricians Ordinary | Electricians W.T. | Signalmen. | Engine Drivers Loco. | Engine Drivers Field | Air Line Men. | Permanent Line Men | Operators, Telegraph | Cablemen | Brigade Section Pioneers | General-duty Pioneers | Signallers | Instrument Repairers | Motor Cyclist | Motor Cyclist Artificers | Telephonists | Clerks | Machine Gunners | Armament Artificers Fitters | Armament Artificers Range Finders | Armourers | Storemen | Privates | W.O.'s and N.C.O.'s (by ranks) not included in trade columns. Cpl. R.A.M.C.(T) | | | | | | | | | | TOTAL to agree with wanting to complete or surplus Officers | TOTAL Other Ranks | Horses Riding | Horses Draught | Horses Heavy Draught | Horses Pack |
|---|---|---|---|---|---|---|---|---|---|---|---|---|---|---|---|---|---|---|---|---|---|---|---|---|---|---|---|---|---|---|---|---|---|---|---|---|---|---|---|---|---|---|---|---|---|---|---|---|---|---|---|---|---|---|---|---|---|---|---|---|---|---|---|---|---|
| CAVALRY— DEFICIENCY | | | | | | | | | | | | | | | | | | | | | | | | | | | | | | | | | | | | | | | | | | | | | | | | | | | | | | | | | | | | | | | | | | |
| SURPLUS | | | | | | | | | | | | | | | | | | | | | | | | | | | | | | | | | | | | | | | | | | | | | | | | | | | | | | | | | | | | | | | | | | |
| R.A.— DEFICIENCY | | | | | | | | | | | | | | | | | | | | | | | | | | | | | | | | | | | | | | | | | | | | | | | | | | | | | | | | | | | | | | | | | | |
| SURPLUS | | | | | | | | | | | | | | | | | | | | | | | | | | | | | | | | | | | | | | | | | | | | | | | | | | | | | | | | | | | | | | | | | | |
| R.E.— DEFICIENCY | | | | | | | | | | | | | | | | | | | | | | | | | | | | | | | | | | | | | | | | | | | | | | | | | | | | | | | | | | | | | | | | | | |
| SURPLUS | | | | | | | | | | | | | | | | | | | | | | | | | | | | | | | | | | | | | | | | | | | | | | | | | | | | | | | | | | | | | | | | | | |
| INFANTRY— DEFICIENCY | | | | | | | | | | | | | | | | | | | | | | | | | | | | | | | | | | | | | | | | | | | | | | | | | | | | | | | | | | | | | | | | | | |
| SURPLUS | | | | | | | | | | | | | | | | | | | | | | | | | | | | | | | | | | | | | | | | | | | | | | | | | | | | | | | | | | | | | | | | | | |
| R.A.M.C.— DEFICIENCY | | | 1 | 2 | | | | | | | 1 | 1 | | | | | | | | | | | | | | | | | | 6 | | | | | | | | | | | | | | | | | | | 14 | 2 | | | | | | | | | 3 | 20 | 2 | 1 | 1 | |
| SURPLUS | | | | | | | | | | | | | | | | | | | | | | | | | | | | | | | | | | | | | | | | | | | | | | | | | | | | | | | | | | | | | | | | | | |
| A.O.C.— DEFICIENCY | | | | | | | | | | | | | | | | | | | | | | | | | | | | | | | | | | | | | | | | | | | | | | | | | | | | | | | | | | | | | | | | | | | |
| SURPLUS | | | | | | | | | | | | | | | | | | | | | | | | | | | | | | | | | | | | | | | | | | | | | | | | | | | | | | | | | | | | | | | | | | |
| A.V.C.— DEFICIENCY | | | | | | | | | | | | | | | | | | | | | | | | | | | | | | | | | | | | | | | | | | | | | | | | | | | | | | | | | | | | | | | | | | | |
| SURPLUS | | | | | | | | | | | | | | | | | | | | | | | | | | | | | | | | | | | | | | | | | | | | | | | | | | | | | | | | | | | | | | | | | | |
| DEFICIENCY | | | | | | | | | | | | | | | | | | | | | | | | | | | | | | | | | | | | | | | | | | | | | | | | | | | | | | | | | | | | | | | | | | |
| SURPLUS | | | | | | | | | | | | | | | | | | | | | | | | | | | | | | | | | | | | | | | | | | | | | | | | | | | | | | | | | | | | | | | | | | |
| DEFICIENCY | | | | | | | | | | | | | | | | | | | | | | | | | | | | | | | | | | | | | | | | | | | | | | | | | | | | | | | | | | | | | | | | | | |
| SURPLUS | | | | | | | | | | | | | | | | | | | | | | | | | | | | | | | | | | | | | | | | | | | | | | | | | | | | | | | | | | | | | | | | | | |

Remarks :—

[signature] Lt Col Signature of Commander.

1/4th Lowland Field Ambulance R.A.M.C. (T) Unit.

52 Division Formation to which attached.

21/12/18 Date of Despatch.

(16523.) Wt. W6016—PP 1432. 1,500m. 3/18. D & S. (E1256) Forms B213a/3. [P.T.O.

**To be made up to and for Saturday in each week**

No. of Report 178

# FIELD RETURN.

Army Form B. 213

(To be furnished by all arms, services, and departments (except A.S.C. units) to the A.G.'s Office at the Base in accordance with Field Service Regulations, Part II.)

RETURN showing numbers (a) Effective strength of Unit. (b) Rationed by Unit. 1/1 LOWLAND FIELD AMBCE. at In the Field 28/12/18 Date.

| Details. | *Personnel: Officers | Other Ranks | | | Animals: Horses: Riding | Draught | Heavy Draught | Pack | Mules: Large | Small | Guns and transport vehicles: Guns, showing description | Ammunition wagons | Machine guns | Aircraft, showing description | Horsed: 4 Wheeled | 2 Wheeled | Mechanical: Motor Cars | Tractors | Lorries, showing description | Trucks, showing description | Trailers | Motor Bicycles | Bicycles | Motor Ambulances | Remarks (Number of Acting W.O.'s and N.C.O.'s included in effective strength to be shown in this column.) |
|---|---|---|---|---|---|---|---|---|---|---|---|---|---|---|---|---|---|---|---|---|---|---|---|---|---|
| Effective Strength of Unit ... ... | (a) 8 | (b) 167 | | | | | | | | | | | | | | | | | | | | | 1 | | (a) 1 @ 1/4 R.S., 1 on leave to U.K.<br>1 @ 1/2 Low. Fd. Amb. 1 @ 1/3 Low. Fd. A.<br>(b) 47 @ 1/2 L.F. Amb.<br>21 @ 1/3 L.F. Amb.<br>10 @ 1st Army P.O.W. Centre<br>1 @ 156 B. H.Q. – 1 at A.D.M.S. – 1 at Div. Train<br>1 @ Convent Pny. 1 on leave to U.K. |
| Details by Arms attached to Unit as in War Establishment ... A.S.C. (H.T.) | | (c) 35 | | | 6 | 16 | (E) 19 | | | | | | | | 13 | 4 | | | | | | | | | (c) 2 on leave to U.K. 2 at 1/2 L.F. Amb. |
| A.S.C. (M.T.) | | (d) 11 | | | | | | | | | | | | | | | | | | | | 2 | | 7 | (d) 2 on leave to U.K. 1 at D.H.Q.<br>1 at 1/2 L.F. Amb.<br>(E) 4 at 1/2 L.F. Amb. |
| Total ... ... | 8 | 213 | | | 6 | 16 | 19 | | | | | | | | 13 | 4 | | | | | | 2 | 1 | 7 | |
| War Establishment ... ... ... | 10 | 231 | | | 8 | 17 | 20 | | | | | | | | 13 | 4 | | | | | | 2 | 1 | 7 | |
| Wanting to complete ... ... (Detail of Personnel and Horses below.) | 2 | 19 | | | 2 | 1 | 1 | | | | | | | | | | | | | | | | | | 15 R.A.M.C.(T) 2 A.S.C.(H.T.) 2 A.S.C.(M.T.) |
| Surplus ... ... (Detail of Personnel and Horses below.) | | 1 | | | | | | | | | | | | | | | | | | | | | | | 1 A.S.C. (H.T.) Farr. Driver |
| †Attached (not to include the details shown above) ... ... ... | | 27 | | | | | | | | | | | | | | | | | | | | | | | Patients |
| Attached for Rations only | 1 | 2 | | | | | | | | | | | | | | | | | | | | | | | Chaplain, Batman, Billet Warden |
| Civilians Employed with and Accompanying the Unit ... | | | | | | | | | | | | | | | | | | | | | | | | | |
| ‡Detached from and struck off effective strength of own Unit ... | | | | | | | | | | | | | | | | | | | | | | | | | |
| ‡Detached from but retained on effective strength of own unit... ... | | | | | | | | | | | | | | | | | | | | | | | | | |
| Total Rationed ... | 5 | 151 | | | 6 | 16 | 15 | | | | | | | | | | | | | | | | | | |

* Blank columns to be used for W.A.A.C. Natives or as may be required.

† In the case of field ambulances, hospitals or depots, the number of patients are to be included here, the names being shown in A.F.A. 36.

‡ These details to be enumerated by arms.

[illegible] Lt. Col. Signature of Commander.

28/12/18 Date of Despatch.

B213 A. S. C. Section. WE 28/12/18

| No. | Rank | Name | Casualty | Date. |
|---|---|---|---|---|
| M2/049901 | Pte. | Hamshaw A.W. | Granted leave to U.K. 14 days. via Calais. 24/12/18 - 7/1/19. Credit Ration allce. @ 2/4 p.d. for that period. | 21 12/18. |

*For information of the A.G.'s Office at the base.*

P.S.C. Sheet attd.

Officers and men who have become casuals, been transferred or joined since last report.

Place In the Field  Date Dec. 28th 1918

| Regtl. Number | Rank | Name | Corps | Nature of casualty, or name of unit from or to which transferred. | Date of being struck off or coming on the ration return. | Remarks * |
|---|---|---|---|---|---|---|
| 316098 | Pte. | Gallacher C. | R.A.M.C.(T.) | Reinforcement from Hospital | 23/12/18 | |
| 316022 | Cpl. | Hislop R. | R.A.M.C.(T.) | Retd. from leave | 23/12/18 | |
| 316221 | Sgt. | Cowan G.P. | -do- | — do — | 25/12/18 | |
| 316003 | Pte. | McGrillies J.D. | -do- | Married Miss Jeanie Glen at 46 Second Avenue Mount Florida Glas. on 25/11/18. Present address of wife c/o Glen, 478 Pollokshaws Road, Glas. | | |
| do. | | — do — | do. | Transfers allotment from mother to wife Mrs Jeanie McGrillies c/o Glen 478 Pollokshaws Road Glasgow, with effect from 25/11/18. | | |
| | Surgeon Lt. Commander | Campbell Ross | R.N. | Reinforcement from 9th Bde. R.F.A. | 26/12/18 | |

Strength: Officers T.F. 6, T.C. 1, R.N. 1, TOTAL 8

| W.O.s N.C.O.s | Men |
|---|---|
| W.O. | 1 |
| Q.M.S. | 1 |
| S. Sgt. | 2 |
| Sgt. | 8 |
| L. Sgt. | 1 |
| Cpls. | 8 |
| L. Cpls. | 4 |
| Pte. | 142 |
| TOTAL | 167 |

All Category A

* State whether absence is of a permanent or temporary nature, adding, in the case of casuals from wounds or disease any available information for communication to the relatives.

*The perforated sheet is not to be used to record casualties; additional sheets, preferably foolscap, to be attached when necessary. These sheets to be carefully numbered and the number of attached sheets to be noted here.*

Additional information regarding "wanting to complete," and sufficient information to explain the difference between the present and previous week's effective strength is to be entered in this space.

Where the return of specific individuals is desired a note is to be made hereon.

No. 316228 Pte. MARTIN M. R.A.M.C.(T.) att. 229 Fd. Amb.

316131. " HENDERSON R. - do - at Base Details

The return of the above men is requested, please.

REMARKS.

Any further remarks necessary may be entered here.

Explanation of R.A. effective strength.

| | Drivers. | Gunners. | Signallers. | Artificers. | N.C.O's. | Total. |
|---|---|---|---|---|---|---|
| | | | | | | |

Perforated Sheet giving detail of personnel and horses wanting to complete or surplus, shown on Army Form B. 213.

No. of Report 178

| Detail of Wanting to Complete or Surplus. | Drivers: R.A. | Drivers: R.E. | Drivers: A.S.C. | Drivers: Car (M.T. A.S.C.) | Drivers: Lorry | Drivers: Steam | Gunners | Gunners Howitzer | Smith Gunners | Range Takers | Farriers: Serjeants | Farriers: Corporals | Shoeing or Shoeing and Carriage Smiths | Cold Shoers | Wheelers: R.A. | Wheelers: H.T. | Wheelers: M.T. | Saddlers or Harness Makers | Blacksmiths | Bricklayers and Masons | Carpenters and Joiners | Fitters & Turners (R.E.): Wood | Fitters & Turners (R.E.): Iron | Fitters: R.A. | Fitters: Wireless. | Plumbers | Electricians: Ordinary | Electricians: W.T. | Signalmen. | Engine Drivers: Loco. | Engine Drivers: Field | Air Line Men. | Permanent Line Men | Operators, Telegraph | Cablemen | Brigade Section Pioneers | General-duty Pioneers | Signallers | Instrument Repairers | Motor Cyclist | Motor Cyclist Artificers | Telephonists | Clerks | Machine Gunners | Armament Artificers: Fitters | Armament Artificers: Range Finders | Armourers | Storemen | Privates | W.O.'s and N.C.O.'s (by ranks) not included in trade columns: S/Sgt R.A.M.C. | | | | | | | | | | | TOTAL to agree with wanting to complete or surplus: Officers | TOTAL: Other Ranks | Horses: Riding | Horses: Draught | Horses: Heavy Draught | Horses: Pack |
|---|---|---|---|---|---|---|---|---|---|---|---|---|---|---|---|---|---|---|---|---|---|---|---|---|---|---|---|---|---|---|---|---|---|---|---|---|---|---|---|---|---|---|---|---|---|---|---|---|---|---|---|---|---|---|---|---|---|---|---|---|---|---|---|---|---|---|
| CAVALRY— Deficiency | | | | | | | | | | | | | | | | | | | | | | | | | | | | | | | | | | | | | | | | | | | | | | | | | | | | | | | | | | | | | | | | | | |
| Surplus | | | | | | | | | | | | | | | | | | | | | | | | | | | | | | | | | | | | | | | | | | | | | | | | | | | | | | | | | | | | | | | | | | |
| R.A.— Deficiency | | | | | | | | | | | | | | | | | | | | | | | | | | | | | | | | | | | | | | | | | | | | | | | | | | | | | | | | | | | | | | | | | | |
| Surplus | | | | | | | | | | | | | | | | | | | | | | | | | | | | | | | | | | | | | | | | | | | | | | | | | | | | | | | | | | | | | | | | | | |
| R.E.— Deficiency | | | | | | | | | | | | | | | | | | | | | | | | | | | | | | | | | | | | | | | | | | | | | | | | | | | | | | | | | | | | | | | | | | |
| Surplus | | | | | | | | | | | | | | | | | | | | | | | | | | | | | | | | | | | | | | | | | | | | | | | | | | | | | | | | | | | | | | | | | | |
| INFANTRY— Deficiency | | | | | | | | | | | | | | | | | | | | | | | | | | | | | | | | | | | | | | | | | | | | | | | | | | | | | | | | | | | | | | | | | | |
| Surplus | | | | | | | | | | | | | | | | | | | | | | | | | | | | | | | | | | | | | | | | | | | | | | | | | | | | | | | | | | | | | | | | | | |
| R.A.M.C.— Deficiency | | | 1 | 2 | | | | | | | | 1 | | | | | | | | | | | | | | | | | | | | | | | | | | | | | | | | | | | | | 13 | 2 | | | | | | | | | | | 2 | 19 | 2 | 1 | 1 | |
| Surplus | | | | | | | | | | | 1 | | | | | | | | | | | | | | | | | | | | | | | | | | | | | | | | | | | | | | | | | | | | | | | | | | | | | | 1 | | | | |
| A.O.C.— Deficiency | | | | | | | | | | | | | | | | | | | | | | | | | | | | | | | | | | | | | | | | | | | | | | | | | | | | | | | | | | | | | | | | | | |
| Surplus | | | | | | | | | | | | | | | | | | | | | | | | | | | | | | | | | | | | | | | | | | | | | | | | | | | | | | | | | | | | | | | | | | |
| A.V.C.— Deficiency | | | | | | | | | | | | | | | | | | | | | | | | | | | | | | | | | | | | | | | | | | | | | | | | | | | | | | | | | | | | | | | | | | |
| Surplus | | | | | | | | | | | | | | | | | | | | | | | | | | | | | | | | | | | | | | | | | | | | | | | | | | | | | | | | | | | | | | | | | | |
| Deficiency | | | | | | | | | | | | | | | | | | | | | | | | | | | | | | | | | | | | | | | | | | | | | | | | | | | | | | | | | | | | | | | | | | |
| Surplus | | | | | | | | | | | | | | | | | | | | | | | | | | | | | | | | | | | | | | | | | | | | | | | | | | | | | | | | | | | | | | | | | | |
| Deficiency | | | | | | | | | | | | | | | | | | | | | | | | | | | | | | | | | | | | | | | | | | | | | | | | | | | | | | | | | | | | | | | | | | |
| Surplus | | | | | | | | | | | | | | | | | | | | | | | | | | | | | | | | | | | | | | | | | | | | | | | | | | | | | | | | | | | | | | | | | | |

Remarks :—

[signature] Signature of Commander.

1/1 LOWLAND FIELD AMBCE. Unit.

52 Div. Formation to which attached.

28/12/18. Date of Despatch.

(16523.) Wt. W6016—PP 1432. 1,500m. 3/18. D & S. (E1256) Forms B2138/3.

[P.T.O.

17

Jan. 1919

52 DIV

Box 2749

1/1 Lowland Fd Amb

VIII 10

140/3490

1/1st Lowland F. A

Instructions regarding War Diaries and Intelligence Summaries are contained in F. S. Regs., Part II. and the Staff Manual respectively. Title pages will be prepared in manuscript.

# WAR DIARY
or
# INTELLIGENCE SUMMARY.
(Erase heading not required.)

525 Army Form C. 2118.

1/1st Lowland Field Ambulance
52nd (Lowland) Division

| Place | Date | Hour | Summary of Events and Information | Remarks and references to Appendices |
|---|---|---|---|---|
| CHAUSSEE N.D. LOUVIGNIES Sh 38 W5b46. | 1/1/19 | | Usual Routine duties. Received A.D.M.S. R 1147/1 dated to-day instructing that guards should be posted to prevent the frequent thefts of Government Property, & arranged to post extra guards. J.W.L. | |
| do. | 2/1/19 | | Sent Commander ROSS to 1/4th R.S. at 1200 to arrange hour of visit to that unit during absence of the M.O. i/c (Capt J.W. BURTON) on 14 days leave to U.K. Attended a Requiem Mass at MONS Cathedral at 1100 in memory of the fallen which was held to-day. Major MACKENZIE & Rev A. MAIN C.F. also attended. J.W.L. | |
| do. | 3/1/19 | | Sent Sgt Cowan to replace Sgt. McMidder with the detachment presently doing duty with 1/2nd L.F.A. at MONS as the latter is required to attend meetings of the sports Committee of this unit. Major MOULTON-BARRETT 52nd Div HQ. inspected improvements carried out by this unit. J.W.L. | |
| do | 4/1/19 | | Received A.D.M.S. R 1167/10 d/3/1/19 to send an officer to 147th Bde R.F.A. at SOIGNIES to see and supervise their sanitation when M.O. went on leave on 9th inst. Sent Pte Austin & 1 motor cycle to report for duty with A.D.M.S. in accordance with his request in R 1166/1 d/3/1/19. J.W.L. | AP 1 A.F. B.213 d 4/1/19 |
| do | 5/1/19 | | Sunday: Weather wet. J.W.L. | |
| do | 6/1/19 | | System of ash bucket collection of rubbish from houses in village commenced to-day. Transport | |

D. D. & L., London, E.C. (A8001) Wt. W1771/M2031 750,000 5/17 Sch. 52 Forms/C2118/14

Instructions regarding War Diaries and Intelligence Summaries are contained in F. S. Regs., Part II. and the Staff Manual respectively. Title pages will be prepared in manuscript.

# WAR DIARY
~~or~~
## ~~INTELLIGENCE SUMMARY.~~
(Erase heading not required.)

526 Army Form C. 2118.

1/1st Lowland Field Ambulance
52nd (Lowland) Division

| Place | Date | Hour | Summary of Events and Information | Remarks and references to Appendices |
|---|---|---|---|---|
| CHAUSSEE N.D. LOUVIGNIES | 6/1/19 (Contd) | | & fatigue men are supplied by this unit for the purpose. Covered ash bins are not available & ashes etc have to be left out at each house in boxes or uncovered receptacles. Hitherto the streets have been kept clean by this unit with some assistance from the civilians. Lieut Rev A Main, Major McKenzie & 3 other ranks to Brussels by ambulance to-day with a view to arranging to send personnel in batches for 3-day educational trips to places of interest in that neighbourhood. They returned at night & reported accommodation obtainable. Jws L | |
| do | 7/1/19 | | Two Officers (Major McKenzie & Capt Downes) 80 O.R. & 6 who ~~are~~ to attend to-morrow to receive ribbons of M.M. from G.O.C. the Division at MONTIGNIES-LEZ-LENS Parade Ground attend a rehearsal parade at that ground to-day. G.S.O. 1 visited this unit Billeting area this forenoon. He visited the cookhouse, Hospital, & some billets & was shown the Log Book kept of work done for farmers etc. & improvements carried out. Jws L | |
| do | 8/1/19 | | The G.O.C. the Division presented ribbons of M.M. to O.R. of the 156th Bde & of the 3 Ambulances at the parade ground V24 a Sh 38. 1/40000 & afterwards the troops marched past in close column of Companies. 80 O.R. 1/1st L.F.A & 12 O.R. from each of 1/2nd L.F.A & 1/3rd L.F.A under Major MACKENZIE & Capt DOWNES of this unit formed the company representing the Divisional R.A.M.C. Capt. & Q.M. REID reported back to unit from short leave to U.K. Jws L | |
| do | 9/1/19 | | Ordinary routine duties carried out. In reply to A.D.M.S. R1214/19 d/7/1/19 ~~asking~~ sent letter stating that (a) this unit was exercising medical & sanitary supervision over 412th Fld Co RE. | |

D. D. & L., London, E.C. (A8001) Wt. W1771/M2031 750,000 5/17 Sch. 52 Forms/C2118/14

527 Army Form C. 2118.

Instructions regarding War Diaries and Intelligence Summaries are contained in F. S. Regs., Part II. and the Staff Manual respectively. Title pages will be prepared in manuscript.

# WAR DIARY
or
~~INTELLIGENCE SUMMARY.~~
(Erase heading not required.)

1/1st Lowland Field Ambulance
52nd (Lowland) Division

| Place | Date | Hour | Summary of Events and Information | Remarks and references to Appendices |
|---|---|---|---|---|
| CHAUSSEE N.D. LOUVIGNIES S.L.38 W.5.6.46 | 9/1/19 (Cont'd) | | 1/4th Royal Scots. 52nd M.G. Batt. 147th Bde R.F.A. at SOIGNIES & from to-day also the 1/7th Royal Scots temporarily during absence of M.O. on leave to U.K.: (b) that sick were being collected from 147th Bde R.F.A. 1/4th & 1/7th Royal Scots. 52nd M.G. Batt. 52nd D.A.C. 412th Fld Coy R.E. & (when necessary) the 52nd L.T.M.B. J.W.L. | |
| do | 10/1/19 | | In accordance with instructions of A.D.M.S. received last night a motor ambulance was sent this morning to DIEST 23 kilos E.N.E. of LOUVAIN to convey a Mme CHIREY aet 77 from civil hospital there to W.I.L.E.S MONS where she will stay the night before being taken on by 42nd M.A.C. to ANZIN. Lt Col J.W. Leitch departs on 14 days leave to U.K. sailing on 13th inst. Major McKenzie takes over temporarily. J.W.L. | |
| | | | N.M. [?] | |
| | 10/1/19 | 1700hrs | Ambce car to DIEST returned having conveyed no patient | |
| do | | | Supply of stone for road repairing authorised by ADMS 52nd Div R1253/2 d/10/1/19 N.M. [?] | App. 2 |
| | 11/1/19 | | M.O. to visit 56 R.F.A. arranged (ADMS [illegible] R1252/4 d/11/1/19 N.M. [?] | A.F. B213 d/11/1/19 |
| | 12/1/19 | | Major Josiah BROWNE South Midland Mtd Bty [?] Fd Ambce att 1/1st Lowland Field Ambce departs & relinquishes acting rank, ADMS 52nd Div No R1251/13 d/10/1/19 ordering his return to civilian practice | |
| | | | ADMS No R791/5 d/11/1/19 orders retention of Surgeon Commander ROSS C. of R.N. Medical Service for service with army but to be available when called upon for service with R.N. N.M. [?] | |
| | 13/1/19 | | nothing to note. N.M. [?] | |

D. D. & L., London, E.C. (a6340) Wt W5300/P713 750,000 3/18 Sch 2688 Forms/C2118/15.

528

Army Form C. 2118.

# WAR DIARY
or
# INTELLIGENCE SUMMARY.
(Erase heading not required.)

1/1st Lowland Fd Ambce
RAMC T
52nd Lowland Division

Instructions regarding War Diaries and Intelligence Summaries are contained in F. S. Regs., Part II. and the Staff Manual respectively. Title pages will be prepared in manuscript.

| Place | Date | Hour | Summary of Events and Information | Remarks and references to Appendices |
|---|---|---|---|---|
| CHAUSEE N.D. LOUVIGNIES Sh 38 W5 646 | 14/1/19 | | Four O.R. for Dispersal Areas, VB & IVA, report to Div Recep Camp under ADMS 52nd Div No R 1292/13 d/13/1/19.<br>ADMS 52nd Div inspected billet area of this unit RBM | |
| | 15/1/19 | | Three O.R. for Dispersal Areas VB & VIII report to Div Receptn Camp under ADMS 52nd Div No R 1308/13 d/14/1/19<br>All mares marked A, B & C. sent for inspection to MONTIGNY-LES-LENS under ADMS 52nd Div No. R 1283/13 d/12/1/19 RBM | |
| do | 16/1/19 | | Nothing to note RBM | |
| do | 17/1/19 | | Recd ADMS. 52nd Div Letter R.1348/18 :— Authy A.G. 6349 (O) d/8/1/19 Alteration of Establishment of Fd. Ambce to two Sections RBM | |
| | 18/1/19 | | Nothing to note. RBM | App. 3 A.F. B.213 d/18/1/19 |
| do | 19/1/19 | | Rev. A. MAIN C.F. off strength proceeded to COLOGNE 2nd Army HQrs RBM<br>Capt. R.A LENNIE and 12 O.R. returned from P. of W. Camp, Mons to HQrs of this unit Authy ADMS 52nd Div R 1373/4 d/18/1/19<br>1/1st Lowland Fd Ambce take over Div. Rest. Stn. LENS from Lt Commander R.O.S.S. Capt RA LENNIE & 20 O.R. posted for duty there RBM | |

D. D. & L., London, E.C.
(10,340) W1 W5300/P713 750,000 3/18 Sch. 2688 Forms/C2118/15.

529

Army Form C. 2118.

# WAR DIARY
*or*
# INTELLIGENCE SUMMARY.
*(Erase heading not required.)*

1/1st LOWLAND FD Ambce RAMC. 52nd (LOWLAND) Division

Instructions regarding War Diaries and Intelligence Summaries are contained in F. S. Regs., Part II. and the Staff Manual respectively. Title pages will be prepared in manuscript.

| Place | Date | Hour | Summary of Events and Information | Remarks and references to Appendices |
|---|---|---|---|---|
| CHAUSEE-N.D-LOUVIGNIES | 20/1/19 | | All school premises occupied by this unit handed over to Civil Authorities under ADMS 52nd Div R 1351/4 d/17/1/19 | |
| Sh 38 W5 b46 | | | Two O.R. detailed to report to 22nd Sanitary Section for temporary duty and instruction under A.D.M.S 52nd Div R 1299/2 d 19/1/19 NDM | |
| do | 21/1/19 | | Nothing to note NDM | |
| do | 22/1/19 | | Remainder of 6 Section Medical Equipment handed in to No 19 ADM Stores VALENCIENNES Authy AG 6349 (Q) d 8/1/19 NDM | |
| do | 23/1/19 | | Nothing to note. NDM | |
| do | 24/1/19 | | Animals classified "Y" three in number sent for Mallein test under ADMS 52nd Div R 1426/13 d22/1/19 NDM | |
| do | 25/1/19 | | A.D.M.S 52nd Div inspected this unit. NDM | App 4 AFB 212 d/25/1/19 |
| | 26/1/19 | | In reply to A.D.M.S 52nd Div wire W151 d 25/1/19 Thirty Electric lights for distribution in offices &c of this unit suggested NDM | |
| | 27/1/19 | | Ten O.R. of this unit attached 1/2nd Low Fd. Ambce temporarily, returned this unit for duty. posted to D.R.S LENS under ADMS 52nd Div R1471/4 d/26/1/19 NDM | |
| | 28 29 30 31 Jany 1919 | | Nothing to report. NDM | |

N Ferguson Mackenzie Major
for O.C. 1/1st Lowland Fd Ambce.

D. D. & L., London, E.C.
(10,140) Wt W5300/P713 750,000 3/18 Sch 2688 Forms/C2118/10.

**To be made up to and for Saturday in each week**

No. of Report 179

# FIELD RETURN.

App. I

Army Form B. 213

(To be furnished by all arms, services, and departments (except A.S.C. units) to the A.G.'s Office at the Base in accordance with Field Service Regulations, Part II.)

RETURN showing numbers (*a*) Effective strength of Unit. (*b*) Rationed by Unit. 1/1 Lowland Field Ambce. at In the Field 4/1/19 Date.

| Details. | *Personnel: Officers | Other Ranks | | | | Animals: Horses: Riding | Draught | Heavy Draught | Pack | Mules: Large | Small | Guns and transport vehicles: Guns, showing description | Ammunition wagons | Machine guns | Aircraft, showing description | Horsed: 4 Wheeled | 2 Wheeled | Mechanical: Motor Cars | Tractors | Lorries, showing description | Trucks, showing description | Trailers | Motor Bicycles | Bicycles | Motor Ambulances | Remarks (Number of Acting W.O.'s and N.C.O.'s included in effective strength to be shown in this column.) |
|---|---|---|---|---|---|---|---|---|---|---|---|---|---|---|---|---|---|---|---|---|---|---|---|---|---|---|
| Effective Strength of Unit ... ... | (a) 8 | (b) 167 | | | | | | | | | | | | | | | | | | | | | | 1 | | (a) 2 on leave to U.K. 1 at 1/3 Low. Fd. Amb. 1 at 1/2 Low. Fd. Amb. (b) 47 @ 1/3 Low. Fd. Ambce. 1 at 1/2 L.F.A. 4 at 155 R. H.Q. 1 at 52 Div. Train – 1 at Concert Party 1 at A.D.M.S. – 1 on leave to U.K. 10 at 1st Army P.o.W. Rest Centre. |
| Details by Arms attached to Unit as in War Establishment ... ... A.S.C. (H.T.) | | (c) 33 | | | | 6 | 16 | 19 | | | | | | | | 13 | 4 | | | | | | | | | (c) 1 on leave to U.K. |
| A.S.C. (M.T.) | | (d) 11 | | | | | | | | | | | | | | | | | | | | | 2 | · | 7 | (d) 1 on leave to U.K. 1 at 52 D.H.Q. 1 at 1/2 Low. Fd. Amb. (e) 1 at 52 Div. M.T. Coy. School Course |
| Total ... ... | 8 | 211 | | | | 6 | 16 | 19 | | | | | | | | 13 | 4 | | | | | | 2 | 1 | 7 | |
| War Establishment ... ... ... | 10 | 231 | | | | 8 | 17 | 20 | | | | | | | | 13 | 4 | | | | | | 2 | 1 | 7 | |
| Wanting to complete ... ... ... (Detail of Personnel and Horses below.) | 2 | 20 | | | | 2 | 1 | 1 | | | | | | | | · | · | | | | | | · | · | · | 15 R.A.M.C. 3 A.S.C.(H.T.) 2 A.S.C.(M.T.) |
| Surplus ... ... (Detail of Personnel and Horses below.) | | | | | | | | | | | | | | | | | | | | | | | | | | |
| †Attached (not to include the details shown above) ... ... ... ... | | 23 | | | | | | | | | | | | | | | | | | | | | | | | Patients |
| Attached for Rations only ... ... | 1 | 1 | | | | | | | | | | | | | | | | | | | | | | | | Chaplain Billet Wardens |
| Civilians Employed with and Accompanying the Unit ... ... | | | | | | | | | | | | | | | | | | | | | | | | | | |
| ‡Detached from and struck off effective strength of own Unit ... | | | | | | | | | | | | | | | | | | | | | | | | | | |
| ‡Detached from but retained on effective strength of own unit... | | | | | | | | | | | | | | | | | | | | | | | | | | |
| Total Rationed ... | 5 | 167 | | | | 6 | 16 | 19 | | | | | | | | | | | | | | | | | | |

* Blank columns to be used for W.A.A.C. Natives or as may be required.

† In the case of field ambulances, hospitals or depots, the number of patients are to be included here, the names being shown in A.F.A. 36.

‡ These details to be enumerated by arms.

[signature] Lt. Col. Signature of Commander. 4 Jan. 1919. Date of Despatch.

B 2/13

| | | A.S.C. Section | | W/E 4/1/19. |
|---|---|---|---|---|
| **No.** | **Rank** | **Name** | **Casualty** | **Date** |
| [illegible]/025?? | A/C.S.M. | Bellchambers | C. To Duty with 12 Army Auxiliary Horse Transport. Authy. R.A.S.C. P.40/16152. [illegible] 6/12/18 | 2-1-19 |
| [illegible]/19200 | A/S.S.M. | Sackley | T From 13 Army Auxiliary Horse Transport for Duty. | 1-1-19 |
| M4/244757 | Dr | Jones | T.A. To Corps Concentration Camp for Demobilisation (Miner) | 31-12-18 |
| /32085 | " | Fox | G.W. Returned from leave | 29-12-18 |
| M1/085646 | Dr. | Joyce | J.W. - do - | 29-12-18 |
| M4/245543 | Dr | Savage | H.T. To A.S.C. Base Depot. Authority First Army. No. 6815 A 17/12/18 | 31-12-18 |

A.S.C. Sheet and.

*For information of the A.G.'s Office at the base.*

Officers and men who have become casuals, been transferred or joined since last report.

Place In the Field Date Jan. 4 1919.

| Regtl. Number | Rank | Name | Corps | Nature of casualty, or name of unit from or to which transferred. | Date of being struck off or coming on the ration return. | Remarks * |
|---|---|---|---|---|---|---|
| | Capt. | Burton J.W. | R.A.M.C. (T) | Granted leave 5/1/19 – 19/1/19 (14 days) | to U.K. via Boulogne | Cross Red Allot. Sea Passage. |
| | Strength: | Officers | T.F. 7 / R.N. 1 / TOTAL = 8 | W.O.s N.C.O.s | Men | |
| | | | | W.O. | 1 | |
| | | | | Q.M.S. | 1 | |
| | | | | S Sgt. | 2 | |
| | | ALL CATEGORY | | Sgt. | 8 | |
| | | | | L Sgt. | 1 | |
| | | | | Cpls. | 8 | |
| | | A1 | | L/cpls. | 4 | |
| | | | | Ptes. | 142. | |
| | | | TOTAL | | 167 | |

* State whether absence is of a permanent or temporary nature, adding, in the case of casuals from wounds or disease any available information for communication to the relatives.

*The perforated sheet is not to be used to record casualties: additional sheets, preferably foolscap, to be attached when necessary. These sheets to be carefully numbered and the number of attached sheets to be noted here.*

Additional information regarding "wanting to complete," and sufficient information to explain the difference between the present and previous week's effective strength is to be entered in this space.

Where the return of specific individuals is desired a note is to be made hereon.

No. 316225 Pte. MARTIN M. R.A.M.C.(T) att 229 Fd. Amb.

316131 · HENDERSON R. -do- at Base Details.

The return of the above men is requested, please.

REMARKS.

Any further remarks necessary may be entered here.

Explanation of R.A. effective strength.

| Drivers. | Gunners. | Signallers. | Artificers. | N.C.O's. | Total. |
|---|---|---|---|---|---|
| | | | | | |

Perforated Sheet giving detail of personnel and horses wanting to complete or surplus, shown on Army Form B. 213.

No. of Report 179

| Detail of Wanting to Complete or Surplus. | Drivers. R.A. | Drivers. R.E. | Drivers. A.S.C. | Drivers. Car M.T. A.S.C. | Drivers. Lorry | Drivers. Steam | Gunners | Gunners Howitzer | Smith Gunners | Range Takers | Farriers Serjeants | Farriers Corporals | Shoeing or Shoeing and Carriage Smiths | Cold Shoers | Wheelers R.A. | Wheelers H.T. | Wheelers M.T. | Saddlers or Harness Makers | Blacksmiths | Bricklayers and Masons | Carpenters and Joiners |
|---|---|---|---|---|---|---|---|---|---|---|---|---|---|---|---|---|---|---|---|---|---|
| CAVALRY— DEFICIENCY | | | | | | | | | | | | | | | | | | | | | |
| SURPLUS | | | | | | | | | | | | | | | | | | | | | |
| R.A.— DEFICIENCY | | | | | | | | | | | | | | | | | | | | | |
| SURPLUS | | | | | | | | | | | | | | | | | | | | | |
| R.E.— DEFICIENCY | | | | | | | | | | | | | | | | | | | | | |
| SURPLUS | | | | | | | | | | | | | | | | | | | | | |
| INFANTRY— DEFICIENCY | | | | | | | | | | | | | | | | | | | | | |
| SURPLUS | | | | | | | | | | | | | | | | | | | | | |
| R.A.M.C.— DEFICIENCY | | | 2 | 2 | | | | | | | | 1 | | | | | | | | | |
| SURPLUS | | | | | | | | | | | | | | | | | | | | | |
| A.O.C.— DEFICIENCY | | | | | | | | | | | | | | | | | | | | | |
| SURPLUS | | | | | | | | | | | | | | | | | | | | | |
| A.V.C.— DEFICIENCY | | | | | | | | | | | | | | | | | | | | | |
| SURPLUS | | | | | | | | | | | | | | | | | | | | | |
| DEFICIENCY | | | | | | | | | | | | | | | | | | | | | |
| SURPLUS | | | | | | | | | | | | | | | | | | | | | |
| DEFICIENCY | | | | | | | | | | | | | | | | | | | | | |
| SURPLUS | | | | | | | | | | | | | | | | | | | | | |

| Detail of Wanting to Complete or Surplus. | Fitters & Turners (R.E.) Wood | Fitters & Turners (R.E.) Iron | Fitters R.A. | Fitters Wireless. | Plumbers | Electricians Ordinary | Electricians W.T. | Signalmen. | Engine Drivers Loco. | Engine Drivers Field | Air Line Men. | Permanent Line Men | Operators, Telegraph | Cablemen | Brigade Section Pioneers | General-duty Pioneers | Signallers | Instrument Repairers | Motor Cyclist | Motor Cyclist Artificers | Telephonists | Clerks | Machine Gunners | Armament Artificers Fitters | Armament Artificers Range Finders | Armourers | Storemen |
|---|---|---|---|---|---|---|---|---|---|---|---|---|---|---|---|---|---|---|---|---|---|---|---|---|---|---|---|
| CAVALRY— DEFICIENCY | | | | | | | | | | | | | | | | | | | | | | | | | | | |
| SURPLUS | | | | | | | | | | | | | | | | | | | | | | | | | | | |
| R.A.— DEFICIENCY | | | | | | | | | | | | | | | | | | | | | | | | | | | |
| SURPLUS | | | | | | | | | | | | | | | | | | | | | | | | | | | |
| R.E.— DEFICIENCY | | | | | | | | | | | | | | | | | | | | | | | | | | | |
| SURPLUS | | | | | | | | | | | | | | | | | | | | | | | | | | | |
| INFANTRY— DEFICIENCY | | | | | | | | | | | | | | | | | | | | | | | | | | | |
| SURPLUS | | | | | | | | | | | | | | | | | | | | | | | | | | | |
| R.A.M.C.— DEFICIENCY | | | | | | | | | | | | | | | | | | | | | | | | | | | |
| SURPLUS | | | | | | | | | | | | | | | | | | | | | | | | | | | |
| A.O.C.— DEFICIENCY | | | | | | | | | | | | | | | | | | | | | | | | | | | |
| SURPLUS | | | | | | | | | | | | | | | | | | | | | | | | | | | |
| A.V.C.— DEFICIENCY | | | | | | | | | | | | | | | | | | | | | | | | | | | |
| SURPLUS | | | | | | | | | | | | | | | | | | | | | | | | | | | |
| DEFICIENCY | | | | | | | | | | | | | | | | | | | | | | | | | | | |
| SURPLUS | | | | | | | | | | | | | | | | | | | | | | | | | | | |
| DEFICIENCY | | | | | | | | | | | | | | | | | | | | | | | | | | | |
| SURPLUS | | | | | | | | | | | | | | | | | | | | | | | | | | | |

| Detail of Wanting to Complete or Surplus. | Privates | W.O.'s and N.C.O.'s (by ranks) not included in trade columns. Sgt. R.A.M.C.T. | | | | | | | | | | | TOTAL to agree with wanting to complete or surplus Officers | TOTAL Other Ranks | Horses Riding | Horses Draught | Horses Heavy Draught | Horses Pack |
|---|---|---|---|---|---|---|---|---|---|---|---|---|---|---|---|---|---|---|
| CAVALRY— DEFICIENCY | | | | | | | | | | | | | | | | | | |
| SURPLUS | | | | | | | | | | | | | | | | | | |
| R.A.— DEFICIENCY | | | | | | | | | | | | | | | | | | |
| SURPLUS | | | | | | | | | | | | | | | | | | |
| R.E.— DEFICIENCY | | | | | | | | | | | | | | | | | | |
| SURPLUS | | | | | | | | | | | | | | | | | | |
| INFANTRY— DEFICIENCY | | | | | | | | | | | | | | | | | | |
| SURPLUS | | | | | | | | | | | | | | | | | | |
| R.A.M.C.— DEFICIENCY | 13 | 2 | | | | | | | | | | | 2 | 20 | 2 | 1 | 1 | |
| SURPLUS | | | | | | | | | | | | | | | | | | |
| A.O.C.— DEFICIENCY | | | | | | | | | | | | | | | | | | |
| SURPLUS | | | | | | | | | | | | | | | | | | |
| A.V.C.— DEFICIENCY | | | | | | | | | | | | | | | | | | |
| SURPLUS | | | | | | | | | | | | | | | | | | |
| DEFICIENCY | | | | | | | | | | | | | | | | | | |
| SURPLUS | | | | | | | | | | | | | | | | | | |
| DEFICIENCY | | | | | | | | | | | | | | | | | | |
| SURPLUS | | | | | | | | | | | | | | | | | | |

Remarks :—

[illegible signature] Lt. Col. Signature of Commander.

1/1 Lowland Field Ambulance. Unit.

52 Div. Formation to which attached.

4-1-19 Date of Despatch.

(16523.) Wt. W6016—PP 1432. 1,500m. 3/18. D & S. (E1256) Forms B2138/3. [P.T.O.

To be made up to and for Saturday in each week

No. of Report 180

App. 2

# FIELD RETURN.

Army Form B. 213

(To be furnished by all arms, services, and departments (except A.S.C. units) to the A.G.'s Office at the Base in accordance with Field Service Regulations, Part II.)

RETURN showing numbers (a) Effective strength of Unit. (b) Rationed by Unit. 1/1 LOWLAND FD. AMB at In the Field 11-1-19 Date.

| DETAILS. | *Personnel | | | | Animals | | | | | | Guns and transport vehicles | | | | | | | | | | | | | | REMARKS (Number of Acting W.O.'s and N.C.O.'s included in effective strength to be shown in this column.) |
|---|---|---|---|---|---|---|---|---|---|---|---|---|---|---|---|---|---|---|---|---|---|---|---|---|---|
| | | | | | Horses | | | | Mules | | | | | | Horsed | | Mechanical | | | | | | | | |
| | Officers | Other Ranks | | | Riding | Draught | Heavy Draught | Pack | Large | Small | Guns, showing description | Ammunition wagons | Machine guns | Aircraft, showing description | 4 Wheeled | 2 Wheeled | Motor Cars | Tractors | Lorries, showing description | Trucks, showing description | Trailers | Motor Bicycles | Bicycles | Motor Ambulances | |
| Effective Strength of Unit ... ... | (a) 8 | (b) 167 | | | | | | | | | | | | | | | | | | | | | 1 | | (a) 1 on leave to U.K. – 1 at 1/3 Low.<br>1 at 1st Army P.O.W. Ret. Camp |
| Details by Arms attached to Unit as in War Establishment ... ... | | | | | | | | | | | | | | | | | | | | | | | | | (b) 46 at 1/2 Low. Fd. Amb.<br>2 at A.D.M.S. – 1 @ 1/3 Low. Fd.<br>1 at 520 … – 1 @ 156 R.H.G.<br>1 at … – 1 at 52 Div. M.T.<br>10 at 1st Army P.O.W. …<br>1 at 22 Corps … |
| A.S.C. (H.T.) | | (c) 33 | | | 6 | 16 | 19 | | | | | | | | 13 | 4 | | | | | | | | | (c) 1 on leave to U.K. |
| A.S.C. (M.T.) | | (d) 11 | | | | | | | | | | | | | | | | | | | | 2 | | 7 | (d) 2 at A.D.M.S. – 1 on leave +<br>(e) 1 on leave to U.K. |
| TOTAL ... ... | 8 | 211 | | | 6 | 16 | 19 | | | | | | | | 13 | 4 | | | | | | 2 | 1 | 7 | |
| War Establishment ... ... ... | 10 | 231 | | | 8 | 17 | 20 | | | | | | | | 13 | 4 | | | | | | 2 | 1 | 7 | |
| Wanting to complete ... ... ... (Detail of Personnel and Horses below.) | 2 | 20 | | | 2 | 1 | 1 | | | | | | | | | | | | | | | | | | 15 R.A.M.C. – 3 A.S.C. (H.T.) 2 A… |
| SURPLUS ... ... (Detail of Personnel and Horses below.) | | | | | | | | | | | | | | | | | | | | | | | | | |
| †Attached (not to include the details shown above) ... ... | | 18 | | | | | | | | | | | | | | | | | | | | | | | Patients |
| Attached for Rations only ... ... | 1° | 3* | | | | | | | | | | | | | | | | | | | | | | | ° Chaplain * … |
| Civilians Employed with and Accompanying the Unit ... ... | | | | | | | | | | | | | | | | | | | | | | | | | |
| ‡Detached from and struck off effective strength of own Unit ... | | | | | | | | | | | | | | | | | | | | | | | | | |
| ‡Detached from but retained on effective strength of own unit... ... | | | | | | | | | | | | | | | | | | | | | | | | | |
| TOTAL RATIONED ... | 6 | 163 | | | 6 | 16 | 19 | | | | | | | | | | | | | | | | | | |

* Blank columns to be used for W.A.A.C. Natives or as may be required.

† In the case of field ambulances, hospitals or depots, the number of patients are to be included here, the names being shown in A.F.A. 36.

‡ These details to be enumerated by arms.

[signature] Signature of Commander.

11-1-19 Date of Despatch.

B. 873

A.S.C. Sect.

W/E 11.1.19

- NIL -

A.S.C.
Sheet Attd.

*For information of the A.G.'s Office at the base.*

Officers and men who have become casuals, been transferred or joined since last report.

Place In the Field Date 11.1.19

| Regtl. Number | Rank | Name | Corps | Nature of casualty, or name of unit from or to which transferred. | Date of being struck off or coming on the ration return. | Remarks * |
|---|---|---|---|---|---|---|
| | Capt. Q.M. | Reid | A.M.K. R.A.M.C.(T) | Retd. from leave | 8.1.19 | |
| 316001 | Pte. | Gallacher | C. R.A.M.C.(T) | Registered as Dispensers as from (23.12.18 Authy. | | O/c. R.A.M.C. Records T.A. Wing Working O.G.18/179 d. 31/12/18 |

Strength Officers T.F. 7
R.N. 1
Total: 8

W.O.s N.C.O.s & Men.

| | |
|---|---|
| W.O. | 1 |
| Q.M.S. | 1 |
| S. Sgts. | 2 |
| Sgts. | 8 |
| L. Sgts. | 1 |
| Cpls. | 8 |
| L. Cpls. | 4 |
| Ptes. | 142 |
| Total: | 167 |

Category A.

* State whether absence is of a permanent or temporary nature, adding, in the case of casuals from wounds or disease any available information for communication to the relatives.

*The perforated sheet is not to be used to record casualties; additional sheets, preferably foolscap, to be attached when necessary. These sheets to be carefully numbered and the number of attached sheets to be noted here.*

# Perforated Sheet giving detail of personnel and horses wanting to complete or surplus, shown on Army Form B. 213.

No. of Report 180

| Detail of Wanting to Complete or Surplus. | Drivers: R.A. | Drivers: R.E. | Drivers: A.S.C. | Drivers: Car (Mt. A.S.C.) | Drivers: Lorry | Drivers: Steam | Gunners | Gunners Howitzer | Smith Gunners | Range Takers | Farriers: Serjeants | Farriers: Corporals | Shoeing or Shoeing and Carriage Smiths | Cold Shoers | Wheelers: R.A. | Wheelers: H.T. | Wheelers: M.T. | Saddlers or Harness Makers | Blacksmiths | Bricklayers and Masons | Carpenters and Joiners | Fitters & Turners (R.E.): Wood | Fitters & Turners (R.E.): Iron | Fitters: R.A. | Fitters: Wireless. | Plumbers | Electricians: Ordinary | Electricians: W.T. | Signalmen. | Engine Drivers: Loco. | Engine Drivers: Field | Air Line Men. | Permanent Line Men | Operators, Telegraph | Cablemen | Brigade Section Pioneers | General-duty Pioneers | Signallers | Instrument Repairers | Motor Cyclist | Motor Cyclist Artificers | Telephonists | Clerks | Machine Gunners | Armament Artificers: Fitters | Armament Artificers: Range Finders | Armourers | Storemen | Privates | W.O.'s and N.C.O.'s (by ranks) not included in trade columns: Sub. R.A.M.C. | | | | | | | | | | | TOTAL to agree with wanting to complete or surplus: Officers | TOTAL: Other Ranks | Horses: Riding | Horses: Draught | Horses: Heavy Draught | Horses: Pack |
|---|---|---|---|---|---|---|---|---|---|---|---|---|---|---|---|---|---|---|---|---|---|---|---|---|---|---|---|---|---|---|---|---|---|---|---|---|---|---|---|---|---|---|---|---|---|---|---|---|---|---|---|---|---|---|---|---|---|---|---|---|---|---|---|---|---|---|
| CAVALRY— DEFICIENCY | | | | | | | | | | | | | | | | | | | | | | | | | | | | | | | | | | | | | | | | | | | | | | | | | | | | | | | | | | | | | | | | | | |
| SURPLUS | | | | | | | | | | | | | | | | | | | | | | | | | | | | | | | | | | | | | | | | | | | | | | | | | | | | | | | | | | | | | | | | | | |
| R.A.— DEFICIENCY | | | | | | | | | | | | | | | | | | | | | | | | | | | | | | | | | | | | | | | | | | | | | | | | | | | | | | | | | | | | | | | | | | |
| SURPLUS | | | | | | | | | | | | | | | | | | | | | | | | | | | | | | | | | | | | | | | | | | | | | | | | | | | | | | | | | | | | | | | | | | |
| R.E.— DEFICIENCY | | | | | | | | | | | | | | | | | | | | | | | | | | | | | | | | | | | | | | | | | | | | | | | | | | | | | | | | | | | | | | | | | | |
| SURPLUS | | | | | | | | | | | | | | | | | | | | | | | | | | | | | | | | | | | | | | | | | | | | | | | | | | | | | | | | | | | | | | | | | | |
| INFANTRY— DEFICIENCY | | | | | | | | | | | | | | | | | | | | | | | | | | | | | | | | | | | | | | | | | | | | | | | | | | | | | | | | | | | | | | | | | | |
| SURPLUS | | | 2 | 2 | | | | | | | | | 1 | | | | | | | | | | | | | | | | | | 6 | | | | | | | | | | | | | | | | | | | 132 | | | | | | | | | | | | 2 | 20 | 2 | 1 | 1 | |
| R.A.M.C.— DEFICIENCY | | | | | | | | | | | | | | | | | | | | | | | | | | | | | | | | | | | | | | | | | | | | | | | | | | | | | | | | | | | | | | | | | | |
| SURPLUS | | | | | | | | | | | | | | | | | | | | | | | | | | | | | | | | | | | | | | | | | | | | | | | | | | | | | | | | | | | | | | | | | | |
| A.O.C.— DEFICIENCY | | | | | | | | | | | | | | | | | | | | | | | | | | | | | | | | | | | | | | | | | | | | | | | | | | | | | | | | | | | | | | | | | | |
| SURPLUS | | | | | | | | | | | | | | | | | | | | | | | | | | | | | | | | | | | | | | | | | | | | | | | | | | | | | | | | | | | | | | | | | | |
| A.V.C.— DEFICIENCY | | | | | | | | | | | | | | | | | | | | | | | | | | | | | | | | | | | | | | | | | | | | | | | | | | | | | | | | | | | | | | | | | | |
| SURPLUS | | | | | | | | | | | | | | | | | | | | | | | | | | | | | | | | | | | | | | | | | | | | | | | | | | | | | | | | | | | | | | | | | | |
| DEFICIENCY | | | | | | | | | | | | | | | | | | | | | | | | | | | | | | | | | | | | | | | | | | | | | | | | | | | | | | | | | | | | | | | | | | |
| SURPLUS | | | | | | | | | | | | | | | | | | | | | | | | | | | | | | | | | | | | | | | | | | | | | | | | | | | | | | | | | | | | | | | | | | |
| DEFICIENCY | | | | | | | | | | | | | | | | | | | | | | | | | | | | | | | | | | | | | | | | | | | | | | | | | | | | | | | | | | | | | | | | | | |
| SURPLUS | | | | | | | | | | | | | | | | | | | | | | | | | | | | | | | | | | | | | | | | | | | | | | | | | | | | | | | | | | | | | | | | | | |

Remarks :—

James Leitch Lt Col Signature of Commander.

1/1 Lowland Fd. Ambce. Unit.

52nd Div. Formation to which attached.

11-1-19 Date of Despatch.

(15523.) Wt. W6016—PP 1432. 1,500m. 3/18. D & S. (E1256) Forms B2138/8. [P.T.O.

**To be made up to and for Saturday in each week**

No. of Report 181 **FIELD RETURN.** App. III Army Form B. 213

(To be furnished by all arms, services, and departments (except A.S.C. units) to the A.G.'s Office at the Base in accordance with Field Service Regulations, Part II.)

RETURN showing numbers (a) Effective strength of Unit. (b) Rationed by Unit. 1/1 Lowland Field Amb. at In the Field 18-1-19 Date.

| Details. | Personnel: Officers | Personnel: Other Ranks | | | | Animals: Horses: Riding | Horses: Draught | Horses: Heavy Draught | Horses: Pack | Mules: Large | Mules: Small | Guns, showing description | Ammunition wagons | Machine guns | Aircraft, showing description | Horsed: 4 Wheeled | Horsed: 2 Wheeled | Mechanical: Motor Cars | Tractors | Lorries, showing description | Trucks, showing description | Trailers | Motor Bicycles | Bicycles | Motor Ambulances | Remarks (Number of Acting W.O.'s and N.C.O.'s included in effective strength to be shown in this column.) |
|---|---|---|---|---|---|---|---|---|---|---|---|---|---|---|---|---|---|---|---|---|---|---|---|---|---|---|
| Effective Strength of Unit ... ... | (a) 7 | (b) 161 | | | | | | | | | | | | | | | | | | | | | | 1 | | (a) 1 at 1st Army P.O.W. Rec. Centre, 2 on leave to U.K. (b) 45 at 1/2 Low. Fd. Amb. 2 at A.D.M.S. – 1 at 1/3 Low. Fd. Amb. 1 at 52 Div. Train – 1 at 155 B.H.Q. 1 at Concert Party – 1 at 52 Div. M.T. 10 at 1st Army P.O.W. Rec. Centre [illegible] (c) 2 [illegible] |
| Details by Arms attached to Unit as in War Establishment ... ... ... | | | | | | | | | | | | | | | | | | | | | | | | | | |
| A.S.C. (H.T.) | | 33 | | | | 6 | 16 | 19 | | | | | | | | 13 | 4 | | | | | | | | | |
| A.S.C. (M.T.) | | (c) 11 | | | | | | | | | | | | | | | | | | | | | 2 | | 7 | |
| Total ... ... | 7 | 205 | | | | 6 | 16 | 19 | | | | | | | | 13 | 4 | | | | | | 2 | 1 | 7 | |
| War Establishment ... ... ... | 10 | 231 | | | | 8 | 17 | 20 | | | | | | | | 13 | 4 | | | | | | 2 | 1 | 7 | |
| Wanting to complete ... ... (Detail of Personnel and Horses below.) | 3 | 26 | | | | 2 | 1 | 1 | | | | | | | | | | | | | | | | | | 21 R.A.M.C. – 3 A.S.C. – 2 A.S.C. (M.T.) |
| Surplus ... ... (Detail of Personnel and Horses below.) | | | | | | | | | | | | | | | | | | | | | | | | | | |
| †Attached (not to include the details shown above) ... ... ... | | 17 | | | | | | | | | | | | | | | | | | | | | | | | Patients |
| Attached for Rations only ... ... | 1 | 1 | | | | | | | | | | | | | | | | | | | | | | | | Chaplain – Billet Warden |
| Civilians Employed with and Accompanying the Unit ... ... | | | | | | | | | | | | | | | | | | | | | | | | | | |
| ‡Detached from and struck off effective strength of own Unit ... ... | | | | | | | | | | | | | | | | | | | | | | | | | | |
| ‡Detached from but retained on effective strength of own unit... ... ... | | | | | | | | | | | | | | | | | | | | | | | | | | |
| Total Rationed ... | 5 | 186 | | | | 6 | 16 | 19 | | | | | | | | | | | | | | | | | | |

* Blank columns to be used for W.A.A.C. Natives or as may be required.

† In the case of field ambulances, hospitals or depots, the number of patients are to be included here, the names being shown in A.F.A. 36.

‡ These details to be enumerated by arms.

[illegible] Major Signature of Commander. 18-1-19 Date of Despatch.

B 713

R.A.S.C. SECTION

W/E 18.1.19

| No. | RANK | NAME | CASUALTY | DATE |
|---|---|---|---|---|
| T4/237009 | Fr. Dvr. | Ramsay W.G. | Returned from leave | 11/1/19 |
| M2/049901 | Pte. | Hampton W.S. | – do – – do – | 12/1/19 |
| T/19300 | T/C.S.M. | Sackley A. | Appointed A.S.S.M. Date of Vacancy 1/1/19. Assumed duties of A.S.S.M. 2/1/19 vice A/C.S.M. Billchamber (T4/102??) transferred to 12 Army Auxiliary Horse Coy. Authy. – R.A.S.C. Records Woolwich C.R. 19609/a/16 – O i/c R.A.S.C. Sect. A.G.'s Office, 3rd Echelon. A.S.S. R. 40/11152/a 13/12/18 | |

[illegible]
Major
for O.C. 1/1st Lowland Fd Ambce R.A.M.C.T.

A.S.C. [illegible]

*For information of the A.G.'s Office at the base.*

Officers and men who have become casuals, been transferred or joined since last report.

Place In the Field    Date 18-1-19

| Regtl. Number | Rank | Name | Corps | Nature of casualty, or name of unit from or to which transferred. | Date of being struck off or coming on the ration return. | Remarks * |
|---|---|---|---|---|---|---|
| – | Lt. Col. | Leitch J.W. | D.S.O. R.A.M.C.(T) | Granted leave to U.K. via Calais 14 days 17-1-19 – 27-1-19 | | Excess Ration allce. for period |
| – | Major | Browne J. | R.A.M.C.(T) | Return to War Office for Civil Employment Authority — Selected wire No. O.A. 30660. A.M.D.1. dated 3/1/19 | | |
| | do. | — do — | do. | Relinquishes acting Rank (on proceeding to War Office) from 13/1/19. | | |
| 316219 | Pte. | Faith J. | R.A.M.C.(T.) | Returned from leave 11/1/19 | | |
| 316038 | " | [illegible] J. | do. | Joined as Reinforcement Lines 52 D.H.Q. | 15/1/19 | |
| 42191 | " | Ward T. | do. | To England for Demobilisation | | 14/1/19 |
| 316044 | " | Pinkerton J. | do. | — do — | — do — | 14/1/19 |
| 3034 | " | Morris E. | do. | do. | do. | 14/1/19 |
| 410023 | L/Cpl. | Reeves F. | do. | do. | do. | 14/1/19 |
| 400014 | Pte. | Beckers J. | do. | do. | do. | 16/1/19 |
| 410054 | " | Parkins W.C. | do. | — do — | do. | 16/1/19 |
| 456092 | Cpl. | [illegible] J. | do. | do. | do. | 16/1/19 |

Strength — Officers  T.F. 6  R.N. 1  TOTAL 7

W.Os. N.C.Os. & men
W.O. 1
Q.M.S. 1
S Sgts 2
Sgts 8
L Sgts 1
Cpls. 7
L Cpls. 3
Ptes. 138
TOTAL 161

ALL CATEGORY "A"

* State whether absence is of a permanent or temporary nature, adding, in the case of casuals from wounds or disease any available information for communication to the relatives.

*The perforated sheet is not to be used to record casualties; additional sheets, preferably foolscap, to be attached when necessary. These sheets to be carefully numbered and the number of attached sheets to be noted here.*

Perforated Sheet giving detail of personnel and horses wanting to complete or surplus, shown on Army Form B. 213.

No. of Report 181

| Detail of Wanting to Complete or Surplus. | Drivers: R.A. | Drivers: R.E. | Drivers: A.S.C. | Drivers: Car M.T.-A.S.C. | Drivers: Lorry | Drivers: Steam | Gunners | Gunners Howitzer | Smith Gunners | Range Takers | Farriers: Serjeants | Farriers: Corporals | Shoeing or Shoeing and Carriage Smiths | Cold Shoers | Wheelers: R.A. | Wheelers: H.T. | Wheelers: M.T. | Saddlers or Harness Makers | Blacksmiths | Bricklayers and Masons | Carpenters and Joiners | Fitters & Turners (R.E.): Wood | Fitters & Turners (R.E.): Iron | Fitters: R.A. | Fitters: Wireless. | Plumbers | Electricians: Ordinary | Electricians: W.T. | Signalmen. | Engine Drivers: Loco. | Engine Drivers: Field | Air Line Men. | Permanent Line Men | Operators, Telegraph | Cablemen | Brigade Section Pioneers | General-duty Pioneers | Signallers | Instrument Repairers | Motor Cyclist | Motor Cyclist Artificers | Telephonists | Clerks | Machine Gunners | Armament Artificers: Fitters | Armament Artificers: Range Finders | Armourers | Storemen | Privates | W.O.'s and N.C.O.'s (by ranks) not included in trade columns: Sgt. R.A.M.C. (H) | W.O.'s and N.C.O.'s: Cpls. " " | W.O.'s and N.C.O.'s | W.O.'s and N.C.O.'s | W.O.'s and N.C.O.'s | W.O.'s and N.C.O.'s | W.O.'s and N.C.O.'s | | | | | TOTAL to agree with wanting to complete or surplus: Officers | TOTAL: Other Ranks | Horses: Riding | Horses: Draught | Horses: Heavy Draught | Horses: Pack |
|---|---|---|---|---|---|---|---|---|---|---|---|---|---|---|---|---|---|---|---|---|---|---|---|---|---|---|---|---|---|---|---|---|---|---|---|---|---|---|---|---|---|---|---|---|---|---|---|---|---|---|---|---|---|---|---|---|---|---|---|---|---|---|---|---|---|---|
| CAVALRY—DEFICIENCY | | | | | | | | | | | | | | | | | | | | | | | | | | | | | | | | | | | | | | | | | | | | | | | | | | | | | | | | | | | | | | | | | | | |
| SURPLUS | | | | | | | | | | | | | | | | | | | | | | | | | | | | | | | | | | | | | | | | | | | | | | | | | | | | | | | | | | | | | | | | | | |
| R.A.—DEFICIENCY | | | | | | | | | | | | | | | | | | | | | | | | | | | | | | | | | | | | | | | | | | | | | | | | | | | | | | | | | | | | | | | | | | |
| SURPLUS | | | | | | | | | | | | | | | | | | | | | | | | | | | | | | | | | | | | | | | | | | | | | | | | | | | | | | | | | | | | | | | | | | |
| R.E.—DEFICIENCY | | | | | | | | | | | | | | | | | | | | | | | | | | | | | | | | | | | | | | | | | | | | | | | | | | | | | | | | | | | | | | | | | | |
| SURPLUS | | | | | | | | | | | | | | | | | | | | | | | | | | | | | | | | | | | | | | | | | | | | | | | | | | | | | | | | | | | | | | | | | | |
| INFANTRY—DEFICIENCY | | | | | | | | | | | | | | | | | | | | | | | | | | | | | | | | | | | | | | | | | | | | | | | | | | | | | | | | | | | | | | | | | | |
| SURPLUS | | | | | | | | | | | | | | | | | | | | | | | | | | | | | | | | | | | | | | | | | | | | | | | | | | | | | | | | | | | | | | | | | | |
| R.A.M.C.—DEFICIENCY | | | 2 | 2 | | | | | | | | 1 | | | | | | | | | | | | | | | | | | 6 | | | | | | | | | | | | | | | | | | | 18 | 2 | 1 | | | | | | | | | | 3 | 26 | 2 | 1 | 1 | |
| SURPLUS | | | | | | | | | | | | | | | | | | | | | | | | | | | | | | | | | | | | | | | | | | | | | | | | | | | | | | | | | | | | | | | | | | |
| A.O.C.—DEFICIENCY | | | | | | | | | | | | | | | | | | | | | | | | | | | | | | | | | | | | | | | | | | | | | | | | | | | | | | | | | | | | | | | | | | |
| SURPLUS | | | | | | | | | | | | | | | | | | | | | | | | | | | | | | | | | | | | | | | | | | | | | | | | | | | | | | | | | | | | | | | | | | |
| A.V.C.—DEFICIENCY | | | | | | | | | | | | | | | | | | | | | | | | | | | | | | | | | | | | | | | | | | | | | | | | | | | | | | | | | | | | | | | | | | |
| SURPLUS | | | | | | | | | | | | | | | | | | | | | | | | | | | | | | | | | | | | | | | | | | | | | | | | | | | | | | | | | | | | | | | | | |
| DEFICIENCY | | | | | | | | | | | | | | | | | | | | | | | | | | | | | | | | | | | | | | | | | | | | | | | | | | | | | | | | | | | | | | | | | | |
| SURPLUS | | | | | | | | | | | | | | | | | | | | | | | | | | | | | | | | | | | | | | | | | | | | | | | | | | | | | | | | | | | | | | | | | | |
| DEFICIENCY | | | | | | | | | | | | | | | | | | | | | | | | | | | | | | | | | | | | | | | | | | | | | | | | | | | | | | | | | | | | | | | | | | |
| SURPLUS | | | | | | | | | | | | | | | | | | | | | | | | | | | | | | | | | | | | | | | | | | | | | | | | | | | | | | | | | | | | | | | | | | |

Remarks :—

[illegible] Signature of Commander.

1/1 Lowland Fld. Amb. Unit.

52 Div. Formation to which attached.

18 - 1 - 19 Date of Despatch.

(16523.) Wt. W6016—PP 1432. 1,500m. 3/18. D & S. (E1256) Forms B213S/3.

[P.T.O.

**To be made up to and for Saturday in each week**

No. of Report 142

# FIELD RETURN.

Army Form B. 213

(To be furnished by all arms, services, and departments (except A.S.C. units) to the A.G.'s Office at the Base in accordance with Field Service Regulations, Part II.)

RETURN showing numbers (*a*) Effective strength of Unit. (*b*) Rationed by Unit. 1/1 Lowland Field Amb^ce^. at In the Field 25-1-19. Date.

App IV

| Details. | *Personnel: Officers | Other Ranks | | | | Animals: Horses: Riding | Draught | Heavy Draught | Pack | Mules: Large | Small | Guns and transport vehicles: Guns, showing description | Ammunition wagons | Machine guns | Aircraft, showing description | Horsed: 4 Wheeled | 2 Wheeled | Mechanical: Motor Cars | Tractors | Lorries, showing description | Trucks, showing description | Trailers | Motor Bicycles | Bicycles | Motor Ambulances | Remarks (Number of Acting W.O.'s and N.C.O.'s included in effective strength to be shown in this column.) |
|---|---|---|---|---|---|---|---|---|---|---|---|---|---|---|---|---|---|---|---|---|---|---|---|---|---|---|
| Effective Strength of Unit ... ... | (a) 7 | (b) 158 | | | | | | | | | | | | | | | | | | | | | | 1 | | (a) 2 on leave to U.K. 2 at Div. Rest Stn. |
| Details by Arms attached to Unit as in War Establishment ... ... ... | | | | | | | | | | | | | | | | | | | | | | | | | | (b) 45 at 1/2 Low. Fd. Amb. 20 at Div. Rest Station 2 at 22 San. Sect. – 2 at A.D.M.S. 1 at 52 Div. Train – 1 at 156 B.H.Q. 1 at Convent Dep. – 1 at 52 Div. M.T. Coy 1 at Corps [illegible] |
| A.S.C. (H.T.) | | (c) 35 | | | | 6 | 16 | (e) 19 | | | | | | | | 13 | 4 | | | | | | | | | (c) 3 at Div. Rest Stn. |
| A.S.C. (M.T.) | | (d) 11 | | | | | | | | | | | | | | | | | | | | | 2 | | 7 | (d) 2 at A.D.M.S. 52 Div. (e) 6 at Div. Rest Stn. |
| Total ... ... | 7 | 202 | | | | 6 | 16 | 19 | | | | | | | | 13 | 4 | | | | | | 2 | 1 | 7 | |
| War Establishment ... ... ... | 8 | 203 | | | | 5 | 13 | 16 | | | | | | | | 10 | 3 | | | | | | 2 | 1 | 7 | |
| Wanting to complete ... ... ... (Detail of Personnel and Horses below.) | 1 | 6 | | | | | | | | | | | | | | | | | | | | | | | | 4 R.A.M.C. – 2 R.A.S.C. (M.T.) |
| Surplus ... ... (Detail of Personnel and Horses below.) | | * 5 | | | | 1 | 3 | 3 | | | | | | | | 3 | 1 | | | | | | | | | * R.A.S.C. (H.T.) |
| †Attached (not to include the details shown above) ... ... ... ... | | 5 | | | | | | | | | | | | | | | | | | | | | | | | Patients |
| Attached for Rations only ... ... | | 1 | | | | | | | | | | | | | | | | | | | | | | | | Billet Warden |
| Civilians Employed with and Accompanying the Unit ... ... | | | | | | | | | | | | | | | | | | | | | | | | | | |
| ‡Detached from and struck off effective strength of own Unit | | | | | | | | | | | | | | | | | | | | | | | | | | |
| ‡Detached from but retained on effective strength of own unit... ... | | | | | | | | | | | | | | | | | | | | | | | | | | |
| Total Rationed ... | 3 | 131 | | | | 6 | 16 | 13 | | | | | | | | | | | | | | | | | | |

* Blank columns to be used for W.A.A.C. Natives or as may be required.

† In the case of field ambulances, hospitals or depots, the number of patients are to be included here, the names being shown in A.F.A. 36.

‡ These details to be enumerated by arms.

[illegible] Major Signature of Commander.

25-1-19 Date of Despatch.

B213

R. A. S. C. SECTION

W/E 25-1-19

— NIL —

R.A.S.C. Sheet Att.

*For information of the A.G.'s Office at the base.*

Officers and men who have become casuals, been transferred or joined since last report.

Place In the Field    Date January 25th 1919

| Regtl. Number | Rank | Name | Corps | Nature of casualty, or name of unit from or to which transferred. | Date of being struck off or coming on the ration return. | Remarks * |
|---|---|---|---|---|---|---|
| 61353 | Pte. | Worsley J. | R.A.M.C. | To U.K. for Demobilisation | | 21/1/19 |
| 104636 | " | Gosling L.J. | do. | do. | do. | 21/1/19 |
| 40126 | " | Partington H. | do. | do. | do. | 21/1/19 |

Strength:- Officers: T.F. 6, R.N. 1, TOTAL 7

W.Os. N.C.Os. & Men

| | |
|---|---|
| W.O. | 1 |
| Q.M.S. | 1 |
| S/Sgts. | 2 |
| Sgts. | 8 |
| L/Sgts. | 1 |
| Cpls. | 7 |
| L/Cpls. | 3 |
| Ptes. | 135 |
| TOTAL | 158 |

* State whether absence is of a permanent or temporary nature, adding, in the case of casuals from wounds or disease any available information for communication to the relatives.

*The perforated sheet is not to be used to record casualties: additional sheets, preferably foolscap, to be attached when necessary. These sheets to be carefully numbered and the number of attached sheets to be noted here.*

Perforated Sheet giving detail of personnel and horses wanting to complete or surplus, shown on Army Form B. 213.

No. of Report 182

| Detail of Wanting to Complete or Surplus. | Drivers. R.A. | Drivers. R.E. | Drivers. A.S.C. | Drivers. Car (M.T.A.S.C.) | Drivers. Lorry | Drivers. Steam | Gunners | Gunners Howitzer | Smith Gunners | Range Takers | Farriers Serjeants | Farriers Corporals | Shoeing or Shoeing and Carriage Smiths | Cold Shoers | Wheelers R.A. | Wheelers H.T. | Wheelers M.T. | Saddlers or Harness Makers | Blacksmiths | Bricklayers and Masons | Carpenters and Joiners | Fitters & Turners (R.E.) Wood | Fitters & Turners (R.E.) Iron | Fitters R.A. | Fitters Wireless. | Plumbers | Electricians Ordinary | Electricians W.T. | Signalmen. | Engine Drivers Loco. | Engine Drivers Field | Air Line Men. | Permanent Line Men | Operators, Telegraph | Cablemen | Brigade Section Pioneers | General-duty Pioneers | Signallers | Instrument Repairers | Motor Cyclist | Motor Cyclist Artificers | Telephonists | Clerks | Machine Gunners | Armament Artificers Fitters | Armament Artificers Range Finders | Armourers | Storemen | Privates R.A.M.C.(T) | W.O.'s and N.C.O.'s (by ranks) not included in trade columns. Cpls. R.A.M.C.(T) | Sgts. R.A.M.C.(T) | Sgts. R.A.S.C. | | | | | | | | | TOTAL to agree with wanting to complete or surplus Officers | TOTAL Other Ranks | Horses Riding | Horses Draught | Horses Heavy Draught | Horses Pack |
|---|---|---|---|---|---|---|---|---|---|---|---|---|---|---|---|---|---|---|---|---|---|---|---|---|---|---|---|---|---|---|---|---|---|---|---|---|---|---|---|---|---|---|---|---|---|---|---|---|---|---|---|---|---|---|---|---|---|---|---|---|---|---|---|---|---|---|
| CAVALRY— DEFICIENCY | | | | | | | | | | | | | | | | | | | | | | | | | | | | | | | | | | | | | | | | | | | | | | | | | | | | | | | | | | | | | | | | | | |
| SURPLUS | | | | | | | | | | | | | | | | | | | | | | | | | | | | | | | | | | | | | | | | | | | | | | | | | | | | | | | | | | | | | | | | | |
| R.A.— DEFICIENCY | | | | | | | | | | | | | | | | | | | | | | | | | | | | | | | | | | | | | | | | | | | | | | | | | | | | | | | | | | | | | | | |
| SURPLUS | | | | | | | | | | | | | | | | | | | | | | | | | | | | | | | | | | | | | | | | | | | | | | | | | | | | | | | | | | | | | | | | | |
| R.E.— DEFICIENCY | | | | | | | | | | | | | | | | | | | | | | | | | | | | | | | | | | | | | | | | | | | | | | | | | | | | | | | | | | | | | | | | | |
| SURPLUS | | | | | | | | | | | | | | | | | | | | | | | | | | | | | | | | | | | | | | | | | | | | | | | | | | | | | | | | | | | | | | | | | |
| INFANTRY— DEFICIENCY | | | | | | | | | | | | | | | | | | | | | | | | | | | | | | | | | | | | | | | | | | | | | | | | | | | | | | | | | | | | | | | | | |
| SURPLUS | | | | | | | | | | | | | | | | | | | | | | | | | | | | | | | | | | | | | | | | | | | | | | | | | | | | | | | | | | | | | | | | | |
| R.A.M.C.— DEFICIENCY | | | 4 | 2 | | | | | | | | | | | | | | | | | | | | | | | | | | 6 | | | | | | | | | | | | | | | | | | | 7 | 2 | 1 | 1 | | | | | | | | | 1 | 19 | | 1 | 3 | 3 |
| SURPLUS | | | | | | | | | | | | | | | | | | | | | | | | | | | | | | | | | | | | | | | | | | | | | | | | | | | | | | | | | | | | | | | | | |
| A.O.C.— DEFICIENCY | | | | | | | | | | | | | | | | | | | | | | | | | | | | | | | | | | | | | | | | | | | | | | | | | | | | | | | | | | | | | | | | | |
| SURPLUS | | | | | | | | | | | | | | | | | | | | | | | | | | | | | | | | | | | | | | | | | | | | | | | | | | | | | | | | | | | | | | | | | |
| A.V.C.— DEFICIENCY | | | | | | | | | | | | | | | | | | | | | | | | | | | | | | | | | | | | | | | | | | | | | | | | | | | | | | | | | | | | | | | | | |
| SURPLUS | | | | | | | | | | | | | | | | | | | | | | | | | | | | | | | | | | | | | | | | | | | | | | | | | | | | | | | | | | | | | | | | | |
| DEFICIENCY | | | | | | | | | | | | | | | | | | | | | | | | | | | | | | | | | | | | | | | | | | | | | | | | | | | | | | | | | | | | | | | | | |
| SURPLUS | | | | | | | | | | | | | | | | | | | | | | | | | | | | | | | | | | | | | | | | | | | | | | | | | | | | | | | | | | | | | | | | | |
| DEFICIENCY | | | | | | | | | | | | | | | | | | | | | | | | | | | | | | | | | | | | | | | | | | | | | | | | | | | | | | | | | | | | | | | | | |
| SURPLUS | | | | | | | | | | | | | | | | | | | | | | | | | | | | | | | | | | | | | | | | | | | | | | | | | | | | | | | | | | | | | | | | | |

Remarks :—

[illegible] Signature of Commander.

1/1 Lowland Field Ambce. Unit.

52 Div. Formation to which attached.

25-1-19 Date of Despatch.

(16523.) Wt. W6016—PP 1432. 1,500m. 3/18. D & S. (E1256) Forms B2138/3.

[P.T.O.

Feb 1919

24

1/1st Low Fd Amb

War Diary

Feb 1919

VR 11

141/3524

530

# WAR DIARY
*or*
# INTELLIGENCE SUMMARY.
(*Erase heading not required.*)

Army Form C. 2118.

1/1st Lowland Fd Ambce R.A.M.C. T.F.
52nd (LOWLAND) Division

Instructions regarding War Diaries and Intelligence Summaries are contained in F. S. Regs., Part II. and the Staff Manual respectively. Title pages will be prepared in manuscript.

| Place | Date | Hour | Summary of Events and Information | Remarks and references to Appendices |
|---|---|---|---|---|
| CHAUSEE-N-D-LOUVIGNIES Sh. 38 W.5.6 4.6. | 1/2/19 | | nothing to report. NBM | |
| | 2/2/19 | | Three O.R. off strength for demobilization NBM | |
| | 3/2/19 | | nothing to note NBM | |
| | 4/2/19 | | do do NBM | |
| | 5/2/19 | | do do NBM | |
| | 6/2/19 | | Recd. ADMS 52nd Div. R1368/8 d/6/2/19:— cadre strength of a Field Amb. no information shown therein as to number of horses on cadre. NBM | |
| | 7/2/19 | | Three O.R. off strength for demobilization. Recd ADMS 52nd Div No. R1584/10 d/7/2/19:— Officers on leave granted extension will be struck off strength on 30th day. NBM | |
| | 8/2/19 | | nothing to note NBM | |
| | 9/2/19 | | do do do NBM | |
| | 10/2/19 | | do do do NBM | |
| | 11/2/19 | | Four totally blind horses evacuated under ADMS R/1600/9 d/9/2/19. Lt. Col. J.W. LEITCH returns from leave. NBM | |
| do | 12/2/19 | | Usual routine duties carried out. Lt Col YOUNG A/ADMS called | JWL |
| " | 13/2/19 | | Visited Div. HQ in Jenlain. ADMS is expected to [illegible] to-day on his return from short leave to U.K. | |
| do | 14/2/19 | | Attended ADMS. Office in [illegible] as A/ADMS. | JWL |
| do | 15/2/19 | | Attended ADMS Office in [illegible] & found that he had returned from leave late last night. Visited D.R.S. at LENS which is carried on by personnel of this Ambulance under command | |

D. D. & L., London, E.C.
(10340) W1 W5300/P713 750,000 3/18 Sch. 2688 Forms/C2118/15.

531 Army Form C. 2118.

Instructions regarding War Diaries and Intelligence Summaries are contained in F. S. Regs., Part II. and the Staff Manual respectively. Title pages will be prepared in manuscript.

# WAR DIARY
~~or~~
# ~~INTELLIGENCE SUMMARY.~~
(Erase heading not required.)

1/1st Lowland Field Ambulance
52nd (Lowland) Division

| Place | Date | Hour | Summary of Events and Information | Remarks and references to Appendices |
|---|---|---|---|---|
| CHAUSSEE N.D. LOUVIGNIES Sh 38 W5 b 4.6 | 15/2/19 (Contd) | | of Surgeon Lt Commander ROSS. J.W.L. | |
| do. | 16/2/19 | | Sunday. Received A.D.M.S. W268 d/15 2/19 "adopt thaw precautions from 0001 hours 16th Feb". ~~Lt~~ Col GREY Special advisor on Scabies (Skin Diseases) to Armies in France visited the Hospital to-day & went over the cases in the Hospital & was shown the baths & arrangements for treatment of scabies. He expressed himself satisfied ~~[illegible]~~ & said he had nothing further to suggest by way of improvement. J.W.L. | |
| do | 17/2/19 | | Nothing to note. 1 Amb. car orderly & driver report for temporary duty to 9th Bde RFA CASTEAU J.W.L. | |
| do | 18/2/19 | | Received ADMS R1687/5 that Lt Col J.W. Leitch D.S.O. RAMC(TF) will under authority of Dshorted Wire DM 32089, AMD1 d/6 2/19 proceed to UK for demobilization on the earliest possible date after handing over to the next senior officer. J.W.L. | |
| do | 19/2/19 | | ~~2 Officers + 6 O.R.~~ One ambulance car, driver, & orderly report to Section 1/2nd LFA GHLIN for temporary duty. J.W.L. | |
| do | 20/2/19 | | ADMS R1719/8 asks for weekly return of Cadre strength on Saturdays. J.W.L. | |
| do | 21/2/19 | | Sent report of medical officer (Major W.F. MacKenzie) detailed by me to report on sanitary condition of chateau at CAMBRON ST VINCENT in accordance with instructions in ADMS ~~[illegible]~~ 1698/2 d/18 2/19. The chateau is occupied by the M.G. Batt. & an explosion of power gas had occurred in Crofoot in the courtyard. J.W.L. | |
| do | 22/2/19 | | Sent suggestions re administration of Cadres of Ambulances to A.D.M.S. in compliance with his | |

D. D. & L., London, E.C.
(10340) Wt W5300/P713 750,000 3/18 S 2688 Forms/C2118/15.

532 Army Form C. 2118.

# WAR DIARY

~~or~~

~~INTELLIGENCE~~ SUMMARY.

(Erase heading not required.)

1/1st Lowland Field Ambulance
52nd (Lowland) Division

Instructions regarding War Diaries and Intelligence Summaries are contained in F. S. Regs., Part II. and the Staff Manual respectively. Title pages will be prepared in manuscript.

| Place | Date | Hour | Summary of Events and Information | Remarks and references to Appendices |
|---|---|---|---|---|
| CHAUSSEE N.D LOUVIGNIES Sh 38 W.S.b.6.6 | 22/2/19 (Contd) | | ~~R.17/19~~ R 1719/8 of even date marked "Sent" | J.W.L. |
| do | 23/2/19 | | Sent to A.D.M.S. roll of 2 horses in this unit called for in his Wire W418 received to-night | J.W.L. |
| do | 24/2/19 | | Received A.D.M.S. R1687/5 d/23/2/19 ~~with~~ and notified him in accordance with instructions that Major a/Lt.Col. J.W. LEITCH would depart from unit en route for U.K. for demobilization on 25/2/19 & would relinquish acting rank with effect from 26/2/19 | J.W.L. |
| do | 25/2/19 | | Nothing to note [initials] | |
| | 26/2/19 | | Report called for under ADMS 52nd Div. R.1779/4 d/26/2/19 submitted on medical treatment ~~of civilians~~ Belgian. During current month there has been an average daily attendance at this unit's Dispensary of six civilians mainly minor ailments of skin such as "Septic abrasions". Average number of visits made to civilians in their homes 1.2 daily. [initials] | |
| | 27/2/19 | | Under ADMS 52nd Div. R.1803/4 d/27/2/19 the practice of registering names of men receiving "Early Treatment" is discontinued, and all ~~records~~ of such names have been destroyed. [initials] ~~One O.R. R.A.S.C. H.T. off strength~~ | |
| | 28/2/19 | | Nothing to note. [initials] | |

[signature] Fergusson Mackenzie
Major
O.C. 1/1st Lowland Fd Ambce

D. D. & L., London, E.C. (a0340) Wt W5300/P713 750,000 3/18 Sch. 52a Forms/C2118/15.

**To be made up to and for Saturday in each week**

Army Form B. 213

No. of Report 163

## FIELD RETURN.

(To be furnished by all arms, services, and departments (except A.S.C. units) to the A.G.'s Office at the Base in accordance with Field Service Regulations, Part II.)

RETURN showing numbers (*a*) Effective strength of Unit. (*b*) Rationed by Unit. 1 Lowland Field Ambulance at In the Field 1-2-19 Date.

| Details. | *Personnel: Officers | Other Ranks | | | | Animals: Horses: Riding | Draught | Heavy Draught | Pack | Mules: Large | Small | Guns and transport vehicles: Guns, showing description | Ammunition wagons | Machine guns | Aircraft, showing description | Horsed: 4 Wheeled | 2 Wheeled | Mechanical: Motor Cars | Tractors | Lorries, showing description | Trucks, showing description | Trailers | Motor Bicycles | Bicycles | Motor Ambulances | Remarks (Number of Acting W.O.'s and N.C.O.'s included in effective strength to be shown in this column.) |
|---|---|---|---|---|---|---|---|---|---|---|---|---|---|---|---|---|---|---|---|---|---|---|---|---|---|---|
| Effective Strength of Unit | (a) 7 | (b) 158 | | | | | | | | | | | | | | | | | | | | | | 1 | | (a) 1 on leave to U.K. – 1 at 1/4 R.S. 2 at Div. Rest Station |
| Details by Arms attached to Unit as in War Establishment | | | | | | | | | | | | | | | | | | | | | | | | | | (b) 35 at 1/2 Low. Fd. Amb. 31 at Div. Rest Station 2 at 22 San. Section – 2 at A.D.M.S. 1 at 52 Div. [illegible] – 1 at Concert Party 1 at 52 Div. M.T. Coy. – 1 at [illegible] |
| A.S.C. (H.T.) | | (c) 35 | | | | 6 | 16 | (e) 19 | | | | | | | | 13 | 4 | | | | – | | | | | |
| A.S.C. (M.T.) | | (d) 11 | | | | | | | | | | | | | | | | | | | | | 2 | | 7 | (c) 3 at Div. Rest Station (d) 2 at A.D.M.S. 52 Div. (e) 6 at Div. Rest Station |
| Total | 7 | 203 | | | | 6 | 16 | 19 | | | | | | | | 13 | 4 | | | | | | 2 | 1 | 7 | |
| War Establishment | 8 | 203 | | | | 5 | 3 | 16 | | | | | | | | 10 | 3 | | | | | | 2 | 1 | 7 | |
| Wanting to complete (Detail of Personnel and Horses below.) | 1 | 6* | | | | | | | | | | | | | | | | | | | | | | | | * 4 R.A.M.C. – 2 R.A.S.C. (M.T.) |
| Surplus (Detail of Personnel and Horses below.) | | 5* | | | | 1 | 3 | 3 | | | | | | | | 3 | 1 | | | | | | | | | * R.A.S.C. (H.T.) |
| †Attached (not to include the details shown above) | | 10 | | | | | | | | | | | | | | | | | | | | | | | | Patients |
| Attached for Rations only | 1 | 1 | | | | | | | | | | | | | | | | | | | | | | | | Chaplains – Billet Warden |
| Civilians Employed with and Accompanying the Unit | | | | | | | | | | | | | | | | | | | | | | | | | | |
| ‡Detached from and struck off effective strength of own Unit | | | | | | | | | | | | | | | | | | | | | | | | | | |
| ‡Detached from but retained on effective strength of own unit | | | | | | | | | | | | | | | | | | | | | | | | | | |
| Total Rationed | 4 | 134 | | | | 6 | 16 | 13 | | | | | | | | | | | | | | | | | | |

* Blank columns to be used for W.A.A.C. Natives or as may be required.

† In the case of field ambulances, hospitals or depots, the number of patients are to be included here, the names being shown in A.F.A. 36.

‡ These details to be enumerated by arms.

[illegible signature] Signature of Commander.

1-2-19 Date of Despatch.

B 213/1

R. A. S. C. Scot.

W/E 1-2-19

— NIL —

1-2-19.

A.S.C.

Shew attd.

*For information of the A.G.'s Office at the base.*

Officers and men who have become casuals, been transferred or joined since last report.

Place In the Field                Date 1 · 2 · 19

| Regtl. Number | Rank | Name | Corps | Nature of casualty, or name of unit from or to which transferred. | Date of being struck off or coming on the ration return. | Remarks * |
|---|---|---|---|---|---|---|
| | | NIL | | | | |
| | | Strength:- Officers T.F. | 6 | | | |
| | | R.W. | 1 | | | |
| | | TOTAL | 7 | W.Os. N.C.Os. & MEN | | |
| | | | | W.O. | 1 | |
| | | | | Q.M.S. | 1 | |
| | | | | S Sgts. | 2 | |
| | | | | Sgts. | 8 | |
| | | | | L Sgts. | 1 | |
| | | | | Cpls. | 7 | |
| | | | | L Cpls. | 3 | |
| | | | | Ptes. | 135 | |
| | | | | TOTAL: | 158 | |

* State whether absence is of a permanent or temporary nature, adding, in the case of casuals from wounds or disease any available information for communication to the relatives.

*The perforated sheet is not to be used to record casualties; additional sheets, preferably foolscap, to be attached when necessary. These sheets to be carefully numbered and the number of attached sheets to be noted here.*

Perforated Sheet giving detail of personnel and horses wanting to complete or surplus, shown on Army Form B. 213.

No. of Report 153

| Detail of Wanting to Complete or Surplus | Drivers R.A. | Drivers R.E. | Drivers A.S.C. | Drivers Car (M.T. R.A.S.C.) | Drivers Lorry | Drivers Steam | Gunners | Gunners Howitzer | Smith Gunners | Range Takers | Farriers Serjeants | Farriers Corporals | Shoeing or Shoeing and Carriage Smiths | Cold Shoers | Wheelers R.A. | Wheelers H.T. | Wheelers M.T. | Saddlers or Harness Makers | Blacksmiths | Bricklayers and Masons | Carpenters and Joiners |
|---|---|---|---|---|---|---|---|---|---|---|---|---|---|---|---|---|---|---|---|---|---|
| CAVALRY—DEFICIENCY | | | | | | | | | | | | | | | | | | | | | |
| SURPLUS | | | | | | | | | | | | | | | | | | | | | |
| R.A.—DEFICIENCY | | | | | | | | | | | | | | | | | | | | | |
| SURPLUS | | | | | | | | | | | | | | | | | | | | | |
| R.E.—DEFICIENCY | | | | | | | | | | | | | | | | | | | | | |
| SURPLUS | | | | | | | | | | | | | | | | | | | | | |
| INFANTRY—DEFICIENCY | | | | | | | | | | | | | | | | | | | | | |
| SURPLUS | | | | | | | | | | | | | | | | | | | | | |
| R.A.M.C.—DEFICIENCY | | | | 2 | | | | | | | | | | | | | | | | | |
| SURPLUS | | | 4 | | | | | | | | | | | | | | | | | | |
| A.O.C.—DEFICIENCY | | | | | | | | | | | | | | | | | | | | | |
| SURPLUS | | | | | | | | | | | | | | | | | | | | | |
| A.V.C.—DEFICIENCY | | | | | | | | | | | | | | | | | | | | | |
| SURPLUS | | | | | | | | | | | | | | | | | | | | | |
| DEFICIENCY | | | | | | | | | | | | | | | | | | | | | |
| SURPLUS | | | | | | | | | | | | | | | | | | | | | |
| DEFICIENCY | | | | | | | | | | | | | | | | | | | | | |
| SURPLUS | | | | | | | | | | | | | | | | | | | | | |

| Detail of Wanting to Complete or Surplus | Fitters & Turners (R.E.) Wood | Fitters & Turners (R.E.) Iron | Fitters R.A. | Fitters Wireless. | Plumbers | Electricians Ordinary | Electricians W.T. | Signalmen. | Engine Drivers Loco. | Engine Drivers Field | Air Line Men. | Permanent Line Men | Operators, Telegraph | Cablemen | Brigade Section Pioneers | General-duty Pioneers | Signallers | Instrument Repairers | Motor Cyclist | Motor Cyclist Artificers | Telephonists | Clerks | Machine Gunners |
|---|---|---|---|---|---|---|---|---|---|---|---|---|---|---|---|---|---|---|---|---|---|---|---|
| CAVALRY—DEFICIENCY | | | | | | | | | | | | | | | | | | | | | | | |
| SURPLUS | | | | | | | | | | | | | | | | | | | | | | | |
| R.A.—DEFICIENCY | | | | | | | | | | | | | | | | | | | | | | | |
| SURPLUS | | | | | | | | | | | | | | | | | | | | | | | |
| R.E.—DEFICIENCY | | | | | | | | | | | | | | | | | | | | | | | |
| SURPLUS | | | | | | | | | | | | | | | | | | | | | | | |
| INFANTRY—DEFICIENCY | | | | | | | | | | | | | | | | | | | | | | | |
| SURPLUS | | | | | | | | | | | | | | | | | | | | | | | |
| R.A.M.C.—DEFICIENCY | | | | | | | | | | | | | | | | | | | | | | | |
| SURPLUS | | | | | | | | | | | | | | | | | | | | | | | |
| A.O.C.—DEFICIENCY | | | | | | | | | | | | | | | | | | | | | | | |
| SURPLUS | | | | | | | | | | | | | | | | | | | | | | | |
| A.V.C.—DEFICIENCY | | | | | | | | | | | | | | | | | | | | | | | |
| SURPLUS | | | | | | | | | | | | | | | | | | | | | | | |
| DEFICIENCY | | | | | | | | | | | | | | | | | | | | | | | |
| SURPLUS | | | | | | | | | | | | | | | | | | | | | | | |
| DEFICIENCY | | | | | | | | | | | | | | | | | | | | | | | |
| SURPLUS | | | | | | | | | | | | | | | | | | | | | | | |

| Detail of Wanting to Complete or Surplus | Armament Artificers Fitters | Armament Artificers Range Finders | Armourers | Storemen | Privates | W.O.'s and N.C.O.'s (by ranks) not included in trade columns: Sgt. R.A.M.C. | Cpl. R.A.M.C. | Sgt. R.A.S.C. (M.T.) | | | | | | | | | TOTAL to agree with wanting to complete or surplus: Officers | TOTAL: Other Ranks | Horses Riding | Horses Draught | Horses Heavy Draught | Horses Pack |
|---|---|---|---|---|---|---|---|---|---|---|---|---|---|---|---|---|---|---|---|---|---|---|
| CAVALRY—DEFICIENCY | | | | | | | | | | | | | | | | | | | | | | |
| SURPLUS | | | | | | | | | | | | | | | | | | | | | | |
| R.A.—DEFICIENCY | | | | | | | | | | | | | | | | | | | | | | |
| SURPLUS | | | | | | | | | | | | | | | | | | | | | | |
| R.E.—DEFICIENCY | | | | | | | | | | | | | | | | | | | | | | |
| SURPLUS | | | | | | | | | | | | | | | | | | | | | | |
| INFANTRY—DEFICIENCY | | | | | | | | | | | | | | | | | | | | | | |
| SURPLUS | | | | | | | | | | | | | | | | | | | | | | |
| R.A.M.C.—DEFICIENCY | | | | | 7 | - | - | | | | | | | | | | 1 | 9 | | | | |
| SURPLUS | | | | | | 1 | 2 | 1 | | | | | | | | | | 8 | 1 | 3 | 3 | |
| A.O.C.—DEFICIENCY | | | | | | | | | | | | | | | | | | | | | | |
| SURPLUS | | | | | | | | | | | | | | | | | | | | | | |
| A.V.C.—DEFICIENCY | | | | | | | | | | | | | | | | | | | | | | |
| SURPLUS | | | | | | | | | | | | | | | | | | | | | | |
| DEFICIENCY | | | | | | | | | | | | | | | | | | | | | | |
| SURPLUS | | | | | | | | | | | | | | | | | | | | | | |
| DEFICIENCY | | | | | | | | | | | | | | | | | | | | | | |
| SURPLUS | | | | | | | | | | | | | | | | | | | | | | |

Remarks :—

[signature] Major Signature of Commander.

1/1 Lowland Field Ambulance Unit.

52 Div. Formation to which attached.

1 - 2 - 19 Date of Despatch.

(16523.) Wt. W6016—PP 1432. 1,500m. 3/18. D & S. (E1256) Forms B2138/8.

[P.T.O.

**To be made up to and for Saturday in each week**

No. of Report 14

# FIELD RETURN.

Army Form B. 213

(To be furnished by all arms, services, and departments (except A.S.C. units) to the A.G.'s Office at the Base in accordance with Field Service Regulations, Part II.)

RETURN showing numbers (*a*) Effective strength of Unit. (*b*) Rationed by Unit. 1/1 Lowland Field Amb[illegible] at [illegible] 8 - 2 - 19 Date.

| Details. | *Personnel: Officers | Other Ranks | | | | Animals: Horses: Riding | Draught | Heavy Draught | Pack | Mules: Large | Small | Guns and transport vehicles: Guns, showing description | Ammunition wagons | Machine guns | Aircraft, showing description | Horsed: 4 Wheeled | 2 Wheeled | Mechanical: Motor Cars | Tractors | Lorries, showing description | Trucks, showing description | Trailers | Motor Bicycles | Bicycles | Motor Ambulances | Remarks (Number of Acting W.O.'s and N.C.O.'s included in effective strength to be shown in this column.) |
|---|---|---|---|---|---|---|---|---|---|---|---|---|---|---|---|---|---|---|---|---|---|---|---|---|---|---|
| Effective Strength of Unit ... ... | (a) 7 | (b) 155 | | | | | | | | | | | | | | | | | | | | | | 1 | | (a) 2 on Leave to U.K. – 1 at 1/4 R.S.<br>1 at Div. Rest Station<br>(b) 35 at 1/2 Low. Fd. Amb. [illegible]<br>29 at [illegible] Rest Station<br>2 at 22 San. Section – 2 at A.D.M.S.<br>1 at 52 Div. [illegible] – 1 [illegible] Coy.<br>1 at 52 Div. M.T. Coy. – 1 at [illegible]<br>(c) 3 at Div. Rest Station – 1 on leave to U.K.<br>(d) 3 at [illegible] 52 Div.<br>(e) 6 at Div. Rest Station. |
| Details by Arms attached to Unit as in War Establishment ... ... | | | | | | | | | | | | | | | | | | | | | | | | | | |
| A.S.C. (H.T.) | | (c) 33 | | | | 6 | 16 | (e) 19 | | | | | | | | 13 | 4 | | | | | | | | | |
| A.S.C. (M.T.) | | (d) 11 | | | | | | | | | | | | | | | | | | | | | 2 | | 7 | |
| Total ... ... | 7 | 199 | | | | 6 | 16 | 19 | | | | | | | | 13 | 4 | | | | | | 2 | 1 | 7 | |
| War Establishment ... ... | 8 | 203 | | | | 5 | 13 | 16 | | | | | | | | 10 | 3 | | | | | | 2 | 1 | 7 | |
| Wanting to complete ... ... ... (Detail of Personnel and Horses below.) | 1 | 9* | | | | | | | | | | | | | | | | | | | | | | | | *7 R.A.M.C. – 2 R.A.S.C. (M.T.) |
| Surplus ... ... (Detail of Personnel and Horses below.) | | 5* | | | | 1 | 3 | 3 | | | | | | | | 3 | 1 | | | | | | | | | *R.A.S.C. (H.T.) |
| †Attached (not to include the details shown above) ... ... ... | | 4 | | | | | | | | | | | | | | | | | | | | | | | | Patients |
| Attached for Rations only ... ... | 1 | 1 | | | | | | | | | | | | | | | | | | | | | | | | Chaplain – Billet Warden |
| Civilians Employed with and Accompanying the Unit ... ... | | | | | | | | | | | | | | | | | | | | | | | | | | |
| ‡Detached from and struck off effective strength of own Unit ... | | | | | | | | | | | | | | | | | | | | | | | | | | |
| ‡Detached from but retained on effective strength of own unit... ... | | | | | | | | | | | | | | | | | | | | | | | | | | |
| Total Rationed ... | 4 | 126 | | | | 6 | 16 | 13 | | | | | | | | | | | | | | | | | | |

* Blank columns to be used for W.A.A.C. Natives or as may be required.

† In the case of field ambulances, hospitals or depots, the number of patients are to be included here, the names being shown in A.F.A. 36.

‡ These details to be enumerated by arms.

[illegible] Major Signature of Commander.

8 - 2 - 19 Date of Despatch.

B 213
No. 144

R.A.S.C. SECTION

W/E 8.2.19

| No. | Rank | Name | Casualty | Date |
|---|---|---|---|---|
| T4/247008 | Dr. | W. Shillaw | Granted leave to U.K. via Calais 8/2/9 - 5/3/9 (28 days) Credit Ration Allce. at 2/4 d. for this period. | 3/2/19. |

*For information of the A.G.'s Office at the base.* A.S.C. Sheet [illegible]

Officers and men who have become casuals, been transferred or joined since last report.

Place In the Field Date 5-2-19

| Regtl. Number | Rank | Name | Corps | Nature of casualty, or name of unit from or to which transferred. | Date of being struck off or coming on the ration return. | Remarks * |
|---|---|---|---|---|---|---|
| – | Capt. | Lennox [illegible] R.A | R.A.M.C. (T) | Granted leave to U.K. 7-2-19 – 21-2-19 (14 days) | | via Calais [illegible] |
| [illegible] | [illegible] | Q Rose D | – do. | To U.K. for demobilization | 3/2/19 | |
| [illegible] | Q Pte. | Q Paterson A | – do. | – do. | 3/2/19 | |
| [illegible] | [illegible] | May J | – do. | – do. | 3/2/19 | |

Summary:- Officers T.F. 6
R.A. 1
TOTAL:- 7

W.O.s N.C.O.s + Men

| | |
|---|---|
| W.O. | 1 |
| Q.M.S. | 1 |
| S Sgts | 2 |
| Sgts | 8 |
| L Sgts | 1 |
| Cpls | 6 |
| L Cpls | 3 |
| Ptes | 133 |
| TOTAL:— | 155 |

* State whether absence is of a permanent or temporary nature, adding, in the case of casuals from wounds or disease any available information for communication to the relatives.

*The perforated sheet is not to be used to record casualties; additional sheets, preferably foolscap, to be attached when necessary. These sheets to be carefully numbered and the number of attached sheets to be noted here.*

Perforated Sheet giving detail of personnel and horses wanting to complete or surplus, shown on Army Form B. 213.

No. of Report 184

| Detail of Wanting to Complete or Surplus. | Drivers R.A. | Drivers R.E. | Drivers A.S.C. | Drivers Car M.T. R.A.S.C. | Drivers Lorry | Drivers Steam | Gunners | Gunners Howitzer | Smith Gunners | Range Takers | Farriers Serjeants | Farriers Corporals | Shoeing or Shoeing and Carriage Smiths | Cold Shoers | Wheelers R.A. | Wheelers H.T. | Wheelers M.T. | Saddlers or Harness Makers | Blacksmiths | Bricklayers and Masons | Carpenters and Joiners |
|---|---|---|---|---|---|---|---|---|---|---|---|---|---|---|---|---|---|---|---|---|---|
| CAVALRY— DEFICIENCY | | | | | | | | | | | | | | | | | | | | | |
| SURPLUS | | | | | | | | | | | | | | | | | | | | | |
| R.A.— DEFICIENCY | | | | | | | | | | | | | | | | | | | | | |
| SURPLUS | | | | | | | | | | | | | | | | | | | | | |
| R.E.— DEFICIENCY | | | | | | | | | | | | | | | | | | | | | |
| SURPLUS | | | | | | | | | | | | | | | | | | | | | |
| INFANTRY— DEFICIENCY | | | | | | | | | | | | | | | | | | | | | |
| SURPLUS | | | | | | | | | | | | | | | | | | | | | |
| R.A.M.C.— DEFICIENCY | | | | 2 | | | | | | | | | | | | | | | | | |
| SURPLUS | | | 4 | | | | | | | | | | | | | | | | | | |
| A.O.C.— DEFICIENCY | | | | | | | | | | | | | | | | | | | | | |
| SURPLUS | | | | | | | | | | | | | | | | | | | | | |
| A.V.C.— DEFICIENCY | | | | | | | | | | | | | | | | | | | | | |
| SURPLUS | | | | | | | | | | | | | | | | | | | | | |
| DEFICIENCY | | | | | | | | | | | | | | | | | | | | | |
| SURPLUS | | | | | | | | | | | | | | | | | | | | | |
| DEFICIENCY | | | | | | | | | | | | | | | | | | | | | |
| SURPLUS | | | | | | | | | | | | | | | | | | | | | |

| Detail of Wanting to Complete or Surplus. | Fitters & Turners (R.E.) Wood | Fitters & Turners (R.E.) Iron | Fitters R.A. | Fitters Wireless | Plumbers | Electricians Ordinary | Electricians W.T. | Signalmen | Engine Drivers Loco. | Engine Drivers Field | Air Line Men | Permanent Line Men | Operators, Telegraph | Cablemen | Brigade Section Pioneers | General-duty Pioneers | Signallers | Instrument Repairers | Motor Cyclist | Motor Cyclist Artificers | Telephonists | Clerks | Machine Gunners |
|---|---|---|---|---|---|---|---|---|---|---|---|---|---|---|---|---|---|---|---|---|---|---|---|
| CAVALRY— DEFICIENCY | | | | | | | | | | | | | | | | | | | | | | | |
| SURPLUS | | | | | | | | | | | | | | | | | | | | | | | |
| R.A.— DEFICIENCY | | | | | | | | | | | | | | | | | | | | | | | |
| SURPLUS | | | | | | | | | | | | | | | | | | | | | | | |
| R.E.— DEFICIENCY | | | | | | | | | | | | | | | | | | | | | | | |
| SURPLUS | | | | | | | | | | | | | | | | | | | | | | | |
| INFANTRY— DEFICIENCY | | | | | | | | | | | | | | | | | | | | | | | |
| SURPLUS | | | | | | | | | | | | | | | | | | | | | | | |
| R.A.M.C.— DEFICIENCY | | | | | | | | | | | | | | | | | | | | | | | |
| SURPLUS | | | | | | | | | | | | | | | | | | | | | | | |
| A.O.C.— DEFICIENCY | | | | | | | | | | | | | | | | | | | | | | | |
| SURPLUS | | | | | | | | | | | | | | | | | | | | | | | |
| A.V.C.— DEFICIENCY | | | | | | | | | | | | | | | | | | | | | | | |
| SURPLUS | | | | | | | | | | | | | | | | | | | | | | | |
| DEFICIENCY | | | | | | | | | | | | | | | | | | | | | | | |
| SURPLUS | | | | | | | | | | | | | | | | | | | | | | | |
| DEFICIENCY | | | | | | | | | | | | | | | | | | | | | | | |
| SURPLUS | | | | | | | | | | | | | | | | | | | | | | | |

| Detail of Wanting to Complete or Surplus. | Armament Artificers Fitters | Armament Artificers Range Finders | Armourers | Storemen | Privates | W.O.'s and N.C.O.'s (by ranks) not included in trade columns. Chls. R.A.M.C. | Sgts. do. | Sgts. R.A.S.C. | | | | | | | | | TOTAL to agree with wanting to complete or surplus Officers | TOTAL Other Ranks | Horses Riding | Horses Draught | Horses Heavy Draught | Horses Pack |
|---|---|---|---|---|---|---|---|---|---|---|---|---|---|---|---|---|---|---|---|---|---|---|
| CAVALRY— DEFICIENCY | | | | | | | | | | | | | | | | | | | | | | |
| SURPLUS | | | | | | | | | | | | | | | | | | | | | | |
| R.A.— DEFICIENCY | | | | | | | | | | | | | | | | | | | | | | |
| SURPLUS | | | | | | | | | | | | | | | | | | | | | | |
| R.E.— DEFICIENCY | | | | | | | | | | | | | | | | | | | | | | |
| SURPLUS | | | | | | | | | | | | | | | | | | | | | | |
| INFANTRY— DEFICIENCY | | | | | | | | | | | | | | | | | | | | | | |
| SURPLUS | | | | | | | | | | | | | | | | | | | | | | |
| R.A.M.C.— DEFICIENCY | | | | | 9 | | | | | | | | | | | | 1 | 11 | | | | |
| SURPLUS | | | | | | 1 | 1 | 1 | | | | | | | | | | 7 | 1 | 3 | 3 | |
| A.O.C.— DEFICIENCY | | | | | | | | | | | | | | | | | | | | | | |
| SURPLUS | | | | | | | | | | | | | | | | | | | | | | |
| A.V.C.— DEFICIENCY | | | | | | | | | | | | | | | | | | | | | | |
| SURPLUS | | | | | | | | | | | | | | | | | | | | | | |
| DEFICIENCY | | | | | | | | | | | | | | | | | | | | | | |
| SURPLUS | | | | | | | | | | | | | | | | | | | | | | |
| DEFICIENCY | | | | | | | | | | | | | | | | | | | | | | |
| SURPLUS | | | | | | | | | | | | | | | | | | | | | | |

Remarks :—

[illegible] Major Signature of Commander.

1/1 Lowland Field Ambce. Unit.

52 Div. Formation to which attached.

8-2-19 Date of Despatch.

(16523.) Wt. W6016—PP 1432. 1,500m. 3/18. D & S. (E1256) Forms B2138/3.

[P.T.O.

**To be made up to and for Saturday in each week**

No. of Report 155

# FIELD RETURN.

Army Form [illegible]213

(To be furnished by all arms, services, and departments (except A.S.C. units) to the A.G.'s Office at the Base in accordance with Field Service Regulations, Part II.)

RETURN showing numbers (*a*) Effective strength of Unit. (*b*) Rationed by Unit. 1/1 LOWLAND FIELD AMBCE at In the Field 15 · 2 · 19 Date.

| Details. | *Personnel: Officers | Other Ranks | Animals: Horses: Riding | Draught | Heavy Draught | Pack | Mules: Large | Small | Guns and transport vehicles: Guns, showing description | Ammunition wagons | Machine guns | Aircraft, showing description | Horsed: 4 Wheeled | 2 Wheeled | Mechanical: Motor Cars | Tractors | Lorries, showing description | Trucks, showing description | Trailers | Motor Bicycles | Bicycles | Motor Ambulances | Remarks (Number of Acting W.O.'s and N.C.O.'s included in effective strength to be shown in this column.) |
|---|---|---|---|---|---|---|---|---|---|---|---|---|---|---|---|---|---|---|---|---|---|---|---|
| Effective Strength of Unit ... | (a) 7 | (b) 149 | | | | | | | | | | | | | | | | | | | 1 | | (a) 1 on leave to U.K. – 1 at 1/4 R. Scots. 1 at Div. Rest Station. |
| Details by Arms attached to Unit as in War Establishment ... | | | | | | | | | | | | | | | | | | | | | | | (b) 35 at 1/2 Low. Fd. Ambce. 2 at 22 Cas. Station – 3 at A.D.M.S. 1 at 52 Div. Train – 1 at Concert Party. 2 on leave in France – 28 on D.R.S.[illegible] |
| R.A.S.C. (H.T.) | | (c) 33 | 6 | 14 | (e) 17 | | | | | | | | 13 | 4 | | | | | | | | | (c) 3 at Divl. Rest Station. 2 on leave to U.K. |
| R.A.S.C. (M.T.) | | (d) 11 | | | | | | | | | | | | | | | | | | 2 | | 7 | (d) 2 at [illegible] 52 Div. |
| Total ... | 7 | 195 | 6 | 14 | 17 | | | | | | | | 13 | 4 | | | | | | 2 | 1 | 7 | (e) 6 at Div. Rest Station |
| War Establishment ... | 8 | 203 | 5 | 13 | 16 | | | | | | | | 10 | 3 | | | | | | 2 | 1 | 7 | |
| Wanting to complete ... (Detail of Personnel and Horses below.) | 1 | 13x | | | | | | | | | | | | | | | | | | | | | x 13 R.A.M.C. – 2 R.A.S.C. (M.T.) |
| Surplus ... (Detail of Personnel and Horses below.) | | 5* | | | | | | | | | | | | | | | | | | | | | * R.A.S.C. (H.T.) |
| †Attached (not to include the details shown above) ... | | 4 | 1 | 1 | 1 | | | | | | | | 3 | 1 | | | | | | | | | Patients |
| Attached for Rations only ... | 1 | | | | | | | | | | | | | | | | | | | | | | Chaplain |
| Civilians Employed with and Accompanying the Unit ... | | | | | | | | | | | | | | | | | | | | | | | |
| ‡Detached from and struck off effective strength of own Unit ... | | | | | | | | | | | | | | | | | | | | | | | |
| ‡Detached from but retained on effective strength of own unit ... | | | | | | | | | | | | | | | | | | | | | | | |
| Total Rationed ... | 5 | 182 | 6 | 14 | 11 | | | | | | | | | | | | | | | | | | |

* Blank columns to be used for W.A.A.C. Natives or as may be required.

† In the case of field ambulances, hospitals or depots, the number of patients are to be included here, the names being shown in A.F.A. 36.

‡ These details to be enumerated by arms.

A D Downes Capt for Lt. Col. Signature of Commander.

15 · 2 · 19 Date of Despatch.

B 213

R.A.S.C. SECTION W E 15 - 2 - 19

| No. | Rank | Name | Casualty | Date |
|---|---|---|---|---|
| TH/247009 | Dr | McDonald D. | Granted leave to U.K. via Calais 15-2-19 - 15-3-19 (28 days) Credit Ration Allce. for that period at 2/4 p.d. | |

No. of W.O's. N.C.O's. men liable to be retained for Armies of Occupation

- NIL -

No of W.O's N.C.O's. men who have volunteered for duty with Armies of Occupation

- NIL -

*For information of the A.G.'s Office at the base:* R.A.S.C. Sheet attd.

Officers and men who have become casuals, been transferred or joined since last report.

Place In the Field    Date Feb. 15th 1919

| Regtl. Number | Rank | Name | Corps | Nature of casualty, or name of unit from or to which transferred. | Date of being struck off or coming on the ration return. | Remarks * |
|---|---|---|---|---|---|---|
| | Lt. Col. | J.D. Leitch D.S.O. | R.A.M.C. (T.F.) | Retd. from leave | 12/2/19 | |
| | do. | do. | do. | Granted extension of leave from 29.1.19 to 2.2.19 Athy. War Office 2.2.19 (A.M.D.1) | | |
| | | | | Further extension of leave 2.2.19 – 9.2.19 Athy. Brig. General i/c Administration London District | | |
| | do. | do. | do. | Credit Ration Allce. for above extension | | |
| 45854 | Pte. | Finlay J. | R.A.M.C. | To U.K. for Demobilization | 8/2/19 | |
| 36059 | " | McEwan H. | do. | do. | 8/2/19 | |
| 41974 | " | Phillips S. | do. | do. | 8/2/19 | |
| 4657 | " | Teal W. | do. | do. | 11/2/19 | |
| 21240 | " | Fenwick W. | do. | do. | 11/2/19 | |
| 316134 | " | Coleridge S. | R.A.M.C. (T.F.) | do. | 11/2/19 | |
| 338053 | " | Marshall G.W. | do. | Granted leave to Abbeville, France 11/2/19–18/2/19 (7 days) Credit Ration Allce. for period at 3/4d. | | |
| 316190 | " | McTavish D.B. | do. | Granted leave to Dunkirk, France. 11/2/19–18/2/19 (7 days) Credit Ration Allce. for period at 3/4d. | | |

Strength. Officers T.F. 6, R.A. 1 — 7

W.Os. N.C.Os. & Men

| | |
|---|---|
| W.O. | 1 |
| Q.M.S. | 1 |
| S. Sgts. | 2 |
| Sgts. | 8 |
| L. Sgts. | 1 |
| Cpls. | 6 |
| L/ Cpls. | 3 |
| Ptes. | 127 |
| | 149 |

All Category "A"

No. of W.O's., N.C.O's & Men liable to be retained for Army of Occupation:- Ptes. 3

No. of W.O's. N.C.O's & Men who have volunteered for Army of Occupation :- Nil

* State whether absence is of a permanent or temporary nature, adding, in the case of casuals from wounds or disease any available information for communication to the relatives.

*The perforated sheet is not to be used to record casualties; additional sheets, preferably foolscap, to be attached when necessary. These sheets to be carefully numbered and the number of attached sheets to be noted here.*

Perforated Sheet giving detail of personnel and horses wanting to complete or surplus, shown on Army Form B. 213.

No. of Report 165

| Detail of Wanting to Complete or Surplus. | Drivers. R.A. | Drivers. R.E. | Drivers. A.S.C. | Drivers. Car | Drivers. Lorry (M.T. R.A.S.C.) | Drivers. Steam | Gunners | Gunners Howitzer | Smith Gunners | Range Takers | Farriers Serjeants | Farriers Corporals | Shoeing or Shoeing and Carriage Smiths | Cold Shoers | Wheelers R.A. | Wheelers H.T. | Wheelers M.T. | Saddlers or Harness Makers | Blacksmiths | Bricklayers and Masons | Carpenters and Joiners | Fitters & Turners (R.E.) Wood | Fitters & Turners (R.E.) Iron | Fitters R.A. | Fitters Wireless. | Plumbers | Electricians Ordinary | Electricians W.T. | Signalmen. | Engine Drivers Loco. | Engine Drivers Field | Air Line Men. | Permanent Line Men | Operators, Telegraph | Cablemen | Brigade Section Pioneers | General-duty Pioneers | Signallers | Instrument Repairers | Motor Cyclist | Motor Cyclist Artificers | Telephonists | Clerks | Machine Gunners | Armament Artificers Fitters | Armament Artificers Range Finders | Armourers | Storemen | Privates | W.O.'s and N.C.O.'s (by ranks) not included in trade columns. Cpl. R.A.M.C.T. | Sgt. do. | Sgt. R.A.S.C. | | | | | | | | TOTAL to agree with wanting to complete or surplus. Officers | TOTAL Other Ranks | Horses Riding | Horses Draught | Horses Heavy Draught | Horses Pack |
|---|---|---|---|---|---|---|---|---|---|---|---|---|---|---|---|---|---|---|---|---|---|---|---|---|---|---|---|---|---|---|---|---|---|---|---|---|---|---|---|---|---|---|---|---|---|---|---|---|---|---|---|---|---|---|---|---|---|---|---|---|---|---|---|---|---|
| CAVALRY— DEFICIENCY | | | | | | | | | | | | | | | | | | | | | | | | | | | | | | | | | | | | | | | | | | | | | | | | | | | | | | | | | | | | | | | | | |
| SURPLUS | | | | | | | | | | | | | | | | | | | | | | | | | | | | | | | | | | | | | | | | | | | | | | | | | | | | | | | | | | | | | | | | | |
| R.A.— DEFICIENCY | | | | | | | | | | | | | | | | | | | | | | | | | | | | | | | | | | | | | | | | | | | | | | | | | | | | | | | | | | | | | | | | | |
| SURPLUS | | | | | | | | | | | | | | | | | | | | | | | | | | | | | | | | | | | | | | | | | | | | | | | | | | | | | | | | | | | | | | | | | |
| R.E.— DEFICIENCY | | | | | | | | | | | | | | | | | | | | | | | | | | | | | | | | | | | | | | | | | | | | | | | | | | | | | | | | | | | | | | | | | |
| SURPLUS | | | | | | | | | | | | | | | | | | | | | | | | | | | | | | | | | | | | | | | | | | | | | | | | | | | | | | | | | | | | | | | | | |
| INFANTRY— DEFICIENCY | | | | | | | | | | | | | | | | | | | | | | | | | | | | | | | | | | | | | | | | | | | | | | | | | | | | | | | | | | | | | | | | | |
| SURPLUS | | | | | | | | | | | | | | | | | | | | | | | | | | | | | | | | | | | | | | | | | | | | | | | | | | | | | | | | | | | | | | | | | |
| R.A.M.C.— DEFICIENCY | | | | 2 | | | | | | | | | | | | | | | | | | | | | | | | | | | | | | | | | | | | | | | | | | | | | 15 | | | | | | | | | | | 1 | 17 | | | | |
| SURPLUS | | | 4 | | | | | | | | | | | | | | | | | | | | | | | | | | | | | | | | | | | | | | | | | | | | | | | 1 | 1 | 1 | | | | | | | | | 7 | - | - | - | |
| A.O.C.— DEFICIENCY | | | | | | | | | | | | | | | | | | | | | | | | | | | | | | | | | | | | | | | | | | | | | | | | | | | | | | | | | | | | | | | | | |
| SURPLUS | | | | | | | | | | | | | | | | | | | | | | | | | | | | | | | | | | | | | | | | | | | | | | | | | | | | | | | | | | | | | | | | | |
| A.V.C.— DEFICIENCY | | | | | | | | | | | | | | | | | | | | | | | | | | | | | | | | | | | | | | | | | | | | | | | | | | | | | | | | | | | | | | | | | |
| SURPLUS | | | | | | | | | | | | | | | | | | | | | | | | | | | | | | | | | | | | | | | | | | | | | | | | | | | | | | | | | | | | | | | | | |
| DEFICIENCY | | | | | | | | | | | | | | | | | | | | | | | | | | | | | | | | | | | | | | | | | | | | | | | | | | | | | | | | | | | | | | | | | |
| SURPLUS | | | | | | | | | | | | | | | | | | | | | | | | | | | | | | | | | | | | | | | | | | | | | | | | | | | | | | | | | | | | | | | | | |
| DEFICIENCY | | | | | | | | | | | | | | | | | | | | | | | | | | | | | | | | | | | | | | | | | | | | | | | | | | | | | | | | | | | | | | | | | |
| SURPLUS | | | | | | | | | | | | | | | | | | | | | | | | | | | | | | | | | | | | | | | | | | | | | | | | | | | | | | | | | | | | | | | | | |

Remarks :—

A D Downes Capt. for Lt. Col. Signature of Commander.

1/1 Lowland Field Ambce. Unit.

52 Div. Formation to which attached.

15 - 2 - 19. Date of Despatch.

(17828.) Wt. W2281—P 1075. 2,750m. 6/18. D & S. (E1256) Forms B2138/11.

[P.T.O.

**To be made up to and for Saturday in each week**

No. of Report 186

# FIELD RETURN.

Army Form B. 213

(To be furnished by all arms, services, and departments (except A.S.C. units) to the A.G.'s Office at the Base in accordance with Field Service Regulations, Part II.)

RETURN showing numbers (*a*) Effective strength of Unit. (*b*) Rationed by Unit. 1st Lowland Field Ambce. at In the Field Date. 22. 2. 19

| Details. | *Personnel: Officers | Other Ranks | | | | Animals: Horses: Riding | Draught | Heavy Draught | Pack | Mules: Large | Small | Guns and transport vehicles: Guns, showing description | Ammunition wagons | Machine guns | Aircraft, showing description | Horsed: † 4 Wheeled | 2 Wheeled | Mechanical: Motor Cars | Tractors | Lorries, showing description | Trucks, showing description | Trailers | Motor Bicycles | Bicycles | Motor Ambulances |
|---|---|---|---|---|---|---|---|---|---|---|---|---|---|---|---|---|---|---|---|---|---|---|---|---|---|
| Effective Strength of Unit ... ... | (a) 7 | (b) 149 | | | | | | | | | | | | | | | | | | | | | | 1 | |
| Details by Arms attached to Unit as in War Establishment ... ... ... | | | | | | | | | | | | | | | | | | | | | | | | | |
| R.A.S.C. (H.T.) | | (c) 32 | | | | 6 | 13 | (d) 1 | | | | | | | | 13 | 4 | | | | | | | | |
| R.A.S.C. (M.T.) | | (d) 11 | | | | | | | | | | | | | | | | | | | | | 2 | | 7 |
| Total ... ... | 7 | 192 | | | | 6 | 13 | 1 | | | | | | | | 13 | 4 | | | | | | 2 | 1 | 7 |
| War Establishment ... ... ... | 8 | 203 | | | | 5 | 13 | 6 | | | | | | | | 10 | 3 | | | | | | 2 | 1 | 7 |
| Wanting to complete ... ... ... (Detail of Personnel and Horses below.) | 1 | 15 × | | | | | | | | | | | | | | | | | | | | | | | |
| Surplus ... ... (Detail of Personnel and Horses below.) | | 4 × | | | | 1 | | 1 | | | | | | | | 3 | 1 | | | | | | | | |
| †Attached (not to include the details shown above) ... ... ... ... | | 8 | | | | | | | | | | | | | | | | | | | | | | | |
| Attached for Rations only ... ... | 1 | | | | | | | | | | | | | | | | | | | | | | | | |
| Civilians Employed with and Accompanying the Unit ... ... ... | | | | | | | | | | | | | | | | | | | | | | | | | |
| ‡Detached from and struck off effective strength of own Unit ... ... | | | | | | | | | | | | | | | | | | | | | | | | | |
| ‡Detached from but retained on effective strength of own unit... ... ... | | | | | | | | | | | | | | | | | | | | | | | | | |
| Total Rationed ... | 5 | 16 | | | | 6 | 13 | 11 | | | | | | | | | | | | | | | | | |

**Remarks** (Number of Acting W.O.'s and N.C.O.'s included in effective strength to be shown in this column.)

(a) 1 on leave to U.K. – 1 at 1/4 R.S.
1 at Div. Rest Station
(b) 33 at [illegible] for Arms.
2 at 22 San. Secn. – 3 at A.D.M.S.
1 at [illegible] – 1 at [illegible]
3 on leave – 28 at D.R. Stn.
6 left unit for demobilization
1 at 9 Bde. R.F.A.
(c) 3 on leave – 3 at D.R. Stn.
(d) 2 at A.D.M.S. – 1 at 9 Bde. R.F.A.
(e) 6 at O.R. Stn.

× 13 R.A.M.C. – 2 R.A.S.C. (M.T.)
× R.A.S.C. (H.T.)
Patients
Chaplain

* Blank columns to be used for W.A.A.C. Natives or as may be required.

† In the case of field ambulances, hospitals or depots, the number of patients are to be included here, the names being shown in A.F.A. 36.
‡ These details to be enumerated by arms.

[illegible] Lt. Col. Signature of Commander.

22. 2. 19. Date of Despatch.

B213

R.A.S.C. SECTION W/E 22.2.19.

| No. | Rank | Name | Casualty | Date |
|---|---|---|---|---|
| T/19200 | SSM | Lackley T. | Granted leave to Paris 6/2/19 – 25/2/19. [illegible] to | period. |
| T4/243601 | Do | Burrows W. | Sick to hospital | 15/2/19 |

No. of W.Os. N.C.Os. & men liable to be retained for Armies of Occupation

– NIL –

No of W.Os. N.C.Os. & men who have volunteered for duty with Armies of Occupation

– NIL –

R.A.S.C.
Sheet attd.

*For information of the A.G.'s Office at the base.*

In the Field 27.2.19

Officers and men who have become casuals, been transferred or joined since last report.

Place ______________________ Date ______________________

| Regtl. Number | Rank | Name | Corps | Nature of casualty, or name of unit from or to which transferred | Date of being struck off or coming on the ration return | Remarks * |
|---|---|---|---|---|---|---|
| [illegible]4 | Pte. | Johnson | R.A.F.M.C.(T.) | 16/2/19 – 23/10 [illegible] | | [illegible] @ 24 p.o. |
| [illegible]100 | Pte. | McTavish | [illegible] | do. | Returned from leave | 19/2/19 |

Drivers T.E. 6
R.N. 1
Total 7

| W.O. N.C.O. & Men | |
|---|---|
| W.O. | 1 |
| Q.M.S. | 1 |
| S. Sgts. | 2 |
| Sgts. | 8 |
| L. Sgt. | 1 |
| Cpls. | 6 |
| L. Cpls. | 3 |
| Ptes. | 127 |
| Total | 140 |

A.1 Category
" " 57

No. of W.Os. N.C.Os. & men liable to be returned for Armies of Occupation: Ptes. 3

No. of W.Os. N.C.Os. & men who have volunteered for duty with Armies of Occupation: NIL

* State whether absence is of a permanent or temporary nature, adding, in the case of casuals from wounds or disease, any available information for communication to the relatives.

*The perforated sheet is not to be used to record casualties; additional sheets, preferably foolscap, to be attached when necessary. These sheets to be carefully numbered and the number of attached sheets to be noted here.*

Perforated Sheet giving detail of personnel and horses wanting to complete or surplus, shown on Army Form B. 213.

No. of Report 196

| Detail of Wanting to Complete or Surplus. | Drivers. R.A. | Drivers. R.E. | Drivers. A.S.C. M.T.-R.A.S.C. | Drivers. Car | Drivers. Lorry | Drivers. Steam | Gunners | Gunners Howitzer | Smith Gunners | Range Takers | Farriers Serjeants | Farriers Corporals | Shoeing or Shoeing and Carriage Smiths | Cold Shoers | Wheelers R.A. | Wheelers H.T. | Wheelers M.T. | Saddlers or Harness Makers | Blacksmiths | Bricklayers and Masons | Carpenters and Joiners | Fitters & Turners (R.E.) Wood | Fitters & Turners (R.E.) Iron | Fitters R.A. | Fitters Wireless. | Plumbers | Electricians Ordinary | Electricians W.T. | Signalmen. | Engine Drivers Loco. | Engine Drivers Field | Air Line Men. | Permanent Line Men |
|---|---|---|---|---|---|---|---|---|---|---|---|---|---|---|---|---|---|---|---|---|---|---|---|---|---|---|---|---|---|---|---|---|---|
| CAVALRY—Deficiency | | | | | | | | | | | | | | | | | | | | | | | | | | | | | | | | | |
| Surplus | | | | | | | | | | | | | | | | | | | | | | | | | | | | | | | | | |
| R.A.—Deficiency | | | | | | | | | | | | | | | | | | | | | | | | | | | | | | | | | |
| Surplus | | | | | | | | | | | | | | | | | | | | | | | | | | | | | | | | | |
| R.E.—Deficiency | | | | | | | | | | | | | | | | | | | | | | | | | | | | | | | | | |
| Surplus | | | | | | | | | | | | | | | | | | | | | | | | | | | | | | | | | |
| INFANTRY—Deficiency | | | | | | | | | | | | | | | | | | | | | | | | | | | | | | | | | |
| Surplus | | | | | | | | | | | | | | | | | | | | | | | | | | | | | | | | | |
| R.A.M.C.—Deficiency | | 3 | 2 | | | | | | | | | | | | | | | | | | | | | | | | | | | | | | |
| Surplus | | | | | | | | | | | | | | | | | | | | | | | | | | | | | | | | | |
| A.O.C.—Deficiency | | | | | | | | | | | | | | | | | | | | | | | | | | | | | | | | | |
| Surplus | | | | | | | | | | | | | | | | | | | | | | | | | | | | | | | | | |
| A.V.C.—Deficiency | | | | | | | | | | | | | | | | | | | | | | | | | | | | | | | | | |
| Surplus | | | | | | | | | | | | | | | | | | | | | | | | | | | | | | | | | |
| Deficiency | | | | | | | | | | | | | | | | | | | | | | | | | | | | | | | | | |
| Surplus | | | | | | | | | | | | | | | | | | | | | | | | | | | | | | | | | |
| Deficiency | | | | | | | | | | | | | | | | | | | | | | | | | | | | | | | | | |
| Surplus | | | | | | | | | | | | | | | | | | | | | | | | | | | | | | | | | |

| Detail of Wanting to Complete or Surplus. | Operators, Telegraph | Cablemen | Brigade Section Pioneers | General-duty Pioneers | Signallers | Instrument Repairers | Motor Cyclist | Motor Cyclist Artificers | Telephonists | Clerks | Machine Gunners | Armament Artificers Fitters | Armament Artificers Range Finders | Armourers | Storemen | Privates Pte. R.A.M.C. | W.O.'s and N.C.O.'s (by ranks) not included in trade columns. Sgt. R.A.M.C. | Sp. R.A.S.C. (H.T.) | | | | | | | | | | TOTAL to agree with wanting to complete or surplus Officers | TOTAL Other Ranks | Horses Riding | Horses Draught | Horses Heavy Draught | Horses Pack |
|---|---|---|---|---|---|---|---|---|---|---|---|---|---|---|---|---|---|---|---|---|---|---|---|---|---|---|---|---|---|---|---|---|---|
| CAVALRY—Deficiency | | | | | | | | | | | | | | | | | | | | | | | | | | | | | | | | | |
| Surplus | | | | | | | | | | | | | | | | | | | | | | | | | | | | | | | | | |
| R.A.—Deficiency | | | | | | | | | | | | | | | | | | | | | | | | | | | | | | | | | |
| Surplus | | | | | | | | | | | | | | | | | | | | | | | | | | | | | | | | | |
| R.E.—Deficiency | | | | | | | | | | | | | | | | | | | | | | | | | | | | | | | | | |
| Surplus | | | | | | | | | | | | | | | | | | | | | | | | | | | | | | | | | |
| INFANTRY—Deficiency | | | | | | | | | | | | | | | | | | | | | | | | | | | | | | | | | |
| Surplus | | | | | | | | | | | | | | | | | | | | | | | | | | | | | | | | | |
| R.A.M.C.—Deficiency | | | | | | | | | | | | | | | 15 | | | | | | | | | | | | 1 | 17 | | | | | |
| Surplus | | | | | | | | | | | | | | | | 1 | 1 | 1 | | | | | | | | | | 6 | 1 | | 1 | | |
| A.O.C.—Deficiency | | | | | | | | | | | | | | | | | | | | | | | | | | | | | | | | | |
| Surplus | | | | | | | | | | | | | | | | | | | | | | | | | | | | | | | | | |
| A.V.C.—Deficiency | | | | | | | | | | | | | | | | | | | | | | | | | | | | | | | | | |
| Surplus | | | | | | | | | | | | | | | | | | | | | | | | | | | | | | | | | |
| Deficiency | | | | | | | | | | | | | | | | | | | | | | | | | | | | | | | | | |
| Surplus | | | | | | | | | | | | | | | | | | | | | | | | | | | | | | | | | |
| Deficiency | | | | | | | | | | | | | | | | | | | | | | | | | | | | | | | | | |
| Surplus | | | | | | | | | | | | | | | | | | | | | | | | | | | | | | | | | |

Remarks :—

John [illegible] Lt. Col. Signature of Commander.

1/1 Lowland Field Ambce. Unit.

52 Div. Formation to which attached.

22. 2. 19. Date of Despatch.

(17828.) Wt. W2281—P 1075. 2,750m. 6/18. D & S. (E1256) Forms B2138/11.

[P.T.O.

14

1st Low. Fd Amb.

Mar. 1919

Vol 12

140/3771

WAR. DIARY

March

1919

533

Instructions regarding War Diaries and Intelligence Summaries are contained in F. S. Regs., Part II. and the Staff Manual respectively. Title pages will be prepared in manuscript.

# WAR DIARY
*or*
# INTELLIGENCE SUMMARY.
(*Erase heading not required.*)

Army Form C. 2118.

1/1st Lowland Fd Amblce
52nd Div

| Place | Date | Hour | Summary of Events and Information | Remarks and references to Appendices |
|---|---|---|---|---|
| CHAUSEE N-D LOUVIGNIES Sh 38 W5646 | 1/3/19 | | Nothing to note RDM | |
| | 2/3/19 | | A.D.M.S. 52nd Div R 1820/9 asks for report as to disposal of AFD books required for historical purposes. RDM Capt Rennie reports from leave, absence explained. | |
| | 3/3/19 | | Capt. Burton off strength, M.O. to 1/4 Roy Scots. Major A.D.M.S. 52nd Div. R1836/9. Five H.D. CZ horses to proceed for sale. RDM | |
| | 4/3/19 | | Report on D.R.S. Lens forwarded citing improvements in accommodation & other changes. RDM | |
| | 5/3/19 | | Nothing to report. RDM | |
| | 6/3/19 | | do do do RDM | |
| | 7/3/19 | | Major A.D.M.S. R1865/1 One NCO. & 19 O.R. detailed for temp'y duty with 1/2nd Low. Fd Amb'ce for temp'y duty. RDM | |

D. D. & L., London, E.C.
(10340) Wt W5300/P713 750,000 3/18 S 2688 Forms/C2118/15.

534

Army Form C. 2118.

Instructions regarding War Diaries and Intelligence Summaries are contained in F. S. Regs., Part II. and the Staff Manual respectively. Title pages will be prepared in manuscript.

# WAR DIARY *or* INTELLIGENCE SUMMARY.

*(Erase heading not required.)*

1/1st Lowland Fd Ambce

| Place | Date | Hour | Summary of Events and Information | Remarks and references to Appendices |
|---|---|---|---|---|
| CHAUSEE N-D LOUVIGNIES Sh 38 W 8646 | 8/3/19 | | Nothing to note NBm | |
| | 9/3/19 | | A.D.M.S. R1415/13 :— One man per day to be held in readiness to proceed to Concent Camp Mons for Demob. NBm | |
| | 10/3/19 | | Nothing to note NBm | |
| | 11/3/19 | | Seven "Z" animals sent to SOIGNIES for Sale NBm | |
| | 12/3/19 | | Nothing to note NBm | |
| | 13/3/19 | | A.D.M.S. R1907/4 Secret, urgent received & acted on. SOIGNIES visited & reported on to A.D.M.S. as to suitable accommodation; ~~Hospital~~ Hospital ~~&~~ Buildings &c for two Cadres & one Fd. Ambce. NBm | |
| | 14/3/19 | | A.D.M.S. R1915/13 embodying "Deported" wire ordering MAJOR W.F. MACKENZIE ~~O.C. 1/1st Lowld Fd Amb~~ to report to W.O. for Demob. NBm | |
| | 15/3/19 | | 15 6.Z. horses proceed to MONS for entrainment | |

D. D. & L., London, E.C. (10340) Wt W5300/P713 750,000 3/18 & 2688 Forms/C2118/15.

N Ferguson [illegible] Major

Instructions regarding War Diaries and Intelligence Summaries are contained in F. S. Regs., Part II. and the Staff Manual respectively. Title pages will be prepared in manuscript.

# WAR DIARY
*or*
# INTELLIGENCE SUMMARY.
*(Erase heading not required.)*

Army Form C. 2118.

535

1/1st Low. Fd. Ambce

| Place | Date | Hour | Summary of Events and Information | Remarks and references to Appendices |
|---|---|---|---|---|
| CHAUSSEE N.D. LOUVIGNIES | 15/3/19 | | Capt R.A. LENNIE, R.A.M.C.(T.F.) assumed command of this Ambce, on departure of A/Major, Capt W.F. MACKENZIE to U.K. for demobilization. RAL | |
| " | 16/3/19 | | Nothing to note RAL | |
| SOIGNIES | 17/3/19 | | Ref ADMS 52nd Div. R 1907/4 instructions this Unit moved to Soignies from Chaussee N.D. Louvignies. Marching in state. Officers 3. O.RANKS 45. R.A.S.C.(H.T.) 18 R.A.S.C.(M.T.) o.Ranks 9. Horses H.D. 2., L.D. 2. 4 wheeled vehicles 13; 2 wheeled vehicles 4. (Horses from Q. Branch 52nd Div. were supplied for haulage purposes) Ambulance Cars 4. RAL<br>The Convent Rue de la STATION, SOIGNIES was taken over as a hospital, and for the housing of the personnel of Ambce RAL<br>Move was completed by 1545 RAL | |
| SOIGNIES | 18/3/19 | | Nothing to note RAL | |
| " | 19/3/19 | | Ref ADMS 52nd Div. instructions R1907/4 billets were alloted by me to Officers and o.Ranks of 1/2, and 1/3 Lowland Fld. Ambces, Cadres. RAL | |
| | 20/3/19 | | Nothing to note RAL. | |
| | 21/3/19 | | Arrival of cadre of 1/3 Lowland Fld Ambce. Conjointly installed with this unit. RAL | |

R.A. Lennie Capt
O.C. 1/1 Lowland Fld Ambce

D. D. & L., London, E.C.
(10340) Wt W5300/P713 750,000 3/18 Sch. 2688 Forms/C2118/15.

536.

Army Form C. 2118.

Instructions regarding War Diaries and Intelligence Summaries are contained in F. S. Regs., Part II. and the Staff Manual respectively. Title pages will be prepared in manuscript.

# WAR DIARY
or
# INTELLIGENCE SUMMARY.
(Erase heading not required.)

1/1st Low. Fd. Ambce.

| Place | Date | Hour | Summary of Events and Information | Remarks and references to Appendices |
|---|---|---|---|---|
| SOIGNIES | 22/3/19 | | Arrival of cadre of 1/2 Lowland Fld. Ambce. Installed with cadres of 1/1st and 1/3rd Lowland Fld Ambces. RAL<br>Hospital run conjointly by personnel drawn from the cadres of the 3 Ambces.<br>Capt. A/Major WALKER R. R. 1/3 Lowland Fld Ambce, acting as S. M. O. RAL | |
| " | 23/3/19 | | ~~Nothing to~~ Ref ADMS 52nd Div. R. 1965/5, CAPT J. EVANS RAMC of this unit, reported to C.R.E. 52nd Div. for duty. RAL | |
| " | 24/3/19 | | CAPT A.D. DOWNES RAMC (T.F.) returned from U.K. leave. RAL | |
| " | 25/3/19 | | Ref ADMS 52nd Div. R1962/5 CAPT A.D. DOWNES RAMC (T.F.) proceeded to UK for Demobilization. RAL | |
| " | 26/3/19 | | Nothing to note RAL | |
| " | 27/3/19 | | Nothing to note RAL | |
| | 28/3/19 | | Nothing to note RAL | |
| | 29/3/19 | | Ref ADMS 52nd Div. R2007/1, 9 Ptes sent to report to O.C. 32nd C.C.S. for tempy duty. RAL | |
| | 30/3/19 | | 9 Ptes above, returned from tempy duty at 32nd C.C.S. | |
| | 31/3/19 | | Nothing to note | |

R A Lennie
Capt
O.C. 1/1 Lowland Fld Ambce

D. D. & L., London, E.C. (10,340) Wt W5300/P713 750,000 3/18 Sch. 52a Forms/C2118/15.

**To be made up to and for Saturday in each week**

No. of Report Nil.

# FIELD RETURN.

Army Form B. 213

(To be furnished by all arms, services, and departments (except A.S.C. units) to the A.G.'s Office at the Base in accordance with Field Service Regulations, Part II.)

RETURN showing numbers (a) Effective strength of Unit. (b) Rationed by Unit. 1/1 Lowland Field Ambce. at Chaussee N. D. 1 - 3 - 19 Date.

| Details. | *Personnel: Officers | Other Ranks | | | | Animals: Horses: Riding | Draught | Heavy Draught | Pack | Mules: Large | Small | Guns and transport vehicles: Guns, showing description | Ammunition wagons | Machine guns | Aircraft, showing description | Horsed: 4 Wheeled | 2 Wheeled | Motor Cars | Tractors | Mechanical: Lorries, showing description | Trucks, showing description | Trailers | Motor Bicycles | Bicycles | Motor Ambulances | Remarks (Number of Acting W.O.'s and N.C.O.'s included in effective strength to be shown in this column.) |
|---|---|---|---|---|---|---|---|---|---|---|---|---|---|---|---|---|---|---|---|---|---|---|---|---|---|---|
| Effective Strength of Unit ... | 6 (a) | 150 (b) | | | | | | | | | | | | | | | | | | | | | | 1 | | (a) 1 at 1/4 R.S. – 1 on leave to U.K. [illegible] 2 at 23 San. Sect. – 3 at R.D.M.S. [illegible] |
| Details by Arms attached to Unit as in War Establishment ... | | | | | | | | | | | | | | | | | | | | | | | | | | (b) 1 at 57 San. Train – 1 at Casualty [illegible] 2 on leave UK – 1 at 9 Bde. R.F.A. 12 [illegible] |
| R.A.S.C. (H.T.) | | 33 (c) | | | | 5 | 10 | 16 (e) | | | | | | | | 13 | 4 | | | | | | | | | (c) 3 on leave – [illegible] |
| R.A.S.C. (M.T.) | | 11 (d) | | | | | | | | | | | | | | | | | | | | | 2 | | 7 | (d) 2 at A.D.M.S. – 1 at 9 Bde. R.F.A. |
| Total ... | 6 | 194 | | | | 5 | 10 | 16 | | | | | | | | 13 | 4 | | | | | | 2 | 1 | 7 | |
| War Establishment ... | 8 | 208 | | | | 5 | 13 | 16 | | | | | | | | 10 | 3 | | | | | | 2 | 1 | 7 | |
| Wanting to complete ... (Detail of Personnel and Horses below.) | 2 | 14 | | | | | 3 | | | | | | | | | | | | | | | | | | | 12 R.A.M.C. – 2 R.A.S.C. (M.T.) |
| Surplus ... (Detail of Personnel and Horses below.) | | 5 | | | | | | | | | | | | | | 3 | 1 | | | | | | | | | 5 R.A.S.C. (H.T.) |
| †Attached (not to include the details shown above) ... | | 15 | | | | | | | | | | | | | | | | | | | | | | | | Patients |
| Attached for Rations only ... | 1 | | | | | | | | | | | | | | | | | | | | | | | | | Chaplain |
| Civilians Employed with and Accompanying the Unit ... | | | | | | | | | | | | | | | | | | | | | | | | | | |
| ‡Detached from and struck off effective strength of own Unit ... | | | | | | | | | | | | | | | | | | | | | | | | | | |
| ‡Detached from but retained on effective strength of own unit ... | | 1° | | | | | | | | | | | | | | | | | | | | | | | 1° | ° R.A.S.C. (M.T.) (32 F.A.) |
| Total Rationed ... | 5 | 165 | | | | 5 | 10 | 16 | | | | | | | | | | | | | | | | | | |

* Blank columns to be used for W.A.A.C. Natives or as may be required.

† In the case of field ambulances, hospitals or depots, the number of patients are to be included here, the names being shown in A.F.A. 36.

‡ These details to be enumerated by arms.

Major [signature] Signature of Commander.

1 - 3 - 19 Date of Despatch.

B 213

R.A.S.C. Section

No 8 1.3.19.

| No. | Rank | Name | Casualty | Date |
|---|---|---|---|---|
| M4/244361. | Dr | Burton W. | Reinforcement ex Hosp. | 23/2/19 |

No. of W.O. [illegible] other ranks liable to be retained for Armies of Occupation.

No. of W.Os. N.C.Os. & Men who have volunteered for duty with Armies of Occupation

NIL.

*For information of the A.G.'s Office at the base.*

Officers and men who have become casuals, been transferred or joined since last report.

Place CHAUSSÉE N. D. Date 1 - 3 - 19

| Regtl. Number | Rank | Name | Corps | Nature of casualty, or name of unit from or to which transferred. | Date of being struck off or coming on the ration return. | Remarks * |
|---|---|---|---|---|---|---|
| | Lt. | [illegible] | D.S.O. R.F.A. [illegible] | [illegible] | 25/2/19 | |
| | - do - | - do - | - do - | [illegible] Rank on 25-2-19 [illegible] | | |
| [illegible] | Pte. | [illegible] | Sd. R.A.M.C. T. | [illegible] | 22/2/19 | |
| [illegible] | " | [illegible] | - do - | [illegible] 52 Div. M.T. [illegible] | 22/2/19 | |
| [illegible] | " | White | - do - | Granted leave to U.K. via Calais 20-2-19 to 13-3-19 (14 days) [illegible] Special [illegible] 52 Div. [illegible] | | Credit [illegible] |

No. of W.O's. N.C.O's & Men liable to be retained for duty with Armies of Occupation :- Ptes. 3

No. of W.O's N.C.O's & Men who have volunteered for duty with Armies of Occupation :- NIL

| | |
|---|---|
| T.F. | 5 |
| [illegible] | 1 |
| | 6 |

W.O. N.C.O. & MEN

| | |
|---|---|
| W.O. | 1 |
| Q.M.S. | 1 |
| S. Sgt. | 2 |
| Sgt. | 4 |
| [illegible] Sgt. | 1 |
| Cpls. | 6 |
| [illegible] | 3 |
| Ptes. | 126 |
| | 150 |

* State whether absence is of a permanent or temporary nature, adding, in the case of casuals from wounds or disease, any available information for communication to the relatives.

*The perforated sheet is not to be used to record casualties; additional sheets, preferably foolscap, to be attached when necessary. These sheets to be carefully numbered and the number of attached sheets to be noted here.*

Perforated Sheet giving detail of personnel and horses wanting to complete or surplus, shown on Army Form B. 213.

No. of Report ____________

| Detail of Wanting to Complete or Surplus. | Drivers. | | | | | | Gunners | Gunners Howitzer | Smith Gunners | Range Takers | Farriers | | Shoeing or Shoeing and Carriage Smiths | Cold Shoers | Wheelers | | | Saddlers or Harness Makers | Blacksmiths | Bricklayers and Masons | Carpenters and Joiners | Fitters & Turners (R.E.) | | Fitters | | Plumbers | Electricians | | Signalmen. | Engine Drivers | | Air Line Men. | Permanent Line Men | Operators, Telegraph | Cablemen | Brigade Section Pioneers | General-duty Pioneers | Signallers | Instrument Repairers | Motor Cyclist | Motor Cyclist Artificers | Telephonists | Clerks | Machine Gunners | Armament Artificers | | Armourers | Storemen | Privates | W.O.'s and N.C.O.'s (by ranks) not included in trade columns. | | | | | | | | | | | TOTAL to agree with wanting to complete or surplus | | Horses | | | |
|---|---|---|---|---|---|---|---|---|---|---|---|---|---|---|---|---|---|---|---|---|---|---|---|---|---|---|---|---|---|---|---|---|---|---|---|---|---|---|---|---|---|---|---|---|---|---|---|---|---|---|---|---|---|---|---|---|---|---|---|---|---|---|---|---|---|---|
| | R.A. | R.E. | A.S.C. | Car | Lorry | Steam | | | | | Serjeants | Corporals | | | R.A. | H.T. | M.T. | | | | | Wood | Iron | R.A. | Wireless. | | Ordinary | W.T. | | Loco. | Field | | | | | | | | | | | | | | Fitters | Range Finders | | | | | | | | | | | | | | | Officers | Other Ranks | Riding | Draught | Heavy Draught | Pack |
| CAVALRY— DEFICIENCY | | | | | | | | | | | | | | | | | | | | | | | | | | | | | | | | | | | | | | | | | | | | | | | | | | | | | | | | | | | | | | | | | | | |
| SURPLUS | | | | | | | | | | | | | | | | | | | | | | | | | | | | | | | | | | | | | | | | | | | | | | | | | | | | | | | | | | | | | | | | | | |
| R.A.— DEFICIENCY | | | | | | | | | | | | | | | | | | | | | | | | | | | | | | | | | | | | | | | | | | | | | | | | | | | | | | | | | | | | | | | | | | |
| SURPLUS | | | | | | | | | | | | | | | | | | | | | | | | | | | | | | | | | | | | | | | | | | | | | | | | | | | | | | | | | | | | | | | | | | |
| R.E.— DEFICIENCY | | | | | | | | | | | | | | | | | | | | | | | | | | | | | | | | | | | | | | | | | | | | | | | | | | | | | | | | | | | | | | | | | | |
| SURPLUS | | | | | | | | | | | | | | | | | | | | | | | | | | | | | | | | | | | | | | | | | | | | | | | | | | | | | | | | | | | | | | | | | | |
| INFANTRY— DEFICIENCY | | | | | | | | | | | | | | | | | | | | | | | | | | | | | | | | | | | | | | | | | | | | | | | | | | | | | | | | | | | | | | | | | | |
| SURPLUS | | | | | | | | | | | | | | | | | | | | | | | | | | | | | | | | | | | | | | | | | | | | | | | | | | | | | | | | | | | | | | | | | | |
| R.A.M.C.— DEFICIENCY | | | | | | | | | | | | | | | | | | | | | | | | | | | | | | | | | | | | | | | | | | | | | | | | | | | | | | | | | | | | | | | | | | |
| SURPLUS | | | | | | | | | | | | | | | | | | | | | | | | | | | | | | | | | | | | | | | | | | | | | | | | | | | | | | | | | | | | | | | | | | |
| A.O.C.— DEFICIENCY | | | | | | | | | | | | | | | | | | | | | | | | | | | | | | | | | | | | | | | | | | | | | | | | | | | | | | | | | | | | | | | | | | |
| SURPLUS | | | | | | | | | | | | | | | | | | | | | | | | | | | | | | | | | | | | | | | | | | | | | | | | | | | | | | | | | | | | | | | | | | |
| A.V.C.— DEFICIENCY | | | | | | | | | | | | | | | | | | | | | | | | | | | | | | | | | | | | | | | | | | | | | | | | | | | | | | | | | | | | | | | | | | |
| SURPLUS | | | | | | | | | | | | | | | | | | | | | | | | | | | | | | | | | | | | | | | | | | | | | | | | | | | | | | | | | | | | | | | | | | |
| DEFICIENCY | | | | | | | | | | | | | | | | | | | | | | | | | | | | | | | | | | | | | | | | | | | | | | | | | | | | | | | | | | | | | | | | | | |
| SURPLUS | | | | | | | | | | | | | | | | | | | | | | | | | | | | | | | | | | | | | | | | | | | | | | | | | | | | | | | | | | | | | | | | | | |
| DEFICIENCY | | | | | | | | | | | | | | | | | | | | | | | | | | | | | | | | | | | | | | | | | | | | | | | | | | | | | | | | | | | | | | | | | | |
| SURPLUS | | | | | | | | | | | | | | | | | | | | | | | | | | | | | | | | | | | | | | | | | | | | | | | | | | | | | | | | | | | | | | | | | | |

Remarks :—

____________ Signature of Commander.

____________ Unit.

____________ Formation to which attached.

____________ Date of Despatch.

[P.T.O.

(17823.) Wt. W2281—P 1075. 2,750m. 6/18. D & S. (E1256) Forms B2138/11.

**To be made up to and for Saturday in each week**

Army Form B. 213

No. of Report 188

# FIELD RETURN.

(To be furnished by all arms, services, and departments (except A.S.C. units) to the A.G.'s Office at the Base in accordance with Field Service Regulations, Part II.)

RETURN showing numbers (a) Effective strength of Unit. (b) Rationed by Unit. 1/1 Lowland Field Amb^ce. Chaussee N.D. Louvignies 4. 3. 19. Date.

| Details | Personnel: Officers | Personnel: Other Ranks | | | Horses: Riding | Horses: Draught | Horses: Heavy Draught | Pack | Mules: Large | Mules: Small | Guns, showing description | Ammunition wagons | Machine guns | Aircraft, showing description | Horsed: 4 Wheeled | Horsed: 2 Wheeled | Motor Cars | Tractors | Lorries, showing description | Trucks, showing description | Trailers | Motor Bicycles | Bicycles | Motor Ambulances | Remarks (Number of Acting W.O.'s and N.C.O.'s included in effective strength to be shown in this column.) |
|---|---|---|---|---|---|---|---|---|---|---|---|---|---|---|---|---|---|---|---|---|---|---|---|---|---|
| Effective Strength of Unit | (a) 4 | (b) 144 | | | | | | | | | | | | | | | | | | | | | 1 | | (a) 1 on leave to U.K. (b) 32 at 1/2 L. F.A. – 3 at A.D.M.S. 1 at 52 Div. Train – 2 at 32 San. Sec. 1 at Corps Rly. – 1 on leave U.K. 7 left Unit for demobilization 1 at 9 Bde R.F.A. – on Course |
| Details by Arms attached to Unit as in War Establishment … R.A.S.C. (H.T.) | | (c) 33 | | | 5 | 10 | 11 | | | | | | | | 13 | 4 | | | | | | | | | (c) 2 on leave U.K. – 1 L/L for demobilization 1 on leave to France |
| R.A.S.C. (M.T.) | | (d) 11 | | | | | | | | | | | | | | | | | | | | 2 | | 7 | (d) 2 at A.D.M.S. – 1 at 9 Bde R.F.A. |
| Total | 4 | 188 | | | 5 | 10 | 11 | | | | | | | | 13 | 4 | | | | | | 2 | 1 | 7 | |
| War Establishment | 8 | 203 | | | 5 | 13 | 16 | | | | | | | | 10 | 3 | | | | | | 2 | 1 | 7 | |
| Wanting to complete (Detail of Personnel and Horses below.) | 4 | 20 x | | | | 3 | 5 | | | | | | | | | | | | | | | | | | x 18 R.A.M.C. – 2 R.A.S.C. (M.T.) |
| Surplus (Detail of Personnel and Horses below.) | | 5 * | | | | | | | | | | | | | 3 | 1 | | | | | | | | | * R.A.S.C. (H.T.) |
| †Attached (not to include the details shown above) | | 12 | | | | | | | | | | | | | | | | | | | | | | | Patients |
| Attached for Rations only | 1 | | | | | | | | | | | | | | | | | | | | | | | | Chaplain |
| Civilians Employed with and Accompanying the Unit | | | | | | | | | | | | | | | | | | | | | | | | | |
| ‡Detached from and struck off effective strength of own Unit | | | | | | | | | | | | | | | | | | | | | | | | | |
| ‡Detached from but retained on effective strength of own unit | | 1° | | | | | | | | | | | | | | | | | | | | | | | 1° A.S.C. M.T. (1/3 L.F.A.) |
| Total Rationed | 4 | 145 | | | 5 | 10 | 11 | | | | | | | | | | | | | | | | | | |

* Blank columns to be used for W.A.A.C. Natives or as may be required.

† In the case of field ambulances, hospitals or depots, the number of patients are to be included here, the names being shown in A.F.A. 36.

‡ These details to be enumerated by arms.

[illegible] Major Signature of Commander.

4. 3. 19 Date of Despatch.

B213

1/1 Low. Field Ambce.
R.A.S.C. Section

W E 5. 3. 19

| No. | Rank | Name | Casualty | Date. |
|---|---|---|---|---|
| T/19200 | R S S M | Sackley T | Returned from leave to Paris | 4/3/19 |
| T4/043531 | Dr | Davis G. L. | Granted leave to BAILLEUL, FRANCE 5/3/19 – 11/3/19 (7 days) Credit Ration Allce. at 2/4 p. d. | 5/3/19 |

R. Bignon Mackenzie
Major
O.C. 1/1 Low. Field Ambce.

4/3/19.

R.A.S.C. Sheet att^d.

*For information of the A.G.'s Office at the base.*

Officers and men who have become casuals, been transferred or joined since last report.

Place CHAUSSEE N. D. LOUVIGNIES    Date 8 - 3 - 19

| Regtl. Number | Rank | Name | Corps | Nature of casualty, or name of unit from or to which transferred. | Date of being struck off or coming on the ration return. | Remarks* |
|---|---|---|---|---|---|---|
| | Capt. | Lennie R.A. | R.A.M.C.(T) | Returned from leave | 3/3/19 | |
| | do. | do. | do. | Granted extension of leave (7 days) Athy. DEPORTED Wire D.M. 32803 Feb. 19 (A.M.D.) 54/19. Credit ration allce. for period. | 21/3/19 - 28/3/19 | Lt. |
| | Capt. | Burton J.W. | R.A.M.C.(T) | To duty with 1/4 Roy. Scots. | 4/3/19 | Athy. A.D.M.S. 52 Div. |
| | Capt. | Downes A.D. | do. | Granted leave to U.K. via Calais 14 days. Credit ration allce. for period | 8/3/19 - 22/3/19 | |
| | Surg. Lt. Commdr. | Ross C. B. | R.N. | Reporting to Admiralty. Athy. Deported Wire D.M. 33112 A.M.D.I. d/3/19 | 5/3/19 | |
| 316074 | Pte. | Johnston A. | R.A.M.C.(T). | Retd. from leave | 4/3/19 | |
| 316003 | " | McKechnie W. | do. | To U.K. for demobilization. Embarked Boulogne | | 24/2/19 |
| 316068 | " | Gourlay W. | do. | do. do. | | do. 24/2/19 |
| 316100 | " | Gough T.C. | do. | do. do. | | do. 24/3/19 |
| 316097 | " | Dickson D. | do. | do. do. | | do. 19/2/19 |
| 316099 | " | Golder J. | do. | do. do. | | do. 19/2/19 |
| 27891 | Cpl. | Edwards J. (M.M.) | do. | do. do. | | do. 20/2/19 |

Strength:- OFFICERS - T.F. 4

W.Os. N.C.Os. - MEN

| | |
|---|---|
| W.O. | 1 |
| Q.M.S. | 1 |
| S/Sgt. | 2 |
| Sgt. | 8 |
| L.Sgt. | 1 |
| Cpls. | 5 |
| L.Cpls. | 3 |
| Ptes. | 123 |
| TOTAL = | 144 |

All CATEGORY A.

W.Os. N.C.Os. & MEN liable to be retained for duty with Armies of Occupation - PTES. 3

W.Os. N.C.Os. & MEN who have volunteered for duty with Armies of Occupation - NIL.

* State whether absence is of a permanent or temporary nature, adding, in the case of casuals from wounds or disease, any available information for communication to the relatives.

*The perforated sheet is not to be used to record casualties; additional sheets, preferably foolscap, to be attached when necessary. These sheets to be carefully numbered and the number of attached sheets to be noted here.*

Perforated Sheet giving detail of personnel and horses wanting to complete or surplus, shown on Army Form B. 213.

No. of Report 88

| Detail of Wanting to Complete or Surplus. | Drivers. R.A. | Drivers. R.E. | Drivers. A.S.C. | Drivers. Car (M.T.A.S.C.) | Drivers. Lorry | Drivers. Steam | Gunners | Gunners Howitzer | Smith Gunners | Range Takers | Farriers Serjeants | Farriers Corporals | Shoeing or Shoeing and Carriage Smiths | Cold Shoers |
|---|---|---|---|---|---|---|---|---|---|---|---|---|---|---|
| CAVALRY—DEFICIENCY | | | | | | | | | | | | | | |
| SURPLUS | | | | | | | | | | | | | | |
| R.A.—DEFICIENCY | | | | | | | | | | | | | | |
| SURPLUS | | | | | | | | | | | | | | |
| R.E.—DEFICIENCY | | | | | | | | | | | | | | |
| SURPLUS | | | | | | | | | | | | | | |
| INFANTRY—DEFICIENCY | | | | | | | | | | | | | | |
| SURPLUS | | | | | | | | | | | | | | |
| R.A.M.C.—DEFICIENCY | | | | 2 | | | | | | | | | | |
| SURPLUS | | | 4 | | | | | | | | | | | |
| A.O.C.—DEFICIENCY | | | | | | | | | | | | | | |
| SURPLUS | | | | | | | | | | | | | | |
| A.V.C.—DEFICIENCY | | | | | | | | | | | | | | |
| SURPLUS | | | | | | | | | | | | | | |
| DEFICIENCY | | | | | | | | | | | | | | |
| SURPLUS | | | | | | | | | | | | | | |
| DEFICIENCY | | | | | | | | | | | | | | |
| SURPLUS | | | | | | | | | | | | | | |

| Detail of Wanting to Complete or Surplus. | Wheelers R.A. | Wheelers H.T. | Wheelers M.T. | Saddlers or Harness Makers | Blacksmiths | Bricklayers and Masons | Carpenters and Joiners | Fitters & Turners (R.E.) Wood | Fitters & Turners (R.E.) Iron | Fitters R.A. | Fitters Wireless. | Plumbers | Electricians Ordinary | Electricians W.T. | Signalmen. | Engine Drivers Loco. | Engine Drivers Field |
|---|---|---|---|---|---|---|---|---|---|---|---|---|---|---|---|---|---|
| CAVALRY—DEFICIENCY | | | | | | | | | | | | | | | | | |
| SURPLUS | | | | | | | | | | | | | | | | | |
| R.A.—DEFICIENCY | | | | | | | | | | | | | | | | | |
| SURPLUS | | | | | | | | | | | | | | | | | |
| R.E.—DEFICIENCY | | | | | | | | | | | | | | | | | |
| SURPLUS | | | | | | | | | | | | | | | | | |
| INFANTRY—DEFICIENCY | | | | | | | | | | | | | | | | | |
| SURPLUS | | | | | | | | | | | | | | | | | |
| R.A.M.C.—DEFICIENCY | | | | | | | | | | | | | | | | | |
| SURPLUS | | | | | | | | | | | | | | | | | |
| A.O.C.—DEFICIENCY | | | | | | | | | | | | | | | | | |
| SURPLUS | | | | | | | | | | | | | | | | | |
| A.V.C.—DEFICIENCY | | | | | | | | | | | | | | | | | |
| SURPLUS | | | | | | | | | | | | | | | | | |
| DEFICIENCY | | | | | | | | | | | | | | | | | |
| SURPLUS | | | | | | | | | | | | | | | | | |
| DEFICIENCY | | | | | | | | | | | | | | | | | |
| SURPLUS | | | | | | | | | | | | | | | | | |

| Detail of Wanting to Complete or Surplus. | Air Line Men. | Permanent Line Men | Operators, Telegraph | Cablemen | Brigade Section Pioneers | General-duty Pioneers | Signallers | Instrument Repairers | Motor Cyclist | Motor Cyclist Artificers | Telephonists | Clerks | Machine Gunners | Armament Artificers Fitters | Armament Artificers Range Finders |
|---|---|---|---|---|---|---|---|---|---|---|---|---|---|---|---|
| CAVALRY—DEFICIENCY | | | | | | | | | | | | | | | |
| SURPLUS | | | | | | | | | | | | | | | |
| R.A.—DEFICIENCY | | | | | | | | | | | | | | | |
| SURPLUS | | | | | | | | | | | | | | | |
| R.E.—DEFICIENCY | | | | | | | | | | | | | | | |
| SURPLUS | | | | | | | | | | | | | | | |
| INFANTRY—DEFICIENCY | | | | | | | | | | | | | | | |
| SURPLUS | | | | | | | | | | | | | | | |
| R.A.M.C.—DEFICIENCY | | | | | | | | | | | | | | | |
| SURPLUS | | | | | | | | | | | | | | | |
| A.O.C.—DEFICIENCY | | | | | | | | | | | | | | | |
| SURPLUS | | | | | | | | | | | | | | | |
| A.V.C.—DEFICIENCY | | | | | | | | | | | | | | | |
| SURPLUS | | | | | | | | | | | | | | | |
| DEFICIENCY | | | | | | | | | | | | | | | |
| SURPLUS | | | | | | | | | | | | | | | |
| DEFICIENCY | | | | | | | | | | | | | | | |
| SURPLUS | | | | | | | | | | | | | | | |

| Detail of Wanting to Complete or Surplus. | Armourers | Storemen | Privates | W.O.'s and N.C.O.'s (by ranks) not included in trade columns. Sjt R.A.M.C.T. | W.O.'s and N.C.O.'s Sjt R.A.S.C. (M.T.) | W.O.'s and N.C.O.'s | W.O.'s and N.C.O.'s | W.O.'s and N.C.O.'s | W.O.'s and N.C.O.'s | W.O.'s and N.C.O.'s | | | | | TOTAL to agree with wanting to complete or surplus Officers | TOTAL Other Ranks | Horses Riding | Horses Draught | Horses Heavy Draught | Horses Pack |
|---|---|---|---|---|---|---|---|---|---|---|---|---|---|---|---|---|---|---|---|---|
| CAVALRY—DEFICIENCY | | | | | | | | | | | | | | | | | | | | |
| SURPLUS | | | | | | | | | | | | | | | | | | | | |
| R.A.—DEFICIENCY | | | | | | | | | | | | | | | | | | | | |
| SURPLUS | | | | | | | | | | | | | | | | | | | | |
| R.E.—DEFICIENCY | | | | | | | | | | | | | | | | | | | | |
| SURPLUS | | | | | | | | | | | | | | | | | | | | |
| INFANTRY—DEFICIENCY | | | | | | | | | | | | | | | | | | | | |
| SURPLUS | | | | | | | | | | | | | | | | | | | | |
| R.A.M.C.—DEFICIENCY | | | 19 | | | | | | | | | | | | 4 | 21 | | 3 | 5 | |
| SURPLUS | | | | 1 | 1 | | | | | | | | | | | 6 | | | | |
| A.O.C.—DEFICIENCY | | | | | | | | | | | | | | | | | | | | |
| SURPLUS | | | | | | | | | | | | | | | | | | | | |
| A.V.C.—DEFICIENCY | | | | | | | | | | | | | | | | | | | | |
| SURPLUS | | | | | | | | | | | | | | | | | | | | |
| DEFICIENCY | | | | | | | | | | | | | | | | | | | | |
| SURPLUS | | | | | | | | | | | | | | | | | | | | |
| DEFICIENCY | | | | | | | | | | | | | | | | | | | | |
| SURPLUS | | | | | | | | | | | | | | | | | | | | |

Remarks :—

[illegible] Major Signature of Commander.

1/1 Lowland Field Ambulance Unit.

52 Div. Formation to which attached.

9. 3. 19 Date of Despatch.

**To be made up to and for Saturday in each week**

No. of Report [illegible]

# FIELD RETURN.

Army Form B. 213

(To be furnished by all arms, services, and departments (except A.S.C. units) to the A.G.'s Office at the Base in accordance with Field Service Regulations, Part II.)

RETURN showing numbers (*a*) Effective strength of Unit. (*b*) Rationed by Unit. [illegible] at [illegible] 15. 3. 19. Date.

| Details | *Personnel: Officers | Other Ranks | | | Animals: Horses: Riding | Draught | Heavy Draught | Pack | Mules: Large | Small | Guns, showing description | Ammunition wagons | Machine guns |
|---|---|---|---|---|---|---|---|---|---|---|---|---|---|
| Effective Strength of Unit ... ... | 5 | 44 | | | | | | | | | | | |
| Details by Arms attached to Unit as in War Establishment ... ... ... | | | | | | | | | | | | | |
| R.A.S.C. (H.T.) | | 33 | | | | 4 | 11 | | | | | | |
| R.A.S.C. (M.T.) | | 11 | | | | | | | | | | | |
| TOTAL ... ... | 5 | 88 | | | | 4 | 11 | | | | | | |
| War Establishment ... ... ... | 8 | [illegible] | | | 5 | 13 | 6 | | | | | | |
| Wanting to complete ... ... ... (Detail of Personnel and Horses below.) | 3 | [illegible] | | | 5 | 9 | [illegible] | | | | | | |
| SURPLUS ... ... (Detail of Personnel and Horses below.) | | [illegible] | | | | | | | | | | | |
| †Attached (not to include the details shown above) ... ... ... ... | | 6 | | | | | | | | | | | |
| Attached for Rations only ... ... | 1 | | | | | | | | | | | | |
| Civilians Employed with and Accompanying the Unit ... ... ... | | | | | | | | | | | | | |
| ‡Detached from and struck off effective strength of own Unit ... ... | | | | | | | | | | | | | |
| ‡Detached from but retained on effective strength of own unit... ... ... | | 1 | | | | | | | | | | | |
| TOTAL RATIONED ... | 5 | 103 | | | | 4 | 11 | | | | | | |

| Details | Guns and transport vehicles: Aircraft, showing description | Horsed: 4 Wheeled | 2 Wheeled | Mechanical: Motor Cars | Tractors | Lorries, showing description | Trucks, showing description | Trailers | Motor Bicycles | Bicycles | Motor Ambulances | REMARKS (Number of Acting W.O.'s and N.C.O.'s included in effective strength to be shown in this column.) |
|---|---|---|---|---|---|---|---|---|---|---|---|---|
| Effective Strength of Unit | | | | | | | | | | 1 | | [illegible] |
| Details by Arms attached to Unit as in War Establishment | | | | | | | | | | | | [illegible] |
| R.A.S.C. (H.T.) | | 13 | 4 | | | | | | | | | [illegible] |
| R.A.S.C. (M.T.) | | | | | | | | | 2 | | 7 | [illegible] |
| TOTAL | | 13 | 4 | | | | | | 2 | 1 | 7 | [illegible] |
| War Establishment | | 13 | 4 | | | | | | 2 | 1 | 7 | |
| Wanting to complete (Detail of Personnel and Horses below.) | | 10 | 3 | | | | | | 2 | 1 | [illegible] | |
| SURPLUS (Detail of Personnel and Horses below.) | | | | | | | | | | | | [illegible] |
| †Attached (not to include the details shown above) | | 3 | 1 | | | | | | | | | [illegible] Patients |
| Attached for Rations only | | | | | | | | | | | | [illegible] |
| Civilians Employed with and Accompanying the Unit | | | | | | | | | | | | |
| ‡Detached from and struck off effective strength of own Unit | | | | | | | | | | | | |
| ‡Detached from but retained on effective strength of own unit | | | | | | | | | | | | [illegible] |
| TOTAL RATIONED | | | | | | | | | | 1 | | |

* Blank columns to be used for W.A.A.C. Natives or as may be required.

† In the case of field ambulances, hospitals or depots, the number of patients are to be included here, the names being shown in A.F.A. 36.
‡ These details to be enumerated by arms.

[illegible] Major Signature of Commander.

15. 3. 19. Date of Despatch.

[illegible]

W.E. 15. 3. 19.

[illegible]

| No. | Rank | Name | Casualty | Date |
|---|---|---|---|---|
| [illegible] | 2nd Lt | [illegible] | [illegible] | 3. 3. 19. |
| [illegible] | Lt | Davis [illegible] | [illegible] | 3. 3. 19. |

[illegible]

— NIL —

Major

[illegible]

*For information of the A.G.'s Office at the base.*

Officers and men who have become casuals, been transferred or joined since last report.

Place ______ Date ______

| Regtl. Number | Rank | Name | Corps | Nature of casualty, or name of unit from or to which transferred. | Date of being struck off or coming on the ration return. | Remarks * |
|---|---|---|---|---|---|---|
| – | [illegible] | [illegible] | [illegible] | [illegible] | [illegible] | |

| | W.O. NCO. | Men |
|---|---|---|
| | W.O. | 1 |
| | QMS. | 1 |
| | S. Sgt. | 2 |
| | Sgt. | [illegible] |
| | L. Sgt. | 1 |
| | Cpl. | 5 |
| | L. Cpl. | 8 |
| | Pte. | 123 |

A1 CATEGORY B

W.Os N.C.Os + Men who are liable to be retained for duty with Armies of Occupation Pres. 3

W.Os. N.C.Os + Men who have volunteered for duty with Armies of Occupation :- NIL

* State whether absence is of a permanent or temporary nature, adding, in the case of casuals from wounds or disease, any available information for communication to the relatives.

*The perforated sheet is not to be used to record casualties; additional sheets, preferably foolscap, to be attached when necessary. These sheets to be carefully numbered and the number of attached sheets to be noted here.*

FIELD RETURN. To be made up to and for Saturday in each week

Perforated Sheet giving detail of personnel and horses wanting to complete or surplus, shown on Army Form B. 213.

No. of Report 90

| Detail of Wanting to Complete or Surplus | Drivers R.A. | Drivers R.E. | Drivers A.S.C. | Drivers Car (MT RASC) | Drivers Lorry | Drivers Steam | Gunners | Gunners Howitzer | Smith Gunners | Range Takers | Farriers Serjeants | Farriers Corporals | Shoeing or Shoeing and Carriage Smiths | Cold Shoers | Wheelers R.A. | Wheelers H.T. | Wheelers M.T. | Saddlers or Harness Makers | Blacksmiths | Bricklayers and Masons | Carpenters and Joiners | Fitters & Turners (R.E.) Wood | Fitters & Turners (R.E.) Iron | Fitters R.A. | Fitters Wireless | Plumbers |
|---|---|---|---|---|---|---|---|---|---|---|---|---|---|---|---|---|---|---|---|---|---|---|---|---|---|---|
| CAVALRY— DEFICIENCY | | | | | | | | | | | | | | | | | | | | | | | | | | |
| SURPLUS | | | | | | | | | | | | | | | | | | | | | | | | | | |
| R.A.— DEFICIENCY | | | | | | | | | | | | | | | | | | | | | | | | | | |
| SURPLUS | | | | | | | | | | | | | | | | | | | | | | | | | | |
| R.E.— DEFICIENCY | | | | | | | | | | | | | | | | | | | | | | | | | | |
| SURPLUS | | | | | | | | | | | | | | | | | | | | | | | | | | |
| INFANTRY— DEFICIENCY | | | | | | | | | | | | | | | | | | | | | | | | | | |
| SURPLUS | | | | 2 | | | | | | | | | | | | | | | | | | | | | | |
| R.A.M.C.— DEFICIENCY | | | 4 | | | | | | | | | | | | | | | | | | | | | | | |
| SURPLUS | | | | | | | | | | | | | | | | | | | | | | | | | | |
| A.O.C.— DEFICIENCY | | | | | | | | | | | | | | | | | | | | | | | | | | |
| SURPLUS | | | | | | | | | | | | | | | | | | | | | | | | | | |
| A.V.C.— DEFICIENCY | | | | | | | | | | | | | | | | | | | | | | | | | | |
| SURPLUS | | | | | | | | | | | | | | | | | | | | | | | | | | |
| DEFICIENCY | | | | | | | | | | | | | | | | | | | | | | | | | | |
| SURPLUS | | | | | | | | | | | | | | | | | | | | | | | | | | |
| DEFICIENCY | | | | | | | | | | | | | | | | | | | | | | | | | | |
| SURPLUS | | | | | | | | | | | | | | | | | | | | | | | | | | |

| Detail of Wanting to Complete or Surplus | Electricians Ordinary | Electricians W.T. | Signalmen | Engine Drivers Loco. | Engine Drivers Field | Air Line Men | Permanent Line Men | Operators, Telegraph | Cablemen | Brigade Section Pioneers | General-duty Pioneers | Signallers | Instrument Repairers | Motor Cyclist | Motor Cyclist Artificers | Telephonists | Clerks | Machine Gunners | Armament Artificers Fitters | Armament Artificers Range Finders | Armourers | Storemen |
|---|---|---|---|---|---|---|---|---|---|---|---|---|---|---|---|---|---|---|---|---|---|---|
| CAVALRY— DEFICIENCY | | | | | | | | | | | | | | | | | | | | | | |
| SURPLUS | | | | | | | | | | | | | | | | | | | | | | |
| R.A.— DEFICIENCY | | | | | | | | | | | | | | | | | | | | | | |
| SURPLUS | | | | | | | | | | | | | | | | | | | | | | |
| R.E.— DEFICIENCY | | | | | | | | | | | | | | | | | | | | | | |
| SURPLUS | | | | | | | | | | | | | | | | | | | | | | |
| INFANTRY— DEFICIENCY | | | | | | | | | | | | | | | | | | | | | | |
| SURPLUS | | | | | | | | | | | | | | | | | | | | | | |
| R.A.M.C.— DEFICIENCY | | | | | | | | | | | | | | | | | | | | | | |
| SURPLUS | | | | | | | | | | | | | | | | | | | | | | |
| A.O.C.— DEFICIENCY | | | | | | | | | | | | | | | | | | | | | | |
| SURPLUS | | | | | | | | | | | | | | | | | | | | | | |
| A.V.C.— DEFICIENCY | | | | | | | | | | | | | | | | | | | | | | |
| SURPLUS | | | | | | | | | | | | | | | | | | | | | | |
| DEFICIENCY | | | | | | | | | | | | | | | | | | | | | | |
| SURPLUS | | | | | | | | | | | | | | | | | | | | | | |
| DEFICIENCY | | | | | | | | | | | | | | | | | | | | | | |
| SURPLUS | | | | | | | | | | | | | | | | | | | | | | |

| Detail of Wanting to Complete or Surplus | Privates | W.O.'s and N.C.O.'s (by ranks) not included in trade columns: Sgt. RAMC | Sgt. RASC MT | | | | | | | | | | | TOTAL to agree with wanting to complete or surplus: Officers | TOTAL: Other Ranks | Horses: Riding | Draught | Heavy Draught | Pack |
|---|---|---|---|---|---|---|---|---|---|---|---|---|---|---|---|---|---|---|---|
| CAVALRY— DEFICIENCY | | | | | | | | | | | | | | | | | | | |
| SURPLUS | | | | | | | | | | | | | | | | | | | |
| R.A.— DEFICIENCY | | | | | | | | | | | | | | | | | | | |
| SURPLUS | | | | | | | | | | | | | | | | | | | |
| R.E.— DEFICIENCY | | | | | | | | | | | | | | | | | | | |
| SURPLUS | | | | | | | | | | | | | | | | | | | |
| INFANTRY— DEFICIENCY | | | | | | | | | | | | | | | | | | | |
| SURPLUS | | 4 | | | | | | | | | | | | 3 | 21 | 5 | 5 | 5 | |
| R.A.M.C.— DEFICIENCY | | | 1 | 1 | | | | | | | | | | | 6 | | | | |
| SURPLUS | | | | | | | | | | | | | | | | | | | |
| A.O.C.— DEFICIENCY | | | | | | | | | | | | | | | | | | | |
| SURPLUS | | | | | | | | | | | | | | | | | | | |
| A.V.C.— DEFICIENCY | | | | | | | | | | | | | | | | | | | |
| SURPLUS | | | | | | | | | | | | | | | | | | | |
| DEFICIENCY | | | | | | | | | | | | | | | | | | | |
| SURPLUS | | | | | | | | | | | | | | | | | | | |
| DEFICIENCY | | | | | | | | | | | | | | | | | | | |
| SURPLUS | | | | | | | | | | | | | | | | | | | |

Remarks :—

[illegible] Major Signature of Commander.

1/8 Lowland Field Amb$^{ce}$ Unit.

52nd Div. Formation to which attached.

15-3-19. Date of Despatch.

**To be made up to and for Saturday in each week**

No. of Report____________

# FIELD RETURN.

Army Form B. 213

(To be furnished by all arms, services, and departments (except A.S.C. units) to the A.G.'s Office at the Base in accordance with Field Service Regulations, Part II.)

RETURN showing numbers (*a*) Effective strength of Unit. (*b*) Rationed by Unit. __________ at __________ Date.

| Details | *Personnel | | | | | Animals | | | | | | Guns and transport vehicles | | | | | | | | | | | Motor Bicycles | Bicycles | Motor Ambulances | Remarks |
|---|---|---|---|---|---|---|---|---|---|---|---|---|---|---|---|---|---|---|---|---|---|---|---|---|---|---|
| | | | | | | Horses | | | | Mules | | | | | | Horsed | | Mechanical | | | | | | | | |
| | Officers | Other Ranks | | | | Riding | Draught | Heavy Draught | Pack | Large | Small | Guns, showing description | Ammunition wagons | Machine guns | Aircraft, showing description | 4 Wheeled | 2 Wheeled | Motor Cars | Tractors | Lorries, showing description | Trucks, showing description | Trailers | | | | (Number of Acting W.O.'s and N.C.O.'s included in effective strength to be shown in this column.) |
| Effective Strength of Unit ... ... | | | | | | | | | | | | | | | | | | | | | | | | | | |
| Details by Arms attached to Unit as in War Establishment ... ... | | | | | | | | | | | | | | | | | | | | | | | | | | |
| Total ... ... | 4 | [illegible] | | | | | 2 | 2 | | | | | | | | 13 | 4 | | | | | | 2 | 1 | 7 | |
| War Establishment ... ... | 8 | [illegible] | | | | 5 | 13 | 16 | | | | | | | | 10 | 3 | | | | | | 2 | 1 | 4 | |
| Wanting to complete ... ... (Detail of Personnel and Horses below.) | 4 | 23 | | | | 5 | 11 | 14 | | | | | | | | | | | | | | | | | | |
| Surplus ... ... (Detail of Personnel and Horses below.) | | 5 | | | | | | | | | | | | | | 3 | 1 | | | | | | | | | |
| †Attached (not to include the details shown above) ... ... | | 11 | | | | | | | | | | | | | | | | | | | | | | | | Patients |
| Attached for Rations only ... | 1 | | | | | | | | | | | | | | | | | | | | | | | | | Chaplain |
| Civilians Employed with and Accompanying the Unit ... ... | | | | | | | | | | | | | | | | | | | | | | | | | | |
| ‡Detached from and struck off effective strength of own Unit ... | | | | | | | | | | | | | | | | | | | | | | | | | | |
| ‡Detached from but retained on effective strength of own unit... | | | | | | | | | | | | | | | | | | | | | | | | | | |
| Total Rationed ... | | | | | | | 2 | 2 | | | | | | | | | | | | | | | | | | |

* Blank columns to be used for W.A.A.C. Natives or as may be required.

† In the case of field ambulances, hospitals or depots, the number of patients are to be included here, the names being shown in A.F.A. 36.

‡ These details to be enumerated by arms.

[illegible signature] Signature of Commander.

22-3-19 Date of Despatch.

A.F. B213

1/1 Lowland Fld Amb^ce — Week ending 17

RASC. HT Section

| No. | Rank | Name | Casualty | Date |
| --- | --- | --- | --- | --- |
| 4/247009 | Dr | McDonald D. | Returned from leave | 18-3-19. |
| T/32085 | Dr | Fox G.W. | Granted 5th rate ASC pay as Shoeing Smith from 24-10-18 vice [illegible] sick to [illegible] Entitled to Shoeing-Smiths pay, original certificate attached from Vet Officer Ref. ASC M19/168 [illegible] Granted [illegible] para 892 [illegible] | |

W.O. NCO & men who are liable to be retained for duty with Army of occupation NIL

W.O. NCO & men who have volunteered for duty with Army of occupation NIL

R.H. [illegible] Capt.

OC 1/1 Lowland Fld Amb

RAMC

22/3/19

*For information of the A.G.'s Office at the base.* RASC. 1st Sheet attached

Officers and men who have become casuals, been transferred or joined since last report.

Place Soignies. Date 22-3-19.

| Regtl. Number | Rank | Name | Corps | Nature of casualty, or name of unit from or to which transferred. | Date of being struck off or coming on the ration return. | Remarks * |
|---|---|---|---|---|---|---|
| | A/Major | W. G. Mackenzie | RAMC | Proceeding to UK on demobilisation | 16/3/19 | |
| | do | do | do | [illegible] on proceeding to UK for demobilisation | | 16-3-19 |
| 31[illegible]29 | Pte | White A | RAMC | Returned from leave 14/3/19 | | |
| 31[illegible]8 | Sgt | [illegible] A | RAMC | (Granted leave to France [illegible] Ration allce for that period [illegible]) | | |
| 31[illegible]66 | Sgt | Campbell J.S. | RAMC | [illegible] demobilisation [illegible] | | 2/3/19 |
| 31[illegible]71 | Pte | Hill J. | RAMC | do do | | do 2/3/19 |
| 3160[illegible] | " | McKellar J.C. | RAMC | do do | | do 2/3/19 |

Strength [illegible] T.F. 5.

| | |
|---|---|
| WO NCO's | MEN |
| W.O. | 1 |
| Q.M.S. | 1 |
| S/Sgt | 2 |
| Sgt | 4 |
| L/Sgt | 1 |
| Cpl | 5 |
| L/Cpl | 3 |
| Pte | 121 |
| TOTAL | 141 |

All Category A

W.O. NCOs & Men liable to be retained for duty with Army of Occupation Pte 3.

W.O. NCOs & Men who have volunteered for duty with Army of Occupation Nil

* State whether absence is of a permanent or temporary nature, adding, in the case of casuals from wounds or disease any available information for communication to the relatives.

*The perforated sheet is not to be used to record casualties; additional sheets, preferably foolscap, to be attached when necessary. These sheets to be carefully numbered and the number of attached sheets to be noted here.*

Perforated Sheet giving detail of personnel and horses wanting to complete or surplus, shown on Army Form B. 213.

No. of Report 190.

| Detail of Wanting to Complete or Surplus. | Drivers. R.A. | Drivers. R.E. | Drivers. A.S.C. | Drivers. Car MT ASC | Drivers. Lorry | Drivers. Steam | Gunners | Gunners Howitzer | Smith Gunners | Range Takers | Farriers Serjeants | Farriers Corporals | Shoeing or Shoeing and Carriage Smiths | Cold Shoers | Wheelers R.A. | Wheelers H.T. | Wheelers M.T. | Saddlers or Harness Makers | Blacksmiths | Bricklayers and Masons | Carpenters and Joiners | Fitters & Turners (R.E.) Wood | Fitters & Turners (R.E.) Iron | Fitters R.A. | Fitters Wireless. | Plumbers | Electricians Ordinary | Electricians W.T. | Signalmen. | Engine Drivers Loco. | Engine Drivers Field | Air Line Men. | Permanent Line Men | Operators, Telegraph | Cablemen | Brigade Section Pioneers | General-duty Pioneers | Signallers | Instrument Repairers | Motor Cyclist | Motor Cyclist Artificers | Telephonists | Clerks | Machine Gunners | Armament Artificers Fitters | Armament Artificers Range Finders | Armourers | Storemen | Privates | W.O's and N.C.O's (by ranks) not included in trade columns. Sgt RAMC | Sgt RASC HT | | | | | | | | | | TOTAL to agree with wanting to complete or surplus. Officers | TOTAL Other Ranks | Horses Riding | Horses Draught | Horses Heavy Draught | Horses Pack |
|---|---|---|---|---|---|---|---|---|---|---|---|---|---|---|---|---|---|---|---|---|---|---|---|---|---|---|---|---|---|---|---|---|---|---|---|---|---|---|---|---|---|---|---|---|---|---|---|---|---|---|---|---|---|---|---|---|---|---|---|---|---|---|---|---|---|---|
| CAVALRY— DEFICIENCY | | | | | | | | | | | | | | | | | | | | | | | | | | | | | | | | | | | | | | | | | | | | | | | | | | | | | | | | | | | | | | | | | | |
| SURPLUS | | | | | | | | | | | | | | | | | | | | | | | | | | | | | | | | | | | | | | | | | | | | | | | | | | | | | | | | | | | | | | | | | | |
| R.A.— DEFICIENCY | | | | | | | | | | | | | | | | | | | | | | | | | | | | | | | | | | | | | | | | | | | | | | | | | | | | | | | | | | | | | | | | | | |
| SURPLUS | | | | | | | | | | | | | | | | | | | | | | | | | | | | | | | | | | | | | | | | | | | | | | | | | | | | | | | | | | | | | | | | | | |
| R.E.— DEFICIENCY | | | | | | | | | | | | | | | | | | | | | | | | | | | | | | | | | | | | | | | | | | | | | | | | | | | | | | | | | | | | | | | | | | |
| SURPLUS | | | | | | | | | | | | | | | | | | | | | | | | | | | | | | | | | | | | | | | | | | | | | | | | | | | | | | | | | | | | | | | | | | |
| INFANTRY— DEFICIENCY | | | | | | | | | | | | | | | | | | | | | | | | | | | | | | | | | | | | | | | | | | | | | | | | | | | | | | | | | | | | | | | | | | |
| SURPLUS | | | | | | | | | | | | | | | | | | | | | | | | | | | | | | | | | | | | | | | | | | | | | | | | | | | | | | | | | | | | | | | | | | |
| R.A.M.C.— DEFICIENCY | | | | 2 | | | | | | | | | | | | | | | | | | | | | | | | | | | | | | | | | | | | | | | | | | | | | 21 | | | | | | | | | | | | 4 | 30 | 11 | 14 | | |
| SURPLUS | | | 5 | | | | | | | | | | | | | | | | | | | | | | | | | | | | | | | | | | | | | | | | | | | | | | | 1 | | | | | | | | | | | | 6 | | | | |
| A.O.C.— DEFICIENCY | | | | | | | | | | | | | | | | | | | | | | | | | | | | | | | | | | | | | | | | | | | | | | | | | | | | | | | | | | | | | | | | | | |
| SURPLUS | | | | | | | | | | | | | | | | | | | | | | | | | | | | | | | | | | | | | | | | | | | | | | | | | | | | | | | | | | | | | | | | | | |
| A.V.C.— DEFICIENCY | | | | | | | | | | | | | | | | | | | | | | | | | | | | | | | | | | | | | | | | | | | | | | | | | | | | | | | | | | | | | | | | | | |
| SURPLUS | | | | | | | | | | | | | | | | | | | | | | | | | | | | | | | | | | | | | | | | | | | | | | | | | | | | | | | | | | | | | | | | | | |
| DEFICIENCY | | | | | | | | | | | | | | | | | | | | | | | | | | | | | | | | | | | | | | | | | | | | | | | | | | | | | | | | | | | | | | | | | | |
| SURPLUS | | | | | | | | | | | | | | | | | | | | | | | | | | | | | | | | | | | | | | | | | | | | | | | | | | | | | | | | | | | | | | | | | | |
| DEFICIENCY | | | | | | | | | | | | | | | | | | | | | | | | | | | | | | | | | | | | | | | | | | | | | | | | | | | | | | | | | | | | | | | | | | |
| SURPLUS | | | | | | | | | | | | | | | | | | | | | | | | | | | | | | | | | | | | | | | | | | | | | | | | | | | | | | | | | | | | | | | | | | |

Remarks :—

R Mennis Capt
Signature of Commander.

1st Lowland Fld. Ambulance Unit.

52nd Division Formation to which attached.

22-3-1919. Date of Despatch.

(17828.) Wt. W2281—P 1075. 2,750m. 6/18. D & S. (E1256) Forms B2138/11.

[P.T.O.

**To be made up to and for Saturday in each week**

No. of Report 191

# FIELD RETURN.

Army Form B. 213

(To be furnished by all arms, services, and departments (except A.S.C. units) to the A.G.'s Office at the Base in accordance with Field Service Regulations, Part II.)

RETURN showing numbers (a) Effective strength of Unit. (b) Rationed by Unit. 1/1 Lan. Fld Amb. at Soignies 29-3-19. Date.

| Details. | *Personnel: Officers | *Personnel: Other Ranks | | | | Animals: Horses: Riding | Horses: Draught | Horses: Heavy Draught | Horses: Pack | Mules: Large | Mules: Small | Guns and transport vehicles: Guns, showing description | Ammunition wagons | Machine guns | Aircraft, showing description | Horsed: 4 Wheeled | Horsed: 2 Wheeled | Mechanical: Motor Cars | Mechanical: Tractors | Mechanical: Lorries, showing description | Mechanical: Trucks, showing description | Mechanical: Trailers | Motor Bicycles | Bicycles | Motor Ambulances | Remarks (Number of Acting W.O.'s and N.C.O.'s included in effective strength to be shown in this column) |
|---|---|---|---|---|---|---|---|---|---|---|---|---|---|---|---|---|---|---|---|---|---|---|---|---|---|---|
| Effective Strength of Unit ... ... | 5 | 122 | | | | | | | | | | | | | | | | | | | | | | | | a 1 at [illegible] a 2 left Unit for Demob. b) 16 at No. 1 CCS 1 at [illegible] 1 at [illegible] |
| Details by Arms attached to Unit as in War Establishment ... RASC (HT) | | 33 | | | | | | | | | | | | | | 13 | 4 | | | | | | | | | 41 left Unit for Demob. c 16 left Unit for Demob. |
| RASC (MT) | | 6 | | | | | | | | | | | | | | | | | | | | | 2 | - | 2 | d) 2 at ADMS. |
| Total ... ... | 5 | 161 | | | | | | | | | | | | | | 13 | 4 | | | | | | 2 | | 2 | |
| War Establishment ... ... ... | 8 | 203 | | | | 5 | 13 | 16 | | | | | | | | 10 | 3 | | | | | | 2 | 1 | 7 | |
| Wanting to complete ... ... (Detail of Personnel and Horses below.) | 3 | 34 | | | | 5 | 13 | 16 | | | | | | | | | | | | | | | | 1 | 5 | +RAMC. |
| Surplus ... ... (Detail of Personnel and Horses below.) | | 5 | | | | | | | | | | | | | | 3 | 1 | | | | | | | | | +RASC HT |
| †Attached (not to include the details shown above) ... ... ... | | 3 | | | | | | | | | | | | | | | | | | | | | | | | Patients |
| Attached for Rations only ... | 1 | | | | | | | | | | | | | | | | | | | | | | | | | Chaplain |
| Civilians Employed with and Accompanying the Unit ... ... | | | | | | | | | | | | | | | | | | | | | | | | | | |
| ‡Detached from and struck off effective strength of own Unit ... ... | | | | | | | | | | | | | | | | | | | | | | | | | | |
| ‡Detached from but retained on effective strength of own unit... ... | | | | | | | | | | | | | | | | | | | | | | | | | | |
| Total Rationed ... | 3 | 83 | | | | | | | | | | | | | | | | | | | | | | | | |

* Blank columns to be used for W.A.A.C. Natives or as may be required.

† In the case of field ambulances, hospitals or depots, the number of patients are to be included here, the names being shown in A.F.A. 36.

‡ These details to be enumerated by arms.

R.H. Lennie Capt. Signature of Commander.

29-3-19. Date of Despatch.

[illegible]

RASC

| No. | Rank | Name | Casualty | Date |
|---|---|---|---|---|
| — | — | — NIL — | — | — |

RASC MT

| No. | Rank | Name | Casualty | Date |
|---|---|---|---|---|
| [illegible] | [illegible] | [illegible] | [illegible] | [illegible] |

NIL

NIL

R.A.S.C. Sheets Attached

*For information of the A.G.'s Office at the base.*

Officers and men who have become casuals, been transferred or joined since last report.

Place Soignies Date 29-3-19

| Regtl. Number | Rank | Name | | Corps | Nature of casualty, or name of unit from or to which transferred. | Date of being struck off or coming on the ration return. | Remarks * |
|---|---|---|---|---|---|---|---|
| | Capt. | Downes | A.D. | R.A.M.C. T. | Returned from leave to UK 22 3/19 | | |
| | " | do. | do. | do | Proceeded to UK. for Demobilization 25 3/19 | | |
| | Capt | Voans | S.D. | R.A.M.C. TC | To C.R.E. 52 Div 23-3-19 | | |
| 316168 | Sgt | Meldrum | A. | R.A.M.C. T | Returned from leave to France 26 3/19 | | |
| 316089 | Pte | Hay | A. | R.A.M.C. T | To Hospital 22 3/19 | | |
| 316229 | Sgt | McGregor | J. | R.A.M.C. (T) | To UK for Demobilization Embarked Boulogne | | 18 3/19 |
| 316230 | Pte | Anderson | J. | do | do | do | 18 3/19 |
| 316101 | " | Graham | R. | do | do | do | 18 3/19 |
| 316231 | " | Strang | A | do | do | do | 18 3/19 |
| 316114 | " | Thomson | A.B. | do | do | do | 18 3/19 |
| 316064 | Cpl. | Lamb | D. | do | do | do | 18 3/19 |
| 316083 | Pte | McGullies | J. | do | do | do | 18 3/19 |
| 316093 | " | Cowie | J | do | do | do | 18 3/19 |
| 325030 | " | Carson | S | do | do | do | 18 3/19 |
| 316159 | " | Carson | W.E | do | do | do | 18 3/19 |
| 316077 | " | McGillivray | W. | do | do | do | 18 3/19 |
| 316219 | " | Faith | J | do | do | do | 15 3/19 |

Strength Officers T.F. 5

ALL CATEGORY A

| WO | NCO | MEN |
|---|---|---|
| | W.O. | 1. |
| | Q.M.S. | 1. |
| | S/Sgt. | 2. |
| | Sgt. | 6 |
| | S/Sgt. | 1. |
| | Cpl. | 4 |
| | L/C. | 3. |
| | Pte. | 104 |
| | TOTALS | 122. |

* State whether absence is of a permanent or temporary nature, adding, in the case of casuals from wounds or disease any available information for communication to the relatives.

*The perforated sheet is not to be used to record casualties; additional sheets, preferably foolscap, to be attached when necessary. These sheets to be carefully numbered and the number of attached sheets to be noted here.*

W.O. NCO & men who are liable to be ~~liable~~ retained for duty with Army of occupation Pte 3.

W.O. NCO & men who have volunteered for duty with the Army of occupation NIL

Perforated Sheet giving detail of personnel and horses wanting to complete or surplus, shown on Army Form B. 213.

No. of Report 191.

| Detail of Wanting to Complete or Surplus. | Drivers: R.A. | Drivers: R.E. | Drivers: A.S.C. | Drivers: Car | Drivers: Lorry | Drivers: Steam | Gunners | Gunners Howitzer | Smith Gunners | Range Takers | Farriers: Serjeants | Farriers: Corporals | Shoeing or Shoeing and Carriage Smiths | Cold Shoers |
|---|---|---|---|---|---|---|---|---|---|---|---|---|---|---|
| CAVALRY— DEFICIENCY | | | | | | | | | | | | | | |
| SURPLUS | | | | | | | | | | | | | | |
| R.A.— DEFICIENCY | | | | | | | | | | | | | | |
| SURPLUS | | | | | | | | | | | | | | |
| R.E.— DEFICIENCY | | | | | | | | | | | | | | |
| SURPLUS | | | | | | | | | | | | | | |
| INFANTRY— DEFICIENCY | | | | | | | | | | | | | | |
| SURPLUS | | | | | | | | | | | | | | |
| R.A.M.C.— DEFICIENCY | | | 5 | | | | | | | | | | | |
| SURPLUS | | | | | | | | | | | | | | |
| A.O.C.— DEFICIENCY | | | | | | | | | | | | | | |
| SURPLUS | | | | | | | | | | | | | | |
| A.V.C.— DEFICIENCY | | | | | | | | | | | | | | |
| SURPLUS | | | | | | | | | | | | | | |
| DEFICIENCY | | | | | | | | | | | | | | |
| SURPLUS | | | | | | | | | | | | | | |
| DEFICIENCY | | | | | | | | | | | | | | |
| SURPLUS | | | | | | | | | | | | | | |

| Detail of Wanting to Complete or Surplus. | Wheelers: R.A. | Wheelers: H.T. | Wheelers: M.T. | Saddlers or Harness Makers | Blacksmiths | Bricklayers and Masons | Carpenters and Joiners | Fitters & Turners (R.E.): Wood | Fitters & Turners (R.E.): Iron | Fitters: R.A. | Fitters: Wireless. | Plumbers | Electricians: Ordinary | Electricians: W.T. | Signalmen. | Engine Drivers: Loco. | Engine Drivers: Field |
|---|---|---|---|---|---|---|---|---|---|---|---|---|---|---|---|---|---|
| CAVALRY— DEFICIENCY | | | | | | | | | | | | | | | | | |
| SURPLUS | | | | | | | | | | | | | | | | | |
| R.A.— DEFICIENCY | | | | | | | | | | | | | | | | | |
| SURPLUS | | | | | | | | | | | | | | | | | |
| R.E.— DEFICIENCY | | | | | | | | | | | | | | | | | |
| SURPLUS | | | | | | | | | | | | | | | | | |
| INFANTRY— DEFICIENCY | | | | | | | | | | | | | | | | | |
| SURPLUS | | | | | | | | | | | | | | | | | |
| R.A.M.C.— DEFICIENCY | | | | | | | | | | | | | | | | | |
| SURPLUS | | | | | | | | | | | | | | | | | |
| A.O.C.— DEFICIENCY | | | | | | | | | | | | | | | | | |
| SURPLUS | | | | | | | | | | | | | | | | | |
| A.V.C.— DEFICIENCY | | | | | | | | | | | | | | | | | |
| SURPLUS | | | | | | | | | | | | | | | | | |
| DEFICIENCY | | | | | | | | | | | | | | | | | |
| SURPLUS | | | | | | | | | | | | | | | | | |
| DEFICIENCY | | | | | | | | | | | | | | | | | |
| SURPLUS | | | | | | | | | | | | | | | | | |

| Detail of Wanting to Complete or Surplus. | Air Line Men. | Permanent Line Men | Operators, Telegraph | Cablemen | Brigade Section Pioneers | General-duty Pioneers | Signallers | Instrument Repairers | Motor Cyclist | Motor Cyclist Artificers | Telephonists | Clerks | Machine Gunners | Armament Artificers: Fitters | Armament Artificers: Range Finders | Armourers | Storemen | Privates |
|---|---|---|---|---|---|---|---|---|---|---|---|---|---|---|---|---|---|---|
| CAVALRY— DEFICIENCY | | | | | | | | | | | | | | | | | | |
| SURPLUS | | | | | | | | | | | | | | | | | | |
| R.A.— DEFICIENCY | | | | | | | | | | | | | | | | | | |
| SURPLUS | | | | | | | | | | | | | | | | | | |
| R.E.— DEFICIENCY | | | | | | | | | | | | | | | | | | |
| SURPLUS | | | | | | | | | | | | | | | | | | |
| INFANTRY— DEFICIENCY | | | | | | | | | | | | | | | | | | |
| SURPLUS | | | | | | | | | | | | | | | | | | |
| R.A.M.C.— DEFICIENCY | | | | | | | | | | | | | | | | | | 34 |
| SURPLUS | | | | | | | | | | | | | | | | | | |
| A.O.C.— DEFICIENCY | | | | | | | | | | | | | | | | | | |
| SURPLUS | | | | | | | | | | | | | | | | | | |
| A.V.C.— DEFICIENCY | | | | | | | | | | | | | | | | | | |
| SURPLUS | | | | | | | | | | | | | | | | | | |
| DEFICIENCY | | | | | | | | | | | | | | | | | | |
| SURPLUS | | | | | | | | | | | | | | | | | | |
| DEFICIENCY | | | | | | | | | | | | | | | | | | |
| SURPLUS | | | | | | | | | | | | | | | | | | |

| Detail of Wanting to Complete or Surplus. | W.O.'s and N.C.O.'s (by ranks) not included in trade columns: Sgt—Ramc. | | | | | | | | | | | TOTAL to agree with wanting to complete or surplus: Officers | TOTAL: Other Ranks | Horses: Riding | Horses: Draught | Horses: Heavy Draught | Horses: Pack |
|---|---|---|---|---|---|---|---|---|---|---|---|---|---|---|---|---|---|
| CAVALRY— DEFICIENCY | | | | | | | | | | | | | | | | | |
| SURPLUS | | | | | | | | | | | | | | | | | |
| R.A.— DEFICIENCY | | | | | | | | | | | | | | | | | |
| SURPLUS | | | | | | | | | | | | | | | | | |
| R.E.— DEFICIENCY | | | | | | | | | | | | | | | | | |
| SURPLUS | | | | | | | | | | | | | | | | | |
| INFANTRY— DEFICIENCY | | | | | | | | | | | | | | | | | |
| SURPLUS | | | | | | | | | | | | | | | | | |
| R.A.M.C.— DEFICIENCY | 1 | | | | | | | | | | | 3 | 34<br>6 | 5 | 13 | 16 | |
| SURPLUS | | | | | | | | | | | | | | | | | |
| A.O.C.— DEFICIENCY | | | | | | | | | | | | | | | | | |
| SURPLUS | | | | | | | | | | | | | | | | | |
| A.V.C.— DEFICIENCY | | | | | | | | | | | | | | | | | |
| SURPLUS | | | | | | | | | | | | | | | | | |
| DEFICIENCY | | | | | | | | | | | | | | | | | |
| SURPLUS | | | | | | | | | | | | | | | | | |
| DEFICIENCY | | | | | | | | | | | | | | | | | |
| SURPLUS | | | | | | | | | | | | | | | | | |

Remarks :—

R. A. Lennie Capt. Signature of Commander.

1/1 Lowland Fld. Ambce. Unit.

52. Division Formation to which attached.

29. 3-19. Date of Despatch.

(17828.) Wt. W2281—P 1075. 2,750m. 6/18. D & S. (E1256) Forms B2138/11.

[P.T.O.

Apl 1919

140/3550

1/1 Lowland F. A.

Instructions regarding War Diaries and Intelligence Summaries are contained in F. S. Regs., Part II. and the Staff Manual respectively. Title pages will be prepared in manuscript.

# WAR DIARY
*or*
~~INTELLIGENCE SUMMARY.~~
*(Erase heading not required.)*

537

Army Form C. 2118.

1/1st Lowland Fld Ambce

Vol 13

| Place | Date | Hour | Summary of Events and Information | Remarks and references to Appendices |
|---|---|---|---|---|
| SOIGNIES | 1/4/19 | | Nothing to note RAL | |
| " | 2/4/19 | | Authority of 52nd Div. Comm. requested by me to wear the badges of the rank of Major re C.D.S 384 Sect II dated Oct 1918 RAL | |
| " | 3/4/19 | | Arrangements made for holding sick-parades of personnel R.Es, and 17th N.F. at Div. hospital, Convent, Rue de la Station RAL | |
| | | | Three O.Rs proceed for Demobilization RAL | |
| " | 4/4/19 | | Instructions recd. A.D.M.S. 52nd Div. Capt + Q.M. A.M. Reid 1/1 L.F.A. completed inspection of 156 Brigade Medical equipment and arranged disposal of surplus RAL | |
| " | 5/4/19 | | Authority Q.M.G. 4003/104 (Q.B.1) dated 29/3/19, all stores surplus to establishment by new Demobilization Store Table returned to Ordnance RAL | |
| | | | Authority for me to wear badges of rank of Major, not granted by Div. Comm. 52nd Div. RAL | |
| " | 6/4/19 | | Nothing to note RAL | |
| " | 7/4/19 | | 3 O.Rs. proceeded for Demobilization today. RAL | |
| " | 8/4/19 | | Leave to U.K. opened for O. Ranks, allotment 4 per Div. Ambces per week RAL | |
| " | 9/4/19 | | Nothing to note RAL | |
| " | 10/4/19 | | Nothing to note RAL | |
| " | 11/4/19 | | Nothing to note RAL | |
| " | 12/4/19 | | Nothing to note RAL | |
| " | 13/4/19 | | 3 O.Rs proceed for Demobilization RAL | |

D. D. & L., London, E.C.
(10540) W1 W5300/P713 750,000 3/18 Sch. 52a Forms/C2118/15.

Army Form C. 2118

5-38

Instructions regarding War Diaries and Intelligence Summaries are contained in F. S. Regs., Part II. and the Staff Manual respectively. Title pages will be prepared in manuscript.

# WAR DIARY
*or*
# INTELLIGENCE SUMMARY.
*(Erase heading not required.)*

1/1st Lowland Fld. Ambce

| Place | Date | Hour | Summary of Events and Information | Remarks and references to Appendices |
|---|---|---|---|---|
| SOIGNIES | 14/4/19 | | Guarantee Letter, A.F.Z.16A. and Medical Certificate for release of 316022 Cpl HYSLOP. 1/1 L.F.A. on Compassionate Grounds, forwarded to A.D.M.S. This N.C.O. is on Cadre Establishment RAL | |
| | | | Capt & Q.M. A.M. REID. 1/1 L.F.A. applied for leave to U.K. RAL | |
| " " | 15/4/19 | | Nothing to note RAL | |
| " | 16/4/19 | | Instructions recd from A.D.M.S. 52nd Div. to demobilize 5, 7, and 5 O.Rs. on 16th and 2 succeeding days RAL. Ref R. 2/095/13 RAL. 5 O Ranks proceed for Demobilization RAL | |
| " | 17/4/19 | | Ref above 7 O.Ranks proceed for Demobilization RAL | |
| " | 18/4/19 | | " " 5 O.Ranks proceed for Demobilization RAL | |
| | | | Ref entry 14th inst above, authority received to demobilize No 316022 Cpl HYSLOP 1/1 L.F.A. RAL | |
| " | 19/4/19 | | Unit now reduced to Cadre Establishment. ADMS 52nd Div. notified. RAL | |
| | | | Applied to RAMC Records Base for Corp. to replace No 316022 Cpl Hyslop - demobilized RAL | |
| " " | 20/4/19 | | Nothing to report RAL | |
| " " | 21/4/19 | | Nothing to report RAL | |
| " " | 22/4/19 | | Nothing to report RAL | |
| " " | 23/4/19 | | Ref. instructions D.A.A.G. 52nd Div. Rev. A.H. FORBES, C.F. 1/1 L.F.A. is ordered to proceed to Labour Commandant No 4 Salvage District. Arras Sub-area for duty. RAL | |
| | | | Orders received from A.D.M.S. 52nd Div. that the Div. would start to entrain for Gailes on 27th inst RAL | |
| " " | 24/4/19 | | Rev. A.H. FORBES C.F. proceeded to Arras Sub-area for duty RAL. | |
| " " | 25/4/19 | | M1/08555 Sergt. TEMP. J. R.A.S.C. M.T. proceeded to CALAIS, for Demobilization in FRANCE. RAL | |
| " " | 26/4/19 | | Nothing to note RAL | |

D. D. & L., London, E.C.
(10340) Wt W5300/P713 750,000 3/18 Sch. 52a Forms/C2118/15.

Instructions regarding War Diaries and Intelligence Summaries are contained in F. S. Regs., Part II. and the Staff Manual respectively. Title pages will be prepared in manuscript.

# WAR DIARY
*or*
# INTELLIGENCE SUMMARY.
*(Erase heading not required.)*

539

Army Form C. 2118.

1/1 Lowland Fld. Ambce

| Place | Date | Hour | Summary of Events and Information | Remarks and references to Appendices |
|---|---|---|---|---|
| SOIGNIES. | 27/4/19 | | 4th + 7th Bns The Royal Scots, and 2 Coys. 52nd M.G.C, whose sick attended at the Hospital, entrained for GAILES. RAL | |
| " " | 28/4/19 | | 7th Battn The Cameronians, (S.R.) and the H.L.I. Brigade, whose sick attended at the Hospital, entrained for GAILES. RAL | |
| " " | 29/4/19 | | Medical inspection of cadre of 17th N.F. RAL | |
| " " | 30/4/19 | | Nothing to note RAL | |

[signature] Capt
O.C. 1/1 Lowland Fld. Ambce.

D. D. & L., London, E.C.
(10340) Wt W5300/P713 750,000 3/18 S. 2688 Forms/C2118/15.

**To be made up to and for Saturday in each week**

No. of Report 192

# FIELD RETURN.

Army Form B. 213

(To be furnished by all arms, services, and departments (except A.S.C. units) to the A.G.'s Office at the Base in accordance with Field Service Regulations, Part II.)

RETURN showing numbers (a) Effective strength of Unit. (b) Rationed by Unit. 1/1 Lowland Field Amb^ce at Soignies 5-4-19. Date.

| Details | *Personnel: Officers | Other Ranks | | | Animals: Horses: Riding | Draught | Heavy Draught | Pack | Mules: Large | Small | Guns and transport vehicles: Guns, showing description | Ammunition wagons | Machine guns | Aircraft, showing description | Horsed: †4 Wheeled | ‡2 Wheeled | Mechanical: Motor Cars | Tractors | Lorries, showing description | Trucks, showing description | Trailers | Motor Bicycles | Bicycles | Motor Ambulances | Remarks (Number of Acting W.O.'s and N.C.O.'s included in effective strength to be shown in this column.) |
|---|---|---|---|---|---|---|---|---|---|---|---|---|---|---|---|---|---|---|---|---|---|---|---|---|---|
| Effective Strength of Unit ... | 4 | 111 | | | | | | | | | | | | | | | | | | | | | | | a 24 left Unit for Demobilisation<br>b 16 at No 1 CCS - 1 at ADMS. |
| Details by Arms attached to Unit as in War Establishment ... | | | | | | | | | | | | | | | | | | | | | | | | | 1 at Concert Pty - 2 at San. Sect.<br>2 on courses - 43 left for Demob. |
| RASC. H.T. | | 33 | | | | | | | | | | | | | 12 | 3 | | | | | | | | | c 16 left Unit for Demob. |
| RASC (M.T.) | | 5 | | | | | | | | | | | | | | | | | | | | 1 | · | 2 | d 1 at ADMS |
| Total ... | 4 | 149 | | | | | | | | | | | | | 12 | 3 | | | | | | 1 | | 2 | |
| War Establishment ... | 8 | 203 | | | 5 | 13 | 16 | | | | | | | | 10 | 3 | | | | | | 2 | 1 | 4 | |
| Wanting to complete ... (Detail of Personnel and Horses below.) | 4 | +49 | | | 5 | 13 | 16 | | | | | | | | | | | | | | | 1 | 1 | 5 | 43 Ramc - 6 RASC MT |
| Surplus ... (Detail of Personnel and Horses below.) | | *5 | | | | | | | | | | | | | 2 | | | | | | | | | | * RASC (HT) |
| †Attached (not to include the details shown above) ... | | 3 | | | | | | | | | | | | | | | | | | | | | | | Patients |
| Attached for Rations only ... | 1 | | | | | | | | | | | | | | | | | | | | | | | | Chaplain |
| Civilians Employed with and Accompanying the Unit ... | | | | | | | | | | | | | | | | | | | | | | | | | |
| ‡Detached from and struck off effective strength of own Unit ... | | | | | | | | | | | | | | | | | | | | | | | | | |
| ‡Detached from but retained on effective strength of own unit ... | | | | | | | | | | | | | | | | | | | | | | | | | |
| Total Rationed ... | 3 | 10 | | | | | | | | | | | | | | | | | | | | | | | |

* Blank columns to be used for W.A.A.C. Natives or as may be required.

† In the case of field ambulances, hospitals or depots, the number of patients are to be included here, the names being shown in A.F.A. 36.

‡ These details to be enumerated by arms.

R M Lennie Capt. Signature of Commander.
OC 1/1 Low Field Amb

5-4-19 Date of Despatch.

B.2[illegible]

Sheet 192

1/1 Lowland Fld Ambce

WE 5-4-19

R.A.S.C. (H.T.)

| No. | Rank | Name | Casualty | Date |
| --- | --- | --- | --- | --- |
| | | NIL | | |

[illegible] Capt

OC 1/1 Lowland Fld Ambce

5/4/19.

WO NCOs & men who are liable to be retained for duty with Army of Occupation NIL

WO NCOs & men who have volunteered for duty with Army of Occupation NIL

Rase 4th Sheet attached

*For information of the A.G.'s Office at the base.*

Officers and men who have become casuals, been transferred or joined since last report.

Place SOIGNIES Date 5-3-19.

| Regtl. Number | Rank | Name | | Corps | Nature of casualty, or name of unit from or to which transferred. | Date of being struck off or coming on the ration return. | Remarks * |
|---|---|---|---|---|---|---|---|
| 130158 | Pte | Gay | A. | RAMC. | To No 2 CCS Valenciennes | | 28 3/19. |
| [illegible] | | [illegible] | W. | RAMC. | To No. 32 CCS | do. | 7 4/19. |
| 112200 | " | Pender. | W. | RAMC | - do - | - do - | 1 4/19 |
| 3[illegible]106 | | McDougall | W | RAMC. | To Hospital | 31-3-19. | |
| 3[illegible]010 | | Campbell | D. | RAMC | To U.K. for Demobilisation Embarked Boulogne, 14 3/19 | | |
| 316140 | " | Neil | A | - do - | - do - | | - do - 14 3/19 |
| 316204 | " | Stanley | R.H. | - do - | - do - | | - do - 14 3/19 |
| 52839 | L/Sgt | Scott | T. | - do - | - do - | | - do - 18 3/19 |
| 316225 | Sgt. | Allison | H.W. | - do. - | - do - | | - do - 20 3/19 |
| 316065 | Pte | Dunlop | D.C.C. | - do - | - do - | | - do - 20 3/19 |
| 316224 | " | Stewart | J.P. | - do - | - do - | | - do - 20 3/19 |
| 316118 | Pte | Wallace | R | RAMC T | Promoted A/Cpl. from 18 3/19 | | |
| | | | | | A/C. AG. 666 SB 19 DDMS M 3 Y2 221 24-3-19. | | |

Strength Officers T.F. 4

| | WO. NCOs | MEN |
|---|---|---|
| | WO. | 1. |
| | QMS | 1 |
| | S/Sgt. | 2. |
| | Sgt. | 5 |
| ALL CATEGORY "A". | L/Sgt. | - |
| | Cpls. | 4 |
| | L/Cpl. | 3. |
| | Pte. | 95 |
| | TOTAL | 111 |

* State whether absence is of a permanent or temporary nature, adding, in the case of casuals from wounds or disease, any available information for communication to the relatives.

*The perforated sheet is not to be used to record casualties; additional sheets, preferably foolscap, to be attached when necessary. These sheets to be carefully numbered and the number of attached sheets to be noted here.*

W.O. NCOs men who are liable to be retained for duty with Army of occupation Nil

" " " who have volunteered for duty with Army of occupation Nil

Perforated Sheet giving detail of personnel and horses wanting to complete or surplus, shown on Army Form B. 213.

No. of Report 192.

| Detail of Wanting to Complete or Surplus. | Drivers: R.A. | Drivers: R.E. | Drivers: A.S.C. | Drivers: Car (MT ASC) | Drivers: Lorry | Drivers: Steam | Gunners | Gunners Howitzer | Smith Gunners | Range Takers | Farriers: Serjeants | Farriers: Corporals | Shoeing or Shoeing and Carriage Smiths | Cold Shoers |
|---|---|---|---|---|---|---|---|---|---|---|---|---|---|---|
| CAVALRY— DEFICIENCY | | | | | | | | | | | | | | |
| SURPLUS | | | | | | | | | | | | | | |
| R.A.— DEFICIENCY | | | | | | | | | | | | | | |
| SURPLUS | | | | | | | | | | | | | | |
| R.E.— DEFICIENCY | | | | | | | | | | | | | | |
| SURPLUS | | | | | | | | | | | | | | |
| INFANTRY— DEFICIENCY | | | | | | | | | | | | | | |
| SURPLUS | | | 0- | 6 | | | | | | | | | | |
| R.A.M.C.— DEFICIENCY | | | | | | | | | | | | | | |
| SURPLUS | | | | | | | | | | | | | | |
| A.O.C.— DEFICIENCY | | | | | | | | | | | | | | |
| SURPLUS | | | | | | | | | | | | | | |
| A.V.C.— DEFICIENCY | | | | | | | | | | | | | | |
| SURPLUS | | | | | | | | | | | | | | |
| DEFICIENCY | | | | | | | | | | | | | | |
| SURPLUS | | | | | | | | | | | | | | |
| DEFICIENCY | | | | | | | | | | | | | | |
| SURPLUS | | | | | | | | | | | | | | |

| Detail of Wanting to Complete or Surplus. | Wheelers: R.A. | Wheelers: H.T. | Wheelers: M.T. | Saddlers or Harness Makers | Blacksmiths | Bricklayers and Masons | Carpenters and Joiners | Fitters & Turners (R.E.): Wood | Fitters & Turners (R.E.): Iron | Fitters: R.A. | Fitters: Wireless. | Plumbers | Electricians: Ordinary | Electricians: W.T. | Signalmen. | Engine Drivers: Loco. | Engine Drivers: Field |
|---|---|---|---|---|---|---|---|---|---|---|---|---|---|---|---|---|---|
| CAVALRY— DEFICIENCY | | | | | | | | | | | | | | | | | |
| SURPLUS | | | | | | | | | | | | | | | | | |
| R.A.— DEFICIENCY | | | | | | | | | | | | | | | | | |
| SURPLUS | | | | | | | | | | | | | | | | | |
| R.E.— DEFICIENCY | | | | | | | | | | | | | | | | | |
| SURPLUS | | | | | | | | | | | | | | | | | |
| INFANTRY— DEFICIENCY | | | | | | | | | | | | | | | | | |
| SURPLUS | | | | | | | | | | | | | | | | | |
| R.A.M.C.— DEFICIENCY | | | | | | | | | | | | | | | | | |
| SURPLUS | | | | | | | | | | | | | | | | | |
| A.O.C.— DEFICIENCY | | | | | | | | | | | | | | | | | |
| SURPLUS | | | | | | | | | | | | | | | | | |
| A.V.C.— DEFICIENCY | | | | | | | | | | | | | | | | | |
| SURPLUS | | | | | | | | | | | | | | | | | |
| DEFICIENCY | | | | | | | | | | | | | | | | | |
| SURPLUS | | | | | | | | | | | | | | | | | |
| DEFICIENCY | | | | | | | | | | | | | | | | | |
| SURPLUS | | | | | | | | | | | | | | | | | |

| Detail of Wanting to Complete or Surplus. | Air Line Men. | Permanent Line Men | Operators, Telegraph | Cablemen | Brigade Section Pioneers | General-duty Pioneers | Signallers | Instrument Repairers | Motor Cyclist | Motor Cyclist Artificers | Telephonists | Clerks | Machine Gunners | Armament Artificers: Fitters | Armament Artificers: Range Finders | Armourers | Storemen | Privates |
|---|---|---|---|---|---|---|---|---|---|---|---|---|---|---|---|---|---|---|
| CAVALRY— DEFICIENCY | | | | | | | | | | | | | | | | | | |
| SURPLUS | | | | | | | | | | | | | | | | | | |
| R.A.— DEFICIENCY | | | | | | | | | | | | | | | | | | |
| SURPLUS | | | | | | | | | | | | | | | | | | |
| R.E.— DEFICIENCY | | | | | | | | | | | | | | | | | | |
| SURPLUS | | | | | | | | | | | | | | | | | | |
| INFANTRY— DEFICIENCY | | | | | | | | | | | | | | | | | | |
| SURPLUS | | | | | | | | | | | | | | | | | | 43 |
| R.A.M.C.— DEFICIENCY | | | | | | | | | | | | | | | | | | |
| SURPLUS | | | | | | | | | | | | | | | | | | |
| A.O.C.— DEFICIENCY | | | | | | | | | | | | | | | | | | |
| SURPLUS | | | | | | | | | | | | | | | | | | |
| A.V.C.— DEFICIENCY | | | | | | | | | | | | | | | | | | |
| SURPLUS | | | | | | | | | | | | | | | | | | |
| DEFICIENCY | | | | | | | | | | | | | | | | | | |
| SURPLUS | | | | | | | | | | | | | | | | | | |
| DEFICIENCY | | | | | | | | | | | | | | | | | | |
| SURPLUS | | | | | | | | | | | | | | | | | | |

| Detail of Wanting to Complete or Surplus. | W.O.'s and N.C.O.'s (by ranks) not included in trade columns. | | | | | | | | | | | TOTAL to agree with wanting to complete or surplus: Officers | TOTAL: Other Ranks | Horses: Riding | Horses: Draught | Horses: Heavy Draught | Horses: Pack |
|---|---|---|---|---|---|---|---|---|---|---|---|---|---|---|---|---|---|
| CAVALRY— DEFICIENCY | | | | | | | | | | | | | | | | | |
| SURPLUS | | | | | | | | | | | | | | | | | |
| R.A.— DEFICIENCY | | | | | | | | | | | | | | | | | |
| SURPLUS | | | | | | | | | | | | | | | | | |
| R.E.— DEFICIENCY | | | | | | | | | | | | | | | | | |
| SURPLUS | | | | | | | | | | | | | | | | | |
| INFANTRY— DEFICIENCY | | | | | | | | | | | | | | | | | |
| SURPLUS | | | | | | | | | | | | 3 | 45 3 | 5 | 3 | 6 | |
| R.A.M.C.— DEFICIENCY | | | | | | | | | | | | | | | | | |
| SURPLUS | | | | | | | | | | | | | | | | | |
| A.O.C.— DEFICIENCY | | | | | | | | | | | | | | | | | |
| SURPLUS | | | | | | | | | | | | | | | | | |
| A.V.C.— DEFICIENCY | | | | | | | | | | | | | | | | | |
| SURPLUS | | | | | | | | | | | | | | | | | |
| DEFICIENCY | | | | | | | | | | | | | | | | | |
| SURPLUS | | | | | | | | | | | | | | | | | |
| DEFICIENCY | | | | | | | | | | | | | | | | | |
| SURPLUS | | | | | | | | | | | | | | | | | |

Remarks :—

R.M. [illegible] Capt. Signature of Commander.

1/3rd Lowland Field Ambulance Unit.

52 Division Formation to which attached.

5-4-19. Date of Despatch.

**To be made up to and for Saturday in each week**

No. of Report 193

# FIELD RETURN.

Army Form B. 213

(To be furnished by all arms, services, and departments (except A.S.C. units) to the A.G.'s Office at the Base in accordance with Field Service Regulations, Part II.)

RETURN, showing numbers (a) Effective strength of Unit. (b) Rationed by Unit. [illegible] Lowland Fd. Amb. at Soignies 12-4-19. Date.

| Details | Personnel: Officers | Personnel: Other Ranks | Personnel | Personnel | Animals: Horses: Riding | Animals: Horses: Draught | Animals: Horses: Heavy Draught | Animals: Horses: Pack | Animals: Mules: Large | Animals: Mules: Small | Guns, showing description | Ammunition wagons | Machine guns | Aircraft, showing description | Horsed: Wheeled 4 | Horsed: Wheeled 2 | Mechanical: Motor Cars | Mechanical: Tractors | Mechanical: Lorries, showing description | Mechanical: Trucks, showing description | Mechanical: Trailers | Motor Bicycles | Bicycles | Motor Ambulances | Remarks (Number of Acting W.O.'s and N.C.O.'s included in effective strength to be shown in this column.) |
|---|---|---|---|---|---|---|---|---|---|---|---|---|---|---|---|---|---|---|---|---|---|---|---|---|---|
| Effective Strength of Unit ... | 3 | 86 | | | | | | | | | | | | | | | | | | | | | | | a. 1 [illegible] unit for Demob. 8 [illegible] at No. 1 C.C.S. – 1 at [illegible] |
| Details by Arms attached to Unit as in War Establishment ... | | | | | | | | | | | | | | | | | | | | | | | | | 2 at San. Sect. for leave |
| | | | | | | | | | | | | | | | | | | | | | | | | | 23 [illegible] for Demob. |
| R.A.S.C. M.T. | | 32 | | | | | | | | | | | | | 11 | 3 | | | | | | | | | 14 [illegible] for Demob. |
| R.A.S.C. M.T. | | 4 | | | | | | | | | | | | | | | | | | | | 1 | | 2 | |
| Total ... | 3 | 122 | | | | | | | | | | | | | 11 | 3 | | | | | | 1 | | 2 | |
| War Establishment ... | 8 | 203 | | | 5 | 13 | 16 | | | | | | | | 10 | 3 | | | | | | 2 | 1 | 7 | |
| Wanting to complete ... (Detail of Personnel and Horses below.) | 5 | 44 | | | 5 | 13 | 16 | | | | | | | | 0 | | | | | | | 1 | 1 | 5 | *40 R.A.M.C. 4 R.A.S.C. M.T. |
| Surplus ... (Detail of Personnel and Horses below.) | | 4 | | | | | | | | | | | | | | | | | | | | | | | * R.A.S.C. M.T. |
| †Attached (not to include the details shown above) ... | | 2 | | | | | | | | | | | | | | | | | | | | | | | Patients |
| Attached for Rations only | 1 | | | | | | | | | | | | | | | | | | | | | | | | Chaplain |
| Civilians Employed with and Accompanying the Unit ... | | | | | | | | | | | | | | | | | | | | | | | | | |
| ‡Detached from and struck off effective strength of own Unit ... | | | | | | | | | | | | | | | | | | | | | | | | | |
| ‡Detached from but retained on effective strength of own unit... | | | | | | | | | | | | | | | | | | | | | | | | | |
| Total Rationed ... | 3 | 62 | | | | | | | | | | | | | | | | | | | | | | | |

* Blank columns to be used for W.A.A.C. Natives or as may be required.

† In the case of field ambulances, hospitals or depots, the number of patients are to be included here, the names being shown in A.F.A. 36.

‡ These details to be enumerated by arms.

R. A. [illegible] Capt. Signature of Commander. 12-4-19 Date of Despatch.

O.C. 1/[illegible] Lowland Fd. Amb.

[illegible] 11-4-19

V.F.S.C. T.T. [illegible]

| No. | Rank | Name | [illegible] | Date |
|---|---|---|---|---|
| [illegible] | [illegible] | Sutton [illegible] | [illegible] | 10-4-19 |

[illegible]

W.O. N.C.O. & men who are liable to be retained for duty with Army of Occupation — NIL —

W.O. N.C.O. & men who have volunteered for duty with Army of Occupation

[illegible]

[illegible] MT

| No. | Name | [illegible] | Remarks | Date |
|---|---|---|---|---|
| [illegible] | [illegible] | [illegible] P.F. | [illegible] MT [illegible] [illegible] | 9-4-19 |

[illegible] Capt.
O.C. [illegible]

12/4/19

Strength officers T.F. 3.

WO. NCO. MEN.

| | |
|---|---|
| W.O. 1st CL. | NIL |
| QMS 2nd CL. | 1. |
| S/Sgt. | 2. |
| Sgt. | 4. |
| L/Sgt. | NIL |
| Cpl. | 4. |
| L/Cpl. | 3. |
| Ptes | 72. |
| TOTAL | 86. |

ALL CATEGORY "A".

12/4/19.

RASC. Sheet attached

*For information of the A.G.'s Office at the base.*

Officers and men who have become casuals, been transferred or joined since last report.

Place SOIGNIES Date 12-4-19.

| Regtl. Number | Rank | Name | Corps | Nature of casualty, or name of unit from or to which transferred. | Date of being struck off or coming on the ration return. | Remarks * |
|---|---|---|---|---|---|---|
| – | Capt. | Downes A.D. | RAMC (TF) | To UK. for Demob. | Embarked. Boulogne | 27 3/19 |
| 316109. | Pte | McDougall W. | RAMC. TF | Reinforcement from Hosp. | 9 4/19. | |
| 316193. | " | Stewart W. | RAMC TF | Returned from 23 VET. HOSP. ST. Omer. | (course) 6-4-19. | |
| 316293 | Cpl. | Donald W. | do. | Returned from 13 VET HOSP. NEUFCHATEL | course 8-4-19. | |
| 316161. | L/c. | Campbell J. | do. | Returned from 52nd Div Concert Pty | 10-4-19 | |
| 316210 | L/c. | Mitchelson D. | do. | Proceeded to UK on 14 days leave. Credit ration all) 14 days at 2/1. £1-9-2. | | |
| 316023. | S/M. | Ritchie D. | do. | To. U.K. for. Demob. | Embarked. Boulogne | 23 3/19 |
| 316238 | Pte | McDonald W.J. | do | do | do. | 23 3/19. |
| 316241. | " | McKean T. | do | do | do | 23 3/19. |
| 316028 | " | Purvis J.A. | do | do | do | 23 3/19. |
| 316084 | " | Rankin J.H.S. | do | do | do | 23 3/19 |
| 316127 | " | White A. | do | do | do | 23 3/19. |
| 495139 | " | Fairbrass G.W. | do | do | do | 23 3/19. |
| 316074 | " | Johnstone A | do | do | do | 23 3/19. |
| 316112 | " | Raeburn A | do | do | do | 28 3/19. |
| 316096 | " | Darkes F. | do | do | do | 28 3/19 |
| 316125 | " | Ovenstone J. | do | do | do | 28 3/19 |
| 316147 | " | Eadie W. | do | do | do | 28 3/19 |
| 316156 | " | Sharp P | do | do | do | 28 3/19 |
| 318164 | " | Hutton E. | do | do | do | 28 3/19 |
| 316191. | " | Stellhouse J. | do | do | do | 28 3/19 |
| 316261. | " | Rennie J. | do | do | do | 28 3/19 |
| 328053 | " | Marshall G. | do | do | do | 28 3/19 |
| 328024 | " | Le Roy H. | do | do | do | 28 3/19 |
| 316285 | " | Campbell W. | do | do | do | 28 3/19 |
| 316296 | " | Hunter J. | do | do | do | 28 3/19 |
| 316291 | " | McIntyre J. | do | do | do | 28 3/19 |
| 316154 | " | Brown R. | do | do | do. | 28 3/19. |
| 316118 | " | Wallace R. | do | do | do | 28 3/19. |
| 316128 | " | Young D.B. | do | do | do | 28 3/19. |
| 316179 | Sgt. | Kenny E.V. | do | do | do | 28 3/19. |
| 316159. | Pte | Tinto A.L. | do | do | do | 28 3/19. |
| 410038 | " | Jackson F.S. | do | do | do | 28 3/19 |
| 410045 | " | Hodgson E.R. | do | do | do | 28 3/19. |
| 316259. | " | Reid J.S. | do | do | do | 29 3/19. |
| 316103 | " | Johnstone R. | do | do | do | 2 4/19. |
| 316148 | " | Laird Dev. | do | do | do | 2 4/19. |
| 316188 | " | Johnstone J.Y. | do | do | do | 2 4/19. |

W.O. N.C.O. & men who are liable to be retained for duty with Army of occupation NIL
" " " who have volunteered for duty with Army of occupation NIL

* State whether absence is of a permanent or temporary nature, adding, in the case of casuals from wounds or disease, any available information for communication to the relatives.

*The perforated sheet is not to be used to record casualties; additional sheets, preferably foolscap, to be attached when necessary. These sheets to be carefully numbered and the number of attached sheets to be noted here.*

Additional information regarding "wanting to complete" and sufficient information to explain the difference between the present and previous week's effective strength is to be entered in this space.

Where the return of specific individuals is desired a note is to be made hereon.

1. Limber Wagon to 1/5th H.L.I. 5. 4. 19.

## REMARKS.

Any further remarks necessary may be entered here.

| Explanation of R.A. effective strength. | | | | | | |
|---|---|---|---|---|---|---|
| | Drivers. | Gunners. | Signallers. | Artificers. | N.C.O's. | Total. |
| | | | | | | |

Perforated Sheet giving detail of personnel and horses wanting to complete or surplus, shown on Army Form B. 213.

No. of Report 93.

| Detail of Wanting to Complete or Surplus. | Drivers: R.A. | Drivers: R.E. | Drivers: A.S.C. | Drivers: Car | Drivers: Lorry | Drivers: Steam | Gunners | Gunners Howitzer | Smith Gunners | Range Takers | Farriers: Serjeants | Farriers: Corporals | Shoeing or Shoeing and Carriage Smiths | Cold Shoers | Wheelers: R.A. | Wheelers: H.T. | Wheelers: M.T. | Saddlers or Harness Makers | Blacksmiths | Bricklayers and Masons | Carpenters and Joiners | Fitters & Turners (R.E.): Wood | Fitters & Turners (R.E.): Iron | Fitters: R.A. | Fitters: Wireless. | Plumbers | Electricians: Ordinary | Electricians: W.T. | Signalmen. | Engine Drivers: Loco. | Engine Drivers: Field | Air Line Men. | Permanent Line Men | Operators, Telegraph | Cablemen | Brigade Section Pioneers | General-duty Pioneers | Signallers | Instrument Repairers | Motor Cyclist | Motor Cyclist Artificers | Telephonists | Clerks | Machine Gunners | Armament Artificers: Fitters | Armament Artificers: Range Finders | Armourers | Storemen | Privates | W.O.'s and N.C.O.'s (by ranks) not included in trade columns | | | | | | | | | | | TOTAL to agree with wanting to complete or surplus: Officers | TOTAL to agree with wanting to complete or surplus: Other Ranks | Horses: Riding | Horses: Draught | Horses: Heavy Draught | Horses: Pack |
|---|---|---|---|---|---|---|---|---|---|---|---|---|---|---|---|---|---|---|---|---|---|---|---|---|---|---|---|---|---|---|---|---|---|---|---|---|---|---|---|---|---|---|---|---|---|---|---|---|---|---|---|---|---|---|---|---|---|---|---|---|---|---|---|---|---|---|
| CAVALRY—DEFICIENCY | | | | | | | | | | | | | | | | | | | | | | | | | | | | | | | | | | | | | | | | | | | | | | | | | | | | | | | | | | | | | | | | | | |
| SURPLUS | | | | | | | | | | | | | | | | | | | | | | | | | | | | | | | | | | | | | | | | | | | | | | | | | | | | | | | | | | | | | | | | | | |
| R.A.—DEFICIENCY | | | | | | | | | | | | | | | | | | | | | | | | | | | | | | | | | | | | | | | | | | | | | | | | | | | | | | | | | | | | | | | | | | |
| SURPLUS | | | | | | | | | | | | | | | | | | | | | | | | | | | | | | | | | | | | | | | | | | | | | | | | | | | | | | | | | | | | | | | | | | |
| R.E.—DEFICIENCY | | | | | | | | | | | | | | | | | | | | | | | | | | | | | | | | | | | | | | | | | | | | | | | | | | | | | | | | | | | | | | | | | | |
| SURPLUS | | | | | | | | | | | | | | | | | | | | | | | | | | | | | | | | | | | | | | | | | | | | | | | | | | | | | | | | | | | | | | | | | | |
| INFANTRY—DEFICIENCY | | | | | | | | | | | | | | | | | | | | | | | | | | | | | | | | | | | | | | | | | | | | | | | | | | | | | | | | | | | | | | | | | | |
| SURPLUS | | | | | | | | | | | | | | | | | | | | | | | | | | | | | | | | | | | | | | | | | | | | | | | | | | | | | | | | | | | | | | | | | | |
| R.A.M.C.—DEFICIENCY | | | | y | | | | | | | | | | | | | | | | | | | | | | | | | | | | | | | | | | | | | | | | | | | | | 40 | | | | | | | | | | | | 3 | 44 | 5 | 13 | 14 | |
| SURPLUS | | | 4 | | | | | | | | | | | | | | | | | | | | | | | | | | | | | | | | | | | | | | | | | | | | | | | | | | | | | | | | | | | 4 | | | | |
| A.O.C.—DEFICIENCY | | | | | | | | | | | | | | | | | | | | | | | | | | | | | | | | | | | | | | | | | | | | | | | | | | | | | | | | | | | | | | | | | | |
| SURPLUS | | | | | | | | | | | | | | | | | | | | | | | | | | | | | | | | | | | | | | | | | | | | | | | | | | | | | | | | | | | | | | | | | | |
| A.V.C.—DEFICIENCY | | | | | | | | | | | | | | | | | | | | | | | | | | | | | | | | | | | | | | | | | | | | | | | | | | | | | | | | | | | | | | | | | | |
| SURPLUS | | | | | | | | | | | | | | | | | | | | | | | | | | | | | | | | | | | | | | | | | | | | | | | | | | | | | | | | | | | | | | | | | | |
| DEFICIENCY | | | | | | | | | | | | | | | | | | | | | | | | | | | | | | | | | | | | | | | | | | | | | | | | | | | | | | | | | | | | | | | | | | |
| SURPLUS | | | | | | | | | | | | | | | | | | | | | | | | | | | | | | | | | | | | | | | | | | | | | | | | | | | | | | | | | | | | | | | | | | |
| DEFICIENCY | | | | | | | | | | | | | | | | | | | | | | | | | | | | | | | | | | | | | | | | | | | | | | | | | | | | | | | | | | | | | | | | | | |
| SURPLUS | | | | | | | | | | | | | | | | | | | | | | | | | | | | | | | | | | | | | | | | | | | | | | | | | | | | | | | | | | | | | | | | | | |

Remarks :—

N. H. Hamil[illegible] — Signature of Commander.

East Lowland Fld Ambce. — Unit.

52nd Division — Formation to which attached.

12-4-19 — Date of Despatch.

**To be made up to and for Saturday in each week**

No. of Report

## FIELD RETURN.

Army Form B. 213

(To be furnished by all arms, services, and departments (except A.S.C. units) to the A.G.'s Office at the Base in accordance with Field Service Regulations, Part II.)

RETURN showing numbers (*a*) Effective strength of Unit. (*b*) Rationed by Unit. at Date.

| DETAILS. | *Personnel: Officers | *Personnel: Other Ranks | *Personnel | *Personnel | *Personnel | Animals: Horses: Riding | Animals: Horses: Draught | Animals: Horses: Heavy Draught | Animals: Horses: Pack | Animals: Mules: Large | Animals: Mules: Small | Guns, showing description | Ammunition wagons | Machine guns | Aircraft, showing description | Horsed: 4 Wheeled | Horsed: 2 Wheeled | Mechanical: Motor Cars | Mechanical: Tractors | Mechanical: Lorries, showing description | Mechanical: Trucks, showing description | Mechanical: Trailers | Motor Bicycles | Bicycles | Motor Ambulances | REMARKS (Number of Acting W.O.'s and N.C.O.'s included in effective strength to be shown in this column.) |
|---|---|---|---|---|---|---|---|---|---|---|---|---|---|---|---|---|---|---|---|---|---|---|---|---|---|---|
| Effective Strength of Unit ... ... | | | | | | | | | | | | | | | | | | | | | | | | | | |
| Details by Arms attached to Unit as in War Establishment ... ... ... | | | | | | | | | | | | | | | | | | | | | | | | | | |
| TOTAL ... ... | | | | | | | | | | | | | | | | | | | | | | | | | | |
| War Establishment ... ... ... | | | | | | | | | | | | | | | | | | | | | | | | | | |
| Wanting to complete ... ... (Detail of Personnel and Horses below.) | | | | | | | | | | | | | | | | | | | | | | | | | | |
| SURPLUS ... ... (Detail of Personnel and Horses below.) | | | | | | | | | | | | | | | | | | | | | | | | | | |
| †Attached (not to include the details shown above) ... ... ... | | | | | | | | | | | | | | | | | | | | | | | | | | |
| Attached for Rations only ... ... | | | | | | | | | | | | | | | | | | | | | | | | | | |
| Civilians Employed with and Accompanying the Unit ... ... | | | | | | | | | | | | | | | | | | | | | | | | | | |
| ‡Detached from and struck off effective strength of own Unit ... ... | | | | | | | | | | | | | | | | | | | | | | | | | | |
| ‡Detached from but retained on effective strength of own unit... ... | | | | | | | | | | | | | | | | | | | | | | | | | | |
| TOTAL RATIONED ... | | | | | | | | | | | | | | | | | | | | | | | | | | |

* Blank columns to be used for W.A.A.C. Natives or as may be required.

† In the case of field ambulances, hospitals or depots, the number of patients are to be included here, the names being shown in A.F.A. 36.
‡ These details to be enumerated by arms.

Signature of Commander. Date of Despatch.

B213. Sheet 1144. 1/1 Lowland Fld. Amb. W.E. 9-4-19

RASC HT

CASUALTIES. — NIL —

12/4/19.

[illegible] Capt.
OC 1/1 Low. Fld. Amb. RAMC

*For information of the A.G.'s Office at the base.*

Officers and men who have become casuals, been transferred or joined since last report.

Place DOIGNIES    Date 19-4-19

| Regtl. Number | Rank | Name | Corps | Nature of casualty, or name of unit from or to which transferred. | Date of being struck off or coming on the ration return. | Remarks * |
|---|---|---|---|---|---|---|
| [illegible] | Pte | [illegible] E. | Lanc F. | [illegible] | | [illegible] |
| | | British Army TF | 3 | | | |
| | | W.O. NCO MEN. | | | | |
| | | Q.M.S. | 1. | | | |
| | | S.Sgt. | 2. | | | |
| | | Sgt. | 4. | | | |
| | | Cpl. | 4 | | | |
| | | L/C. | 3 | | | |
| | | Pte. | 42 | | | |
| | | TOTAL | 86 | | | |

CATEGORY A

WO NCO & Men who are liable to be retained for duty with Army of occupation NIL

WO NCO & MEN who have volunteered for duty with Army of occupation NIL

* State whether absence is of a permanent or temporary nature, adding, in the case of casuals from wounds or disease any available information for communication to the relatives.

*The perforated sheet is not to be used to record casualties; additional sheets, preferably foolscap, to be attached when necessary. These sheets to be carefully numbered and the number of attached sheets to be noted here.*

Perforated Sheet giving detail of personnel and horses wanting to complete or surplus, shown on Army Form B. 213.

No. of Report 194

| Detail of Wanting to Complete or Surplus. | Drivers: R.A. | Drivers: R.E. | Drivers: A.S.C. | Drivers: Car | Drivers: Lorry | Drivers: Steam | Gunners | Gunners Howitzer | Smith Gunners | Range Takers | Farriers: Serjeants | Farriers: Corporals | Shoeing or Shoeing and Carriage Smiths | Cold Shoers | Wheelers: R.A. | Wheelers: H.T. | Wheelers: M.T. | Saddlers or Harness Makers | Blacksmiths | Bricklayers and Masons | Carpenters and Joiners | Fitters & Turners (R.E.): Wood | Fitters & Turners (R.E.): Iron | Fitters: R.A. | Fitters: Wireless. | Plumbers | Electricians: Ordinary | Electricians: W.T. | Signalmen. | Engine Drivers: Loco. | Engine Drivers: Field | Air Line Men. | Permanent Line Men | Operators, Telegraph | Cablemen | Brigade Section Pioneers | General-duty Pioneers | Signallers | Instrument Repairers | Motor Cyclist | Motor Cyclist Artificers | Telephonists | Clerks | Machine Gunners | Armament Artificers: Fitters | Armament Artificers: Range Finders | Armourers | Storemen | Privates | W.O.'s and N.C.O.'s (by ranks) not included in trade columns. | | | | | | | | | | | TOTAL to agree with wanting to complete or surplus: Officers | TOTAL to agree with wanting to complete or surplus: Other Ranks | Horses: Riding | Horses: Draught | Horses: Heavy Draught | Horses: Pack |
|---|---|---|---|---|---|---|---|---|---|---|---|---|---|---|---|---|---|---|---|---|---|---|---|---|---|---|---|---|---|---|---|---|---|---|---|---|---|---|---|---|---|---|---|---|---|---|---|---|---|---|---|---|---|---|---|---|---|---|---|---|---|---|---|---|---|---|
| CAVALRY— DEFICIENCY | | | | | | | | | | | | | | | | | | | | | | | | | | | | | | | | | | | | | | | | | | | | | | | | | | | | | | | | | | | | | | | | | | |
| SURPLUS .. | | | | | | | | | | | | | | | | | | | | | | | | | | | | | | | | | | | | | | | | | | | | | | | | | | | | | | | | | | | | | | | | | | |
| R.A.— DEFICIENCY | | | | | | | | | | | | | | | | | | | | | | | | | | | | | | | | | | | | | | | | | | | | | | | | | | | | | | | | | | | | | | | | | | |
| SURPLUS .. | | | | | | | | | | | | | | | | | | | | | | | | | | | | | | | | | | | | | | | | | | | | | | | | | | | | | | | | | | | | | | | | | | |
| R.E.— DEFICIENCY | | | | | | | | | | | | | | | | | | | | | | | | | | | | | | | | | | | | | | | | | | | | | | | | | | | | | | | | | | | | | | | | | | |
| SURPLUS .. | | | | | | | | | | | | | | | | | | | | | | | | | | | | | | | | | | | | | | | | | | | | | | | | | | | | | | | | | | | | | | | | | | |
| INFANTRY— DEFICIENCY | | | | | | | | | | | | | | | | | | | | | | | | | | | | | | | | | | | | | | | | | | | | | | | | | | | | | | | | | | | | | | | | | | |
| SURPLUS .. | | | | | | | | | | | | | | | | | | | | | | | | | | | | | | | | | | | | | | | | | | | | | | | | | | | | | | | | | | | | | | | | | | |
| R.A.M.C.— DEFICIENCY | | | | 4 | | | | | | | | | | | | | | | | | | | | | | | | | | | | | | | | | | | | | | | | | | | | | 45 | | | | | | | | | | | | 5 | 35 | 5 | 13 | 16 | |
| SURPLUS .. | | | 4 | | | | | | | | | | | | | | | | | | | | | | | | | | | | | | | | | | | | | | | | | | | | | | | | | | | | | | | | | | 4 | | | | |
| A.O.C.— DEFICIENCY | | | | | | | | | | | | | | | | | | | | | | | | | | | | | | | | | | | | | | | | | | | | | | | | | | | | | | | | | | | | | | | | | | |
| SURPLUS .. | | | | | | | | | | | | | | | | | | | | | | | | | | | | | | | | | | | | | | | | | | | | | | | | | | | | | | | | | | | | | | | | | | |
| A.V.C.— DEFICIENCY | | | | | | | | | | | | | | | | | | | | | | | | | | | | | | | | | | | | | | | | | | | | | | | | | | | | | | | | | | | | | | | | | | |
| SURPLUS .. | | | | | | | | | | | | | | | | | | | | | | | | | | | | | | | | | | | | | | | | | | | | | | | | | | | | | | | | | | | | | | | | | | |
| DEFICIENCY | | | | | | | | | | | | | | | | | | | | | | | | | | | | | | | | | | | | | | | | | | | | | | | | | | | | | | | | | | | | | | | | | | |
| SURPLUS .. | | | | | | | | | | | | | | | | | | | | | | | | | | | | | | | | | | | | | | | | | | | | | | | | | | | | | | | | | | | | | | | | | | |
| DEFICIENCY | | | | | | | | | | | | | | | | | | | | | | | | | | | | | | | | | | | | | | | | | | | | | | | | | | | | | | | | | | | | | | | | | | |
| SURPLUS .. | | | | | | | | | | | | | | | | | | | | | | | | | | | | | | | | | | | | | | | | | | | | | | | | | | | | | | | | | | | | | | | | | | |

Remarks :—

[illegible] Capt Signature of Commander.

Lowland Fd. Ambce Unit.

52nd Divn Formation to which attached.

19-11-19 Date of Despatch.

[P.T.O.

(17828.) Wt. W2281—P 1075. 2,750m. 6/18. D & S. (E1256) Forms B2138/11.

R.A.S.C. Stat attached

**To be made up to and for Saturday in each week**

No. of Report 95

# FIELD RETURN.

Army Form B. 213

(To be furnished by all arms, services, and departments (except A.S.C. units) to the A.G.'s Office at the Base in accordance with Field Service Regulations, Part II.)

RETURN showing numbers (*a*) Effective strength of Unit. (*b*) Rationed by Unit. 1st Lowland Fld. Ambce at SOIGNIES 26-4-19 Date.

| DETAILS. | *Personnel: Officers | Other Ranks | | | | Animals: Horses: Riding | Draught | Heavy Draught | Pack | Mules: Large | Small | Guns and transport vehicles: Guns, showing description | Ammunition wagons | Machine guns | Aircraft, showing description | Horsed: 4 Wheeled | 2 Wheeled | Mechanical: Motor Cars | Tractors | Lorries, showing description | Trucks, showing description | Trailers | Motor Bicycles | Bicycles | Motor Ambulances | REMARKS (Number of Acting W.O.'s and N.C.O.'s included in effective strength to be shown in this column.) |
|---|---|---|---|---|---|---|---|---|---|---|---|---|---|---|---|---|---|---|---|---|---|---|---|---|---|---|
| Effective Strength of Unit ... ... | 3 | [illegible] | | | | | | | | | | | | | | | | | | | | | | | | [illegible] |
| Details by Arms attached to Unit as in War Establishment ... ... ... | | | | | | | | | | | | | | | | | | | | | | | | | | [illegible] |
| | | | | | | | | | | | | | | | | | | | | | | | | | | 2 on leave to U.K. |
| | | | | | | | | | | | | | | | | | | | | | | | | | | 18 at No. CCS - [illegible] |
| RASC H.T. | | 32 | | | | | | | | | | | | | | 11 | 3 | | | | | | | | | 14 [illegible] |
| RASC M.T. | | 4 | | | | | | | | | | | | | | | | | | | | | | | 1 | 1 [illegible] U.K. |
| TOTAL ... ... | 3 | 108 | | | | | | | | | | | | | | 11 | 3 | | | | | | | | 1 | |
| War Establishment ... ... ... | 8 | 203 | | | | 5 | 13 | 16 | | | | | | | | 10 | 3 | | | | | | 2 | 1 | 4 | |
| Wanting to complete ... ... ... (Detail of Personnel and Horses below.) | 5 | 99 | | | | 5 | 13 | 16 | | | | | | | | | | | | | | | 2 | 1 | 6 | 92 R.A.M.C. [illegible] R.A.S.C. (M.T.) |
| SURPLUS ... ... (Detail of Personnel and Horses below.) | | 4 | | | | | | | | | | | | | | 1 | | | | | | | | | | R.A.S.C. H.T. |
| †Attached (not to include the details shown above) ... ... ... | | 1 | | | | | | | | | | | | | | | | | | | | | | | | Patient |
| Attached for Rations only ... ... | | | | | | | | | | | | | | | | | | | | | | | | | | |
| Civilians Employed with and Accompanying the Unit ... ... ... | | | | | | | | | | | | | | | | | | | | | | | | | | |
| ‡Detached from and struck off effective strength of own Unit ... ... | | | | | | | | | | | | | | | | | | | | | | | | | | |
| ‡Detached from but retained on effective strength of own unit... ... ... | | 1 | | | | | | | | | | | | | | | | | | | | | | | | R.A.S.C. M.T. [illegible] duty. |
| TOTAL RATIONED ... | 2 | 142 | | | | | | | | | | | | | | | | | | | | | | | | |

* Blank columns to be used for W.A.A.C. Natives or as may be required.

† In the case of field ambulances, hospitals or depots, the number of patients are to be included here, the names being shown in A.F.A. 36.

‡ These details to be enumerated by arms.

[illegible] Capt. Signature of Commander. 26-4-19. Date of Despatch.

O.C. 1st Lowland Fld. Ambce.

B213 Sheet 195. 1/1 Lowland Field Ambce W.E. 26-4-19

R.A.S.C.

| No. | RANK | NAME | | CASUALTY | DATE |
|---|---|---|---|---|---|
| M2/135099 | Pte | Blackwell | G.T. | To U.K. on leave (14 days) Credited Ration all. 14 days @ 2/- 1-9-2 | 21-4-19. |
| M1/09555 | Sgt | Yems | J. | To M.T. Workshops Cologne on demob. | 24-4-19. |
| M2/134510 | Cpl | Lawson | P.F. | Reinforcement from M.T. Workshops Cologne. | 24-4-19. |
| | | | | | |

26/4/19.

Capt.
OC 1/1 Lowland Fld Ambce

W.O. NCO & men who are liable to be retained for duty with Army of occupation Nil

W.O. NCO & men who have volunteered for duty with Army of occupation

*For information of the A.G.'s Office at the base.*

Officers and men who have become casuals, been transferred or joined since last report.

Place [illegible] Date [illegible]-4-19

| Regtl. Number | Rank | Name | Corps | Nature of casualty, or name of unit from or to which transferred. | Date of being struck off or coming on the ration return. | Remarks * |
|---|---|---|---|---|---|---|
| 316000 | Pte | Lawton H. | R.A.M.C. (T) | Retained in the Service under M.S. act 1916, Session [illegible] from 20-4-19. | | |
| | | | | £15 Bounty | claimed | |
| 3160[illegible]11 | Pte | Miller J. | R.A.M.C. (T) | [illegible] for Demobilization [illegible] | | [illegible] 28 3/19 |
| 3[illegible]954 | " | Southern G. | do | do | | do 1 4/19 |
| 316149 | " | Carson J.B. | do | do | | do 6 4/19 |
| 316235 | " | McCartney J. | do | do | | do 6 4/19 |
| 3161[illegible] | " | McMenemy R. | do | do | | do 6 4/19 |
| 316204 | " | Edmiston A. | do | do | | do 6 4/19 |
| 316256 | " | Nisbet A. | do | do | | do 6 4/19 |
| 42136 | " | Terry C.A. | do | do | | do 6 4/19 |
| 316185 | " | McGregor M.R. | do | do | | do 29 3/19 |
| 316136 | " | Muir A. | do | do | | do 29 3/19 |
| 3160[illegible]4 | " | McAllister G. | do | do | | do 29 3/19 |
| 316021 | " | Craig J. | do | do | | do 28 3/19 |
| 3160[illegible] | " | Brown W. | do | do | | do 28 3/19 |
| 316124 | " | [illegible] J. | do | do | | do 28 3/19 |
| C.F. | Rev. | [illegible] A.H. | A.C.D. | Transferred to [illegible] | | 24-4-19 |

Strength Officers T.F. 3.

W.O. N.C.O. Men

| | |
|---|---|
| Q.M.S. | 1 |
| S.S. | 2 |
| Sgt | 4 |
| Cpl. | 4 |
| L/Cpl. | 3 |
| Pte | 58 |
| Total | 72 |

ALL CATEGORY "A".

W.O. N.C.O. & men who are liable to be retained for duty with Army of occupation NIL

W.O. N.C.O. & men who have volunteered for duty with Army of occupation NIL

* State whether absence is of a permanent or temporary nature, adding, in the case of casuals from wounds or disease any available information for communication to the relatives.

*The perforated sheet is not to be used to record casualties ; additional sheets, preferably foolscap, to be attached when necessary. These sheets to be carefully numbered and the number of attached sheets to be noted here.*

Perforated Sheet giving detail of personnel and horses wanting to complete or surplus, shown on Army Form B. 213.

No. of Report 95

| Detail of Wanting to Complete or Surplus. | Drivers. R.A. | Drivers. R.E. | Drivers. A.S.C. | Drivers. Car | Drivers. Lorry RASC M.T. | Drivers. Steam | Gunners | Gunners Howitzer | Smith Gunners | Range Takers | Farriers Serjeants | Farriers Corporals | Shoeing or Shoeing and Carriage Smiths | Cold Shoers | Wheelers R.A. | Wheelers H.T. | Wheelers M.T. | Saddlers or Harness Makers | Blacksmiths | Bricklayers and Masons | Carpenters and Joiners | Fitters & Turners (R.E.) Wood | Fitters & Turners (R.E.) Iron | Fitters R.A. | Fitters Wireless. | Plumbers | Electricians Ordinary | Electricians W.T. | Signalmen. | Engine Drivers Loco. | Engine Drivers Field | Air Line Men. | Permanent Line Men | Operators, Telegraph | Cablemen | Brigade Section Pioneers | General-duty Pioneers | Signallers | Instrument Repairers | Motor Cyclist | Motor Cyclist Artificers | Telephonists | Clerks | Machine Gunners | Armament Artificers Fitters | Armament Artificers Range Finders | Armourers | Storemen | Privates | W.O's and N.C.O's (by ranks) not included in trade columns. | | | | | | | | | | | TOTAL to agree with wanting to complete or surplus. Officers | TOTAL Other Ranks | Horses Riding | Horses Draught | Horses Heavy Draught | Horses Pack |
|---|---|---|---|---|---|---|---|---|---|---|---|---|---|---|---|---|---|---|---|---|---|---|---|---|---|---|---|---|---|---|---|---|---|---|---|---|---|---|---|---|---|---|---|---|---|---|---|---|---|---|---|---|---|---|---|---|---|---|---|---|---|---|---|---|---|---|
| CAVALRY—DEFICIENCY | | | | | | | | | | | | | | | | | | | | | | | | | | | | | | | | | | | | | | | | | | | | | | | | | | | | | | | | | | | | | | | | | | | |
| SURPLUS | | | | | | | | | | | | | | | | | | | | | | | | | | | | | | | | | | | | | | | | | | | | | | | | | | | | | | | | | | | | | | | | | | | |
| R.A.—DEFICIENCY | | | | | | | | | | | | | | | | | | | | | | | | | | | | | | | | | | | | | | | | | | | | | | | | | | | | | | | | | | | | | | | | | | | |
| SURPLUS | | | | | | | | | | | | | | | | | | | | | | | | | | | | | | | | | | | | | | | | | | | | | | | | | | | | | | | | | | | | | | | | | | | |
| R.E.—DEFICIENCY | | | | | | | | | | | | | | | | | | | | | | | | | | | | | | | | | | | | | | | | | | | | | | | | | | | | | | | | | | | | | | | | | | | |
| SURPLUS | | | | | | | | | | | | | | | | | | | | | | | | | | | | | | | | | | | | | | | | | | | | | | | | | | | | | | | | | | | | | | | | | | | |
| INFANTRY—DEFICIENCY | | | | | | | | | | | | | | | | | | | | | | | | | | | | | | | | | | | | | | | | | | | | | | | | | | | | | | | | | | | | | | | | | | | |
| SURPLUS | | | | | | | | | | | | | | | | | | | | | | | | | | | | | | | | | | | | | | | | | | | | | | | | | | | | | | | | | | | | | | | | | | | |
| R.A.M.C.—DEFICIENCY | | | | | 4 | | | | | | | | | | | | | | | | | | | | | | | | | | | | | | | | | | | | | | | | | | | | 92 | | | | | | | | | | | | 6 | 99 | 5 | 13 | 16 | |
| SURPLUS | | | | 4 | | | | | | | | | | | | | | | | | | | | | | | | | | | | | | | | | | | | | | | | | | | | | | | | | | | | | | | | | | 4 | | | | |
| A.O.C.—DEFICIENCY | | | | | | | | | | | | | | | | | | | | | | | | | | | | | | | | | | | | | | | | | | | | | | | | | | | | | | | | | | | | | | | | | | | |
| SURPLUS | | | | | | | | | | | | | | | | | | | | | | | | | | | | | | | | | | | | | | | | | | | | | | | | | | | | | | | | | | | | | | | | | | | |
| A.V.C.—DEFICIENCY | | | | | | | | | | | | | | | | | | | | | | | | | | | | | | | | | | | | | | | | | | | | | | | | | | | | | | | | | | | | | | | | | | | |
| SURPLUS | | | | | | | | | | | | | | | | | | | | | | | | | | | | | | | | | | | | | | | | | | | | | | | | | | | | | | | | | | | | | | | | | | | |
| DEFICIENCY | | | | | | | | | | | | | | | | | | | | | | | | | | | | | | | | | | | | | | | | | | | | | | | | | | | | | | | | | | | | | | | | | | | |
| SURPLUS | | | | | | | | | | | | | | | | | | | | | | | | | | | | | | | | | | | | | | | | | | | | | | | | | | | | | | | | | | | | | | | | | | | |
| DEFICIENCY | | | | | | | | | | | | | | | | | | | | | | | | | | | | | | | | | | | | | | | | | | | | | | | | | | | | | | | | | | | | | | | | | | | |
| SURPLUS | | | | | | | | | | | | | | | | | | | | | | | | | | | | | | | | | | | | | | | | | | | | | | | | | | | | | | | | | | | | | | | | | | | |

Remarks :—

W A Lennie Capt. Signature of Commander.

O/c Lowland Fld. Ambce. Unit.

52nd Division Formation to which attached.

26-4-19 Date of Despatch.

(17828.) Wt. W2281—P 1075. 2,750m. 6/18. D & S. (E1256) Forms B2138/11. [P.T.O.